Jewish Virtue Ethics

SUNY series in Contemporary Jewish Thought

Richard A. Cohen, editor

Jewish Virtue Ethics

Edited by

GEOFFREY D. CLAUSSEN,
ALEXANDER GREEN, and
ALAN L. MITTLEMAN

SUNY
PRESS

Published by State University of New York Press

Printed in the United States of America

For information, contact State University of New York Press, Albany, NY
www.sunypress.edu

Library of Congress Cataloging-in-Publication Data

Names: Claussen, Geoffrey D., editor. | Green, Alexander, editor. | Mittleman, Alan L., editor.
Title: Jewish virtue ethics / Geoffrey D. Claussen, Alexander Green, and Alan L. Mittleman, editors.
Description: Albany : State University of New York Press, [2023] | Series: SUNY series in Contemporary Jewish Thought | Includes bibliographical references and index.
Identifiers: ISBN 9781438493916 (hardcover : alk. paper) | ISBN 9781438493923 (ebook) | ISBN 9781438493909 (pbk. : alk. paper)
Further information is available at the Library of Congress.

10 9 8 7 6 5 4 3 2 1

Contents

Acknowledgments ix

Foreword xi
Julia Annas

Introduction 1
Geoffrey D. Claussen, Alexander Green, and Alan L. Mittleman

Chapter 1. Biblical Literature 9
Amanda Beckenstein Mbuvi

Chapter 2. Philo of Alexandria 23
Carlos Lévy

Chapter 3. Titus Flavius Josephus 37
Clifford Orwin

Chapter 4. Rabbinic Literature 51
Deborah Barer

Chapter 5. Baḥya Ibn Paquda 65
Diana Lobel

Chapter 6. Solomon Ibn Gabirol 81
Sarah Pessin

Chapter 7. Maimonides 97
Kenneth Seeskin

Chapter 8. Elazar of Worms 111
Joseph Isaac Lifshitz

Chapter 9. Naḥmanides 123
Jonathan Jacobs

Chapter 10. The *Zohar* 137
Eitan P. Fishbane

Chapter 11. Gersonides 149
Alexander Green

Chapter 12. Ḥasdai Crescas 163
Roslyn Weiss

Chapter 13. Joseph Albo 173
Shira Weiss

Chapter 14. Isaac Arama 185
Baruch Frydman-Kohl

Chapter 15. Moses Cordovero 199
Eugene D. Matanky

Chapter 16. Baruch Spinoza 213
Heidi M. Ravven

Chapter 17. Moses Ḥayyim Luzzatto 227
Patrick Benjamin Koch

Chapter 18. Moses Mendelssohn 241
Elias Sacks

Chapter 19. Menaḥem Mendel Lefin 255
Harris Bor

Chapter 20. Ḥayyim of Volozhin 269
Esti Eisenmann

Chapter 21. Naḥman of Bratslav 283
Shaul Magid

Chapter 22. Isaac Bekhor Amarachi 297
Katja Šmid

Chapter 23. Israel Salanter 311
Sarah Zager

Chapter 24. Simḥah Zissel Ziv 325
Geoffrey D. Claussen

Chapter 25. Hermann Cohen 337
Shira Billet

Chapter 26. Abraham Isaac Kook 353
Don Seeman

Chapter 27. Martin Buber 369
William Plevan

Chapter 28. Mordecai Kaplan 383
Matthew LaGrone

Chapter 29. Eliyahu Eliezer Dessler 395
Esther Solomon

Chapter 30. Joseph Soloveitchik 409
Yonatan Y. Brafman

Chapter 31. Hannah Arendt 425
Ned Curthoys

Chapter 32. Emmanuel Levinas 441
Richard A. Cohen

Chapter 33. Abraham Joshua Heschel 455
Einat Ramon

Chapter 34. Jewish Feminism 469
Rebecca J. Epstein-Levi

Chapter 35. Jewish Environmentalism 483
Hava Tirosh-Samuelson

Afterword 497
Alan L. Mittleman

List of Contributors 503

Index 511

Acknowledgments

We are grateful to James Peltz, Associate Director and Editor in Chief at SUNY Press, and Richard A. Cohen, editor of the SUNY series in Contemporary Jewish Thought, for their support of this project. We also acknowledge the generous financial support of the Office of the Provost of the Jewish Theological Seminary; Sergey Dolgopolski and the Gordon and Gretchen Gross Professorship in Jewish Studies in the Department of Jewish Thought at SUNY, University at Buffalo; and the Office of the Provost, the Office of the Dean of the College of Arts and Sciences, and the Lori and Eric Sklut Endowed Professorship in Jewish Studies at Elon University.

Foreword

JULIA ANNAS

In the late twentieth century there was a striking revival of virtue ethics, and it made a great impact. In philosophy departments virtue ethics was initially resisted as an unfamiliar outsider, but it is now well established as one of the three major ethical theories (the others being Kantianism and consequentialism, usually in the form of utilitarianism). It's notable that, unlike the other two, virtue ethics has spread all over the place, to areas considered "applied" rather than "pure"—to bioethics, legal ethics, environmental ethics, and many more, where answers are needed to the ethical problems that arise in the lives we lead.

To begin with, contemporary virtue ethics was tied closely to Aristotle's version of it. This is not surprising, since Aristotle is the first (Western) philosopher to lay out the structure of virtue ethics in a clear way, giving an account of how we develop the virtues though learning and habituation—through aspiring to become a better person as we come to understand how and why the good people in our community do what they do and say the things they say. His central insights about virtue are not, though, tied to details like his "doctrine of the mean," or, more importantly, his account of the virtuous person's overall aim, which he takes to be a development of rational human nature. This has appealed to contemporaries who have welcomed an account friendly to naturalism and secularism; but Aristotle himself preserves an alternative account in which the good life is located in contemplation of what transcends human nature, and Plato as well as later thinkers took the aspiration of the virtuous person to involve more than human achievement. The earliest thinker to appreciate that the accounts of virtue and the good life, from Aristotle onwards, were well adapted to a religious tradition, was Philo of Alexandria, whose own account demonstrates the superiority of Jewish virtues over those of the pagans.

Aristotle takes his ethics to answer to the philosophically defensible aspects of the way thoughtful and reflective people think about ethics, and so it is not surprising to find that, whether in Aristotelian or non-Aristotelian form, the long and exceptionally rich Jewish philosophical and intellectual tradition features virtue prominently in its ethical reflections. It is a tradition in which there is always a strong emphasis on ethics, and on a way of life in which virtue is developed in the context of a life lived in accordance with Jewish tradition. Virtue is developed in a socially embedded way—and in a way in which there is no dividing line between, in modern terms, "sacred" and "secular"; awareness of transcendent values, and of the importance of studying the scriptures and the scholarly traditions that interpret them, is woven into everyday life in a seamless way. It is a tradition in which commandments and rules are central, but it is never a tradition of mere obedience to rules; rules structure the passage through life, but it is not mere adherence to rules that is centrally important, rather doing so in the right way, with awareness of the role of rules in developing character and virtue. Here is plenty of room for reflections on the importance of different ways of teaching and learning, of the relative roles of ideal figures (like those of revered rabbis), narratives, arguments, and scholarly study of scripture.

The Jewish intellectual and philosophical tradition is abundant in reflections about virtue and related issues about its development, its importance, and its resources for enlarging our thinking. We find great philosophical figures like Philo, Spinoza, and Arendt, well-known outside the Jewish tradition, and also many less famous figures who wrote for their students, their congregations, their wider audiences in flourishing and in difficult times. The reader of this book will be introduced to a dazzling series of thinkers, differing in their historical circumstances and in their emphasis on different aspects of the tradition, but unified by their concern with ethics in the Jewish tradition, and thus, in differing and often disparate ways, with virtue.

Introduction

GEOFFREY D. CLAUSSEN, ALEXANDER GREEN
AND ALAN L. MITTLEMAN

What is good character? What are the traits of a good person? How should good character traits—virtues—be cultivated? How should negative character traits—vices—be avoided? The history of Jewish literature is filled with reflection on questions of character and virtue such as these.

This volume explores that history, focusing on virtues. We understand virtues broadly, as good character traits, or "excellences of character."[1] Virtues are dispositions that require refinement or cultivation, and for which it is appropriate to hold agents responsible should they fail to cultivate them. In the history that we explore in this volume, Jews have pointed to this sort of concept with Hebrew words such as *ma'alot, de'ot,* or *middot tovot,* Greek words such as *aretai,* Arabic words such as *akhlaq,* Latin words such as *virtutes,* German words such as *Tugenden,* as well as related words in other languages. Jewish thinkers have also written about "virtue" in the singular—excellent moral character in general. And they have written about many particular virtues, such as love, reverence, wisdom, humility, temperance, generosity, justice, courage, and holiness.

The thinkers discussed in this volume all see virtues as significant and essential. As such, their ethical approaches are all forms of "virtue ethics," broadly defined as forms of moral thought wherein virtues are central to morality.[2] However, other elements—such as laws, rules, and principles—may *also* be central to morality in Jewish thought. These different emphases have not been separated to the extent that they have been in contemporary moral philosophy. Some of the thinkers in this volume may well be characterized as deontologists or as consequentialists, and many of them see virtues and rules as working together in a mutually reinforcing way.[3] But all of them see virtue as central to ethics, and so we are placing them under the rubric of "Jewish virtue ethics" in this broad sense.

This book covers thousands of years of Jewish literature, reflecting a wide range of contexts and influences. Though some readers may primarily think of Aristotle's influence when they think of "virtue ethics," ancient traditions about virtue that are invoked in this volume include not only Aristotelian traditions but also Platonic traditions and a wide range of biblical and rabbinic traditions. The medieval and modern traditions discussed within this volume typically look back to one or more of these traditions, although they also chart new paths and reflect many other sorts of influences. The volume points to the diversity of approaches to virtue throughout Jewish intellectual history, while also showing some common themes that have united many of these diverse approaches.

We feature thirty-five influential approaches in this volume, focusing on individual thinkers, while also considering some movements and bodies of literature. Chapter 1 introduces diverse perspectives from the Hebrew Bible itself, a body of literature that is foundational for the other thinkers and approaches in the volume. We then consider the Stoic approach taken by Philo of Alexandria (chapter 2), the politically focused approach of Josephus (chapter 3), and the Torah-focused models developed within classical rabbinic literature (chapter 4).

A number of the chapters that follow consider medieval examples of what is often called "musar literature," literature that focuses directly on virtue and character, including the writings of Baḥya Ibn Paquda (chapter 5) and Solomon Ibn Gabirol (chapter 6), both eleventh-century Spanish thinkers shaped by Neoplatonism and a range of Jewish and Islamic traditions. The volume then continues with a chapter on the twelfth-century philosopher Moses Maimonides (chapter 7), whose ethics reflect an Aristotelian framework. A number of subsequent chapters feature fourteenth- and fifteenth-century philosophers in Spain and France who engage with and respond to Maimonides, including Levi Gersonides (chapter 11), Ḥasdai Crescas (chapter 12), Joseph Albo (chapter 13), and Isaac Arama (chapter 14).

Other chapters focused on medieval thinkers consider alternative models, rooted in esotericism and mysticism. These models include those developed by Elazar of Worms in thirteenth century Germany (chapter 8), Naḥmanides in thirteenth-century Spain (chapter 9), the authors of the *Zohar* in thirteenth- to fourteenth-century Spain (chapter 10), and Moses Cordovero in the land of Israel in the sixteenth century (chapter 15).

The volume then transitions into the modern era with chapters on the seventeenth-century Dutch philosopher Baruch Spinoza (chapter 16) and the eighteenth-century Italian kabbalist Moses Ḥayyim Luzzatto (chapter 17). Subsequent chapters consider ideas of virtue encouraged by leaders of the eighteenth- and nineteenth-century Haskalah (Jewish Enlightenment): Moses Mendelssohn (chapter 18) in Germany and Menaḥem Mendel Lefin (chapter 19) in Poland. We also consider Eastern European thinkers steeped in Kabbalah and opposed to the Haskalah, namely, the Lithuanian traditionalist Ḥayyim of Volozhin (chapter 20) and one of the rabbis from the Hasidic movement, Naḥman of Bratslav, in Ukraine (chapter 21). Moving further south to Salonika, Greece, the following chapter considers the nineteenth-century Sephardi author Isaac Bekhor Amarachi, who wrote and translated musar literature into Ladino. We also include two chapters on early leaders of the nineteenth-century Musar movement, a Lithuania-based movement that emphasized the study of musar literature, Israel Salanter (chapter 23) and Simḥah Zissel Ziv (chapter 24).

Turning to figures who rose to influence in the twentieth century, we consider a range of influential figures who wrote extensively about virtues: the German neo-Kantian philosopher Hermann Cohen (chapter 25); the first Ashkenazi chief rabbi of Mandatory Palestine, Religious Zionist thinker Abraham Isaac Kook (chapter 26); the dialogic thinker Martin Buber (chapter 27); the American pragmatist Mordecai Kaplan, founder of the Reconstructionist movement (chapter 28); Eliyahu Eliezer Dessler, scion of the Musar movement, who shaped contemporary Haredi Judaism (chapter 29); Joseph Soloveitchik, a major influence on centrist and modern Orthodoxy in America (chapter 30); the moral-political thinker Hannah Arendt, who aligned herself with a Jewish "pariah tradition" (chapter 31); the French philosopher Emmanuel Levinas, for whom ethics was fundamental as "first philosophy" (chapter 32); and the theologian Abraham Joshua Heschel, who has had a profound influence on non-Orthodox movements in the United States (chapter 33).

The volume concludes with two approaches that emerged in the latter part of the twentieth century and have flourished in the twenty-first century: Jewish feminism (chapter 34) and Jewish environmentalism (chapter 35).

Each of the chapters in this volume addresses four common questions: (1) In what ways are virtues important to the thinker, work, or movement under discussion? (2) Which particular virtues, or kinds of virtues, are especially important to them? (3) How do they think that virtues can be cultivated, and are there exemplars of virtue? (4) How does their conception of virtue affect their interpretation of Judaism or of Jewish identity?

This set of questions provides a way into the analysis of the place of virtue across the range of Jewish moral thought; it also provides a common template for the various chapters. It is our hope that the chapters—and the thinkers that they treat—may be compared with one another, given their shared attention to the prompts.

We can see, from the chapters in the volume, that virtues may be important in a wide variety of ways. Some thinkers stress the importance of virtue for a community, while others stress how virtue leads to individual flourishing or transcendence. Some speak of immediate communities, while others offer a cosmopolitan vision. Some stress flourishing in this world, while some speak of rewards in the world to come, and others reject any talk of consequences for the self altogether. Some stress how virtues combat injustices on earth, while others stress how virtues strengthen the divine realm. Some stress how virtue leads to intimacy with God, while in other models intimacy with the divine does not seem possible, and in some models God plays little if any role at all. Some models focus on moderation, while others frame ideal virtue as a kind of extreme. Some stress the rational character of the virtues, while others are more suspicious of claims of rationality. And some reflect a negative assessment of human nature, while others offer a more positive assessment.

The chapters also point to the importance of a variety of particular virtues. Humility, justice, and love for others are singled out across a particularly wide range of chapters. Courage, fear (or awe) of God, generosity, and temperance (or moderation) also receive some particular attention. Love of God, friendship, holiness, piety, and wisdom are among the other virtues that are singled out in both premodern and modern contexts. But many other virtues highlighted in particular chapters are mentioned nowhere else in the volume. Some are uniquely tied to particular thinkers: for example, the virtue of receptivity to God's goodness in the thought of Solomon ibn Gabirol (chapter 6), the virtue of dialogical responsiveness and openness in the thought of Martin Buber (chapter 27), or the virtue of realism in the thought of Hannah Arendt (chapter 31).

Both premodern and modern thinkers discussed in the volume see the performance of the Torah's commandments (*mitzvot*) as a means for cultivating virtue, though they often stress different aspects of the commandments, sometimes emphasizing the ways that virtue is cultivated through the performance of actions and sometimes emphasizing, as in the case of Baḥya Ibn Paquda (chapter 5), "the duties of the heart."

Many chapters also point to practices of study, though these practices are often of very different kinds. Ancient rabbinic literature (chapter 4) often emphasizes how virtue is developed through the legal argumentation carried out by sages. Gersonides (chapter 11) stresses the importance of studying the Torah's narratives. Isaac Bekhor Amarachi (chapter 22) advises spending an hour each day studying musar literature. Israel Salanter (chapter 23) recommends ritualized, emotional study of musar literature within a particular sort of communal environment. We also find models of how storytelling shapes virtue, including the intergenerational storytelling found in the book of Deuteronomy (chapter 1) and Hannah Arendt's model of historically grounded storytelling (chapter 31). In Rebecca Epstein-Levi's discussion of Jewish feminism (chapter 34), we see practices of citation cultivating virtue.

Other chapters point to other sorts of practices. Elazar of Worms (chapter 8), for example, offers a model of seeking to embarrass oneself so as to develop greater modesty. Moses Mendelssohn (chapter 18) explains how poetry and music may foster virtue. Menaḥem Mendel Lefin (chapter 19) advances a system for focusing on one trait at a time and charting one's progress with that trait. Naḥman of Bratslav (chapter 21) requires submission to the *zaddik*. Simḥah Zissel Ziv (chapter 24) recommends visualization exercises that cultivate empathy. Eliyahu Eliezer Dessler (chapter 29) and Emmanuel Levinas (chapter 32) describe how acts of generosity and responsibility cultivate those virtues.

Many of the thinkers and works discussed in this volume also point to exemplars of virtue. Moses and Abraham are especially well-represented, although different thinkers see these figures as exemplifying very different virtues. Even when they are associated with the same sort of virtue, these virtues are often imagined in very different terms: for example, the *Zohar*'s model of how Abraham exemplifies justice (*tzedek*, in chapter 10) is very different from Mordecai Kaplan's model of how Abraham exemplifies justice (chapter 28). The volume also refers to a number of other exemplary biblical characters and rabbis, as well as other pious figures and philosophers, both those who are Jewish and those who are not (Socrates, for example, appears as an exemplar in four different chapters). Some thinkers also point to God as the ultimate exemplar of virtue.

The various conceptions of virtue in this volume are linked with various understandings of Judaism / Torah and Jewish / Israelite identity. Each thinker under discussion sought to advance certain ideas about identity and tradition, and these ideas shape and are shaped by the thinker's ideas about virtue.

Virtue ethics has been a burgeoning field of moral inquiry among academic philosophers in the postwar period. Although Jewish ethics has also flourished as an academic (and practical) field, attention to the role of virtue in Jewish thought has been underdeveloped. This volume seeks to illuminate its centrality not only for readers primarily interested in Jewish ethics but also for readers who take other approaches to virtue ethics, including within the Western virtue ethics tradition. It is our hope that the essays gathered here will provide hitherto unrecognized or unknown sources for philosophical reflection.

Notes

1. Rosalind Hursthouse and Glen Pettigrove, "Virtue Ethics," in *The Stanford Encyclopedia of Philosophy (Winter 2018 Edition)*, ed. Edward N. Zalta, https://plato.stanford.edu/archives/win2018/entries/ethics-virtue.

2. For some approaches to defining "virtue ethics," see Julia Annas, "Virtue Ethics," in *The Oxford Handbook of Ethical Theory*, ed. David Copp (New York: Oxford University Press, 2006), 515–36; Rosalind Hursthouse, *On Virtue Ethics* (Oxford: Oxford University Press, 1999); Martha C. Nussbaum, "Virtue Ethics: A Misleading Category?," *Journal of Ethics* 3, no. 3 (1999): 163–201.

3. Alan L. Mittleman, *A Short History of Jewish Ethics: Conduct and Character in the Context of Covenant* (Chichester, UK: Wiley-Blackwell, 2012), 7. For

a general treatment of this problem, see Onora O'Neill, *Towards Justice and Virtue: A Constructive Account of Practical Reasoning* (Cambridge: Cambridge University Press, 1996).

Chapter 1

Biblical Literature

AMANDA BECKENSTEIN MBUVI

The Hebrew Bible is not monolithic. Although contemporary readers typically encounter it as a single volume—the Tanakh, the Jewish Bible, the Hebrew Bible, the Old Testament, or simply "the Bible"—it is actually a compilation of texts that contain distinct genres and points of view. The oldest known biblical manuscripts are from the second century BCE, but the biblical texts came to us through a process that spanned (at least) hundreds of years and that involved people in a variety of historical and cultural contexts, with less known about those contexts than about, say, the Greco-Roman world. Accordingly, basic facts about the biblical texts' history and background remain matters of considerable debate. These circumstances complicate any topical analysis of the Bible.

This chapter will not attempt to harmonize or catalogue the Bible's relationship to virtue across all of those differences. Rather than making a systematic or comprehensive statement, it will offer a way into thinking about virtue in biblical literature. It will devote special attention to the Torah (Genesis-Deuteronomy) because of its foundational position and role, and it will give some consideration to the way subsequent parts of the canon carry forward trajectories that begin there. The texts discussed here are not intended to represent the Bible as a whole. Biblical literature is vast and contains many more facets than this chapter can explore. These reflections present just a few of the many things that can be said about virtue in relation to biblical literature. Readers are encouraged to use them as inspiration for considering other aspects of biblical literature not discussed here.

This chapter examines biblical literature as its own discrete collection of voices. When read independently, biblical literature does not always resemble the versions of the Bible created through subsequent reception. Despite its embrace by proponents of Western Civilization, and despite the formative role that embrace has played in the West's process of self-definition,[1] biblical literature is not Western. At least most biblical literature precedes Plato and Aristotle and derives from a cultural context distinct from theirs. Even the characterization "Jewish" is not quite accurate, because the term "Jew" was not yet used the way it is used now.[2] Biblical literature reflects an earlier way of assigning identity and conceptualizing peoplehood. Accordingly, biblical literature does not exactly engage in what this volume identifies as Jewish virtue ethics, though it does provide an important foundation for that enterprise. One of biblical literature's most helpful contributions to a contemporary consideration of Jewish virtue ethics is the way that it challenges the assumptions that many readers bring to considerations of virtue. This chapter will build on that challenge.

Virtue in the Bible

The biblical texts celebrate many of the same qualities that others label as virtues. However, they show less interest in abstract conceptions of the good than in the qualities and behaviors that reflect the identity of B'nai Yisrael (the people Israel) as the people of YHWH and that facilitate the practical matters of hosting the presence of YHWH and living in the promised land. For example, the Torah (Genesis-Deuteronomy) focuses on the particular rather than the abstract and universal. While the narratives depict certain behaviors and tendencies in a positive light, they generally do not bother to name the qualities that they reflect. Such labeling is more likely to be found for negatively regarded attitudes and behaviors. At the same time, in contrast to the directly articulated morals of works like Aesop's Fables, the Torah features stories that do not declare their import. Many of the stories present morally complex situations without clearly specifying intended takeaways for readers.

The Bible's relationship to virtue can be compared to the parent whose cultural frame of reference precludes the idea of making declarations of love, but who demonstrates depth of care and concern for their children in other ways. As there are many different ways to conceptualize and express love, so too are there many ways to conceptualize and express moral excellence. The Bible includes a number of different moral paradigms, each with its own language and logic. Although these paradigms correspond in many ways to source critical analyses of the biblical texts, the goal here is to delineate some of the different conceptual worlds within the received text, not to speculate about their origins. In the Bible, these paradigms cooperate and coexist.

One biblical paradigm for moral excellence is the paradigm of *family*, whose prominence in Genesis gives it a foundational role in the rest of the Bible. It foregrounds story and genealogy and emphasizes identity, community, and memory. Key features include genealogies and family stories—narratives and anecdotes that define what it means to be B'nai Yisrael and that transmit that understanding to subsequent generations. As a framework for moral excellence, it emphasizes the importance of living in accordance with one's familial identity and role.

Like the paradigm of family, the paradigm of *covenant* also conceives moral excellence in relational terms, prizing loyalty above all. In the ancient Near Eastern context from which the biblical texts originated, the language and rituals of covenant were a familiar way of conveying allegiance, though usually in the political sphere.[3] Deploying language commonly found in treaties, Deuteronomy frames the commandments as a means of demonstrating commitment to YHWH and not as an expression of freestanding moral standards.[4] That is not to say that Deuteronomy actively denies the existence of such standards, only that it approaches moral excellence from a different direction.

In contrast to the accessible, analytical language associated with covenant, the *priestly* paradigm operates in accordance with a symbolic world that it assumes its audience will understand through analogy rather than argument.[5] Stretching the bounds of what moderns recognize as relevant to morality, it attributes a kind of objective reality to impurity, so that even inanimate objects become like moral subjects liable to atonement. Moreover, as S. Tamar Kamionkowski observes, biblical writers "described the land as analogous to a human body with the agency and vulnerabilities of human bodies. . . . Both the land and the people have their own covenantal relationships with God."[6] In texts like Leviticus, the priestly voice focuses on the necessary conditions for hosting the presence of YHWH and living in the promised land. It foregrounds holiness, purity, ritual, and craftsmanship, and emphasizes clear distinctions between categories.[7]

These paradigms are best understood as culturally rooted means of expressing moral concepts. Translation between paradigms is possible—moral concepts expressed in terms of one could be recast in terms of another. Such translation could reflect a shift in values, or it could bring out values that were implicit in another mode of reckoning.

Particular Virtues

Because the biblical texts do not directly address virtue in the way that texts from another cultural context might, it is often left to the interpreter to provide the labels for the moral qualities that they celebrate. One virtue that plays an important role in the Bible might be termed rootedness in *toledot,* after the word for genealogy. It consists of a kind of communal groundedness: knowing YHWH and understanding one's place in creation and community. Genesis applies genealogy to the cosmos (2:4), thus placing B'nai Yisrael's relationship to the natural world under the auspices of family. Situating the origins of B'nai Yisrael in the midst of a story that begins before the call of Abram and that extends beyond the line of Jacob, Genesis presents a familial network that leaves no human outside of the range of B'nai Yisrael's responsibility. The book pairs acts of divine election with an emphasis on relationship and reconciliation across the differences thus created (as with Jacob and Esau, for example).[8] In this way, it suggests that the flourishing of B'nai Yisrael is bound up with the flourishing of all humanity. The expansive conception of family in Genesis means that embracing one's familial role goes beyond one's household, beyond B'nai Yisrael, and even beyond humanity.[9]

Another virtue that plays an important role in the Bible is memory—the (appropriate) apprehension of the past as a guide for present behavior, as exemplified by the injunction to "befriend the stranger, for you were strangers in the land of Egypt" (Deut. 10:19). In contrast to the modern preoccupation with historicity, this way of engaging the past is less concerned with "what really happened" than with the way that stories structure ways of being in the world. As a biblical virtue, memory upholds the importance of remaining mindful of certain pivotal events, correctly identifying their implications, and living accordingly.

An important virtue in the paradigm of covenant, a disposition to heed YHWH, derives from the same grammatical root as the word *shema*. The opening of the Shema (Deut. 6:4) is typically rendered in English as "hear," but the virtue might be better translated as "heeding" to capture the dual implications of listening and complying. The key illustration of the virtue is a negative one: Saul loses his kingship for failing to manifest it. The prophet Samuel conveys to Saul God's instruction to wage holy war to "exac[t] the penalty for what Amalek did to Israel" (1 Sam. 15:2). Saul undertakes the raid but does not do so in accordance with the dictates of holy war. When Samuel confronts him with that point, Saul argues that his actions were sufficient, especially since his intention for the livestock he unlawfully captured is to perform sacrifices to YHWH. Samuel, however, declares otherwise:

> Does the LORD delight in burnt offerings and sacrifices
> As much as in [heeding] the LORD's command?
> Surely, [heeding] is better than sacrifice
> Compliance than the fat of rams. (1 Sam. 15:22)

Samuel's point here is not so much a dig at priestly approaches to moral excellence as it is an insistence that doing something for YHWH is no substitute for doing what YHWH commands. Loyalty to YHWH's word takes precedence above all, above the merit of particular actions as independently evaluated, and above the intention of the individual.

Ḥokhmah emerges as an important virtue in the priestly paradigm. Contemporary usage most frequently equates *ḥokhmah* with wisdom. However, in keeping with the tendency of biblical Hebrew to use the same word to describe something concrete and something abstract (as in *ruaḥ* for wind and for spirit), the biblical texts give the word a wider semantic range. The priestly paradigm uses it to characterize the essential quality of the artisans who construct the Tabernacle and its furnishings (e.g., Exod. 31:1–6), presenting craftsmanship as a virtue and thereby blurring what moderns perceive as the distinction between virtue and skill.

The extensive description of the Tabernacle should not be understood as instructions for building a set to serve as a backdrop for what really matters, namely, the action. Rather, the physical attributes of the Tabernacle play an important role in communicating a particular understanding of YHWH and Israel.[10] Moreover, "the details that are lavished on the building of the desert tabernacle carry a doctrinal principle in the gradations of quality. Menahem Haran points out that the gradations of holiness are expressed in the quality of the sacred furniture."[11] In that symbolic language, doing craftsmanship is doing theology. The priestly paradigm takes that idea so seriously that, Mary Douglas argues, "Leviticus is a sacred text designed on the proportions of a temple." As she explains, "Narrative, whether literary or dramatic, must unfold in space of some kind. If the theme is complex, systematic reference to a known structure supplies a framework. Temple architecture tends to carry heavy cosmological symbolism."[12] The association between word, space, and self is further underscored by the way in which the performance of animal sacrifice in Leviticus invokes the spatial design of the Tabernacle.[13] Although the modern imagination associates the priestly with the otherworldly in opposition to the material world, the priestly paradigm in the biblical texts depicts virtue in a way that is literally visceral. Accordingly, it prizes the ability to shape the material world and labels that quality with the same term used to describe the ability to order the mental world and skillfully interpret experience and structure understanding.

How Virtue Is Cultivated

Deuteronomy provides a rich opportunity to examine ways that the biblical texts think virtues are cultivated. It includes vivid depictions of moral formation, with the Shema being the most famous example: "Take to heart these instructions with which I charge you this day. Impress them upon your children. Recite them when you stay at home and when you are away, when you lie down and when you get up. Bind them as a sign on your hand and let them serve as a symbol on your forehead; inscribe them on the doorposts of your house and on your gates" (6:6–9). These verses encapsulate a number of the book's primary strategies for moral formation: intergenerational storytelling, dramatic recitation, and physical engagement with its words. They also illustrate Deuteronomy's tendency to think holistically about the acts that perpetuate moral formation, considering both the process of creation and the process of reception, in keeping with the book's emphasis on the community rather than the individual.

The instruction to "impress [these instructions] upon your children" regards moral formation as an intergenerational act. As discussed above in relation to the virtue of memory, the Torah uses storytelling to glean from the past inspiration for a particular way of being in the world. When parents engage in storytelling with their children, they reinforce their own commitment to this identity and reproduce it in future generations. Through storytelling, children come to understand what it means to be B'nai Yisrael and identify accordingly. In these ways, storytelling both reflects and reinforces the links that bind the community. Deuteronomy emphasizes its own role in being recounted to help the community maintain its identity, and to inspire similar storytelling practices within the families that make up the community.

A variety of sensory approaches provide the means for B'nai Yisrael to assimilate its teachings. The auditory is most prominent, as reflected in the injunction to hear (*shema*). Inscriptions on the doorposts and gates provide visual cues. Tactile reinforcement comes in the form of bindings on the hand and a "symbol" on the forehead. Deuteronomy mandates these acts in such a way as to emphasize, for example, both the tactile experience of making inscriptions and the visual experience of seeing them. True to its Hebrew name (*Devarim*, literally "words"), Deuteronomy emphasizes words. For people unable to read or write, like most of Deuteronomy's earliest audience, the multisensory engagement the book prescribes helps them connect with holy scripture and afford it a prominent place in their lives.

Deuteronomy's approach to the cultivation of virtue should also be understood in terms of the emphasis on loyalty in the paradigm of covenant and its political background. For example, its depiction of storytelling not only illuminates the cultivation of virtue in the paradigm of family, but also reflects the convention of discussing the history between the parties to certain kinds of ancient Near Eastern treaties. Another relevant convention concerns the elaboration of blessings and curses that will result from fidelity to or violation of the covenant, as found in Deuteronomy 27–28. The precise function of Deuteronomy's blessings and curses remains a matter of debate. As Richard Elliott Friedman observes, "The curses are four times the length of the blessings. . . . This list may convey that threats of punishment were thought to be more effective than promises of reward. Or it may convey the opposite: that threats are *less* effective, and therefore more are required."[14] In any case, Deuteronomy 27–28 manifests two strategies for moral formation. One involves the power of rhetoric: the emotional impact and motivational force generated by the numerousness of the blessings and curses and the vividness with which they are described. The other involves a performance in which tribes positioned on different mountains recite the blessings or the curses, dramatizing the choice between directions. Once again, a biblical text renders an abstract concept in material terms.

King David as an Exemplar of Virtue

When it comes to biblical exemplars of virtue, King David presents an interesting case study, because different paradigms construe his moral excellence in different ways. As found in the books of Samuel and Kings, the paradigm of covenant emphasizes David's loyalty to YHWH while readily depicting his flaws. In contrast, the priestly paradigm found in 1-2 Chronicles maintains sharp moral distinctions by depicting David as a man of impeccable character and always casting his actions in a positive light.

Samuel-Kings presents David as YHWH's handpicked king. After rejecting Saul, YHWH declares an intention to "seek out a man after His own heart" (1 Sam. 13:14) and sends Samuel to the house of Jesse to anoint one of his sons as king. Although David holds such low status in his own family that he is not initially included in Samuel's visit, YHWH explains, "For not as a man sees [does the LORD see]; man sees only what is visible, but the LORD sees into the heart" (1 Sam. 16:7) and identifies David as the chosen one. David displays moral excellence as envisioned by the paradigm of covenant, upholding YHWH's honor (e.g., 1 Sam. 17:46–47) and demonstrating devotion (e.g., 2 Sam. 6:21–22). YHWH expresses special love and loyalty toward David, pledging "I will be a father to [your offspring who reigns after you] and, he shall be a son to Me. When he does wrong, I will chastise him with the rod of men and the affliction of mortals; but I will never withdraw my favor from him as I withdrew it from Saul, whom I removed to make room for you. Your house and your kingship shall ever be secure before you; your throne shall be established forever" (2 Sam. 7:14–16).

This strong endorsement might lead readers to assume the best of David in narratives that could also be construed as critical. (It remains a matter of debate whether Samuel-Kings presents David as someone who maintained integrity even in difficult circumstances, or as someone akin to the head of a criminal organization, whose enemies conveniently disappeared while his hands ostensibly remained clean.) However, Samuel-Kings presents a particularly disturbing episode as a turning point in David's life. As summarized in the word of YHWH through the prophet Nathan:

> It was I who anointed you king over Israel and it was I who rescued you from the hand of Saul. I gave you your master's house and possession of your master's wives; and I gave you the House of Israel and Judah; and if that were not enough, I would give you twice as much more. Why then have you flouted the command of the LORD and done what displeases Him? You have put Uriah the Hittite to the sword; you took his wife and made her your wife and had him killed by the sword of the Ammonites. Therefore the sword shall never depart from your House—because you spurned me by taking the wife of Uriah and making her your wife." (2 Samuel 12:7–10)

Contemporary readers might focus on David's transgression of moral standards and identify such criminal and immoral acts as adultery and murder, among others. This prophetic utterance takes a different approach. In keeping with the paradigm of covenant, it emphasizes the way in which David's behavior constitutes disloyalty toward YHWH: "you spurned me." In keeping with the logic of the blessings and curses in Deuteronomy 27–28, this failure has consequences. David and his family suffer great turmoil.[15] Nevertheless, it does not sever the powerful bond between David and YHWH.

While the paradigm of covenant focuses on the ongoing imperative to live in accordance with the covenant relationship to YHWH and embraces moral ambiguity, the priestly paradigm operates with clearly differentiated categories. Thus, Chronicles clearly specifies

Saul's shortcomings as the reason that he lost the kingship (1 Chron. 10:13–14) but makes no mention of any fault of David's. The book includes YHWH's declaration of support for David (1 Chron. 17:7–14) but makes no mention of David's predatory acquisition of Bathsheba, a stark contrast to the prominence of that incident in Samuel-Kings. The portrayal of David in Chronicles is unequivocally positive.

In keeping with its priestly focus, Chronicles takes a greater interest than Samuel-Kings in the Ark of the Covenant's journey to Jerusalem, emphasizing David's ritually appropriate behavior. For example, "David gave orders that none but the Levites were to carry the Ark of God, for the LORD had chosen them to carry the Ark of the LORD and to minister to Him forever" (1 Chron. 15:2). The seemingly minor detail of David's attire also illustrates the way in which the priestly paradigm construes him as an exemplar of virtue. In Chronicles' rendition of the Ark's procession, "David . . . wore a robe of fine linen and a linen ephod. This rather dignified apparel does not fit well with the picture of the king leaping and dancing, thereby incurring the contempt of his wife Michal in 15:29 (cf. 2 Sam 5:20–23)."[16] Since Chronicles most likely draws on the narratives of Samuel-Kings, the inclusion of a detail that does not suit its narrative context thus provides a window into the distinctive perspective of the later text.

Conclusion

Qualities from the family paradigm for moral excellence like memory and being rooted in *toledot* are not often considered in contemporary discussions of moral formation, perhaps because of the modern tendency to regard identity as a passively received inheritance rather than as an active construction of individuals and communities. Nevertheless, those qualities do play a central role in structuring Jewish communal practices that emerge in later centuries. Memory and *toledot* are frequently invoked in prayer (e.g., references to "memory of the exodus from Egypt" and "our God and the God of our ancestors"). Genealogies are recited during services when calling people to the Torah and when offering prayers for healing. Memory plays a prominent role not only in Yahrzeit observances and other rituals of mourning, but also in the strategic way that the story of the Jewish people is recounted both formally (as in a Passover Seder) and informally (as in a D'var Torah about Juneteenth) to reinforce the community's identity, structure its relationship to its context, and guide its behavior.

The individualistic conception of religion that often prevails in Eurocentric contexts can lead people to overlook the importance of community in biblical literature.[17] As Joel Kaminsky explains, biblical texts that emphasize individual responsibility nuance rather than displace communal perspectives. He concludes,

> Individuals are important to God, but their individuality is derived from membership in the community at large. God is not concerned with the individual qua individual, but with the individual as a member of a particular nation, Israel. To see that this is the case one need only look through the Pentateuch, the deuteronomistic history, or the prophetic corpus to see that the fate of various individuals who are discussed in the text is always related to the history of the nation as a whole.[18]

In contrast, contemporary Jewish texts on moral formation frequently have an exclusive focus on individual attitudes and behaviors, not considering what it might look like for a community to be virtuous.[19]

The absence of the communal perspective in many contemporary texts reflects not only shifting cultural norms, but also the way that white privilege has shaped the reading of Jewish tradition. For example, in the context of the contemporary USA, being an individual is a privilege accorded to white people, but not to others, who are construed as representatives of the racial groups to which they belong and treated accordingly (as evidenced in the internment of Japanese-Americans but not German-Americans during World War II, for example). People whose experience is so profoundly shaped by the implications of their minoritized racial identity tend to be mindful of their social role and the ways in which it is enforced. In contrast, whiteness easily escapes conscious thought, all the more so because of the way in which it functions as an unmarked racial identity (i.e., white people are just called people while members of other racial groups are labeled as such). White privilege derives from social norms that obscure their own presence and impact and thereby do not register as subject to personal moral accountability. It thus contributes to a perspective on virtue that focuses on the individual as an isolable unit whose social position does not require explicit consideration. Reflecting different social norms, biblical literature can inspire contemporary readers to think beyond the individual and reckon with the collective identities that govern so much of their experience.

Biblical literature engages moral excellence from diverse social locations, another contribution that it makes to contemporary discussions of Jewish virtue ethics. For example, David's social location changes dramatically over the course of his story, from his obscure beginnings, through his rise to prominence under the capricious eye of Saul, to his exile, his eventual ascendance to the kingship, and the declining potency of his later years. Joseph and Moses experience similar shifts. Not all biblical exemplars of virtue eventually attain political power, however. The heroic midwives of Exodus 1 defy Pharaoh's order to kill Hebrew babies from an extremely vulnerable position. Not only are they not powerful; they may not even be Israelites. Exodus leaves it unclear whether they are Hebrews or Egyptians who work with Hebrews. Other texts present explicitly non-Israelite figures as exemplars of Israel's most cherished virtues. For example, 2 Samuel emphasizes that Uriah, the husband that David has killed in order to make Bathsheba his wife, is both a Hittite and David's moral superior. The diversity of these figures and their experiences provides a range of points of identification for readers, and it draws attention to the role of social location in the narratives through which they engage biblical conceptions of virtue.

Biblical literature is central to the development of Jewish thought, and many of the virtues discussed in this chapter have been central to Jewish communities. When considered on their own, however, biblical texts approach virtue in ways that are often very different from the ways that they are approached by many subsequent Jewish readers. There is much to learn from considering biblical literature independently of the ways it has been repackaged by later readers.

Notes

1. Jonathan Sheehan, *The Enlightenment Bible: Translation, Scholarship, Culture* (Princeton, NJ: Princeton University Press, 2005), x.

2. Shaye J. D. Cohen, *The Beginnings of Jewishness: Boundaries, Varieties, Uncertainties* (Berkeley: University of California Press, 1999), 104.

3. As Juha Pakkala remarks, "The influence of political and loyalty treaties on Deuteronomy is uncontested, but the exact nature and date of this influence is controversial," "The Influence of Treaties on Deuteronomy, Exclusive Monolatry, and Covenant Theology," *Hebrew Bible and Ancient Israel* 8, no. 2 (2019): 159. Pakkala suggests that Deuteronomy derived the concept of exclusive monolatry from the treaties (183).

4. Sara J. Milstein explains, "By prescribing the same penalty for a disobedient son, an adulterous woman, or a worshiper of celestial bodies, these later scribes innovatively imported the concept of law into the religious sphere." *Making a Case: The Practical Roots of Biblical Law* (New York: Oxford University Press, 2021), 88. Milstein describes Deuteronomy as "a pseudo-'law collection' that had as its primary interest not law but instead the mandate of exclusive monolatry" (156). In other words, the book deploys legal material for the theological purpose of encouraging loyalty to YHWH.

5. Mary Douglas, *Leviticus as Literature* (Oxford: Oxford University Press, 2000), 18.

6. S. Tamar Kamionkowski, *Leviticus* (Collegeville, MN: Liturgical Press, 2018), 199.

7. Contemporary interpreters often put priestly texts to ethical use in a way that does not reflect the distinct interests of those texts. For example, regarding the sexual prohibitions of Leviticus 18, Alex Weissman remarks, "There may be a moral valence in these prohibitions, but the emphasis remains primarily on maintaining Israelite distinctiveness. Sexual morality, if present at all, is simply a means to an ethic of distinctiveness." In Kamionkowski, *Leviticus*, 180.

8. Joel S. Kaminsky, *Yet I Loved Jacob: Reclaiming the Biblical Concept of Election* (Nashville: Abingdon Press, 2007), 74.

9. Amanda Beckenstein Mbuvi, *Belonging in Genesis: Biblical Israel and the Politics of Identity Formation* (Waco, TX: Baylor University Press, 2016).

10. Nahum M. Sarna, *Exploring Exodus: The Heritage of Biblical Israel* (New York: Schocken, 1986), 203–204.

11. Douglas, *Leviticus as Literature*, 57, citing Menahem Haran, *Temples and Temple-Service in Ancient Israel* (Oxford: Clarendon Press, 1977), 165.

12. Douglas, *Leviticus as Literature*, 58.

13. Douglas, *Leviticus as Literature*, 79.

14. Richard Elliott Friedman, *Commentary on the Torah, with a New English Translation* (San Francisco: Harper Collins, 2001), 648.

15. This narrative reflects a cultural perspective according to which suffering for another family member's crime made as much sense as an entire sports team facing negative consequences because of a foul committed by a single player.

16. John J. Collins, *Introduction to the Hebrew Bible*, 3rd ed. (Minneapolis: Fortress, 2018), 447.

17. Cf. Joel S. Kaminsky, *Corporate Responsibility in the Hebrew Bible* (Sheffield, UK: Sheffield Academic Press, 1995), 179.

18. Kaminsky, *Corporate Responsibility*, 137.

19. Cf. Kaminsky, who remarks, "The biblical writers were aware that our individuality can only be understood in relation to the various collectivities in which we participate and that being human means that we are linked to other people through the consequences of their actions. But this does not mean that the Bible ignores the importance of the individual. In fact . . . the Bible has a very nuanced theology of the relationship between the individual and the community. Rather than playing off the more individualistic passages within the Bible against those that espouse a more corporate view, one can see the way in which these elements qualify and complement each other. Inasmuch as the biblical view of the relationship between the individual and the community takes account of both poles, but places more emphasis upon the community and the individual's responsibility to that community, it can provide a much needed corrective to current ethical thinking that seems to treat society as nothing more than a collection of unrelated individuals who just happen to live together." *Corporate Responsibility*, 187–88.

Chapter 2

Philo of Alexandria

CARLOS LÉVY

Philo's life is both a mystery and a paradox. He wrote a huge number of treatises and had a prominent role in the life of his community, but we know very little about his biography. Even his dates are debated, perhaps 20 BCE–45 CE. As was stressed by Greg E. Sterling in his general introduction to the Philo of Alexandria Series, we are much better informed about his family than about him.[1] He was born into one of the most powerful Jewish families in Egypt. His brother Julius Gaius Alexander, among many other activities, was an *alabarch,* a word that means "general controller of taxes." As his name indicates, he had Roman citizenship. This did not prevent him from being a citizen of the *polis* of Alexandria, which had a special status in Egypt. Alexander had close relations both with the Roman imperial family and with the Herodian dynasty. He was himself a quite generous donor to Jewish institutions, covering the Temple doors of Jerusalem with gold and silver. His older son, Tiberius Julius Alexander, had an incredible career. He held many Roman governorships, and he was Titus's chief of staff during the Jewish war (66–70 CE). Philo himself seems to have had a much more discrete life. Nonetheless, he was a prominent figure in his community, since he was designated to lead the Jewish delegation to Rome after the first pogrom in Alexandria in 38 CE. For the first time in history, Jews were confined to a ghetto where they suffered ill-treatment and large-scale massacres. The description by Philo of his confrontation with Caligula, perhaps the most insane of the Roman emperors, is an absolutely fascinating text, since it symbolizes the confrontation between two wholly heterogeneous worlds.[2] When Caligula, after a long delay, agreed to receive the two embassies, that of the Greeks and that of the Jews, the first thing he asked the Jews was: "Are you the god-haters who do not believe me to be a god, a god acknowledged among all the other nations, but [who believe a god] not to be named by you?" (*Legatio* 353). Though a psychopath, the emperor knew that this question was the most critical one, the one that could most easily destabilize his interlocutors. Philo and the other ambassadors were allowed to go back to Alexandria after Caligula's death and this temporarily put an end to a dramatic situation.

The Representations of Virtue: Rachel and Sarah

There are many passages in Philo in which the superiority of men over women is affirmed in a manner that is shocking for us, but quite common in his time, as an allegory for the relationship of the active virtues to the virtues of the senses. As an example, he says in *Quod omnis probus liber sit,* 117 that women and adolescents have only a limited reason. We find the same kind of assertion in *Legatio ad Gaium,* 319–20, where he says that generally women are unable to go beyond sensations in their thoughts. When he wants to make an exception about Julia Augusta, Augustus' wife, he says that she managed to "masculinize" her reason, so that it was able to perceive intelligible items as clearly as sensitive objects. At the same time, while the word "virtue" has a Latin root, *virtus,* which alludes to the generic difference between a man and a woman, and to the superiority of the man, the Geek term *aretē* only means the perfection of a nature. But Philo is a master of allegory who, though never expressing a doubt about the historical reality of the biblical characters, turns them into symbols of ethical and spiritual principles.[3] For example, in his allegorical system, Rachel represents the senses and the unreasoning part of our nature, but she is their virtue, that is, the most reasonable form of them. This implies that, although "Rachel" is far from ethical perfection, "she trains us to despise all that should be held of little account, [such as] reputation and wealth and pleasure, which the vulgar mass of ordinary men who accept the verdict of dishonest hearsay and the equally dishonest court of the other senses, judge worthy of their admiration and their efforts."[4] The difference between the sensitive virtues and the active virtues is clear. The former is a kind of auto-regulation of sensations. The later require the intervention of reason.

As a virtue, although being the virtue of the irrational parts of the soul, Rachel was deemed worthy to marry Jacob, the symbol of the active virtues.[5] Their son, Joseph, is of a mixed nature, such that he will never reach the perfection of his father: "For there is manifest in him, on the one hand, the rational strain of self-control, which is of the masculine family, fashioned after his father Jacob: manifest, again, is the irrational strain of sense-perception, assimilated to what he derives from his mother."[6] This passage shows the complexity of Philo's position on the problem, much debated in Hellenistic schools, of the predispositions to virtue: Was it necessary to stress heredity, nature, or education? While in the case of Abraham, or in that of Moses, nothing is said of their heredity, in the case of Joseph, to be the son of Rachel was the main obstacle on the way to wisdom, but it did not prevent him from achieving political virtue.

Actually, there is a Philonic paradox: although women are psychologically and ethically devalued, they are used for the representation of ethical virtue. It is said of Leah that she is the symbol of the rational part of soul, since "she teaches us to avoid the rough and uneven path, impassable to virtue-loving souls, and to walk smoothly along the level highway where there are no stumbling-blocks or aught that can make the foot to slip."[7] Still more interesting is the case of Sarah. As demonstrated by Dorothy Sly, when Philo evokes her as a historical character, he strips her of both her strong personality and her feminine characteristics.[8] And when her biblical image is different from his own conception of femininity, for example when she gives an order to Abraham, he masculinizes or transforms her into the symbol of virtue. In *De Abrahamo* 247, he writes about her: "Many a story I could relate in praise of this man (*tēs anthrōpou*)." He does not use the word *anēr*, which means "a man" in a biological sense, but *anthrōpos*, which is more ambiguous, since it can either mean "a human being," or can be a synonym of *anēr*. When she becomes the symbol of wisdom, Sly says, "the effect of allegory is both to elevate her and to dissolve her."[9] Can we say, however, that "the person Sarah whom Philo allows to emerge is only a shadow of the Biblical

Sarah"?[10] It seems less excessive to affirm that through that person he tries to elaborate a reflection on the perfection of human nature through the contradictory archetypes of masculinity and femininity.

Cardinal Virtues in the *Treatise of Virtues*

Philo's main elucidation of the virtues is in his *Treatise of Virtues* (*De virtutibus*),[11] where he combined the four cardinal virtues, while adapting it to the philosophy of its time and allowing openings toward specifically Jewish conceptions, as with regard to repentance. The *Treatise of Virtues,* to which many different titles are assigned by the manuscripts, belong to the *Exposition of the Law,* one of the three great series of Philonic works, with the *Allegorical Commentary* and the *Quaestiones in Genesim et Exodum.* Its date is uncertain, although it is generally accepted that it was written in a period of intense tension between the Jewish community and the Alexandrian Greeks. This is an element that could lead to the conclusion that it was redacted during the civil unrest of 38–41 CE. In any case, Philo's reflection is not an abstract one; it deals with the problem of the tension between particularism and universalism. The four "discreet sections" generally admitted by editors, although with a lot of interrogations are "On Courage," "On Humanity," "On Repentance," and "On Nobility." The division of the virtues in *Treatise of Virtues* is different from the quadripartite one—justice, courage, prudence and moderation—that the Stoics have inherited from Plato and Aristotle.[12] In many places Philo is giving an answer to those who accused the Jews of hating the rest of humanity, this accusation arising especially among the political and cultural Greek aristocracy of Alexandria, Stoicism had a predominant place in the Alexandrine philosophical panorama, as we can guess from characters such as Apion or Chaeremon, who both had an eminent role in the cultural and political life of their city. Philo's strategy aims at the subversion of Stoic concepts.

(1) "On Courage": The treatise on courage, defining it, in the Socratic and Stoic tradition, as a serene and thoughtful response to danger, can be interpreted in the context of antisemitic riots, the climax of which was the awful pogrom of 38 CE. Courage is the full expression of reason in front of dangers. The aim is to prevent physical strength and the use of violence from being confused with this virtue. Philo's

theoretical conception of courage is generally a very intellectualistic one. When in *De vita Mosis*. 1.44, he praises Moses for having killed a bloodthirsty Egyptian, he says that it was a good action (*euages*), not a brave action. The only mention of courage in the *De vita Mosis* occurs in 2.216, where Philo says that synagogues are the real schools of all virtues, among which is courage.

(2) "On Nobility": The question of nobility (*euphuia*) was much debated in this school. The problem was to define precisely the respective roles of innate and acquired characteristics. It became more crucial in the Hellenistic role, where *phusis*, nature, was the only criterion. Some Stoics gave importance to the good nature, while others preferred to stress the role of education. Philo does not enter into this debate; he connects nobility neither with social prestige nor with natural predispositions, but with the practice of virtue, which can conflict with nature, as when Abraham accepted the sacrifice of his son.[13]

(3) "On Repentance": Divergences from Stoic virtues include repentance, *teshuva*, which is considered a Jewish virtue, but it was certainly not a Stoic one. In Stoicism, to live wisely is to live in the present, such that those who prefer hope or repentance to lucid reflection on the moment were considered as beings subjected to passion, and therefore in some way insane. For Philo, repentance is the ability to recognize one's fault, to confess it, and to admit that God has no responsibility for the fault (*Legum allegoriae* 2.78). Repentance is always the victory of reason over passions, but it needs the help of God, who prefers to give time to the sinner instead of punishing him or her immediately (*Legum allegoriae* 2.106)

(4) "On Humanity": Last, but certainly not least, is the virtue of humanity (*philanthrōpia*). Here Philo's method is subtly and fiercely dialectical. For the Stoics, a human being was always the center of a set of concentric circles: family, city, nation, and finally humanity. The principle was that each human being had to be considered as a brother/sister, not from a biological point of view, but because of their common rationality. Philo does not reject this principle. He strives to demonstrate with many arguments that the Law of Moses is the best example of *philanthrōpia*, since the prophet recommends one to love not only Jews, but foreigners as well. He adds many examples proving that Moses loved all humanity equally. All this could have been approved by a Stoic philosopher who would have concluded that Moses had had the same intuitions as Zeno, the founder of Stoicism,

many centuries before him. But Philo was not content with parallelism; he wanted to show Mosaic *influence* on Zeno. In the *Probus* 57, he says that "[w]e may well suppose that the fountain from which Zeno drew this thought was the law-book of the Jews." In order to show that the Jewish *philanthrōpia* was much greater than the Stoic one, he extends it to animals and even vegetables. This was absolutely contrary to the Stoic dogma of *oikieiōsis,* whereby for a human being there can be no duty of justice or humanity toward an animal. In the rivalry with Stoicism, Philo goes beyond controversy, he raises a fundamental objection: Why would animals be excluded from human duties? His own response as a Jew is that naturalism limits the human possibilities, while the word of God opens greater possibilities for benevolence and justice.

The Paths of Virtue

Progress and Perfection

As a Jew, Philo did not discuss the ethical perfection of the patriarchs. But as a man raised in the *paideia,* the Greek educational system, he had to give a conceptual explanation of the ways leading to perfection.

In Stoicism, ethical progress does not have a simply linear route. It is not because the person in progress accomplishes all the acts in harmony that he or she becomes ethically perfect. The sage is the exceptional human being whose individual reason is in perfect harmony with the perfection of the universe. In Philo, however, ethical progress is not a matter of nature. In the *De sacrificiis* 120, he explains that Reuben, the first son of Jacob, will not be given precedence even though he is the eldest son of Jacob. It will instead be given to Levi, just as it was given to Jacob, who had precedence over the firstborn Esau. Why? because Reuben represented only the natural abilities of a human being, while Levi's life was one of perfect virtue. Reuben can strive and progress without attaining the service of God. In other words, Reuben lacks the transcendent dimension that Levi, as God's servant, represents. Another example is that of Jacob in the *De ebrietate* 82. Jacob, as we have seen, is for Philo "the Man of practice," and in this passage he is said to "be in the last bout of his exercises of virtue." But the achievement of his progress does not depend on him, or at least not only on him. It is God who decides to change his name, saying that he will no more be called Jacob, but Israel, since "He had willed to plant eyes in his understanding that he might see clearly what before he had grasped by hearing, for sight is more trustworthy than the ears." Philo does not despise the importance of nature in the process of ethical progress. Rather, he denies that nature is the *alpha* and *omega* of the reflection on ethics, which is always subordinated to the acceptation of divine transcendence.

JUDAISM AND POLITICS: JOSEPH, THE STATESMAN

Joseph is probably the most complex of Biblical individuals in Philo's work. As a son of Jacob, symbol of the active virtues, he embodies his father's resistance to evil in the famous episode of Potiphar's wife. At the same time, however, Joseph remained in Egypt, that is, for Philo in a land of sin, where animals were worshipped. For Philo, this was the greatest abomination imaginable. Joseph gets a taste for politics, he is a good and just ruler, but he lives in a world that is not that of truth but that of only plausible and probable appearances. His political virtue means to bring justice and prosperity to the whole Egyptian nation. The complexity of his character is expressed by Philo through the contradiction between two treatises. His image is very positive in the *De Josepho,* where he is the type of the excellent ruler, both forward-looking and concerned about the well-being of Pharaoh's subjects. On the other hand, in the treatise about dreams (*De somniis*) Philo is extremely harsh on him. He says that Joseph means "addition," and he presents him as someone who lives in dreams, "who to what is genuine adds what is counterfeit, to what is appropriate what is alien, to what is true what is false, to what is sufficient what is excessive, to vitality, debauchery, to life's maintenance, vanity." It is easier to understand Philo's interpretation of the character of Joseph if we compare the statesman with the representation of Moses. While Joseph decided to remain in Egypt and to govern the country, Moses, though having been adopted by the family of Pharaoh, led his people out of this country. In the exodus, he took with him the bones of Joseph, who had left the request to be buried outside Egypt. Joseph humanely applied the laws of Pharaoh, while Moses applied the Law of God. In Philo's work, Joseph is an anticipation of Moses, an imperfect and in some aspects a disappointing anticipation.

The Role of the Virtues in Philo's Worldview

Philonic Virtue and Greek Philosophy

The *Thesaurus Linguae Graecae* counts 673 occurrences of the word *aretē* in Philo. It is without any doubt a central concept in his thought, perhaps the main one. *Aretē* and *virtue* are semantically different. The Latin word *virtus* originally means the highest quality of a man, *qua* man. It implies force in all the meanings of the term, while *aretē* means the perfection of human nature, in the most general meaning. The problem for Philo was that he stood at the crossroads of three different conceptions of *aretē*.

Being a Jew with very little knowledge of Hebrew, he had to define how the Jewish concept of a virtuous man, that is, a man living in accord with the precepts of the Torah, could be expressed with the words of the Greek language, so deeply imbued with philosophy. For him the translation of the Law in Greek was as essential as the gift of Torah on the Sinai.[14] In his work the characters who embody the virtues are Jewish, but their attitudes are expressed and interpreted with Greek notions.

As an inhabitant of the Roman Empire, where Stoicism had become predominant, he had to face an immanentist system in which the rational nature of the universe was the one God. In this doctrine, nature arranged everything in order to make the human being, the only other rational being in the universe, as perfect as God. How then to explain imperfection? The Stoics said that there was no other ontological reason for human imperfection than a misuse of human liberty. In their absolutely deterministic doctrine, there was a very complex universal network of causes, with different statuses. Some of them were main causes; the others auxiliary causes. That distinction was used by them in order to create a space for human liberty. The *sophos*, the Stoic sage was said by them to be extremely rare but absolutely perfect.

Though Platonism is much less systematic than Stoicism, it can be said that in general it establishes an ontological difference between human nature and perfection. In the *Timaeus*, the universe was created by the Demiurge as a copy of transcendent Forms. To be a philosopher, a *philosophos*, was to be a lover of wisdom, to strive for a perfection that is not of this world.

Three words are helpful in order to understand Philo's similarities and differences with respect to Greek ethics: (1) *nomos* (law), (2) *oikeiōsis* (adaptation), (3) *omoiōsis* (imitation). (1) As to *nomos*, Philo was immensely proud of the law given by God to Israel. He says in *De vita Mosis* 2.44 that if historical circumstances became better for the Jewish people, "each nation would abandon its peculiar ways, and, throwing overboard their ancestral customs, turn to honouring our laws." The idea of a cosmopolis gathering all humans under a unique law had strong Stoic resonances but nobody before the Alexandrian Jews had thought that the law revealed by God to a particular nation could become a law for all mankind.[15] There are in Philo many elements that seem to be close to Stoic universalism, but the background is different, since no Stoic had never imagined a special relation between God and a particular nation.

(2) As to adaptation, for the Stoics nature was like a house (*oikos*) in which everything was planned to guide the human being to perfection, and thus to happiness, by adapting himself or herself to the universal rationality of the world. Wisdom, virtue, and happiness are totally synonymous in Stoicism. They are all the three founded on the idea of a progressive adaptation to the universal rationality of the world. Philo was reluctant to use the concept of *oikeiōsis*. He used it rarely and always with significant semantic differences. For him *logos* was only one of the powers of an absolutely transcendent God, Whom he never confused with nature.

(3) As to imitation, a keyword in Platonism, Plato wrote in his *Theaetetus* (176b) a sentence that became the key to the ethics of Middle Platonism, the period of dogmatic Platonism corresponding to the two first centuries of Christian era: "We ought to try to escape from earth to the dwelling of the gods as quickly as we can; and to escape is to become like God, so far as this is possible; and to become like God is to become righteous and holy and wise." Philo quotes this passage in his *De fuga* (63), where he says that it was written by "a man highly esteemed." But if it is true that he feels unquestionably closer to the Platonic transcendence than to Stoic immanence, for him this flight is not a purely theoretical concept, nor simply a personal attitude. It cannot be considered without a reference at least two worldly flights: that of Abraham and the exodus of the Jewish people. Plato couldn't imagine the flight of a whole nation, nor was it possible to him to imagine it without connecting it directly to the quality of an individual

soul. By contrast, the Philonic reflection on virtues, at the same time that it is expressed with Greek philosophical concepts, never strays from the ethical models given by the Bible.

VIRTUES IN THE BIBLICAL CONTEXT

These are the main elements of Philo's use of the Greek philosophical concepts that he needed to develop his conception of virtues. But what about his reading of the Biblical creation stories and the inclusion of the virtues in his account of the creation? Consider *On the Creation* (*De opificio mundi*), Philo's retelling of the Genesis story.[16]

In section 81, he gives a very pessimistic view of the life of human being in a world where incessant natural disasters force him or her to work hard in order to earn his livelihood. This disorder of nature, he says, is similar to the chaos in human souls. But he adds that if human beings were more virtuous and succeeded in overcoming negative passions, "we might entertain the hope that God, who is a lover of virtue and fine behaviour and is moreover well disposed to humankind, will cause the good things of life to be supplied to the race spontaneously and ready for consumption" (81). This gives a very special responsibility to humans. God intervenes in their human life. He is the one who can change the laws of nature, but human beings have to deserve it and, in any case, the divine liberty is absolute. Humans can only have "hope."

In section 153, we find a fine description of the Garden of Eden, about which he says: "In the case of the divine garden of delights all the plants in fact possess soul and reason, bearing fruit in form of the virtues and in addition uncorrupted understanding and keenness of mind by which what is good and what is evil is recognized, as well as life without disease and indestructibility and whatever is of a similar kind to these."[17] Most interesting is the fact that fruits bear the form of virtues in a world where all the plants possess soul and reason. This proves that one of the functions of virtue is to unify the world, as if the ontological distinctions that seem to structure the world are merely illusions.

The main aspect of the inclusion of virtues in a biblical context is, however, Philo's most famous division of three types of men who strive towards the good.[18] In this exegesis Abraham represents the effort to know, since he abandoned astrology to migrate to "real nature study"; that is, he went from the world to the maker of the world.[19] Jacob is the symbol of the active virtue. He goes first to Laban, then he leaves Laban's house, which is a symbol of a materialist perception of world, to go toward Isaac. And Isaac himself "belongs to the new race, superior to reason and truly divine" (*De Fuga et inuentione* 168). He does not have to undergo the same trials as the other patriarchs. At the same time Philo adopts the Platonic and Stoic idea that one cannot have one virtue without having them all. From this point of view, the division of three types of perfect men is above all a kind of phenomenology of perfection in scripture, rather than the positing of an ontological distinction.

Conclusion: A Transcendent Humanism

What kind of Jew was Philo? Certainly a deeply sincere one, who thought that the Bible was wholly true and that the truth of God's word could be read both with a literal interpretation and with an allegorical one, in Greek or in Chaldean, a term he uses to refer to the Hebrew language. He respected the laws of Shabbat and the Jewish festivals. He had an intense love of the people of Israel, *ahavat* Israel, in all the dimensions of the concept: the love of his Alexandrian community, which he bravely defended in front of Caligula, and of all the Jews who lived in Egypt, especially the *therapeutai* whose ascetic life he describes in the *On the Contemplative Life* (*De vita contemplativa*); the love of Jerusalem and of its Temple; the love of the whole diaspora; the love of all mankind, since he thought that one day all the humans would adopt the Law of Moses. At the same time, Philo's faith is in a Judaism without messianism and it is difficult to discern his model of the afterlife.[20] Under this condition, virtue was for him the main, and perhaps the one, access road to transcendence, an itinerary during which the individual had to perceive its *oudeneia,* that is, its nothingness when it tries to exist by itself, without understanding that everyone depends on God. For rabbinic Judaism, the attempt to integrate Greek philosophy in the interpretation of the Bible, itself translated into Greek, was an error, tragically demonstrated by the disappearance of the Jewish community of Alexandria, ca. 117 CE. But even if it was an error, let us remember Rabbi Nachman who stressed that going astray could sometimes be necessary to find the true way.

Notes

1. Mireille Hadas-Lebel, *Philo of Alexandria: A Thinker in the Jewish Diaspora* (Leiden: Brill, 2012), 54–58; Greg E. Sterling, "General Introduction: The Philo of Alexandria Commentary Series," in Walter T. Wilson, *Philo of Alexandria: "On Virtues"* (Leiden: Brill, 2011), ix–xiv; Maren Niehoff, *Philo of Alexandria: An Intellectual Biography* (New Haven, CT: Yale University Press, 2018), 1–68.

2. E. G. Huzar, "Emperor Worship in Julio-Claudian Egypt," in *Aufstieg und Niedergang der römischen Welt*, part 2, vol. 18.5 (Berlin: de Gruyter, 1995), 3092–43; Louis H. Feldman, *Jew and Gentile in the Ancient World* (Princeton, NJ: Princeton University Press, 1993); Ellen Birnbaum, "Philo on the Greeks: A Jewish Perspective on Culture and Society in First Century Alexandria," *Studia Philonica Annual* 13 (2001): 37–58; Pieter W. van der Horst, *Philo's Flaccus: The First Pogrom* (Leiden: Brill, 2003), 22–24.

3. On Philo's use of allegory, see David Runia, "Etymology as an Allegorical Technique in Philo of Alexandria," *Studia Philonica Annual* 16 (2004): 101–21.

4. Philo, *De congressu eruditionis gratia* 27.

5. On Jacob, see Elisa Uusimäki, "A Mind in Training: Philo of Alexandria on Jacob's Spiritual Exercises," *Journal for the Study of the Pseudepigrapha* 27, no. 4 (2018): 265–88.

6. Philo, *De somniis* 2.15–16.

7. Philo, *De congressu* 28. See William Loader, *Philo, Josephus, and the Testaments on Sexuality: Attitudes towards Sexuality* (Grand Rapids, MI: Eerdmans, 2011), 163.

8. Dorothy Sly, *Philo's Perception of Women* (Atlanta, GA: Scholars Press, 2020), 152: "The effect of allegory thus is to elevate and to dissolve her."

9. Sly, *Philo's Perception*, 152.

10. Sly, *Philo's Perception*, 154.

11. See the introduction to, translation of, and commentary on *On Virtues* in Wilson, *Philo of Alexandria*.

12. Philo adopts this division in *Leg.* 1.57, where the four rivers of paradise represent the four traditional virtues.

13. Philo, *Abr.* 193.

14. Philo, *Mos.* 2.37–38.

15. On the question of Philo's universalism, see Katell Berthelot, *Philanthrōpia judaica: Le débat autour de la "misanthropie" des lois juives dans l'Antiquité* (Leiden: Brill, 2003).

16. A new interpretation of the *De opificio mundi* as a general introduction to the whole Philonic work is given by E. Matusova, "Genesis 1–2 in *De opificio mundi* and Its Exegetical Context," *Studia Philonica Annual* 31 (2019): 57–94.

17. Some manuscripts record *adiaphtoros* ("uncorrupted") and others *adiaphoforos* (neutral).

18. See Carlos Lévy, "Philo's Ethics," in *The Cambridge Companion to Philo*, ed. Adam Kamesar (Cambridge: Cambridge University Press, 2009), 164–65.

19. Philo, *Quis rerum divinarum heres sit* 98.

20. The thesis of Philo as a thinker of reincarnation has been defended by Sami Yli-Karjanmaa, *Reincarnation in Philo of Alexandria* (Atlanta, GA: SBL Press, 2015), but it is controversial.

Chapter 3

Titus Flavius Josephus

CLIFFORD ORWIN

> For those who think rightly must observe with exactness their own laws of piety, while not reviling those of others.
>
> —Josephus, *Against Apion* 2.144[1]

> While it is true that Josephus emphasizes, in his Preface to the *Antiquities* (1.14), that the main lesson to be learned from his work is that G-d rewards those who obey him and punishes those who do not. . . . Josephus thereafter generally downgrades the role of G-d in order to emphasize the virtues and achievements of his biblical heroes.
>
> —Louis H. Feldman, *Josephus's Interpretation of the Bible*[2]

Yosef ben Mattityahu (ca. 37–ca. 100 CE) was born in Jerusalem, the son of a father of the upper priestly caste and of a mother of royal (i.e., Hasmonean) descent.[3] Presumably educated as a Sadducee, he was acclaimed (according to his own account) a child prodigy of learning.[4] While still an adolescent, however, he decided to make a trial of all

The author thanks Logan M. Gates for invaluable research assistance in preparing this chapter.

three main Jewish sects of the time. Despite prolonged study with a desert master, he declared himself a Pharisee.[5] As a young man he participated in an important embassy to Rome.[6] As hostilities loomed, he was assigned to organize the defenses of turbulent Galilee.[7] After many ups and downs, he surrendered to the Romans at Jotapata in 69 CE.[8] He lived thereafter as a client of the Flavian dynasty, first in Judaea as a privileged prisoner in the retinues of Vespasian and his son and successor in command, Titus.[9] After the war he lived at Rome as an imperial freedman, taking as custom required the *praenomen* and *nomen* of his emancipator Vespasian, Titus Flavius, to which he added the Latinized Josephus. He wrote prolifically in Greek, first the enormously influential *Jewish War*, later *Antiquities of the Jews* and *Against Apion,* in which he defended the Jews against their pagan detractors, and his *Life,* in which he defended himself against his (mostly) Jewish ones. Lost to the Jewish tradition, his works were preserved by Christianity.

The Importance of Ethics to Josephus

You had never thought of Flavius Josephus as a proponent of virtue ethics? Nor, before our editors had prodded me, had I. Yet there is a strong prima facie case for doing so. For Alasdair MacIntyre, the most celebrated proponent of virtue ethics in our time, the very model of a tradition of such ethics is the classical and teleological one that reaches its perfection in Aristotle. As is clear from Josephus's writings, this tradition played a major role in shaping him as a teacher of ethics. At the same time MacIntyre, as a Christian and eventually a Thomist, promotes a synthesis of the classical tradition and the Christian one. This would require reconciling the Bible and Aristotle by showing how "only a life constituted by obedience to law could be such as to exhibit fully those virtues without which humans can't reach their *telos*."[10] According to MacIntyre this merger of the pagan and prophetic traditions was the project of St. Thomas Aquinas. Yet it had also been that, mutatis mutandis (i.e., substituting the Hebrew Bible for the Christian one) of Josephus, as later it would be that of Thomas's illustrious predecessor Maimonides. We can say then not only that Josephus remains, after Philo of Alexandria (ca. 20 BCE–ca. 50 CE), our earliest extant Jewish practitioner of virtue ethics in its classical sense, but also (again after Philo) the earliest extant attempt to elaborate a distinctly Jewish version of such an ethics by merging it with the Torah.

True, Josephus presents himself as a historian, not a philosopher, and composed no treatise on ethics. Still, he was a defender of the Torah and, as we might say, the Jewish way of life, and to defend the Torah one must interpret it. At the core of the Torah, in Josephus's understanding as in our own, is a teaching concerning virtue. Whether the Torah may be said to teach virtue ethics was the concern of an earlier chapter of this volume. Yet such was certainly the claim of Josephus. While a Jewish writer first and last, his interpretation of the Jewish tradition owed much to Hellenic thought. And Hellenic ethics, whether as presented by Plato, Xenophon, Aristotle, and Theophrastus or by the Hellenistic schools that succeeded them, was the very model of a virtue ethics. Josephus's thought, which presents itself as syncretic, either finds this approach in the Torah or seeks to reconcile the two.[11]

Josephus wrote not treatises but narratives, including two counternarratives, apologetic writings devoted to refuting the narratives of others. Despite differences of genre and emphasis among his works, all fall into the category that Aristotle would describe as history, which is to say accounts of sequences of actual particular events. (These include the nine books of the *Antiquities* that retell the events of the Hebrew Bible as part of a history of the Jewish people up to Josephus's own time, in which Josephus has thus assimilated a collection of Hebrew books to a Hellenic genre.) His writings therefore contain systematic treatments neither of virtue as such nor of any particular virtue. He treats these subjects as befits a historian. They figure in his writings as they affect the fates of both peoples and individuals.

In his treatment of virtue Josephus thus conforms to the classical historical tradition, which privileged the virtues of statesmanship and the primacy of the political. He also follows his classical models in attending above all to the question of the regime, the comprehensive ordering of a society from which its distinctive character follows, including its prevailing virtues and vices. Josephus's remarkable innovation is to reinterpret the Torah as such a regime. It is the Torah so considered—its founding, its vicissitudes, its fall, and its [future] redemption—that is the ultimate subject of each of his narratives.[12] The virtues and vices of his particular characters relate to their roles in this grand narrative of Jewish history from Creation to his day (and beyond). His argument on behalf of the Torah is that it originated in the highest virtue (whether divine or human) and that it has surpassed all other systems of legislation in inculcating virtue in its practitioners. Josephus's loftiest praise of the Torah in this regard occurs in *Against Apion*, where he responds to pagan charges that the Torah has bred only vices. His virtue ethics is therefore inseparable from his praise of the Jewish law and the way of life dictated by it.

The Virtues Most Important to Josephus, the Manner of Their Cultivation, and Their Exemplars

As suggested, Josephus's fundamental criterion for virtue is political, but political in an exalted sense. On the one hand, for him as for other classical writers, virtue serves the political regime, as the sum of those qualities that tend to its preservation, and therefore is relative to that regime. On the other hand, for him as for these other writers, politics also aims at virtue in a more exalted sense. This is virtue as the full development of human capacities and with it the achievement of human happiness. Virtue in this sense does not simply serve the regime: on the contrary the regime should serve it. Society exists not only to preserve the lives, property, and freedom of the citizens, but also to achieve the good life through the moral education of the citizens.

Josephus's claim is that no regime has met these exacting criteria so well as the Jewish one prescribed by the Torah. This claim is the key to his strategy as an apologist. Through it he seeks to turn pagan hatred of the Jews on its head. For the enemies of the Jews in those days had argued that the Jews were uniquely perverse and vicious not because they had departed from their laws but from their very schooling in them.[13] The Jews, their laws, the vices or virtues of their way of life: as these themes had been inseparable for Josephus's adversaries, so must they be for him.

Among other things the enemies of the Jews had impugned and misrepresented the sacrificial cult. Josephus devotes considerable energy to defending it. So, for example, in the *Jewish War*, as Michael Tuval has recently stressed, Josephus emphasizes violations of ritual law as the crucial transgressions of the warring factions in Jerusalem during the Great Rebellion. According to Tuval this demonstrates that at this stage of Josephus's career his standards remain priestly. In the later writings, by contrast, all written with apologetic intention at a greater remove from the catastrophe of 70 CE, Josephus stresses rather the "ethical" aspect of Judaism. (Tuval casts this as Josephus's transition from "Jerusalem priest" to "Diaspora Jew.")[14]

Tuval's reading has much to be said for it. There are certainly differences of emphasis between the *War* and Josephus's later writings. Yet if only because Josephus's treatment of virtue remains so fragmentary in the *War*, it is questionable whether we can draw conclusions from it as firm as Tuval's. We could argue, moreover, that the broader problem that Josephus presents as fatal to the defense of Jerusalem is its subversion by the *stasis* or civil strife that rages inside the city. The transgressions of ritual law are primarily the consequences of this strife.[15] So viewed they still signal the primacy of piety for Josephus, but of piety in a much broader sense than respect for the ritual law: piety as the foundation of civic virtue as such.

This interpretation of the debacle of 70 CE would bridge much of the gap between Josephus's earlier and later teachings. Fatal would have been the rebels' lack not of different virtues than those praised in the later writings but of the very same ones. According to Josephus, his account of the Jewish regime (*politeuma*) in *Against Apion* intends to show that the Jews possess "laws excellently designed to foster piety, community among themselves and humanity toward everyone else, as well as justice, fortitude in toils, and contempt of death."[16] Clearly the rebels had persisted in the last two of these virtues, while proving deficient in the first four.

This passage furnishes Josephus's first statement of the virtues demanded of Jews as such, which the Torah seeks to inculcate. It is not his last: at 2.170, he will list "justice, good sense (or moderation: Greek *sōphrosynē* can denote either an 'intellectual' virtue or a 'moral' one), fortitude, and agreement in all things among fellow citizens." The omission of piety from this second list signals not its dismissal but its promotion. It now figures as the master virtue of which those listed are deemed aspects: the laws of Moses "did not make piety a part of virtue, but all these others parts of piety." This claim more than any other informs Josephus's praise of Moses as lawgiver. He credits him, first, with grasping the primacy for education of exemplarity,[17] second, with the recognition of the necessity just noted that all virtue be presented to the people under the aspect of piety,[18] third, with grasping that all education in ethics requires a blend of precept and practical habituation,[19] fourth, that frequent recitation of the law should deprive any of the excuse of ignorance of it.[20] In all these respects Josephus presents Moses as unique among legislators.

One cannot stress too much that Josephus's case for the ethical superiority of Jewish life is a case for the superiority of the law. Josephus's understanding of the character of virtue is thus inseparable from that of the means of inculcating it. Josephus agrees with the Pythagorean Xenophilus that if you want your son to receive the best education, you should raise him in a city with good laws.[21] Good laws must be not only necessary but also sufficient for civic virtue; if they are not, they cannot qualify as good. As we have already seen, Josephus's innovation is to reinterpret the Torah as furnishing good laws in this politically exacting sense. Only on the basis of this claim can he declare the imagined ancestral Jewish regime a "theocracy."[22] Where laws that instill virtue prevail, there God rules.

We children of liberal society recoil from the notion of the law as a pervasive and overarching guide to life; it strikes us as "totalitarian." Yet for Josephus as for his models both classical and Jewish, every adequate code of law (and a fortiori the supremely excellent one) is necessarily illiberal in this sense. The ultimate goal of legislation is habituation in the practice of virtue. Teachers in the usual sense take their worthy but subordinate place in this sublime exercise.

Because the virtue of the Jewish people as such is identical with its dogged adherence to law, its conclusive or most convincing demonstration is the privations that it shows itself willing to undergo for the sake of that law, thereby affirming its unshakable authority for them.[23] Josephus goes so far as to suggest that it is this unshakable authority that more than anything else confirms the divine provenance of the law.[24] Practically speaking, then, it is the willing submission to martyrdom that is the peak of virtue ethics as practiced by the people. The Greek term for education to virtue ethics was *paideia:* "Jewish *paideia,* Josephus shows, is *paideia* for martyrdom."[25] Martyrdom properly understood is to be distinguished from the mass suicide enjoined on the besieged Sicarii at Masada by their leader Eleazar ben Jair: it expresses not despair but faith in God's ultimate triumph.[26]

So much for the high level of virtue to be expected of the ordinary Jew, and the means of its inculcation. As for the virtue of the extraordinary human being, it is of a different stripe entirely. This fact may be obscured by the loftiness of Josephus's praise of everyday

Jewish virtue. Still, he clearly presents this last as law bred, which as such falls far short of the virtue of the exceptional individual. While the excellence of ordinary virtue is that of the law on which it depends, extraordinary virtue, Josephus's supreme exemplar of which is Moses, soars far above the law. The virtue of the ordinary human being (and here Josephus explicitly mentions women and children) is conservative. It consists of deep piety, hence immovable fidelity to the received law.[27] That of the founder is transformative or revolutionary. There could not be a starker contrast between the two.

In transcending law, this superior virtue transcends inculcation. Nor does Josephus anywhere ascribe it to divine infusion. It is inborn in the rare individuals who display it. Those fit to teach others in the comprehensive sense of legislating for them do not require to learn from anyone themselves.

Josephus and the Jewish Tradition

The question of how Josephus's understanding of virtue affects his interpretation of the Jewish tradition raises the sixty-four-thousand-dollar question concerning his thought. Ultimately his understanding of virtue and his interpretation of the tradition are inseparable. As we have seen, he defends the Jewish law as the product of the highest individual virtue and as promoting the highest virtue feasible for a community. The latter, as we have also seen, is relatively clear and unproblematic: the virtue of a community consists in its profound fidelity to its law. This fidelity attests above all to its piety: it conceives its law as God-given and obedience to it as the core of submission to His will. Josephus presents most leading members of the community from the Abrahams and the Samuels of early times to the failed moderate leaders of the Great Revolt as exemplifying this fidelity as well as demanding it of the people.

Yet while remaining within these acceptable bounds, Josephus's presentation of the virtues of his protagonists tends toward Hellenization. Abraham, for example, while still outstanding for his faith, has shed the nomadic simplicity that had served to underline that faith. On the contrary, he is a cosmopolitan and a savant, who brings the geometry and astronomy of his native Chaldea to the previously clueless Egyptians.[28] The first of a line of such characterizations in the *Antiquities,* this clearly anticipates Maimonides's argument that the prophets were as such also philosophers.[29]

In general Josephus's vindication of the Jewish way of life in terms of virtue ethics rests on a notion of virtue that is highly syncretic. The least we must say is that, in fulfilling his task of justifying Jewish ways to educated Gentiles, Josephus takes to its limit the rationalizing implications of Deuteronomy 4:6. The goodness of the law must be fully intelligible to any reader with eyes to see. A crucial implication of this is that pagan (Hellenic or Roman) virtues define the framework for the exposition of Jewish ones: the Torah is praised for its success at inculcating those virtues most respected by (reasonable) pagans.

These tensions are most obvious in Josephus's presentation of the supreme model of human virtue, rising even above that of an Abraham or a Joseph: Moses. The Torah praises Moses for one virtue and one virtue only: his unsurpassed humility (Num. 12:3). This is the virtue of the human being who is most faithful to God's commands, because he makes no claim to superiority such as might ground ambitions of his own. If either brother resembles a statesman it is Aaron (Exod. 4:14–17). Yet Aaron's stint as the de facto ruler of the Israelites culminates in the episode of the Golden Calf. Moses undertakes no such initiatives; it is not he but the Lord who rescues the Israelites from Egypt. Moses is merely his instrument, and as such his primary virtues are faith and obedience.

Josephus, by contrast, presents Moses as the statesman par excellence. He does not explicitly reject the view that he was the faithful servant of God, and as such entirely dependent on His providence. Yet he offers glimpses of what can only be called an alternative Moses.

Consider, for examples, *Antiquities* 2.238–53, which offers an episode from the life of Moses unfounded in Scripture. It presents him early in his career, before his initial expulsion from Egypt and sojourn among the Midianites. He figures as a pagan prince, the heir apparent to the throne of Pharaoh and general of Egypt's armies. In a war with Egypt's longtime foe the Ethiopians, he wins a total and stunning victory. He does so against all odds and all expectations, so that the triumph of the Egyptians is no less complete—and no less improbable—than the Israelites' subsequent triumph over the Egyptians themselves. Yet Josephus does not ascribe this astonishing reversal to God or His Providence. It is entirely the doing of Moses.

This episode reinforces a certain peculiarity in Josephus's treatment of miracles. To be sure, in his account of the exodus Josephus not only recounts the Biblical plagues inflicted on the Egyptians, but embroiders them lavishly. So too his account of the passage through the Red Sea. Yet he proceeds to undermine the plausibility of these events in the course of his very vindication of them. Anticipating some readers' skepticism concerning the last of these marvels, he adduces a more recent and therefore supposedly more credible such instance, of the withdrawal of the Pamphylian Sea in Asia Minor before the army of Alexander the Great.[30] He thus offers an event drawn from profane history to vouch for the credibility of one known only from sacred history. He further comments, and not of the Pamphylian but of the Red Sea that it had behaved as it did "either by the will of God or on its own (*kata tautomaton*)."[31] He thus suggests that this might have occurred without divine intervention from some unknown natural cause. This paves the way for a stunning further concession: Josephus grants that reasonable readers might reject the supernatural aspects of his narrative entirely: "Let these things be received as seems good to each."[32] Similar phrases recur throughout the retelling of the biblical account, none with greater impact than at 3.322, where the premise in question is the divine inspiration of the Mosaic legislation.

Obviously, this issue of the role of the divine in human affairs is crucial for the interpretation of Moses's virtue and of virtue in Josephus generally. If we were to subtract the wonders from Josephus's account of the Exodus, what remained would resemble in the decisive respect Moses's defeat of the Ethiopians. There Josephus had not only ascribed Moses's victory entirely to his own virtue but had raised the possibility of so interpreting the Exodus as well. He remarked that just as the "sacred scribes" of the Egyptians had rejoiced at Moses's acceptance of the command against the Ethiopians because "they hoped to prevail over their enemies through his virtue," so those of the Hebrews had "fore[seen] that they might escape the Egyptians through the generalship of Moses."[33] They had thus imagined an Exodus accomplished by the great but merely human capacities displayed by Moses in his waging of the Ethiopian campaign.

The rest of Josephus's account of Moses displays this same ambiguity. Whereas the Torah, as already noted, praises Moses for his humility, and no other virtue, there is no corresponding passage in Josephus. Rather Moses's father-in-law Reuel admires him for his manly virtue (*andragathia*), the core of virtue according to the Hellenic tradition. What is more, he bids Moses be mindful of his virtue or excellence (*aretē*) as something setting him above others and not to be wasted on their trivial affairs.[34] (It should go without saying that there is no corresponding exhortation to pride in the Torah original.) Throughout Josephus's account, relics of the Torah's humble Moses (e.g., 3.212, albeit with the suggestion that Moses adopted this pose for statesmanly reasons) vie with indications of a different more Hellenically inflected one.[35]

We could say much more of Josephus's presentation of Moses, as of those of such other of his models as Joseph, Samuel, David, and Solomon, not neglecting his surprisingly sympathetic rendering of Saul. It is enough to grasp that the two possible readings of these characters imply two diametrically opposed versions of virtue ethics: one anchored in humility and the other in pride or self-reliance. They further imply two possible readings of Josephus's works as a whole and their implications for the life of the reader. Readers who accept his reiterated affirmations of prophecy and other works of Divine Providence will be led to a return to the Torah in a somewhat Hellenized version of the original. Those skeptical of these affirmations who accept Josephus's invitation to read the narrative as purged of them will be led elsewhere. Not to rejection of the Torah or the virtue ethics that according to Josephus it implies. Quite the contrary. But the two readerships will understand that Torah and its ethics differently. The question of whether either of these perspectives on the tradition, the prophetic and the rationalizing, is to be taken for Josephus's own is beyond our modest scope. It suffices for our purposes merely to note these complexities.[36]

Notes

1. Throughout I refer to Josephus's works by book and chapter, so as be to intelligible to readers regardless of the editions that they may use. Translations are my own.

2. Louis H. Feldman, *Josephus's Interpretation of the Bible* (Berkeley: University of California Press, 1998), 664.

3. Josephus, *Life* 1.1–4.
4. Josephus, *Life* 2.9.
5. Josephus, *Life* 2.10–12.
6. Josephus, *Life* 3.
7. Josephus, *Life* 7.29; *War* 2.568.
8. Josephus, *Life* 8–74; *War* 2.569–3.398.
9. Josephus, *War* 3.399–407, 408, 410, 434–39; 4.622–29.

10. Alasdair MacIntyre, *After Virtue: A Study in Moral Theory* (1981; New York: Bloomsbury Academic, 2020), 323.

11. The study of Josephus has suffered from lack of attention to him as a thinker. In a welcome trend of recent decades, however, leading scholars have come to take him more seriously as one. Consider, for example, Tessa Rajak, "Josephus," in *Cambridge History of Greek and Roman Political Thought*, ed. Christopher Rowe and Malcolm Schofield (Cambridge: Cambridge University Press, 2000), 585–96; "The *Against Apion* and the Continuities in Josephus' Political Thought," in *Understanding Josephus: Seven Perspectives*, ed. Steve Mason (Sheffield, UK: Sheffield Academic Press, 1998), 222–46; Daniel R. Schwartz, "Josephus on the Jewish Constitutions and Community," *Scripta Classica Israelitica*, 7 (1983): 30–52; "Rome and the Jews: Josephus on 'Freedom' and 'Autonomy,'" in *Representations of Empire: Rome and the Mediterranean World*, ed. Alan K. Bowman, Hannah M. Cotton, Martin Goodman, and Simon Price, *Proceedings of the British Academy* 114 (Oxford: Oxford University Press, 2002), 65–81. More recent have been Michael S. Kochin's contributions to this project of retrieval as well as my own. Michael S. Kochin, "Education after Freedom," in *In Search of Humanity*, ed. Andrea Radasanu (Lanham, MD: Lexington Books, 2015), 129–48; "Freedom and Empire in Josephus," *History of Political Thought* 39, no. 1 (2018): 16–32. Clifford Orwin, "The Wedding of *Logos* and *Ergon*: Josephus' Defense of the Torah in *Against Apion*," in *Prinicìple and Prudence in Western Political Thought*, ed. Christopher Lynch and Jonathan Marks (Albany: State University of New York Press, 2016), 91–109; "The Melancholy of Departure: The Mirage of Aristocracy in Josephus' *Judaean War*," in *Flavius Josephus: Von Jerusalem nach Rom*, ed. Judith Goeppinger (forthcoming from Brill, 2023). In a class by itself is Pierre Vidal-Naquet, "Du bon usage de la trahison," in Flavius Josèphe, *La guerre des Juifs*, tr. Pierre Savinel (Paris: Éditions du Minuit, 1977) 9–115.

12. All scholars of Josephus's reading of the Bible owe an enormous debt to the late Louis H. Feldman, quoted at the head of this article. Feldman, may his memory be for a blessing, made it his task to expound in detail all the differences between the Biblical text and Josephus's recapitulation of it, including, therefore, those between its presentation of the virtues of its characters and Josephus's. He thus laid the magnificent groundwork for all subsequent efforts to interpret these differences.

Due to adverse circumstance, I was unable to consult Harold W. Attridge, *The Interpretation of Biblical History in the "Antiquitates Judaicae" of Flavius Josephus* (Missoula, MT: Scholars Press, 1976).

13. Josephus, *Against Apion* 2.145–47.

14. Michael Tuval, *From Jerusalem Priest to Roman Jew: On Josephus and the Paradigms of Ancient Judaism* (Tübingen: Mohr Siebeck, 2013).

15. Compare Thucydides, *Peloponnesian War* 2.16.

16. Josephus, *Against Apion* 2.146.

17. Josephus, *Against Apion* 2.159.

18. Josephus, *AA* 2.170–71.

19. Josephus, *Against Apion* 2.171–74.

20. Josephus, *Against Apion* 2.175–78.

21. Diogenes Laertius, *Lives of the Philosophers* 8.16.

22. Josephus, *Against Apion* 2.165. This is the earliest extant instance of this term, which Josephus introduces with an apology that suggests that it is his coinage, intended to distinguish the Jewish regime from all others (or at rate from any others that do not share its rationality). Cf. Orwin, "Wedding," 97–100.

23. Josephus, *Antiquities* 3.317–22.

24. Josephus, *Antiquities* 3.22.

25. Kochin, "Freedom and Empire," 31. The most perfect example of this education to martyrdom is that practiced by the Essenes, whose unflinching willingness to face death is supported by an extrabiblical doctrine of the immortality of the soul (*War* 2.151–58). The lengthy praise of the Essenes of which these passages form the climax casts them as the paragons of popular Jewish virtue ethics. That this praise is hyperbolic is confirmed by the contradiction between *War* 2.158 and *Life* 2.10–12.

26. Josephus, *War* 7.320–401. Kochin, "Freedom and Empire," 31.

27. Josephus, *War* 2.179–83.

28. Josephus, *Antiquities* 1.154–57, 166–68.

29. Feldman, *Interpretation*, 662–63.

30. Josephus, *Antiquities*, 2.347–48.

31. Josephus, *Antiquities* 2. 347–48.

32. Josephus, *Antiquities* 2.347–48.

33. Josephus, *Antiquities* 2.243.

34. Josephus, *Antiquities* 3.65, 69.

35. Consider the tension between the consecutive sentences of *Antiquities* 3.64 and 3.65, and the implication of the final sentence of 3.273 (of which there are numerous parallels throughout the account of the Mosaic legislation). On the negotiatiopn of this issue of prophecy versus (human) legislation in *Against Apion* see Orwin, "Wedding."

36. There is another side of Josephus's presentation of virtue ethics that stands apart from his presentation of the Jewish tradition, but that would have to be integrated with it to grasp his perspective on virtue as a whole. This is his presentation of the virtue of the Romans. I mean here not his praise of Vespasian and Titus in the pages of the *Jewish War*, which is for obvious reasons suspect. I mean, rather, his praise of a strain of Roman virtue that refuses submission to emperors, namely, civic or republican virtue. On this subject and a suggestion as to its relation to Josephus's treatment of Jewish virtue, see Kochin, "Freedom and Empire," 28–30.

Chapter 4

Rabbinic Literature

DEBORAH BARER

After the fall of the Second Temple in 70 CE, the Jewish sages of late antiquity, known collectively as the rabbis (or sages), laid the foundations for Judaism as we know it today. Their work both preserved and transformed the traditions of Second Temple Judaism through biblical interpretation (*midrash*), legal innovation, and the transmission of teachings by earlier authorities. The center of rabbinic life was originally in Palestine but eventually shifted to Babylonia; over time, rabbinic instruction also shifted from smaller discipleship circles to larger, more institutionalized academies. While the initial influence of the early rabbis was marginal, and their world was not representative of the average Jew or Jewish experience, the rabbinic movement came to exert significant cultural, ritual, and legal authority, and their teachings are at the center of later Jewish study and practice.

Most works dating to the classical rabbinic period (ca. 10–600 CE)[1] were originally transmitted orally but were later recorded in writing. These works include the Mishnah (ca. 200 CE), the Tosefta,[2] the Palestinian Talmud (ca. 400 CE), the Babylonian Talmud (ca. 600 CE), and several midrashic compilations. The Babylonian Talmud (hereafter, BT or, simply, "the Talmud") is the most widely studied of these texts.

While some rabbis undoubtedly read Greek literature, there is no evidence that rabbinic conceptions of virtue or the good life were directly influenced by Greek philosophy. Instead, rabbinic literature articulates its own ideal—that of the righteous sage, who embodies Torah for his community—and its own curriculum for attaining that ideal. Certain aspects of this vision and approach have strong parallels in Greco-Roman culture. For example, rabbinic education in Palestine, like its Greco-Roman and early Christian counterparts, centered on the imitation of teachers and exemplars.[3] In some ways, these rabbinic exemplars resemble the Aristotelian man of virtue; Rabbi Akiva (who I discuss at length below) was often celebrated as embodying the mean between two potential extremes.[4] In other ways, however, the rabbinic curriculum and its ethical ideals differ markedly from their Greco-Roman counterparts. Above all else, the sage is celebrated for his[5] learning and love of Torah, but his passion for Torah may overwhelm other classical virtues, such as temperance or prudence, and may impede upon norms of good conduct. In some examples, the zeal or righteous anger of a sage literally burns or otherwise destroys objects within his path;[6] while such passion is potentially disruptive, and even dangerous, it is also revered.

In this respect, rabbinic culture elucidates different virtues from those found in Greek philosophy. Indeed, the entire goal of rabbinic formation is different from that of an Aristotelian virtue ethic.[7] The student of Aristotle strives to achieve a life of virtue and balance, with the goal of attaining human flourishing (*eudaimonia*) in this world; the student of the rabbis strives to center every aspect of his life around Torah—a task that may require restraint in some circumstances and more extreme behavior in others—with the goal of attaining a place in the world to come (*olam ha-ba*).

Virtues and Their Cultivation

Rabbinic literature is deeply interested in character formation and the cultivation of specific dispositions and behaviors. Unlike Greek literature, however, rabbinic texts do not tend to enumerate a list of virtues, but rather promote the cultivation of specific skills or dispositions necessary to the life of the sage. A few works, such as Pirkei Avot and Avot de Rabbi Nathan, contain ethical maxims designed to promote a process of reflection that will cultivate sagely attitudes and behaviors.[8] However, across the rabbinic corpus, the cultivation of sagely capacities largely focuses on two aspects of life. Disciples learn proper social and ritual conduct through direct imitation of their masters, or through reading narratives about the behavior of other sages. Rabbis also cultivate discernment and insight through partnered learning, where they hone their skills at textual interpretation and legal argumentation. I briefly consider each of these aspects of the rabbinic curriculum in turn.

Imitation

Rabbinic formation centers heavily on the process of discipleship. Numerous rabbinic stories describe a disciple following his master and asking questions about his behavior. A famously provocative set of narratives involve a disciple observing his master in the bathroom and bedroom, intruding on his master's most intimate moments in order to learn proper conduct.[9] Rabbinic teachers were aware that they were on display, at times explicitly modifying their actions to communicate proper behavior more effectively.[10] This sense of being on display correlates with concerns about shame and shaming. The virtuous sage knows how to properly correct or rebuke his fellow and how to disagree with his colleagues in a way that does not cause embarrassment. While rabbinic education centered more heavily on direct imitation during the early rabbinic period in Palestine, explicit teachings about shaming are especially prominent in the Babylonian Talmud. This may reflect the fact that the Babylonian academies were far more competitive and hierarchical, increasing opportunities for public embarrassment and yielding more severe social consequences and loss of status for public mistakes.[11]

Argumentation and Interpretation

Torah was the central framework through which rabbis negotiated the world and shaped Jewish practice. Rabbis thus needed to be able to interpret the various possible implications of Torah verses, as well as to analyze their practical and halakhic (legal) implications. Emphasizing these skills, BT Sanhedrin 17a states that in order to sit as a judge on the Sanhedrin (the highest court), a person must know "how to render a carcass of a creeping animal pure by Torah law," even though the Torah explicitly states that such animals are impure (Lev. 11:41–43).[12] This qualification may seem counterintuitive—why would the ability to argue *against* the explicit teaching of the Torah be valued? One possible answer is that this qualification is not designed to subvert the Torah, but rather to ensure the judge is able understand the matter at hand from all possible angles, allowing the law to be adapted and applied to a continuously changing world. This qualification for judges thus highlights the importance of interpretive and analytical mastery.

And yet, while such skills and insight were prized, they needed to be tempered by clarity about the actual substance of the text and its implications, as well as an ability to teach in a way that others are able to understand. Practical wisdom, as displayed in the ability to balance intellectual dexterity with the demands of the world, was thus a central virtue of the rabbinic world, albeit one that even the most revered sages struggled to attain. As BT Eruvin 13b notes, Rabbi Meir had an unequalled intellect in his generation, but rabbinic law was not always established in accordance with his opinion precisely because he was so good at argumentation. Since he could argue an issue well from both sides, his colleagues could not always ascertain which side was correct. Such intellectual virtuosity, while respected, must be balanced by prudential judgment.

To develop their interpretive skills and capacities for judgment, rabbis learned in pairs with a friend or *ḥavruta*, relying on questions or challenges from their study partners to help sharpen their reasoning. The importance of this mode of study is highlighted in a famous story about Rabbi Yoḥanan and Resh Lakish. In the course of a legal argument, the two quarrel and Rabbi Yoḥanan levels an ad hominem attack at Resh Lakish, reminding him of his past life as a bandit. Resh Lakish is so insulted that he dies, and the sages assign to Rabbi Yoḥanan a new study partner, Eliezer ben Pedat. Instead of arguing against Rabbi Yoḥanan, as Resh Laskish did, Eliezer ben Pedat works to find teachings that support his new study partner's positions. While one might expect him to be gratified, Rabbi Yoḥanan is distressed and cries, "Can you be compared to the son of Lakish [i.e., Resh Lakish]? With the son of Lakish, when I would state a matter, he would raise twenty-four difficulties against me, and I would answer him with twenty-four responses, and the halakhah [law] would be broadened and clarified. . . . Don't I already know the merit of what I say?"[13] This story highlights the value placed on rabbinic insight; critique and debate were beneficial to everyone, since through this process "the halakhah would be broadened and clarified." Rather than reaching agreement about the substance of the law and its practical application, the chief goal of study was often to understand the Torah in all its nuance and from all possible angles.[14]

The rabbinic curriculum thus emphasized intellectual dexterity, attentiveness to practical demands, argumentative skill, and norms of interpersonal conduct, including respect for others and the avoidance of shaming. The disciple who attained these skills and correctly balanced them would not only display knowledge and insight, in the sense of understanding fundamental Torah teachings and being able to exposit them further, but also practical wisdom, or the ability to assess the implications of those teachings when applied in the world and whether specific applications would further the ultimate goals and values of the Torah.

The Virtuous Sage: Rabbi Akiva as Exemplar

It is notable that, much like the heroes of the Hebrew Bible, rabbinic sages are presented as both revered and highly flawed human beings, and the specific virtues or qualities prized by the rabbis shift over time. The early rabbis, or *tannaim* (ca. 10–200 CE), often appear as archetypes who embody different virtues or capacities. As noted above, of these early sages, Rabbi Akiva often appears as the one who embodies not only wisdom in the sense of knowledge and intellectual dexterity, but also practical wisdom. In the language of Aristotelian ethics, he achieves the mean, enabling him to balance numerous different skills and qualities. Although Aristotle often presents virtue as the mean between two vices, each of the extremes discussed below are valued qualities in and of themselves; they become problematic only when a sage pursues them to the exclusion of all else. Two of the earliest sages, Rabbi Eliezer ben Horkanus and Rabbi Elazar ben Azariah, illustrate the problem.[15]

According to Pirkei Avot 2:8, Rabbi Eliezer ben Horkanus had an incredible ability to retain and transmit received teachings; he is described as a "cistern who never loses a drop." His colleague, Rabbi

Elazar ben Azariah, has a similarly impressive ability to generate new teachings and insights; he is described as "an overflowing spring." Neither rabbi, however, is the ideal model for the sage, who must be able to transmit the substance of tradition accurately while also adding his own insights and generating new teachings. Rabbi Eliezer is unable to innovate or generate new insights, while Rabbi Elazar does not remember what he has learned. Their colleague, Rabbi Akiva, emerges as the archetype who is able to both retain his learning and generate new insights; he finds the balance or mean between these two potential extremes. He is acclaimed not only for his learning but for the virtues he embodies. He is also the only sage to engage in a specific path of mystical contemplation (described as entering the *pardes*) and emerge unscathed; his companions either die, go insane, or become heretics.[16]

Two famous Talmudic narratives illustrate how Rabbi Akiva comes to master the two core elements of the rabbinic curriculum: proper behavior and Torah learning. The first, known colloquially as the "Oven of Akhnai" (BT Bava Metzi'a 59a–b), records a dispute between Rabbi Eliezer ben Horkanus and the rest of the sages, represented by Rabbi Joshua, over an obscure issue in the laws of purity and impurity. The story makes it clear that Rabbi Eliezer's position is technically the correct one; the "cistern" recalls tradition accurately, and several miracles—including a divine voice from heaven!—affirm that he is correct. And yet, the sages reject his position, arguing that one cannot rely on miracles or divine voices to determine the law. Since the Torah was given to humanity, the power to interpret it is in the hands of the community, who should follow the majority position. Rabbi Joshua bases his claims on a rather audacious reading of Exodus 23:2; in its original context, the verse he cites actually cautions *against* following the majority. Nonetheless, the story affirms his position; in a narrative postscript, the reader learns that when Rabbi Joshua issued his pronouncement, "The Holy One Blessed be He smiled and said, 'My children have defeated me.' "[17] The majority view carries the day. Rabbi Eliezer, however, refuses to cede, and is excommunicated as a result.

While this narrative is fertile ground to explore the construction of rabbinic power and authority, it does not end with the dramatic debate over the oven. Instead, the story goes on to describe the disastrous effects of Rabbi Eliezer's excommunication, and it is here that Rabbi Akiva plays an important role.

> The Sages said, "Who will go and inform him?" Rabbi Akiva said to them, "I will go, lest an unsuitable person go [and inform him in an insensitive manner] and he would thereby destroy the entire world." What did Rabbi Akiva do? He wore black and wrapped himself in black [a sign of mourning] and sat before him at a distance of four cubits [the distance one is to maintain from an ostracized person]. Rabbi Eliezer said to him, "Akiva, what is different about today from other days?" Rabbi Akiva said to him, "My teacher, it appears to me that your colleagues are distancing themselves from you."[18]

Rabbi Akiva here breaks the news gently to his colleague and teacher, demonstrating that he is grieved over what has happened. In doing so, he embodies the virtue of compassion.

Compassion, it seems, is a virtue that many rabbis struggled to attain. Rabbi Akiva worries that if one of his other colleagues informs Rabbi Eliezer of his excommunication, they might not do so in a sensitive manner. His concerns are not unwarranted; several stories describe rabbis who are dismissive or callous toward those who they view as inferior, due either to a presumed lack of learning or to other personal qualities, including appearance.[19] While Rabbi Akiva's careful and compassionate handling of the matter helps mitigate Rabbi Eliezer's response—he does not "destroy the whole world"—even he cannot completely forestall the impact of Rabbi Eliezer's anger and shame over his treatment: "His [Rabbi Eliezer's] eyes shed tears, and the entire world was afflicted: one-third of the olives, and one-third of the wheat, and one-third of the barley. And some say that even dough spoiled in a woman's hands. It is taught: There was great anger on that day, as any place that Rabbi Eliezer fixed his gaze was burned."[20] The affliction does not end with the natural world but strikes directly at the heart of the rabbinic community. The story concludes with the death of Rabban Gamliel, who, as the *nasi* (patriarch) and the head of the rabbinic community, is held responsible for Rabbi Eliezer's suffering. The text makes it clear that Rabban Gamliel dies as a direct result of Rabbi Eliezer's distress and his pleading with God over his mistreatment. Here, Rabban Gamliel's failure to handle the situation delicately is contrasted with Rabbi Akiva's masterful and compassionate treatment of Rabbi Eliezer.

In addition to his exemplary behavior, Rabbi Akiva is revered for his insight and skill at interpreting Torah. These qualities are all the more impressive because he does not begin his learning until the age of forty.[21] A famous Talmudic story suggests that even God is impressed by his interpretive abilities:

> When Moses ascended on High [to receive the Torah], he found the Holy One, Blessed be He, sitting and tying crowns on the letters. Moses said before Him, "Master of the Universe, who is detaining your hand [i.e., why do you delay in giving the Torah]?" God said to him, "There is a man who is destined to be born after several generations, and Akiva ben Yosef is his name; he is destined to derive from each and every thorn of these crowns mounds and mounds of *halakhot* [laws]."[22]

In this story, Moses asks God why he is willing to delay the giving of the Torah in order to add what appear to be purely decorative flourishes. Surely, the Torah should be given to the people as quickly as possible, so that they can begin to follow God's teachings! God replies that even these apparently insignificant minutiae contain hints of meaning, and from them Rabbi Akiva will be able to unlock myriad new teachings and laws. In a show of deference to Rabbi Akiva's immense interpretive abilities, God is willing to delay the revelation of the Torah itself.

While interpretive skill is celebrated, the righteous sage must also learn how to employ his skills appropriately, and the ways that Rabbi Akiva chose to display his virtuosity was not without its critics. Some of his colleagues argued that he reached conclusions without a sufficient textual basis, conclusions that may carry serious consequences. On one occasion, Rabbi Ishmael lambasts Rabbi Akiva's interpretation of Leviticus 21:9, which discusses the penalty for the adulterous daughter of a priest. Based on the fact that the verse begins with the *vav* consecutive (a grammatical way of linking Hebrew phrases together, but that can also be read as an inclusive "and"), Rabbi Akiva concludes that both the married daughter of the priest *and* the daughter who is merely betrothed are punished with death by burning. This interpretive move by Rabbi Akiva closely models the type of intensive reading for which he is praised in the story above; he is extracting new *halakhot* on the basis of minute textual details, in this case, the presence of a single letter. Rabbi Ishmael's response is at once damning and derisive, asking, "Should we take this woman out to be burned on the basis of a *vav* [lit. because you distinguish between *bat* and *u-bat*]?"[23] For Rabbi Ishmael, at least, Rabbi Akiva's interpretive skill has crossed the line from virtue into vice.[24]

Rethinking Virtue: The Flawed but Righteous Sage

As we have seen, even Rabbi Akiva, the virtuous sage par excellence who masters the core skills and capacities of the rabbinic curriculum, remains an imperfect figure, subject to critique by his colleagues. These imperfections, such as they are, help to distinguish the rabbinic ideal of the righteous sage from Aristotle's man of virtue. It is significant that Rabbi Akiva is particularly remembered for his role in the failed Bar Kochba revolt. While his participation and identification of Bar Kochba as a messianic figure could be seen as representing a massive error in judgment, Rabbi Akiva is typically revered for the way he displays extreme piety at the time of his death. As he undergoes a horrifically painful execution at the hand of the Roman government, he recites the Shema, the prayer that affirms God's unity. This recitation is understood as an acceptance of God's will and of his own fate. Nevertheless, his students are shocked.

> His students said to him, "Our master, even now [you recite the Shema]?" He said to them, "All my days, I have been troubled by this verse: [*You shall love the Lord your God with all your heart, with all your might, and*] *with all your soul* (Deut. 6:5)—even if he takes your soul. I said to myself: When will I have the opportunity to fulfill this verse? Now that I have the opportunity, shall I not fulfill it?" He lengthened his recitation of the word "One," until his soul left his body as he recited "One." A voice descended from Heaven and said, "Happy are you, Rabbi Akiva, that your soul left your body as you recited 'One.' "[25]

In this narrative, Rabbi Akiva departs from the model of the temperate sage. He is not praised for his interpretive skills, or his ability to find a balance in his conduct. On the contrary, he is praised—by a voice from heaven itself—for the very extremes of his piety. He is not only willing to sacrifice his life, but he embraces it as a chance to serve God in a new way. Here, while Rabbi Akiva remains an exemplary sage, he has drifted far from the Aristotelian ideal of virtue as the mean, embodying instead the rabbinic ideal of devotion to Torah and to God, even in his death.

To distinguish it from Greek conceptions of virtue, I refer to this rabbinic ideal instead as *righteousness*. Like Aristotle's man of virtue, the righteous sage has distinct capacities and qualities. He lives his life in strict adherence to divine teaching. He exhibits a passionate love for Torah, devoting himself to Torah study and to living as the Torah dictates. Rabbinic education and formation are designed to cultivate the skills and qualities that support this, including intellectual dexterity and interpretive ability, treating others with honor and compassion, extensive Torah knowledge, and practical wisdom. A sage's zeal for Torah, however, can sometimes come into conflict with other rabbinic virtues; it does not always belie a temperate character or lead to the most prudential judgments, as the case of Rabbi Akiva attests. When such conflicts arise, love for Torah trumps all else; as the case of Rabbi Akiva shows, it is this virtue—his passion for Torah, and a willingness to adhere to it even unto death—that not only elicits communal respect but also divine approval.

Indeed, most rabbinic figures, including many not mentioned here, are memorable precisely for their extremes of behavior, or for qualities that make them unusual or exceptional in some way. Often, these are not qualities that the reader is expected to imitate. For example, Rabban Gamliel has delicate sensibilities that prompt him to grant himself certain legal leniencies (BT Berakhot 16b), while Rabbi Shimon bar Yoḥai becomes an ascetic, isolating himself with his son in a cave for many years (BT Shabbat 33b). Resh Lakish, as we have seen, is famous for having been a bandit before becoming a rabbi (BT Bava Metzi'a 84a). Students of the Talmud are often especially drawn to the figure of Elisha ben Abuyah, also known as *Aḥer* (lit. "Other"). Famous for his heresy and subsequent abandonment of the rabbinic path, Aḥer provides the classic example of the model one should *not* follow. And yet, while one might expect him to be vilified as a result, rabbinic tradition presents Aḥer as a complex and compelling character, who retains ties to his rabbinic colleagues long after he has officially left their ranks. His heresy is tragic, not villainous.[26]

The early rabbinic sages are deeply complex and imperfect characters. They are men who strive to follow God's teachings and spread Torah, but they are also subject to fits of pettiness and pique, overly concerned about rank, dismissive of those they disagree with, and liable to lash out when they feel threatened. Far from equanimity, the rabbinic disposition is often fiery, but when properly directed, their passionate zeal burns for God and Torah, eliciting approval from heaven and communal respect. Rabbinic teaching strives to help restrain the sages' troublesome human tendencies and redirect their energies toward learning and Torah. It is perhaps ironic, then, that many of the rabbis' most troublesome behaviors also emerge in the course of Torah study. Their zeal for Torah can lead the sages to be callous toward their fellow human beings. As a result, to truly achieve a life of righteousness, the sage's love of learning must be tempered by good behavior, proper etiquette, and compassion for those around him.

Conclusion

The dynamic and imperfect human who struggles to live a life oriented around God and Torah is a compelling model indeed, and one of the reasons the sages of the Talmud remain fascinating to readers today. Their model is at once inaccessible and attainable. The depths of their learning and interpretive skill require years of study, but their passion and liveliness invite the reader into a dynamic world. It is precisely because that world is populated by flawed characters that it seems inviting. The rabbinic vision is one that accommodates human weakness, and that acknowledges the tensions that may arise between the strict demands of Torah and ideals of interpersonal conduct. Their model is one of striving, not attainment. Perfect righteousness is not something that a person can ever fully achieve in this life. If we think of virtue as an *orientation* toward certain goods, however, then its pursuit becomes accessible.

While the rabbinic fellowship circles and academies were not open to all Jews, their vision of the good life was. Any Jew could choose to orient his or her[27] life around the pursuit of Torah and good deeds. A person could strive to learn and follow rabbinic teachings, and to model one's actions on rabbinic exemplars. Jews could place the love of God and Torah at the center of their lives. There was no assumption that doing so would necessarily lead to the perfection of one's character, or the achievement of *eudaimonia* (flourishing) in this world. As the martyrdom of Rabbi Akiva poignantly illustrates, following the rabbinic path did not guarantee success or long life in this world, nor should one follow that path in pursuit of an earthly reward.[28] If one's love of Torah and efforts to lead a life in accordance with God's teaching were sincere, however, it could earn that person something much more valuable: a place in the world to come.[29]

Notes

1. Most scholars correlate the end of this period with the redaction of the Babylonian Talmud, although the timeline of this redaction process remains a topic of debate.

2. The dating of the Tosefta is contested. While some claim that the Tosefta comments on and expands upon the Mishnah, others argue that it predates the Mishnah, perhaps commenting on a proto-Mishnah. See Judith Hauptman, *Rereading the Rabbis: A Woman's Voice* (Boulder, CO: Westview Press, 1998).

3. For a discussion of the role of exemplars in both late Greco-Roman and early Christian education, see Peter Brown, "The Saint as Exemplar in Late Antiquity," *Representations*, no. 2 (Spring 1983): 1–25. Later, in Jewish Babylonia, rabbinic education shifts to more formal instruction in the academies, although the master-disciple relationship remains important.

4. In the *Nichomachean Ethics*, Aristotle repeatedly represents a virtue as the mean between two vices. See, for example, his discussion of courage as the mean between the vices of cowardice or fear and overconfidence (3.6–9, esp. 3.6.1).

5. In the classical rabbinic period, all rabbis were men. As a result, my discussion of the ideal sage and rabbinic notions of virtue will assume a male actor.

6. Cf. BT Shabbat 33b, BT Bava Metzi'a 59b.

7. While numerous other Greek and Roman thinkers articulate ideas of virtue, my primary interlocutor here will be Aristotle, as his ethics has a significant impact both on later Jewish thinkers, such as Maimonides, and on the virtue ethics tradition articulated and developed by many philosophers today.

8. See Jonathan Wyn Schofer, *The Making of a Sage: A Study in Rabbinic Ethics* (Madison: University of Wisconsin Press, 2005).

9. BT Berakhot 62a.

10. See Moshe Simon-Shoshan, "'People Talking Without Speaking': The Semiotics of the Rabbinic Legal Exemplum as Reflected in Bavli Berakhot 11a," *Law and Literature* 25, no. 3 (2013): 446–65.

11. Jeffrey L. Rubenstein, "Shame," in *The Culture of the Babylonian Talmud* (Baltimore: Johns Hopkins University Press, 2003), 67–79.

12. Lev. 11 further makes clear that the carcass of an impure animal transmits impurity.

13. BT Bava Metzi'a 84a. All translations my own.

14. Bamidbar Rabbah 13:15 poetically describes the Torah as having "seventy faces" to emphasize the many different angles through which it can be understood.

15. I am grateful to my teacher Leah Rosenthal, who first introduced me to the ways these sages represent different paradigms of rabbinic learning.

16. BT Ḥagigah 14b.

17. BT Bava Metzi'a 59b.

18. BT Bava Metzi'a 59b.

19. See, for example, the exchange between Rabbi Elazar and the ugly man in BT Ta'anit 20b.

20. BT Bava Metzi'a 59b.

21. Avot de Rabbi Natan 6:2. For a more complete discussion of Rabbi Akiva's life, see Barry W. Holz, *Rabbi Akiva: Sage of the Talmud* (New Haven, CT: Yale University Press, 2017).

22. BT Menachot 29b.

23. BT Sanhedrin 51b

24. There are several complicating factors to this story. Although the framing of the story appears dramatic—Rabbi Akiva is willing to kill a woman over a *vav*!—the actual disagreement between Rabbi Akiva and Rabbi Ishmael is much less stark. Both agree that the woman in question would be subject to the death penalty, they simply disagree on the *method* by which she should be executed, since burning was perceived to be a more severe form of capital punishment than other alternatives. Furthermore, Rabbi Akiva and Rabbi Ishmael both represent different hermeneutic schools. Thus Rabbi Ishmael's critique is not only leveled at Rabbi Akiva's decision in this instance, but at his broader approach to reading the Torah; this is only one in a series of interpretive differences between them. For more on their respective schools, see Azzan Yadin, *Scripture as Logos: Rabbi Ishmael and the Origins of Midrash* (Philadelphia: University of Pennsylvania Press, 2004); Azzan Yadin-Israel, *Scripture and Tradition: Rabbi Akiva and the Triumph of Midrash* (Philadelphia: University of Pennsylvania Press, 2015).

25. BT Berakhot 61b.

26. See BT Ḥagigah 15a-b. Aḥer's heresy stems both from a confused mystical vision and from an inability to reconcile the tragedies of the world with divine justice. He maintains ties to his rabbinic colleagues, who suc-

cessfully petition for him to be judged and then eventually admitted to the world to come after his death.

27. Although rabbinic texts are primarily directed toward a male audience, and the rabbis themselves were all men, rabbinic teachings also established norms and ideals for the community writ large.

28. See Pirkei Avot 1:3.

29. The rabbinic idea of the world to come (*olam ha-ba*) is typically correlated with the afterlife, a desirable realm that the deserving person inhabits after death, or with a future messianic age. While the rabbis do sometimes imagine life in *olam ha-ba*, and discuss the idea of a reward that realm, conceptions of the afterlife in rabbinic literature are not always clearly or fully developed.

Chapter 5

Baḥya Ibn Paquda

DIANA LOBEL

Baḥya Ibn Paquda of Saragossa, Spain is author of the Judeo-Arabic classic *Guidebook to the Duties of the Heart* (*Kitāb al-Hidāya ilā farā'iḍ al-qulūb*) (ca. 1050–1080 CE)—translated into Hebrew by Judah Ibn Tibbon in 1160 as *Ḥovot ha-Levavot* (*Duties of the Heart*)—a work that reflects traditional Jewish and Islamic piety, philosophical spirituality, Islamic asceticism, and Sufi mystical devotion. Baḥya argues that duties of the *heart* (which comprises the entire inner being—mind, feeling, and will) are as important as external religious duties.

We know very little about the biography of Baḥya; we have little historical evidence external to his work *Duties of the Heart* and several devotional poems. In his Hebrew introduction, Ibn Tibbon informs us that Baḥya was a *dayyan*, a judge of the rabbinical court. "One of the scholars of Spain was our Rabbi (Rabbenu) Baḥya *ha-dayyan*, son of Joseph." (The epithet "Rabbenu," our rabbi, has remained with Baḥya until the present day.) We know that Baḥya lived in Muslim Spain, and it has been confirmed that he lived in Saragossa, but the precise dates that Baḥya lived and worked are not known. For some time, there was debate as to whether he lived in the second half of the eleventh century, or the beginning of the twelfth. A. S. Yahuda, who published an Arabic edition of *The Duties* in 1912, argued for a twelfth-century date for Baḥya, based on a precise literary coincidence between Baḥya's work and a short work of the eleventh-century Islamic pietist al-Ghazālī.[1] More recently, D. Z. Baneth showed that Baḥya and Ghazālī in fact drew from a common source, a work belonging to the end of the tenth century, and definitely written before 1058.[2] Further, a work by Moses Ibn Ezra mentions Baḥya's creativity as belonging to an earlier generation than Ibn Ezra's own work (ca. 1090), and following that of Jonah Ibn Janah (ca. 1050–1055). Scholars thus generally locate Baḥya's period of creativity between 1050 and 1090.[3] Since we have so little biographical information about Baḥya, scholars look to other clues to his social and intellectual context, such as literary sources for his ideas. We find sources in the early Islamic pietist al-Muḥāsibī (ca. 781–857), Saadya Gaon (882–942), the tenth-century Muslim encyclopedists known as the Brethren of Purity (*Ikhwān al-ṣafā'*), and the poetry and ethical work of Solomon Ibn Gabirol (d. 1070).

The Centrality of Inner Virtues

As noted, Baḥya's work integrates several streams of medieval Jewish and Islamic thought: rabbinic Judaism, Mu'tazilite rationalist theology (*kalām*), Neoplatonic philosophy, Islamic asceticism (*zuhd*), and mysticism (Sufism).[4] Baḥya lived before the full absorption of Aristotelian ideas into Jewish philosophy—an absorption that was adumbrated by the critique of Judah Halevi (1075–1141) in the *Kuzari*. Thus Baḥya's work does not belong to the category of Aristotelian virtue ethics. However, virtues are central to Baḥya's thought; his work is a guidebook to the inner life. Written in the manner of a Sufi devotional manual, the book includes ten gates, each describing an inner duty to God. Baḥya's duties include Sufi virtues such as reliance on God, humility, and love; and philosophical obligations such as proving for oneself the existence and unity of God and contemplation of God's wisdom in creation. He is both a philosophical rationalist and a mystical and ascetic pietist.

A word should be said about asceticism (*zuhd*) in the Islamicate sphere. Ehud Krinis is currently engaged in writing a monograph contextualizing Baḥya's work within the broader framework of the attitude of ascetic renunciation known as *zuhd*. This will broaden the work of Amos Goldreich, who identified al-Muḥāsibī, a key early Islamic pietist emphasizing *zuhd* themes, as an important source for

Baḥya. While Goldreich contextualized both al-Muḥāsibī and Baḥya within Sufism, Krinis contextualizes both thinkers within the *zuhd* framework.[5] Krinis's insight accounts well for the somber tone of Baḥya's writing, and for the fact that Baḥya shows little interest in history, and focuses almost exclusively on the inward sphere. On the attitude of *zuhd*, Sara Sviri writes:

> In general terms, *zuhd* in Islam, especially within the Ṣūfī lore, focuses on "attitude" and "states of mind" rather than on "activity" and extreme conduct. . . . To this, one may add such notions as *ḥusn al-ẓann*, thinking well [in particular of Allāh's decree], and hence cultivating an attitude of acceptance (*riḍā*), reliance (*tawakkul*), gratitude (*shukr*), perseverance (*ṣabr*) and submission (*islām, istislām*). In Ṣūfī parlance this has led to the pre-eminence of "the actions of the hearts" (*aʿmāl al-qulūb*) over "the actions of the bodily organs" (*aʿmāl al-jawāriḥ*).[6]

This characterization is quite appropriate for Baḥya's work.

Baḥya's work is also considered the first of a new genre of ethical literature in medieval Judaism.[7] The central question of his introduction is why there have been no works devoted to the cultivation of inner duties. Baḥya thus sees the cultivation of virtue as an obligation, no less important than the performance of external duties. It is a duty to love, trust, and be devoted to God. In the Eighth Gate, he refines his typology, defining three categories of duties: external duties, whose performance does not require internal intention; mixed duties, such as prayer, that involve both external performance and internal intention; and pure duties of the heart, which require no particular outward expression (8:3, Ninth Way).[8] The cultivation of a virtuous inward character is thus a central goal of religious life.

Scholars have debated whether Baḥya's duties of the heart represent the dimension of intention in carrying out other religious obligations or whether they represent an entire new set of obligations parallel to the 613 commandments of Jewish law.[9] What is clear is that Baḥya's duties of the heart encompass the entire inward sphere accompanying actions, including intentions, theological beliefs, and motivations.[10] Baḥya thus emphasizes the inner dimension of virtue. As in Aristotelian ethics, for Baḥya, virtues are states of character.

For Baḥya, they are not only dispositions to act in a certain way, but constitute autonomous values. Rabbinic thought interprets the obligation to love God as acting in ways that express love.[11] This is true for Baḥya as well. However, while Baḥya does not deny the importance of carrying out external duties (which he calls duties of the limbs), he emphasizes that the ultimate value of action lies in the inner sphere of intention (duties of the heart), and that inner states of love, reliance, and devotion—the pure duties of the heart—are of supreme value.[12]

Baḥya's Central Virtues

Many of Baḥya's virtues emphasize the intellectual and theological spheres. Like Saadya, Baḥya emphasizes that it is a religious duty to prove for oneself philosophical truths about the divine. Thus his first Gate is purifying one's understanding of God's unity, and his second Gate is devoted to contemplation of creation, to find within it traces of the divine. Baḥya parallels early figures in Islam such as Ḥasan al-Baṣrī (641–727) and al-Muhāsibī (ca. 781–857) who bridge mysticism and rationalist theology.[13] For Baḥya, there is also a close connection between purification of one's conception of God's oneness and purity in one's acts of devotion. Socrates, Plato, and Aristotle emphasize the unity of the virtues; the goal for these thinkers is a unified state of character that expresses itself in virtues such as justice, moderation/temperance, piety, courage, and wisdom. Likewise, each of Baḥya's virtues mirrors and complements the others; Baḥya's aim is an integrated state of character unified by the oneness of God and the singularity of devotion.

Baḥya is steeped in the Sufi tradition of absolute reliance on God and the complex of virtues associated with asceticism (*zuhd*). His focus on reliance on God and passive quietism is somewhat in tension with rabbinic emphasis on activism; Baḥya may even veer toward the Islamic view that all is determined by the divine.[14] In contrast to the Aristotelian emphasis on the mean and moderation, Baḥya argues that reason calls for an extreme of humility, self-abasement, and asceticism, even while he acknowledges that the Torah tempers the rational imperative to ascetic renunciation with a call for moderation, so as to maintain the social order of the world (3:3).[15]

Nevertheless, the key virtue that is the culmination of his path is not asceticism but love.[16] Here, too, he focuses on the extreme love for

God that is willing to sacrifice all (10:4).[17] He draws a key distinction that Maimonides will echo between two kinds of fear: fear of punishment, and reverence and awe that calls us to serve God simply because God is worthy of service.[18] His culminating virtue of love even moves toward union with the divine; he defines love as a yearning of the soul to be attached to the divine light (10:1).[19] Likewise in the chapter on self-reckoning, he describes a state of divine infusion in which God acts through the servant (8:3, Tenth Way).[20] Baḥya's emphasis is clearly on the theological goal of connection with God, to which the anthropological relationship between humans is but a stepping stone.

Baḥya describes the states of fear or reverence and love as intimately intertwined. He argues that fear of God is of two kinds. One is fear of God's punishment and trials; this falls short of the level of people who revere God. A leitmotif through his work is the rabbinic statement that one should not serve God as servants who seek reward (Pirkei Avot 1:3). In one passage, he connects this rabbinic statement with the words of a pious person: "I would be ashamed before my Lord to serve him in expectation of reward or in fear of punishment, because then I would be like a bad servant, who only does his work when he fears or hopes, but otherwise not. I however want to serve him because he is worthy of it."[21] The eleventh-century theologian al-Ghazālī attributes this and similar statements to several Sufi thinkers, including Rabi'a al-'Adawiyya (d. 752), a key figure in early Sufi pietism. When asked what for her constitutes the truth of faith, Rabi'a answered, "I have never served God out of fear of hell or out of yearning for Paradise, because then I would be just like a bad servant; I only serve him out of love and longing for him."[22] We thus see in Baḥya the seamless integration of rabbinic and Sufi ideals of pure, disinterested devotion.

Baḥya goes on to describe a second type of fear based on awe, reverence, and magnification of the power of God, which accompanies a person and is inseparable from one as long as one lives. This is the highest level of the fear of God, which the Torah describes as *yirah*; it is the gate to the pure love and intense, unsettling yearning for God. Whoever reaches this level of fear of God will not fear or be frightened by anyone other than God. Baḥya cites an anecdote in which one of the virtuous (*al-sāliḥīn*) described that he found a pious person laying down in a desert land. He said to him, "Don't you fear the lions in your lying down in a place like this?" The man replied, "I would be ashamed before my Lord that he would see me fearing anything other than him" (10:6).[23] The final saying, "I would feel ashamed before my Lord if I feared something other than him," is attributed to the second Islamic Caliph, 'Umar I, and appears in the tenth-century Sufi manual of Qushayrī.[24] Once again, Baḥya is deeply immersed in the language of both rabbinic and Sufi piety, which hold pure love and awe of God above all other values. Baḥya artfully integrates Sufi and rabbinic expressions of this common ideal.

For Baḥya, then, love and awe are two intertwined states that partake of the same quality. The higher reverence is not fear of punishment, but recognition of God's awesome grandeur, which is not very different from love. One loves God because God represents the ultimate value, intrinsically worthy of reverence. However, love as portrayed by Baḥya also reflects an element of longing; awe is the gateway to intense, unsettling yearning for union with God.

Love is thus clearly the culmination of all the virtues; the single virtue that encompasses all others.[25] Love is cultivated through a spiritual path. Baḥya does not present stages and states in the same sense as do the systematic Sufi thinkers of his time. In classical Sufi thought, a stage or a station (*maqām*; pl. *maqāmāt*) is cultivated through a path of spiritual effort, while a state (*ḥāl*; pl. *aḥwāl*) is a gift from God.[26] In their manuals, systematic Sufi thinkers created a hierarchical progression for the cultivation of these virtues. By contrast, the gates of Baḥya's book do not correspond to a precise hierarchy, although Baḥya does add conceptual order to the gates. This is because he is creating an intellectual system as well as a spiritual system, and is committed to showing conceptual relationships and affinities between the virtues. While love is the culminating virtue or synthesis of all duties of the heart, each duty entails and mirrors the others. One can see Baḥya's work as guiding the spiritual seeker on a path that culminates in integration of the duties of the heart, all the spiritual and intellectual virtues.

The Cultivation of Virtue: Baḥya's Moral and Spiritual Ideal

What then is Baḥya's conception of the ideal person; what is the character that a person is striving to cultivate by means of this spiritual path? Although we have said that the culminating virtue is love, the guiding concept along the path is obedience (*ṭā'a*). Baḥya inherits this virtue from both Mu'tazilite rational theology and Sufi and ascetic (*zuhd*) piety; Baḥya's ideal person is both a rationalist and a pietist. He or she studies the Torah, but also contemplates nature and uses reason to prove for him or herself the existence and oneness of God and the obligation of obedience. One will then see the wisdom of absolute surrender to and reliance upon the divine, entrusting to God affairs of both this world and of the next. Most importantly, the pious person strives for purity of intention and integration between intention and action. One must be on guard against spiritual pride and aim for genuine humility and submission. Baḥya even takes into account the approach of ascetics such as the *Malamātiyya,* a Sufi group that would engage in blame-worthy actions in order to combat spiritual pride.[27] Baḥya, however, argues that to abstain from virtuous actions on account of what people might think is just another form of religious exhibitionism (*riyā',* being aware of being seen).[28]

Baḥya and the Jewish, Sufi, and Ascetic (*Zuhd*) Traditions

It is clear that much of the tenor of Baḥya's ethics is Sufi and ascetic (*zuhd*) in character, and he is not hesitant to cite extensive examples from the full range of Islamic literature, without mentioning any Islamic texts or thinkers by name.[29] His cited prooftexts are all from Jewish literature, both Biblical and rabbinic. One gets the impression that he is unselfconscious in his integration of streams of thought—Islamic and Jewish, rabbinic, philosophical, and theological. Subsequent generations who have read Baḥya in Hebrew translation have read this as a purely Jewish pietistic work, often unaware of its deep indebtedness to Islamic literature and modes of thought. Baḥya clearly believes that the Jewish path of *mitsvot* is meant to create an integrated spiritual character, one of humility, gratitude, and obedience to God, trusting and relying on the divine alone, repentant, shunning wealth and luxury, deeply devoted to God with a pure love. Baḥya's extensive citations from Biblical and rabbinic texts suggest that this is his genuine spiritual and pietistic reading of the Jewish tradition. His final gate on the true love of God is a meditation on the central assertion of God's unity in the Shema prayer. He cites as exemplars Biblical figures from Abraham to Job, along with tales of numerous unnamed pious figures culled from Islamic *hadīth*, ascetic, and Sufi literature.[30]

A later thinker who was also deeply influenced by Sufism, Abraham son of Maimonides (1186–1237), is more self-conscious in his borrowing from and relationship to Sufi traditions. He states that he grieves when he sees Jews imitating Islamic traditions, when the practices of the Sufis are themselves borrowed from the Biblical prophets.[31] Baḥya makes no such apologetic or self-conscious statement. He never mentions the Sufis or Islamic ascetics by name, citing their exemplars in Arabic as "one of the righteous/pious ones [*al-sāliḥīn*]" or "one of the virtuous [*al-afāḍil*]." He does argue that he is filling an obvious lacuna in Jewish works written on duties, since he had not found any that expressed the most central, binding, and continuous duties, namely, the internal duties, the duties of the heart (introduction).[32] For Baḥya, to be a Jew is not primarily a matter of practice, but of belief, emotion, and total life orientation or attitude. In contrast to Judah Halevi, who emphasizes the particularity of Jewish practice, Baḥya stresses the universal way of inward religious devotion.[33] He argues that the Jewish system of *mitsvot* was given as a special grace to enable Jews to more fully express gratitude to God and receive appropriate reward (3:3, 3:6).[34]

Duties of the Heart: Virtue, Law, and the Supreme Goal

Baḥya presents a novel approach to the relationship between virtue and law, building upon Saadya's distinction between rational and revelational commandments. For Saadya, rational commandments are mainly social and ethical, relations between human beings, while revelational commandments pertain to duties toward God.[35] By contrast, for Baḥya, rational commandments include all the duties of the heart, the inward spiritual states that are the heart of human beings' relationship to the divine.

While the duties of the limbs are finite, the duties of reason are infinite and constantly expanding. This raises the question of the relationship between the 613 commandments and the duties of the heart; it seems that the two categories are overlapping. Some of the 613 commandments are duties of the heart; some duties of the heart are included within the 613 commandments. But the duties of the heart also branch off infinitely. The 613 commandments offer a baseline minimum, but we can always find new ways to serve, love, and be devoted to God (3:3, 10:7).[36] The law of revelation commands virtue; all the more so does the law of reason. Baḥya thus extends the realm of obligation. The obligation to cultivate a virtuous character is broader than that enjoined by the Torah; its reach is almost infinite. Whereas for Baḥya, as for Saadya, the law supplied by reason needs positive revelatory law to supply details and implementation, the law enjoined by reason also entails obligations not given by the positive law of the Torah alone.

In Baḥya's initial listing in the introduction to the book, he divides commandments into those that are received and those that are rational, and says that all duties of the heart are rational. Here he draws upon Saadya's distinction between rational and received commandments, whose source is Mu'tazilite. When the Mu'tazilites speak of reason, they are not thinking of abstract logic, but of a natural moral instinct. Saadya writes, "[I]n regard to all the things which [God] commands us to do, he has implanted approval of them in our reason, and in regard to all the things that he forbids us to do, he has implanted disapproval of them in our reason."[37] The prime example Saadya gives of a rational moral cognition is gratitude; he sees this as the root of prayer and all acts of divine service.

Received knowledge, in contrast, is that which is received by "hearing" from an external source. Thus while human beings immediately intuit the evil of lying and stealing, they must hear from the received law about forbidden foods. The received laws are thus termed laws that are "heard," in contrast to the rational laws, which are cognized.

Baḥya accepts Saadya's epistemology with minor variations, and with it the distinction between rational and received obligations, although he uses the term "duties" rather than "laws." He weaves this distinction together with another one: the distinction between duties of the heart and duties of the limbs, which, as Amos Goldreich has shown, was articulated in a form close to that of Baḥya by the ninth-century Islamic pietist al-Muḥāsibī.[38] Religious knowledge is divided into two parts. One is knowledge of the duties of the limbs, which is the external knowledge; the second is knowledge of the duties of the heart, which is the hidden knowledge or knowledge of the inner (introduction).[39]

The duties of the limbs are in turn divided into two categories. One consists of duties that reason would make obligatory, even if Scripture had not declared their obligation. The second category consists of revelational duties, those that reason in itself neither necessitates nor prohibits, such as the prohibition of eating milk with meat. Duties of the heart, he asserts, are all rational; reason declares these duties incumbent, even if they are not ordained by Scripture (introduction).[40] The two axes—rational and received commandments, duties of the heart and duties of the limbs—are thus overlapping. All duties of the heart are recognized by reason; some are among the 613 commandments of the Torah.

Of note here is that Baḥya's mind and heart are not two separate categories; Baḥya makes no distinction between beliefs and virtues. Baḥya moves smoothly between the categories: from belief in a creator who created the world from nothing to the virtue of absolute trust, from contemplation of creation to dedication of action to God. His work thus expresses the unity of the intellectual and moral virtues; any duty whose locus is the inner dimension is a duty of the heart.

Baḥya had wondered why the inner duties have not been discussed in classical guides to the commandments. Nevertheless, he concludes that not only are they not optional or supererogatory; they are indeed foundational to all the other duties. Since the inner realm of the mind and heart is the most noble dimension of a human being, surely humans must be held accountable not only for outer actions, but also for the inner life. Moreover, none of one's outer actions can be properly carried out without the cooperation of the inner being. If the inner being were not convinced that the heart has obligations to God, it could not rouse in the body the motivation to act. By the same token, not only do human beings have a duty to perform actions of divine service; they are also obliged to have proper intentions. Thus surely God would not have left the inner realm free of obligation (introduction).[41]

In the Eighth Gate, Baḥya develops three categories of commandments: duties of the limbs, duties of the heart, and duties that include both limbs and heart. Among duties of the limbs alone, he includes laws such as observing festivals, Sabbaths, and fast days, and performing outer actions of religious observance. Among duties of heart and limbs together, he includes commandments such as prayer, reading the Torah, glorifying and praising God, spreading knowledge of God, commanding the good, and prohibiting evil. The duties that are purely of the heart are those that have no outward manifestation, being purely internal and known to the person and God alone. These include pure affirmation of God's oneness, reliance on God, the resolution to take upon oneself obedience to God, dedicating one's actions to God alone, humility before both God and humans, repentance, an abstinent heart, and love for God. Among negative duties of the heart, he includes refraining from envy, the inclination to disobey God, and attachment to things of this world.

We see how radical is Baḥya's reconfiguration of the realm of obligation in Judaism.[42] Baḥya has in effect created an entirely new category of obligation. Moreover, if we think of these internal spiritual states as virtues, Baḥya has in effect argued that the rational law commands us to cultivate a virtuous character. Virtue is for Baḥya primarily an internal state. To those who would conceive of Judaism as purely a religion of outward behavior, Baḥya argues that the Torah's goal is to promote an inward spirituality, a virtuous inner life.

This life culminates in the supreme goal of connection with the divine light, promised in the next world and adumbrated in this world. We can have intimations of this state in this world:

> If this point [that God is aware of one's inner being] is repeated in the mind of the believer, and he constantly reflects upon it in his soul, God will always be present with him in his consciousness, and he will see Him with the eyes of the intellect. . . . If he continues to do this, God will soothe him and keep him company in his spiritual loneliness; he will acquaint him with the secrets of His wisdom and open the door of knowing Him. . . . He will take it as His task to manage and direct him, not leaving him alone to himself and to his own devices, as it is said in the psalm of David, "the Lord is my shepherd, I shall not want" [Ps. 23:1], to the end of the psalm. And he will become in the highest ranks of the companions of God, and in the most exalted of the levels of the pure, and he will see with no eye, and hear with no ear, and converse with no tongue, and feel things with no senses, and sense these things with no need of logic.
>
> He does not prefer one thing to another; he does not wish for a situation other than the one in which he finds

> himself. For God has chosen all for him, and he has tied his own satisfaction to that of God and connected his love to God's love, so that he loves what God loves, and hates what is hateful to Him. Of him said the Sage [Prov. 8:34–35]: "Happy is the man that harkens to me, watching daily at my gates, waiting at the posts of my door. For whoever finds me finds life, and obtains favor of the Lord."[43]

The path of inner virtue thus culminates in a mystical experience of infusion with the divine, being guided in a loving, intimate relationship with a personal companion. For Baḥya, virtue is a necessary and sufficient goal for the supreme goal, the culminating virtue of love for God, both in this life and the next.

Notes

1. A. S. Yahuda, ed., *Al-hidāja'ilā farā'iḍ al-qulūb des Bachja Ibn Josef Ibn Paqūda* (Leiden: Brill, 1912), 63ff.

2. D. Z. Baneth, "The Common Teleological Source of Baḥya Ibn Paquda and al-Ghazālī" [Hebrew], in *Sefer Magnes*, ed. F. Baer et al. (Jerusalem: Hebrew University Press, 1938).

3. See P. K. Kokowzov, "The Date of the Life of Baḥya Ibn Paquda," in *Livre d'hommage à la mémoire du Dr. Samuel Poznanski* (Warsaw: Comite de la Grande Synagogue a Varsovie, 1927): 19–20.

4. See Sara Sviri, "*Zuhd* in Islamic Mysticism: Conduct and Attitude," in *Perspectives on Early Islamic Mysticism: The World of al-Ḥakīm al-Tirmidhī and His Contemporaries* (New York: Routledge, 2020), 38. Cf. Amos Goldreich, "Possible Arabic Sources for the Distinction between 'Duties of the Heart' and 'Duties of the Limbs' " [Hebrew], *Te'udah* 6 (1988): 179–208.

5. Krinis presented the outline of his book in progress, tentatively titled *Stranger in This World: Baḥya Ibn Paquda and the Turn Inward in Islamic and Judeo-Arabic Asceticism (Zuhd)* at the Harvard University Starr seminar, March 17, 2021. Cf. Goldreich, "Possible Arabic Sources.' "

6. See Sviri, "*Zuhd* in Islamic Mysticism," 38.

7. Joseph Dan, *Jewish Mysticism and Jewish Ethics* (Northvale, NJ: Jason Aronson, 1996), 25–26.

8. Baḥya Ibn Paquda, *Kitāb al-Hidāya ilā farā'iḍ al-qulūb (Torat Ḥovot ha-Levavot)*, ed. and trans. Joseph Qafiḥ (Jerusalem: Central Committee of Yemenite Jews, 1973), 341–42; *Book of Direction to the Duties of the Heart*, trans.

Menahem Mansoor (London: Routledge and Kegan Paul, 1973), 364; *Sefer ha-Hadrakhah el Ḥovot ha-Levavot*, trans. Binyamin Abrahamov (Ramat-Gan: Bar Ilan University Press, 2019), 264.

9. Amos Goldreich, "Possible Arabic Sources," 179–80.

10. Cf. Bernard Septimus, "What Did Maimonides Mean by *Madda'*?," in *Me'ah She'arim: Studies in Medieval Jewish Spiritual Life in Memory of Isadore Twersky*, ed. G. Blidstein et al. (Jerusalem: Hebrew University Magnes Press, 2001), 108–10.

11. See Sifrei Deuteronomy, Pisqa 32.

12. On the relationship between intention and action in Baḥya, see Hannah Kasher, "A Hypothetical Dialogue between Judah Halevi and Baḥyā Ibn Paqūda," *Studies in Arabic and Islamic Culture* 2 (2006): 57–86, esp. 59, 71.

13. Cf. Diana Lobel, *A Sufi-Jewish Dialogue: Philosophy and Mysticism in Baḥya Ibn Paquda's "Duties of the Heart"* (Philadelphia: University of Pennsylvania Press, 2007), 198–200. Speaking about knowledge of the heart, al-Makkī, *Qūt al-qulūb* teaches that Ḥasan was the first to "set people upon the path of this knowledge, and start tongues [talking] about it, to articulate its matters, reveal its lights and uncover its veil. He spoke in it of things that had never been heard by any of his peers." The Sufis thus regard Ḥasan as their founder: "Ḥasan is our *imām* in this doctrine that we represent. We walk in his footsteps and follow his ways; from his lamp we have our light." See al-Makkī, *Qūt al-qulūb* (Cairo, 18921893), 1:149–50. Cf. English translation in *Knowledge of God in Classical Sufism*, trans. John Renard (Mahwah, NJ: Paulist Press, 2004), 175–76.

14. See R. J. Zvi Werblowsky, "Faith, Hope and Trust: A Study in the Concept of *Biṭṭaḥon*," *Papers of the Institute of Jewish Studies* 1 (1964): 95–139, esp. 126; Alexander Altmann, "The Religion of the Thinkers: Free Will and Predestination in Saadia, Baḥya, and Maimonides," in *Religion in a Religious Age*, ed. S. D. Goitein (Cambridge, MA: Association for Jewish Studies, 1974): 33–35.

15. *Duties* 3:3; 139 (Qafiḥ); 185 (Mansoor); 118 (Abrahamov). See Howard Kreisel, "Asceticism in the Thought of R. Baḥya Ibn Paquda and Maimonides," *Da'at* 21 (1988): 5–22, at 7–13; Allan Lazaroff, "Baḥya's Asceticism against Its Rabbinic and Islamic Background," *Journal of Jewish Studies* 21 (1970): 31, 36–38.

16. It is of note that the ascetic pietist al-Muḥāsibī also places love at the apex of the pietist path, as does al-Ghazālī. See Margaret Smith, *Readings from the Mystics of Islam* (London: Luzac, 1972), sources 13, 16; Christopher Melchert, "The Transition from Asceticism to Mysticism in the Middle of the Ninth Century C.E.," *Studia Islamica*, no. 83 (1996): 54, citing Abū Nu'aym 10:78; Binyamin Abrahamov, *Divine Love in Islamic Mysticism: The Teachings of al-Ghazālī and al-Dabbāgh* (London: Routledge, 2003), 28 and 41, citing al-Ghazālī, *Iḥyā' 'ulūm al-dīn, Kitab al-maḥabba; Iḥyā'* vol. 4, book 6.

17. *Duties* 10:4; 418 (Qafiḥ); 433 (Mansoor); 321 (Abrahamov).

18. See Maimonides, *Mishneh Torah, Hilkhot Yesodei ha-Torah* 2:1–2; *Hilkhot Teshuvah* 10:1–10.

19. *Duties* 10:1; 410 (Qafiḥ); 427 (Mansoor); 315 (Abrahamov).

20. *Duties* 8:3, Tenth Way; 347–48 (Qafiḥ); 369 (Mansoor); 268 (Abrahamov).

21. *Duties* 10:6; 420 (Qafiḥ); 436 (Mansoor); 323 (Abrahamov).

22. Al-Ghazālī, *Iḥyā' 'ulūm al-dīn* 4:222.

23. *Duties* 10:6; 420 (Qafiḥ); 436 (Mansoor).

24. Al-Qushayrī, *Al-Risāla al-Qushayrīya fī 'ilm al-taṣawwuf*, 129, lines 10ff, cited by Yahudah, *Al-Hidāja*, 90.

25. See Georges Vajda, *La théologie ascétique de Baḥya Ibn Paquda* (Paris: Imprimerie Nationale, 1947), 22–23.

26. See Michael Sells, *Early Islamic Mysticism* (Mahwah, NJ: Paulist Press, 1996), 102.

27. Sara Sviri, "*Hakīm Tirmidhī* and the *Malāmatī* Movement in Early Sufism," in *Classical Persian Sufism from its Origins to Rumi*, ed. Leonard Lewisohn (Oxford: Oneworld, 1999), 583–613.

28. Lobel, *A Sufi-Jewish Dialogue*, 160–63, 166–67, 170–75. Ehud Krinis contextualizes these themes as characteristic of the broader movement of *zuhd*.

29. For a comprehensive survey for Baḥya's Islamic sources, see Binyamin Abrahamov, "The Sources Used by Rabbi Baḥya Ibn Paqūda in *Ḥovot ha-Levavot*" [Hebrew], *Oreshet* 9 (2020): 7–38.

30. See Abrahamov, "The Sources," 21–30.

31. Maimonides, *The High Ways to Perfection of Abraham Maimonides*, ed. Samuel Rosenblatt (New York and Baltimore: Johns Hopkins Press, 1938), 2:322; cf. 266, 320, 420.

32. *Duties*, introduction; 18 (Qafiḥ); 88–89 (Mansoor); 27–28 (Abrahamov).

33. See Sara Sviri, "Spiritual Trends in Pre-Kabbalistic Judeo-Spanish Literature: The Cases of Baḥya Ibn Paquda and Judah Halevi," *Donaire* 6 (April 1996): 78–84; Ehud Krinis, "Radical Judeo-Andalusian Thinkers in Conflict: The Cases of Baḥya Ibn Paqūda and Judah Halevi," *Frankel Institute Annual*, vol. 2019, 25–27.

34. *Duties* 3:3; 141 (Qafiḥ); 187 (Mansoor); 119 (Abrahamov); 3:6; 163–64 (Qafiḥ); 204 (Mansoor); 135 (Abrahamov); Hannah Kasher, "A Hypothetical Dialogue," 82–83.

35. Lazaroff, "Baḥya's Asceticism," 25.

36. *Duties* 3:3; 137–38 (Qafiḥ); 184 (Mansoor); 117 (Abrahamov); cf. 10:7; 428 (Qafiḥ); 443 (Mansoor); 329 (Abrahamov); Lobel, *A Sufi-Jewish Dialogue*, 188–89.

37. Saadya Gaon, *Kitāb al-mukhtār fī'l-amānāt wa'l-i'tiqādāt* (*Sefer ha-Nivḥar ba-Emunot u-va-De'ot*), 3:1, ed. and trans. J. Qafiḥ (Jerusalem: Sura Institute for Research and Publication, 1970), 118; *Book of Beliefs and Opinions*, trans. Samuel Rosenblatt (New Haven, CT: Yale University Press, 1948), 40.

38. Goldreich, "Possible Arabic Sources"; Lobel, *A Sufi-Jewish Dialogue*, 196–98.

39. *Duties*, introduction; 15–16 (Qafiḥ); 87 (Mansoor); 25 (Abrahamov).

40. *Duties*, introduction; 16 (Qafiḥ); 87 (Mansoor); 25 (Abrahamov).

41. *Duties*, introduction; 19 (Qafiḥ); 89 (Mansoor); 28 (Abrahamov).

42. See Dan, *Jewish Mysticism and Jewish Ethics*, 26; Krinis, "*Radical Judeo-Andalusian Thinkers in Conflict*."

43. *Duties* 8:3, Tenth Way; 347–48 (Qafiḥ); 369 (Mansoor); 268 (Abrahamov). On this passage, see Lobel, *A Sufi-Jewish Dialogue*, 47–50; Diana Lobel, "On the Lookout: A Sufi Riddle in Sulamī, Qushayrī, and Baḥya Ibn Paquda," in *Studies in Arabic and Islamic Culture* 2 (2006): 107–12.

Chapter 6

Solomon Ibn Gabirol

SARAH PESSIN

Solomon Ibn Gabirol (Abū Ayyūb Sulaimān Ibn Yaḥyā Ibn Jabīrūl, known in the Latin West as Avicebron [Hebrew: Shelomoh ben Yehudah Ibn Gabirol) was born in 1021 or 1022 in Malaga, spent time in Saragossa, and died in 1054–1058, 1069, or 1070, likely in Valencia. A brilliant poet and philosopher-theologian, Ibn Gabirol was influenced by biblical and other Jewish texts alongside Pythagorean, Aristotelian, and Plotinian materials. He was the author of over three hundred poems, including his magisterial philosophical *Kingdom's Crown*, the ethical treatise *On the Improvement of the Moral Qualities* (in Arabic, *kitab iṣlāḥ al-akhlāq*), and his philosophical magnum opus *The Fountain of Life*, written in Judeo-Arabic in the eleventh century (*yanbū' al-ḥayāt*) and translated into Latin (*Fons Vitae*) in the twelfth century. The Latin version was influential on centuries of Christian scholastics who took it to be the work of an Augustinian Christian—a confusion cleared up in the 19th century when Salomon Munk located a thirteenth-century Hebrew summary of the text (*mekor ḥayyim*) and identified "Avicebron" as the well-known Jewish poet.

Virtues and Worldview

In his concern for virtuous life, Ibn Gabirol follows a Greco-Islamo-Jewish set of sensibilities according to which humans and the world in which we live are a "microcosm" (little world, or little order) in relation to a "macrocosm" (big world, or big order) itself taken sometimes as the divine mind and sometimes as the universe as a product of the divine mind. In his particularly emanationist frame—rooted in the Neoplatonic works of third-century Greek thinker Plotinus by way of such texts as *The Theology of Aristotle* (a misleadingly titled Arabic edition of books 4–6 of Plotinus's *Enneads*)—Ibn Gabirol additionally envisions a "universal intellect" as a first creation and emanating source in which the rest of existence is sustained. Referred to as the "sphere of Intellect" (Hebrew, *galgal ha-sekhel*) in his *Keter Malkhut* poem,[1] this repository of divine truths serves as a boundary between God's unity and the rest of reality and, as such, as a God-appointed source and sustaining cause of existence and order in the world. All of which is to say that in an emanationist context, a "macrocosm/microcosm" framing takes on a heightened intensity as the "little world"—the entire universe but also each human soul—is not only said *to mirror* but *to take its root in* a higher reality that is its source.

In such an intimate relation to a higher world, humans are at once rooted in and fallen from pure order, wisdom, and goodness. Resonating with a Jewish discourse on *teshuvah* (repentance, from the Hebrew root "return"), and very much on par with the at once descriptive and prescriptive implications of *imitatio dei* (i.e., descriptively we are said to be like God—at least in relation to our best ultimate state; prescriptively we are called to be like God so as to reach our best ultimate state), we find a Greek emanationist emphasis on a "return" in which humans are called upon to recover their root in wisdom and goodness. Framed by "turning" and "returning" directives in both a Jewish and Greco-Islamic philosophical key, Ibn Gabirol sees the cultivation of goodness, wisdom, and a host of other virtues as a path to reclaiming our connection to the higher realities in which we are ultimately grounded and from which we are always falling away.

Because there is an order to things—moreover, an order that is nothing less than a product and mark of God's goodness—to live in the world is to aim to "return" oneself and the world to its perfect order. In the case of humans, this involves properly ordering our souls, which includes cultivating wisdom and other virtues that either extirpate or tame our bodies' recalcitrant tendencies toward maximum disorder. While Ibn Gabirol speaks of a positive sense of matter (more on that below), he also follows in a range of Greek philosophical traditions that see matter—and, in particular, corporeal, terrestrial matter—as a privation of goodness: matter in this sense is a marker of our fall away from the perfection of God's pure goodness and the perfect order that follows from it.

In such a context, metaphysical and cosmological analyses are always ethical for Ibn Gabirol: because God and Intellect root the universe—including individual human souls—in the fullness of goodness and wisdom, all theological, philosophical, scientific, and even logical and mathematical inquiry will always involve reordering our souls on our path back to goodness. Very much aligning with calls to *imitatio dei,* Ibn Gabirol is part of a Greco-Islamic tradition that sees God's pure goodness as both that which ultimately grounds us and as that towards which we must constantly strive. Ibn Gabirol is in this respect attuned to our striving after something of the goodness of God—a theme that emerges throughout his philosophical writing. We can also see this theme in his ethical treatise where he references a number of biblical verses, including King David's calling out to God "Make with me a covenant for goodness" (Ps. 86:17, "*aseh imi ot le-tovah*") along with the reminder that the heights of such goodness are granted to those who "walk uprightly and work righteousness" (Ps. 15:2, "*holekh tamim u-foel tzedek*").

And it is within this broader context that he turns to twenty particular virtues in his *On the Improvement of the Moral Qualities.* Engaging themes that occur in a range of Greek and Islamic philosophical, scientific, and medical traditions, Ibn Gabirol sees the details of human constitution in microcosmic relation to the four elements: in relation to earth, air, fire, and water, the human is made of black bile, blood, yellow bile, and phlegm (*al-balghām*)[2]—the four humours that we find in Hippocrates through Galen and that are broadly associated with the four elements across a wide range of Greek thinkers. But while many Greek traditions tie imbalances of earth/black bile, air/blood, fire/yellow bile, and water/phlegm to four groupings of human conditions—the melancholic, sanguine, choleric, and phlegmatic in turn—Ibn Gabirol divides up the virtues and vices into five groupings of four traits that he aligns with the five senses broadly and even metaphorically construed in relation to biblical texts. While not found as such in either Plato or the Brethren of Purity (*Ikhwān aṣ-Ṣafā*), it is worth considering Ibn Gabirol's emphasis on the five senses in comparison to and contrast with the microcosmic analysis of the human body in relation to the cosmos in Plato's *Timaeus*,[3] and the analysis of the five senses' relation to planets in the Ikhwān's Islamic cosmological-ethical writings that, we might add, use the same Arabic phrase that appears in Ibn Gabirol's title—*iṣlāḥ al-akhlāq*—to highlight the importance of improving one's moral qualities.[4]

We will summarize Ibn Gabirol's twenty sense-by-sense correlated virtues/vices below. But we will also probe into the depths of his *Fons Vitae* philosophy to recommend a twenty-first "hidden virtue"—the virtue of receptivity that sits at the core of all the other virtues and that sits at the core of the call to return to goodness. Especially in a context where cosmology is inherently ethical, but also in light of what we will see is a uniquely apophatic sensibility to Ibn Gabirol's emanationist project, we are well-served to find our way to a hidden virtue that quietly and repeatedly announces itself across his unusual discourse on reality as an iterative series of matters upon matters upon matters—including a materiality at the core of even intellect. In its content and in its form, Ibn Gabirol's "metaphysics of matter" gives rise to a virtue theoretical emphasis on the value of receptivity at the heart of theology and ethics.

Which Virtues?

Let's start with the twenty virtue/vice constellations that Ibn Gabirol lays out in his ethical treatise. He divides these into groups of four with one group for each of the five senses, in this way embarking on something of a "sensory virtue theory" (see table 6.1).[5]

The first thing to note is how he connects a sensory virtue theory to a theology. This should come as no surprise given what we have already seen about his Greek, Jewish, and Islamic microcosm/macrocosm contexts:

> [M]an ought to consider carefully the qualities which belong to his senses and not employ them except when it is necessary; for God, exalted be He, has so constituted them in man that he can wisely order them, since through them he guards the normal condition of his life. By their means he sees colors, hears sounds, tastes food (flavors),

Table 6.1. Virtues and vices in *On the Improvement of the Moral Qualities*

sight	hearing	smell	taste	touch
pride (*ash-shamkh*) >*shamakha*- to be lofty; to disdain; form 6= to be boastful, to put on airs	**love** (*al-ḥubb*) > *ḥabba*= to love, to like	**wrath** (*al-ghaḍab*) > *ghaḍiba*= to be or become angry, mad, irritated	**joy** (*al-faraḥ*) > *fariḥa*= to be happy, to rejoice	**generosity** (*sakhā'*) > *sakhā*= to be generous
humility (*al-khushū'*) > *khasha'a*= to be submissive, humble	**hate** (*al-bughḍ*) > *baghiḍa*= to be hated; to be hateful	**contentment** (*ar-riḍā'*) > *raḍiya*= to be satisfied; to be pleased; form 10= to try to gain good will or favor	**grief** (*al-hamm*) > *hamma*= to make uneasy, to fill with anxiety; to worry; form 8= to be distressed, grieved	**stinginess** (*al-bakhal*) or: **greed** (*al-bukhl*) > *bakhala*= to be stingy, to scrimp, to give reluctantly
shyness, timidity (*al-ḥayā'*) > *ḥayiya*= to live; to experience; to be ashamed; form 10= to be embarrassed; to be shy	**mercy** (*ar-raḥma*) > *raḥima*= to have mercy; to have compassion; to spare; form 6= to show human understanding for one another; to love and respect one another	**jealousy** (*al-ghayra*) > *ghāra*= to be jealous	**tranquility** (*aṭ-ṭumā'nīna*) > ṭam'*ana*, ta'*mana*= to calm; form 4= to become still; to be sure, to trust	**courage** (*ash-shajā'a*) > *shaju'a*= to be courageous, brave

continued

Table 6.1. Continued.

sight	hearing	smell	taste	touch
shamelessness; impudence; insolence; sauciness (*al-qiḥa*) > *waqaḥa*= to be shameless, impudent, insolent	**hard-heartedness, hardness, harshness, sternness, severity, cruelty, mercilessness** (*al-qaswa*) > *qasā*= to be harsh, stern, cruel, merciless, remorseless; to treat harshly; form 2= to harden the heart	**liveliness, vivacity** (*an-nashāṭ*) > *nashiṭa*= to be lively, animated, spirited, active, eager, keen, energetic; to attend (to something) actively	**remorse, repentance, regret** (*an-nadam*) > *nadima*= to repent	**cowardice** (*al-jubn*) > *jabuna*= to be a coward, to be fearful, to shrink (from something)

Source: Author provided.

> smells odors, distinguishes between hard and soft, and all other things which are necessary to his life; and many which are useful we will mention when we commence (the subject), please God. We will now describe the senses and the various advantages to be derived from their use and the necessity of refraining from the use of them when they would cause harm.[6]

We may in this regard speak of a theological-moral-sensory interface in which divine design orders human life such that the embodied activities of everyday life through which we aim to attain goodness are themselves grounded in and supervenient upon the basic sensory ways we engage our world.

We may in this spirit speak of a framework that moves us organically albeit in complex ways from color to courage to covenant.

But even beyond this, Ibn Gabirol's theological-moral-sensory frame is also a creatively hermeneutical one—a hybrid physiognomic-literary mode of interpretation and analysis that is at once biological and metaphorical, embodied and textual. To see this, consider Ibn Gabirol's invocation of an Ecclesiastes-meets-Exodus-meets-physiognomy framing just prior to the above insight in his introductory essay. After recounting the connection between the four elements and the four humours and clarifying that each human organ and sense is microcosmically ordered by God in relation to the cosmic whole, he adds the following about the senses in particular:

> Solomon the Wise alludes to them when he says (Ecclesiastes 9:11) "I returned and saw under the sun"; "seeing" here means to observe carefully, the general term for "seeing" being here used in the place of the specific term, "observing carefully" as in saying "under the sun" he means whatever the sun encircles. In the saying, "The race is not to the swift" he hints as the sense of smell, which is (situated in) the nose, because running is impossible except through the inhalation of air from without to cool the natural heat which is within man. The inhalation is accomplished by the sense of the nose, and if there were no nose there could be no breathing which causes motion. In saying "Nor is the battle to the strong," he wishes to indicate the sense of hearing; just as we see that war consists of crying and of hearing in battles, as it is said (Exod. 32:17) "There is a noise of war in the camp." In saying "Nor yet riches to the understanding," he refers to the sense of touch, which is of a kind with the understanding: the latter is of the category of the inner senses, which are concealed in the nature of the soul, as for example, perception, thought, and understanding. In saying, "Nor is there favor to men of skill," he wishes to indicate the sense of sight, which does not become knowledge except through prolonged attention to scripture and continuous study of books.[7]

Here, the implication of speaking of the five external senses is quickly expanded in at least three different senses, each of which deepens the complexity of the hermeneutical method at play: (1) in a jointly quantitative-qualitative expansion, speaking of the five external senses now includes referencing *internal* senses; (2) moving from ethics to religion and from the universality of the former to the narrower particularisms of the latter, a sensory virtue theory is now connected to a study of Torah—a link seen both in his own use of Biblical proof-texts, and in the content of his claim in the last line; and lastly, (3) he signals that his sensory virtue theory will engage something of a scientific-moral-metaphorical hermeneutic in which we can move from the term "nose" to a consideration of all manner of human motions and doings, and from the term "hearing" to an inquiry into the human experience of war. That said, these moves are not merely metaphorical: for example, in his further remarks on smell's relation to wrath and jealousy, and returning to the Greek medical framing of temperaments in relation to ratios of bodily humours, he speaks of how these vices stem from a "heated temperament" and how the countervailing virtue of vivacity "consists in the movements of a man and results from the ordering of the organs of breathing, which are pivotal to the sense of smell." To be sure, the method here is complex and deserves careful attention. One takeaway is that when it comes to ancient or contemporary debates over cognitive or noncognitive, theological or affective aspects of moral life, Ibn Gabirol's method invites us to avoid simplistic approaches that are so God-dependent as to leave no room for bodies or human reason, so body-dependent as to leave no room for cognitive or divine factors, or so cognition-driven as to leave no room for God or body. Ibn Gabirol's sensory virtue theory weaves in roles for God, reason, and body—and it is perhaps this vexing intersection of factors that leads him to engage a metaphorical frame in relation to a broadly apophatic impulse that he shares with a range of Greek, Islamic, and Jewish thinkers.

Here we might add that Ibn Gabirol sees reason not only as providing the yardstick by which we measure justice and goodness but, as such, as providing direction on how to improve the moral qualities and reorient the soul. Furthermore, beyond Ibn Gabirol's describing each of the twenty qualities as species falling under the five senses as their genera, in his broadest logics he appears to root each of the virtue/vice constellations in moral-meets-sociopolitical questions of truth and justice: Sight is connected to pride, humility, shyness, and shamelessness because it connects us to the social world in ways that can tempt us away from the goodness of virtue to the pursuit of pleasure—the allure of whatever is shiniest, as it were, over the demands of the day. To the extent that we fall prey to such "sight failures" we become the types of people who chase our every whim in flights of shameless, prideful self-indulgence; to the extent that we overcome such "sight failures," we dispose ourselves to serve others in humble responsibility. Hearing is connected to love, hate, mercy, and cruelty in a similar spirit: where Greco-Islamic traditions of political philosophy—from Plato and Aristotle to al-Farabi and Maimonides—reflect on the potential dangers (albeit alongside the potential benefits) of imagination-fueled spaces of rhetoric (in contrast to reason-fueled spaces of philosophy), in his own commentary on "ears," Ibn Gabirol calls on us to avoid being persuaded down unjust paths. In its link with food and, in turn, an allegorical sense of Adam and Eve's sin pointing us to the dangers of unbridled bodily appetites, taste points to the broad need to train ourselves to discipline our desires. And so on.

Without recounting in further detail his analyses of the twenty moral qualities and their relation to the senses, we may say that in his sensory virtue theory Ibn Gabirol approaches the senses not merely as a sense-scientist, but through a complex physiology-meets-theology-meets-psychology-meets-politics-meets-metaphor method. In such a frame, sight is sight—and it is also more than sight; and so too for the other senses and their relation to the moral qualities and what is involved in improving them.

And to the twenty moral qualities, we can add a hidden twenty-first virtue. Here, we turn to Ibn Gabirol's *Fons Vitae* and its unusual description of layers upon layers of matter at the core of reality. One way this idea gets summarized—and rejected—among medieval Christian scholastics is as a "Doctrine of Universal Hylomorphism." Leaving aside its supporters who saw in the text an anti-emanationist Augustinian doctrine of spiritual matter and Divine Will, its detractors summarized the "matter layers" at worst as a misunderstanding of Aristotelian metaphysics and at best as a spurious and unjustified extension thereof. In short, Aristotle is known for a doctrine of hylomorphism that—drawing on the Greek *hyle* meaning matter and *morphē* meaning form—refers to his analysis of all *corporeal* substances as composites of matter and form. Ibn Gabirol's account is seen as a "universal" hylomorphism in that it attributes matter to even *incorporeal* substances (including Intellect)—a move that gets criticized as ill-informed.

Leaving aside the fuller details here,[8] the best response to such criticisms is to note that Ibn Gabirol's analysis is not best seen through an Aristotelian lens but a Neoplatonic one—and, in particular, an emanationist one framed by apophasis. Apophasis (the Greek term for "denial" or "negation," with *apo+phasis* literally signaling "unsaying") refers to "negative theological" moments in texts in which language's very failure to capture God is on display. Common examples include "hyper-predication"—claims that emphasize God's being hyper-x or beyond-y; paradoxical logics in which God is described in opposing ways; or metaphorical/analogical logics in which descriptions of God are qualified with the reminder that they are not precise descriptions—itself meant in a range of ways, some of them more content than others to acknowledge the depths of our inability to know divine details, but all of them pulsing with a sense of God's presence: even the staunchest proponents of apophasis who think we can know next to nothing about God are of course not atheists. On the contrary, in their very preoccupation with telling us how much they can't tell us about God, we can discern a rather evocative nod to the sheer fullness of their actual lived experience of the divine; we can in this regard speak of even their apophatic feats in terms of *kataphasis*, or "affirmation." In part following this logic, we may approach emanationism not so much as a doctrine about a cosmic causal mechanism but as a form of apophatic-kataphatic discourse in which a description of God and the divine realm is at least in part a silent—we might even say prayerful—nod to the paradox of divine unity: where God is a site of pure unified goodness and also the source of the plurality all around us, emanation—in its metaphorical description of the "flowing forth" of realities from other realities in relation to God as source—can be seen as a discourse that marks that mystery. In such a context, Ibn Gabirol's supplementing an emanationist discourse with "layers of matter" can be approached as something of a phenomenological dive into the iterative depths of the universe's dependencies on the gifts of its source. Devoid of the negative implications of lower corporeal matter in any number of Platonic and Aristotelian contexts (including in Ibn Gabirol's own treatment of lower corporeal matter), Ibn Gabirol's description of layers of spiritual matter at the heart of Souls and even at the heart of the Universal Intellect just outside of God pulses with a sense of receptivity, mystery, and desire. While Aristotle indeed describes matter as a desire for and receptivity to form—a set of insights undoubtedly at play in Ibn Gabirol—he does so at the intersection of natural science questions (e.g., "prime matter" is posited in response to questions about elemental change) and a set of metaphysical inquiries in which God is "cause of motion," not a source or sustainer of being. Indeed, for Aristotle, asking where being comes from or on what being relies are ill-formed questions. Not so for emanationists for whom the mystery of the reliance of all being and beings ultimately on and from a divine source is the framing impulse. Its Aristotelian resonances notwithstanding, Ibn Gabirol's discourse of matter is part of an emanationist frame. Less a failed attempt at natural science or even at metaphysics in the strictly Aristotelian sense, Ibn Gabirol's metaphysics-of-matter is best approached as an apophatic-kataphatic response (but not in the sense of a solution) to divine mystery and the paradoxes that arise from the reliance of multiple beings upon an utterly unified divine source. Ibn Gabirol's metaphysics-of-matter is in this regard an iterative inquiry into fragile receptivities at the heart of life within the context of a Neoplatonic frame that views all of life as dependent on divine life. Emphasizing the utter-dependence of reality that follows from within such a frame, Ibn Gabirol discerns in the logic of materiality a kind of grounding receptivity and desire at the core of life. And he amplifies this insight in at least four ways: (1) he describes all non-God substances in terms of multiple material layers—a discourse of receptivities upon receptivies, (2) he inverts classic hierarchies of forms-over-matters to highlight higher realities in their roles "as matters" sustaining lower realities (thereby associating matter with what is more sublime, not less), (3) he speaks of a universal (incorporeal) matter just outside of God at the heart of Universal Intellect, and (4) he even goes so far as to root that sublime matter in the hidden Divine Essence.

From the depths of Ibn Gabirol's own silent desire to know an unknowable God emerges a discourse on God's own hidden Essence giving rise to an iterative flow of matters. On the one hand, this signals how higher realities like Intellect and Soul carry on their own sustaining relations to lower effects in ways that mirror God's ultimate sustaining role: Intellect sustains Soul and Soul sustains Nature in the way that matter sustains form—lower beings are in this sense sustained like form. And it also signals just how deeply all things outside of God stand ready to desire after and receive something of His goodness—lower beings are in this sense receptive like matter.

There is a poetry in all of this, to be sure—and it manifests not simply as an "apophatic" site of negation, but as a "kataphatic" positive relation to a divine source; perhaps we may even speak of Ibn Gabirol's material metaphysics as a mode of prayer. To say that Universal Intellect—and each human intellect in turn—is "made up of matter" is not to make a confused Aristotelian claim about corporeal mereology; it is, rather, to humbly engage in reflection on the hidden mystery of God's goodness and the ways that all things are nothing if they are not first sites of receptive desire for something of that goodness. It is in this spirit that we may rethink Ibn Gabirol's *Fons Vitae* and its many differences from scholastic Aristotelian metaphysics.[9] And it is also in this spirit that we may speak of Ibn Gabirol's sense of receptivity—and the corresponding desire for goodness—as a hidden twenty-first virtue linking us to nothing less than God's own hidden core.

Exemplars: From Universal Matter to Divine Essence

In his enumeration of moral qualities, Ibn Gabirol connects virtues to various biblical exemplars—such as the prophet Moses in his own humility, and so on. More broadly—both in relation to the hidden virtue of receptivity and in relation to the pursuit of all virtues in the context of a microcosm/macrocosm frame—Ibn Gabirol roots virtue in the divine goodness. In the spirit of *imitatio dei,* God is the ultimate exemplar of virtues because God is the purity of goodness after whose goodness we strive and on the basis of whose goodness we live. Here, we are well-served to hear in Ibn Gabirol's emanationism a nod to a Greco-Islamic tradition of creation in the spirit of Plato's *Timaeus* 29e where God is described as sharing forth goodness because He is "without jealousy." In effect, while Plato does not speak in emanationist terms, this insight sits at the heart of emanation in Plotinus and his followers: God is so good that He cannot but share His goodness forward—a kind of ultimate freedom completely free of external limitations and pressures. His goodness, in other words, is already a principle of sharing-goodness-forward. Here, not unrelated to our inquiries into apophasis-as-kataphasis above, emanation is less a cosmic mechanism than a way of referencing God's lack of jealousy—God's pure goodness as a site of pure sharing-forth-of-goodness. And whereas we spoke above of the virtue of receptivity—a striving after something of God's goodness—we may here add two supplements: (1) in the spirit of *imitatio dei,* if we are striving to emulate a divine goodness that shares itself forward, then we are also striving to live lives in which we share goodness forward; and, relatedly, (2) this is not simply about sitting in search of God but about living virtuous lives in relation to our fellow humans and in relation to all living creatures and the world around us—all of which, for Ibn Gabirol as for a range of Greco-Islamic emanationists, has its source in God's bounty. Indeed, we may say that in Ibn Gabirol, God's own reality is an exemplar for living in such a way that we share goodness forward. And in related spirit, Ibn Gabirol highlights a material receptivity at the core of all beings, starting, of course, with Intellect itself as the primary site of being's desire for and striving after God. From a "material cosmology" of receptivity and desire emerges a call to live receptively—not just in relation to God but in relation to all fellow creatures—in the hopes of receiving and transmitting, returning to and paying forward something of that very goodness. We might go so far as to say that living receptively "as matter," so to speak, is the only real way to access something of the divine goodness and, as such, the only real way to be in the position of sharing goodness forward. While God is not matter in Ibn Gabirol, we can perhaps capture the spirit of this insight in a dual call to "be like matter" so you can "be like God." *Imitatio materiae* (imitation of matter), as it were, as a precondition for *imitation dei* (imitation of God). It is a material phenomenology of life lived in receptive desire after something of the goodness of God.

Greco-Jewish Phenomenology of Concrete Life

In such a "material phenomenology," might we not discern something of a Buberian rebuke of "theomania," the condition in which people ignore or harm neighbors and the world as they work to "find God"? Following emanationist frames in Plotinus and Greco-Islamic-Jewish traditions of microcosm/ macrocosm thinking, Ibn Gabirol's "virtue of receptivity" invites us to a twofold approach to life in which divinity cannot be experienced directly and in which honoring divine goodness comes through living virtuously in the concrete world. Also, not unlike the depth of lived experience more commonly associated with the Buberian I-Thou (see chapter 27 in this volume), Greco-Jewish emanationism is in part a deep sense of the presence-and-promise of divine goodness in the folds of everyday life. Such lived experience fuels a hunger for acting virtuously alongside a sense of intellect's gifts but also its limits as we navigate a world permeated by hidden openings of goodness—a point not lost, for example, on a thinker like Levinas (see chapter 32), who in his own radical ethical phenomenology frequently nods to Plato's and Plotinus's sense of a "goodness beyond being" at the core of life.[10]

Reflecting on the prayerful contours of Ibn Gabirol's own emanationist, matter-inflected phenomenology, it is perhaps most fitting to end with his own poetic call to virtuous life in our own hidden bond with divine goodness:

> . . . your life is like unto God's life
> hidden, like you yourself are hidden;
> if thine own maker be pure
> know too your own purity and marvel.[11]

Notes

1. See cantos 24–26. For facing Hebrew-English, see Ibn Gabirol, *The Kingly Crown*, trans. Bernard Lewis (Notre Dame, IN: University of Notre Dame Press, 2003), 76–83.

2. Wise translates "white moisture" for phlegm and "gall" for "bile"; I retranslated to better indicate the Greek humours as commonly translated. See Ibn Gabirol, *Improvement*, 32 (Arabic section, 3, line 7).

3. For a sense, see *Timaeus* 29d–35b, 44d–46a, 48e–53c, 64a–73a, 81e–92c.

4. On the Brethren of Purity, see Majid Fakhry, *Ethical Theories in Islam* (Leiden: Brill, 1991), 93–99; Seyyed Hossein Nasr, *An Introduction to Islamic Cosmological Doctrines* (Albany: State University of New York Press, 1993), 23–104 on Brethren (with body-part-to-planet correlations on 101), and 236–74 for related themes in Avicenna; Godefroid de Callataÿ and Bruno Halflants, eds., *Epistles of the Brethren of Purity: On Magic* (Oxford: Oxford University Press, 2011), 149n216, on their use of the phrase *iṣlāḥ al-akhlāq*.

5. For the chart in Arabic, see Ibn Gabirol, *Improvement* (Arabic section), 15 (reading "shīn" in *al-khushū'* in column 1, row 2). I provide Arabic roots and translations based on Ibn Gabirol's biblical examples alongside Hans Wehr and Lane Arabic lexicons; my goal here is to convey the phenomenological-lexical ranges of these qualities.

6. Ibn Gabirol, *Improvement*, 35.

7. Ibn Gabirol, *Improvement*, 33.

8. For my fuller analysis see my *Ibn Gabirol's Theology of Desire: Matter and Method in Jewish Medieval Neoplatonism* (Cambridge: Cambridge University Press, 2013); for my comparison of Ibn Gabirol's emanationist approach to "matter layers" in contrast with medieval scholatic mereology, see "When a Part Is Not a Part? Hylomorphic Emanationist Mereology in Ibn Gabirol," in *On What There Was: Parts and Wholes*, ed. Andrew Arlig (Turnhout, Belgium: Brepols, forthcoming); for my analysis of apophasis in relation to emanation, see *Ibn Gabirol's Theology of Desire*, 131–39, on the idea of the "doubly apophatic"; for my distinction between "apophatic metaphysics" and "apo-metaphysics," see "Jewish Emanationisms," *Oxford Handbook of Jewish Philosophy*, ed. Paul Franks and Yitzhak Melamed (Oxford: Oxford University Press, forthcoming); and for reflection on Ibn Gabirol, Derrida, and Levinas, see my "Khoric Apophasis: Matter and Messianicity in Islamo-Judeo-Greek Neoplatonism," in *Negative Theology as Jewish Modernity*, ed. Michael Fagenblat (Bloomington: Indiana University Press, 2017), 180–97.

9. For a fuller contrast between Ibn Gabirol's material metaphysics and scholastic mereologies of matter, see Pessin, "When a Part Is Not a Part."

10. On Levinas and Ibn Gabirol, see Pessin, "Khoric Apophasis," and Pessin, "Bonomythy and the Goodward Life: Sacred-Ethical Invitations to Pause, Prayer, and Politics in Plotinus and Levinas," in "Constructive Jewish Theology," ed. Stephen Kepnes, special issue (early view), *Modern Theology*, August 2022, https://doi.org/10.1111/moth.12813.

11. From Ibn Gabirol's *"reshut le-neshamah"*; for Hebrew, see Zangwill 1923/44, poem 41, 69, lines 3, 5–6; my translation.

Chapter 7

Maimonides

KENNETH SEESKIN

Moses ben Maimon (known to English speaking audiences as Maimonides and Hebrew speaking audiences as Rambam) was born in Cordoba, Spain, in 1138 and died in Fostat, a section of Cairo, in 1204. He is generally regarded as the greatest Jewish philosopher of the medieval period not only for the *Mishneh Torah,* a fourteen-volume compendium of Jewish law but for the *Guide of the Perplexed,* a philosophic analysis of the Hebrew Bible, which he characterized as an investigation of "the science of the Law in its true sense." This science is summed up by the first two commandments, which mandate belief in the existence of an incorporeal God.

He is also known for his rationalistic interpretation of Jewish law according to which every commandment either promotes a true opinion, such as belief in God, inculcates a noble quality, such as justice, or prevents wrongdoing. Although the rationale for some commandments may not be apparent, he insisted that we are obliged to seek it. He was and remains a controversial thinker. His critics argue that he abandoned the traditional understanding of God by bringing in material from Greek and Islamic sources. His defense was to say that Judaism is committed to the search for truth and that we should accept truth no matter where we find it. Regardless which side of the controversy one takes, there is no denying that Maimonides had a lasting impact on Jewish self-understanding.

It is customary to divide Maimonides's ethical writing into three stages: one highlighted by "Eight Chapters," one by the *Mishneh Torah,* and one by the *Guide of the Perplexed.* I will take these works up to show that after being a staunch supporter of Aristotelian virtue ethics, Maimonides came to have doubts on the grounds that it could not account for exceptional degrees of piety or the highest form of intellectual achievement. Although Maimonides never abandoned Aristotelian virtue ethics completely, in the last analysis, his thinking about it was mixed.

"Eight Chapters"

"Eight Chapters" is a section taken from Maimonides's *Commentary on the Mishnah* and often published as a free-standing essay.[1] The challenge Maimonides faced in writing it was how to reconcile Jewish law with prevailing scientific opinions of the day, many of which were derived from Aristotle, who is often viewed as the founding father of virtue ethics.[2]

Looked at superficially, Jewish law is comprised by a list of commandments (according to tradition, 613 in all). They cover everything from how to eat, cook, clean, celebrate holidays, treat other people, distribute property, go to war, and engage in sexual relations. Even so, there are gaps. While the Torah is relatively clear what animals can be eaten and what cannot, it says nothing about how much to eat or how to maintain a healthy diet. Or, to take another example, it typically prohibits rash or excessive behavior but says nothing about how to achieve the mean between rashness on the one hand and cowardice or irresolution on the other. Although the rabbis offered extensive commentaries on Torah legislation, there is nothing in rabbinic literature that takes up questions like "What is virtue?" or "What is the nature of the human soul?" The closest one gets to such a discussion is the Mishnaic tractate Pirkei Avot (often translated as *Ethics of the Fathers*), which is mainly a collection of aphorisms.

It would seem therefore that Jewish sources are more conducive to a law-based ethics than to a virtue-based ethics. To Maimonides, however, Jewish law is more than just a list of dos and don'ts but a system designed to bring about the best in human beings. The question he faced was how to articulate and defend the systematic character of Jewish law and in so doing show that it rests on a firm, scientific foundation.

Maimonides begins by saying that, rather than going into commandments one at a time, he will deal with the principles on which they are based. Just as a doctor must know the parts of the body as well as what things make it sick and what things healthy, Maimonides argues that one who wants to instill sound moral habits in the soul needs to know its parts as well. He proceeds to divide the soul into five parts: nutritive, sentient, imaginative, appetitive, and rational. Like Aristotle, Maimonides divides the rational part of the soul into the productive, deliberative, and theoretical. A soul that does not develop its rational part is for that reason defective.

Transgressions and commandments are concerned with the sentient and appetitive parts. Again like Aristotle, Maimonides distinguishes moral from intellectual virtue. The moral virtues, which include moderation, liberality, justice, gentleness, humility, contentment, and courage, are found in the appetitive part, and the corresponding vices consist in excess or deficiency of these qualities. Thus virtue or the healthy disposition of the soul is a matter of attaining the right balance between extremes. In chapter 4, Maimonides describes the various extremes that the moral virtues avoid. We do not have to go into them in detail to remark how close Maimonides is to Aristotle's account of moral virtue in books 3 and 4 of the *Nicomachean Ethics*. He even agrees that moral virtue is a habit developed by frequent repetition.

For people who are naturally inclined to one extreme or the other, the remedy is to aim for the opposite extreme so that the soul will wind up near the middle. This is analogous to a body that must take on more than the normal amount of water because it is too dry or more than the normal amount of heat because it is too cold. It follows that while it may look as if virtuous people are going to extremes, they are only counterbalancing potentially harmful inclinations in their character. Maimonides therefore concludes chapter 4 by saying: "If a man continually weighs his actions and aims at the mean, he is in the highest of human ranks. In that way, he will come close to God and will attain what belongs to him."

Despite the confidence with which Maimonides presents his arguments, it is obvious that his attempt to reconcile Jewish law with Aristotelian virtue ethics faces several problems. With no explicit mention of a mean in Jewish sources, Maimonides relies on Psalm 19:8

("The Law of the Lord is perfect, restoring the soul; the testimony of the Lord is sure, making wise the simple"). How exactly does one restore the soul? Maimonides argues that one does so by following the mean and avoiding extremes. Yet as anyone can see, this interpretation goes beyond anything contained in the original text. Why should we believe that the psalmist was referring to the doctrine of the mean unless we are already convinced of its truth? Maimonides finds additional support at Zechariah 7:9: "Execute true judgment and show loving-kindness and compassion, every man to his brother." But this is open to the same objection.

The reason Maimonides could take such liberties with the biblical text is that he made an assumption that few modern scholars would share: that truth as established by reason cannot contradict truth as expressed in scripture. It follows that if reason can show that virtue consists of the mean between extremes, then it must be the case that scripture affirms the same view. While we may think that Maimonides is taking enormous liberties by reading Aristotelian virtue theory into the Psalms, he would answer that scripture does not assert anything that is untrue.

It is clear, however, that in trying to bring scripture into conformity with established science, Maimonides faced a number of problems. Though he is on solid ground in saying that Jewish law does not ask people to starve themselves, beat themselves, refrain from alcohol, or practice celibacy, it is far from clear that it sought to instill a psychic condition analogous to bodily health. In fact, as Raymond Weiss points out, most of the virtues Maimonides discusses in "Eight Chapters" have no corresponding term in biblical or rabbinic Hebrew.[3]

The central problem Maimonides faced is that Jewish law and Aristotelian virtue ethics emerged out of vastly different cultures. Aristotle reflects the ideals of an aristocratic culture that values people who occupy high places in society, lead armies into battle, or decide weighty matters of state. By contrast the rabbis reflect the ideals of a religious culture based on quiet virtues such as mercy, repentance, and devotion to God. Their model is the *ḥasid,* a humble, studious person of exceptional piety. According to Pirkei Avot (4.4), a person should be "exceedingly humble in spirit." This coheres with Numbers 12:3, which says that Moses was among the meekest of people. Both are a far cry from Aristotle's *megalopsychos* (great souled man), who is too proud to care what others think about him.

In chapter 4, Maimonides lists humility as a mean between arrogance and self-abasement, but he goes on to say that due to caution and restraint, pious men sometimes deviate from the mean and take modesty to the point of extreme humility.[4] Aristotle too admitted that there are cases where the doctrine of the mean does not apply. For him (*Nicomachean Ethics* 1107a7–27), these cases include spite, shamelessness, and envy, among character traits, and adultery, theft, and murder, among actions. Note, however, that these are vices, whereas humility for Maimonides is an important virtue, arguably the most important. The difference between the two thinkers will become more pronounced when Maimonides takes up the subject of character traits in the *Mishneh Torah*.

Finally, there is the issue of treating God as a moral exemplar. The Torah clearly endorses the principle of *imitatio dei*. Leviticus 19:2 says, "Speak to the entire assembly of Israel and say to them: 'Be holy because I, the LORD your God, am holy." Along similar lines, Deuteronomy 28:9 commands the people to walk in God's ways. There is little doubt that *imitatio Dei* is one of the foundations of Jewish self-understanding. The problem is that God does not face anything like the challenges we do, for example, danger, exhaustion, emotional distress, lack of knowledge, or insufficient material resources. At *Nicomachean Ethics* 1178b11–12, Aristotle asks whether it makes sense to ascribe moral virtues to God at all. If God is characterized as self-thinking thought, the answer would be no. God would be an exemplar of intellectual virtue but not moral virtue as we normally understand it.

One could reply by saying that the divine qualities revealed to Moses at Exodus 34, for example, mercy, graciousness, and slowness to anger, exhibit more than self-thinking thought and are moral in character. In fact, the text of the preceding chapter (Exod. 33: 19) has God say: "I will make all My goodness pass before you." This means that if God is merciful, we should be merciful; if God is gracious, we should be gracious, and so on.

Appealing as this implication is, it does little to solve the theoretical problem posed by *imitatio dei*. In the first place, it is not clear whether mercy, graciousness, and so on, are best understood as adhering to a mean. In the second, Maimonides himself will argue later on that the subject of these virtues is not God himself but the natural world that God has created.[5] He will also argue that even people without training in philosophy should be taught that God has no emotions or moral dispositions.[6] If this is true, then it makes no sense to suppose that God either cultivates or embodies the health of the soul as its exists in humans. Although "Eight Chapters" does not raise all these issues, we will see that, over time, Maimonides could not ignore them.

The Mishneh Torah

That brings us to the *Mishneh Torah*, Maimonides fourteen-volume compendium of Jewish law, especially the section entitled "Laws of Character Traits" (*Hilkhot Deot*). Once again, by identifying character traits as a separate category, Maimonides was departing from rabbinic tradition by trying to find a scientific justification for Jewish law. Not surprisingly, he begins his presentation with the issues discussed earlier in "Eight Chapters." Without mentioning Aristotle by name, he points out that character traits follow a pattern: the extremes are undesirable and the best path is the middle way "which is equidistant from either of the extremes, without being close to either of them."[7] That is why "[t]he sages of old commanded that a man continuously appraise his character traits and evaluate them and direct them in the middle way so that he will become sound of body."[8] Thus a wise person should not be easily angered or be like the dead without any feeling at all. Rather a wise person should follow the middle course and display anger only when something important is a stake.

Already in the first chapter of "Laws of Character Traits," Maimonides distinguishes between the wise person (*ḥakham*), who avoids pride and displays humility by reaching the mean, and the pious person (*ḥasid*), who avoids pride by going to the other extreme and carrying himself lowly at all times. This implies that extreme humility is not just a way of counteracting an undesirable inclination but an end in itself.

He enlarges on this point in the second chapter by saying that there are a number of cases where the doctrine of the mean does not apply. Among them are arrogance, where a person should not simply be humble but exceedingly humble. Another is anger. Here Maimonides says that a person should train himself not to become angry even when he is justified in being so. If there are circumstances where a person must show anger to children or other members of the community, Maimonides thinks he should present an angry face to the public but remain calm within. Thus: "This is the way of the righteous: They accept humiliation but do not humiliate others; listen when they are shamed but do not answer. Moreover, they do so with love and take joy in their suffering."[9]

Maimonides treatment of anger contrasts sharply with Aristotle's (*Nicomachean Ethics* 1126a3–6), which maintains that only a fool would fail to show anger when it is justified or fail to show it in the right way, at the right time, and toward the right person. Moreover, feigning anger when one does not really feel it would be evidence of deception. According to David Shatz, Aristotle's virtuous person must exhibit harmony between inner feeling and outer act, because that is part of what virtue demands.[10] Here, then, is another point where the two thinkers part company.

Not only does Maimonides now value behavior that reaches for an extreme, he admits that there are a number of such cases. He continues to uphold the doctrine of the mean by saying that it holds as a general principle.[11] But there is no question that he also recognizes a higher standard of behavior. He justifies the higher standard by invoking the rabbinic doctrine of action beyond the measure of the law (*lifnin meshurat ha-din*), which means in effect supererogation.[12] The problem is that, once supererogation is introduced, we go beyond what Aristotelian virtue ethics can support. In simple terms, Maimonides has begun to part company with Aristotelian virtue ethics and incline toward what can only be described as a rabbinic ethics.

Another area where Maimonides inclines toward a rabbinic ethics is his treatment of repentance (*teshuvah*). Maimonides's position on repentance as well as his continuity with rabbinic thought is summed up in the following passage:

> Let not the penitent [*ba'al teshuvah*] suppose that he is kept apart from the degree attained by the righteous because of the iniquities and sins that he has committed. This is not so. He is beloved by the Creator . . . as if he had never sinned. Moreover, his reward is great; since, though having tasted sin, he renounced it and overcame his evil passions. The sages say, "Where the penitents stand, the completely righteous cannot stand." This means that the degree attained

> by penitents is higher than those who have never sinned, the reason being that the former have had to put forth a greater effort to subdue their passions than the latter.[13]

Although Aristotle mentions remorse at one point, there is nothing in his thought comparable to Maimonides's position as expressed in this passage.[14] To take this a step further, Maimonides describes repentance as an action that runs counter to what a person has done in the past rather than a character trait she has developed over a period of time. Indeed, the possibility of repentance implies that character traits are not definitive of a person's behavior since the penitent has decided to strike out in a whole new direction. That is why the penitent enjoys a higher status than a person who has never sinned at all.

There are, however, respects in which both Aristotle and Maimonides depart from virtue ethics as we normally understand it. In the *Mishneh Torah,* Maimonides claims that one of the reasons Moses is superior to the other prophets is that he "separated himself from women and everything of that nature forever" and bound his mind entirely to God.[15] Later he claims that to study the Torah properly, one must give his life for it "constantly straining his body to the point of discomfort."[16] Since God does not experience anger or laughter, joy or sorrow, it is hard to see how we can become like God by balancing such extremes. As Maimonides emphasizes throughout "Laws of the Principles of the Torah," God is pure intellect. If so, then the primary way we can become like God is to develop our own intellect.

In the *Guide of the Perplexed,* Maimonides will argue that moral virtues are not valuable as ends in themselves but only as means necessary for developing the intellect. In other words, a person whose appetites push her to extremes of behavior, who cannot control her-temper, or who takes poor control of her body is unlikely to have the time or patience to focus on physics, logic, or mathematics, let alone metaphysics.

We saw that Aristotle worked himself into a similar predicament. If God has no moral virtues, then adhering to the mean cannot be a direct way of approaching God. In book 10 of the *Nicomachean Ethics,* he points out (1) that political and military actions surpass all other moral virtues in nobility and grandeur, (2) that they do not involve leisure and are not chosen for their own sake, (3) that contemplation (*theoria*) is of greater value and aims at no end beyond itself, and (4) that intellectual activity constitutes the complete happiness of human beings.[17] But the next thing he says is that such a life would be more than human.

So while contemplation is the supreme end of life, it remains a goal we can strive for and in our better moments achieve but can never fully embody. This accords well with Maimonides's description of Moses at *Guide* 1.51, a leader who served other people with his limbs only when all the while his heart was focused on God. It could be said, therefore, that both thinkers were aware that the doctrine of the mean is limited, because, in the end, intellectual fulfilment takes precedence over moral action.

The Guide of the Perplexed

Having produced an exhaustive codification of Jewish law in the *Mishneh Torah,* Maimonides set out to discuss "the science of the Law in its true sense" in the *Guide of the Perplexed* (1. intro.), which he identifies with physics and metaphysics. It is hardly surprising, then, that the *Guide* takes a strong stance on the superiority of intellectual to moral virtue. In his words: "His [human] ultimate perfection is to become rational *in actu,* I mean to have an intellect *in actu;* this would consist in his knowing everything concerning all the beings that it is within the capacity of man to know in accordance with his ultimate perfection. It is clear that to this ultimate perfection there do not belong either actions or moral qualities and that it consists only of opinions toward which speculation has led and that investigation has rendered compulsory."[18]

The same sentiment is repeated at *Guide* 3.54. As to how Moses and the Patriarchs were able to achieve intellectual perfection when they were charged with leading a whole community, he invokes the view that they served others in a perfunctory manner with their limbs only.[19] This does not mean that Maimonides completely abandoned the doctrine of the mean. As Herbert Davidson points out, the *Guide* contains passages that continue to equate "righteous" with "balanced."[20] But this equation is compatible with saying that, however necessary, righteousness is not the ultimate end of human life.

Like Aristotle, Maimonides claims that intellectual virtue, which is an end in itself, is achieved mostly in solitude and isolation from other people.[21] But as one might expect, he goes even further. At *Guide* 2.36, he tells us that the person who aspires to noble things "will have detached his thought from, and abolished his desire for, bestial things—I mean the preference for the pleasures of eating, drinking, sexual intercourse."[22] Later, at *Guide* 3.33, he praises the Nazirite, who undertakes a voluntary pledge of abstinence, despite having labeled such behavior excessive in "Eight Chapters" and the *Mishneh Torah*. Finally, at *Guide* 52, he claims that "perfect men" put contact with other people in the same category as secret conduct with their wives and in latrines.

When it comes to God, Maimonides must find a way to account for the meaningfulness of statements like "God is merciful" or "God is gracious" without attributing emotions or moral dispositions to God. He does so by proposing a particular interpretation of Exodus 33–34. In the former chapter, when Moses asks to see God's glory (*kavod*), God answers that no mortal can see the divine face and live but that if Moses stands behind a rock, God will cause all of his goodness to pass by. At *Guide* 1.54, Maimonides takes this to mean that while Moses cannot know the essence of God, he can know the ways and works of God, that is, the goodness God has produced in the created order.

This assumes, of course, that the created order is a well-designed system in which each animal species is given the means to protect itself and search for food. It follows that when we imitate God by undertaking merciful or gracious actions, we are not imitating what God is but rather what God has made or done. Accordingly: "The meaning here is not that He possesses moral qualities, but that He performs actions resembling the actions that in us proceed from moral qualities—I mean from aptitudes of the soul; the meaning is not that He . . . possesses aptitudes of the soul." Thus Maimonides refrains from saying that God *is* merciful or gracious but says instead God *is called* merciful or gracious. Put otherwise, it is not that God possesses a merciful or gracious disposition but that the consequences or effects of divine activity resemble the merciful or gracious actions performed by humans.

What, then, should we do if we want to imitate God? Maimonides explains: "It behooves the governor of a city, if he is a prophet, to acquire similarity to these attributes, so that these actions may proceed from him according to a determined measure and according to the deserts of the people who are affected by them and not merely because of his following a passion." If a judge is going to grant mercy, the reason should not be that she is acting from a merciful disposition herself but that the prisoner merits merciful treatment on his or her own. Once again this represents a shift from an emphasis on moral virtue to an emphasis on intellectual virtue. If Maimonides is right in saying that development of the latter requires one to disparage contact with other people or to treat them in a perfunctory manner, then it is hard to avoid the conclusion that the two kinds of virtue are not compatible. So while the person who imitates God might exemplify mercy or graciousness, these qualities would proceed from an enhanced level of discernment rather than a disposition or character trait.

Conclusion

The problem with Maimonides's intellectualism is its exclusivity. As he surely knew, the number of people who could emulate Moses and the Patriarchs is miniscule. In fact, he claims that it is a level to which even he cannot aspire.[23] Much the same can be said of the *ḥasid*, who never feels anger and achieves an extreme degree of humility. It is not that these people have learned how to control their emotions and offset inclinations that point in one direction with actions directed to another but that, like God, they have risen above emotion altogether. We can characterize their actions as virtuous, but the kind of virtue we are talking about takes us well beyond the Aristotelian account of moral virtue.

This does not mean that Maimonides has abandoned Aristotle altogether. Any society that hopes to produce such people would have to teach its citizens to inculcate good habits and aim for the mean. For these people, taking pleasure in good actions and abhorring bad ones would be decisive. As Maimonides wrote in "Eight Chapters," a wise ruler will prescribe actions and moral habits that must be repeated until they are no longer burdensome and become part of a person's character. If a person develops the wrong habits and goes to excess, the ruler "must follow the same course in treating it as in the medical treatment of bodies," which is to reestablish equilibrium. While this alone will not produce people of exceptional piety or intellectual acumen, it is likely to produce a civil and orderly state. Nonetheless Maimonides held out the hope that in such a state, a few leaders would approach the level of perfection achieved by Moses and the Patriarchs by focusing entirely on the intellect. This emphasis on the intellect above everything else takes us beyond the rabbinic tradition as well.

Notes

1. For an available English translation with notes and commentary, see Maimonides, *Ethical Writings of Maimonides*, ed. Raymond L. Weiss and Charles Butterworth (New York: Dover, 1975), 59–104.

2. In a famous letter, Maimonides said that except for the prophets, Aristotle represents the highest point of human intellectual achievement. See Alexander Marx, "Texts by and about Maimonides," *Jewish Quarterly Review*, n.s., 25, no. 4 (1935): 378–80.

3. Raymond L. Weiss, *Maimonides' Ethics* (Chicago: University of Chicago Press, 1991), 27.

4. Daniel Frank, "Humility as a Virtue: A Maimonidean Critique of Aristotle's Ethics," in *Moses Maimonides and His Time*, ed. Eric Ormsby (Washington, DC: Catholic University Press of America, 1989), 97. Also see Frank, "Anger as a Vice: A Maimonidean Critique of Aristotle's Ethics," *History of Philosophy Quarterly* 7, no. 3 (1990): 269–81.

5. See Maimonides, *The Guide of the Perplexed*, trans. Shlomo Pines (Chicago: University of Chicago Press, 1963), 1.54, 124–25.

6. See Maimonides, *The Guide of the Perplexed*, 1.35–36, 81–82; 1.54, 124–25.

7. Maimonides, "Laws of Character Traits," *Mishneh Torah* 1.1.4. For an English translation, see Maimonides, "Laws concerning Character Traits," in *Ethical Writings of Maimonides*, 28–58.

8. Maimonides, "Laws of Character Traits," in *Mishneh Torah* 1.1.4.

9. Maimonides, "Laws of Character Traits," in *Mishneh Torah*, 1.2.3. For rabbinic precedents, see Babylonian Talmud, *Shabbat* 88b and *Yoma* 23a.

10. David Shatz, "Maimonides' Moral Theory," in *The Cambridge Companion to Maimonides*, ed. Kenneth Seeskin (Cambridge: Cambridge University Press, 2005), 177.

11. Maimonides, "Laws of Character Traits," in *Mishneh Torah* 1.2.7.

12. Maimonides, "Laws of Character Traits," in *Mishneh Torah* 1.1.5.

13. Maimonides, "Laws of Repentance," in *Mishneh Torah* 1.7.4. The rabbinic quote is taken from BT Berakhot 34b. For further discussion of how Maimonides's view of repentance sets him apart from Aristotle, see Jonathan Jacobs, "Aristotle and Maimonides on Virtue and Natural Law," *Hebraic Political Studies* 2, no. 1 (2007): 51–56.

14. Aristotle, *Nicomachean Ethics* 1110b17–24.

15. Maimonides, "Laws of the Principles of the Torah," in *Mishneh Torah* 1.7.6.

16. Maimonides, "Laws for the Study of the Torah," in *Mishneh Torah* 1.3.12.

17. Aristotle, *Nicomachean Ethics* 1177b16–26.

18. Maimonides, *The Guide of the Perplexed,* 3.27, 511. Although this is the prevailing view of Maimonides, some have questioned it on the grounds that Maimonides seems to bring moral virtues back into the picture on the last three pages of the book in connection with Jeremiah 9:22–23. For a full discussion, see Shatz, "Maimonides' Moral Theory."

19. Maimonides, *The Guide of the Perplexed,* 3.51, 624.

20. Herbert Davidson, "The Middle Way in Maimonides' Ethics," *Proceedings of the American Academy for Jewish Research* 54 (1987): 46–47.

21. Maimonides, *The Guide of the Perplexed,* 3.51, 621.

22. Maimonides, *The Guide of the Perplexed,* 2.36, 371.

23. Maimonides, *The Guide of the Perplexed,* 3.51, 624.

Chapter 8

Elazar of Worms

JOSEPH ISAAC LIFSHITZ

Throughout the twelfth and thirteenth centuries a pietistic movement arose among the Jews in Germany. It was not a large movement, and probably not homogenous in its theology and its ethics. Among these pietists, the most renowned, and probably most influential, are Rabbi Shmuel He-Hasid, his son, Rabbi Judah He-Hasid, and Judah's disciple, Rabbi Elazar of Worms, all of them descended from the Kalonymus family who immigrated from northern Italy.

Shmuel and his son Judah lived in Speyer and moved later to Regensburg.[1] Judah is known as the author of *Sefer Hasidim,* a collection of customs, laws, and ethics. His disciple, Elazar, was born in Mainz in 1180 and lived most of his life in Worms, where he died in 1240. Judah's most prolific disciple, Elazar wrote biblical and Talmudic commentary, commentary on the Jewish prayer book, poetry, halakhah and mystical works. He is best known for his influential book *Sefer ha-Rokeaḥ,* a book of Jewish law, which includes some ethics and theology.[2]

What unites these pietists, as well as other pietists in Germany, are manifestations of ascetism as acts of self-denial, self-humiliation, and pronounced stringency in ritual matters.[3] Yet different protagonists among the Hasidim focused on different issues. Judah He-Hasid's *Sefer Hasidim* gave extensive attention to ethical issues, including charitable behavior, equality,[4] mercy, and concern for other human beings as well as for nonhuman animals. *Sefer Hasidim* also teaches self-control, restraint, honesty, and modesty. Elazar of Worms wrote comparatively less on ethics, but when he did, he focused mainly on modesty.[5]

Given this focus, this chapter will present the different aspects of the virtue of modesty in Elazar's writings. I will claim that Elazar's discussion of modesty is strongly related to his mystical and theological theory. Unlike other Jewish thinkers in the Middle Ages who analyzed the virtue of modesty primarily in ethical terms, Elazar found four dimensions in this virtue; in addition to the ethical/religious dimension, modesty has theological, social, and mystical aspects. Modesty as a *social virtue* is the way for the pious to withstand social criticism. Very often, especially in a homogeneous society, many criticize any individual who chooses to adopt a way of life that is more stringent, or that appears more moralistic. Such behavior seems to the many as critical of their own behavior and, in response, it is natural for them to criticize one who stands out. A devout person who is concerned about how others view him may feel pressure to conform. That is why Elazar considered it essential for a pious person to disregard his honor and concern himself with his religious obligations only.

Modesty as a *theological virtue* is the consequence of the devout person's understanding of God. Because God is the Creator of the world and is above all his creatures, man is obliged to live with an attitude of modesty. Awareness of the existence of God should depress one's own egocentricity. Thus, modesty is not necessarily directed toward other people but toward God, but from this, modesty toward human beings follows.

Modesty as an *ethical/religious virtue,* is what I refer to as a practice of penance. A pious person may seek self-effacement in order to receive divine mercy. Social humiliation is worse than physical suffering, and therefore counts as atonement for his bad deeds. Thus, a devout person should welcome the opportunity to be humiliated or at least shown disrespect.

Modesty is also regarded as a *mystical virtue,* mainly due to the danger of vanity. Mysticism is power. When a person has knowledge of the mystical world, he has theurgic power that may mutate into vengeance, into hurting others. The mystic is obliged, therefore, to restrain himself from anger, and above all, from vanity, so that he will not abuse the power he gains against others.

The virtue of modesty is not, in Elazar's thought, inherently good. The virtue of modesty is instrumental. It is about achieving higher theologically oriented virtues. How the virtuous dimensions of modesty serve the theological end will be the focus of this paper.

Modesty as a Social Virtue

Fritz (Yitzhak) Baer noticed, already in 1938, the weight that was given to modesty in the writings of Hasidei Ashkenaz.[6] Baer thought that their religio-social thought was influenced by contemporary Christianity. We indeed find similar expressions among the Franciscans and other Christian pietists. Social equality, low self-image, low interest in earthly desires—these were common to both the Jewish Hasidim and medieval Christian pietists.

Rabbi Elazar builds on the teaching of his rabbi, Judah He-Hasid. Let us briefly consider the latter's teaching before turning to Elazar. In *Sefer Hasidim*, Judah He-Hasid describes modesty as the greatest of all moral virtues, and one especially important for Torah scholars.[7] He suggests that the pietists acquire modesty so that they will be able to withstand criticism, and instructs them not to be proud of their virtue:

> The root of modesty, in a place where there is greatness and honor, is that one should distance himself and not include himself with other human beings. . . . Anything that a man can do to diminish his own honor in order to increase the honor of God-fearing people, he has to do. As it is written in Psalms: "For whom a contemptible man is abhorrent, but who honors those who fear the Lord" [15:4]. And if he will recognize that others are boasting about their own modesty, and he gets embarrassed for being less modest than they, he should listen to them. For instance, when these people are considered greater than he and they refuse to stand before him (as they deserve) in order to show off their modesty. In such a case, he gets embarrassed for they will criticize his arrogance (even though it was they who sent him to stand at the front). Yet he should do so and receive the embarrassment, for the sake of their honor, and they will get punished for receiving honor on his account.[8]

In this rather puzzling text, modesty is entangled in complicated social relations. When modesty becomes a popular virtue, people may boast of their own modesty, and thereby cease to be modest. It becomes a vicious circle. Once a person is aware of his own modesty, he may realize the status that it confers on him within a society that prizes the virtue. He may become proud of it. To that extent, he obliterates his own modesty. Nonetheless, *Sefer Hasidim* suggests in such a case that the really modest man, aware of his own tendency to be proud of his modesty, act with arrogance in order to appear to others as a person who does *not* deserve their respect. Thus, suggests *Sefer Hasidim*, the pietist will correct himself and reach true modesty.

Judah He-Hasid also considers modesty as the root of all other moral virtues. The modest man, because of his low self-image, will be less tempted to get angry. His low self-image will help him to forgive others, and, even more so, to be resolute in the face of the criticism of others (which seems to be a common event), as we may notice in this passage of *Sefer Hasidim*:

> That is why it is right to stay far from anger, and to get accustomed to ignoring any sense of self-hurt, even when being offended. That is the good path. An angry man is left with his anger, and he finds himself saying things that he will regret later, even towards God. Leaving the path of anger will lead one to the path of modesty, as can be concluded from the acts of Hillel the Elder. There wasn't anyone who was more modest than he was, and it was his modesty that caused converts to come under the Indwelling. A person should not be angry in his own home, otherwise his servants might feed him non-kosher food, because of the fear of his anger, and he will never find out.[9]

A modest man is a person with many ethical virtues, but it is his modesty that generates those virtues in him. Modesty makes it easier for a humble person to acquire self-control. It enables him to forgive others, to be a loving person, to maintain high levels of pietism, and to ignore the criticism of others.

In the writings of Elazar of Worms, we find a similar approach. Elazar also claims that modesty is a virtue because it enables the Hasid to have greater self-control and greater power to withstand criticism.

Elazar repeats the same reasons for modesty as his mentor, Judah, but in addition, bases them on sources from the Bible and Talmud. Moses, King David, as well as Hillel the Elder, are all examples of modesty:

> Therefore, flesh and blood, you came from soil and the spirit will return to [the One] who gave it. Attach yourself to loving your creator before your candle will die. Block your desire and stick to modesty, so you will never answer to a person who embarrasses you. "When they were in Hazeroth, Miriam and Aaron spoke against Moses, because of the Cushite woman he married: 'He married a Cushite woman.' . . . Now Moses was a very humble man, more so than any other man on earth" [Num. 12:1–3], because he never answered back. Similarly as we find in the Talmud [BT Hullin 89]: "the one who shut his mouth at time of quarrel." [BT Kiddushin 71:] "Silence in Babylon is considered a sign of good lineage." [BT Shabbat 17:] "Hillel was sitting bent down in front of Shammai, and because of that he merited that the law should be decided according to his interpretation." Likewise, [BT Eruvin 13] "law was decided according to Hillel's school because they were reciting the opinion of their opponent, the school of Shammai, before the opinion of their own." [BT Shabbat 31] relates the modesty of Hillel. Gideon as well: "And the men of Ephraim said to him, 'why did you do that to us? . . .' But he answered them, 'After all, what have I accomplished compared to you? . . .' And when he spoke in this fashion, their anger against him abated" [Judges 8:1–3]. With King David as well, we find the virtue of modesty: "O Lord, my heart is not proud nor my look haughty; I do not aspire to great things or to what is beyond me" [Ps. 131:1]. There is no merit like that of the one who is humble [and not for the sake of a reward]. He will merit four things—fear of God, wealth, honor, and life. Who is the one who merits life in the world to come? The modest, as it says, "Let the faithful (humble) exult in glory" [Psalms 149:4]. And finally, in Hullin: "for the merit of modesty the world stands, because the modest considers himself as nothing, and the world is hanging on nothing."[10]

Modesty, for Elazar, is the greatest virtue. Like Judah He-Hasid, Elazar also emphasizes that modesty helps to sustain the Hasid despite criticism. In a small and provincial community in medieval Ashkenaz (Germany), tolerance for different styles of religiosity was not that common. The Hasid had often to insulate himself against the criticism of less rigorous members of his social world:

> "The beginning of wisdom is the fear of the Lord" [Ps. 111:10], because the first steps to becoming a Hasid are difficult. Many make fun of him and his blood is spilt. He must listen and not answer back. "Incline Your ear, O Lord, for I am poor and needy. Preserve my life, for I am steadfast" [Ps. 86:1–2]. And after he is accustomed to being steadfast, even if people will pay him to leave his ways, he will not do so just because of shame.[11]

Elazar also thought that modesty endows the modest person with power. Thus, the modest Hillel's interpretations became authoritative and the biblical war hero Gideon, who declined the offer of kingship, was victorious against his opponents. Of course, thinking of the power that modesty provides would show a lack of modesty. As the sages said: "be not like servants who serve for the sake of receiving a reward; instead, be like servants who serve their master not for the sake of receiving a reward" (Pirkei Avot 1:3). Elazar himself considers a righteous man as one who is not to be completely righteous.[12]

Modesty as a Theological Value

> Keep your mouth from being rash and let not your throat be quick to bring forth speech before God. For God is in heaven and you are on earth; that is why your words should be few
>
> —Ecclesiastes 5:1

Modesty as a theological virtue is the effect of the pious' perception of God as the Creator of the world. Perceiving God as the Creator generates a sense of humiliation before God. Awareness of the existence of God should mitigate egocentricity. Thus, modesty is not necessarily humbling oneself before other human beings but before God, and from this modesty stems modesty vis-a-vis human beings. By being modest, man augments the image of God.

This theological aspect of modesty is most important for Elazar of Worms. Morality is only valuable, if it has a theological value as well, if it serves to bring the pietist close to the Divine Presence. Modesty and humility are important not because of their intrinsic moral value but because they serve to enhance the perception of God. As Elazar writes:

> And when he (the pious) reads Torah, Prophets, the Writings and the Talmud, and he will see the reward and punishment and know that his bad actions are many, and he should humble and lower himself and soften his heart and be afraid of the punishment, and he should repent, as did Josiah who tore his clothes. And God answered him: "because your heart was softened and you humbled yourself before the Lord" [2 Kings 22:19]. Humbling is modesty. He who controls his acts and soul, when people despise him, he could avenge himself, but because of his modesty he declines to do so. He stays silent and suffers. If anything bad will happen to him, to himself, his estate, his children, his relatives, he will justify God and shut his mouth from speaking complaints against God, and [prevent] his heart from thinking bad thoughts, as did Aaron "and Aaron was silent" [Lev. 10:3]. If men will praise him, he will tell them—do not praise me, because I know my sins. If he will learn Torah the whole day, he will praise God and thank him, and [yet] will suspect that God may be upset with him. "Who asked that you trample my courts" [Isa. 1:12]. "And to the wicked, God said: Who are you to recite My laws and mouth the terms of My covenant" [Ps. 50:16].[13]

Elazar appreciates the moral value modesty, but he finds this value an aftereffect of its theological value. Because man humbles himself before the Lord, he becomes a moral person. Morality is always an effect, a derivative, not the principal value itself.

At the same time, we should not deny the existence of moral values in the thought of Elazar. We should note that what makes God great is His righteousness, unlike man who is a sinner and unable to follow the demands of God. God's righteous commandments are by themselves a testimony to His moral perfection. If what defines the greatness of God is the moral distance between man and God, modesty, as well as any other moral value, is attributed to God as well. Because of this attribution, moral virtues receive a theological virtue.

As Elazar quotes from *Pirkei Heikhalot*:

> Rabbi Ishmael said: Thus, Metatron, Sar ha-Panim, told me: Before they appointed me to serve the throne, the Lord opened for me six thousand gates of knowledge, three thousands of wisdom, three thousands of life . . . three thousands of modesty and three thousands of fear of God. Since this time, He added to me knowledge to knowledge, wisdom to wisdom, . . . modesty to modesty . . . I was honored by these good and praised values more than all saintly figures.[14]

Modesty is not just an ethical value; its full meaning develops in the context of the relationship between God and the pietist. Modesty is compared to wisdom, to the knowledge of God. It is as infinite and as eternal as they are. Modesty before God is the deepest verification of the difference between God and man. More than a philosophical declaration, an emotional attitude toward God that diminishes the self and augments God is the supreme expression of faith. When this is understood, when modesty is perceived to be the embodiment of faith, modesty receives value that is tantamount to all of the great attributes of man by which he perceives God.

Modesty as a Religious Value (Modesty as Penance)

Modesty is a religious virtue for the pious, because it is considered as a means of penance.[15] The pain of having a low image in society can bestow on the pietist the merit of receiving divine mercy for his sins. Social humiliation is worse than physical suffering and therefore counts as atonement for his bad deeds. Thus, a pious person should be happy for the opportunity to be humiliated or at least disrespected. The pietist may seek to humble himself in order to achieve mercy from God.

As we have already witnessed, Elazar suggests that the pious embarrass himself by behaving with vanity in front of great people. As I explained above, the reason for doing so is to achieve an authentic modesty.

Reward and punishment for psychological pleasures are greater than for materialistic pleasures. Pleasures of success, honor, and satisfaction are all greater than physical pleasures, and suffering from lack of all of those is by far greater than physical suffering. Whoever suffers in this world is rewarded in the world to come. That is why the truly modest person, who avoids any respect and honor, deserves merit in the world to come. Elazar urges the pious to seek out embarrassment so he will gain in the next world:

> He (the pious) should be mindful of reward and punishment and know that his bad actions are many, and he should surrender and lower himself and soften his heart and be afraid of the punishment, and he should repent as did Josiah who tore his clothes. And God answered him: "because your heart was softened and you humbled yourself before the Lord" [2 Kings 22:19]. Humbling is modesty. He who controls his acts and his soul [is one who], when people despise him, could take revenge, but because of his modesty he declines to do so; he stays in silence and suffering. If anything bad will happen to him, to his person, his estate, his children, his relatives, he will justify God and shut his mouth from talking (against God), and his heart from thinking bad thoughts, as did Aaron "and Aaron was silent" [Lev. 10:3]. If men will praise him, he will tell them—do not praise me, because I know my sins. If he will learn Torah the whole day, he will praise God and thank him and yet will suspect that God may be upset with him. "Who asked that of you to trample my courts" [Isa. 1:12]. "And to the wicked, God said: Who are you to recite My laws and mouth the terms of My covenant" [Ps. 50:16]. If he will be in a quarrel with his neighbor, he should submit to him. As it says: "She is more in the right than I" [Gen. 38:26]. If his neighbor was lying about him, he should not embarrass him and not get angry with him. If he is rich and honorable, he should lower his spirit.[16]

Modesty as a Mystical Virtue

As was suggested by Ivan G. Marcus and others, according to Elazar of Worms various modes of pietistic thought and behavior could prepare an individual for mystical thought, study, and experience, which have spiritual value in and of themselves.[17] Elazar does not mention the mystical aspect when he discusses modesty in *Sefer ha-Rokeaḥ*. But in the beginning of his *Book of the Name,* he instructs the pious and his students how to transmit mystical knowledge. He warns against teaching such knowledge to a person who is not worthy. Among the virtues that are demanded, he cites modesty and the control of anger. I find this demand to be crucial. Mystical knowledge, as noted above, can be dangerous. Modesty and the control of anger must work in tandem, rooted in a sense of responsibility. Elazar is afraid of the power that may be directed to revenge in times of anger. That is why virtues like control of anger and the modesty that helps to facilitate it are so valuable for the mystic:

> His specific name, we shall explain its meaning as far as it is possible to. . . . The Merciful may forgive us as we shall explain it. It is revealed to him that I am writing for the sake of knowing His might. One may not give this knowledge to anyone unless they are pious and are not getting angry, modest and have a fear of God, and are observing His commandments. The specific name is only delivered on waters, as it says: "The voice of the Lord is over the waters" [Ps. 29:3].[18]

Thus, modesty as well as control of anger are necessary traits for whoever gains power of the great names of God. Purity, fear of God, and following God's commandments are all important traits, and are necessary conditions for achieving a level of mystical knowledge and experience. Yet, the harm that a mystic may cause, demands a proper personality as well. A mystic should be a person of self-control, so he will not use his power when he loses his temper, and he should be modest so he will not want to harm his opponents.

At the same time, we should consider here as well, the theological value of modesty. The fact that Elazar listed modesty together with fear of God shows that what concerned him was also a proper perception of God, which is only achieved by the modest, who humbles himself in order to leave room for God. Only a modest man can truly perceive God in his greatness, and only a modest man can truly understand the name of God.

Conclusion

Unlike the great Jewish scholars of medieval Spain such as Maimonides, Judah Halevi, Naḥmanides, Rabbenu Baḥya, and others, Elazar of Worms did not consider ethical virtues as intrinsically valuable. Or, more precisely, he did not consider them as deserving of a primarily ethical treatment or exposition. Their value depends on their theological context, on their serving an ultimately theological purpose. That is why we do not find many discussions regarding ethics as such in his vast writings. There is one ethical virtue that is an exception to this rule—modesty. As I have explained, modesty serves several important theological purposes. Modesty enables pietistic life by helping the pietist to ignore criticism from an intolerant society; modesty is welcomed as penance; modesty is a necessary virtue for the mystic so he will not harm others with the power he achieves.

According to Elazar, the most important purpose of modesty is to create more room for God and to augment his presence. I find this aspect of modesty to be its core value. The rest of the values associated with modesty are practical reasons that may help to persuade people to achieve this virtue. Modesty as a theological value is an embodiment of faith, and thus Elazar perceives it as the pearl of all values.

Notes

1. See Ephraim Shoham-Steiner, "Exile, Immigration and Piety: The Jewish Pietists of Medieval Germany, from the Rhineland to the Danube," *Jewish Studies Quarterly* 24, no. 3 (2017): 234–60.

2. See Joseph Isaac Lifshitz, "Nefesh Ha-Hayyim and its Sources in Hasidei Ashkenaz," [Hebrew] *Daat*, no. 79/80 (2015): 77–93.

3. Ephraim Kanarfogel, *"Peering through the Lattices": Mystical, Magical, and Pietistic Dimensions in the Tosafist Period* (Detroit: Wayne State University Press, 2000), 33–37. For a full bibliography see Kanarfogel, 33n1.

4. Considering the context of the Middle Ages, Hasidei Ashkenaz were much more egalitarian than scholars like Halevi. See Yitzhak Baer, "Ha-Megama ha-Datit ha-Hevratit shel Sefer Hasidim," [Hebrew] *Zion* 3 (1937): 1–50, esp. 38–41.

5. For self-humiliation as a general interest of the German Pietists see Kanarfogel, *Peering through the Lattices*, 33–37.

6. Baer, "Ha-Megama ha-Datit," 50–51.

7. Judah He-Hasid, *Sefer Hasidim*, ed. Reuben Margaliyot [Hebrew] (Jerusalem: Mosad Harav Kook, 1957), 16, 70–71.

8. *Sefer Hasidim*, 15–17.

9. *Sefer Hasidim*, 145, 150.

10. Elazar of Worms, *Sefer ha-Rokeaḥ*, Laws of Hasidut, "The Root of Modesty" [Hebrew] (Jerusalem, 2009), 1–24.

11. Elazar of Worms, *Sefer ha-Rokeaḥ*, Hasidut, 1–24.

12. Elazar of Worms, *Sefer ha-Shem* (Jerusalem, 2004), 201.

13. Elazar of Worms, *Sefer ha-Rokeaḥ*, "The Root of Modesty," 6–8.

14. Elazar of Worms, *Sodei Razai*, Hilchot Mitatron (Jerusalem, 2004), 2–3.

15. See Kanarfogel, *Peering through the Lattices*, 34–35.

16. Elazar of Worms, *Sefer ha-Rokeaḥ*, "The Root of Modesty," 7–8.

17. Ivan G. Marcus, *Piety and Society: The Jewish Pietists of Medieval Germany* (Leiden: Brill, 1981), 21–22, 36, 117–18; Eliot Wolfson, "The Mystical Significance of Torah-Study in German Pietism," *Jewish Quarterly Review* 84, no. 1 (1993): 44n4; Haym Soloveitchik, "Three Themes in the Sefer Ḥasidim," *AJS Review* 1 (1976): 321n27; Kanarfogel, *Peering through the Lattices*, 36.

18. Elazar of Worms, *Sefer ha-Shem*, 1.

Chapter 9

Naḥmanides

JONATHAN JACOBS

Rabbi Moses ben Naḥman (Ramban or Naḥmanides; ca. 1194–1270) was born to a distinguished family in Gerona, Catalonia (Christian Spain), where he remained for most of his life. Although earning his living as a physician, Naḥmanides was also the head of the Jewish community, a decisor of Jewish religious law (halakhah), a commentator on the Torah and Talmud, kabbalist, philosopher, and poet. His teachers included Rabbi Judah bar Yakar, head of the Barcelona yeshiva, and Rabbi Nathan ben Meir of Trinquetaille. Naḥmanides had an excellent reputation among non-Jews, and was a close friend of King James I of Aragon (Jaume el Conqueridor; reigned 1213–1276). In 1263, he was summoned to Barcelona for a public disputation with scholars of Christianity in the presence of the king and his ministers. We have two records of the event: Naḥmanides's own documentation in Hebrew, and corresponding documentation distributed by the church in Latin. It seems Naḥmanides won the disputation; as a result, he was dragged through a series of trials that eventually forced him to flee Spain. In 1267, he left Spain and immigrated to the land of Israel. Naḥmanides visited Jerusalem, sent a letter to his son Naḥman from there, and reestablished the decimated Jewish community. Apparently, he established his permanent residence in Acre, where he joined the Tosafists who had immigrated and settled there several decades earlier. He died in Acre in 1270.

Naḥmanides's literary output is wide-ranging and very impressive. His oeuvre includes a commentary on the Talmud, commentaries on the Torah and on the Book of Job, halakhic monographs, polemics defending earlier commentators ("Rishonim"), books of Jewish and religious thought, and sermons (including a sermon on Ecclesiastes).

The scholar who wishes to clarify Naḥmanides's thought on virtue ethics is faced with a number of problems:

1. Naḥmanides did not write any books of philosophy, so his statements of a philosophical character do not always coalesce into a single clear statement.[1] This fact makes it difficult for scholars of Naḥmanides to point to any systematic treatment of ethical questions in his work.
2. The subject of the virtues does not constitute a central topic in Naḥmanides's work, nor does any substantial discussion devoted to this topic appear in his writings. Nonetheless, his elevated moral consciousness is clearly recognizable in his Torah commentary, and it is reflected among other things in his approach to the question of "reasons for the commandments."[2]

In what follows, therefore, the suggestions I shall make with regard to his ideas about virtue ethics should be regarded as tentative. Let me begin by presenting the virtues that Naḥmanides prescribed with regard to oneself, and then proceed to a virtue that Naḥmanides prescribed in one's relationships with others.

"You Shall Be Holy"

For Naḥmanides, the Torah—despite all its precise details—does not fully suffice to guide one's behavior. Therefore, alongside all of the many specific commandments, the Torah issues a command about general ethical guidelines that the individual must fill with practical content. Naḥmanides points to two commandments that express wide-ranging demands for virtue: the commandment "You shall be holy, for I, the LORD your God, am holy" (Lev. 19:2), and the commandment "Do what is right and good" (Deut. 6:18).[3]

Naḥmanides viewed the commandment "You shall be holy" (Lev. 19:2) as requiring a certain degree of abstinence, that is, a fundamental overcoming of one's physical desires—for having sex, for eating meat, and for drinking wine. On these points this virtue demands abstinence above and beyond the explicit commands of the Torah:

> The Torah proscribes immoral sexual relationships and forbidden foods, but it permits intercourse between man and wife, eating meat, and drinking wine. So there is license for a man of appetite to steep himself in lust with his wife (or his many wives), or to "be of those who guzzle wine, or glut themselves on meat" (Prov. 23:20), or to discuss all sorts of vile things, as long as they involve something that the Torah does not explicitly prohibit. One could therefore be a scoundrel with the full permission of the Torah.
>
> So after giving the details of those things that are specifically prohibited [in ch. 18], the Torah now gives us a general commandment to restrain ourselves from excess even in those things that are permitted: to limit intercourse to that which is necessary to fulfill the commandments . . . and to limit our intake of wine. Notice that the Nazirite [of Num. 6], who may not drink wine, is referred to as "holy," and the Torah presents the evils of wine in its stories about Noah and Lot.[4]

Following this comment, Naḥmanides broadens the demand for additional kinds of holiness that are not linked to physical desires and are not mentioned explicitly in the Torah, such as distancing oneself from uncleanness and refraining from excessive speech:

> We must keep ourselves separate from uncleanness even if it is something not specifically forbidden elsewhere. Again, the fact that the Nazirite—who avoids contact with the dead—is described as "holy" provides an example. Similarly, one must keep from defiling one's mouth and tongue by overeating of gross foods and from foul speech. . . . One should sanctify oneself in this way until one reaches the level of restraint of Rabbi Ḥiyya, who never spoke an idle word in all his days.

Naḥmanides concludes the list with a demand for personal conduct that includes physical cleanliness: "This general commandment actually goes so far as to include cleanliness as an aspect of holiness. . . . It is in fact the essence of the text to insist that we keep ourselves clean, pure, and separate from the mass of humanity, who soil themselves with all sorts of perfectly permissible ugliness." It must be emphasized that Naḥmanides does not require anyone to completely refrain from physical pleasure. The appropriate level of abstinence (in his view) is not expressed by mortification of the body. Man needs to have control over his desires so that his physical actions are employed only in the service of God and not for personal pleasure. Holiness requires that one be cleansed of all immoderate desire. Elsewhere he wrote: "'And serve Him alone,' according to the Sages, means to act before Him at all times like a slave serving his master, treating his owner's demands as central and his own needs as incidental, to the extent demanded by the Sages [Pirkei Avot 2:12]: 'Let all your deeds be for the sake of heaven'—even his own physical needs should be satisfied only for the sake of serving God. He should eat and sleep and do whatever it takes to maintain his body for God's service. And this is indeed a correct explanation" (commentary to Deut. 6:13). In a *derashah* on Ecclesiastes, he similarly writes: "One must not pursue worldly pleasures, which are ephemeral and fade swiftly. . . . All worldly pleasures and desires are worthless. One must uproot them from one's mind and forget them completely. . . . One must occupy oneself in this world entirely for the sake of heaven and in fear of God and not indulge oneself with luxuries, using only what is necessary. That is the only true pleasure."[5]

In sum, one who adopts the virtue of abstinence in accordance with the general commandment to "be holy" will know that one must be punctilious in areas of personal ethics: eating, drinking, sex, impurity, hygiene, speech. This level of refinement is demanded of everyone. It does not demand that one detach oneself from ordinary life, which is an attribute only of the most virtuous.[6]

Humility

Alongside the general demand for abstinence, there is an additional character trait that is most important for Naḥmanides. The work in which he presents in most detailed form his views on the necessary ethical traits is the *Iggeret ha-Musar* (Epistle on Ethics), which he sent in his old age from the land of Israel to his son, Naḥman, who was living at that time in Catalonia.[7] In this short epistle, Naḥmanides guides his son in the ways of proper behavior. The epistle begins with a warning against anger: "Make sure always to speak pleasantly to everyone at all times, and in this way you will be saved from anger, the vice that causes sin. Our Sages of blessed memory said the same: 'All kinds of hell hold sway over one who is angry' (BT Ned. 22a)." Immediately afterward Naḥmanides clarifies that avoiding anger is not a goal in itself, but is just one step on the path to acquiring the virtue of humility: "And when you are saved from anger you ascend to the virtue of humility, *which is the best of all virtues*." According to this statement of Naḥmanides, humility is the most important ethical character trait.

The prohibition of pride is for Naḥmanides a commandment of the Torah. It is derived from the text's warning the king of Israel "not to act haughtily toward his fellows" (Deut. 17:20):

> This implies that haughtiness in general is forbidden by the Torah. If the text curbs the king's haughtiness, how much more is this true for others, who can have no pretensions to act haughtily. For the text cautions even one who is deservedly exalted to lower himself beneath his less deserving fellows. In fact, haughtiness is a quality despised by God even in a king, for greatness and exaltation belong to the Lord alone. Praise too belongs only to Him, and humanity should boast of none but Him.

Though this verse is about the king, the prohibition of pride affects not only the king but everyone: The king has good reason to be proud, and yet it is forbidden him. Simple people have no such reasons for pride and so must certainly not fall into this vice.

Intimacy with God

Both abstinence and humility are personal ethical traits that one must develop with regard to oneself. Nonetheless, for Naḥmanides the development and improvement of the personality was not a goal in itself. Its great importance was that these traits are a necessary stage on the way to mystical intimacy with the Creator, which is one of the basic pillars of Jewish philosophy and mystical tradition in the Middle Ages. Examination of mystical intimacy with God as the goal of human existence and as a spiritual ideal for the medieval sages in general and Naḥmanides in particular demands inquiry into the esoteric teachings of the exegetes and Jewish thinkers, but that is outside the scope of this chapter.[8] In the present context I will address only the overt level and not the theurgic dimension in Naḥmanides's understanding of the reason for the commandments. *Devekut* is described by Naḥmanides as follows: "Remembering God and loving Him always, never letting your thoughts leave Him 'when you lie down and when you get up' [Deut. 11:19], to the extent that even when speaking with other people one's thoughts are not with them but remain before God. It could be that the lives of people who are on that level are 'bound up in the bundle of life' [1 Sam. 25:29] even while they are still alive, being themselves a habitation for the *Shekhinah*" (comment to Deut. 11:22). It would seem that this comment does not address the kind of mystical intimacy demanded of the masses, but only that of the spiritual elite, who must commune directly with the *Shekhinah* by means of extreme concentration and purification of the body. Yet even the ordinary person must attain a certain level of intimacy with God. According to Adam Afterman, Naḥmanides thought that intimacy with God was structured on a pyramidal basis: "At its base are the masses who commune with the sages; at its apex are those unique individuals who achieve direct intimacy with the *Shekhinah,* at various levels, while they are still living. In between are found the people of integrity: once, the prophets; now, the sages."[9]

Both in *Iggeret ha-Musar* and in his comment to the commandment to "be holy," Naḥmanides wrote that positive character traits serve as rungs by which to ascend higher and higher in one's service of the Holy One, with the ultimate goal of mystical intimacy with God.

In *Iggeret ha-Musar,* after identifying humility as "the best of all the virtues," he writes:

> Through humility, the trait of fear will enter his heart . . . and when he behaves humbly, being ashamed before others and fearing sin and rejoicing in the worship of the Omnipres-

> ent and *cleaving to His will, His Shekhinah will rest upon him* . . . and now, my son, know and see that everyone whose pride exalts him over others rebels against the kingdom of heaven, for he glorifies himself with the garment of God's kingdom . . . so make yourself small and let the Omnipresent exalt you.

The proud man distances himself from his Creator and rebels against Him. In contrast, the man who acquires the virtue of humility can achieve the fear that will assist him in concentrating upon God and lead to mystical intimacy with Him—which is the aim of human existence and its ultimate goal.

In his commentary on the commandment to "be holy" Naḥmanides similarly emphasizes that the final aim of the added holiness that comes to expression through abstinence is mystical intimacy with the Holy One. At the end of those comments, he writes this: "'For I the Lord your God am holy' means that by being holy ourselves, we achieve intimacy with Him." It is clear, then, that Naḥmanides understood the virtues necessary in one's personal life—humility and abstinence—as merely a stage on the journey to the goal of mystical intimacy with the Creator.[10]

"Beyond the Letter of the Law"

So far, we have discussed the virtues that have to do with personal morality. The second general commandment (according to Naḥmanides) has to do with the pursuit of what is good and right in the realm of interpersonal relations. Naḥmanides deals with this topic in a number of places. At the end of his comment to the verse "be holy," discussed above, he offers two examples of general commandments, of which one stems from the verse "Do what is right and good" (Deut. 6:18):[11]

> It is in fact the way of the Torah to conclude a series of specific prohibitions with a general commandment of the same kind. After giving the specific details of how business is to be conducted fairly—"you must not steal" [Exod. 20:15], "you must not defraud" [Lev. 19:13], "you must not wrong anyone" [Lev. 19:33] and the like—the Torah concludes, "Do

> what is right and good in the sight of the Lord" [Deut. 6:18], inserting a positive commandment to behave with upright behavior and equity and actually go beyond the letter of the law, acting in a way that will win the approval of others, as I shall explain when I reach that text.

The examples cited by Naḥmanides here deal with business matters. Beyond the explicit prohibitions—not to steal, not to overcharge the customer—the Torah demands upright behavior "beyond the letter of the law," that is, business dealings based on self-restraint and thoughtfulness. This is also the meaning of his statement, "They said in the Mekhilta: Doing 'what is upright in His sight'—this refers to business dealings. It teaches that anyone whose word is reliable, with whom people are happy to do business, is considered as if he had fulfilled the entire Torah. I will expand on this when I reach 'Do what is right and good' [Deut. 6:18] if the good God is good to me" (from his comment to Exod. 15:26).

Yet in his actual comment to "Do what is right and good" Naḥmanides did not restrict himself to restraint in business dealings and financial matters; he expanded the ethical demand to all interpersonal relationships:

> The Sages have a lovely approach to this, saying that it means one should go beyond the letter of the law. The previous verse [Deut. 6:17] already said to obey the commandments, decrees, and laws that [God] has enjoined upon you; now the text is telling us, "Even outside the realm of the commandments, make sure to do what is right and good, for God loves the right and the good." This is in fact something of major importance. It is impossible for the Torah to include every potential human interaction, social, commercial, and political. But once it has mentioned a number of them—such as these from Leviticus 19: "You shall not go about as a talebearer" [16], "You shall not take vengeance or bear a grudge" [18], "Do not stand idly by the blood of your fellow" [16], "You shall not insult the deaf" [14], "You shall rise before the aged and show deference to the old" [32], and the like—it repeats the instruction to do what is good, honest, and upright, encouraging people

> to voluntarily yield some of their prerogatives, so that one is known as someone of honesty and integrity in every aspect of behavior.

One who accustoms oneself to doing "what is right and good" will know how to treat others justly and with integrity. The requirement is that one behave with moderation and consideration in all one's relations with others. At every stage of interaction with other people, one must live with concern for others.[12]

Models of Ethical Behavior

Which biblical characters—in Naḥmanides's opinion—serve as models of ethical behavior? Abstinence and refraining from the idle pleasures of this world was in Naḥmanides's view the province of Abraham, Isaac, and David. In his comment to "Abraham breathed his last, dying at a good ripe age, old and contented" (Gen. 25:8), Naḥmanides wrote, " 'Old and contented'—He had gotten everything he asked for, and all his wants were completely satisfied. So too was Isaac 'contented with days' [Gen. 35:29]. He was not waiting for the coming days to bring him anything he did not already have. We read the same of David: 'He died at a ripe old age, contented with days, riches and honor' [1 Chron. 29:28]. That is the story both of God's kindness to the righteous and of their own virtue in not desiring anything they do not need: 'You have granted him the desire of his heart' [Ps. 21:3]. It is not so with others: 'A lover of money never has his fill of money' [Eccles. 5:9]." These righteous men serve as examples of people for whom a small amount is enough, who had no need for luxuries.[13] Naḥmanides also attributed this quality to Job, who said, "Did I rejoice in my great wealth, in having attained plenty?" (Job 31:25). In his commentary to Job, Naḥmanides wrote, "And it may be possible to explain 'Did I rejoice in my great wealth?' as Job praising his own frugality. He announced that he did not put his trust in silver or gold, that he took no great pleasure in his vast wealth, but that he rejoiced in his lot to the full extent of what he had, with no desire for anything more" (comment to Job 35:28).

The biblical character who serves as the best example of attaining the virtue of humility is, of course, Moses—the most complete human being ever, from a religious perspective, of whom it is said, "Moses was a very humble man, more so than any other man on earth" (Num. 12:3). Naḥmanides characterized Moses as a man who shunned pride and remained humble even when his humility is not explicitly recorded in the text, as for example in the following cases.

In the first encounter between Moses and God, at the burning bush (Exod. 3–4), Moses rejected God's request that he inform the elders of Israel about the exodus from Egypt, finishing by saying, "Please, O Lord, send by the hand You will send" (Exod. 4:13). Naḥmanides begins his explanation of Moses's words with three explanations, from the Targum and Rashi, that interpret Moses's words in various ways. He then writes, "But I think it means 'by the hand of whomever You wish to send—for there is no one in the world who would not be better suited for this mission than I.' Now Moses's reason for such obstinacy was that he was 'a very humble man, more so than any other man on earth' [Num. 12:3]. For he did not dare aggrandize himself enough to tell the king, 'The Lord sent me,' nor go to the Israelites to take them out of Egypt and become their king." Moses's humility was so great that he thought everyone more worthy than him to bring the word of the Lord to the people of Israel.

Elsewhere Naḥmanides argued that Moses's humility won him the opportunity to play a role comparable to that of the Holy One. After the Holy One assigned Moses as His agent to bring the word of the Lord to Pharaoh (Exod. 6:29), Moses replied, "See, I am of impeded speech" (Exod. 6:30), and the Holy One responded, "See, I place you in the role of God to Pharaoh, with your brother Aaron as your prophet" (Exod. 7:1). The commentators suggest various interpretations of the difficult phrase "I place you in the role of God to Pharaoh." In his comment to Exodus 6:13, Naḥmanides suggests a daring interpretation that takes the verse at face value: "'You will go before Pharaoh and command Aaron, but Pharaoh will not hear your words. Aaron, on assignment from you, will utter your words to him, just as God commands a prophet and the prophet utters His words and reproves the people with them.' This was a promotion for Moses, which he earned by his great humility in being embarrassed on account of his impeded speech." According to Naḥmanides, Moses was originally intended to speak directly to Pharaoh. But by virtue of his humility he rose to a level like that of the Lord: just as God speaks to the prophet and the prophet transmits His words to the people, Moses too would speak to Aaron, who would transmit his words to Pharaoh.

The humility of Moses was expressed not only in his encounters with the Holy One but also in his encounters with human beings. For example, after Moses came down from Mount Sinai and saw the Golden Calf, he asked Aaron, "What did this people do to you that you have brought such great sin upon them?" (Exod. 32:21). Naḥmanides asks why Moses accused Aaron only of the people's sin and did not task him with his own sin: "Moses ought to have first castigated him for his own sin, and only then for that of the people: 'How could you commit this great sin against God, and make so many others stumble in the same way?' " Naḥmanides's explanation is that Moses, out of his great humility, did not want to remind Aaron of his own sin, because Aaron was his older brother. "But Moses, in his great humility, was careful to respect his older brother, and mentioned only the people's sin." In all three of these cases and in others as well,[14] Naḥmanides characterizes Moses as a humble man even when the text itself does not explicitly say so or even call for such an explanation.

At one point, Naḥmanides compares the humility of Moses to that of Aaron—both of them avoid strife because of their humility. Of Moses, Naḥmanides writes in connection to the accusations of Aaron and Miriam: " 'Now Moses was a very humble man' [Num. 12:3]. God had to be jealous on Moses's behalf. He himself would never respond to a quarrel of this kind even if he had known about it"; about Aaron Naḥmanides writes, " 'Korah fell on his face' [Num. 16:4]. But Aaron did not. He did not say a word during this entire dispute, being both too sacred and too disciplined to do so. He kept silent, as if admitting that Korah's status was greater than his own, but that he was simply doing what Moses said and obeying the king's decree."[15]

To conclude: Naḥmanides made ethical demands that touch both on thought and on action, both in one's relationship with God and in one's relationship to other people. The goal of the commandment "Do what is right and good" is to employ justice in order to make society whole again; the goal of the commandment "be holy" is abstinence that would ultimately lead to mystical intimacy with the Creator. This commandment is linked with the demand for humility, whose goal is likewise intimacy with the Creator. The processes of perfection, transcendence, and purification will eventually lead to intimacy between man and God.

Notes

1. For example, Moshe Idel, "Nahmanides: Kabbala, Halakha and Spiritual Leadership" [Hebrew], *Tarbiz* 64 (1995): 559–60; Moshe Halbertal, *By Way of Truth: Naḥmanides and the Creation of Tradition* [Hebrew] (Jerusalem: Shalom Hartman Institute, 2006), 14.

2. Halbertal, *By Way of Truth*, 284.

3. See also Chaim Henoch, *Nachmanides: Philosopher and Mystic* [Hebrew] (Jerusalem: Torah Laam, 1978), 123–31; Moshe Halbertal, *Interpretative Revolutions in the Making: Values as Interpretive Considerations in Midrashei Halakhah* [Hebrew] (Jerusalem: Magnes Press, 1997), 30–32; Halbertal, *By Way of Truth*, 286–90; Oded Yisraeli, " 'Taking Precedence over the Torah': Vows and Oaths, Abstinence and Celibacy in Naḥmanides's Oeuvre," *Journal of Jewish Thought and Philosophy* 28, no. 2 (2020): 133–34 and n28.

4. See also his explanation of the sin of the "wayward and defiant" son: "He commits two violations: one, cursing his father and mother and rebelling against them; and two, being a glutton and a drunkard, which violates Lev. 19:2, 'You shall be holy, for I, the LORD your God, am holy' " (comment to Deut. 21:18).

5. Naḥmanides, *Writings of R. Moses ben Naḥman*, ed. C. B. Chavel (Jerusalem: Mossad Harav Kook, 1963), 190–91.

6. On abstinence in Naḥmanides's thought and its reflection in his Torah commentary and in his personal life, see further in Yisraeli, "Taking Precedence over the Torah," 133–39.

7. The question of the *Iggeret*'s authorship is much discussed in the scholarly literature. The accepted view today is that it is completely authentic. See Oded Yisraeli, *Rabbi Moses b. Nachman (Nachmanides)—Intellectual Biography* [Hebrew] (Jerusalem: Magnes Press, 2020), 326–27. Quotations from the *Iggeret* are based on the Hebrew of MS Parma-Palatina 2784/28 (De Rossi 1390; F 13633), which was copied in 1286, just fifteen years after Naḥmanides's death.

8. On the idea of mystical intimacy with God and its development among the thinkers of the Middle Ages, see the study of Adam Afterman, *Devekut: Mystical Intimacy in Medieval Jewish Thought* [Hebrew] (Los Angeles: Cherub, 2011). On mystical intimacy in Naḥmanides's thought see further there, 286–333, with bibliography of earlier research on this topic at 286n2.

9. Afterman, *Devekut*, 296; see the full discussion on 296–302.

10. On abstinence as a stage on the way to mystical intimacy see Yisraeli, "Taking Precedence over the Torah," 140–45.

11. The other general commandment mentioned there is the commandment to keep the Sabbath, which is not directly connected to ethical traits.

12. See also his comment to "[b]e careful to heed all these words" (Deut. 12:28): "There is no specific mention here of laws, rules, injunctions, or commandments. It just says 'all these words' to include something more general in the statement, that is, 'what is good and right.' See my comment to Deut 6:18." It is interesting to note that in his comment to Deuteronomy 6:18 all the examples of specific prohibitions are taken from Lev. 19.

13. This apparently does not contradict Naḥmanides's claim that the Patriarchs were extremely wealthy; see his comment to Gen. 25:34. See also Miriam Sklarz, "The Terms 'Error' and 'Enticement' in Naḥmanides' Rebuke of Ibn Ezra" [Hebrew], *Studies in Bible and Exegesis* 8 (2008): 567–68.

14. The humility of Moses is mentioned also in Naḥmanides's comments to Exod. 16:6, Num. 11:28, and Deut. 1:12.

15. Naḥmanides added these words to his commentary only after reaching Israel. See Yosef Ofer and Jonathan Jacobs, *Naḥmanides' Torah Commentary Addenda Written in the Land of Israel* [Hebrew] (Jerusalem: World Union of Jewish Studies, 2013), 448–49.

Chapter 10

The *Zohar*

EITAN P. FISHBANE

The *Zohar* is the masterpiece of Kabbalah, though the latest consensus among scholars is that what came to be known as *Sefer ha-Zohar* (The Book of Radiance) is the amalgamation of a diverse range of manuscript sources ranging numerous decades and reflecting the authorial involvement of a group of several, perhaps many, other mystics (and in all probability a series of groups).[1]

What is typically referred to as *guf ha-Zohar* (the main body of the *Zohar*) appears to have been written in the Castille-León region of what is now Spain between the years 1270 and 1330. A pseudepigraphic work, the *Zohar* was attributed to the second-century tannaitic sage Rabbi Shimon bar Yoḥai, despite the fact that scholarship has conclusively demonstrated that the text was written by late thirteenth- and early fourteenth-century Iberian kabbalists. Written in an invented variation of Aramaic, while the norm for kabbalistic works written at this time was Hebrew, the authors of the *Zohar* sought to emulate and evoke the Aramaic usage of ancient and late antique rabbinic works (though often erring in their assumptions about how tannaitic mystics would have expressed mystical matters), thereby seeking to relocate the *Zohar* in space and time from medieval Castille to ancient land of Israel. This Aramaic came to be essential to the rhetoric of the *Zohar* beyond the mere cloak of pseudepigraphic attribution; I contend that it functions to cast a spell of spiritual mystery and poetic wonder over the reader. Seen most generally, the *Zohar* may be divided into two umbrella genres that are interspersed and woven together throughout the voluminous pages of text (first published in Italy in the 1550s from a myriad of manuscripts, and typically printed in three thick volumes): (1) the episodic fictional tale (though not presented as fiction!) of Rabbi Shimon bar Yoḥai and his disciples wandering through the ancient Galilee in quest of mystical wisdom, often discovering it in the mouths of wondrous strangers they meet along the way; and (2) the mystical-midrashic speeches uttered by Rabbi Shimon, his disciples, and these mysterious strangers encountered along the path of their sojourn. These discourses emulate classical midrashic form, but the vast majority of their content centers on a mystical conception of Divinity and the ways in which that metaphysical reality is encoded in a symbolic reading of the Torah and the many other books of the Hebrew Bible.

The Cultivation of Virtue in the *Zohar*

If virtue ethics here is to be understood along Aristotelian lines—that is, that right action is grounded in the cultivation of paradigmatic character traits (or, as Rosalind Hursthouse has put it:[2] "What sort of a person should I be?" in contrast to the question—more typical of Kantian and Utilitarian theories—"What sorts of actions should I perform?" or "what choice should I make in a given circumstance?")[3]—then it is fair to say that the *Zohar* formulates such an ethical vision through its engagement with the two primary literary genres that structure its textual landscape. The first is the representation of virtue through the fictional narrative of the putatively tannaitic mystics wandering through the terrain of ancient Galilee. The second is the exposition of virtue within the mystical-midrashic discourses spoken by the characters. In the case of the first genre (narrative), this is a modality of narrative exemplum ethics—discernment from represented relationships, interactions, and exempla of a cluster of virtuous character traits. In the case of the second genre (mystical midrash, mythic theology), the presentation of virtuous ideals flows from symbolically infused reflections on specific biblical figures—what these personalities allude to within the Divine Self (i.e., the inner-divine *sefirot*), and what traits they constitute to be emulated by the human being: Abraham as hospitable, Jacob as grateful and peaceful, Joseph as a model of sexual restraint and forgiveness, Moses as humble, and so on.

Virtue ethics in the fictional scenes of the *Zohar* is anchored in the quest for (kabbalistic) wisdom, piety, love, and friendship. I mention the last two *both* with an eye to how they were central for Aristotle's vision of the good life, along with his virtue ethics descendants in philosophers such as Martha Nussbaum,[4] Hursthouse, Iris Murdoch,[5] and Alexander Nehamas,[6] *and* in regard to the way in which such interpersonal relational ideals are understood by the authors of the *Zohar* as phenomena of human flourishing that are directly tied to a revelatory encounter with the Divine. The relational encounter is itself a moment in which God's face, the face of *Shekhinah,* shines in presence to the beholding friend.[7]

This bridging of the physical and the metaphysical in the moment of relational encounter is essential to understanding piety, virtue, and pursuit of the good in the *Zohar*: that the life well-lived is a realization of *tzelem Elohim,* of the human being as an embodied refraction, perhaps even *incarnation,* of the Divine Self. In this sense, moral choice—which flows from an ingrained character trait—is fundamentally theological for the kabbalists of the *Zohar,* perhaps even *theomorphic* (as opposed to *anthropomorphic*) in the emulation of the divine paradigm of perfection, the ultimate exemplum. So framed, if *eudaemonia* in the Aristotelian legacy indicates that good is an end in itself, the correlative equivalent of such eudaemonic perfection in the kabbalistic/zoharic sense is the fulfillment of the attributes and dimensions of the Divine Self. This is developed further in sixteenth- and seventeenth-century kabbalistic *musar* texts like Moses Cordovero's *Tomer Devorah,* Eliyahu de Vidas's *Reishit Hokhmah,* and Yishayahu Horowitz's *Shenei Luḥot ha-Berit,* and then in the mystical-moral dimensions of eighteenth through twentieth century Hasidic homiletics, but it is also very much characteristic of the thirteenth century zoharic moral vision.

The cultivation of virtuous character and its traits is, for the *Zohar* and its later kabbalistic descendants, bound up in a theological conception of perfection to which the human life aspires. Thus virtue ethics for the *Zohar* is entwined with a vision of piety and devotion: to act in a virtuous manner is to embody certain theological ideals and to express a particular mode of pious, spiritual devotion. This deep intersection between ideals of moral righteousness and paradigmatic theological states is also reflected in several key passages that are worth citing and paraphrasing here as examples of envisioned ethical perfection and the manner in which that is inextricable from metaphysical dynamics. Let us consider, for example, one of the earliest biblical juxtapositions of virtue versus vice—*Kayin ve-Hevel* (Cain and Abel)—how the *Zohar* discusses them as paradigms of the good and its opposite, and how this polarity is cast in metaphysical-mythic terms. For the most part in these instances, the virtuous-evil dichotomy is presented in general, all-encompassing terms, as opposed to addressing specific virtues/character traits as we will observe in the next section. Speaking in the voice of one of its main protagonists, Rabbi Abba, the *Zohar* states: "Come and see: When one follows the path of truth [*azil be-oraḥ qeshot*] he tends toward the right [*azil le-yemina*], drawing upon himself a supernal holy spirit [*ruḥa qadisha ila'ah*] from above. The spirit ascends in holy desire to unite above, cleaving to supernal holiness irremovably. But when one follows the path of evil and strays [*azil be-oraḥ bish ve-satei orḥoi*], he draws upon himself an unsure spirit of the left side, defiling him, so he becomes defiled."[8]

While the authors of the *Zohar*, through the homiletic voice of Rabbi Abba, do not yet clarify just what constitutes the good, virtuous life—structured by "the path of truth"—a human life conducted with ideal goodness and adherence to that "true way" (*oraḥ qeshot*) is connected and causally guided toward to the right side of Divinity (right in its directional sense, the opposite of the left). This right side of God—the *yemina*—is well established in the *Zohar* and in kabbalistic lore more broadly as the side of *Ḥesed* (love/kindness) and of *Raḥamim* (compassion/love). It is further notable that this path of human behavior—in which one is aligned with a certain side and force within Divinity—is presented as the opposite of an undesired state of behavior, the inverse of virtue, the path of evil (*oraḥ bish*). In the mythology and anthropology sketched above in the *Zohar*, there is a metaphysical consequence—an event of theurgy—that follows directly from whether the person conducts themselves in the way of *qeshot* as opposed the way of *bish*, the latter characterized as a waywardness, a straying from the paradigmatic path (*ve-satei orḥoi*). When the "path of truth" is followed, the "supernal holy spirit from above" is drawn down onto him—a classic kabbalistic formulation for positive theurgical stimulation—and, inversely, when one follows the path of evil, he becomes "defiled" and "impurified" by the downflow of "the impure spirit of the left side" onto him. Conduct deemed virtuous or unvirtuous here reverberates in the upper realms, and a positive or a negative spirit comes to dwell upon that person. As the *Zohar* goes on to elaborate, this primordial dichotomy of virtue and evil was the root cause for the metaphysical divergence between Cain and Abel; while Abel was born infused with the pure holy spirit that resulted from the righteousness and adherence to the "path of truth" by biblical Adam, Cain was conversely born into an evil state that likewise was caused by the primordial sin of Adam, one that caused the "slime" of the demonic Other Side to insert the evil character of the Left into Eve, resulting in the unvirtuous condition of Cain.

Let us consider one other presentation of virtuous character in the *Zohar*, modeled on the biblical figure of Abraham:

> Rabbi Abba opened, "Listen to me, you stubborn-hearted, who are far from צדקה (*tzedaqah*), righteousness (Isa. 46:12) [*reḥoqim mi-tzedaqah*]. Listen to me, you stubborn-hearted. How hardened are the hearts of sinners, who see the paths and ways of Torah yet do not contemplate them! Their hearts are hardened (*libaihu taqifin*): not turning back in repentance (*de-la mehadrin be-tiyuvta*) to their Lord, they are called stubborn-hearted.
>
> *Far from righteousness*, for they keep themselves far from Torah.
>
> Rabbi Ḥizkiyah said, "for they keep themselves far from the blessed Holy One (*de-mitraḥaqei mi-Qadosh Barukh Hu*), so they are *far from righteousness*. Being *far from righteousness*, they are far from peace, for they have no peace, as it is written: *There is no peace, says YHVH, for the wicked* (Isa. 48:22). Why? Because they are *far from righteousness*.
>
> Come and see: Abraham sought to draw near the blessed Holy One and was drawn near, as it is written: *You loved* צדק (*tzedek*), *righteousness, and hated wickedness* (Ps. 45:8). Because he loved *tzedek, righteousness*, he was drawn near צדקה (*tzedakah*), *righteousness*. So it is written, *Abraham, My lover* (Isa. 41:8). Why *My lover*? Because *you loved righteousness*—love of the blessed Holy One, whom Abraham loved more than all his contemporaries, who were *stubborn-hearted* and *far from righteousness*, as has been said.[9]

This passage is particularly remarkable in its symbolic references to dimensions of Divinity that are relatively veiled to the uninitiated reader of the *Zohar,* the way in which the virtuousness of Abraham is bound up with his spiritual bondedness—indeed, his devotional love or *eros*—toward one of those divine *sefirot*. According to Rabbi Abba, stubbornness, or perhaps hard-heartedness (*libaihu taqifin*), causes the sinners to not see the deeper mysteries of the Torah beneath the surface level. Were they to see the divine reverberations within the Torah, the text suggests, surely they would "turn back in repentance" (*mehadrin be-tiyuvta*). Spiritual perception thus leads to penitence and the transformation of vice. The state of wickedness—the converse of the virtuous character—stems from a hardened refusal to spiritually contemplate the divine secrets, presumably implying that coming closer to God—characterized as a state of love between Abraham and God—would lead naturally to a condition of virtue.

In kabbalistic symbolism, צדקה (*tzedakah*), *righteousness*, indicates the male *sefirah* known as *Tif'eret*, while צדק (*tzedek*), (also) righteousness, refers to the female *sefirah*, *Shekhinah*. Abraham loved *Shekhinah*, and consequently was drawn close to *Tif'eret*. Notably, in ethical terms, the devotional attachment to *tzedek* is a connection to a virtuous condition, while *tzedakah* would instead indicate a modality of behavior, the manifestation of the righteous character-state through acts of righteousness. What is more, the word צדקה (*tzedakah*) is most commonly used to refer to virtuous actions of charitable giving toward the less fortunate.

Core Virtues Reflected in the *Zohar*

As mentioned above, one of the primary genres that the *Zohar* utilizes to articulate its vision of ideal character, its unsystematic implementation of virtue ethics, is that of *narrative ethics*—a nexus of literature and philosophy, or in the case of the *Zohar*, of theology, literature, and philosophy.[10] I have dealt with this genre as it is reflected in the *Zohar*, along with more extensive references, in my previous work.[11] I shall not reiterate what was developed there, except to distill several character traits of virtue ethics that are discernible in that corpus and worthy of underscoring here in this shorter essay.

Insofar as *wisdom* has been identified by interpreters of Aristotle and contemporary virtue ethicists as a central trait in the cultivation of character, in quest of the life well-lived, this rises to the fore among medieval kabbalists in general, and for the authors of the *Zohar* in particular. For the *Zohar*, to be wise—to live out the virtue of wisdom—is, to be sure, notably different from the understanding of classical Greek philosophers such as Aristotle, as well as medieval Jewish philosophers. For the medieval kabbalists, the ideal of wisdom is fundamentally theologically and metaphysically oriented (often also true of medieval Jewish philosophers), characterized as *ḥokhmat ha-nistar*—the wisdom of the hidden, of the concealed matters—which typically refers to insight into the mysteries of Divinity and the ways in which God is alluded to symbolically in the world, the human self, and the Torah. Indeed, it is mystical-metaphysical wisdom about Torah and its secrets. This cultivation of wisdom—the attainment of a character extolled as a sage of mystical secrets—is the ground of what might be labeled *eudaemonia* in the *Zohar*, reflected in the oft-repeated exclamation of *zaka'ah ḥulqana* ("happy is our portion!") uttered by various mystic companions upon hearing a great kabbalistic teaching. This formulation and its significance for the much broader concept of happiness in the history Jewish thought and philosophy (and in relation to the Aristotelian legacy regarding *eudaemonia*) was studied in depth by Hava Tirosh-Samuelson.[12]

This state of wisdom as a virtuous condition is specifically imbued with the conviction that reality must be probed for deeper divine meanings that are present beneath the surface, never being satisfied with the surface-level perceptions of truth presented at first glance. As we find in the exclamatory statement by Rabbi Shimon bar Yoḥai in *Zohar* 1:83a: "Rabbi Shimon was walking on the road, and with him were Rabbi Elazar his son, Rabbi Abba, and Rabbi Yehudah. While they were walking, Rabbi Shimon said: "I am stunned how people of the world do not look to understand the words of Torah and upon what they stand!" Indeed, if a life of virtue is understood to be a realization of flourishing and the ideals of how a human life ought to be lived, the *Zohar* correspondingly asserts its belief that proper perception and awareness is one in which Torah and the world roundabout are understood to be permeated by divine allusions and mysteries. Wisdom, according the kabbalists in general and the *Zohar* in particular, is a state of mind in which the divine spiritual underpinnings and symbolic markers are discerned in the mundane realm.

Though the following elements of virtuous character as articulated by the *Zohar* are not meant to be exhaustive, they do reflect the core structure of this zoharic vision: (1) In a manner parallel to the way friendship was correlated to virtue ethics by Aristotle, Montaigne, and others, the *Zohar* likewise raises up the ideal form of this interpersonal dynamic as a grounding feature of a kabbalistic vision of human flourishing. Like Aristotle, and Plato before him, this idealization of friendship in the *Zohar* was an expression of a certain kind of love, a certain mode of *eros*.[13] Like the ancient Greek model, this was fundamentally a love between male friends, and for the *Zohar*, this male friendship was bound up in a shared spiritual quest for mystical wisdom and revelatory encounter with Divinity. Notably, the *Zohar* frequently characterizes the revelation of the divine face to the male mystic as the embodiment of the female divine potency (*Shekhinah*) in the face of the fellow male mystic friend. This is expressed in variations of exclamations such as (paraphrased) "How wonderful it is to see the face of the *Shekhinah*!" And, even more erotically: "I have been blessed to kiss the the face of the *Shekhinah*!" Such expressions, which pervade the zoharic stories, reflect the strong undercurrent of love and passion that runs through the emotional texture of zoharic representations of interpersonal relationships; the revelatory connection between human mystic and deity; and the inner-divine eros and sexuality that anchors the mythology of zoharic metaphysics and theology. Among other key works of scholarship, this theme is developed evocatively by Yehuda Liebes in his classic essay, "*Zohar* and Eros,"[14] and by Elliot R. Wolfson in several publications.[15] Thus, it is the emotion of love—in this sense of love that is grounded in the passion of discipleship and fellowship oriented around the sharing of mystical wisdom about God—that drives and ultimately defines a vision of the good, ideal life, a sense of spiritually inflected virtue that is the *Zohar*'s version of *eudaemonia*. The flourishing life is one that takes place in the context of kabbalistic community, loving friendship in shared pursuit of the mysteries of the Torah, the wisdom of the hidden.

(2) Remaining with the motif of love and—thinking with the philosophy of Martha Nussbaum—its outgrowth into empathy and compassion, I turn to what I consider a second major element of zoharic virtue ethics: *eschewing judgmentalism based on superficial*

appearances, instead graciously *giving the benefit of the doubt* to each person one encounters—that they potentially contain deep mystical wisdom (viz., not assuming that the other person who is encountered is devoid of deep mystical wisdom, but instead *cultivating openness and generosity of spirit, a magnanimity in seeing the potential good and depth of the other*).[16] This virtuous ideal is bound up in the frequent zoharic use of *anagnorisis* (the term influentially used by Aristotle in his *Poetics*) in its narrative constructions, the poetics of recognition[17] in which the protagonists repeatedly encounter seeming simpletons and fools during their peregrinations throughout the Galilee and the broader land of Israel. In each case, the main characters—members of the *ḥavrayya,* the spiritual friendship circle who are disciples of the great Rabbi Shimon bar Yoḥai—happen upon a stranger who is first assumed by the protagonists to be unworthy of their time and attention based on the assumption that this stranger could not possibly have something profound to teach them in matters of mystical Torah, the ultimate goal of their travels. In each case, this assumption is turned on its head, and the donkey-driver (a frequent example of a presumptively unlearned worker), the child, or the apparently simple Jew turns out in truth to be the exact opposite of what he is assumed to be. The presumed simpleton reveals himself to be a great mystic sage who expounds a learned kabbalistic discourse, dramatically overwhelming the protagonists with the brilliance of his unexpected teaching.[18] This motif of *anagnorisis* was utilized by a range of other non-kabbalistic practitioners, Jewish and non-Jewish, in the medieval art of the frame-tale.[19]

(3) If *love, generosity,* and *care* constitute a core axis of virtue ethics in the *Zohar,* this is extended to the idealized behavior of charity—of compassion and the enactment of care toward the poor and the vulnerable—framed also in regard to the practice of hospitality. Here two cases are particularly relevant. In the first instance, found in *Zohar* 2:61a–b,[20] an exemplum tale is told about a recurrent mystical master in the zoharic stories, one Rabbi Yeisa, who makes the effort to *notice* the misfortune of a poor man who was neglected and ignored by the other people of the town. His moral act is one of deliberately not looking away, of *seeing* the suffering of poverty and vulnerability, and then acting to rectify it by restoring the spirit of the ailing poor man with fig juice. This exemplum story is utilized by the zoharic authors to assert the paradigmatic principle, the moral

value, of caring for the vulnerable and not looking away from the face of suffering. The second case I shall mention here briefly involves a prominent passage in the *Zohar* (3:103b–4a) in which it is asserted that while the mystic seeks to theurgically draw down the spirit-Presences of the Divine Guests (the *ushpizin*) from on high into the *sukkah*, such an invocation of heavenly presence is only of value if the virtue of hosting and feeding the impoverished hungry in one's community, feeding them the physical portion of those supernal Divine Guests, is enacted.[21]

(4) Lastly, let me mention in highly truncated fashion two other virtues that prove quite important for the authors of the *Zohar*. The first of these (a) is *the principle of pure and unilateral forgiveness* (an intention that must be made explicit prior to going to sleep at night), the letting go of resentment over having been wronged without any quid pro quo, and also without the shade of narcissism, a sense of superiority, over having benevolently granted this forgiveness to the other (here I gesture toward arguments to this effect made by Moshe Halbertal and Martha Nussbaum).[22] The second of these last zoharic virtues that I shall mention here is (b) *the ideal of avoiding, subduing, and controlling one's own anger and that of others*.[23] In this regard, the *Zohar* expands upon the much earlier rabbinic assertion that one who gives in to the pernicious emotion of anger acts as nothing less than an idolator in that moment.[24] For the authors of the *Zohar*, the adaptation of this rabbinic dictum is characterized as the tearing of one's heavenly soul and the invocation of the demonic Other Side into one's inner self. To indulge in rageful behavior is to embody the ferocity of the unrestrained Left Side of Divinity, *Gevurah* and *Din* unbalanced by love and compassion. What is more, through its use of exemplum narrative ethics, the *Zohar* also idealizes one who steps into the breach to restrain the potentially harmful anger of another person and who works to soothe and cool the fires of the other's rage.

In conclusion, albeit with extreme brevity, in this paper I have sought to demonstrate the strong degree to which the category and characteristics of virtue ethics are integral to the nature and texture of the *Zohar*. The vision of the mystical life presented by the medieval kabbalists is fundamentally theomorphic, seeking to articulate the ideals of moral piety whereby the human being may realize their essential character as manifestations of the divine form, a true *tzelem Elohim*.

Notes

1. See Daniel Abrams, *Kabbalistic Manuscripts and Textual Theory* (Jerusalem: Magnes Press; Los Angeles: Cherub, 2010), 224–428; Ronit Meroz, *The Spiritual Biography of Rabbi Shimon bar Yoḥai* [Hebrew] (Jerusalem: Mossad Bialik, 2018), throughout.

2. Rosalind Hursthouse, *On Virtue Ethics* (Oxford: Oxford University Press, 1999), 26.

3. It is worth noting Martha Nussbaum's critique of this divide in ethical theory, arguing that both Kantian deontology and utilitarianism involve key elements of virtue at their core as well. See Nussbaum's reconsideration of her early position as influenced by Aristotle (her original view articulated in her 1978 monograph on Aristotle) in Martha C. Nussbaum, "Virtue Ethics: A Misleading Category?," *Journal of Ethics* 3, no. 3 (1999): 163–201; and now in the preface to the 2001 revised edition of Nussbaum, *The Fragility of Goodness: Luck and Ethics in Greek Tragedy and Philosophy* (Cambridge: Cambridge University Press, 2001), xxiv–xxv.

4. See both the Nussbaum publications cited above and her discussion of love and compassion in her more recent writings such as *Upheavals of Thought: The Intelligence of Emotions* (New York: Cambridge University Press, 2001), and *Political Emotions: Why Love Matters for Justice* (Cambridge, MA: Harvard University Press, 2013).

5. See, for example, Iris Murdoch, *The Sovereignty of Good* (Abingdon, UK: Routledge, 2001).

6. With particular regard to the nexus between virtue and friendship in classical sources, a correlation integral to the medieval *Zohar*, see Alexander Nehamas, *On Friendship* (New York: Basic Books, 2016), 21–27. Also see Lorraine Smith Pangle, *Aristotle and the Philosophy of Friendship* (Cambridge: Cambridge University Press, 2002), e.g., 54.

7. See Eitan P. Fishbane, "God in the Face of the Other: Mystical Friendship in the *Zohar*" in *Friendship in Jewish History, Religion, and Culture*, ed. Lawrence Fine (University Park: Pennsylvania State University Press, 2021), 38–54.

8. *Zohar* 1:54a. For our purposes here I have provided the translation of Daniel C. Matt (with minor adaptations), *The Zohar: Pritzker Edition* (Stanford, CA: Stanford University Press, 2004), 1:301.

9. *Zohar* 1:76b–77a. I again provide the translation of Daniel C. Matt (with minor adaptations), *The Zohar: Pritzker Edition*, 2:1–2.

10. Notable, albeit select, examples of this work include Adam Zachary Newton, *Narrative Ethics* (Cambridge, MA: Harvard University Press, 1995); Martha C. Nussbaum, *Love's Knowledge: Essays on Philosophy and Literature* (New York: Oxford University Press, 1992); and Nussbaum, *Upheavals of Thought*.

11. Eitan P. Fishbane, *The Art of Mystical Narrative: A Poetics of the Zohar* (New York: Oxford University Press, 2018), 280–335.

12. Hava Tirosh-Samuelson, *Happiness in Premodern Judaism: Virtue, Knowledge, and Well-Being* (Cincinnati: Hebrew Union College Press, 2003).

13. See, for example, David Bolotin, *Plato's Dialogue on Friendship: An Interpretation of the Lysis, with a New Translation* (1979; Ithaca: Cornell University Press, 1989); Lorraine Pangle Smith, *Aristotle and the Philosophy of Friendship* (Cambridge: Cambridge University Press, 2002).

14. Yehuda Liebes, "Zohar and Eros" [Hebrew] *Alpayyim* 9 (1994): 67–119.

15. See, in particular, the section entitled "Mystical Fellowship as the Constitution of the Divine Face," in Elliot R. Wolfson *Through a Speculum that Shines: Vision and Imagination in Medieval Jewish Mysticism* (Princeton, NJ: Princeton University Press, 1994), 367–77.

16. On love, empathy, and compassion as key emotions in the cultivation of justice and moral philosophy, see Nussbaum, *Upheavals of Thought*, 297–456; Nussbaum, *Political Emotions*, 137–60; 378–98. Also see the earlier reflections of Iris Murdoch, *The Sovereignty of Good*, e.g., 60–61.

17. For an extensive study of this motif and literary technique in the broader terrain of comparative literature, see Terence Cave, *Recognition: A Study in Poetics* (Oxford: Oxford University Press, 1988).

18. On this motif in the *Zohar*, see Yechiel Shalom Goldberg, "The Foolishness of the Wise and the Wisdom of Fools in Spanish Kabbalah: An Inquiry into the Taxonomy of the Wise Fool," *Journal for the Study of Sephardic and Mizrahi Jewry* 1, no. 2 (2007): 42–78; Eitan P. Fishbane, *The Art of Mystical Narrative*, 128–52; Melila Hellner-Eshed, *A River Flows from Eden: The Language of Mystical Experience in the Zohar* (Hebrew edition, 2005; Stanford, CA: Stanford University Press, 2009), 146–53.

19. See Fishbane, *The Art of Mystical Narrative*, 128–52, 357–80.

20. Discussed in greater depth in Fishbane, *The Art of Mystical Narrative*, 296–307.

21. See Fishbane, *The Art of Mystical Narrative*, 317–24.

22. For an expanded analysis, see Fishbane, *The Art of Mystical Narrative*, 286–95.

23. See Fishbane, *The Art of Mystical Narrative*, 324–35.

24. See BT Shabbat 105b and Pirkei Avot 5:11.

Chapter 11

Gersonides

ALEXANDER GREEN

Rabbi Levi ben Gershom (1288–1344) is one of the most original and innovative Jewish philosophers of the Middle Ages after Moses Maimonides. He is known either in Rabbinic circles through the acronym Ralbag or in academic studies through the latinized name Gersonides. Despite the fact that he lived in Provence during the period when it was the center for Jewish intellectual and scientific study, very little is known about Gersonides's personal life.

His major accomplishment in the history of Jewish thought is his advocacy for a form of Aristotelian Judaism, a position that he took further than any of his predecessors. He studied Aristotle's writings through the Hebrew translation of Averroes's commentaries. All his writings were written in Hebrew, though scholars debate whether he had reading knowledge of Latin. His writings demonstrate a synthesis of Maimonides's philosophic Judaism with Averroes's naturalism. While Maimonides's philosophy is tempered with skepticism about many of his own scientific proofs, Gersonides's project was to synthesize reason and faith "without any doubt" (*be-ofen she-lo yishaer bo safek*). Or, stated differently, "adherence to reason is not permitted if it contradicts religious faith."[1]

Gersonides's writings reflect a wide range of intellectual interests and activities. Besides being a philosopher, he was an experimental scientist whose conclusions were attained by empirical observation. For example, his interest in astronomy led him to invent a tool that he called "Jacob's Staff," which was designed to measure the distance between celestial objects. His earliest writings were Hebrew supercommentaries on the Hebrew translations of Averroes's scientific commentaries on Aristotle. Gersonides's major theological writing is his treatise *Wars of the Lord* (*Sefer Milḥamot Hashem*). In this work, he presents a series of issues that (by implication) he believed Maimonides did not get right in his *Guide of the Perplexed*. It is the organization and boldness of such an independent treatise to rival the *Guide* that was likely a factor in the longevity of Gersonides's influence. Gersonides also wrote commentaries on much of the Hebrew Bible, some of which were printed in early versions of the Rabbinic Bible, the *Mikraot Gedolot*.

Virtue and Human Teleology

Gersonides argues that one of the purposes of the Torah as a divine law is the cultivation of moral virtues in its adherents.[2] His understanding of the moral virtues was influenced by Aristotle's *Nicomachean Ethics*, to which he likely had access through Samuel ben Judah of Marseilles's translation of Averroes's *Commentary on Aristotle's Nicomachean Ethics* into Hebrew in the early 1320s.[3] However, the justification to read the Torah as a vehicle for becoming trained in the Aristotelian moral virtues had already become central to the Jewish philosophical curriculum through many of Maimonides's works. Gersonides continues the tradition of virtue ethics derived from both Aristotle and Maimonides through advocating that the ideal character traits are a mean between two extremes of behavior. However, his empirical astronomical studies inspired him to reach beyond this model and eventually led him toward a new way of understanding the purposes of human striving.

Gersonides's understanding of God and the universe is ordered and teleological, such that everything in nature has a purpose. God is thus the soul or intellect of the universe and is its efficient, formal, and final cause who emanates incorporeal intellects that move the celestial spheres. A part of God's order (but in no way encompassing it) is the Agent Intellect, which is the law and order of the corporeal world.[4] The Agent Intellect is created by God, which means that whatever the Agent Intellect knows, God knows in a more perfect manner.

The particulars in the corporeal world are produced by the heavenly bodies, God's instruments, which prepare the material and accidental natures of sublunar phenomena (e.g., shape, size, temperament).[5] God's knowledge of particulars is knowledge of the general patterns laid out astrologically by the heavenly bodies that were created by God. As a result, Gersonides presents God as one who is ignorant of particulars *as* particulars due to the superiority of His knowledge of universals. According to this view, God does not know for sure how particular human beings will decide to act in particular instances. He knows your probable choice, but cannot determine with certainty whether you will make the choice toward which you are inclined.[6]

Following from this, there are two distinct goals for humanity, related to their body and soul: to achieve preservation of one's physical self and, more importantly, to achieve immortality of the soul through perfection of the intellect. The preservation of the body is rooted in the practical intellect, which, for humans, is a more developed biological survival mechanism than that possessed by other animals. Gersonides views God's providence in the fact that all living beings are biologically endowed with the tools for their self-preservation, whether human or nonhuman. Nonhuman creatures have this survival instinct in the form of bodily organs, instinctual desires, or innate skills or mental powers. Human beings do not have these highly developed physical organs or instincts, but instead have the power of reason, specifically in the form of the practical intellect that can create arts or perfect certain virtues of physical self-preservation.[7] This is especially relevant since, according to Gersonides, the heavenly bodies largely guide human affairs, even though astronomers have not been successful in tracing the exact movements of the heavenly bodies and using them as perfect guides to predict human behavior.[8] Thus, instead of trying to comprehend and overcome the stars, the practical intellect is able to focus its efforts on achieving physical self-preservation through cultivating arts and virtues to withstand the impact of the whims of fortune or avoid its decree as predetermined by the stars.[9]

The highest goal for humanity is to acquire as much knowledge as one can, since the afterlife represents a continuous contemplation of everything acquired in this life, but in the afterlife one cannot acquire new knowledge after death. To achieve happiness in the next world, one must be focused on acquiring knowledge in this world. The knowledge one acquires is not of abstract forms, but begins by contemplating material particulars. As Gersonides posits, the outcome of such study through astronomy leads to an awareness of how God beneficently constructed the heavens for human benefit.[10] These conclusions do not lead to social isolation and ignorance of humanity, but to an ethics of altruism. If the contemplation of nature leads to the conclusion that God constructed it selflessly for the benefit of the lower beings, then humans must imitate God by altruistically benefitting others who are in a weaker position than them.[11] Altruistically helping others as an outcome of reaching a high level of knowledge, according to Gersonides, is carried out by individuals who in every generation imitate God in rationally desiring to direct others to perfection. This, according to Gersonides, explains the prominence of the role of the shepherd and the prophet described in every generation in the Bible. These unique individuals understand their place in the cosmos as fulfilling the same role as that of the stars relative to God, by imitating God's beneficence in disseminating wisdom to those lacking it. They do so through teaching and writing books and, through them, they present the best means to guide other individuals toward achieving knowledge of God, nature, and also their eternality.[12] It is also carried out in actions in interpersonal relations that imitate God's construction of the heavenly bodies through acts of human justice to restore the just ordering of nature. Moreover, it is achieved in actions that improve human life beyond what is necessary in the same way that aspects of nature are given to various species that go beyond what is necessary to survive.

The Virtues of Physical Preservation and the Virtues of Altruism

Gersonides constructs two new categories of virtues that correspond to the perfection of body and soul, what I refer to as the virtues of physical preservation and the virtues of altruism.[13] The virtues of physical preservation, whose purpose is to preserve the body from the negative determinations of the stars and promote worldly thriving, are endeavor (*hishtadlut*), diligence (*ḥaritzut*), and cunning (*hiteḥakmut*) in crafting stratagems (*taḥebulot*). The virtues of altruism, whose purpose is to imitate God's beneficent construction of the heavenly bodies (and by effect other parts of nature) for human benefit, are loving-kindness (*ḥesed*), grace (*ḥaninah*), and beneficence (*hatavah*).

Endeavor (*hishtadlut*) is the striving to successfully obtain goods that are part of the natural biological cycle, such as having and maintaining the health of children, safeguarding the well-being of one's family, and ensuring proper burial. Endeavor is an imitation of nature that is constructed to preserve the existence of its creatures and does so with greater strength the more complex the organism.[14] Thus Gersonides expands upon Averroes's statement that "nature endeavors [*yishtadel ha-teva*]" to bring about "the greatest possible perfection."[15] Nature's endeavor is in giving superior organs for superior beings to preserve (*shemirah*) their existence more effectively within the hierarchy of nature. The means for humans to achieve these goals with the practical intellect are multiple and variable, depending on the contingencies of particular situations. Consequently, Gersonides gives a list of practical maxims to guide endeavor:

- Use whatever means necessary to obtain one's goal, especially those that will make success likely.
- Do not settle for a less complete good.
- Attempt to obtain a next best good when one cannot obtain a perfect good.
- Avoid those obstacles that lead one away from obtaining a right end.
- Act to obtain a good in advance of when you need it.
- Initiate an action and then complete it.

It is important to note that endeavor is morally neutral, cultivated by the good and the bad alike.

Diligence (*ḥaritzut*) is the quickness in acting to acquire the necessary material goods of property, wealth, and food.[16] The psychological basis of this virtue can be found in the *Supercommentary on De Anima*, where *ḥaritzut* refers to the quickness of reception of the appetitive soul in receiving motion from the imaginative faculty, leading to quickness of individuals to act based upon the plans in the imagination.[17] Cunning (*hiteḥakmut*) is the use of slyness and ingenuity by means of ruses, deceptions, and tricks. Gersonides shows how this virtue is used in saving a life, in business, and in war. Stratagems can also be used to remove or minimize evil. One fundamental reason that ingenuity in crafting stratagems is so crucial for good people is that those striving to do evil and hurt others have been proficient at cultivating them as well.

Loving-kindness (*ḥesed*) is an imitation of God's creating the heavenly bodies for human beings with no self-interested benefit to God through human acts of teaching and justice. God's loving-kindness is expressed in his construction of the heavenly bodies, which are designed to benefit the sublunar world in the best possible way. The celestial bodies are created anthropocentrically as reflected in their perfect structure, motion, and rays.[18] The primary way for people to imitate God's loving-kindness is by teaching those who know less to help increase the intellectual perfection of those beings, a form of imitation of the loving altruism of the celestial bodies that emanate knowledge to lower levels of reality.[19] The second way humans can imitate God's loving-kindness is by actions that strive to equalize an imbalance in power that unjustly occurred in the world. God ordered the celestial bodies with the goal of preserving a balanced equilibrium between the different elements, though sometimes there is an accidental imbalance of one element.[20] Acts of justice that correct accidental imbalances are also a form of loving-kindness by restoring God's original equilibrium. Grace (*ḥaninah*) and beneficence (*hatavah*) operate together, as God's grace is imitated in people through acts of beneficence. If loving-kindness is creating an ordered system and maintaining its well-ordered nature, grace, and beneficence are the acts of providing an object to another that is not necessary to live, but improves one within that system. Therefore Gersonides expounds how God's "activity that derives from him—beneficence (*hatavah*) and grace (*ḥaninah*)—is i.e. giving form to existent things in [a] most perfect way."[21] The nature of God's grace and beneficence is evident to Gersonides in his creation of animal biology. God does so in such a way that endows animals with many parts that are not necessary for their existence, but yet improves them. Consequently, in describing God's thirteen attributes, he defines grace (*ḥanun*) as "[h]e gives to some of the beings certain things by way of graciousness, that is, things that are not necessary for their existence but are present in them by way of betterment, as demonstrated in the *Book of Animals* [*Generation of Animals* 2.1.731b]."[22] In imitating God's construction of nature, Gersonides provides some guidelines for beneficent giving:

- Acts of beneficence should be universal, meaning that one should give to everyone, whether friend or enemy. However, it is preferable to only benefit enemies whom one thinks have the potential to be improved, while those who are hopelessly wicked should be avoided.
- Acts of beneficence must work to improve the receiver of the gift.
- The gift should not serve as a burden on the receiver.
- In giving, the self-interest for the giver should not serve as the primary motive of the gift.

There are, however, many cases in which one must simply avoid the possibility of being in a dangerous situation. Gersonides states the principle that "it is not appropriate to put oneself in danger" and that it is "appropriate to run away from even the smallest possibility of life threatening danger."[23] Gersonides thus presents us with numerous ways to overcome or avoid the forces of chance, but ultimately admits to the necessity of fleeing danger due to the inability to truly comprehend the possible causes and outcomes of future chance events. Hence, the prudent person keeps out of trouble.

Virtue and Biblical Narrative

Gersonides makes a case that the virtues are best taught and learned through narrative. In Gersonides's introduction to his *Commentary on the Torah,* he describes the Torah as guiding its adherents by means of three different methods: (1) commandments (*mitzvot*), (2) political philosophy through inculcating correct character traits (*middot*), and (3) (theoretical) knowledge of existence (*deot*). He introduces the second path with a justification for the Bible teaching ethics and political philosophy through its use of narrative. Indeed, he comes to the novel but decisive conclusion that practical matters are more effectively discussed through examples of the lives and actions of individuals in a narrative form than in a scientific commentary or through the commandments of the law.

He offers two reasons for this conclusion. The first is for the sake of imitation and the imagination: ethical lessons are best instructed through imitation of the life and actions of specific individuals and the most effective way to do so is through stories rather than through rules. This is because stories about the deeds of biblical personalities appeal to the imagination, inspiring people to "follow in their footsteps and to conduct ourselves in their ways."

The second is for the sake of simplicity and variability: the narratives are based on a choice number of examples that if systematized in scientific treatises would have too many different cases and examples for people to follow without failure. The number of different potential cases to which the virtues could be applied is vast and would likely lead to confusion if listed. Of course, the narratives are merely examples that do not claim to cover every single ethical dilemma; rather, they help train the individual in practical reasoning that can be applied to cases that are not mentioned in the narrative.

In other words, Gersonides advocates that ethics is best presented in narrative form like those in the Torah over reading a treatise such as the *Nicomachean Ethics* because its stories successfully present characters that exemplify in their actions the outcome of the cultivation of moral virtues.[24]

Virtue and Torah

In Gersonides's conception, the Torah is the product of the deepest philosophic contemplation of nature by the prophets, such that studying the Torah's narratives and following its laws leads to perfection of body and soul. This philosophic contemplation was achieved by empirically studying nature, of which the Torah is the "empirical data" that resulted.[25] In observing the successes and failures of the Israelites throughout their history, the prophets concluded that the Israelites succeeded as a nation when they learned to perfect both the virtues of physical preservation and the virtues of altruism in striving to overcome their predetermined astrological fate in this life and survival of their soul in the afterlife.

Gersonides views the early chapters of Genesis (4–10), from the story of Cain and Abel to the Tower of Babel, as demonstrating man's limited attempt to pursue physical preservation through the construction of arts. At this early stage, human beings lacked the virtues of endeavor, diligence, and cunning and were deficient in loving-kindness and beneficence for others. He regards Cain and Abel as "great sages" (*ḥakhamim gedolim*) of their day, since Cain developed the art of agriculture and Abel the art of animal husbandry through experimentation. Yet ultimately Abel was more successful, leading to Cain's jealousy and murder of him. The scientific progress was lost, though Cain's descendants rediscovered it many generations later.[26] The culmination of these early forms of science was the Tower of Babel, which was supposed to provide the ideal means of human preservation and safety. The Tower would serve as a focal point for human civilization, so that individuals could see the building from afar and know not to wander off into other dangerous lands. God's destruction of the Tower (which is a metaphor for being vulnerable to the forces of the constellations) was to teach them that it is in fact more practical to spread throughout the world to preserve humanity more effectively, since if loss happens in one place, the rest will survive.[27] The implied lesson is that one cannot predict the way the heavenly bodies will affect human life, and thus practical wisdom must be prepared for all eventualities.

It is Abraham who, in Gersonides's view, properly understood the nature of God and the heavenly bodies and is thus an exemplar of the virtues of self-preservation and beneficence. In particular, Abraham recognized the importance of perfecting the moral virtues according to the mean. Gersonides points out that Abraham acted with courage (*gevurah*, as a mean between fear and rashness) in leading soldiers into battle against the four kings and in confronting Abimelech. Abraham also acted with contentedness (*histapkut*, a mean between avarice and slothful indifference with respect to money) in not taking booty from the four kings and was satisfied with the amount of possessions he already had after parting with Lot.[28] But Abraham understood that, while the mean is necessary, it is not sufficient. He acted with creative endeavor (*hishtadlut*) to obtain goods that are part of the natural biological cycle, such as having progeny. For example, although Abraham's original intention was to have children with Sarah, Sarah understood that one must think creatively and proposed Hagar as a substitute, considering the possibility that she may have greater biological potency for becoming pregnant.[29] In addition, Abraham exhibited diligence (*ḥaritzut*) in acquiring property and preserving it to the best of his ability by transporting all his possessions from Canaan to Egypt to ensure maximal maintenance of them.[30] Abraham also acted with cunning (*hiteḥakmut*) in developing military tactics to effectively battle the four kings.[31] Lastly, Abraham showed beneficence (*hatavah*) by generously welcoming the three guests into his tent without any knowledge of who they are or why they have come.[32]

In Gersonides's reading, Abraham's virtuous behavior also demonstrates that acting with practical wisdom requires weighing competing moral goods to determine the right course of action. For example, God commanded Abraham to leave Ur of the Chaldees to go to Canaan (Gen. 12:1), but shortly after, he left Canaan for Egypt because of the famine (Gen. 12:10). Gersonides points out two potential obstacles that might have deterred Abraham from remaining in Canaan: (1) he would be ignoring God's original command to settle in Canaan; (2) going to Egypt required potentially putting his wife in danger of being defiled by Pharoah. Abraham justified his decision to leave Canaan and go to Egypt, according to Gersonides, because (1) God's command can be ignored in this case since the necessities of nourishing the body take temporary priority over God's command; (2) one should not follow the example of the "foolish pietist" (*ḥasid shoteh*) who is pious in meticulously following ritual laws, while ignoring basic human necessities, such as a man who witnesses a woman drowning in the river, but will not rescue her since he would have to immodestly look at her body (BT Sotah 21b). The lesson derived from this story is that the necessity of survival overrules the laws of modesty.[33]

Moreover, as Gersonides illustrates, Israelites were successful when they strove to cultivate the virtues to overcome the decrees of the constellations. Otherwise they were fated to live by chance and potentially suffer a negative decree. For example, God told Abraham in a prophecy that the Israelites would be slaves in Egypt (Gen. 15:13); however, according to Gersonides, this prediction was a contingent one, such that the decree of the stars could have been overcome. In other words, if the Israelites would have been more dedicated to perfecting the physical and altruistic virtues rather than competing over physical goods, they could have avoided being enslaved to Pharaoh in Egypt.[34] Thus, in Gersonides's reading, the inner corruption of the Israelites was a contributing factor to their enslavement in Egypt. In fact, Gersonides traces the moral decay back to when Jacob's sons made the pursuit of pleasure a central aim, by searching for a place to graze for their flocks in Shechem, while ignoring the dangers surrounding them. There is a difference between increasing possessions for the sake of diligence and pursuing possessions purely for pleasure.[35]

Gersonides views the political model advocated by the Torah as an attempt to perfect the physical and altruistic virtues on a national scale. In Gersonides's conception, a political community can help its members achieve physical preservation and knowledge leading to eternality through a divided institution of kingship and priesthood. Gersonides describes the institution of the kingship as the political representation of the practical intellect with its ethics focused on self-preservation; hence, the kingship is ultimately aimed at preserving physical existence on a collective level. The executive role of the king is put into practice through fighting wars and accumulating wealth.[36] The institution of the priesthood is the political representation of the material intellect with its ethics of altruistic enlightenment, whereby the priests are philosophers and teachers dedicated to spreading knowledge to others and helping them achieve immortality.[37] Since Gersonides regarded the Temple and its rituals as a metaphor for the laws and structure of the universe, he saw the priests who are responsible for these rituals as having a unique understanding of the structure of the cosmos.[38] In fact, he viewed the priests as the ones who study the philosophical secrets behind the structure of the tabernacle, Temple, and sacrificial laws and are able to pass on this knowledge from one generation to the next.[39]

Conclusion

Gersonides continues the tradition of virtue ethics derived from Aristotle in the *Nicomachean Ethics* and developed by Maimonides in the *Commentary on the Mishnah* and the *Mishneh Torah*. However, the uniqueness of Gersonides's model is that he places a greater emphasis on virtues of physical preservation and virtues of altruism, than do Aristotle or Maimonides. Gersonides also advocates that ethics is better presented in narrative form like the stories in the Torah over reading a philosophical treatise or legal code. He shows through his biblical interpretations how the characters strive and fail in the cultivation of these virtues.

Notes

1. Gersonides, *Wars of the Lord*, trans. Seymour Feldman, vol. i (Philadelphia: Jewish Publication Society, 1984), 226 (1.14). The standardized book and chapter numbers in *Wars of the Lord* are in parentheses.

2. Gersonides, *Commentary on the Torah: Genesis*, ed. Baruch Braner and Eli Freiman (Jerusalem: Maaliyot, 1993), 2.

3. Averroes, *Middle Commentary on Aristotle's Nicomachean Ethics in the Hebrew Version of Samuel ben Judah*, trans. and ed. Lawrence V. Berman (Jerusalem: Israel Academy of Science and Humanities, 1999). For a study of Samuel ben Judah of Marseilles, see Lawrence V. Berman, "Greek into Hebrew: Samuel ben Judah of Marseilles: Fourteenth Century Philosopher and Translator," in *Jewish Medieval and Renaissance Studies*, ed. Alexander Altmann (Cambridge: Cambridge University Press, 1967), 289–320. Gersonides explicitly cites the *Nicomachean Ethics* (*Sefer Ha-Middot*) at Gersonides, *Commentary on the Torah: Genesis*, 5, 85, 86; *Commentary on the Torah: Deuteronomy*, eds. Baruch Braner and Carmiel Cohen (Jerusalem: Maaliyot, 2017), 81; and *Commentary on Job*, trans. Abraham L. Lassen (New York: Bloch, 1946), 20.

4. Gersonides, *Wars*, vol. iii, 137 (5.3.5).

5. Gersonides, *Wars*, vol. ii, 34–37 (2.2).

6. Gersonides, *Wars*, vol. ii, 135–36 (3.6).

7. Gersonides, *Wars*, vol. ii, 176–79 (4.5).

8. Gersonides, *Wars*, vol. ii, 33 (2.2).

9. Gersonides, *Wars*, vol. ii, 34–36 (2.2) and 177 (4.5).

10. Gersonides, *Wars*, vol. iii, 39–42 (5.2.3).

11. Gersonides, *Wars*, vol. ii, 55 (2.5).

12. Gersonides, *Commentary on Song of Songs*, trans. Menachem Kellner (New Haven, CT: Yale University Press, 1998), 22, 30, 52, 63.

13. For an expanded discussion of this topic, see Alexander Green, *The Virtue Ethics of Levi Gersonides* (New York: Palgrave-Macmillan, 2016), 19–90 (chs. 1–2).

14. This has been developed in two recent studies on Gersonides's supercommentary on Averroes's commentary on the *Book of Animals*. See Warren Zev Harvey, "Gersonides and Spinoza on Conatus," *Aleph* 12, no. 2 (2012): 273–97; Ahuva Gaziel, "Gersonides' Naturalistic Account of Providence in Light of the *Book of Animals*," *Aleph* 12, no. 2 (2012), 243–71.

15. Aristotle, *Generation of Animals* 3.2.760a–b and *Supercommentary on Averroes' Commentary on De Animalibus*, referenced by Harvey, "Gersonides and Spinoza on Conatus," 278 (ch. 17, MS Vatican, 127a).

16. Gersonides, *Commentary on the Torah: Genesis*, 267, 274, 298, 308.

17. Gersonides, *Supercommentary on Averroes' Commentary on De Anima*, ed. and trans. Stephen Jesse Mashbaum, in "Chapters 9–12 of Gersonides'

Super-commentary on Averroes' Epitome of the De Anima: The Internal Senses," by Stephen Jesse Mashbaum (PhD diss., Brandeis University, 1981), 183.

18. Gersonides, *Wars*, vol. iii, 39–42 (5.2.3).

19. Gersonides, *Wars*, vol. I, 97 (intro).

20. Gersonides, *Wars*, vol. ii, 168–69 (4.3).

21. Gersonides, *Wars*, vol. iii, 232 (6.1.4).

22. Gersonides, *Commentary on the Torah: Exodus*, vol. 2, ed. Baruch Braner and Carmiel Cohen (Jerusalem: Maaliyot, 2001), 424 (on Exod. 34:6). Thank you to Warren Zev Harvey for this translation. See Harvey, "Gersonides and Spinoza on Conatus," 286.

23. Gersonides, *Commentary on the Torah: Genesis*, 440, 503.

24. Gersonides, *Commentary on the Torah: Genesis*, 2.

25. For an analysis of Gersonides's understanding of the Torah as "empirical data," see Charles Manekin, "Conservative Tendencies in Gersonides' Religious Philosophy," in *The Cambridge Companion to Medieval Jewish Thought*, ed. Daniel Frank and Oliver Leaman (Cambridge: Cambridge University Press, 2003), 305, 315–16.

26. Gersonides, *Commentary on the Torah: Genesis*, 123–29.

27. Gersonides, *Commentary on the Torah: Genesis*, 183–84.

28. Gersonides, *Commentary on the Torah: Genesis*, 212–13, 293.

29. Gersonides, *Commentary on the Torah: Genesis*, 227.

30. Gersonides, *Commentary on the Torah: Genesis*, 194.

31. Gersonides, *Commentary on the Torah: Genesis*, 212–13.

32. Gersonides, *Commentary on the Torah: Genesis*, 269.

33. Gersonides, *Commentary on the Torah: Genesis*, 202–203.

34. Gersonides, *Commentary on the Torah: Exodus*, vol. 1, ed. Baruch Braner and Carmiel Cohen (Jerusalem: Maaliyot, 1999), 20, 26–27; Robert Eisen, *Gersonides on Providence, Covenant, and the Chosen People: A Study in Medieval Jewish Philosophy and Biblical Commentary* (Albany: State University of New York Press, 1995), 55–72.

35. Gersonides, *Commentary on the Torah: Genesis*, 455.

36. Gersonides, *Commentary on the Torah: Deuteronomy*, ed. Baruch Braner and Carmiel Cohen (Jerusalem: Maaliyot, 2017), 257, 270.

37. Gersonides, *Commentary on the Torah: Exodus*, 2:350.

38. Gersonides, *Commentary on the Torah: Exodus*, 2:289–90.

39. Gersonides, *Commentary on the Torah: Leviticus*, vol. 1, ed. Baruch Braner and Eli Freiman (Jerusalem: Maaliyot, 2003), 39–41; *Commentary on the Torah: Numbers*, ed. Baruch Braner and Eli Freiman (Jerusalem: Maaliyot, 2009), 55.

Chapter 12

Ḥasdai Crescas

ROSLYN WEISS

Ḥasdai Crescas was born in or around 1340, in Barcelona, Spain. He is descended from a long line of Torah scholars and was a student of the great Talmudist Rabbi Nissim ben Reuben Gerondi (Ran). In the first period of his life, he was a student at the local yeshiva in Barcelona, where he studied Bible and Talmud, as well as Kabbalah, science, and philosophy. In his twenties, Crescas was a merchant and communal leader.

In 1387, Joan I of Aragon, along with his French queen, Violant de Bar, appointed Crescas chief judge of the Jews of Aragon. Crescas then relocated to Saragossa. In 1391, the Jews of Barcelona fell victim to horrific pogroms. Thousands of Jews were killed and, within a short time, about one hundred fifty thousand Jews—almost half the Jews of Spain—were Christian. Crescas lost his only son to these vicious pogroms.

Crescas's first known work was an epistle to the Jewish community of Avignon chronicling the slaughter of 1391. In 1397–1398 he composed *Refutation of the Principles of the Christians* (*Bittul Ikkarei ha-Notzerim*), seeking to discredit ten basic principles of Christianity. *Sermon on the Passover* is likely Crescas's as well. During his last years he wrote his magnum opus, *Light of the Lord*, in which he counters several of the views Maimonides presents in the *Guide of the Perplexed*, including its emphasis on intellect as the surest—indeed, the only—path to God. Although Crescas intended to produce a work (to be called *Lamp of the Commandment*) to rectify what he regarded as problematic in Maimonides's *Mishneh Torah,* he was unable to do so. Until his death late in 1410 or 1411, Crescas remained the spiritual head of Spanish Jewry.

The Virtues

Crescas's discussion of the virtues appears in *Light of the Lord* 2.6.1, within the context of a consideration of the Torah's final end. On the assumption that the Torah necessarily has but one final end, how is the perfection of virtues to be viewed: Is perfection in virtues the final end or is it one end among several? Is it a first end or an intermediate end? Crescas recognizes four perfections toward which the Torah directs us: perfection in virtues, in views, in bodily happiness, and in psychic happiness.[1] Crescas lists them in this order as if they form an obvious hierarchy, taking up the perfection of the virtues first (206–209),[2] suggesting that this perfection is lowest in the hierarchy.

Indeed, as Crescas begins his discussion of the relationship between the four perfections and the Torah's final end, as well as the perfections' relationship to each other, he presents a familiar scheme in which the final end for man is the eternal bliss enjoyed by the intellect when, at death, the soul, along with the intelligibles it has acquired that constitute it,[3] is at last rid of the body. On the assumption that this end is the Torah's end, Crescas presents the virtues as a prelude to and as preparation for higher, intellectual achievement: the virtues, as purifiers of the soul and its light, removing the dross of impurity in the form of lusts, jealousies, and contentiousness that extinguish the soul's light, prepare the soul for loftier attainments (210). Not only are the virtues merely preparatory, he observes, but they are also temporary, and, so, like the excellences of the body through whose organs the soul operates and that must therefore be in optimal condition, they cannot begin to compare in excellence to the eternity of uninterrupted and unalloyed pleasures of the intellect. The perfection of views is, from the perspective of a hierarchy with intellectual attainment at its summit, thought to be most essential to the end of man thus conceived (210). Among the "views" conveyed by the Torah, Crescas lists the following: that God exists, that He is one, that He is neither a body nor a force in a body, that He is all-knowing, that there is Divine Providence, and that God has enormous power as evidenced by creation, miracles, and prophecy (209).

Although this is the beginning of Crescas's story, it is by no means its end. Having presented a plausible account of the relationship among the four perfections to which the Torah guides us—as if he himself is persuaded of its truth—Crescas proceeds to undermine it. Although Crescas begins by positing all deeds and views in the Torah, as well as material reward, as inferior to, and in service of, the acquisition of intelligibles as their aim, what he concludes is that not this but rather love and fear of God and devoted service to Him in the form of the observance of the Torah's commandments with joy and zeal are the Torah's ultimate end. Observance of the commandments is the direct path to eternal life in the Divine Presence for it is the soul of the righteous that endures—not the intellect of thinkers and the intelligibles that constitute their intellects.

The Particular Virtues (*Middot*)

For Crescas the virtues to which the Torah guides us are of two kinds: (1) virtues of conduct, that is, the virtues of conducting oneself properly vis-à-vis oneself, the members of one's household, and one's fellow-citizens; and (2) virtues of character, that is, the virtues that are one's formed dispositions or character traits. Crescas looks to both the Torah and the Rabbinic tradition as his sources for the virtues.

Virtues of Conduct

With respect to one's conduct toward oneself (206), the Torah forbids certain sexual relations as well as the eating of those foods that promote bad character traits[4] and extinguish the light of the intellect that perfects the soul.[5] The Torah also requires the avoidance of things that are impure, in order to foster cleanness and purity in the soul.

The household comprises a man's wife, children, and servants. With respect to a man's wife (206–207), the Torah requires of her husband that he meet her every need—both while he lives and after he dies. So, too, the needs of her daughters. In addition, a man must set down in writing what his wife's sons are to inherit. It is incumbent upon a wife to serve her husband; the fruits of her labor and her property are his. A wife is freed from the performance of time-bound commandments, presumably so that she may fulfill her duties to her husband. (Crescas appears to admit to be guessing here, as there is indeed no ancient source that states the purpose of this leniency.) She is not exempt from commandments that are not time bound, as these may be performed at any time. She is similarly not exempt from the negative commandments, as these do not require the taking of any action. Of primary concern to the Torah and the tradition is the fostering of a peaceful home. To this end, the Rabbis demand of a man that he honor his wife more than himself.

With respect to children (207), a man is enjoined to have intercourse with his wife in a holy way. A father must ensure the fitness of his child's body and soul—the former by providing sustenance and teaching his son a craft, the latter by circumcision. Children are required to revere and honor their parents. In order to improve the conduct of children, the Torah goes so far as to demand the death of a rebellious child. (One can only surmise that this commandment is intended as no more than a warning, as the child's actual death would hardly serve to improve his conduct.)

Crescas next considers what the Torah enjoins with respect to slaves—Hebrew and Canaanite (207–208). With respect to Israelite slaves, they are not to be worked "with rigor" (an expression borrowed from the Torah where it refers to the mistreatment the children of Israel suffered at the hands of their Egyptian masters—Exod. 1:13; also Lev. 25:43), so as not to subject them to humiliation. They must be nourished in the same way as their master. At their departure, they are to be generously provided for. Female Israelite slaves are accorded particular care. Once they show signs of puberty they are to be set free, lest they suffer degradation as they mature. They must be protected in childhood. Either the father or the son must see to their betrothal, lest their marriage prospects diminish on account of their having been slaves. The commandment to betroth female slaves takes precedence even over the commandment to redeem slaves.

Canaanite slaves are to be brought "under the wings of the Divine Presence" (208). They are to observe the same commandments as women—they, like women, are to be exempt from time-bound commandments, presumably for the same reason, namely, to be free to work and serve. Once these slaves are freed, they are as Israelites. They must be immediately freed if they sustain damage to their limbs. Any slave who escapes slavery and seeks refuge in the land of Israel is to be granted his freedom, in accordance with the Talmudic interpretation of the verse Deuteronomy 23:16: "You shall not return unto his master a servant who has escaped."

With respect to fellow-citizens (208), the Torah provides guidance concerning the virtues of justice and equity through commandments and through stories about the Patriarchs. The Torah encourages distancing oneself from having recourse to subtleties that undermine equity. It holds courts of law in esteem, and forbids the taking of a bribe even to acquit the innocent.

In setting out rules for proper conduct, in *commanding* the acts that promote appropriate relations, the Torah locates virtues of conduct in the deeds themselves. The Torah demands of people that they treat themselves and others in the way it prescribes; doing so is in itself virtuous. Virtues of conduct, the first category of virtues that Crescas considers, are virtues of action. Even if they help people to avoid bad character traits and indeed even inculcate good ones, Crescas clearly wants to distinguish them from the virtues in his second category, virtues of character, whose direct aim is to shape character.

Virtues of Character

Turning next to virtues of character (208–209), Crescas singles out three virtues in particular. The first, courage, is exemplified by Abraham as he waged wars against mighty armies. The second is generosity: the Torah mandates the giving of charity and gifts to the poor; it designates sabbatical years and the jubilee year as times in which the land must lie fallow, debts are remitted, and the produce of the land is freely available to the needy; it also prohibits usury. Furthermore, the Torah encourages one to go beyond what is strictly required in one's treatment of colleagues. Here, too, it is Abraham whose conduct with respect to kings sets the standard. The third is humility. Moses is the paradigm for this virtue. Crescas further notes in this connection that arrogance is forbidden to kings, and flattery is generally proscribed in favor of rebuking others for wrongdoing. The Torah goes so far as to prohibit hatred, revenge, and bearing a grudge. Its aim is to foster love within communities (209).

The Role of the Virtues in Fostering the Torah's True Final End

Since Crescas opposes in the most vehement terms the intellectualist understanding of man's final end—and, a fortiori, of the Torah's final end—he must find a place for the virtues within a different conception of the Torah's final end. He has many reasons, both from the point of view of speculation and from the point of view of the Torah, for disputing the notion that the final end is the freeing of the intellect to revel in its intellection. From the perspective of the Torah, a person secures eternal life through the performance of commandments (211). Of course, if it were the case that the intellect is constituted by intelligibles, it would surely not be the case that it is constituted by commandments, so that if the final end were the release of the intellect, the commandments would be useless for the attainment of man's final end. Similarly, reward and punishment for merits and transgressions would have no place, nor would the martyrdom that is so highly valued in Judaism, in which a man sacrifices his very life to sanctify God's name (211–12). Indeed, even the notion of wickedness would have no place. The end of the Torah for man, Crescas argues, has to be for man qua man, not for man qua intellect—and intellect, as he observes, is not man (212–13). The soul of man is a spiritual substance; it is not pure intellect. Moreover, as Crescas contends, reward and punishment can only be assigned for serving God or for rebelling against Him. The love and pleasure one feels in serving God are reflections of one's perfection; indeed, a separate intellect cannot experience pleasure. Love and pleasure, moreover, are quite distinct from intellection (215). Thus the end of the Torah is captured neither by deeds nor by views absolutely, but rather by the love and fear of God that accompanies them.

Noteworthy, too, with regard to the matter of the Torah's final end, is Crescas's insistence that the Torah leads *all* those who hold fast to it—whether they are perfected or deficient—to human happiness and the "yearned-for end" (305). The Torah provides, Crescas says, "the most excellent guidance toward the perfection of the virtues of character and intellect,[6] as well as the utmost rousing of service to God" (306).

Taking on Maimonides

The discussion of the final end of the Torah and of the whole of existence is explicitly directed against Maimonides who, as Crescas observes, at least appears to regard it as pointless to seek such a final end (205).[7] Crescas, for his part, sees it as obligatory to seek the final end of the Torah. Insofar as all rational productivity manifests purpose, how could the Torah lack a final end? Crescas expresses his confidence that once the end of the Torah is understood, so, too, will the reasons for even the most baffling commandments. As Crescas's consideration of the end of the Torah and existence draws to a close, he seeks to reconcile his own firm conviction that seeking such an end is necessary and important with Maimonides's seemingly opposite view. He concludes that what Maimonides must mean is that it is *very difficult* to know this purpose; he surely cannot mean that there is none (240–41).

Although Crescas does not explicitly defy or reproach Maimonides with respect to the views he expresses in his discourse on virtue known as "Eight Chapters,"[8] the glaring absence in Crescas's *Light of the Lord* of anything resembling the Aristotelian and Maimonidean notion of virtue as a mean between extremes is telling. Crescas's conception of virtue, whether of conduct-virtue or of character-virtue, is always and only rooted in the Torah—either in the commandments or in its representations of exemplary biblical figures. There is indeed only one reference made in *Light of the Lord* to "Eight Chapters," and that is to Maimonides's discourse in chapter 5 concerning the commandment to "love the Lord your God with all your heart and with all your soul . . ." (Deut. 6:5). For Maimonides, the intensity of the love that this verse demands is such that one may love nothing else unless one loves it for the sake of this love. But where Maimonides speaks of the duty to love God in terms of a duty to know Him, Crescas speaks in terms of service.

Two Further Related Ideas

The Torah's First Commandment

Crescas mentions twice (291, 306) that the first commandment in the Torah is the prohibition of meat-consumption, deriving it no doubt from the verse Genesis 2:16, where God *commands* the man, saying: "Of every tree of the garden you may freely eat."[9] As Crescas interprets this verse, it implies that the eating of anything else is forbidden. Crescas does not indicate—though he might have—that he regards this prohibition as an ideal such that the subsequent permission to eat meat granted to the sons of Noah and, following that, to the Hebrew nation, amounts to a concession to their deficiency. Since Crescas does indeed regard Adam, despite his having sinned grievously, as "the handiwork of God and disposed to perfection to the greatest extent" (161), it would not be unthinkable for him to see the first commandment as having been addressed to Adam as a superior human being.[10] Be that as it may, the two contexts in which Crescas cites this first commandment are: (1) the question of whether God promises spiritual reward in addition to corporeal, material, "illusory," reward—considering that, after all, the Torah speaks almost exclusively of material reward, and (2) the question of whether the Torah we have is eternal.

In the course of considering the first of these questions, Crescas notes that no reward—neither corporeal reward nor spiritual reward—accompanied this commandment; it was simply taken for granted, and rightly so, that *spiritual* reward would follow its observance. Crescas then concludes that it is specifically material reward that needs to be promised explicitly because it is material reward that does not go without saying (291).

In considering the second question, Crescas asks if one ought not to conclude from the fact that the Torah was given at a certain time to a specific people, that had the recipients at the time been either more perfect or more deficient, a different Torah would have been given. After all, it certainly seems to be the case that meat-consumption was forbidden to the people of Adam's generation but was permitted first to the sons of Noah and then subsequently to the Israelites, who received a far greater number of commandments than the seven prescribed to the sons of Noah. Yet Crescas concludes that our current Torah is at the height of perfection inasmuch as it addresses the needs of both perfect and deficient alike. It contains, he says, not only the perfection of wisdom for thinkers and the elite, but the perfection of the virtues, the awakening of hearts to serve God, to become attached to Him, and so to enjoy the love for God that is eternal happiness (306).

The Four Elements

In book 4 of *Light of the Lord*, issue 6 (345–46), Crescas takes up the question of the existence and nature of demons. In this context Crescas registers his belief that the four elements—earth, water, air, and fire—and the proportions in which they are mixed in people, have a profound effect on people's character. In demons, Crescas contends, the light elements—fire and air—dominate and generate extremes of arrogance, anger, and envy, to the point that demons seek to propel people to evildoing. In human beings, an excess of the element earth engenders such undesirable traits as anger, envy, and the coveting of honor and prestige. The best character traits are produced when the four elements combine in equal measure. It would seem, then, that one's character, in Crescas's view, is determined in part by one's disposition as a result of the distribution of the four elements[11] and in part (the larger part?) by one's observance of the commandments and by one's emulation of the biblical paragons of the various virtues.

Conclusion

For Crescas, since the final end of Creation, of Torah, of man, is not the acquisition of intelligibles for the sake of an eternity of intellection by one's purified intellect, it follows that neither views nor deeds are primary or essential to its attainment. Primarily and essentially, the part of the Torah directed to its highest end—and to ours—is one that is "small in quantity but large in quality" (215), the part that concerns neither views nor deeds absolutely, but is "the love of God and the true fear of Him" (215). This is what ensures the end in every respect, not only according to the Torah and the tradition, but also, Crescas maintains, according to speculation as well.

Notes

1. "Psychic" translates the Hebrew *nafshi,* and means "of the soul." Crescas has another term *ruḥani,* for which "spiritual" is the closest English equivalent.

2. Page references are to Ḥasdai Crescas, *Light of the Lord,* trans. Roslyn Weiss (Oxford: Oxford University Press, 2018).

3. "Intelligibles" translates the Hebrew term *muskalot* and refers to that which is accessible to and known by the intellect alone. For some thinkers, these are limited to the truths of mathematics and logic; for others, metaphysical truths qualify as well.

4. These bad traits are later identified as cruelty, indifference, and lust (231–32). Eating the prohibited foods and engaging in illicit sexual relations also cause disturbances and unclarity in the intellect, and are harmful to both soul and body.

5. Crescas sees in these prohibitions evidence of God's providence and guidance.

6. The perfection of the virtues of intellect refers to the perfection of views mentioned earlier. The Torah guides people to truth.

7. See chapter 69 of part 1 of Moses Maimonides, *Guide of the Perplexed*, trans. Shlomo Pines, 2 vols. (Chicago: University of Chicago Press, 1974).

8. Moses Maimonides, *The Eight Chapters of Maimonides on Ethics (Shemona Perakim): A Psychological and Ethical Treatise*, trans. Joseph I. Gorfinkle (New York: Columbia University Press, 1912).

9. Crescas does not explicitly cite his source for this "first commandment." In Gen. 1:29, God informs the human beings that He has provided them "for eating" (*leokhlah*) every herb bearing seed and every fruit tree whose fruit bear seeds. But it is not until Gen. 2:16 that the eating of the fruit of the trees of the Garden is framed as a commandment: "And God commanded the man, saying. . . ."

10. The alternative would be that the sons of Noah and Abraham and his descendants were superior to Adam and his generation in piety so that the prohibition on meat-consumption would therefore be for them an unnecessary and excessive stringency.

11. Crescas does not relate his notion that the mixture of the four elements in the human soul bears significantly on one's character to his broader discussion of free will in 3.5. The two kinds of necessitation he considers there are causal necessitation and necessitation attributable to divine foreknowledge. He rejects out of hand the suggestion that human action might be subject to "in itself"-necessity, the kind of necessity that is intrinsic and depends on nothing outside itself.

Chapter 13

Joseph Albo

SHIRA WEISS

Minimal details are known about Joseph Albo's life. Born in Monreal, a town in Aragon, sometime before 1380,[1] Albo studied with Ḥasdai Crescas of Saragossa.[2] Albo served as rabbi and preacher in the community of Daroca in Christian Spain and assumed a leadership role in a hostile period in Jewish history. He moved to a rabbinic position in Soria in Castile, possibly as a result of the destruction of his community in Daroca (1415), and completed his major philosophical treatise, *Sefer ha-Ikkarim* (*Book of Principles*). Cognizant of the hardships encountered by his generation until his death in approximately 1444, Albo sought to lead his own community, as well as the larger Jewish community in the preservation of their religious commitments amid persecution. His status as a rabbinic leader can be further understood from his participation as a defendant of the Talmud in the Tortosa Disputation and from his sole surviving halakhic responsum, as the Spanish Jewish community looked to Albo for guidance.

The Importance of Virtue

In *Sefer ha-Ikkarim,* one of the most popular Hebrew books within the corpus of medieval Jewish philosophy, Albo sought to teach the dogmas of Judaism and enable his coreligionists to discern the truth of the Law of Moses and the authenticity of Judaism in an effort to inculcate such values into their character despite the accusations of their persecutors. Albo maintained that only the Torah could give humanity full knowledge of how to obey God's will and achieve human perfection. Virtue ethics was, therefore, taught throughout his work, as Albo aimed to help his readers develop as moral individuals who can discern right from wrong through understanding true beliefs and adhering to proper observance. In a medieval period of turmoil, tension, and religious disputation, fifteenth-century Jews were in need of a universal system of dogma that they could internalize to substantiate and uphold their commitments against religious attacks and coercion. Albo's exposure to the Tortosa Disputation, Christian philosophical propaganda, and polemics motivated him to counteract his opponents' arguments by teaching his generation the truths of Judaism, which he considered to be the exclusive divine law.

Albo emphasized obedience to Jewish law as a means of achieving virtue and perfection and, in *Sefer ha-Ikkarim,* presented a rationalistic defense of Judaism by proving that the Law of Moses is the only law that fulfills the definition of divine law in general, demonstrating its uniqueness within the context of the universal law that connects humanity with God. Albo felt that no other Jewish philosophical work had satisfactorily dealt with the general principles of religion and that there was no universally accepted delineation of dogma; rather, numerous works were composed that varied with regard to the obligatory nature and number of the principles.[3] Albo was dissatisfied with his predecessors' failure to distinguish between the principles regarding divine legislation common to all religions, and special principles unique to a particular religion. As a result, in his introduction to *Sefer ha-Ikkarim,* Albo articulated his objective of explicating principles of divine law to teach correct opinions and to identify the divine character of the Law of Moses: "I have composed this book and called it *The Book of Principles,* because it investigates the principles of laws generally, and especially the principles of divine law. . . . Then it investigates the principles of the Law of Moses, concerning the divine character of which all agree, and shows that it has general principles, appertaining to it in virtue of its character as divine, and special principles, appertaining to it as being the particular divine law that it is."[4] Albo explained that a divine law is recognized as genuine if it fulfills two criteria: (1) if it is in accordance with three *Ikkarim* (principles): God's Existence, Revelation, and Reward and Punishment,[5] and (2) if it has been proven that it was transmitted by a genuine divine messenger in a direct manner from God. Albo demonstrated that the Law of Moses is the only law that corresponds to the definition of divine law, thereby proving its uniqueness in the context of the universal laws.[6]

Albo argued that limitations of the human intellect require divine law to guide the individual to both truth and proper conduct. In contrast to divine law, he criticized Aristotle for giving too much flexibility to practical wisdom in establishing conventional laws and for not specifying the proper time, place, or measure of virtuous acts,[7] since humans cannot determine such matters and must rely upon divine specification. For Albo, Aristotle discussed virtues in a general manner, defining temperance as a mean between excessive indulgence and abstinence in eating, drinking, and sexual and other pleasures, but with no precise instruction.[8] Albo argued that, without a doubt, if humanity had the capacity to determine virtues precisely, Aristotle would have written as much. Rather, Albo concluded, "divine help alone can do it,"[9] by which he meant that only divine law can provide the appropriate specifications to instruct humanity to achieve virtue; however, it is up to the individual to exercise one's choice to obey divine law and achieve virtue. Albo quoted Psalms 19:9, "The commandment of the Lord is pure like the sun enlightening the eyes," guiding adherents on the path of righteousness, and he provided examples of such specifications, supported by biblical or rabbinic prooftexts. For instance, divine law inculcates the virtue of moderation (*yirat ḥet*) by dictating that the proper purpose of sexual intercourse is to procreate with one's wife when she is ritually pure. Divine law also prohibits drinking immediately before divine service or prayer in order to allow for necessary concentration. Divine law habituates the proper amount of courage (*gevurah*) by identifying appropriate times to risk one's life when sanctifying God's name or fighting idolaters. Albo, again citing the Psalmist in Psalms 19, asserted that observance of divine law affords theoretical perfection regarding truth and falsehood, moral perfection, and perfection of the useful and the pleasurable. Judaism, the authentic divine law, equipped adherents to distinguish between right and wrong and pursue a life of virtue in accordance with God's commands.

The Importance of Spiritual over Intellectual Virtue

Due to diverse influences, Albo's general philosophic approach lies between that of the rationalists (most notably Maimonides) who argue that the Torah aims at intellectual perfection and that of philosophers, such as Halevi and Crescas, who prioritize humanity's spiritual rather than intellectual worship of God. Albo agreed with the rationalists that the human is the noblest creation in the sublunar world whose purpose is to perfect himself, thus reflecting the influence of Aristotle's thought and that of Maimonides and Gersonides within the Jewish Aristotelian tradition. Albo did not, however, conceive of perfection in theoretical understanding, but rather in finding favor with God. Whereas Aristotle (and Maimonides) argued that the individual can develop his intellect to apprehend theoretical truths, which is the ultimate human end,[10] Albo rejected Aristotle's and Maimonides's conclusion that human perfection is intellectual, since, he claimed such perfection would not be attainable by the majority of humanity, and God would not set the desired purpose of humanity to only be achievable by a small minority.[11] Therefore, Albo argued that through performance of divine commands, individuals of every intellectual capacity have the ability to reach perfection, as the entire nation of Israel achieved prophecy at Mount Sinai,[12] stressing divine recompense and individual providence consequent upon moral and religious practice rather than intellectual achievement.[13]

Albo maintained that only the Torah, the exclusive divine law, can give humanity comprehensive instruction for obeying God's will to achieve virtue and human perfection, representing the Jewish anti-Aristotelian school of thought of Halevi, Naḥmanides, Rashba, Ritba, and Nissim ben Reuben Gerondi (RaN), as well as his teacher, Ḥasdai Crescas. Albo, like Crescas, emphasized observance of divine commandments as a means toward human perfection, as opposed to the Maimonidean notion that rational speculation constitutes the purpose of Torah. Albo asserted that performance of commandments, proper intention of fulfilling the Divine will,[14] and fear of God[15] can merit the reward of miracles, divine union,[16] immortality,[17] and prophecy.[18] However, Albo cautioned that observance of the precepts must not be achieved for the sake of receiving such rewards, but rather trust or hope in God must be maintained continuously even in adversity, as Psalms 62:9 states, "Trust in Him at all times."[19] Albo explained how such virtues foster each other, "Hope in God, far from weakening the heart, strengthens it, for if one hopes in God and his heart truly relies on the Holy One of Israel, trusting that He will grant his request, he gets stronger and more courageous."[20] Trust, according to Albo, referred to hope for divine mercy, not for reward, "Particular hope means that a man should hope that God in His compassion and abundant mercy will make his way straight, will deliver him from harm and will choose what is good and suitable for him, by putting it in his heart to choose the good and reject the evil. . . . [F]or God's providence always comes to those who hope for mercy, not to those who hope for reward."[21] Alan Mittleman argues that such hope reveals virtue, since unlike hope for reward, which is a natural disposition of giving and taking, continuous hope in God constitutes excellence and "manifests a courage that repudiates despair."[22] Despair reflects the willingness to succumb to hardship, as opposed to the virtue of hope, which cultivates trust in God despite adverse circumstances. Albo asserts, "Therefore, I do not despair that I will emerge from my troubles."[23]

This distinction is similar to Albo's differentiation between "repentance out of fear of God," which is achieved due to free choice and conveys a general awe of God as the source of both reward and punishment, and "repentance out of fear of punishment" in which the affliction of the punishment coerces the sufferer to submit in repentance. Albo concluded that repentance necessitates freedom and, thus, one who is coerced by fear of punishment does not merit forgiveness,[24] whereas one who is motivated by the awe of the constant awareness of divine providence achieves atonement. Hope and atonement are only associated with repentance out of fear of God, a recognition that God is responsible for everything, good and evil. Such virtues are also related to courage, as Albo argued that the plagues in Egypt that preceded the exodus caused cowardice, which explains Pharaoh's desire to succumb to the Israelites' request for liberation or "repent" out of fear of punishment. Therefore, God hardened, or emboldened Pharaoh's heart in order to afford him courage to overcome the cowering effects of the plagues and arrive at a free decision whether or not to repent. Albo wrote, after the suffering from the plagues was alleviated, Pharaoh "took courage" and pursued the Israelites, proving that his initial repentance (liberation of the Israelites) was due to the compulsion of the afflictions caused by the plagues.[25] As a result, his ultimate punishment was just, since he could have chosen to repent freely and courageously and achieve forgiveness and virtue, yet he instead refused on repeated occasions. Albo's conception deviates from Maimonides's understanding of courage in "Eight Chapters,"[26] which is based on Aristotle's view in *Nicomachean Ethics* 3.6, as a mean between the extremes of fear and rashness, since humans are naturally predisposed to fear and cowardice.[27] Even if Pharaoh naturally cowered due to the afflictions of the plagues, according to Albo, God's hardening gave him the courage, which he may not have been able to muster otherwise, to choose freely whether or not to repent.

The Cultivation of Virtue

For Albo, virtue is cultivated by following divine law, which guides one on the proper course. He described the dual motivations behind performance of commandments: love of God and fear of God (resulting from reflecting upon the divine sublimity and worth). These intentions, necessary for the proper observance of divine law, contribute to the development of character, and ultimately, human perfection. Albo explained that one should strive to be glad and rejoice despite the challenge and toil involved in serving God. Abraham exemplified such virtue and was, therefore, called "God-fearing" at the end of his trials, as well as "Abraham, My friend" (Is. 41:8).[28] Albo wrote, "This is why the patriarch Abraham was praised for this kind of love more than others; and the Bible calls him, "Abraham, My friend," because he had no other purpose in mind than to do the will of God whom he loved."[29]

Albo maintained human free choice and explained that when a benefit is determined in favor of a person as a divine reward, it is conditional upon a certain degree of right conduct in obedience of divine commandments, just as when an evil is determined to befall a person as a divine punishment, it is similarly conditional upon his being wicked or sinful to a certain degree. If the wickedness or virtue changes, the predetermined fate also necessarily changes for the better or the worse. The choice to do good contributes to the reception of the divine influence or the annulment of a divine decree. Every sinner has the ability to choose to repent and thereby become another person, concerning whom no such divine decree was made.

Albo cited Abraham as a paradigm for human emulation in his voluntary observance of divine commandments and achievement of virtue. Abraham was praised for obeying God's command at the Binding of Isaac, which he freely chose to do solely out of love of God. "Nor was there any other cause compelling him to do this. . . . Not even the command of God was a compulsion."[30] Abraham, according to Albo, did not act out of fear of punishment or love of reward, but rather submitted to God's will out of recognition of the sublimity and awe of God. That awareness, Albo argued, constituted the true fear of God for which Abraham was praised: "Now I know that you are a God-fearing man" (Gen. 22:12).[31] Albo maintained that Abraham had complete free choice, and neither God's command nor foreknowledge of Abraham's actions determined the outcome of the trial. Abraham's decision to bind Isaac was free since he was conscious of his option to show compassion for his son by choosing to not heed the divine commandment, which would have been justified as an effort to fulfill God's promise for Isaac to be his lineage.[32] Yet he acted out of no other motivation than to do the will of God. "The expression, 'Now I know,' is used because it was then that the actual incident occurred which showed what He knew already, namely, that Abraham was God-fearing and served God from love and not from fear of punishment."[33]

Conclusion

In *Sefer ha-Ikkarim,* Albo sought to convince his generation that despite the compulsion by the Christians, Judaism was the only true divine law, and encouraged his coreligionists to retain their religion. He was successful in fulfilling his chief objective to defend Jewish dogma. Collete Sirat argues, "[*Sefer ha-Ikkarim*] perfectly accomplishes the task for which it was conceived . . . namely, to show that the Law of Moses was the only one that corresponds to the definition of divine law, and therefore to establish its particularism in the larger context of the universal laws that tie man to God."[34] Albo's delineation of principles enabled Jews to discern the truth by distinguishing Judaism from other faiths and provided Jews with the theological commitments necessary to observe their religion properly. They needed such a uniform and accepted system of beliefs to bolster their identity and character and sustain Jewish tradition against the attacks and coercion of persecutors. Albo attempted to provide his fellow Jews with an understanding of the nature of God and His relation to humanity, and to His nation, in particular. He wanted to foster within them the appropriate intentions to observe God's commandments, motivated by love and fear of God, hope, trust, and courage, to guide them in their achievement of virtue. The popularity of *Sefer ha-Ikkarim*[35] and its classification as the last of the philosophical and theological classics of medieval Judaism, belonging to the same genre of literary works as *The Book of Doctrines and Beliefs, Duties of the Heart, Kuzari, The Exalted Faith, Guide of the Perplexed, Wars of the Lord,* and *Light of the Lord,*[36] not only testifies to the reception of his work by his generation, but reflects Albo's enduring impact upon the cultivation of virtue through Jewish belief and practice.

Notes

1. Heinrich Graetz, *History of the Jews* (Philadelphia: Jewish Publication Society, 1894); Emil Hirsch, "Joseph Albo," in *The Jewish Encyclopedia* (New York: Funk and Wagnalls, 1906); Alexander Altmann, "Joseph Albo," in *Encyclopedia Judaica* (Jerusalem: Keter, 1971), 535–37.

2. Joseph Albo, *Sefer ha-Ikkarim Book of Principles* 1:18, 1:9; *Sefer ha-Ikkarim* [*Book of Principles*], trans. Isaac Husik (Philadelphia: Jewish Publication Society of America, 1930), 1:200; 3:148.

3. "For while they all agree that it [the Law of Moses] is divine, they differ not a little concerning the number of its basic principles, some saying they are thirteen (Maimonides), some that they are twenty-six (David bar Yom Tov ben Bila), and some that they are only six (Crescas). But there is not one of these learned men who made any effort to explain those principles which pertain to a divine law generally . . . nor to whether there can be only one divine law. . . ." Albo, *Sefer ha-Ikkarim,* introduction; Husik trans. 1:36.

4. Albo, *Sefer ha-Ikkarim* introduction; Husik trans. 1:37.

5. According to Albo, the criteria for a believer were not solely acceptance of the three *ikkarim* (principles of divine law), but also derivative principles, *shoreshim* (roots). From Albo's first *ikkar,* Existence of God, are derived: God's Unity, Incorporeality, Independence from Time, and Freedom from Defects. From his second *ikkar,* Revelation, are derived: God's Knowledge, Prophecy, and Authenticity of God's Messenger. From his third *ikkar,* Reward and Punishment, is derived: Divine Providence. In addition to the three fundamental and eight derivative principles of divine legislation, Albo specified six dogmas of lesser status *anafim* (branches), which must be believed by every Jew:

Creation ex nihilo, Superiority of the Prophet Moses, Immutability of Torah, Achievement of human perfection by any one of the Torah's commandments, Resurrection, and Messiah.

6. Albo argued against the divinity of Christianity since the Catholic religion's doctrine of the Trinity contradicts divine unity, which is essential to the principle of the existence of God. Similarly, Islam's messenger does not fulfill the criteria necessary for transmission of divine law, since it was not demonstrated that Mohammed was directly addressed by God and commissioned with a divine message. Furthermore, a mass revelation comparable to that of Moses at Sinai was not achieved by Jesus or Mohammed, who both claimed to have superseded Judaism.

7. Aristotle, *The Nicomachean Ethics,* trans. by H. Rackman (Cambridge: Harvard University Press, 1956), 2.6.

8. Aristotle, *Nicomachean Ethics* 3.10.

9. Albo, *Sefer ha-Ikkarim* I:8; Husik trans. 1:84.

10. While there is a clear focus on the intellect (which is not as pronounced in the thought of Albo), Aristotle's and Maimonides's conceptions of human perfection have been debated by scholars. The ambiguity of *Guide of the Perplexed* 3.54 has led to various interpretations of Maimonides's position. See Menachem Kellner, *Maimonides on Human Perfection* (Atlanta: Scholars Press, 1990).

11. Albo, *Sefer ha-Ikkarim* 3:3.

12. Albo, *Sefer ha-Ikkarim* 3:11. Albo proceeded to pose the problem: "It would seem, then that all the commandments and admonitions found in the Torah are essential to the attainment of human perfection, else God would not have commanded them. But such a proposition is very strange and hard. For if this were the case, no man would be able to acquire the perfection in question, "For there is not a righteous man upon the earth, that doeth good, and sinneth not" (Eccles. 7:20)" (*Sefer ha-Ikkarim* 3:29; Husik trans. 3:270). Albo responded that observance of one commandment alone is sufficient for human perfection (*Sefer ha-Ikkarim* 3:29). In a later treatise, Albo offered a different solution: Since "'there is not a righteous man upon earth, that doeth good and sinneth not (Eccles. 7:20),' it follows that all men should be punished eternally for any sin they have committed or for disobedience of God's command of which they are guilty, though the nature of punishment can be different. How then can anyone escape eternal punishment according to this mode of determination, and how can a mortal merit spiritual reward, whether temporary or eternal? . . . It seems to me that the difficulty may be solved by saying that . . . punishment is made temporary by divine grace, though according to strict justice it should be eternal" (*Sefer ha-Ikkarim* 4:38; Husik trans. 4:374). Despite the differences, Albo argues in both that human perfection and immortality are accessible to every individual (either because

all of humanity can obey at least one command or because everyone can be afforded divine grace to alleviate deserved punishment), in contrast to Maimonides's exclusive perfection for the intellectual elite.

13. Herbert Davidson, "Medieval Jewish Philosophy in the Sixteenth Century," in *Jewish Thought in the Sixteenth Century*, edited by Bernard Cooperman (Cambridge: Harvard University Press, 1983), 112.

14. Albo, *Sefer ha-Ikkarim* 3:28.

15. Albo, *Sefer ha-Ikkarim* 3:27.

16. "Belief in God and in His Torah gives perfection of the soul. . . . Through faith the soul rises high above the things of nature, and can therefore control them. . . . This is why we find that miracles are performed for men of faith, and not for men of speculative knowledge, so as to show that faith stands higher than speculation and the things of nature. Therefore, one may through it attain true union with God during life after death." (*Sefer ha-Ikkarim* 1:21; Husik trans. 1: 176–78).

17. "Divine righteousness decrees that those who believe should obtain that degree of eternal life which is promised in the Torah, because they trust and believe in His Torah, though they are not able to acquire an intellectual comprehension." (*Sefer ha-Ikkarim* 2:15; Husik trans. 2:98).

18. "We never find the gift of prophecy in any one of the philosophers, though they were wise men in theoretical speculation; whereas we do find prophecy among the Jewish people. This shows that it is not a natural phenomenon associated with theoretical speculation. For if it were so, why should this gift have been kept from the other nations, so that their wise men despite their perfection of intellect and imagination are devoid of the prophetic inspiration?" *Sefer ha-Ikkarim* 3:8; Husik trans. 3:71.

19. Albo, *Sefer ha-Ikkarim* 4:46; Husik trans. 4:450.

20. Albo, *Sefer ha-Ikkarim* 4:49; Husik trans. 4:469.

21. Albo, *Sefer ha-Ikkarim* 4:48; Husik trans. 4:464.

22. Alan Mittleman, *Hope in a Democratic Age* (Oxford: Oxford University Press, 2009), 58.

23. Albo, *Sefer ha-Ikkarim* 4:48; Husik trans. 4:465.

24. Albo, *Sefer ha-Ikkarim* 4:25.

25. Albo, *Sefer ha-Ikkarim* 4:25; Husik trans. 4:227.

26. Moses Maimonides, "Eight Chapters," in *Ethical Writings of Maimonides*, ed. Raymond L. Weiss and Charles Butterworth (New York: New York University Press, 1975), 69.

27. For an analysis of Maimonides's conception of the virtue of courage, see Alexander Green, "Maimonides on Courage," *Jewish Studies Quarterly* 22, no. 2 (2015): 162–83. Maimonides, in *Guide of the Perplexed* 2.38, describes Moses in courageous terms for boldly, with "no fear or dread," demanding from Pharaoh the Israelites' liberation from Egyptian slavery.

28. Albo, *Sefer ha-Ikkarim* 3:34; Husik trans. 3:314.

29. Albo, *Sefer ha-Ikkarim* 3:36; Husik trans. 3:332.

30. Albo, *Sefer ha-Ikkarim* 3:36; Husik trans. 3:332.

31. Albo, *Sefer ha-Ikkarim* 3:32.

32. Gen. 22:12.

33. Albo, *Sefer ha-Ikkarim* 4:13; Husik trans. 4:127.

34. Collete Sirat, *A History of Jewish Philosophy in the Middle Ages* (Cambridge: Cambridge University Press, 1990), 381.

35. Over seventeen editions of Albo's Hebrew text were subsequently published and translated into Latin, English, German, and Italian in order to accommodate the demand of readers unable to understand the original editions.

36. Husik, translator's introduction to *Sefer ha-Ikkarim,* 1:xvii.

Chapter 14

Isaac Arama

BARUCH FRYDMAN-KOHL

The life of Isaac (Yitzhaq) ben Moses Arama (Spain, ca.1420–Naples, 1494) coincided with the last years of Spanish Jewry. He served as the head of a Talmudic academy in Zamora in Castille, taught and preached in three communities in Aragon—Tarragona, Fraga, and Calatayud—and, after the Expulsion of 1492, spent his final years in Naples.[1] His sermons, recast into an extended commentary to the Torah, *Akedat Yitzḥak,* discuss both textual and conceptual issues and became quite popular.[2] He composed a polemical work, *Ḥazut Kashah,*[3] as well as commentaries on the *megillot* of Song of Songs, Esther, Ruth, Lamentations, and Ecclesiastes. *Yad Avshalom,* his commentary on the Book of Proverbs, was written last and dedicated to the memory of his son, Solomon.[4]

The fifteenth century saw the broadening of religious thought beyond the savants of the community through the use of sermons to bring significant Jewish ideas to a wide audience. Arama used his sermons and commentaries to argue for the possibility of salvational felicity for the general Jewish public through loyalty to the observance of traditional *mitzvot* and the cultivation of personal and social virtues. Arama indicated that his sermons, no doubt in a more abbreviated form, were motivated by recognition that Jews, whether invited or compelled, listened to Christian sermons and noted that their preachers "search enthusiastically for religious and ethical content, using all appropriate hermeneutical techniques." Accordingly, unlike some scholars who sought "only to explain the grammatical forms of words and the simple meanings of the stories and the commandments," Arama undertook to "exalt the image of our Torah to our own people by regaling them with gems from its narratives and laws."[5] Aware of the capacity of Christian preachers to interest listeners, Arama responded by providing both a textually probing (*perishah*) and a theologically discursive (*derishah*) exposition of biblical texts, similar to the *thema* in Christian sermons.[6] These became the basis for his Torah commentary, *Aqedat Yitzhaq*.

Crisis and Creativity: Cultivation of Virtue

The defenders and interpreters of the naturalism and intellectualism of Arab Aristotelianism remained part of Sephardic intellectual culture into the fifteenth century, even though there remained a long history of discontent with those philosophical ideals among Spanish Jewish intellectuals.[7] Arama was among those religious thinkers who sought to decouple the content and path of faith from that of demonstrative knowledge. He turned from his predecessors' stress on science and metaphysics to an emotional-spiritual conception of faith (Latin, *fides*), such that the eternal felicity of soul would be dependent on the love and fear of God.[8]

Although concerned about the excesses of the radical thinkers he called *mitpalsefim*, who "corrupt the path of Torah, undermine its laws, and deny miracles, divine knowledge, providence and prophecy,"[9] Arama realized that only philosophy had "the depth, subtlety and precision" that he and his audience wanted.[10] Accordingly, Arama creatively introduced rabbinic texts into a conversation with philosophical sources, demonstrating respect (with reservations) for Maimonides's *Guide of the Perplexed* and general disagreement with Gersonides.[11] He contended that the moral and metaphysical teachings of Judaism were superior to Greco-Arabic rationalism, went beyond the natural and limited capacity of philosophical epistemology, and served as a more reliable source for personal flourishing and felicity.[12] The true beliefs taught by Torah required acceptance by conscious, willful decision and involved devotion to the performance of the commandments. These would lead to a deeper relationship with God. Despite his disagreement with the metaphysical claims of Jewish Aristotelianism, Arama displayed admiration for the "political philosophy which is well-known from the [*Nicomachean*] *Ethics,* whose words are all correct, which lead to the lights of the candelabra of the pure Torah and which shine and enlighten with opinions and discipline."[13]

Arama also disagreed with Christian theology, arguing that the teachings of Torah were more rational than the beliefs of the dominant religion of Spain. At one point, he recounts a debate, using the scholastic question and answer style, with a Christian theologian, and indicates that he bested that scholar by demonstrating that political (social) philosophy disproved Christian teaching about divine grace.[14] Nonetheless, Arama also expressed appreciation for Christian theologians who displayed deference to faith over philosophy. In *Ḥazut Kashah,* he indicates that "a group of Christians"—probably scholastic theologians—"accepted the value of philosophy . . . but whatever contradicted their religion they uprooted root and branch."[15]

Arama's multileveled, sophisticated, and nuanced approach sought to defeat what he perceived to be disloyalty by extreme rationalists, while also opposing charges of heresy hurled at the philosophers by their anti-philosophical detractors. He validated the usefulness of philosophy, respectfully responded to Christian conversionary efforts, and provided an old-new path to faith based on biblical and rabbinic texts. Because it would foster both a stronger connection to the people of Israel and the ultimate flourishing of soul, Arama's approach also served to strengthen the fidelity and faith of those who remained loyal to Judaism.[16]

A Manual for Virtue

Arama's commentary to the Torah is expansive and covers many topics. His commentary on Proverbs, however, is more focused on moral content and direction. Although Arama discusses issues related to virtue ethics in *Aqedat Yitzẖaq* and his commentaries to the various *megillot,* it is appropriate to characterize the Proverbs commentary, *Yad Avshalom,* as a manual for virtue. With its recurrent references to awe or "fear of YHVH," Proverbs presented Arama with a theological base from which to develop his ideas. Arama seeks to demonstrate the rhetorical beauty, practical virtues, and religious depth of the Book of Proverbs. As in *Aqedat Yitzhaq*, Arama offers textual and thematic explanations, dividing the book into major sections, subdividing some chapters, and joining other chapters together in a topical and rhetorical reorganization. He presents Proverbs as a manual for the political and personal virtues that constitute overt (*niglah*) practical wisdom along with a concealed (*nistar*) deeper message about the danger of philosophical excess, the value of theoretical wisdom and the significance of theological truths.

In Arama's analysis of the opening verses of Proverbs, he identifies five key benefits (*to'aliyyot*) of the moral and intellectual virtues found in this biblical book.

(1) "To learn wisdom and lessons" (Prov. 1:2), as both intellectual wisdom (*sekhel v'i'yyun*) and moral virtue are acquired through proper behavior (*derekh eretz*) and lead to the flourishing of the soul.

(2) "Understanding words of discernment" (1:2), for the true comprehension of a proverb and its lesson involve the development of the soul by habituation.

(3) "Acquiring disciplined knowledge of righteousness, justice, and equity" (1:3), since a proverb teaches righteousness in personal practice, justice in relation to others, and fairness/equity in all of one's affairs.

(4) "Endowing the simple with shrewdness" (1.4), teaching lessons by garbing the concept in an accessible form, so that even the less educated can grasp them.

(5) "The wise one, hearing them, will gain more wisdom" (1.5), as the epistemological method of Proverbs is to lead one to initially grasp an expression or metaphor, habituate personal behavior and then gradually acquire a more complex concept.

According to Arama, personal and political (social) virtues such as the moderate mean, friendship and love, equity in judgment, prudence and temperance, kindness, humility and hope are "mother's teaching" (*torat imekha*).[17] These "virtues and the practical wisdom essential to the flourishing of society and soul, are conveyed through Bible stories with ethical lessons."[18] "When properly established, the outcome of organizing a home and society is a necklace of beauty for the [woman's] neck."[19] The political and personal virtues associated with practical wisdom identified with "mother's teaching" set the table for greater intellectual knowledge or theoretical wisdom, which is an important stage in the development of faith. The "father's instruction" (*musar avikha*) requires an environment that the Virtuous Woman, *eshet ḫayyil*, can provide. She encompasses a totality of behavior that lays the groundwork for the intellectual knowledge important for the proper understanding of Torah.[20]

Although personal and political virtues derive from home, mother, and Bible, Arama often refers to Aristotle as a supportive thinker. Thus, for Aristotle, virtue is not only a state of character, but also the balance between excess and deficiency, "a kind of mean." In his discussion, Arama cites Aristotle, but also attributes the source of this idea to Jewish sources.[21] When explaining the two marital matches mentioned in Talmud (BT Sotah 2b), a subject to which he devotes attention in his commentary to both Torah and Proverbs, Arama indicates that his understanding of marital love is related to Aristotle's theory of friendship.[22] When commenting on the appointment of virtuous men to adjudicate legal matters (Exod. 18:21) and the nature of decision making, Arama refers to Aristotle's discussion of *epeikeia*, equity or fairness in judgement.[23] In a similar way, Arama noted Aristotle's statement about the importance of clarity of vision and effort to achieve a naturalistic good in conjunction with his discussion of the religious-spiritual goal, "Let all your actions be for the sake of heaven."[24]

Sarah Heller-Wilensky identifies the following theological virtues as critical to Arama: awe or fear of God; faith in, love for, service of, and prayer to the divine; and repentance. They are conveyed through the acting out of *mitzvot* that teach theological truths.[25] As was commonly taught within Christian Scholastic circles, Arama thought that theological truths are beyond the limitations of philosophical knowledge. "It is impossible to attain felicity [through philosophy]. Even if a person were to grow in wisdom to know all that Aristotle and his associates knew," contingent knowledge based on the material and natural world would lack certainty.[26] However, another form of knowledge, which stems from the perfect supernal realm, enables humans to know truths that exceed the grasp of the human mind. For Arama, these are conveyed by ritually enacted theology. Belief in Creation is conveyed by observance of the Sabbath. Divine power and will are learned from the practices associated with Passover and the redemption from Egypt. Prophecy and revelation are associated with Shavuot, the festival celebrating the giving of Torah. Rosh Hashanah, with its emphasis on God's awareness of human deeds, teaches the belief in Divine providence. The possibility of *teshuvah,* repentance and forgiveness of sin, is acted out on Yom Kippur. Sukkot with its messianic overtones transmits the belief in the world to come.[27]

Arama then points to the essential theological virtue that he sees as the base for true knowledge and belief: "The fear of the Eternal is the beginning of knowledge" (Prov. 1:7). "Without this virtue, neither proverbs nor study have value." He links this theological virtue to a particular belief: "There is no fear or awe without a belief in the willed divine act of creation from non-existence, which the divine Torah teaches about Genesis."[28] Elsewhere, Arama writes that only awe/fear "can bring one to [a state of] faith."[29] He returns to this idea many times, most forcefully in the conclusion of Proverbs, where he notes a literary *inclusio* that links the last chapter to the first chapter. The idealized Virtuous Woman (*eshet ḥayyil*) is to be praised, because she embodies all the virtues, especially the essential one, "fear of the Eternal" (Prov. 31:30). Although many people have human virtues, there are inadequacies and gaps in all of them. "Many women have acted with virtue" (Prov. 31:29)—other religions and philosophies have "sought to be virtuous through analytical wisdom and actions"—but "the Virtuous Woman 'exceeds them all' . . . because she directs people to the flourishing of the soul, which is the supreme purpose of all wisdom and knowledge."[30]

Cultivation of Virtue

The virtues associated with practical wisdom and the observance of *mitzvot* create the capacity for theoretical wisdom. When not carried to extremes, they clarify the limits of human knowledge, illuminate the dimension of religious faith and "inevitably lead to a deeper understanding of God and thereby contribute to human felicity."[31] Arama's exposition of virtues essential for home and social life is an important aspect of the attention he gives to human flourishing rooted in fidelity to commandments, loyalty to a community, and faithful "attachment" to God.[32] When the limitations of human wisdom are reached, the commitment to follow God's demand, even if it conflicts with reason, is a higher stage of faith based on awe, fear of the Divine (*yirah*).

How does one develop the virtues that Arama admired? We have already mentioned the cultural community of the home with "mother's teaching" and the study of Biblical narratives with moral lessons. Arama also believed that it was essential to avoid falling into a pattern of problematic practices and beliefs. "They who have left the path of rectitude to follow the ways of darkness and who rejoice in doing evil have habituated themselves to erroneous opinions."[33] Because "the soul is cultivated by habituation," correct wisdom and knowledge with repeated and guided practice in moral actions lead to a virtuous life, a practice that Aristotle wrote "makes a very great difference, or rather all the difference."[34] Intention and proper direction is also a significant factor in the cultivation of virtue. "All one's analyses should be to know God . . . who desires, knows and acts on everything."[35]

Temptations, however, abound. In images from Proverbs, they lurk near windows, walk the streets, and even enter the homes of the unsuspecting. And Arama sees philosophical claims as the tempting eye candy for his generation.[36] Arama dramatizes an encounter, portraying the Strange Woman as if garbed in material status, out for the evening, enticing a man with the illusion that the path of philosophical wisdom is beneficial. In response, Arama notes that the structure of city and home, symbolic for Aristotle of a well governed polity and society, are partial protection against dangerous ideas.[37] The historic integrity of the Spanish Jewish community is a safeguard against dangerous ideas and an important way to convey historic virtues during a challenging time.

Often, a mother's advice for a good life is to choose good friends. For Arama, proper associations are important for the development of virtues. Avoid people, pursuits, and passions that are the sources of vice and seek the wisdom and presence of those who uphold virtuous behavior. "One needs friends to support resistance to the wickedness of this [Strange] Woman." These friends are "Wisdom and Understanding."[38] When referring to theologically reliable beliefs that remain within the framework of faith, Wisdom is a source of strength and virtue. However, just as the Woman of Virtue is an exemplar of virtue, the Strange Woman, associated with "natural" or philosophical Wisdom, has a personality and allure that loom large as a source of vice.[39] This need for good friends is similar to Aristotle's observation that "the supremely happy man will need friends of this sort, since his purpose is to contemplate worthy actions and actions that are his own, and the actions of a good man who is his friend have both these qualities."[40]

Arama emphasizes the significance of freedom of choice in relationship to the possibility of divine reward and punishment.[41] However, despite human effort (*hishtadlut*), there are too many things that interfere and make it impossible to find what God wants through reason alone. Since "science has already established regarding the final truth of human felicity and flourishing that ultimate perfection is a gift from God,"[42] the divine commandments structure a framework for the cultivation of virtue and become a beneficent path to significant theological truths.

While Arama emphasized the importance of acts rather than analysis, he explained that the ethical ideas of Aristotle, "who did not know the light of Torah," were not deficient because he did not know "the wonders of religion." Aristotle and his followers could not understand that just as moral actions lead to moral virtues, so divine religion provides a path of the perfection of moral virtues, political (social) virtues and spiritual felicity.[43] Arama explains:

> After [Solomon, the author of Proverbs,] investigated all human activity and aspects of human action in the manner of Aristotle—who said that in all work, study, act and decision, one should see that it is for a good goal—he did not find any [ultimate] human purpose . . . until he explained that these Torah deeds, which include an aspect of the intellectual that is correct from the perspective of the divine Torah, "this is the essence of a human." This matter escaped Aristotle and all who followed him.[44]

As Heller-Wilensky has argued, the virtues that Arama claims escaped Aristotle's analysis were religious ones, taught by prophetic revelation, beyond the ken of naturalistic inquiry.[45] Moreover, "while human ethics require something to be done with love and generosity, it is preferable to fulfil it out of awe. That is, the awe that can bring one to [a state of] faith."[46]

Arama emphasizes the virtue of awe above all others and sees it as essential to true belief and faith. He denigrates philosophers "who are wise in their eyes, but had no awe/fear of God;"[47] instead "awe of the Eternal is the beginning of knowledge" (Prov. 1:5). Arama's emphasis on awe as the defining theological virtue plays an important role in the individuals he chooses to valorize as exemplars of this and other virtues. Notwithstanding the rabbinic ambivalence about Noah, Arama saw him as a model for a generation that had erroneously given primacy to philosophical insight and now sought a return to faith. Noah is described in the Torah as "righteous and wholehearted" (*tamim*)[48] and Arama indicates that Noah's personality was *tamim* in reference to his relationship with God. "He believed according to the tradition that he already had from his father without any [philosophical] analysis. . . . This is the intent of the divine Torah, which says, "You shall be *tamim* with the Eternal your God" (Deut. 18:13)."[49] In Arama's portrayal, Noah had a wholehearted faith, received from his ancestors, and "without complete knowledge from philosophical inquiry . . . he heard from a prophet and believed without troubling himself with speculative analysis. . . . Faith received from a religious [tradition] or a prophet is called *temimut*."[50] That "simple faith"—which one might find among the uneducated masses of Spanish Jewry—is superior to speculative inquiry that exhibits unreliability, uncertainty, and limited scope.

However, as we have seen, Arama does not completely reject philosophical inquiry and analysis that can serve a basis for an alternate path to faith. This "road less traveled," which begins with philosophical analysis and then transcends the limitations of such speculation, may be what he offers to an intellectual elite in his community. This path also reflects Arama's historiography of faith that imagines the revelation of Torah as a corrective to earlier philosophical efforts to understand the divine.[51] For Arama, who adopts the Maimonidean narrative of Abraham's philosophic passage to recognition and understanding of the divine, Abraham exemplifies this more difficult path that revelation at Sinai would make accessible to the entire Jewish people.[52]

To grow in faith, Abraham would have to make a decisive break with his intellectual past. This reach beyond rationalism involved a personal struggle.[53] Abraham is called to be *tamim*, wholehearted like Noah, but to attain this faith in a different way. While philosophers see *mishpat*, the unwavering rule of nature, as characteristic of the divine, Abraham would be "extricated from reliance on astral speculation" by the promise of future progeny. He was called to see *ḫesed*, divine grace, as characteristic of the miraculous and providential incursion of God into the world.[54] The next step in his "pilgrim's progress" was circumcision, which is "done as a commandment [given] by a commander in accordance with a superior and remarkable knowledge, without human considerations, intolerable to philosophical knowledge."[55] This act signifies for Arama a belief and relationship that transcends human understanding. The Binding of Isaac was the final step in the transformation of Abraham from philosopher to "faithful believer," animated by the awe of God. Scornfully, Arama comments, "No philosopher [really understands the meaning of] awe, for they do not fear that any evil will come to them from [God]. . . . Philosophers have no faith in anything! They know what they know. What they do not know, they deny and say [that it] is nothing."[56] For Arama, awe reflects a belief in the possibility of reward and punishment for fulfilment of the commandments and represents a higher stage of faith.

Virtue for Tradition and Life

The awe-filled faith that Arama identifies as the essential virtue has cosmic consequences for the world and redemptive repercussions for the Jewish people. In *Yad Avshalom,* he characterizes four types of Jewish believers. The *Peti* (simple one) believes what has been taught by tradition without questions. The *Arum* (clever one) accepts Torah as long as it does not conflict with reason. The *Kesil* (fool) relies on reason alone. The *Ḥakham* (wise one) believes even when there is a conflict with reason.[57] Reflecting a sense that faith and the fulfilment of the commandments have ultimate and universal implications, Arama decries the groups whose teachings conflict with Torah and says that "these flawed groups destroy the world with their ideas."[58] Arama's message to the Jews who have remained loyal to virtues rooted in the covenant and practices of Judaism is that their fidelity has significant universal implications.

For Arama, human faith and deeds will lead to personal felicity and will restore God to a redemptive role in history.[59] At the conclusion of *Yad Avshalom,* Arama reminds his readers that the promises of God and this larger redemptive vision are dependent on the attitudes and actions of the Jewish people. "The end is like the beginning in this book. It starts with 'Fear of the Eternal is the beginning of wisdom' and concludes 'A woman who fears the Eternal is to be praised.' . . . This awe/fear includes true faith . . . which will be great assistance to reach flourishing."[60] Rather than messianic activism in the face of national despair, Arama calls for spiritual rejuvenation through the personal and social virtues that grow from the observance of the commandments and lead to the theological virtue of awe of heaven and faith in God.

Notes

1. Hayyim Yosef Pollock, "The Life of Rabbi Yizhaq Arama," in Isaac ben Moses Arama, *Aqedat Yizhaq*, ed. Hayyim Yosef Pollock (Pressburg, 1849; repr. Jerusalem, 1964) (hereafter, *AY*). The full-length study by Sarah Heller-Wilensky, *The Philosophy of Isaac Arama in the Framework of Philonic Philosophy* [Hebrew] (Jerusalem: Bialik Institute, 1956), remains the finest exposition of Arama's thought. Also see Chaim Pearl, *The Medieval Jewish Mind: The Religious Philosophy of Isaac Arama* (Bridgeport, CT: Hartmore House, 1972), who fails to cite Heller-Wilensky.

2. Israel Bettan, *Studies in Jewish Preaching: Middle Ages* (1939; repr. Lanham, MD: University Press of America, 1987), 130–91; Marc Saperstein, *Jewish Preaching 1200–1800: An Anthology* (New Haven, CT: Yale University Press, 1989), 17–18, 392–93; James Robinson, "Philosophy and Science in Medieval Jewish Commentaries on the Bible," in *Science in Medieval Jewish Cultures*, ed. Gad Freudenthal (Cambridge: Cambridge University Press, 2011), 471, 475.

3. Isaac ben Moses Arama, *Ḥazut Kashah* (hereafter, *HQ*), in *Aqedat Yitzhaq*, vol. 6 (first printing Savionetta 1552).

4. Isaac ben Moses Arama, *Yad Avshalom: Commentary on Proverbs* (Leipzig: Izaak Frieman, 1858; repr. Jerusalem, 1968) (hereafter, *Yad*).

5. *AY*, introduction, 1–2. Translated in Saperstein, *Jewish Preaching*, 393.

6. Jonathan Adams and Jussi Hanska, *The Jewish-Christian Encounter in Medieval Preaching* (London: Routledge, 2020), 5–6.

7. Eric Lawee, "Sephardic Intellectuals: Challenges and Creativity (1391–1492)," in *The Jew in Medieval Iberia*, 1100–1500, ed. Jonathan Ray (Boston: Academic Studies Press, 2011), 350–91.

8. Shalom Rosenberg, "The Concept of 'Emunah' in Post-Maimonidean Jewish Philosophy, in Isadore Twersky, ed. *Studies in Medieval History and Literature*, v.2 (Cambridge: Harvard University Press, 1984), 299; Hava Tirosh-Samuelson, *Happiness in Premodern Judaism: Virtue, Knowledge, and Well-Being* (Cincinnati: Hebrew Union College Press, 2003).

9. *AY*, introduction, 4.

10. Bernard Septimus, "Yitzhaq Arama and Aristotle's Ethics," in *Jews and Conversos at the Time of the Expulsion*, ed. Yom Tov Assis and Yosef Kaplan (Jerusalem: Zalman Shazar Center, 1999), 1–24.

11. Menachem Kellner, "Gersonides and His Cultured Despisers: Arama and Abravanel," *Journal of Medieval and Renaissance Studies* 6, no. 2 (1976): 269–96.

12. Septimus, "Arama and Aristotle," 6.

13. *AY*, introduction, 4. On the reception in the fifteenth century of Aristotle's *Nicomachean Ethics* by Jewish scholars, see Septimus, "Arama and Aristotle," 11–12; also see Heller-Wilensky, *The Philosophy of Isaac Arama*, 191–206.

14. *HQ* 4. On this ambivalent attitude toward Christianity, see Eric Lawee, "Changing Jewish Attitudes towards Christian Society: The Case of Spain in the Late Middle Ages," *York University Centre for Jewish Studies Annual* 3 (2001): 1–15, and " 'The Beautiful People of Edom': Differing Jewish Approaches to Spanish Christian Culture at the End of the Medieval Period" [Hebrew], *Jewish Studies, Internet Journal* 14 (2018), https://jewish-faculty.biu.ac.il/files/jewish-faculty/shared/JSIJ14/lawee.pdf. On the accusation of the irrationality of Christianity, see Daniel Lasker, *Jewish Philosophical Polemics against Christianity in the Middle Ages* (New York: Ktav and Anti Defamation League, 1977).

15. *HQ* 7. Septimus, "Arama and Aristotle," 14n56, terms this a "two-plane scheme." I think there are three levels to his epistemology.

16. Baruch Frydman-Kohl, "H̲azut Qasha: Faith, Felicity and Fidelity in the Thought of Yis̲haq Arama" (unpublished thesis, Jewish Theological Seminary, 2004).

17. *Yad* 6b on Prov. 1:9.

18. *Yad* 75b on Prov. 23:25. On practical wisdom (*phronesis*) and theoretical or philosophical wisdom (*theoria*) in Aristotle, see *Nicomachean Ethics* 1.7.1098a16; 6.7.1141a20–22; 6.11.1143b14–17; 10.7.1177a12–18 and 1177b31–34.

19. *Yad* 7a on Prov. 1:8.

20. *Yad* 103a on Prov. 31:10. For a discussion of gender in Arama, see Julia Schwartzmann, "Gender Concepts of Medieval Jewish Thinkers and the Book of Proverbs," *Jewish Studies Quarterly* 7, no. 3 (2000): 183–202.

21. Aristotle, *Nicomachean Ethics* 2.6.1106a14–b28. *AY* 77.46a. See also 27.227b. See Heller-Wilensky, *The Philosophy of Isaac Arama*, 184–85.

22. *AY* 8.82a cites Aristotle regarding pleasure and emotional bonding. In *AY* 72.4b, he states, "The political philosopher has explained that the source of love is similarity and partnership." For Arama, marital love (*ḥibbah*) is based on similarity, attributed to the formation of woman from man in Genesis, as well as affection and attraction, which grow over time. On this and differences from Aristotle, see Julia Schwartzmann, "Isaac Arama and His Theory of Two Matches (*Zivvugim*)," *Jewish Studies Quarterly* 13, no. 1 (2006): 27–49.

23. *AY* 43.95b. Arama cites the obligation to do what is "good and right in the sight of God and human" (Deut. 12:28; Sifre Devarim 79.5) indicating that Torah incorporates the possibility of natural justice and flexibility into divine legislation. He recognizes that a righteous person follows *tzedek*, the general rule, while the *h̲asid* responds to the particulars of a situation,

24. *AY* 72.2b citing Pirkei Avot 2:12 in dialogue with *Ethics* 1.2 to be "like archers who have a mark to aim at."

25. Heller-Wilensky, *The Philosophy of Isaac Arama*, 194–205. The idea that matters of faith are enacted by the performance of mitzvot derives from Ḥasdai Crescas, "*haemunah hanitlet b'mitzvah*" *Or Hashem* 3:2, *Light of the Lord*, tr. Roslyn Weiss (Oxford: Oxford University Press, 2018) 321.

26. *AY* 27.209a. See Thomas Aquinas, *Summa Contra Gentiles* 3.16–55 and *Summa Theologiae* 1–2, q1–22.

27. *AY* 67.99a–b. See Heller-Wilensky, *The Philosophy of Isaac Arama*, 88–96. Hava Tirosh Rothschild, "Jewish Philosophy on the Eve of Modernity," in *History of Jewish Philosophy*, ed. Daniel Frank and Oliver Leaman (London: Routledge, 1997), 510, suggests that Arama's "distinct contribution to Jewish dogmatics was the association of each of these beliefs with a particular ritual."

28. *Yad* 5a–b on Prov. 1:1.

29. Arama, *ḤQ* 3.6b.

30. *Yad* 107a–b on Prov. 31.

31. Ari Ackerman, "Jewish Philosophy and the Jewish-Christian Philosophical Dialogue in Fifteenth-Century Spain," in *The Cambridge Companion to Medieval Jewish Philosophy*, ed. Daniel H. Frank and Oliver Leaman (Cambridge: Cambridge University Press, 2003), 378.

32. Arama refers to *middot mediniyot*, which I translate as social, as well as political ethics.

33. *Yad* 11a on Prov. 2:13.

34. *Yad* 6a on Prov. 1:3; Aristotle *Nicomachean Ethics* 2.1.1104b26.

35. *Yad* 12a on Prov. 3:6. For Aristotle, see *Nicomachean Ethics* 1.2.1094a24–25.

36. *Yad* 24b on Prov. 8:1.

37. *Yad* 23b on Prov. 7:5–10. Arama refers to Aristotle, *Nicomachean Ethics* 7.9.1151a5: "Even a clever man can be intemperate, imagining that this is something that one ought to do."

38. *Yad* 23a on Prov. 7:4.

39. *Yad* 3a, introduction, and 103a–108b on Prov. 31. Regarding the Strange Woman and Arama's identification of Wisdom with her, see Schwartzmann, "Gender Concepts," 195. Also see Esperanza Alfonso, "Late Medieval Readings of the Strange Woman in Proverbs," in *Medieval Exegesis and Religious Difference*, ed. Ryan Szpiech (New York: Fordham University Press, 2015), 187–99.

40. Aristotle, *Nicomachean Ethics* 9.9.1170a6.

41. *Yad* 26b on Prov. 8:19.

42. *AY* 16.137; see *Yad*, 96a–b on Prov. 30:5.

43. *ḤQ* 7.14b; *AY*, 46.118b.

44. *AY* 33.62b. Also *Yad* 10b on Prov. 2:6: "This is also what he said in Ecclesiastes: 'The last thing is to fear God, which is a great principle for the flourishing of the human.'"

45. Heller-Wilensky, *The Philosophy of Isaac Arama*, 194–205.

46. *HQ* 3.6b, rejecting Maimonides position that one should ideally relate to the Divine out of love.

47. *Yad* 12a on Prov. 3:6.

48. Gen. 6:9. Other translations for *tamim* include "perfect" and "blameless."

49. *HQ* 2.5a.

50. *AY* 13.139a.

51. *HQ* 8.15b.

52. Maimonides, *Mishneh Torah: Laws of False Worship* 1.1–3.

53. *HQ* 2.5a–b. Septimus, "Arama and Aristotle," 23–24n95, sees this as a reward for Abraham's philosophical achievements.

54. *HQ* 8.19b.

55. *HQ* 2.5b.

56. *HQ* 3.6 a–b. Note the sharp disagreement with Maimonides (*Guide* 3.27–29) and Gersonides (*Commentary to Torah,* Deut. 6:24) who conceptualize awe as recognition of the grandeur and transcendence of the divine, and Arama's reliance on Joseph Albo, *Iqqarim* 3.31.

57. *Yad* 44b–45a on Prov. 14:16–19.

58. *AY* 19.159b.

59. *HQ* 12.34b.

60. *Yad* 107b–8a on Prov. 31:30.

Chapter 15

Moses Cordovero

EUGENE D. MATANKY

Moses Cordovero (Cordoeiro) (1522–1570), active in the Galilean town of Safed, was the preeminent kabbalist prior to the ascent of Isaac Luria. His surname implies that his family originated in the town of Cordova, Spain, but due to its spelling, they presumably resided in Portugal before their eventual immigration to Safed.[1] While scant details are known concerning his early years,[2] from his scattered autobiographical statements we may discern that he studied Jewish exoteric material with Joseph Karo and that he began to study Kabbalah with Solomon Alqabeṣ—his brother-in-law—at the age of twenty and within six years completed his work *Pardes Rimonim* (Orchard of Pomegranates), a masterful overview of key kabbalistic topics.[3] Of primary concern in this composition was the theosophical conception of the Godhead,[4] expressed through sefirotic entities and divine names. Determining the precise configuration and interconnectedness of the Godhead was of particular importance for Cordovero. A prolific writer, his oeuvre demonstrates his command of almost the entire Jewish corpus; from his earliest composition until his more mature works such as *Or Yaqar*, a systematic commentary on the entire *Zohar*, *Tefillah le-Moshe*, a prayerbook replete with kabbalistic commentary and intentions, and *Sefer Elimah*, a complex work exploring theosophical, theurgical, and mystical aspects of Kabbalah.

Cordovero believed that, for redemptive purposes, his historical period was one that necessitated the dissemination and learning of the Jewish esoteric doctrine of Kabbalah.[5] To this end, Cordovero embarked on a number of literary trajectories; one of the most important being his *Tomer Devorah* (The Palm Tree of Deborah),[6] as well as the various musar works written by his students and spiritual heirs.[7] In *Tomer Devorah,* Cordovero explored the relation between the individual and the divine realm; both in stature and in virtues. Cordovero, following kabbalistic tradition, conceived the person as a microcosm and the divine stature and sefirotic realm a macrocosm.[8]

Furthermore, Cordovero understood the human person as possessing theurgical abilities in relation to the supernal realm. For example, when individuals perform a commandment in the mundane realm with a bodily limb, they strengthen that same divine limb within the supernal realm; conversely, when individuals transgress in the mundane realm with a bodily limb, they weaken that limb within the supernal realm. This understanding of human-divine interaction creates an earthly arena of cosmic consequences. While halakhah (Jewish law) does not cover every aspect of daily life, Cordovero's approach does. For Cordovero, every moment is seen as deciding between divine harmony or discord. This hypernomian tendency is well documented within this genre of literature.[9] Toward this end, the proper cultivation of virtues (*middot*) was crucial for Cordovero's understanding of human destiny. While non-kabbalistic conceptions of Judaism may only require a "religious behaviorism,"[10] Cordovero required the total commitment of the Jewish practitioner beyond the "four cubits of halakhah" (BT Berakhot 8a).

Concerning *Tomer Devorah,* it is important to keep Charles Mospik's advice in mind. Mopsik wrote that it "should be read as one reads *Pardes Rimonim* or *Elimah Rabbati* otherwise you will not understand it or miss out on what is most profound and essential. It is above all a kabbalistic book."[11] While *Tomer Devorah* is thought of as a kabbalistic-musar treatise, it is mistaken to think that Cordovero intended it to be read in a purely populistic manner.[12] This insight is well demonstrated throughout the treatise, which was purposefully constructed with the deepest kabbalistic elements in mind.

Cordovero structured his *Tomer Devorah* according to the zoharic section known as the *Idrot* (Assemblies).[13] This zoharic section is of the earliest strata and rife with anthropomorphic imagery, discussing at length the various measurements of the divine body. Cordovero, like other kabbalists, walked a very fine line between anthropomorphic language and actual corporeal conceptualization of the divine.[14] The reticence on the part of kabbalists to employ unapologetic corporeal language is due to the Maimonidean influence on classic kabbalistic thought.[15] Similar to Maimonides's *The Guide of the Perplexed,* which explained how seemingly corporeal depictions of the divine found in the Bible were in fact equivocal, Cordovero prepared a lengthy introduction to the *Idrot* in order to explain away, to some extent, its overtly corporeal terminology. Of note is that he began this introduction with an explanation of the equivocal term *middot,* which may mean measurement, *sefirot,* and attributes or virtues.[16] This shared semantic field is vital to our understanding of virtue ethics within this kabbalist's thought, for virtues are interrelated with the very construction and materialization of the divine itself. This correlation of *sefirot* and *middot* creates an ontological connection between the divine realm and the human realm, in which the *sefirot,* which reflect the divine essence, are parallel to human virtues, which reflect the soul.

In part of the *Idrot* section (*Zohar* 3:131b–35a), we find that Micah 7:18–20 are accredited as representing the thirteen attributes of mercy and are employed as a rectification of the beard of *Arikh Anpin* (The Long Countenance).[17] It should be noted that within non-kabbalistic texts, the thirteen attributes of mercy are to be found in Exodus 34:6–7. The difference between the respective sets of verses should be highlighted by contrasting them:

Micah 7:18–20	Exodus 34:6–7
[1] Who is a God like You, [2] removing iniquity [3] and passing over the transgression [4] of the remnant of His people? [5] He does not retain His wrath forever, [6] for He delights in love. [7] He will return and have compassion upon us; [8] He will subdue our iniquities; [9] and You will cast all their	[1] The Lord! [2] The Lord! [3] a God [4] compassionate [5] and gracious, [6] slow to anger, [7] abounding in kindness [8] and faithfulness, [9] extending kindness to the thousandth generation, [10] forgiving iniquity, [11] transgression, [12] and sin; [13] yet He does not remit all

sins into the depths of the sea. [10] You will grant truth to Jacob, [11] love to Abraham, [12] as You swore to our fathers [13] from days of old.	punishment, but visits the iniquity of parents upon children and children's children, upon the third and fourth generations.[18]

Whereas in the Micah verses there is no mention of judgment, within the Exodus verses judgment remains an inherent and concluding element.[19] The preference in the *Zohar,* which Cordovero follows, for the former set of verses is due to the conceptualization of the highest persona of the anthropomorphic Godhead—the Ancient One or *Arikh Anpin,* which is identified by Cordovero as the *sefirah* of *Keter*[20]—with the attribute of pure mercy without any hint of judgment.[21] It is this aspect of the Godhead that must be emulated according to Cordovero.

To fully realize the radical nature of divine imitation that Cordovero is extolling,[22] we must discuss the nature of the highest gradation of the Godhead. Within kabbalistic thought, the divine is understood as infinite (*ein sof*), which contains all—including contradictory forces. Yet this does not mean that kabbalists understood the *ein sof* in a completely nondualistic manner; rather, the negative side, which includes the qualities of judgment and femininity, is entirely effaced within the positive side, which includes the qualities of mercy and masculinity. While it may seem impossible to speak of a right side without a left side, lightness without darkness, masculinity without femininity, it is precisely this conceptualization that the kabbalists employed to discuss the infinite and the first emanation: *Keter*.[23] Thus, Cordovero's demand of the individual to emulate the highest gradation, "the ontic source wherein all things are unified in an identity of in-difference,"[24] is a demand to emulate the divine gradation in which difference, whether ontological or ethical,[25] has yet to be formulated.

This emulation tasks the individual to have a superhuman ability to tolerate insult and their fellow's evil deeds.[26] This conceptualization of nondifferentiation is likewise expressed in Cordovero's statement concerning the interconnectedness of the divine and the Jewish people.[27] Lastly, Cordovero explicitly invokes this notion in his closing subsection of this chapter, in which the individual is called upon to imitate the aspect of "from days of old," which is kabbalistically understood as the persona of the "Ancient of Days," which being the highest gradation of the Godhead "embraces all other [qualities]."[28]

Ultimately, the individual is employed to imitate the divine in this manner for this aspect of divinity is a "concealed concealment," thus, when they act in accordance with an aspect of this wholly compassionate disposition, it is disclosed within this world, so that it "may not be hidden."[29]

If the first chapter of *Tomer Devorah* is to be read as a rectification and imitation of the highest gradation of the Godhead, then the following chapters may be read as continuing this rectification of the entirety of the Godhead. Of supreme importance is the attribute correlated with the highest *sefirah* of *Keter*—humility—for "this is the key to them all for it is the chief of them all."[30] Another virtue of note is that of repentance, which is correlated with the third *sefirah* of *Binah*. Cordovero proffers in this treatise that the secret of repentance is not merely the negation of evil acts, but their transformation into good. Even the archetypical sin of Cain, which within Jewish tradition is connected to the sin of Adam, could have been transformed into merit, if Cain so desired to repent.[31] Similarly, in his discussion of the *sefirah* of *Gevurah*, which is associated strongly with judgment and evil, Cordovero instructs that one must enlist the evil inclination that stems from this *sefirah*. The trace of evil found here may be transmuted by employing it for one's spouse.[32] As Cordovero wrote:

> In truth the evil inclination should be bound and tied down so that it is not incited to any bodily act whatsoever, not for the desire of cohabitation. . . . However, for his wife's sake he should gently bestir his evil inclination in the direction of the sweet Powers, . . . he should intend to sweeten all those rectifications (*tiqqunim*) with the good inclination and to really perform the rectification for Her [*Shekhinah*] . . . for the sake of the Supernal Union.[33]

As with the virtue of repentance, which may transform past misdeeds into good, so too the channeling of one's desire toward a sanctified purpose—the supernal unification of *Tiferet* and *Shekhinah*—can sweeten the negative, but vital, energy drawn from *Gevurah*. Lastly, Cordovero's advice concerning the attribute of *Malkhut*—the last *sefirah*—is especially interesting: complete empathetic identification with her exiled state. The individual is implored to: "Carry out exiles, by exiling himself from his house of rest constantly, after the fashion of Rabbi Simeon and his company who divorced themselves to study the Torah. And how much better if he bruises his feet wandering from place to place without horse and chariot."[34] Just as the *Shekhinah* is exiled while the Jewish people are exiled, so too the kabbalist is to exile himself from the comforts of his home and community and wander without reprieve to empathize with her condition.[35] These aforementioned virtues do not encompass all the virtues that Cordovero suggested that the adherent follow, but they do represent important kabbalistic virtues.

Cordovero, besides the prescriptions and proscriptions that he wrote in *Tomer Devorah*, was personally involved in a Safedian confraternity, in which the members were given several rules to follow.[36] We find that members were to transform their hearts in to "a dwelling place for the *Shekhinah*," "avoid anger altogether," and, among other directives, "refrain from speaking derogatorily about any person."[37] Many of the principles of behavior listed in this document may find direct correlatives in Cordovero's *Tomer Devorah*. Although not explicitly stated, seemingly these traits and virtues were to be cultivated by continuous practice and reinforced through living within the confraternity. In fact, three of the prescriptions of the confraternity were:

> 14. Let a person commune with one of the Associates every day for the purpose of conversing about devotional concerns.
>
> 15. A person ought to discuss with the same Associate, every Sabbath eve, what he did each day of that past week. From there he should go forth to welcome the Sabbath Queen.
>
> . . .
>
> 29. An individual should be careful about confessing his transgressions prior to eating and before going to sleep.[38]

The first two ordinances demonstrate the importance of peer-reinforcement for virtuous living. While the last directive shows the importance of self-reinforcement. Through the creation of a confraternal space in which individuals may ask for direction and create an environment in which they are held accountable by their peers, in addition to self-regulatory practices, Cordovero's confraternity nurtured an optimal atmosphere for the cultivation of virtues and the rejection of unwanted traits.

Within the sophisticated kabbalistic symbolism that Cordovero employed, these virtues are interconnected within a web of semiotic meaning, for each attribute is related simultaneously to various biblical verses, figures, zoharic passages, human and divine attributes, and human and divine corporeal features. Thus, each virtue draws upon multiple sources that are all interconnected. This is especially the case for a thinker as systematic as Cordovero. For example, in *Pardes Rimonim* concerning the word "repentance," Cordovero writes that it is related to the *sefirah* of *Binah*, as is found in *Tomer Devorah*, but it also related to the *sefirah* of *Malkhut*.[39] Similar ambiguity can be found concerning almost every attribute—each receiving an appropriate prooftext culled from the many pages of the *Zohar*. Thus, within Cordovero's conceptualization of any virtue, alongside the seemingly straightforward instructions, like "When man is born it is necessary to provide him with all his food,"[40] are numerous intentions and implications concerning the divine emanation. Thus, this directive not only concerns the provision of sustenance for others, but it also includes a command to help the *sefirah* of *Tiferet*, which has an admixture of mercy and judgment, to come closer to the side of mercy than that of judgment. Offering of proper nourishment, that is, fulfillment of commandments, facilitates the proper alignment of *Tiferet*.

As we have seen, Cordovero's conception of virtue is to be found throughout every plane of existence. The identification of the ethical with the ontological—how one ought to live is coeval with how one truly exists—perforce charged the topic with a certain gravity. One may even claim that the purpose of disseminating the kabbalistic-ethical treatise of *Tomer Devorah* was not only to introduce the masses to kabbalistic ideas, but concretely to affect their behavior to align with these ideals. As noted above, Cordovero saw his generation as particularly suitable for redemption and, therefore, the increased revelation of esoteric literature was a necessity. However, this could not only be accomplished through such works as his *Or Ne'erav*, which introduced kabbalistic basics to Jewish individuals,[41] but rather an entire transformation of Jewish identity was necessary. The reorganization of Jewish life and tradition to reflect the kabbalistic ideals developed and presented in Cordovero's approach was of the highest order. However, these kabbalistic ideals contain within them certain radical elements inherent in a mystical system that conceptualized the divine as an infinite entity, discussed above.[42] It is precisely the understanding of virtue within this mystical conceptualization that we will turn to now.

The attuned reader will be able to detect the hypernomian tendency within Cordovero's presentation of virtues to be imitated by the ardent believer.[43] This disposition does not entirely align with halakhic behavior, as halakhah is based on a dichotomous view of reality in which there exists conceptions of good and evil, mercy and judgment. However, as mentioned, the first section of *Tomer Devorah,* when read with Cordovero's exposition of the zoharic section on which it is based, is entirely concerned with the virtue of pure mercy without giving any voice to judgment. Thus, Cordovero's path goes "beyond the normative categories of good and evil."[44] For instance, Cordovero writes that a person should not rebuke his fellow, "[e]ven when it is permitted to chastise."[45] Although admonishing one's fellow is a commandment that, when permitted, must be performed, Cordovero instructs the reader to always be merciful. This going beyond the law in accordance with virtuous living is well captured in Timothy Chappell's example concerning the place of rules within virtue ethics. Chappel wrote: "Justice and love plausibly contrast as to the place in them of substantive and specific rules. Justice is all about adjudicating what follows from the rules; love is about caring for someone or something else; love may involve rules, but seems likely to deploy them less centrally than justice."[46] It is precisely these elements of justice and love that may be fruitfully identified with Cordovero's conception of judgment and mercy, found in most kabbalistic texts. Even more so, Cordovero's conception of mercy has no rules and its primary characteristic is that of boundlessness.[47]

The kabbalistic conceptualization of the infinite as beyond all dichotomies renders its imitation a hypernomian venture: "An ethos beyond the duality of good and evil . . . that emulates the plane of being wherein opposites converge and binary logic is transcended."[48] The individual is required to embody the contradictory virtues of pure mercy and self-annihilation. The former represents the surplus of selfhood and the latter the very absence of it. Becoming entirely merciful the individual is able to relate to all Jews as part of one body, while the individual who undergoes self-annihilation is able to contain all other traits.[49] Although deriving from opposite sides of the ontological spectrum, surplus in contrast to absence, they ultimately lead to a state of nondifferentiation. It is due to this conceptualization that Cordovero is able to state that repentance is able to transform sinful past acts into meritorious deeds. For the only shred of evil that is found within the sefirotic realm is that which is connected to the *sefirah* of *Binah*—which has roots in the *sefirah* of *Keter*. By returning, which in Hebrew is etymologically related to repentance, these acts to their roots, one brings them into this realm of pure mercy.[50] Thus, within Cordovero's mystically enrooted virtue ethics, we find a radical formulation of what it means to imitate the divine qua infinite and thereby what it means to be virtuous.

Notes

1. See Zohar Raviv, *Decoding the Dogma within the Enigma: The Life, Works, Mystical Piety and Systematic Thought of Rabbi Moses Cordoeiro (aka Cordovero, Safed, Israel, 1522–1570)* (Saarbrücken: VDM, Verlag Dr. Müller, 2008), 51–52.

2. See Solomon Schechter, *Studies in Judaism: Second Series* (Philadelphia: Jewish Publication Society of America, 1908), 237; Bracha Sack, *The Kabbalah of Rabbi Moshe Cordovero* [Hebrew] (Beer Sheva: Ben Gurion University of the Negev Press, 1995), 11–32; Raviv, *Decoding the Dogma within the Enigma*, 18–93.

3. Both referenced in his introduction to *Pardes Rimonim*.

4. See at length Joseph Ben-Shlomo, *The Mystical Theology of Moses Cordovero* [Hebrew] (Jerusalem: Bialik Institute, 1965).

5. See Sack, *The Kabbalah of Rabbi Moshe Cordovero*, 18, 38–39. Also, see Gershom Scholem, *Major Trends in Jewish Mysticism* (New York: Schocken, 1941), 244; Ira Robinson, *Moses Cordovero's Introduction to Kabbalah: An Annotated Translation of His Or Ne'erav* (New York: Michael Scharf Publication Trust of the Yeshiva University Press, 1994), xi–xii; Boaz Huss, *The Zohar: Reception and Impact*, trans. Yudith Nave (Oxford: Littman Library of Jewish Civilization, 2016), 201–202.

6. On this work, see Mordechai Pachter, "Homiletic and Ethical Literature of Safed in the 16th Century" [Hebrew] (PhD diss., Hebrew University, 1976), 356–62; Joseph Dan, *Jewish Mysticism and Jewish Ethics* (Seattle: University of Washington Press, 1986), 83–87; Eitan P. Fishbane, "A Chariot for the Shekhinah: Identity and the Ideal Life in Sixteenth-Century Kabbalah," *Journal of Religious Ethics* 37, no. 3 (2009): 400–404; Alan Mittleman, *A Short History of Jewish Ethics: Conduct and Character in the Context of Covenant* (Malden, MA: Wiley-Blackwell, 2012), 139–44; Patrick B. Koch, "Approaching the Divine

by *Imitatio Dei*: *Tzelem* and *Demut* in R. Moshe Cordovero's *Tomer Devorah*," in *Visualizing Jews through the Ages: Literary and Material Representations of Jewishness and Judaism*, ed. Hannah Ewence and Helen Spurling (New York: Routledge, 2015), 48–61; Patrick B. Koch, *Human Self-perfection: A Re-assessment of Kabbalistic Musar-Literature of Sixteenth-Century Safed* (Los Angeles: Cherub Press, 2015), 78–103.

7. Notably, Elijah de Vidas's *Reshit Ḥokhmah*, Isaiah Horowitz's *Shenei Luḥot ha-Berit*, and Abraham Azulai's *Ḥesed le-Avraham*.

8. This view is not Cordovero's innovation, but rather has much precedence within Jewish literature, see Alexander Altmann, "The Delphic Maxim in Medieval Islam and Judaism," in *Biblical and Other Studies*, ed. Alexander Altmann (Cambridge, MA: Harvard University Press, 1963), 196–232. Divine stature refers to the kabbalistic understanding of God's anthropomorphic dimensions, such as his forehead, eyes, nose, mouth, beard, and so on; see Gershom Scholem, *On the Mystical Shape of the Godhead: Basic Concepts in the Kabbalah*, ed. Jonathan Chipman (New York: Schocken, 1991), 15–55. The sefirotic makeup refers to the conception of the divine essence as mediating itself through ten *sefirot*, which may be understood as vessels of sorts that contain divinity.

9. Concerning the term hypernomian, see Elliot R. Wolfson, *Venturing Beyond: Law and Morality in Kabbalistic Mysticism* (Oxford: Oxford University Press, 2006), 199–285. Wolfson succinctly defines hypernomian as "extending beyond the limit of the law to fulfill the law" (109). Extending beyond the law can manifest itself in seemingly antinomian behavior, in which the abrogation of the law is in fact its fulfillment, or within extreme pietistic kabbalistic literature, in which the practitioner is required to go beyond the strict delineated boundaries of "the normative categories of good and evil" (262).

10. See Abraham Joshua Heschel, *God in Search of Man: A Philosophy of Judaism* (New York: Farrar, Straus and Giroux, 1955), 320–35, esp. 327: "The ultimate requirement is to act beyond the requirements of the law. Torah is not the same as law, as *din*. To fulfill one's duties is not enough. One may be a scoundrel within the limits of the law."

11. Charles Mopsik, introduction to *Le Palmier de Débora*, ed. Charles Mopsik (Paris: Verdier, 1985), 28. Similarly, see Koch, *Human Self-Perfection*, 82.

12. As has been demonstrated, the genre of kabbalistic-musar is only defined much later; see Patrick B. Koch, "'Many Books on Issues of Divine Service': Defining Musar in Early Modernity," *Journal of Jewish Studies* 71, no. 1 (2020): 1–24.

13. On the *Idrot*, see Yehuda Liebes, *Studies in the Zohar* (Albany: State University of New York Press, 1993), 74–84, 95–98; Pinchas Giller, *Reading the Zohar: The Sacred Text of the Kabbalah* (New York: Oxford University Press,

2001), 89–173; Melila Hellner-Eshed, *Seekers of the Face: Secrets of the Idra Rabba (the Great Assembly) of the Zohar* (Stanford: Stanford University Press, 2021).

14. See, for example, Moses Cordovero, *Pardes Rimonim* (Krakow / Nowy Dwor: Isaac ben Aaron Prostitz, 1591), 1.3, 8–9 [Hebrew]. All references to *Pardes Rimonim* are according to gate and chapter.

15. Concerning Maimonides's influence on Kabbalah, see Moshe Idel, "Maimonides and Kabbalah," in *Studies in Maimonides*, ed. Isadore Twersky (Cambridge: Harvard University Press, 1990), 31–81; Elliot R. Wolfson, "Beneath the Wings of the Great Eagle Maimonides and Thirteenth-Century Kabbalah," in *Moses Maimonides (1138–1204): His Religious, Scientific, and Philosophical "Wirkungsgeschichte" in Different Cultural Contexts*, ed. Görge K. Hasselhoff and Otfried Fraisse (Würzburg: Ergon Verlag, 2004), 209–37; Jonathan V. Dauber, "Competing Approaches to Maimonides in Early Kabbalah," in *The Cultures of Maimonideanism: New Approaches to the History of Jewish Thought*, ed. James T. Robinson (Leiden: Brill, 2009), 57–88; Elliot R. Wolfson, " 'Via Negativa' in Maimonides and Its Impact on Thirteenth-Century Kabbalah," *Maimonidean Studies* 5 (2008): 393–442.

16. Moses Cordovero, *Sefer ha-Zohar im Peirush Or Yaqar*, 23 vols. (Jerusalem: Aḥuzat Yisra'el, 1962–1995), 21:83–84 [Hebrew]. Furthermore, see Moshe Idel, *Kabbalah: New Perspectives* (New Haven, CT: Yale University Press, 1988), 128–34; Moshe Idel, *Absorbing Perfections: Kabbalah and Interpretation* (New Haven, CT: Yale University Press, 2002), 226–334. Cf. Koch, *Human Self-perfection*, 109–12. Also, see Mopsik, introduction to *Le Palmier de Débora*, 29. Cf. Moses Maimonides, *The Guide of the Perplexed*, 2 vols., trans. Shlomo Pines (Chicago: University of Chicago Press, 1963), 1.54, 123–28.

17. Concerning this development, see Giller, *Reading the Zohar*, 118–19.

18. This is a traditional numbering found among such Jewish thinkers as Naḥmanides and Abraham ibn Ezra. It should be noted that Cordovero has a different system found in Cordovero, *Sefer ha-Zohar im Peirush Or Yaqar*, 22:12. Cf. Koch, *Human Self-Perfection*, 94. Translations are based on the NJPS Bible.

19. It should be noted that judgments (*dinim*) within kabbalistic theosophical thought are correlated with the left side of emanation—the roots of evil. A common trope within zoharic literature is "sweetening the judgment," which means the dilution and eventual transformation / reversion of evil back to its holy source. Likewise, due to the correlation of the feminine and judgments, this trope implies an effacement of the feminine, see Elliot R. Wolfson, *Circle in the Square: Studies in the Use of Gender in Kabbalistic Symbolism* (Albany: State University of New York Press, 1995), 93–94.

20. Concerning Cordovero's identification, see Cordovero, *Sefer ha-Zohar im Peirush Or Yaqar*, 22:21. Also, see Sack, *The Kabbalah of Rabbi Moshe Cordovero*, 131n65.

21. See Elliot R. Wolfson, *Language, Eros, Being: Kabbalistic Hermeneutics and Poetic Imagination* (New York: Fordham University Press, 2005), 177–89; Elliot R. Wolfson, *Luminal Darkness: Imaginal Gleanings from Zoharic Literature* (Oxford: Oneworld, 2007), 1–28.

22. Concerning Cordovero's thought on *imitatio dei,* see Mopsik, introduction to *Le Palmier de Débora,* 30–41; Dan, *Jewish Mysticism and Jewish Ethics,* 85; Wolfson, *Venturing Beyond,* 197–98; Fishbane, "A Chariot for the Shekhinah," 401–404; Mittleman, *A Short History of Jewish Ethics,* 140–41; Koch, "Approaching the Divine by Imitatio Dei"; Koch, *Human Self-Perfection,* 78–103.

23. See Wolfson, *Venturing Beyond,* 220–21, concerning Cordovero's formulation in *Elimah Rabbati.*

24. Elliot R. Wolfson, *Alef, Mem, Tau: Kabbalistic Musings on Time, Truth, and Death* (Berkeley: University of California Press, 2006), 92.

25. Elliot R. Wolfson, *Open Secret: Postmessianic Messianism and the Mystical Revision of Menaḥem Mendel Schneerson* (New York: Columbia University Press, 2010), 231–40.

26. See Moses Cordovero, *The Palm Tree of Deborah,* trans. Louis Jacobs (London: Vallentine, Mitchell, 1960), 47–50.

27. Cordovero, *The Palm Tree of Deborah,* 53. It should be noted that Cordovero, like many kabbalists, believed there to be an ontological differentiation between Jews and non-Jews, see at length Wolfson, *Venturing Beyond,* 17–185.

28. Cordovero, *The Palm Tree of Deborah,* 68.

29. Cordovero, *The Palm Tree of Deborah,* 69.

30. Cordovero, *The Palm Tree of Deborah,* 76. Concerning the importance of this attribute, see Wolfson, *Venturing Beyond,* 286–316; Fishbane, "A Chariot for the Shekhinah," 385–418.

31. Cordovero was greatly perturbed by the existence of evil, see Kalman P. Bland, "Neoplatonic and Gnostic Themes in R. Moses Cordovero's Doctrine of Evil," *Bulletin of the Institute of Jewish Studies* 3 (1975): 103–29; Joseph Dan, "'No Evil Descends from Heaven': Sixteenth-Century Jewish Concepts of Evil," in *Jewish Thought in the Sixteenth Century,* ed. Bernard D. Cooperman (Cambridge, MA: Harvard University Press, 1983), 97–100; Sack, *The Kabbalah of Rabbi Moshe Cordovero,* 83–102.

32. It should be noted that Cordovero, like other kabbalists, wrote for a purely male audience and his views may be defined as phallocentric, see Wolfson, *Language, Eros, Being,* passim.

33. Cordovero, *The Palm Tree of Deborah,* 102–104. Also, see Mittleman, *A Short History of Jewish Ethics,* 143–44.

34. Translation based on Cordovero, *The Palm Tree of Deborah,* 115. Cordovero wrote a treatise about his revelatory experiences that he received in his self-exiled exhibitions: *Sefer Gerushin.* On this work, see Raviv, *Decoding the Dogma within the Enigma,* 243–355.

35. For this practice in Safed, see Marla Segol, "Performing Exile in Safed School Kabbalah," *Magic, Ritual, and Witchcraft* 7, no. 2 (2012): 131–63.

36. See Schechter, *Studies in Judaism*, 292–94; Lawrence Fine, *Safed Spirituality: Rules of Mystical Piety, the Beginning of Wisdom* (New York: Paulist Press, 1984), 30–39.

37. Fine, *Safed Spirituality*, 34–35.

38. Fine, *Safed Spirituality*, 36–37.

39. Cordovero, *Pardes Rimonim*, 23.22.

40. Cordovero, *The Palm Tree of Deborah*, 92.

41. Robinson, *Moses Cordovero's Introduction to Kabbalah*.

42. Wolfson has even referred to *ein sof* as meontological, meaning neither being, nor nonbeing, but rather being-not. In other words, the infinite is a nonreifiable entity, see Wolfson, *Open Secret*, 107–14.

43. See at length, Wolfson, *Venturing Beyond*, 286–316.

44. Wolfson, *Venturing Beyond*, 262.

45. Cordovero, *The Palm Tree of Deborah*, 54.

46. Timothy Chappell, "Virtues and Rules," in *The Handbook of Virtue Ethics*, ed. Stan van Hooft (Durham, UK: Acumen, 2014), 82.

47. However, this boundlessness has one limitation: the non-Jew. As the non-Jew within Cordovero's thought lacks ontological existence, they are only able to be included within this merciful disposition through effacement, see Elliot R. Wolfson, "Heeding the Law beyond the Law: Transgendering Alterity and the Hypernomian Perimeter of the Ethical," *European Journal of Jewish Studies* 14, no. 2 (2020): 243–48.

48. Wolfson, *Venturing Beyond*, 306,

49. Cordovero, *The Palm Tree of Deborah*, 76.

50. Cordovero, *The Palm Tree of Deborah*, 86–89. Concerning the hypernomain understanding of pure mercy, see Wolfson, "Heeding the Law beyond the Law," 215–63.

Chapter 16

Baruch Spinoza

HEIDI M. RAVVEN

The Mind has no other power than that of thinking.

—Spinoza, *Ethics*, part 5, Proposition 4 Scholium[1]

Desire is the very essence of man.

—Spinoza, *Ethics*, part 3, Definition of the Affects 1

Independence of Mind is a private virtue.

—Spinoza, *Political Treatise* 1.6

Baruch Spinoza was born in Amsterdam in 1632 and died in the Hague in 1677. His parents and ancestors had been crypto-Jews (Marranos) who had maintained their Jewish allegiance in the face of the forced conversions to Christianity that had swept the Iberian Peninsula beginning in Spain in 1391, finally reaching the remaining

---

I wish to dedicate this paper to the memory of my exalted teacher, Professor Alexander Altmann, may his memory be a blessing, who mentioned to me nearly a half century ago that Spinoza, not Freud, should be regarded as the great founder of psychotherapeutic praxis and theory. I hope I have offered some reflection here on the truth and importance of that insight.

Jews of Portugal in 1497, where persecution had till then not been as intense. The Netherlands became a refuge for Portuguese Jews who had remained in the Iberian Peninsula and were still under the threat of the Catholic Inquisition when Holland achieved its independence from Spain in 1609, after a war of independence that had lasted nearly one hundred years. Baruch Spinoza was thus of the first generation of former Marranos to be born in the Netherlands, a member of the Portuguese (Jewish) community. In the Netherlands, former crypto-Jews could renew their Jewish commitments openly and return to a Jewish communal life. Spinoza had a strong Jewish education and was educated in the Jewish philosophical tradition as passed down in the Sephardic world. He was particularly influenced by Maimonides, Gersonides, Crescas, and Hebreo Leone. The influence of Maimonides and Judaeo-Arabic scientific naturalism is evident throughout Spinoza's works, especially in his assessment of the relation, even identity, of the knowledge of God and the love of God. A free thinker whose philosophic inquiry pushed him beyond customary bounds, Spinoza was excommunicated at age twenty-four from the still precariously established Jewish community of Amsterdam. He never joined another religious community, turning down the Chair in Philosophy at Heidelberg, a post requiring a religious test. Holland was widely known to be the most tolerant country in Europe and a haven not only for persecuted Jews but for philosophers and other free thinkers escaping suppression in their own countries, Hobbes and Descartes among them. Spinoza took five years off from writing his major philosophic work, the *Ethics*, to write the *Theological Political Treatise* in response to what he felt as an urgent demand of his time, the growing threat to liberty of conscience and thought, tolerance and freedom of worship in the Netherlands. It was the only one of his books to be published in his lifetime and it instantly became the subject of enormous controversy and widespread vilification. The overriding concern in that work is how to lessen the dangers of religious fanaticism upon burgeoning democratic institutions. It is a plea for democracy and religious pluralism, a blueprint for how both ought to be made the guiding principles of all modern liberal, nondenominational states. Spinoza envisioned freedom of conscience and freedom of speech as cardinal virtues and principles of the modern state, reflecting not only his personal history but also a Dutch society that had already become religiously pluralist and increasingly diverse in the wake of expansionist New World and

Asian trade and settlement. In the *Ethics*, his major philosophical work and statement, Spinoza focused on the moral transformation of the individual rather than on the principles, laws, and institutions of the polity. Nevertheless, as in *The Theological Political Treatise*, he set as the aim of a life well lived the attainment of *freedom*. Personal freedom is the goal and fulfillment of a life of *virtue*. How Spinoza makes this argument, and what he means by the freedom that is identical with virtue, are the subjects of this essay.

Spinoza and Ethics

As the title of his major work suggests, ethics is at the center of Spinoza's philosophical project. What he first called "my philosophy" he later changed to the *Ethics*, so we see in this the centrality of ethics to Spinoza's overall philosophical project and thinking. Another indication of the centrality and perhaps pervasion of all philosophy by ethics in Spinoza's understanding emerges from the book in a different way: a book titled the *Ethics* actually begins with metaphysics and God and Nature and it ends with spiritual transformation, the human approach to God. So either everything is ethics in some Spinozistic sense, or ethics has come to be something else in the course of the book than what we thought it was at the beginning. Some interpreters have insisted that only part 4 of the *Ethics* is *actually* "ethics," or ethics proper, and it alone should be considered Spinoza's contribution to the philosophy of ethics.[2] For part 4 begins with definitions of "good" and "bad," contains a theory of the origin and nature of "virtue" in Proposition 22 and its Corollary, introduces in the middle principles of moral valuation and many specific moral valuations, offers a theory of evil in Proposition 64, an exemplary moral model of virtue, the free man, in Propositions 67–73, and then ends with an appendix that enumerates thirty-two moral rules. However appealing to our contemporary sensibilities it might be to regard Spinoza's ethical theory as contained only or principally in part 4, we should, nevertheless, take Spinoza at his word. Hence, we should try to discover why *all* philosophy was ethics to him.

Perhaps he was right and it is *we* moderns or postmoderns who are wrong to compartmentalize ethics in one discrete domain among many, separating it from cosmology, metaphysics, theology, epistemology, biology, and psychology, all of which contribute to ethics in his understanding. Spinoza makes clear that the assimilation of all philosophy to ethics in some yet to be determined sense is not be found in any simple moralizing of the universe, that is, in theorizing a universe created by a just God where things turn out morally right in the end, the just rewarded and the unjust punished. For Spinoza famously embraced the phrase, God or Nature, an equivalence whose weight is on the second term. To clarify, he ended part 1 of the *Ethics* with an extended attack on the error of attributing teleology (purpose, moral or otherwise) to nature. He regarded the view that nature has inherent purposes and aims as intellectually suspect and mythic. Instead, he argued that nature follows strict and impersonal causal and logical sequences and is played out in natural laws that manifest the myriad interactions of forces. Its operation is the necessary deterministic working out of impersonal laws, like gravity or the second law of thermodynamics (to give contemporary examples), laws that cannot be disobeyed, because they are descriptive rather than regulatory. It is these impersonal causal principles and natural laws of science and metaphysics that Spinoza proposed express the divine attributes. Spinoza regarded the image of a Just Law Giver in the Sky as an anthropomorphism that he rejected and derided as much as Maimonides did in *The Guide of the Perplexed*.

All Virtue Is Intellectual Virtue

We need to ask ourselves how, in such an impersonal, natural universe of cause and effect, does Spinoza derive ethics, an account of virtue? How can knowing the laws of physics, for example, transform us morally and spiritually? The link turns out to be intellectual, for it is both the breadth of knowledge and the integrity and honesty of the search that demarcate the line between the ethical and the nonethical. That is so, Spinoza argues at great length in the *Ethics*, insofar as we include self-knowledge in our scientific endeavor, extending from the self proper infinitely out into the universe and back. Perhaps Spinoza is the greatest practitioner and interpreter since Socrates of the Delphic maxim, Know Thyself, as the beginning of wisdom. For Spinoza's ethical theory, his account of virtue, identifies all moral principles as specifications of, and all moral actions as flowing from, the integration of a searingly honest self-reflection with a push outward toward rigorous scientific investigation of all things in the universe. The "highest good," that is, virtue, Spinoza tells us in the beginning of the early *Treatise on the Emendation of the Intellect,* his first, aborted, attempt at writing his philosophy, can be discovered only in "the knowledge of the union that the mind has with the whole of Nature." This is the goal and the project from which Spinoza never strayed. That attainment was "as difficult as it was rare" and he believed he had accomplished it in the *Ethics,* a work he regarded as perhaps not the most beautiful philosophy but the true one. For Spinoza demonstrated in the *Ethics* that the scientific method of the tracing of causes and the discovery of causal principles—which he outlined in the the *Theological Political Treatise* (ch. 7) as the general method of rigorous scientific inquiry—and the integration of the resulting bodies of knowledge into an overall universal explanatory framework, as he attempted in the *Ethics,* could and ought to be applied to the understanding of oneself as well. What distinguished the search as ethical rather than narrowly scientific is the application of broad theoretical natural causal explanations to the self—mind as well as body—that is, the inclusion of the self within the universal framework of natural causes.

Hence, it is where the exploration begins and ends, not its content per se, that renders the scientific method a *moral* praxis. Its ethical power to transform lies in its capacity to engage and modify one's self-understanding. Hence, for Spinoza, ethics is the path of knowledge-of-self-in-world and world-in-self, thereby transforming a person from nonmoral or premoral to moral, from opaque to oneself to self-conscious and self-aware, a kind of knowledge that has profound implications for action. Spinoza harks back to an ancient Greek moral sensibility of sin as a form of ignorance. He writes in part 4, Proposition 23: "Insofar as a man is determined to some action from the fact that he has inadequate ideas, he cannot be said, without qualification, to be acting from virtue; he can be said to do so only in so far as he is determined from the fact that he understands." Yet Spinoza is calling our attention not to an innocent ignorance but to what we today designate, "motivated ignorance." He writes of it (part 5, Proposition 42 Scholium) that "the ignorant man . . . lives as if he were unconscious of himself, God, and things." It is a subterranean ignorance that disguises an unconscious or not fully conscious psychology of the uncritical acceptance of prevailing beliefs, even devolving at times into a denial justifying the dishonest embrace of self-serving illusions that skirt hard truths about self and world. It is here that desire comes into the picture, for ignorance of this kind is more an *affective* failure than it is a cognitive one. While ethics is a matter of understanding and self-understanding, it is desire—one's motives, pleasures, and emotions—that drive self-related knowledge. Thus, desire is the wellspring of virtue for it is the source of the capacity for intellectual honesty—and also marks its failure.

"Desire Is the Essence of Man"

Spinoza, the great advocate of the supremacy of intellectual virtue as the foundation of all virtues, at the same time and not as paradoxically as it at first may appear, defines human beings by their affective nature and not principally by their cognitive capacity, as was and is the standard wont of the philosophical tradition from Plato onward. "Desire," he writes, "is the very essence of man" (*Ethics*, part 3, Definition of the Affects 1). A basic desire, a striving for survival and self-furthering, permeates all our endeavors and capacities, rather than being one among a range of human capacities and faculties. This desire especially permeates and drives our thinking, Spinoza contends.[3] He bases this claim on a deeper metaphysical principle, that "mind and body," in contrast to Descartes's philosophy, "are one and the same thing," albeit understood in two different ways (*Ethics*, part 3, Proposition 2 Scholium). This is so because Nature, the universe, is psychophysical; it is one thing described and explained in two ways (the only ones available to the human mind of the infinite ways). Desire resides in a unitary human being—really, in all beings—permeating all capacities and activities, mental and physical. Hence thinking is affectively laden and expressive, and action is the necessary outcome of desires of the mind-body each of us is. In seventeenth-century philosophic terminology, Spinoza calls the basic desire that is our essence, the "conatus." "The conatus with which each thing endeavors to persist in its own being is nothing but the actual essence of the thing itself," he writes (*Ethics*, part 3, Proposition 7).

If we are desiring entities in a world of other desiring entities, engaging in both cooperative projects and also competing for supremacy and resources, to promote cooperation over competition is a task of the education of desire—on a societal level and on a personal, individual one. The *Ethics* is about the latter and the *Theological Political Treatise* is about the former. Spinoza introduces the project of the *Ethics* in part 4, Proposition 22 Corollary: "The conatus [desire] to preserve oneself is the primary and sole basis of virtue." It is with the transformation of the conatus, he goes on, that virtue must engage, "[f]or no other principle can be conceived prior to this one . . . and no virtue can be conceived independently of it." The conatus can be transformed, and the only path to such transformation, Spinoza argues, is through understanding. "The greatest striving [conatus] of the Mind, and its greatest virtue is understanding," Spinoza writes (*Ethics*, part 5, Proposition 25) and, hence, "things are good only insofar as they aid man to enjoy the life of the Mind," and, conversely, "an emotion is bad or harmful only insofar as the mind is thereby hindered from being able to think" (part 5, Proposition 9 Demonstration). The search for truth in principle fulfills human desire, that is, human nature, and also results in virtue. But first, how does Spinoza make the case that intellectual virtue brings about personal fulfillment, that honesty in science and honesty in self-understanding are fulfilling? And second, how does he make the case that intellectual virtue amounts to what the designation "ethics" promises, namely, that we come to care for each other and for the world? How does Spinoza make these two moves, from perfected intellect to the fulfillment of desire and from self to other?

To begin to answer these questions, let's call to mind the principle of the "highest good" that Spinoza introduced in the *Treatise on the Emendation of the Intellect*: that the ultimate goal is "the knowledge of the union that the mind has with the whole of Nature." That principle would seem to imply that we can become one with the universe in some sense, extending our minds to embrace it, and hence to embrace all others together as one. Moreover, the attainment of that consummate virtue, Spinoza further informs us here, gives us "joy to all eternity," a spiritual ecstasy. Philosophy, *his own philosophy*, is the route to such transformation—a goal that is intellectual, spiritual, moral, and psychological. The immediate motivation, however, according to Spinoza is neither the search for pleasure nor for virtue. It is, instead, the search for *freedom*, for the previrtuous life, the nonmoral and even immoral life, is a life of *bondage*. The unexamined life, lacking honest self-awareness and world-understanding, is both unfree and unvirtuous.

Of Human Bondage

Spinoza titles part 4 of the *Ethics* "Of Human Bondage," and he explains what he means by that in the subtitle, "Or the Strength of the Emotions." Later in part 4, in Proposition 66 and its Scholium, Spinoza explains further his claim of the slavery of ignorance:

> [W]e shall readily see the difference between the man who is guided only by emotion or belief and the man who is guided by reason. The former, whether he will or not, performs actions of which he is completely ignorant. The latter does no one's will but his own, and does only what he knows to be of greatest importance in life, which he therefore desires above all. So I call the former a slave and the latter a free man.

The bondage Spinoza is pointing to is clearly psychological; it is a state of psychic disempowerment and even at times flailing. Our slavery is to our own memories, for "it is not within the free power of the mind to remember or to forget anything." Memory dominates our present and our future, for "[w]e can take no action from mental decision unless memory comes into play" (*Ethics*, part 3, Proposition 2 Scholium). We are slaves to our own pasts, to our own culture, to our families of origin, and even to the present context. Memory locks us into a world we inherit, shaping our understanding and desires through inherited belief and practical, social, and political incentives and disincentives."[4]

We cannot free ourselves by a mere act of will, Spinoza insists, for the idea that we have freedom of will is mistaken. He derides such a notion: "A baby thinks that it freely seeks milk, an angry child that it freely seeks revenge, and a timid man that he freely seeks flight. Again, the drunken man believes that it is from free decision of the mind that he says what he later, when sober, wishes he had not" (*Ethics* part 3, Proposition 2 Scholium). Instead, the mind in all its capacities is as causally deterministic and determined as everything else in nature, for the mind, according to Spinoza, is as natural as the body. "Mental decisions arise in the mind from the same necessity as the ideas of things existing in actuality," Spinoza writes, "and those who believe that they . . . do anything from free mental decision are dreaming with their eyes open" (part 3, Proposition 2 Scholium). It is only because we "are conscious of [our] actions [but] ignorant of the causes by which they are determined" that we harbor the illusion of free will, a magical capacity to escape and transcend deterministic causal chains (part 2, Proposition 2 Scholium). Hence, we cannot simply pull ourselves out of our bondage and choose beyond memory and the motives shaped by memory. For all thinking is affective, motivated and emotional, in its very embodied nature, and cannot be independent of body and world since "[t]he mind and body are one and the same thing," albeit understood and explained in two different ways (part 3, Proposition 2 Scholium). Our knowledge and beliefs and thoughts, including our reason, are also states of desire, emotion, and motivation—and memory. Hence, "mental decisions are nothing more than the appetites themselves" (part 3, Proposition 2 Scholium). For "mental decision on the one hand, and the appetite and physical state, on the other hand, . . . are one and the same thing which, when considered under the attribute of Thought . . . we call decision, and when considered under the attribute of Extension . . . we call a physical state." Nevertheless, we have one avenue of freedom, and it is our power to understand ourselves and to gain knowledge of the world: "the Mind has no other power than that of thinking and forming adequate ideas" (part 5, Proposition 4). We discover that embodiment can be a source of strength and not only weakness, because transforming our beliefs, insofar as they are driven by deeply emotional memories about ourselves and the world, can bring us freedom.

The Freedom, Power, and Virtue of the Mind

Spinoza defines emotions as "the affections of the body by which the body's power of activity is increased or diminished, assisted or checked, together with the ideas of these affections." Hence emotions span body and mind, registering psychophysical states on a scale from weakness to strength, which Spinoza terms from "passivity" to "activity." They indicate the degree of a person's passive or active posture in the world. Even beliefs and thinking, as the cognitive component of emotion, indicate such a posture. So thinking is not only true or false, but, crucially, either unexamined passive reflection, acceptance, of the world as found (according to "the common order of nature," Spinoza calls it) or active reconstruction of it via rigorous causal investigation and explanation. Thinking does not *reflect* reality, in Spinoza's view, but *enacts* it just as much as material causes do. Hence thinking whether active or passive is, and results in, a form of action because it is motivated engagement with and in the world. Thought-emotion-action is a unit. "We are active when something takes place, in us or externally to us, of which we are the adequate cause; . . . we are passive when something takes place in us, or follows from our nature, of which we are only the partial cause" (*Ethics*, part 3, Definition 2).

The mind in understanding, because it originates in and expresses the power of the mind to reconstruct its own experience in terms of the causal system of the universe operative in both self (mind and body) and in the world, is active. It grasps (in principle) the causal sequences that encompass the entire universe that resulted in oneself. But as a result, those infinite causes are *internalized* in one's mind as *self* and *self-explanatory*. There are in principle no causes outside the self to which it is passive. To know oneself is to know the entire universal causal system, mental and physical, within oneself that gave rise to this me at this time. The boundaries of (the causal systems of) self and world have become intertwined, indistinguishable. And that has affective consequences as well as motives. For if we are each fundamentally a self-perpetuating desiring unit, that unit has burst its bounds! It has broken free.

Attaining independence of mind amounts to developing one's own interpretation of one's experience based on a searingly honest self-examination of one's own motives and emotions and memories, integrating it into a broader rigorous causal understanding of one's world moving outward ultimately to all of nature. Such active self-reflection and self-understanding make possible distancing from passive acceptance of the life dominated by the commonplaces and incentives of the local. Spinoza's free man has become a cosmopolitan citizen of the universe. His virtue is his freedom to see his own self-perpetuation, his conatus, as part and parcel of the perpetuation of the eternity of the universe. Spinoza famously writes in part 5 of the *Ethics* (Proposition 23 Scholium): "We feel and experience that we are eternal. For the mind senses those things that it conceives by its understanding just as much as those which it has in its memory. Logical proofs are the eyes of the mind. . . . [W]e . . . sense that our mind, in so far as it involves the essence of our body under a form of eternity, is eternal."

Because our mind actively reproduces the causal system of the world, of nature, mentally in the mind *as self*, it unites the individual mind with its infinite origins and eternal effects in Nature or God.

The human mind's striving for unity with the divine mind's ongoing producing of Nature—Spinoza's Nature Naturing, *natura naturans*—harks back to Maimonides's account in the *Guide* of the knowledge of God as communion through Reason with (the sublunar domain of) God's Attribute of Action, an ecstatic Intellectual Knowledge of God that is at the same time the Love of God. Spinoza's final words in the *Ethics* could be a fitting ending to the *Guide* and is inspired by it: "Blessedness is not the reward of virtue, but virtue itself. . . . Blessedness consists in love towards God, a love that arises from . . . knowledge . . . and therefore it is virtue itself." Spinoza's theory of activity, that all virtue "must be related to the mind in so far as the mind is active," his theory of emotion, of the identity of mind and body, and finally of the identification of God with Nature were all innovations Maimonides could not have envisioned. Nevertheless we discern Spinoza's wrestling with Maimonides's great insight that the knowledge of God engenders in us the love of God—which both thinkers take as a love for, and an understanding of, God's natural creation—and thereby fulfills human nature, brings ecstatic joy, renders us eternal in the only way possible, and makes of us virtuous people who desire the good of all. "Because we enjoy blessedness," Spinoza concludes his final proposition of the *Ethics* in a Maimonidean key, "we are able to keep our lusts in check." Nevertheless, Spinoza's theory of intellectual virtue both naturalizes and psychologizes Maimonides's vision while also breaking new ground. For Spinoza points us toward modernity in his ideal of independence of mind, of achieving personal freedom from narrow aspects of one's past and provincial origins appropriate to citizenship in a pluralist cosmopolitan polity, and of finding joy and peace and beneficence towards all, virtue, through a psychotherapeutic praxis of deep and honest self-reflection upon the specificities of memory when brought into the broader universe of understanding.

A Final Note on the Jewishness of Spinoza's Philosophy

Spinoza's greatest homage to his Jewish heritage might be his recommendation in the *Theological Political Treatise* (chs. 17–18) of the

Ancient Israelite Commonwealth as a model of government that the endangered Dutch Republic ought to embrace, because it enshrined democracy, freedom of speech and conscience, and checks and balances. The Jewish biblical state was a model he pleaded ought to be embraced by all modern polities, and someday might even inspire a revived Jewish commonwealth, a prescient nod to a future Zionism (*Theological Political Treatise*, ch. 3). We might also discern in both Spinoza's universalizing of ethics as encompassing all Philosophy and in his embrace of intellectual virtue as the wellspring of moral personality tributes to a deeply Jewish value and sensibility: *Torah Lishma*, learning for its own sake, which transforms the soul.[5]

Notes

1. All quotations from the *Ethics* will be based on the Shirley translation, *Baruch Spinoza: The Ethics and Selected Letter*, trans. Samuel Shirley, ed. and introd. Seymour Feldman (Indianapolis: Hackett, 1982).

2. Those interpreters who have attributed an ultimate ethical status to Spinoza's model of human nature in *Ethics* part 4 include Edwin Curley, "Spinoza's Moral Philosophy," in *Spinoza: A Collection of Critical Essays*, ed. Marjorie Grene (New York: Anchor, 1973), 354–76); Robert McShea, "Spinoza: Human Nature and History," in *Spinoza: Essays in Interpretation*, ed. Maurice Mandelbaum and Eugene Freeman (LaSalle, IL: Open Court, 1975), 101–15; McShea, "Spinoza's Human Nature Ethical Theory," in *Proceedings of the First Italian International Congress on Spinoza (1982)*, ed. Emilia Giancotti (Naples: Bibliopolis, 1985), 281–90); McShea, "Spinoza in the History of Ethical Theory," *Philosophical Forum* 8, no. 1 (1976): 59–67); Paul Eisenberg, "Is Spinoza an Ethical Naturalist?," in *Speculum Spinozanum, 1677–1977*, ed. Siegfried Hessing (London: Routledge and Kegan Paul, 1977), 145–64; Herman DeDijn, "Naturalism, Freedom, and Ethics in Spinoza," *Studia Leibnitiana*, 22, no. 2 (1990): 138–50.

3. The late neuroscientist and founder of Affective Neuroscience, Jaak Panksepp, has provided evidence that Spinoza was right about the claim of the affective pervasion by a basic desire for survival and perpetuation. Panksepp discovered seven basic emotional circuits in the midbrain. The one he terms SEEKING pervades all the rest and he identifies it with Spinoza's conatus. Panksepp maintains that the SEEKING capacity underlies the Darwinian competitive striving and it accounts for it. See, for example, Jaak Panksepp, Richard D. Lane, Mark Solms, and Ryan Smith, "Reconciling Cognitive and Affective Neuroscience Perspectives on the Brain Basis of Emotional Experience," in *Neuroscience and Behavioral Reviews* 76, pt. B (2017): 187–215.

4. *Ethics,* part 2, Proposition 18 Scholium: "Memory . . . is simply a linking of ideas involving the nature of things outside the human body, a linking which occurs in the mind parallel to the order and linking of the affections of the human body."

Ethics, part 2, Proposition 17 Corollary: "The mind is able to regard as present external bodies by which the human body has once been affected, even if they do not exist and are not present."

5. See, my "Spinoza's Rupture with Tradition—His Hints of a Jewish Modernity," in *Jewish Themes in Spinoza's Philosophy,* ed. Heidi M. Ravven and Lenn E. Goodman (Albany: State University of New York Press, 2002), 187–223.

Chapter 17

Moses Ḥayyim Luzzatto

PATRICK BENJAMIN KOCH

What the materiality of nature seeks to erase from our mind, reading and reflection will call to memory.

—Moses Ḥayyim Luzzatto, *Mesillat Yesharim*

In "The Young Man from Padua," the writer Ḥayyim Naḥman Bialik (1873–1934) describes the protagonist of his essay as a "man of contrasts, but not of vicissitudes."[1] The figure behind this title, the polymath Moses Ḥayyim Luzzatto (also known by his acronym Ramḥal), was indeed a personality with many faces and talents.[2] Born in Padua in 1707 to one of the oldest and most reputable Italian Jewish families, he received, according to his own account, divine revelations from an angelic mentor and other supernal entities since the age of twenty.[3] He wrote seminal works on Lurianic Kabbalah and a "second" *Zohar*,[4] and he was equally well versed in philosophy and contemporary Italian

This research was made possible by the generous support of the German Research Foundation (DFG), in the framework of the Emmy Noether project "Jewish Moralistic Writings of the Early Modern Period: 1600–1800" (Project No. 320105005).

scientific and cultural discourse, as reflected in his treatises on rhetoric and logic and not least in his poetry and play scripts, which have led some to call him the first modern Hebrew writer.[5] Persecuted as an alleged Sabbatean during his lifetime—an accusation that inter alia forced him to leave Padua and relocate to Amsterdam in 1735—he was posthumously celebrated by *maskilim*, *ḥasidim*, and *mitnaggedim* alike, all of whom identified with his spiritual-intellectual legacy in their own individual ways.[6] Last but not least, Luzzatto, who headed a pietistic confraternity with messianic and redemptive inclinations while still in Padua, authored books dealing with moral edification (musar).[7] In 1743, he left Amsterdam for the Holy Land, where he died approximately three years later in Acre during an outbreak of a plague.

The Place of Virtue in Luzzatto's Thought

Virtues are firmly embedded in Luzzatto's worldview and constitute a central aspect of his conception of human self-perfection. He repeatedly argues—in an implicitly Platonic manner—that God's essence is absolute perfection and the true good, and that a person must strive for this good by doing that which is pleasing to God.[8] In his systematic account of the basic principles of Jewish faith outlined in *Derekh ha-Shem*, he specifies that God's "purpose in creation was to bestow His good to another."[9] However, a member of the community of Israel can only achieve this good if he attains it through his own efforts, through the perfection of his intellect, and the cultivation of virtues (*middot tovot*).[10] Bringing oneself closer to God ultimately culminates in a state of prophecy, one that Luzzatto describes as a degree in which the individual "clearly realizes that the One to whom he is bound is God."[11]

In many respects, Luzzatto's moral instruction in *Mesillat Yesharim* complements his rather philosophical discussion in *Derekh ha-Shem*, both of which he composed during his time in Amsterdam.[12] While the latter includes detailed explanations of the different levels and qualities of divine inspiration, the former only mentions these effects of self-perfection in passing.[13] In contrast, the main discussion of *Mesillat Yesharim* is dedicated to the different virtues that need to be mastered on the path of attaining perfection (an issue only marginally addressed in *Derekh ha-Shem*).[14] These qualities constitute the human efforts that prepare the ground for God bestowing His sanctity on the individual.[15] Luzzatto adopts his set of virtues from the "rungs" of the famous rabbinic dictum (*baraita*) attributed to the second-century Tannaitic figure Pinḥas ben Ya'ir in the following sequence: vigilance (*zehirut*), alacrity (*zerizut*), blamelessness (*neki'ut*), separateness (*perishut*), purity (*taharah*), piety (*ḥasidut*), humility (*anavah*), fear of sin (*yirat ḥet*), and sanctity (*kedushah*).[16] Furthermore, he establishes a continuity between the *baraita* and the biblical exhortations of Deuteronomy 10:12–13 ("And now, O Israel, what does the Lord your God demand of you? Only this: to revere the Lord your God, to walk only in His paths, to love Him, and to serve the Lord your God with all your heart and soul, keeping the Lord's commandments and laws, which I enjoin upon you today, for your good"). For Luzzatto, they are identical in content, but follow a different ordering principle. He explains their differences by pointing out that, "whereas Moses arranged them in accordance with the kinds of duties we have, . . . the Sages . . . arranged them in the order in which we acquire them."[17]

Luzzatto's Hierarchy of Virtues

Luzzatto joins the long list of authors who have used the *baraita* as a template to promote their program of self-improvement.[18] However, while most of Luzzatto's predecessors only loosely follow the various gradations, *Mesillat Yesharim* offers a systematic treatment of the characteristics and different elements of each virtue, the question of how to acquire them, and the factors that adversely affect their cultivation. Luzzatto focuses mainly on the psycho-spiritual aspects of enhancing one's conduct and character, or what Kristján Kristjánsson refers to as "virtuous emotions."[19] This attitude is expressed particularly clearly when he laments that only a "few belong to the type that devotes regular thought and study to the perfection of [divine] service, love and fear [of God], communion [with Him], and all other elements of piety"[20]—which is not necessarily to be understood as an indication of the elitist nature of this way of life, but rather as a polemic against those who indulge only in the theoretical study of religious and secular topics.[21] It also shows that Luzzatto uses "piety" (*ḥasidut*) both in a generic sense—as an umbrella term for the different components of the path to perfection—and more specifically in order to refer to one particular rung in one's quest for closeness to God.[22] Accordingly, he designates those people who master the path of perfection as *ḥasidim*.[23]

In general, it can be stated that the inner dimension of self-perfection—or the "[proper] intention of the heart and correct thought" (*kavvanat ha-lev ve-yosher ha-maḥshavah*)[24]—occupies a central position in Luzzatto's thought. In the final part of *Derekh ha-Shem*, he establishes a hierarchical order between four different types of action (*ma'aseh*); namely, those that are continuous, daily, periodic, and circumstantial.[25] He gives the love and the fear of God as two examples of those actions that an individual must constantly bear in mind.[26] In the further course of the discussion, he stresses how difficult it is to stand before God's greatness in awe,[27] a statement that he also echoes in *Mesillat Yesharim*, where he writes that "only someone who has already acquired all the previously mentioned traits is prepared to attain" this penultimate stage.[28] Against this background, it can be concluded that the sequence of virtues to be mastered follows a clear hierarchical order. However, while discussing the question of how to acquire the first and lowest rank of vigilance (*zehirut*), Luzzatto also asserts that "the ultimate form of this level is called fear of sin (*yirat ḥet*)."[29] In order to resolve this alleged contradiction, it has been argued that Luzzatto refers to two different types of *yirat ḥet*.[30] It seems more likely, however, that he points here to an ongoing cyclical process of spiritual refinement, one that reconnects the lowest of virtues with the highest and demands a continuous effort as outlined in the first category of actions in *Derekh ha-Shem*. From this vantage point, Luzzatto's understanding of the substance of vigilance, namely, "to monitor all one's deeds and supervise all one's ways, so as not to retain a bad habit or trait, much less a transgression or sin,"[31] seems to constitute a Judaized version of the Stoic attitude of *prosoche*. The latter has been described by Pierre Hadot as "a continuous vigilance and presence of mind, self-consciousness which never sleeps, and a constant tension of the spirit," and as a "concentration on the present moment."[32] In contrast to the Stoic stance, however, Luzzatto embeds the highest level of mindfulness in a culture of fear that can be understood as specifically Jewish for two reasons: It is based not only on an overly developed anxiety of transgressing the Torah's positive and negative commandments. The Torah (which also marks the first rung in the *baraita* of Pinḥas ben Ya'ir) is at the same time the main object of study for cultivating yet another, more elevated type of awe, the awe of God's sublimity (*yirat ha-romemut*). Accordingly, while elaborating on the permanent need of being in a state of contemplation and reflection to acquire the fear of sin, he writes that "there is no training in fear other than through constant, uninterrupted occupation with the Torah and its ways."[33] Since this highest of virtues is not only the most difficult to achieve, but one that can also be easily lost, Luzzatto calls for a permanent and cyclic "reading and reflection" of *Mesillat Yesharim*. It represents a strategy that "will call to memory" "what "the materiality of nature seeks to erase from our mind."[34] At the same time, it may also reflect his personal messianic intentions and an attempt to "perpetuate the union with the [divine feminine attribute named] *Shekhinah*" and "refine his purity during the period awaiting the final redemption," as has been suggested by Elisheva Carlebach.[35]

In sum, then, it can be stated that the virtues that a person is capable of actively acquiring should all be considered equally important for mastering the various steps on the path to perfection. What distinguishes them, however, is the degrees of difficulty in putting them into practice.

The Cultivation of Virtues in Luzzatto

According to Luzzatto, an action is considered good when a person does "that which is pleasing to the Creator."[36] This vague definition is somewhat narrowed down by specifying those factors that are detrimental to the virtues one ought to cultivate. He states, for example, that a preoccupation with worldly affairs, jesting and mockery, and evil company prevent one from attaining the virtue of vigilance, and he adopts one of the classical pair of opposites promoted in musar literature that juxtaposes humility with pride.[37] Still, it must be noted that *Mesillat Yesharim* as a whole lacks instructions for concrete actions, despite the fact that Luzzatto gave each individual virtue a separate chapter that ostensibly deals with its proper acquisition. As Emil Hirsch already aptly remarked more than a century ago, *Mesillat Yesharim* constitutes one of the few examples among the many works of musar that sheds "light on the foundations rather than on the facts of consecrated conduct," and that considers "practice . . . as the outflow of principle."[38] This method surfaces more clearly in Luzzatto's philosophical writings, which were also composed during his time in Amsterdam, and particularly in his "gradation rule," which prioritizes general principles (*kelalim*) over specific details (*peratim*).[39] In this sense, Luzzatto can be defined as a virtue theorist rather than a virtue ethicist.

On a more practical level, Luzzatto's approach reflects his acknowledgment of an infinite multitude of human capabilities. With this in mind, he explains that "every individual requires direction and guidance that accord with his trade or vocation . . . not because piety varies. . . . But inasmuch as the bearers [of piety] vary, the means that get them to that goal cannot but vary with the individual."[40] In order to implement these principles, Luzzatto promotes a method of cultivating a particular state of mind circumscribed by the term *hitbonenut*—a process that Jonathan Garb has poignantly described as an "engaged reflection amidst the travails of daily life."[41]

In accordance with his focus on principles rather than actions, didactic stories that exemplify the conduct of perfected individuals are virtually absent in *Mesillat Yesharim*.[42] However, similar to Baḥya Ibn Paquda's musar classic *Duties of the Heart*, Luzzatto makes frequent use of biblical and rabbinic quotations in order to support his psycho-spiritual vision of self-perfection. In this respect, citations from the book of Psalms play a particularly central role in *Mesillat Yesharim*, and the biblical figure of King David is accordingly stylized as an exemplar of *ḥasidut*.[43] Moreover, and in contrast to some of his predecessors, Luzzatto does not necessarily perceive the cultivation of virtues as an imitation of the Godhead.[44] Rather, as mentioned above, he presents the acquisition of these "good qualities" as an expression of reverence for God. At the same time, it constitutes a sort of "awakening from below," which, when executed properly, can potentially induce a transformation process that is initiated by means of divine support in which a person transcends his natural boundaries and achieves an angelic state of being.

Luzzatto's Conception of Virtue and Its Impact on His Interpretation of Judaism

Luzzatto's focus on principles and the deliberate ambiguity resulting therefrom appear to have been a decisive factor in *Mesillat Yesharim*'s great success among the different ideological branches of modern Judaism. In terms of its reception, Luzzatto's path to virtue can therefore be considered a universal one that thanks to its multivocality has managed to provide the moral underpinnings for very different lifestyles.

As far as Luzzatto's own agenda is concerned, scholars have offered a variety of readings.[45] What most of them share, however, is their acknowledgment of the central place that habituation occupies in Luzzatto's path to virtue. In *Mesillat Yesharim,* he stresses again and again that the acquisition of a virtue does not come naturally, but rather over time and as a result of self-reflection and constant practice. It is this very process that transforms the traits that Luzzatto outlines from something unnatural into "a second nature"[46] for the person who cultivates them. The importance of this type of self-conditioning is also reflected in the general tone of *Mesillat Yesharim,* which switches from a "sober-minded" discourse in the first half of the book to an increasingly personal and intimate language that becomes most articulate in the last third of the book.[47]

Although Luzzatto was undoubtedly a kabbalist and the author of several kabbalistic works, his moral treatise *Mesillat Yesharim* is decidedly non-kabbalistic. Some have argued that Luzzatto felt compelled to conceal the kabbalistic dimension of the former due to the prohibition on publishing esoteric writings in the wake of the accusations of being a Sabbatean. Accordingly, some attempts have been made to reveal the supposedly hidden message of *Mesillat Yesharim.* However, and as rightly noted by Jonathan Garb, such interpretations should be regarded primarily as part of the reception history rather than providing information about the actual content of this work.[48] In fact, *Mesillat Yesharim* differs from many of the highly popular kabbalistic-ethical books, which became one of the most dominant literary forms of musar since its Safedian revival in the sixteenth century. Compared to Moses Cordovero's *Tomer Devorah* or Elijah de Vidas's *Reshit Ḥokhmah*—both of which systematically draw parallels between virtues and the *Sefirot* and devote much of their discussion to the impact of human virtuous conduct on the divine structure by means of theurgy—Luzzatto's approach appears to be more akin to those of medieval non-kabbalistic books of musar, such as Ibn Paquda's *Duties of the Heart* or the anonymous *Orḥot Tzaddikim.*

In sum, it can be concluded that Luzzatto's "moral psychology" is a call to a personal, lived holiness that promotes permanent contemplation and reflection by means of engagement in Torah. In doing so, it is an open criticism of a Judaism that pays little attention to this spiritual dimension and instead focuses merely on the theoretical exploration of things, a trend that is epitomized in *Mesillat Yesharim* by the figure of the talmudist-scientist. At the same time, Luzzatto opposes those who, by reason of misguided zeal, exaggerate in their bodily self-mortifications, a group he depicts by the image of the hypocritical false ascetic.[49] One might be tempted to deduce from his dismissive attitude toward these rather extreme and one-sided orientations that Luzzatto himself opted for a golden mean in the Aristotelian sense. However, the opposite is the case. In *Mesillat Yesharim* and *Derekh ha-Shem*, he presents a radical way of life, one that suggests striving for perfection by means of cultivating a permanent state of mindfulness. The ultimate goal of this path is to achieve a state of true attachment (*hitddabekut amiti*[*t*]) and to become receptive for divine inspiration (*ruaḥ me-marom*) that transforms the adept "quite literally [into] an angel of God."[50] Put differently, if for Aristotle, virtue is the excellence at being human, for Luzzatto, it is a prerequisite of becoming a vessel for the divine.

Notes

1. Ḥayyim Naḥman Bialik, "Ha-Baḥur mi-Padua," Bialik House Archive, IL-BIAL-7246, https://www.nli.org.il/en/archives/NNL_ARCHIVE_AL997009626766405171/NLI.

2. For an overview of Luzzatto's life and works, see Joseph Dan and Joelle Hansel, "Luzzatto, Moses Ḥayyim," in *Encyclopaedia Judaica*, 2nd ed., ed. Fred Skolnik and Michael Berenbaum (Detroit: Thomson Gale, 2007), 13:281–86. See also Rachel Puterman, "Moshe Hayyim Luzzatto 1707–1747," *Jewish Affairs* 51, no. 4 (1996): 24–34. For a comprehensive intellectual biography, see Jonathan Garb, *Kabbalist in the Heart of the Storm: R. Moshe Hayyim Luzzatto* [Hebrew] (Tel Aviv: Haim Rubin Tel Aviv University Press, 2014).

3. See Elisheva Carlebach, "Redemption and Persecution in the Eyes of Moshe Hayim Luzzatto and His Circle," *Proceedings of the American Academy for Jewish Research* 54 (1987): 1–29, esp. 3–4, 14–15; as well as Garb, *Kabbalist in the Heart of the Storm*, 101–27.

4. Moses Ḥayyim Luzzatto, *Zohar Ramḥal*, ed. Yosef Avivi (Alon Shavut: Hoza'at Tevunot, 2009). Cf., however, Jonathan Garb, "The Authentic Kabbalistic Writings of Moses Hayyim Luzzatto" [Hebrew], *Kabbalah* 25 (2011): 165–222, who claims that much of what Avivi has published is not by Luzzatto.

5. See, for example, Yeruḥam Fishel Lachower, *Al Gevul ha-Yashan ve-he-Ḥadash* (Jerusalem: Mossad Bialik, 1951), 29–96.

6. On Luzzatto's persecution, see Elisheva Carlebach, *The Pursuit of Heresy: Rabbi Moses Hagiz and the Sabbatian Controversies* (New York: Columbia University Press, 1990), 195–255. See also Carlebach, "Redemption and Persecution," 22–27. On the wide acceptance of *Mesillat Yesharim*, see Garb, *Kabbalist in the Heart of the Storm*, 271.

7. On this confraternity, see David Sclar, "Perfecting Community as 'One Man': Moses Ḥayim Luzzatto's Pietistic Confraternity in Eighteenth-Century Padua," *Journal of the History of Ideas* 81, no. 1 (2020): 45–66. On his messianism, see Isaiah Tishby, *Messianic Mysticism: Moses Hayim Luzzatto and the Padua School*, trans. Morris Hoffman (Oxford: Littman Library of Jewish Civilization, 2008); as well as Elliot R. Wolfson, "*Tiqqun Ha-Shekhinah*: Redemption and the Overcoming of Gender Dimorphism in the Messianic Kabbalah of Moses Ḥayyim Luzzatto," *History of Religions* 36, no. 4 (1997): 289–332.

8. See, for example, Moses Ḥayyim Luzzatto, *Da'at Tevunot—The Knowing Heart*, trans. Shraga Silverstein (Jerusalem: Feldheim, 1982), 16–17. For a short summary of Platonistic virtue ethics, see, Rosalind Hursthouse and Glen Pettigrove, "Virtue Ethics," in *The Stanford Encyclopedia of Philosophy*, Winter 2018 ed., ed. Edward N. Zalta, https://plato.stanford.edu/archives/win2018/entries/ethics-virtue/.

9. Moses Ḥayyim Luzzatto, *Derekh ha-Shem—The Way of God*, trans. Aryeh Kaplan, 3rd ed. (Jerusalem: Feldheim, 1981), 37; Moses Ḥayyim Luzzatto, *Derekh Ḥokhmah—The Path of Wisdom*, trans. E. R. Spring (Emanuel: Shaarei Chochmah Institute, 1992), 50. Cf. also Jonathan Garb, "Shame as an Existential Emotion in Modern Kabbalah," *Jewish Social Studies* 21, no. 1 (2015): 100.

10. Luzzatto, *Derekh ha-Shem*, 102–103, 42–43 (see also 332–33); Luzzatto, *Derekh Ḥokhmah*, 40. See also Moses Ḥayyim Luzzatto, *The Complete Mesillat Yesharim: Dialogue and Thematic Version*, ed. and trans. Avraham Shoshana (Cleveland: Ofeq Institute, 2007), 302–303, where he writes that "true perfection lies only in cleaving to Him, blessed be He. . . . For that alone is [true] good, while everything else that people deem to be good is but vanity and deceptive lie." In this context, I prefer to translate the term *adam* as "member of the community of Israel," since Luzzatto dedicates an entire chapter in *Derekh ha-Shem* to the question of "Israel and the Nations," in which he argues that the actions of the nations have no impact whatsoever on the state of creation or divine revelation (Luzzatto, *Derekh ha-Shem*, 142–43).

11. Luzzatto, *Derekh ha-Shem*, 206–207. See also 214–17, where Luzzatto clarifies that one draws closer to God by means of devotion, good deeds, and self-purification. Aryeh Botwinick reads Luzzatto's notion of prophecy against the background of the naturalistic approach of Maimonides: see Botwinick, "A Maimonidean Reading of Luzzatto's *Mesillat Yesharim*," *Jewish Studies Quarterly* 7, no. 3 (2000): 203–22, esp. 205–207. 212. See also Avraham Shoshana, who

in his introduction to *The Complete Mesillat Yesharim* writes that "we are convinced that there exist clear parallels between Ramchal's thought in Mesillat Yesharim and Rambam's teachings" (xxxii). On the impact of Maimonides on Luzzatto's thought, see also Yeshayahu Leibowitz, *Conversations on Mesillat Yesharim of Ramḥal* [Hebrew] (Jerusalem: Hamad Printing, 1997).

12. See Garb, *Kabbalist in the Heart of the Storm*, 85. Though we do not have an exact date for the completion of *Derekh ha-Shem*, *Mesillat Yesharim*'s dialogue version (hereinafter referred to as SV) mentions in the colophon that it was completed on Wednesday, Elul 25, 5498 (1738). The later thematic version (hereinafter referred to as SP) was first printed in Amsterdam in 1740. See Luzzatto, *Complete Mesillat Yesharim*, xxii–xxiii.

13. Luzzatto, *Derekh ha-Shem*, 205–35; Luzzatto, *Complete Mesillat Yesharim*, 285–86 (SV), 519–22 (SP).

14. For a comprehensive discussion of *Mesillat Yesharim*, see Garb, *Kabbalist in the Heart of the Storm*, 271–319.

15. Cf. Luzzatto, *Complete Mesillat Yesharim*, 515 (SP). This idea is more explicitly articulated in the dialogical version, where it reads: "For what nature denies him, [God's] munificence (blessed be He) will bestow upon him, and assist him [to achieve]" (279 [SV]).

16. Luzzatto, *Complete Mesillat Yesharim*, 42 (SV), 299 (SP). There are many extant varieties of this particular *baraita*. In the dialogical order (42), Luzzatto follows the standard printed version of BT Avodah Zarah 20b. In the thematically structured printed book, he only mentions "Torah leads to vigilance, etc." (299; and see fol. 2a in the 1740 Amsterdam edition). A different order (and partly different virtues) can be found for example in PT Shekalim 14b. See also PT Shabbat 9a, Songs of Songs Rabbah 1:1, and Midrash Mishle 15. The interconnections of the *baraita*'s traits are based on biblical proof-texts that focus on ritual matters or cultic laws as recorded in the Torah, as well as on psychological matters adopted from the Prophets and Writings. See Lev. 16:20, 12:8, 16:9; Isa. 57:15; Prov. 22:4; Ps. 86:2, 89:20; Ezek. 37:14; Mal. 3:23; and cf. Peter Schäfer, *Die Vorstellung vom heiligen Geist in der rabbinischen Literatur* (Munich: Kösel Verlag, 1972), 120. For a comprehensive discussion of the *baraita* in its rabbinic context, see Aharon R. E. Agus, "The Ladder of R. Pineḥas ben Yair, or: The Body of Life," in *Hermeneutic Biography in Rabbinic Midrash: The Body of This Death and Life* (Berlin: de Gruyter, 1996), 83–201.

17. Luzzatto, *Complete Mesillat Yesharim*, 42 (SV). This explanation is missing in the more popular thematic version. It is noteworthy that the sixteenth-century Safedian kabbalist Elijah de Vidas opens the second gate of his musar anthology *Reshit Ḥokhmah* with a discussion of Deut. 10:12. See Vidas, *Reshit Ḥokhmah ha-Shalem*, ed. Yosef Ḥayyim Waldman (Jerusalem, 1984), Gate of Love, introduction, 1:343, and see also 1:599–647, for a discussion of the *baraita* of Pinḥas ben Ya'ir.

18. For a comprehensive discussion of the *baraita*'s singnificance in musar literature, see Patrick B. Koch, *Human Self-perfection: A Re-assessment of Kabbalistic Musar-Literature of Sixteenth-Century Safed* (Los Angeles: Cherub Press, 2015), 46–77.

19. Kristján Kristjánsson, *Virtuous Emotions* (Oxford: Oxford University Press, 2018). See also Gopal Sreenivasan, *Emotion and Virtue* (Princeton, NJ: Princeton University Press, 2020).

20. Luzzatto, *Complete Mesillat Yesharim*, 292.

21. On the polemical tone of *Mesillat Yesharim*, see also David Sclar, "Adaptation and Acceptance: Moses Ḥayim Luzzatto's Sojourn in Amsterdam among Portuguese Jews," *AJS Review* 40, no. 2 (2016): 354–56.

22. For a comprehensive discussion of the importance of the notion of *ḥasidut* in musar literature, see Koch, *Human Self-perfection*, 196–212. For the centrality of *ḥasidut* in *Mesillat Yesharim* (with a focus on its kabbalistic meaning), see Mordekhai Ḥayyim Chriqui, "Sha'ar ha-Mesillah: Sod le-Yesharim," in *Mesillat Yesharim le-Or Kitvei ha-Ramḥal*, ed. Mordekhai Ḥayyim Chriqui (Jerusalem: Makhon Ramḥal, 2000), 28–41.

23. See, for example, Luzzatto, *Complete Mesillat Yesharim*, 510, where he presents conduct that is befitting for "each and every man of piety" (*kol ḥasid ve-ḥasid*), or his reference to the "circle of pietists" (*kat ha-ḥasidim*) that he mentions at the very beginning of the dialogue version (1).

24. Luzzatto, *Complete Mesillat Yesharim*, 9.

25. It is noteworthy that in *Derekh Ḥokhmah*, Luzzatto also establishes a hierarchy of four types of study that forms another aspect of his holistic vision of the pursuit of perfection.

26. Luzzatto, *Derekh ha-Shem*, 238–39.

27. Luzzatto, *Derekh ha-Shem*, 253. He furthermore specifies that the person who is in a constant state of awe is considered "purified of the darkness associated with the physical body" and "enveloped by the Divine Presence."

28. Luzzatto, *Complete Mesillat Yesharim*, 503. It is noteworthy that even though *yirat ḥet* is described as the penultimate rung, it actually constitutes the highest degree that a person can accomplish without divine help.

29. Luzzatto, *Complete Mesillat Yesharim*, 320 (SP), and cf. 66 (SV).

30. Luzzatto, *Complete Mesillat Yesharim*, 265–66n3. Note that Luzzatto in fact distinguishes between three different types of fear: the fear of punishment, the fear of God's majesty, and the fear of sin. He does not, however, distinguish between two different types of the fear of sin, as suggested by Avraham Shoshana. For a detailed discussion of the notions of fear and awe in Luzzatto, see Jonathan Garb, "From Fear to Awe in Luzzatto's *Mesillat Yesharim*," *European Journal of Jewish Studies* 14, no. 2 (2020): 287. On the centrality of "fear" in musar literature, see also Ilaria Briata, "Repentance through Fear: Cosmic and Body Horror in *Shevet Musar*," *European Journal of Jewish Studies* 14, no. 2 (2020): 264–84.

31. Luzzatto, *Complete Mesillat Yesharim*, 61 (SV), 313–14 (SP). On the detrimental factors that keep one from vigilance and eventually lead to sin, see also 81 (SV) and 335 (SP).

32. Pierre Hadot, *Philosophy as a Way of Life: Spiritual Exercises from Socrates to Foucault*, ed. and introd. Arnold I. Davidson, trans. Michael Chase (Malden, MA: Blackwell, 1995), 84. Interestingly, Luzzatto refers to two aspects that characterize the ideal form of fear of sin, namely, to worry about what one is doing in the present, and reflecting in what one has done in the past. Luzzatto, *Complete Mesillat Yesharim*, 271 (SV), and see also 267 (SV).

33. Luzzatto, *Complete Mesillat Yesharim*, 275 (SV), and for a slightly different version 512 (SP).

34. Luzzatto, *Complete Mesillat Yesharim*, 300 (SP). On the difficulties of achieving a permanent state of the fear of sin, see 268 (SV) and 512 (SP). For Luzzatto's instruction to repeatedly study the work, see 291 (SP).

35. Carlebach, "Redemption and Persecution," 29. On *tikkun ha-shekhinah* as the central doctrine in Luzzatto's thought, see Wolfson, "*Tiqqun Ha-Shekhinah*," esp. 329. See also Garb, *Kabbalist in the Heart of the Storm*, 209–16.

36. Luzzatto, *Complete Mesillat Yesharim*, 287 (SV), 523 (SP).

37. Luzzatto, *Complete Mesillat Yesharim*, 80 (SV), 332 (SP). On the juxtaposition of humility and pride, see 244 (SV) and 484 (SP). On an earlier, rather comprehensive discussion of pride, see 145–48 (SV) and 394–98 (SP).

38. Emil G. Hirsch, "R. Moses 'Hayim Luzzato's 'Path of the Righteous,' " in *Studies in Jewish Literature Issued in Honor of Professor Kaufmann Kohler on the Occasion of His Seventieth Birthday*, ed. David Philipson, David Neumark, and Julian Morgenstern (Berlin: Reimer, 1913), 147, 148.

39. Moses Ḥayyim Luzzatto, *Derekh Tevunot ha-Shalem* (Jerusalem: Makhon Ramḥal, 2017), 19; as well as Dan and Hansel, "Luzzatto," 283.

40. Luzzatto, *Complete Mesillat Yesharim*, 287 (SV), 523 (SP).

41. Garb, "From Fear to Awe," 295.

42. That said, it is important to mention that Luzzatto does dedicate an entire chapter to Moses as a prophet in *Derekh ha-Shem* (see 228–35). There is good reason to believe that Luzzatto himself did identify with his biblical namesake. A document preserved in his own handwriting indicates that he considered his marriage to his wife Zipporah, daughter of R. Finzi of Mantua, to signify the union between the biblical Moses and Zipporah. See Dan and Hansel, "Luzzatto," 282; Carlebach, "Redemption and Persecution," 12. For a detailed analysis of Luzzatto's kabbalistic (and redemptive) interpretation of his marriage, see Wolfson, "*Tiqqun Ha-Shekhinah*," 302–303, 318–23.

43. See Garb, *Kabbalist in the Heart of the Storm*, 291–92. Concerning Luzzatto's use of the book of Psalms, Garb refers to an unpublished seminar paper by Avishai Bar-Asher (292n48).

44. Such as, for example, the sixteenth-century kabbalist Moses Cordovero (1522–1570) in his kabbalistic musar treatise *Tomer Devorah*. See Patrick B. Koch, "Approaching the Divine by *Imitatio Dei*: *Tzelem* and *Demut* in R. Moshe Cordovero's *Tomer Devorah*," in *Visualizing Jews through the Ages: Literary and Material Representations of Jewishness and Judaism*, ed. Hannah Ewence and Helen Spurling (New York: Routledge, 2015), 48–61; Koch, *Human Self-perfection*, 78–103.

45. For a good overview of the different readings of *Mesillat Yesharim*, see Garb, *Kabbalist in the Heart of the Storm*, 271–81.

46. Luzzatto, *Complete Mesillat Yesharim*, 177 (SV), 426 (SP).

47. It has been argued that the first part of *Mesillat Yesharim* constitutes a nomian discourse suitable for a mainstream readership, whereas the second half promotes what Elliot Wolfson has described in a different context as "hypernomian" conduct—namely, behavior that strives for a law beyond law. See, for example, Garb, *Kabbalist in the Heart of the Storm*, 297 (and 297n64); 300–301. On hypernomianism, see Elliot R. Wolfson, *Venturing Beyond: Law and Morality in Kabbalistic Mysticism* (Oxford: Oxford University Press, 2006); and more recently, Wolfson, "Heeding the Law beyond the Law: Transgendering Alterity and the Hypernomian Perimeter of the Ethical," *European Journal of Jewish Studies* 14, no. 2 (2020): 215–63.

48. Garb, *Kabbalist in the Heart of the Storm*, 277–78 (for a summary of three kabbalistic readings of *Mesillat Yesharim*, see 277–81).

49. On musar as "moral psychology," see Alan Mittleman, *A Short History of Jewish Ethics: Conduct and Character in the Context of Covenant* (Chichester, UK: Wiley-Blackwell, 2012), 7.

50. Luzzatto, *Complete Mesillat Yesharim*, 520 (SP).

Chapter 18

Moses Mendelssohn

ELIAS SACKS

> The universal laws of nature have this makeup: Revere the Creator! Love virtue, flee vice! Control your passions, submit your desires to reason!
>
> —Moses Mendelssohn, "On Evidence in Metaphysical Sciences"

These words appear in Moses Mendelssohn's "On Evidence in Metaphysical Sciences," a 1763 German essay that famously edged out a submission by Immanuel Kant for first place in a contest held by the Prussian Royal Academy of Sciences.[1] Often described as the founder of modern Jewish thought and a leading figure in the German Enlightenment, Mendelssohn (1729–1786) was born in rural Prussia and moved to Berlin at the age of fourteen, eventually becoming a partner in a silk enterprise while pursuing a wide range of literary and communal activities. After acquiring various languages, he began to write in German on metaphysics and aesthetics, including an acclaimed treatise on immortality that earned him the sobriquet "the German Socrates." He also published works on Judaism in both German and Hebrew, ranging from biblical commentaries to the first modern Hebrew journal to writings on topics such as Jewish law.

His fame led him to become involved in political affairs, including conflicts between Jewish communities and non-Jewish authorities and emerging debates regarding Jewish civic rights.[2]

My essay takes up the themes Mendelssohn invokes in his remarks from "On Evidence." More specifically, I will show that a concern with the cultivation of virtue plays a central role in his thought, shaping his understanding both of the Jewish tradition and of the human condition.

Anthropology and Virtue

Mendelssohn's account of virtue is rooted in his philosophical anthropology, which ascribes to the human being the "vocation" of pursuing "perfection" or "flourishing"—a condition, ultimately unattainable, in which an individual has properly cultivated and rendered harmonious the faculties of her soul and body. On this view, an action is good insofar as it promotes the pursuit of perfection and evil insofar as it impedes this task. For example, while economic pursuits can be good if treated as opportunities to refine our faculties, such pursuits become evil if they distract us from properly developing our bodies and intellects.[3]

This position leads Mendelssohn to explore the mechanisms behind good acts. Holding that we assess the goodness of actions through rational reflection by the faculty of cognition or comprehension, he writes in "On Evidence" that it is vital for this reflection to produce "effective and lively knowledge which passes over into the capacity to desire and incites . . . practical decisions." In particular, he continues, because "human beings possess, in addition to reason, sense and imagination, inclinations and passions," it is crucial that reason "either subdue the lower powers of the soul, or also include them to their advantage."[4] The idea here is that we will be more likely to perform acts deemed good if we reflect on moral questions in ways capable of shaping our desires, and that this will occur if our reflection counteracts opposing impulses that also influence those cravings. For example, while we might act in ways cognition deems evil if our senses produce powerful inclinations for such actions and determine the content of our desires, we will act in ways cognition deems good if we engage in reflection that somehow overcomes those inclinations and produces yearnings for the good.

Virtue is one way in which this effective knowledge emerges. Stating in "On Evidence" that "virtue is a proficiency [*Fertigkeit*] in performing good actions,"[5] Mendelssohn continues:

> Ethics puts into our hands the means of maintaining the harmony of the lower powers of the soul with reason. . . . [For example,] there is *practice*. The more we reflect on certain reasons and the more we derive motives for our action from them, the livelier the impression is which they leave on the mind, and the easier it is for them to include the lower parts of the soul as well. If this practice is continued long enough for the action to become easy for us, we then say that we have acquired a proficiency in doing something. Habit and practice rule despotically in our hearts, and by their help one can subdue the most obstinate inclinations and bring the most stubborn passions under the yoke of reason; or, rather, by their help one can produce inclinations and passions that have the same ultimate purpose as the precepts of reason.[6]

Having defined virtue as a proficiency, Mendelssohn frames this as a condition in which "action" becomes "easy" because we have "practice . . . reflect[ing]" and thereby "produce inclinations and passions that have the same ultimate purpose as the precepts of reason." On this model, we acquire a virtue when, through recurring reflection on moral topics, our rational judgments become so ingrained that they generate "inclinations" for behavior deemed good that counteract opposing drives, determining the substance of our desires and making it "easy" to act in morally praiseworthy ways. Put more simply, a virtue is a condition in which our rational judgments have become so deeply entrenched that they shape our desires and dispose us to pursue the good.

Mendelssohn advances similar claims elsewhere. An earlier German essay calls on each individual to "ponder . . . inferences of practical philosophy frequently" and "continue practicing until . . . he is no longer conscious of his rules, in other words, until his principles have turned into inclinations and his virtue appears to be more natural instinct than reason."[7] His Hebrew commentary on the Pentateuch—the *Bi'ur* or "Elucidation"—uses the term "dispositions" (*tkhunot*):[8]

> The connection between the faculties of comprehension and desire produces the soul's character traits, which are dispositions to do evil or good, toward oneself or others. They all emerge in accordance with an individual's comprehension and capacity for distinguishing between good and evil, as well as in accordance with the faculty of desire that leads him to do good and refrain from evil. Part of the perfection of the rational being is the presence within him of a harmonious relation and proportion between the faculty of desire and the faculty of comprehension, producing the virtues. For the more powerfully the faculty of comprehension recognizes the good and the evil, the more desire grows, and love for the good and hatred for the evil gain strength as the rational being is stirred to cleave to the good.[9]

Echoing his German works' focus on the alignment of desire and reason, Mendelssohn's Hebrew commentary casts virtues as "character traits" emerging when cognition acts so "powerfully" that its judgments determine our yearnings and leave us "stirred to cleave to the good." One dimension of Mendelssohn's anthropology, then, is an account of virtue as a proficiency or disposition—a character trait in which our rational judgments have become so deeply ingrained that they are capable of shaping desires and dispose us to act in ways that promote perfection.[10]

Identification or Cultivation?

Although Mendelssohn occasionally invokes specific virtues, he devotes less attention to the details of these traits than to the processes by which they are cultivated. For instance, while "On Evidence" considers the nature of justice and describes it as a virtue, this discussion appears not in the account of ethics cited above, but rather in a passage on philosophical language—a passage that shows how a careful analysis of terms used in a Platonic definition of justice yields a Leibnizian interpretation of this trait.[11] By contrast, the account of ethics discussed earlier offers its treatment of how virtues are cultivated—of how "practice" reflecting on moral topics yields new "inclinations"—without discussing the details of specific traits.[12]

Another example appears in Mendelssohn's Hebrew commentary on Maimonides's *Treatise on Logic*. One of the Maimonidean selections that Mendelssohn discusses alludes both to virtues that yield "actions" and to "intellectual virtues" involving "the conception of intelligibles." This taxonomy would seem to provide an opportunity to discuss specific instances of each category, but, rather than do so, Mendelssohn's comments stress the need for diligence when cultivating these traits, noting that "one must learn to train oneself to choose good without sloth or weakness, and to despise evil with all one's heart," and that we should attend to "the preparation that takes place in the soul and will, and the persistence and diligence given to that preparation to the point that the disposition endures."[13] Mendelssohn thus seems to treat the cultivation of virtues as a more pressing issue than their identification. Building on the idea that virtues involve rational judgments becoming so deeply ingrained that they shape desires and yield actions, he focuses less on the specific character traits that fall within this category, and more on the means by which reason's judgments achieve this level of practical efficacy.

Practice, God, and Aesthetics

As we have seen, on Mendelssohn's view, we acquire virtues through "practice"—through reflecting so frequently on ethics that our judgments generate inclinations for behavior deemed good, influencing our desires and making moral action "easy." Beyond emphasizing the frequency of moral reflection, however, he also ascribes importance to the content of our rational deliberation, offering this example of the "inferences of practical philosophy" that an individual should "ponder . . . frequently": "One should learn to consider every human action in connection with the ever-present lawgiver of nature and in relation to eternity. One should get used to having these considerations before one's eyes in every act that one performs. If one does this, a wholesome enthusiasm for virtue will be awakened in us, and each reason motivating us to be virtuous will attain an ethical majesty through which its influence and its effectiveness on the will is strengthened."[14] The background is Mendelssohn's view that God wishes for us to act in morally praiseworthy ways, since "the wisest and most benevolent being" cannot "have any other intention than the perfection of creatures": if actions are good insofar as they promote the pursuit of perfection, then God will wish for us to perform such deeds, since an omniscient and benevolent deity will recognize, and wish for us to pursue, perfection as our proper vocation.[15]

Mendelssohn's point in the passage quoted above is to link frequent reflection on this type of deity to the cultivation of virtue, arguing that if we "consider every human action in connection with the ever-present lawgiver of nature" and have "these considerations before [our] eyes in every act," the result will be a passionate orientation toward or "wholesome enthusiasm for virtue." If we create recurring opportunities to reflect on God as we act, we will recognize that this deity wishes for us to behave in morally praiseworthy ways, and we will be motivated to ask, again and again, whether our deeds meet this standard—to engage in the recurring ethical reflection that leaves our judgments so deeply ingrained that they pave the way for moral behavior. Frequent reflection on a deity who endorses the good implants virtuous dispositions *for* the good.

Mendelssohn also stresses "the utility of fine arts and sciences for ethics": "Rational grounds convince the intellect of the splendidness of virtue, and the fine arts wrest the imagination's approval. . . . One sees, then, what is involved if the principles of practical ethics are to have the proper effect on what we do . . . and if they are to bring about an enduring and constant readiness for virtue. They must be enlivened by *examples,* supported by the force of *pleasant sentiment,* kept constantly effective by *practice,* and finally transformed into a *proficiency.*"[16] Taking the "pleasant sentiment" generated by poetry, music, and other aesthetic forms to exercise a powerful influence on nonrational faculties such as the imagination, Mendelssohn argues that aesthetically moving presentations of moral content can orient those faculties toward virtue, generating impulses for the good that shape desires and deeds. For example, rather than simply presenting an abstract philosophical argument for the importance of justice, poems and songs might offer portrayals of this trait that are so aesthetically pleasing that they capture our imagination and inspire desires to act in a similar manner, aligning our yearnings with reason and producing virtuous dispositions. For Mendelssohn, then, virtue emerges not only from recurring rational reflection on ethics or on a deity who endorses the good, but also from encounters with stirring presentations of moral content in aesthetic media such as poetry and music.

Although we will see that Mendelssohn discovers these paths to virtue in the Jewish tradition, it is notable that he does not frame these modes of cultivation as being the exclusive province of any one religion. He associates virtue not with the doctrinal claims of any specific tradition, but with rational reflection on various topics and the "fine arts" in general.[17] Given this emphasis on the universal accessibility of virtue, then, it should not be surprising that Mendelssohn often cites non-Jewish individuals as exemplars of these traits. For instance, one of his German writings on tolerance and Judaism suggests that "a Confucius or a Solon" might serve as an example of an individual who "guides people to virtue in this life."[18] Similarly, his treatise on immortality—a rewriting of Plato's *Phaedo*—includes a preface on "the life and character of Socrates" that repeatedly casts the Greek philosopher as a teacher and model of virtue.[19]

Judaism and Virtue

Mendelssohn's approach to the cultivation of virtue also shapes his conception of Judaism, beginning with his account of halakhah or Jewish law.[20] One of his best-known claims, appearing across his writings, is that this legal system generates frequent reflection on eternal truths accessible through reason, such as God's existence and divine providence. On this view, insofar as Jewish law requires the performance of actions in diverse spheres of life (from diet to worship to dress), and insofar as these actions are understood as in some sense connected to God, the enactment of halakhically required practices can direct attention to their divine source, creating recurring opportunities to reflect on this deity's existence and attributes.[21]

Mendelssohn takes up the ethical implications of this view in the conclusion of the *Bi'ur* on Exodus, which discusses the frequent reflection on God generated by halakhic norms:[22] "By means of this, the person will always set it upon his heart to distinguish between the good and the evil, between the beneficial and the harmful, and he will not go whoring after the arrogance of his whoring heart and pile gluttony upon thirst."[23] Mendelssohn elsewhere uses the language of "distinguishing between the good and the evil" for the rational assessment of actions' goodness;[24] his image of "going whoring after the arrogance of [a] whoring heart and piling gluttony upon thirst" draws on Deuteronomy 29:18, which he reads as a reference to an individual who desires evil actions—who "augments natural desires with wanton ones," is characterized by "wickedness of the inclination," and engages in "sin."[25] When Mendelssohn discusses the halakhically animated contemplation of God in these terms, then, he is highlighting the moral significance of halakhic observance. If an individual is motivated by halakhah to reflect on a God who desires the good, then this individual "will always . . . distinguish between the good and the evil" and avoid "the arrogance of [a] whoring heart," assessing the fit between her deeds and God's wishes with a frequency that protects her from becoming the sort of person who craves evil—with a frequency that leaves her judgments so deeply ingrained that they combat "wickedness of the inclination," shape her "desires," and orient her away from "sin." And while Mendelssohn does not explicitly use the term "virtue" here, the force of his argument is clear. If (according to the *Bi'ur*) halakhah generates recurring reflection on God and ethics that aligns yearnings with reason, and if (according to his other writings) this harmonious relation between cognition and desire grounds virtuous dispositions, then Jewish law serves as a means of inculcating these character traits. Halakhah fosters precisely those cognitive processes that Mendelssohn links to the cultivation of virtue.

The *Bi'ur* on Exodus 15 advances a similar claim about biblical aesthetics, casting the poetry of the Hebrew Bible as a source of "virtues and excellent dispositions":[26] "[Such poetry involves] excellence that arises from arranging content and statements in a beautiful way intended for the end desired in [poetry]—namely, that the words enter not only the listener's ear, but also his heart. They should remain engraved on the tablets [of his heart] . . . firmly establishing within him the virtues and excellent dispositions like goads and nails that have been planted, like a stake that will not be dislodged."[27] On one level, this is an argument about pleasure. Mendelssohn proceeds to note that biblical poetry lends itself to musical recitation,[28] and we have seen that he takes the pleasant sentiment arising from fine arts and sciences to influence nonrational faculties and foster virtue.

On another level, though, this is a claim about religious and ethical reflection:

> [The poet's] art and purpose was to subdue the faculties of the soul, rule over its character traits, and transform its dispositions. . . . So that the poem's words might serve this end, our ancestors would cut every utterance into parts and divide each part into short clauses nearly equal in their quantity. Therefore, you will not find in any one of these clauses more than four or fewer than two words. . . . When a short clause contains content and meaning that enter the heart, this content easily becomes orally preserved, memorized, and enduringly familiar.[29]

For Mendelssohn, biblical poetry is organized not into rhyming couplets or lines with fixed numbers of long or short syllables, but into units of short, parallel clauses. For example, Exodus 15:11 contains two units consisting of parallel clauses of four and two words, respectively:

Unit A:

mi	*khamokhah*	*ba'elim*	*adonay*
Who	is-like-you	among-the-powers	O-Eternal?
mi	*kamokhah*	*nedar*	*bakodesh*
Who	is-like-you	glorified	in-holiness?

Unit B:

nora	*thilot*
Formidable	in-praise,
oseh	*fele*
doer	of-wonders![30]

Mendelssohn advances two claims about this parallelism.

He argues, first, that biblical poetry's structure renders its "content . . . memorized" and "enduringly familiar." His claim is that the Bible's short, parallel clauses can easily become lodged in our memories, and that these words and their content might therefore become "enduringly familiar"—that we may find ourselves reflecting, again and again, on biblical poems and their claims. With Exodus 15:11, for instance, short phrases such as "formidable in-praise" and "doer of-wonders" will naturally stick in our minds, and we may thus find ourselves thinking, over and over, about the deity such words describe. Moreover, Mendelssohn continues, this structure allows biblical poems to "transform . . . dispositions" and "establish . . . virtues." If biblical poetry's parallelism promotes frequent reflection on God, and if this religious contemplation aligns desire with reason to produce virtuous dispositions, then biblical poetry—like Jewish law—serves to cultivate these character traits. Embedding descriptions of God in the minds of its audience through the use of short, parallel clauses, biblical poetry can lead individuals to reflect so frequently on the deity that they acquire inclinations for the good.[31]

This focus on the cultivation of virtue extends beyond Mendelssohn's account of biblical poetry to his treatment of biblical narrative. The *Bi'ur*'s overview of virtue—its explanation of how the "connection" between cognition and desire yields "dispositions to do . . . good"—appears in a gloss on Genesis 2:9, focused on the tree of knowledge of good and evil in the Garden of Eden. The *Bi'ur* begins with two medieval interpretations of what happened when the first humans ate from this tree: Naḥmanides's claim that this incident endowed humans with the capacity for choice, paving the way for myriad sins; and Maimonides's claim that this incident diverted the first humans from metaphysical contemplation, replacing a situation in which they were exclusively focused on rational truths with one in which they were also concerned with conventions such as moral custom.[32]

Mendelssohn offers an alternate view, rooted in his account of virtue: "God formed Adam upright on the earth and established a harmonious relation and proper proportion between his cognition and his desire. Had Adam remained in this upright disposition, he would not have deviated at all from the path of the good through the strengthening of the faculty of craving, except through limited comprehension—that is, when thinking that the good is evil and that the evil is good, which would occur only rarely."[33] Having described virtues as dispositions arising from the alignment of reason and desire, Mendelssohn now suggests that Adam[34] was created with precisely "this upright disposition" and "harmonious relation": he naturally engaged in rational reflection capable of shaping his yearnings, and thus naturally possessed the virtuous character traits emerging from this "harmonious relation." Adam's reason might occasionally misidentify evil acts as good, but he would always be disposed to choose whichever deeds his cognition deemed praiseworthy.

This changed, however, when he ate from the tree:

> It belonged to the nature of the tree of knowledge to strengthen and add vigor to the faculty of desire. . . . With regard to man . . . this was a great evil, since compared to his limited comprehension, his faculty of desire gained strength beyond the proper proportion and relation. From this issue all the vices. . . . A person will sink and drown in the mire of the imaginary good, turning to what is beautiful and pleasant to the senses or the imagination.[35]

On Mendelssohn's' reading, the forbidden tree added "vigor to the faculty of desire," disrupting "the proper . . . relation" between cognition and desire by elevating "what is . . . pleasant to the senses or the imagination." Rather than create free will or distract from metaphysics, the tree strengthened the faculty of desire in the sense of allowing it to be shaped more vigorously by inclinations rooted in nonrational sources, with the result that Adam was no longer uniformly disposed to act in accordance with his cognition: endowed with a faculty of desire increasingly susceptible to influence by sources such as the senses, Adam found himself in a condition where his rational judgments might be unable to overcome competing impulses and incline him toward the good. The tree thus replaced a situation in which an "upright disposition" was natural with a situation in which "vices" were possible—with a situation in which cognition's "proper . . . relation" to desire might be absent, and in which virtue therefore could no longer be assumed but instead would have to be cultivated.

The Human Condition

I began this essay by citing Mendelssohn's call to "love virtue" and "submit . . . desires to reason." We have now seen that these themes are central to his thought. Defining virtues as character traits in which reason's judgments have become so deeply ingrained that they shape the content of our desires and dispose us to pursue the good, Mendelssohn's German and Hebrew writings repeatedly reflect on the cultivation of these dispositions, raising this issue when exploring topics ranging from Jewish law to biblical poetry to the Garden of Eden.

Yet this is not all. Before outlining his interpretation of the tree of knowledge, Mendelssohn explains the hermeneutic that animates his reading:

> The entire account of creation, as well as all that scripture recounts regarding what happened to Adam, Eve, Cain, and Abel, is all true and reliable. . . . In addition, however, these stories contain an allusion to and model for what will happen to the entire human species in general. What happened to Adam and his children in particular is what happens to the entire species in general. For this reason, scripture describes at length the details of their [lives], on the basis of which a wise individual will understand all that happens to human beings, from the time they were created to the end of all the generations.[36]

More than an account of Eden, Mendelssohn sees the narrative he is discussing as a "model for what will happen to the entire human species . . . from the time they were created to the end of all the generations." When he claims that Adam found himself in a condition where virtue could not be assumed but instead would have to be cultivated, then, Mendelssohn is making a point not only about a primeval garden, but also about an enduring feature of human existence. In contrast to those among his eighteenth-century contemporaries who take history to involve progress toward moral perfection,[37] he insists that an imbalance between reason and desire will remain an ever-present possibility, and that individuals will therefore always be faced with the task of pursuing this balance and orienting themselves toward the good. For Mendelssohn, we might say, part of what it means to be human is to be the sort of creature who must strive to acquire virtuous dispositions. A concern with the cultivation of virtue shapes his understanding not only of the Jewish tradition, but also of the human condition.

Notes

1. Moses Mendelssohn, "On Evidence in Metaphysical Sciences," in *Philosophical Writings*, ed. and trans. Daniel Dahlstrom (Cambridge: Cambridge

University Press, 1997), 301; the German is *Gesammelte Schriften Jubiläumsausgabe*, ed. Fritz Bamberger et al., 24 vols. (Stuttgart-Bad Canstatt: Frommann, 1971–) (hereafter, *JubA*), 2:323.

2. See Alexander Altmann, *Moses Mendelssohn: A Biographical Study* (Tuscaloosa: University of Alabama Press, 1973).

3. See *JubA* 6.1:19–65, 143–48, 152; 2:166; 13:65–66; 15.2:23, 26, et al. On Mendelssohn's anthropology more generally, see Anne Pollok, *Facetten des Menschen: Zur Anthropologie Moses Mendelssohns* (Hamburg: Meiner, 2010).

4. Mendelssohn, "On Evidence," 304–305; *JubA* 2:326.

5. Mendelssohn, "On Evidence," 299; *JubA* 2:320. "Virtue" translates the German *Tugend* throughout my article.

6. Mendelssohn, "On Evidence," 305; *JubA* 2:327.

7. Mendelssohn, "Rhapsody or additions to the Letters on sentiments," in *Philosophical Writings*, 165–66; the German is *JubA* 1:421–22.

8. This commentary is part of a broader work that also includes a German translation of the Pentateuch. Mendelssohn composes the entire translation, the Exodus commentary, and sections of the other commentaries, including the discussions of Genesis 2 and Deuteronomy 29 below.

9. *Bi'ur* on Genesis 2:9 (*JubA* 15.2:23), following my translation in *Moses Mendelssohn: Writings on Judaism, Christianity, and the Bible*, ed. Michah Gottlieb (Waltham, MA: Brandeis University Press, 2011) (hereafter, *WJCB*), 209. "Virtues" translates the Hebrew *midot nikhbadot* (literally, "noble character traits"), linked in Mendelssohn's earlier writings (*JubA* 14:116, 118) to a phrase—*midot me'ulot* (literally, "excellent character traits")—that he identifies as the Hebrew for the German *Tugend*. The *Bi'ur* on Genesis 2 also contrasts *midot nikhbadot* with *midot pḥutot* (literally, "inferior character traits"), equated by Mendelssohn (*JubA* 14:118) with the German *Laster* (vices).

10. On Mendelssohn's sources, see Paul Guyer, "Kantian Perfectionism," in *The Virtues of Freedom* (Oxford: Oxford University Press, 2016), 77–79; Ned Curthoys, "Moses Mendelssohn and the Character of Virtue," in *Representing Humanity in the Age of Enlightenment*, ed. Alexander Cook et al. (London: Routledge, 2016), 65–78; Melissa Merritt, "Mendelssohn and Kant on Virtue as a Skill," in *The Routledge Handbook of Philosophy of Skill and Expertise*, ed. Ellen Fridland and Carlotta Pavese (London: Routledge, 2020), 88–99.

11. Mendelssohn, "On Evidence," 273–74; *JubA* 2:291–92.

12. Mendelssohn does allude back to his discussion of justice: "On Evidence," 300; *JubA* 2:321.

13. *Bi'ur Milot Hahigayon* (*JubA* 14:115–16), following *Moses Mendelssohn's Hebrew Writings*, ed. Edward Breuer and David Sorkin, trans. Breuer (New Haven, CT: Yale University Press, 2018), 101–102.

14. Mendelssohn, "Rhapsody," 165; *JubA* 1:421.

15. Mendelssohn, "On Evidence," 298; *JubA* 2:318.

16. Mendelssohn, "On Evidence," 305–306; *JubA* 2:327–28.

17. Reflection on God, however, would seem to be restricted to theists.

18. Mendelssohn, "Open Letter to Lavater," in *WJCB* 10–11; *JubA* 7:12.

19. See, for example, *Phädon*, in *JubA* 3.1:13, 15–17, 23, 28.

20. This reading draws on my "Law, Ethics, and the Needs of History: Mendelssohn, Krochmal, and Moral Philosophy," *Journal of Religious Ethics* 44, no. 2 (2016): 355–62. I look forward to Sarah Zager's treatment in "'I Will Sing of Love and Justice': Jewish Responses to the Theological Roots of Contemporary Virtue Ethics" (PhD diss., Yale University, forthcoming).

21. Mendelssohn also posits additional mechanisms, which lie beyond this article.

22. See my "Law, Ethics, and the Needs of History." Mendelssohn also links this reflection to the biblical tabernacle.

23. *Bi'ur* on conclusion of Exodus (*JubA* 16:407; translation mine). The "this" in "by means of this" refers to ensuring that "all . . . deeds are for the sake of heaven," presented by Mendelssohn as a situation in which individuals "devote all their deeds and hearts' thoughts to the Height"—in which individuals repeatedly contemplate God.

24. *Bi'ur* on Genesis 2:9 (*JubA* 15.2:23), following *WJCB* 208.

25. *Bi'ur* on Deuteronomy 29:18 (*JubA* 18:496; translation mine, following Mendelssohn's German rendering).

26. This reading draws on my "Poetry, Music, and the Limits of Harmony: Mendelssohn's Aesthetic Critique of Christianity," in *Sara Levy's World*, ed. Nancy Sinkoff and Rebecca Cypess (Rochester, NY: University of Rochester Press, 2018), 131–36. See also Gottlieb, "Aesthetics and the Infinite: Moses Mendelssohn on the Poetics of Biblical Prophecy," in *New Directions in Jewish Philosophy*, ed. Aaron Hughes and Elliot Wolfson (Bloomington: Indiana University Press, 2010), 326–53; Grit Schorch, *Moses Mendelssohns Sprachpolitik* (Berlin: de Gruyter, 2012), 96–140.

27. *Bi'ur* on Exodus 15 (*JubA* 16:126), following *WJCB* 212–13; on the Hebrew (*midot nikhbadot*) rendered as "virtues," see note 9.

28. *Bi'ur* on Exodus 15 (*JubA* 16:126), following *WJCB* 213–14.

29. *Bi'ur* on Exodus 15 (*JubA* 16:126), following *WJCB* 213–14.

30. I follow Mendelssohn's German translation (*JubA* 16:141).

31. Mendelssohn ascribes a similar role to the accents governing the Bible's liturgical chanting: see my "Poetry, Music, and the Limits of Harmony."

32. *Bi'ur* on Genesis 2:9 (*JubA* 15.2:22–23).

33. *Bi'ur* on Genesis 2:9 (*JubA* 15.2:23), following *WJCB* 210.

34. Mendelssohn discusses Eve in similar terms.

35. *Bi'ur* on Genesis 2:9 (*JubA* 15.2:24), following *WJCB* 211.

36. *Bi'ur* on Genesis 2:9 (*JubA* 15.2:23), following *WJCB* 208.

37. See, for example, Mendelssohn's rejection of moral progress in *Jerusalem* (*WJCB* 85–87; *JubA* 8:161–64).

Chapter 19

Menaḥem Mendel Lefin

HARRIS BOR

Transitional characters are always fascinating. Rabbi Menaḥem Mendel Lefin (1749–1826) was one such character. Sandwiched between the still-medieval Judaism of his native Eastern Europe and the Berlin Haskalah (Jewish Enlightenment), he was not fully at home in either but attempted to bridge the gap.

Lefin was born in Satanów, Podolia, a region in Poland (currently Ukraine). He had a traditional Jewish religious upbringing but, like many of his contemporaries, was drawn to Berlin, the heartland of the nascent Haskalah. There, he formed a friendship with Moses Mendelssohn (1729–1806), who became the father of the movement (see chapter 18 in this volume). Unlike other Eastern European Jews who made the journey to Berlin in search of inspiration, Lefin returned to the East aiming to develop a Haskalah that sought to encourage educational reform through a blend of practical reason with strict adherence to tradition.

Lefin's acknowledged influences include Moses Maimonides (1138–1204), the US founding father Benjamin Franklin (1706–1790) and the philosophers Immanuel Kant (1724–1804) and Adrien Helvétius (1715–1771). His writings also display a debt to other Enlightenment thinkers, such as the English philosopher John Locke (1632–1704), and the physician David Hartley (1705–1757).[1]

Lefin was fortunate to have the financial backing of Prince Adam Kazimierz Czartoryski (1734–1823), a landowner and major figure of the Polish Enlightenment. With his patronage secured, Lefin had time to write books and pamphlets and to influence discussion at senior levels on Jewish politics. His works include *Epistles of Wisdom* (*Moda le-Binah*) dealing with natural science (1789), *Healing of the People* (*Refu'at ha-Am*) (1794), which encouraged the study of science, *Moral Accounting* (*Ḥeshbon ha-Nefesh*) (1808), an ethical work, a translation of parts of Maimonides's *Guide of the Perplexed* into Mishnaic Hebrew (1829), and didactic works in German and Yiddish. The focus of this chapter will be his *Ḥeshbon ha-Nefesh,* as this work best encapsulates the place of virtue in his thinking.[2] It also profoundly influenced Rabbi Israel Salanter (1810–1883), the founder of the Musar movement (see chapter 23) as well as many of Salanter's students.[3]

The Role of Virtue

Virtue is central to Lefin's outlook, as it was to the Enlightenment more generally. In recent years, the image of the Enlightenment has shifted. No longer is it seen as a singular event, secular and fanatical about reason and progress, but as a series of developments arising out of an engagement with religion that spread across Western and Central Europe "in a sequence of cross-confessional and cross-national influence and filiation."[4] Some of these Enlightenments were antithetical toward religion; others embraced it.

Ideas associated with the Religious Enlightenment include tolerance, moderation, reasonableness, a focus on practical works over metaphysics, and an incorporation of modern scientific learning into the religious worldview.[5] Those associated with Mendelssohn's circle had similar interests to many Christian Enlighteners, but additionally aimed at reconnecting Judaism to its textual heritage and the wider culture.[6]

Ḥeshbon ha-Nefesh is not a philosophical text but a manual aimed at achieving religious virtue. It is primarily targeted at men, not just in their role as fathers but as husbands and friends too. Lefin advises fathers to monitor the moral progress of their sons from ages thirteen to fifteen until they are ready to progress unaided.[7] He also counseled men to work on virtue with their wives or to find a male study partner for the same purpose.[8]

Lefin's Method

The method that Lefin adopts is not his own but taken from the second part of the memoirs of Benjamin Franklin, which was possibly inspired by Cotton Mather's *Bonifacus: An Essay upon the Good* (1710). Franklin was also influenced by Locke. Despite his strict Calvinist upbringing, Franklin was for a time an ardent proponent of Deism, which rejected the idea of revelation and sought to know God from reason and nature. Franklin, however, came to see a personal God as essential to the all-important task of cultivating virtue, although it is not clear whether he viewed God as a supernatural interventionist deity or a useful fiction.[9]

Lefin introduces Franklin's method after bemoaning the absence of personal accounts from the sages detailing their path to virtue.[10] Following Franklin, Lefin recommends focusing on thirteen character-traits. Each week, one focuses on one of these traits to a greater degree than the other twelve. Thus, over a period of thirteen weeks all the traits will have been covered, and over the period of fifty-two weeks, an individual will have focused on each trait four times. The individual is encouraged to formulate short maxims to encapsulate each trait and to keep a notebook to record the progress made using weekly grid charts, detailing the traits in the columns and the days of the week along the rows.

Lefin's book contains a handful of chapters introducing the method. The remaining chapters deal with the thirteen traits (i.e., equanimity, patience, order, decisiveness, cleanliness, humility, righteousness, frugality, diligence, silence, calmness, truth, and separation). These are the same traits promoted by Franklin, but Lefin is keen to encourage readers to replace his list of virtues with others more suited to their specific needs.[11] Lefin's work also differs from Franklin's by introducing references to the Talmud and other rabbinic literature to inspire his readers. For example, falsehood is bad not only because it undermines trust and brings shame on the perpetrator but also because it is hateful to God, who is described as the "God of truth."

Lefin also reminds the reader of the insults directed at false witnesses in the Talmud.[12]

Views of the Self

Lefin's program is underpinned by a new understanding of child development. In the eighteenth century, it was believed that young children had only limited moral capabilities, but, as they mature, they develop a rational comprehension of their moral duties. This notion led to more specialized approaches to education. In Germany, Philanthropinism, an educational movement founded by Johann Bernhard Basedow (1723–1790), drew on Locke's *Some Thoughts Concerning Education* (1693) and the writings of Jean-Jacques Rousseau (1712–1778). There are strong parallels between Franklin's and Basedow's educational programs and the schools they inspired. Philanthropinism focused on all aspects of the person: the sciences, the arts, virtue, well-being, and development of rationality. Its aims included fostering religious tolerance and preparing students for real life. Basedow sought to generate enthusiasm and discouraged rote learning. Children needed to be inspired toward education and virtue rather than pressurized into obedience.[13]

In this period, the human psyche was still associated with the immaterial, immortal soul of religious tradition, but was now also seen as an object of scientific enquiry and aligned to the science of medicine.[14] An understanding of its workings was viewed as a prerequisite to the attainment of virtue. As Joachim Heinrich Campe (1746–1818), an educator associated with the Philanthropine, wrote, just as natural history must be studied before physics, so "psychological lessons should introduce morality and religion."[15] Lefin held a similar view.

Lefin's psychology is based on sensationalism, the idea popularized by Locke that the mind is formed by impressions from external objects and our reflection on them.[16] For Locke, the mind has no innate ideas. It is a *tabula rasa,* a clean slate, on which external objects imprint themselves. As Locke put it: "These two I say, external material things, as objects of sensation, and the operations of our minds within, reflection, are to be the only originals from whence all our ideas take their beginnings."[17]

For Locke, an understanding of the senses can lead to a better understanding of religious duty, but not to perfect knowledge, which is "beyond the comprehension of any finite being."[18] He also thought reason to be a weak motivator. There is a place for unquestioning belief, especially for the masses who require "plain commands," obedience, and practice.[19]

Locke's ideas, as mediated by Enlightenment pedagogues, were useful to the early proponents of the Jewish Enlightenment (*maskilim*), like Lefin, who used them to adapt approaches within traditional Jewish ethical literature (*musar*) to the goals of the Haskalah. Fear of punishment was replaced with awe at God's majesty, often associated with appreciating the divine in nature. Readers were encouraged to understand their inner workings and develop positive habits. The *yetzer ha-ra* (evil inclination) became passions to be tamed or directed. The ultimate goal of these books was to shape souls who would be respected, virtuous, and religiously committed.[20] A focus on practical virtue allowed these moderate Maskilim to demote philosophical speculation from its position as an ideal, and to protect faith.[21]

In *Ḥeshbon ha-Nefesh*, Lefin describes the psyche as comprising two opposing units. One he terms the intellectual soul (*nefesh sikhlit*), and one he terms the animal soul (*nefesh beheimit*). The animal soul is not identical with the traditional evil inclination but is more neutrally described as a passive entity. Lefin likens the animal soul to standing reeds that have no active force, but that are bent by the power of the wind.[22] In a further, more developed analogy, the animal soul is likened to a giant elephant that needs to be goaded and cajoled into human service. Without being directed, the animal soul moves sluggishly: "She is engrossed in a profound sleep from which she is unable to move herself." What moves her are external forces alone. These are associated with the evil inclination whose onslaught she cannot withstand unless a stronger force is applied. The evil inclination is thus externalized and not evil at all. As for the animal soul, this can only see that which "is near and at hand," is drawn to immediate gratification, and has no patience. It cannot be motivated by command, by argument or by considering long term outcomes.

Virtue comes from learning to harness and manipulate this animal power. Lefin uses this discussion to interest his reader in the natural world. Birds can be taught to hunt, and the ox can be put under the yoke and made to plough. The mighty elephant itself is "lured into traps by the hundreds and thousands." Lefin does not view this as an abuse as we might do today, but as a display of our "God given ability" to "control" the elephant, "to train it to exact his master's commands, to accept the yoke which he places upon it and to serve man with all its strength."[23] To "profit" from animals in this way, one must know how to train them. One needs to become an expert in "subterfuge" and to understand their psychology, and so it is with the animal soul.[24]

In contrast to the animal soul, the intellectual soul is an active force that makes use of categories of thinking, which are traditionally described as wisdom, discernment, and understanding (*ḥokhmah, binah,* and *da'at*).[25] The intellectual soul is not tempted by immediate gratification but can calculate the long term consequences of action: "It enables man to forgo immediate gratification so as to be able to receive something more valuable in the future."[26] The intellectual soul uses reason to find purpose, and can evaluate truth claims about the past, and detect falsehood: "One who has understanding . . . can recognize what really transpired in the past by examining the claims of parties to proceedings as well as the lies they tell now."[27] The intellectual soul can also connect ideas and makes associations that go beyond the literal. For example, when one hears the beating of a drum it might conjure up images of war or something more peaceful. The intellectual soul can also make use of symbols, as evidenced by the doctor's use of medical symbols or sign language used by the deaf.[28] However, it is the intellectual soul that spreads the "light of knowledge" through the white nerves that spread out from the brain and spinal cord.[29]

There are parallels between Lefin's analysis of the animal and intellectual souls and ideas found in *The Chimp Paradox* by Steve Peters, a British psychiatrist. This practical guide describes a rational mental function it calls the "human," which it contrasts with our impulsive, emotional side referred to as the "chimp," which responds only to stimulus. The chimp is neither good nor bad, but simply requires training. We also have an aspect called the "computer," which can be programmed by the human and used to embed habits within the chimp.[30]

Basing himself on the sensationalist ideas described, Lefin explains that every sensation that we experience leaves an impression or trace in our memory, however weak. On encountering such sensation again, the new impression combines with the original trace to strengthen the overall intensity of the experience: "From this you can understand how habits strengthen impressions that have become weak."[31] The impression can be created by intellectual as well as physical objects.[32]

Each time a person battles a desire, an impression is created in his memory that is reawakened with even greater force when that desire is encountered again. Through repeated encounters with desires, one builds up strength that enables him to overcome the passions. This is so even if specific battles are lost. The mere attempt to exercise restraint builds resistance.[33]

As numerous contemporary books dealing with the practice of habits point out, habit formation should start small, and one should work with ones' passions rather than against them.[34] Lefin shares these insights. He sees a parallel between building physical strength and moral strength. One who practices carrying a one-pound weight each day, eventually ought to be able to carry a twelve-pound weight for an hour.[35] Tiny habits have compound effects. Lefin also recognizes the power of motivation to push boundaries and compel the animal soul to undertake tasks that would otherwise be unthinkable: "[A]lthough one might be unable to lift forty pounds in a state of calm, when angry or excited he might be able to throw sixty pounds."[36] Lefin's reference to weightlifting, might be read as an encouragement toward physical activity, characteristic of Locke, Rousseau, and the Philanthropine.[37]

Lefin further conveys the subtle impact of thoughts and the passions they evoke on our actions, and how quickly thoughts can be replaced by other thoughts that have a different physical effect. He describes a confident gentleman, strolling along with his head lifted high, taking care with his steps and "rolling his walking stick in the tips of his fingers," but that same person may become deflated when he encounters someone whose presence challenges his self-worth, and this change becomes evident in his posture, which might suddenly slump.

Lefin is further aware of how we pick out from the world those objects that most interest us and tend to ignore everything else. An artisan, smith, shoemaker, or shopkeeper may all be looking at the same bustling market, but each will be drawn to those sights and sounds that concern him in his profession.[38] Lefin wants us to use these insights to understand how we might influence thoughts by focusing on specific virtues within his regimen, and thereby develop habits to direct the animal soul in the path of virtue.[39]

Lefin, however, appreciates that not everything can be controlled. Luck or chance plays a central role in his system. Traits become refined in the face of real-life challenges, but sometimes the right opportunities do not arise. We should hope for an opportunity to address each week's trait but refrain from actively seeking out such opportunity.[40] Lefin here is taking a traditional approach. The Talmud states that true repentance occurs when one resists a temptation to which one has previously succumbed.[41] However, it is considered wickedness for a person to expose himself to such a temptation, even if he believes that, this time, he will be able to resist it.[42]

Lefin further recognizes that character development will not be a continuous progression. It will involve periods of stagnation, steep drops, and steady climbs.[43] A lapse should not be taken as a sign of failure nor progress as a sign of success. Each might simply reflect the external realities one is facing at any given moment. Lefin further appreciates that serendipity dictates our moral journey. The friends we keep, the business we engage in, the property we own, and our family, test us in different ways.[44] Change, too, is always afoot. New life situations disturb our equanimity. New social situations or encountering the unfamiliar present challenges. To face these, we need to prepare ahead.[45] Such preparation is particularly important when we are forced into large changes, like getting married or moving to a different city.[46] In flagging these changes, Lefin might have been addressing the anxieties of his age; adjusting to a partner in a world of weakening faith in arranged marriages or adjusting to a new city or community in a time of increasing mobility and greater diversity in outlook.

Chance also plays a part internally. Desires arrive without our choosing. Some desires can be spotted from a distance. They grow stronger as they approach us and are more easily dealt with than those that ambush us without warning "awakening the passions with great intensity."[47] There are people who become destabilized by good news or bad, unexpected pleasure or pain. Lefin describes how some people become disturbed by the slightest change in their regular routine or by a chair or table out of place, and how others develop phobias such as a fear of public speaking or leading a prayer service.[48] He recommends tackling these issues by focusing on the trait of equanimity (*menuchat nefesh*), inner balance.[49] But when it comes to those things we cannot avoid, we need patience (*savlanut*).[50]

Lefin, however, is far from a fatalist. Human endeavor is all important. He encourages each person to start each day by focusing on the trait that he is going to work on that day, and to plan all his material and worldly pursuits in advance, including the proper order in which each task is to be tackled.[51] If Lefin were alive today, he would be reaching for productivity handbooks such Nir Eyal's *Indestractable* or Cal Newport's *Deep Work*.[52] But Lefin's central goal is the attainment of virtue and promoting Jewish religious practice. Lefin encourages a constant review of progress by using charts, and personal adjustments as new traits suggests themselves for focus. Progress must be measured.[53] Lefin also shares with the productivity hacks a desire for order (*seder*). Order involves "fixing for every thought and concept a fixed time and turning to each thing in isolation, to demarcate its boundaries, so one thing does not impinge upon another."[54] For Lefin this is not just about personal success, but communal betterment. He berates men of learning and good character traits who live chaotic lives when it comes to their household, worldly, and spiritual affairs.[55]

A Place for God

In Lefin's scheme, God is forever present, manifesting Himself in three ways: through nature, wisdom, and kindness. He writes that the measure of God's glory "fills the entire world, for there is not even a grain of sand in the entire world that does not contain within it an aspect of higher wisdom."[56] God is the permanence and stability on which the fluidity of earthly existence and cycles of nature stand. His wisdom is manifest in the animal and intellectual souls. Lefin encourages his readers to take pleasure in understanding and experiencing nature; the colors, sounds, smells, and sweet tastes that abound. But the greatest pleasure of all is the "sublime pleasure of acting righteously."[57]

Lefin's God is also intensely personal. In the traditional mode, Lefin calls on each person to praise God even in the midst of suffering. God is described as the "faithful lover," "the exalted bestower of kindness, may He be blessed," who created suffering only for each person's benefit.[58]

Elsewhere, Lefin encourages *imitatio dei*, encapsulated in the injunction to *"walk in his ways"* (Deut. 28:9). But in *Ḥeshbon ha-Nefesh*, God is more often portrayed as a source of moral encouragement, the helper of those who help themselves.[59] This is an aspect of the divine to which Benjamin Franklin was also drawn. In his autobiography, he recounts that, having conceived God to be the Fountain of Wisdom, "I thought it right and necessary to solicit his assistance for obtaining it." Franklin composed a short prayer to this end asking God to strengthen his resolve to perform what wisdom dictates.[60]

What kind of person then does Lefin seek to mold? His ideal appears to be the man or woman (although primarily man) who displays faith, equanimity, and control. He encourages individuals to be sensitive to their rational and animal aspects, capable of working with, not against, their passions, respectable, efficient, industrious, and kind. Lefin has a place for God, but not the God of the medieval mystics or the Hasidim of his own day, against whom he polemicizes. As Nancy Sinkoff writes, all of Lefin's "philosophical, psychological, and ethical works were part of Lefin's overarching effort to safeguard traditional Ashkenzic piety and structures of religious authority from what he believed to be Hasidic subversion."[61] Where Hasidism encourages ecstasy and a preoccupation with kabbalistic ideas, Lefin encourages virtue and ethical self-transformation. Lefin was highly critical of Hasidic Rebbes or *Zaddikim*, who he saw as manipulative and hypocritical.[62] For him, the individual must be directed by his own assessment of the traits on which he needs to work, rather than authority figures.[63]

It is this focus on the ethical over the mystical, and on the programmatic, psychological approach to ethical training that most likely endeared Lefin's *Ḥeshbon ha-Nefesh* to the proponents of the nineteenth-century Musar movement, although the latter retained a place for religious passion.[64] Lefin's God does not call from the depths, or demand sacrifice, like Soloveitchik's Adam 2 (*homo religiosus*) (see chapter 30), but helps those who help themselves to achieve the virtuous life, rooted in the world.

However, reading Lefin today, in our age of commercialized self-help and lifehacking, one can't help wondering: Is practical virtue in the mode of the Religious Enlightenment enough to sustain the life of the soul, to keep the fires of religious enthusiasm burning? Or is it the start of a spiritual decline; the first steps toward a sterile bourgeois morality where goodness is equated with civility, self-fulfilment, material betterment, and productivity; and where God ceases to be *Our Father, Our King*, or the ultimate underpinning of all creation, but takes on the role of a life coach, before disappearing altogether?[65]

Notes

1. Nancy Sinkoff, *Out of the Shtetl: Making Jews Modern in the Polish Borderlands* (Providence, RI: Brown Judaic Studies 336, 2020), 115, 126–27, 136–37.

2. Nancy Sinkoff, "Lefin, Menaḥem Mendel," *YIVO Encyclopedia of Jews in Eastern Europe*, August 23, 2010, https://yivoencyclopedia.org/article.aspx/Lefin_Menahem_Mendel.

3. Immanuel Etkes, *Rabbi Israel Salanter and the Mussar Movement: Seeking the Torah of Truth* (Philadelphia: Jewish Publication Society, 1993), 118, 123–26. Salanter's teacher, Rabbi Zundel of Salant, may have brought the book to his attention. At Salanter's instigation, *Ḥeshbon ha-Nefesh* was republished in 1844.

4. David J. Sorkin, *The Religious Enlightenment: Protestants, Jews, and Catholics from London to Vienna* (Princeton, NJ: Princeton University Press, 2018), 3–6.

5. Sorkin, *Religious Enlightenment*, 3–19.

6. Sorkin, *Religious Enlightenment*, 167.

7. Menaḥem Mendel Lefin (Menahem Mendel Levin), *Cheshbon ha-Nefesh* [*Ḥeshbon ha-Nefesh*], prepared by Dovid Landesman and trans. Shraga Silverstein (Jerusalem: Feldheim, 1995), sec. 40. In this chapter, I have taken a nonliteral approach to translation, using or adapting Silverstein's translation.

8. Lefin, *Cheshbon ha-Nefesh*, sec. 44–45.

9. Kerry Walters, "Franklin and the Question of Religion," in *The Cambridge Companion to Benjamin Franklin*, ed. Carla Mulford (Cambridge: Cambridge University Press, 2009), 91–103.

10. Lefin, *Cheshbon ha-Nefesh*, sec. 19.

11. Lefin, *Cheshbon ha-Nefesh*, sec. 111.

12. Lefin, *Cheshbon ha-Nefesh*, sec. 103. See Jeremiah 10:10; BT Shabbat 55a; BT Sanhedrin 29a.

13. Jürgen Overhoff, "Franklin's Philadelphia Academy and Basedow's Dessau Philanthropine: Two Models of Non-denominational Schooling in Eighteenth-century America and Germany," in *Paedagogica Historica* 43, no.6 (2007): 801–18.

14. Christa Kersting, *Die Genese der Pädagogik im 18. Jahrhundert: Campes "Allgemeine Revision" im Kontext der neuzeitlichen Wissenschaft* (Weinheim: Deutscher Studien Verlag, 1992), 127; Martin L. Davies, *Identity or History? Marcus Herz and the End of the Enlightenment* (Detroit: Wayne State University Press, 1995), 122–34.

15. Joachim Heinrich Campe, *Kleine Seelenlehre für Kinder* (Berlin, 1783); translated as *Elementary Dialogues for the Improvement of Youth* (London, 1792), ii–iii.

16. Cassirer maintains that in the eighteenth-century this idea was "exalted to the rank of an indubitable principle." Ernst Cassirer, *The Philosophy of the Enlightenment,* trans. Fritz C. A. Koelln and James P. Pettegrove (Princeton, NJ: Princeton University Press, 1951), 98.

17. John Locke, *An Essay Concerning Human Understanding,* ed. Peter H. Nidditch (Oxford: Oxford University Press, 1975), 2.1.4.

18. Locke, *Essay Concerning Human Understanding,* 1.28, 1.401.

19. John Locke, *The Reasonableness of Christianity, as Delivered in the Scriptures,* trans. John C. Higgins-Biddle (Oxford: Clarendon Press, 1999), 14, 157–58. Benedict Spinoza (1632–1677) (chapter 16 in this volume) held similar views about the masses' inability to be guided by reason, see *Theological-Political Treatise,* ed. Jonathan Israel (Cambridge: Cambridge University Press, 2007), 16.7, 199. For other similarities between Locke and Spinoza see Wim Klever, "Locke's Disguised Spinozism," https://huenemanniac.files.wordpress.com/2009/01/lockes-disguised-spinozism.pdf.

20. For works that fall within this category see Isaac Satanov's *Sefer ha-Midot* (Berlin, 1784), and Naphtali Herz Wessely's *Sefer ha-Midot* (Berlin, 1786?). On the Haskalah's transformation of the *Musar* more generally see Harris Bor, "Moral Education in the Age of the Jewish Enlightenment" (PhD diss., University of Cambridge, 1997); Bor, "Enlightenment Values, Jewish Ethics: The Haskalah's Transformation of the Traditional Musar Genre," in *New Perspectives on the Haskalah,* ed. Shmuel Feiner and David Sorkin (London: Littman Library of Jewish Civilization, 2001), 48–63.

21. In one manuscript, Lefin writes that philosophic knowledge "brings no benefit in the matter of doing good for one's fellow creatures." Joseph Perl Archive, JNULA, 4° 1153/130, 55. Sinkoff, *Out of the Shtetl,* 132.

22. BT Taanit 20b. See Sinkoff, *Out of the Shtetl,* 138.

23. Lefin, *Cheshbon ha-Nefesh,* sec. 1.3.

24. Lefin, *Cheshbon ha-Nefesh,* sec. 1.4; See also sec. 14.

25. Lefin, *Cheshbon ha-Nefesh,* sec. 91.

26. Lefin, *Cheshbon ha-Nefesh,* sec. 92.

27. Lefin, *Cheshbon ha-Nefesh,* sec. 92, footnote.

28. Lefin, *Cheshbon ha-Nefesh,* sec. 96. By 1720, the British manual alphabet had essentially found its present form. It was adopted in Germany. "History of Sign Language," Wikipedia, https://en.wikipedia.org/wiki/History_of_sign_language.

29. Lefin, *Cheshbon ha-Nefesh,* sec. 67. A physiological account of human psychology is found in David Harvey's writings, and elsewhere in Lefin. See Sinkoff, *Out of the Shtetl,* 116–17.

30. Steve Peters, *The Chimp Paradox* (London: Vermillion, 2012).
31. Lefin, *Cheshbon ha-Nefesh*, sec. 53.
32. Lefin, *Cheshbon ha-Nefesh*, sec. 55.
33. Lefin, *Cheshbon ha-Nefesh*, sec. 55–57.
34. Brian J. Fogg, *Tiny Habits: The Small Changes That Change Everything* (London: Virgin Digital, 2019). See also James Clear, *Atomic Habits: An Easy and Proven Way to Build Good Habits and Break Bad Ones* (London: Random House Business Books, 2018).
35. Lefin, *Cheshbon ha-Nefesh*, sec. 58.
36. Lefin, *Cheshbon ha-Nefesh*, sec. 60.
37. Dorinda Outram, Theodore M. Brown, and Elizabeth Free, "An Enlightenment View of School Health," *American Journal of Public Health* 96, no. 9 (2006): 1560.
38. Lefin, *Cheshbon ha-Nefesh*, sec. 42.
39. Lefin, *Cheshbon ha-Nefesh*, sec. 43.
40. Lefin, *Cheshbon ha-Nefesh*, sec. 23.
41. BT Yoma 86b. See also Maimonides, MT Hilkhot Teshuvah 2:1.
42. BT Bava Batra 57b.
43. Lefin, *Cheshbon ha-Nefesh*, sec. 29.
44. Lefin, *Cheshbon ha-Nefesh*, sec. 31.
45. Lefin, *Cheshbon ha-Nefesh*, sec. 34.
46. Lefin, *Cheshbon ha-Nefesh*, sec. 35.
47. Lefin, *Cheshbon ha-Nefesh*, sec. 52.
48. Lefin, *Cheshbon ha-Nefesh*, sec. 69.
49. Lefin, *Cheshbon ha-Nefesh*, sec. 67.
50. Lefin, *Cheshbon ha-Nefesh*, sec. 76.
51. Lefin, *Cheshbon ha-Nefesh*, sec. 21.
52. Nir Eyal, *Indistractable: How to Control Your Attention and Choose Your Life* (London; Bloomsbury, 2019); Cal Newport, *Deep Work* (London; Piatkus, 2016).
53. Lefin, *Cheshbon ha-Nefesh*, sec. 30.
54. Lefin, *Cheshbon ha-Nefesh*, sec. 79.
55. Lefin, *Cheshbon ha-Nefesh*, sec. 80.
56. Lefin, *Cheshbon ha-Nefesh*, sec. 72. This is likely a reference to Genesis Rabbah 10:7: "There is not a blade of grass below that does not have an angel above, striking it and commanding it 'Grow!' "
57. Lefin, *Cheshbon ha-Nefesh*, sec. 74. The idea that God can be sensed from nature is found in many Jewish medieval sources, including Maimonides and other of Lefin's writings. See Sinkoff, *Out of the Shtetl*, 121–24.
58. Lefin, *Cheshbon ha-Nefesh*, secs. 74–76.
59. Joseph Perl Archive, JNULA, 4° 1153/130, 55; cited in Sinkoff, *Out of the Shtetl*, 132.

60. Benjamin Franklin, *The Autobiography of Benjamin Franklin*, ed. Leonard Woods Labaree (New Haven, CT: Yale University Press, 2003). See also Shai Afsai, "Benjamin Franklin's Influence on Mussar Thought and Practice: A Chronicle of Misapprehension," *Review of Rabbinic Judaism* 22, no. 2 (2019): 235.

61. Sinkoff, *Out of the Shtetl*, 114. The reference to *Chochmah, Binah*, and *Da'at* may have been aimed at reclaiming these ideas from the ChaBaD school of Hasidim whose name is an acronym of these words. Sinkoff, *Out of the Shtetl*, 154, 158. See also Hillel Levin, "Between Hasidism and Haskalah: On a Disguised Anti-Hasidic Polemic," in *Peraqim Betoldot Hahevrah Hayehudit Biymei Habeinayim uVa'et Hahadashah*, ed. Immanuel Etkes and Joseph Salmon (Jerusalem: Zalman Shazar Center, 1980), 189.

62. Sinkoff, *Out of the Shtetl*, 146–48.

63. Lefin, *Cheshbon ha-Nefesh*, secs. 41 and 59.

64. Etkes, *Rabbi Israel Salanter*, 320–22. The later Musar leader, Rabbi Joseph Josel Horowitz (1847–1919) of Navardok, considered that ecstasy and the emotions allowed one to transcend the physical. See Dov Katz, *Tenuat Hamusar*, vol. 4 (New York: Feldheim, 1996), 234.

65. A move toward viewing religion in terms of civility and virtue can be detected in Lefin's speculation that even the commandments between man and God were given to enhance relations between human beings. In this, he observes how making blessings over food and other enjoyable things fosters a greater appreciation for others and desire to benefit them. Joseph Perl Archive, JNULA, 4° 1153/130, 53; see Sinkoff, *Out of the Shtetl*, 134.

Chapter 20

Ḥayyim of Volozhin

ESTI EISENMANN

Rabbi Ḥayyim of Volozhin was born in Volozhin on 7 Sivan 5509 (May 24, 1749), to Yitzhak ben Ḥayyim Itskovits, the community leader, and his wife Rivka ben Yosef Rappaport, himself the son of Rabbi Simḥa Hacohen Rappaport. The young Ḥayyim studied in Minsk and then, from age nineteen, with the Vilna Gaon. Around 1774, he returned to Volozhin, where he served as town rabbi (except for one year in Vilkomir) until his death on 14 Sivan 5581 (June 14, 1821).[1] Ḥayyim was viewed as the Vilna Gaon's successor in the battle against Hasidism and the rehabilitation of Torah study.[2] His crowning glory was the establishment of the Etz Ḥayyim yeshiva in Volozhin early in the nineteenth century—which earned him the title of the "father of the Lithuanian yeshivot."[3] Unlike the yeshivot of the Middle Ages, which were small local institutions supported by the community, Etz Ḥayyim was pedagogically and financially independent.[4] In the early nineteenth century, a group of the Gaon's disciples immigrated to Palestine; Ḥayyim's share in their initiative is not clear. It is known that he provided substantial assistance to the immigrants and served as the rabbinic authority for the organization in Vilna that provided financial support to the Lithuanian Jews in Palestine (known as the

This research was supported by Herzog Academic College.

Perushim) and their kollel, Aderet Eliyahu.[5] Ḥayyim's most important works, aside from halakhic responsa, are *Nefesh ha-Ḥayyim*, a treatise of kabbalistic theology that expounds the Lithuanian anti-Hasidic (*mitnagged*) worldview,[6] and *Ruaḥ ha-Ḥayyim*, which is a commentary on Pirkei Avot.

The Role of Moral Self-improvement in Ḥayyim's Teachings

Ḥayyim saw Torah study and observance of the precepts as the totality and sole goal of a Jewish man's life.[7] This means Torah study of a practical and halakhic nature that includes deep study of the Talmud, including the commentators, especially Rashi and the Tosafists, in order to understand a passage and its various aspects.[8] Drawing on kabbalistic ideas,[9] he asserted that observance of the precepts and especially Torah study[10] support and preserve the world, which would be destroyed without them. To ethical improvement—which he referred to as "fear of the Lord"—he attached secondary importance, as a means only.[11] For Ḥayyim, the Torah is all-inclusive and makes ethical self-improvement almost wholly superfluous. Hence he called for concentrating on traditional Torah study rather than spending time with books on ethics (musar).

As Ḥayyim saw things, Torah study had been declining over the generations and then suffered a grievous blow in his generation.[12] There were two reasons why Torah study had reached such a low ebb. The first was the material hardships of daily life—the need to make a living and the troubles of life in exile. These prevented people from devoting time to Torah study. The second reason was ideological—the emphasis being placed on the "fear of the Lord." People were spending their time poring over musar texts instead of engaging in classic Torah study.[13]

Ḥayyim warned against the focus on ethical improvement and fear of the Lord: all the time spent reading musar works was apt to come at the expense of talmudic study. He did not believe, however, that ethics should be totally discarded, inasmuch as "the beginning of wisdom is Fear of the Lord" (Ps. 111:10), which means that fear of the Lord is a prerequisite for acquiring wisdom.[14] This is why in later generations, when the rabbis saw that their students had totally abandoned the idea of ethical improvement, they took to writing books on that topic even though the previous generation had engaged exclusively in Torah study.[15] Still, even in a generation lacking fear of the Lord, its cultivation must be seen as a preparation and preliminary for Torah study and limited accordingly.

In Ḥayyim's two books, drawing on the talmudic sages,[16] he compares fear of the Lord to a storehouse where grain is kept[17] and models the proper relationship between Torah study and ethical self-improvement on that between growing the grain and building the storehouse. If the latter task is neglected, the grain will rot in the field and all the effort devoted to raising it will be for naught. On the other hand, it is totally absurd for people to spend all their energy and money on the storehouse and never fill it with grain. Similarly, fear of the Lord is the granary meant to hold the acquisition of wisdom. If there is no work on ethical behavior, Torah study is apt to be in vain, but the means must never replace the goal, with ethics viewed as the main thing. In *Ruaḥ ha-Ḥayyim,* Ḥayyim suggests the ratio of the time to be invested in each of these pursuits. Drawing on the same talmudic midrash, he concludes that one should devote five minutes to ethics for every fifteen hours of Torah study.[18]

As mentioned, for Ḥayyim the Torah is all-inclusive and makes ethical self-improvement almost wholly superfluous. There are two aspects to this. First, the Torah guards a man against sinning and envelops him in a light that preserves him from sin.[19] A man who learns Torah is exempt from the need to spend much time cultivating fear of the Lord, thanks to the preservative power of the Torah.[20] This is why human beings are permitted to engage in Torah study even if they do so "not for its own sake." Ultimately, illuminated by the light of Torah, they will rise to the level of study "for its own sake."[21] In keeping with this idea, Ḥayyim attacks people who deride those who do not learn for the sake of learning. Not only do the critics fail to understand that the Torah has the power to raise a person to the level of study for its own sake, they also deter such students and reduce the scale of Torah study among the Jews.[22] He sees the idea that fear of the Lord is the supreme value to be a provocation by the Evil Impulse aimed at putting an end to Torah study.[23] Accordingly, the serious student of Torah is exempt from the need to develop his fear of heaven, inasmuch as Torah study protects an individual and ipso facto fashions his fear of heaven. Nevertheless, as noted, ab initio it is forbidden to totally set aside efforts aimed at ethical self-improvement: "In any case, both of them are necessary for a man—Torah and fear"[24]—but he must devote minimal time to the latter.

The second reason why ethical self-improvement is almost superfluous is that after the giving of the Torah, all good actions and virtues are specified by halakhah.[25] Because the Torah includes everything, even acts of human kindness, which are sometimes identified with ethical conduct and ethical self-improvement, are part of the Torah. So too, fear of the Lord is one of the 613 precepts, meaning that its performance, for all its importance, does not stand out above the observance of the [other] precepts.[26] As is the way of halakhah, it stipulates that one must not devote too much time to developing it, but only to Torah study.[27]

There is no doubt that in Ḥayyim's war against those who emphasized musar at the expense of Torah study there was an echo of the Hasidic criticism of classic scholarship, which held that there is a gap between the student's intellectual achievements and his fear of heaven. This critique is why Hasidism posited a new scale of values, with devotion to God at the center.[28] Ḥayyim rejected this criticism and asserted that Torah study works automatically and fashions fear of heaven; it is only in the very first stage of study, which is deemed "not for its own sake," that it is possible for a student to lack fear of heaven. The talmudic sages permitted such study in the knowledge that Torah has the power to lead an individual to true fear of the Lord.

The Definition of the Virtues

Intellectual Virtues and Their Connection to Spiritual Virtues

Even though Ḥayyim assigns almost exclusive value to Torah study, nowhere in his books does he deal with intellectual achievement. What is more, he considers knowledge to be a gift that is bestowed on individuals by divine bounty.[29] As a result, the prime virtues that a man should cultivate with regard to Torah study are perseverance (*kevi*ʿ*ut*),[30] serious effort (*yegi*ʿ*ah*), and Torah study without outside interests (*peniyah*), which strives to achieve full comprehension of the entire Torah (*Torah lishmah*).[31] Perseverance also means ensuring that there are students who will carry on Torah study in the next generation.[32] A person who diligently studies Torah through constant intensive study will acquire not only knowledge of the plain meaning of the Torah but also its arcane and the secrets of existence.[33]

The fact that perseverance, serious effort, and study without self-interest are the intellectual virtues that a person must adopt in his Torah study and that the actual acquisition of knowledge is dependent on divine grace restores fear of the Lord to its special place in the service of the Lord. Ḥayyim's notion of the fear of the Lord, as we shall see, also includes the demand that human beings understand that even though their role in this world is to study Torah and observe the precepts, they must not congratulate themselves for studying and observing the precepts but must give thanks to God that He permitted them to draw near to him and study His Torah.

Fear of the Lord as a Spiritual Virtue

What, then, is "fear of the Lord" for Ḥayyim? He distinguishes two types—fear of punishment, which is of lesser rank, and true fear of the Lord, which is most excellent. This is evident in his commentary on the dictum of Antigonus of Socho, in Pirkei Avot 1:3: "Do not be like slaves that serve the master in order to receive a reward."[34]

We are inclined to honor our superiors purely on account of their high rank; but also to show respect to those of lower rank if they are responsible for law and order or if they support us financially. Because God is an exalted king, who also observes our every action and also supplies our physical needs, we must honor Him for all three reasons. However, we must exalt God and serve him out of recognition of His greatness, and not due to fear or hope of a reward.[35] Recognition of His greatness is accompanied by a sense of shame, which is an important component of Ḥayyim's fear of the Lord:

> Now among the types of fear, several types are immeasurably great. But the imperative fear is that stated by Rabbi Yoḥanan ben Zakkai (BT Berakhot 28): "May it be His will that the fear of heaven be on you as much as the fear of flesh and blood." Know that when a man commits a sin and says nobody will see me, this is fear on account of shame. . . . He should feel shame and embarrassment vis-

> à-vis his creator, who stands constantly alongside him and no place is devoid of Him. If another person was with him he would not do it, so how then can he do it when he is with the King, the King of the king of kings, the Holy One Blessed Be He, in His work? This kind of fear is certainly useful for turning away from evil and guarding against the snare. But there is also shame when performing a precept, because it is not as a man imagines, namely, that he is doing some great good when he performs some precept or studies Torah and for this he should inherit the world and everything in it. In truth, though, it is just the opposite: what great and important for us is that we have been granted the merit of performing precepts and studying His Torah, as we say, "Who Sanctified us in His precepts" and "You brought us near, our King, to Your service." Every time a man performs a precept or studies for where is it his strength that he came to cleave to the King, the Lord of Hosts, in the Torah, which is His delight, and it is neither a title for him nor glory for him to stand in the sanctuary of the King, the Temple of the Lord. And even were he pure of sin and cleansed of transgression, what are his deeds? All the more so should he be ashamed of his sins and transgressions against the Lord who raises him up. Hence he should resolve to abandon his path from now on and never return to his folly, and entreat the Lord in His loving-kindness to help him learn Torah and understand its depths and realize that he is asking for something great.[36]

Thus a man's shame before his Creator is twofold: he is ashamed to transgress in His presence, knowing that He is watching him all the time; and he is ashamed of himself that, even though he is a lowly and sinful creature, God has honored him and made it possible for him to serve Him and study His Torah.[37] If so, the fear of God includes repenting one's sins, on the one hand, and resolving to perform sincere and genuine service of God, out of recognition of the privilege human beings enjoy of serving God. Because fear of heaven is perpetual repentance and recognition of the privilege that we have been granted, Ḥayyim adopts the view that humility is the greatest virtue of all that a man must cultivate, in that it is the loftiest virtue that leads to sincere fear of heaven.

The Importance of Humility as a Means to Attain Fear of Heaven

Humility is the most important virtue in Ḥayyim's project of ethical self-improvement.[38] As noted, its importance derives from the fact that it leads one to fear of God[39] and incorporates all the virtues.[40] The recognition of man's nullity and of the privilege granted him to serve God obligates him to move away from every sin and the lures of the Evil Impulse. Commenting on the dictum by Rabbi Levitas of Yavne (Pirkei Avot 4:4), "Be exceedingly low of spirit," Ḥayyim writes: "One should not think that he is fulfilling the precept of humility by being lowly in his own eyes; he must truly believe that he is nothing, that 'man's hope is only a worm' and he has nothing to be proud of."[41] Humility causes a man to negate himself, to devote himself wholly to Torah study, and makes it possible for him to cleave to and be one with the deity that is found in every place, until the deity speaks from his own throat as it were.[42]

As we have seen, Ḥayyim considered the fear of the Lord to be a means to store up wisdom and study the Talmud. In his view, the coarser the vessel the larger the volume it occupies, leaving less room for filling it with content.[43] Thus the excellence of humility is it prepares a man to minimize his ego and leaves more room to be filled by the light of Torah. Note that Ḥayyim's humility is not a virtue that relates to other people, but to the Creator. However, when a person makes himself small before his Creator he ipso facto does so with regard to other human beings. On Ben Zoma's statement (*Avot* 4:1), "Who is wise? He who learns from all men. . . . Who is mighty? He who subdues his nature. . . . Who is rich? He who rejoices in his portion," Ḥayyim commented as follows:

> This means that the main thing, to merit divine inspiration, comes only through humility. . . . Now a person lacking in excellent qualities, even if he abases himself he cannot be called "humble," because it counts for nothing if he has nothing to be proud of. But someone who has excellent qualities and nevertheless does not feel them at all and has

> a low spirit—he is called "humble." And it is in accordance with the number and magnitude of his excellent qualities that the magnitude of his humility is measured. . . . All the virtues in the world are included in these three—wisdom, strength, and wealth. And this is what he said, namely, that the divine presence rests only on one who is wise, strong, and wealthy, but even so he is humble.[44]

For Ḥayyim, wisdom, strength, and wealth do not depend on a person; rather, all of them are divine gifts that are determined at birth.[45] A man who is aware of this will not be arrogant toward others because of his wisdom and strength and will share his wealth with the poor. In his view, because wisdom is a sort of trouvaille, God can cause even a lowly man to discover a windfall, so the wise man has no cause to avoid learning from him. It follows that humility is not primarily a moral quality that shapes the relations between a man and his fellows, but is first and foremost a cognitive and mental quality that pertains to the relationship between human beings and God and from which the ethical treatment of others derives.

Moses as the Ideal Exemplar of Humility

Although Ḥayyim emphasizes that all of the Patriarchs, Tanna'im, and Amora'im can serve as paragons of humility,[46] there is no doubt that Moses is the exemplar of the highest form of that virtue.[47] Moses abased himself totally and had no self-importance whatsoever. Abraham, too, minimized his own worth and said, "I am dust and ashes" (Gen. 18:26)—but dust, however lowly, remains a substance. Moses, by contrast, protested, "what are we?" (Exod 16:7–8), totally negating himself. Drawing on kabbalistic ideas, Ḥayyim explains that even though every individual's soul resides in his body, throughout his life its root remains planted in the upper realms. The body is the cause of a partial severance and imperfect connection between the soul and its root. For Moses, however, who accounted himself as nothing, the root of his soul was not separated from the rest by his body. He explains the divine injunction "Remove your shoes from your feet" (Exod. 3:5) as symbolizing the removal of Moses's physical nature and the creation of a direct link between the soul and its root, with no break between them. This continuity was made possible by his humility.[48]

We should note that Ḥayyim did not only preach, but also followed his principles, and was extremely self-effacing. In a letter written in early 1802, addressed to "all lovers of the Torah," which described the pathetic state of Torah learning in order to raise funds to establish his yeshiva, his humility leads him to protest people's habit of presenting him as the disciple of the Vilna Gaon. "I see myself obligated to make it clearly known in Israel that I must not detract from the honor of our great and holy rabbi, his soul in Eden, and have my name associated with his."[49]

The Path to Acquiring Fear of the Lord and Humility

With regard to the path that leads to fear of the Lord and humility, Ḥayyim stipulates both the time to be devoted to it and the means for doing so. He recommends that one spend several minutes to acquire fear of the Lord before beginning Torah study, though he allows that one may interrupt one's learning from time to time and return to focusing on fear of the Lord.

As for the means to be employed, Ḥayyim believes that the most important device for acquiring fear of the Lord is introspection and reflection (*hirhurei teshuvah*) about a man's sins and nullity as compared to God and the mission assigned him—studying and observing the Torah.[50] " 'Say little and do much'—that is, always say and think that despite all the Torah you have learned so far, and all the precepts you have observed, you have so far achieved only the minimum of the minimum. Bestir yourself to learn and do much much more."[51] For Ḥayyim, even the confession of sins, which from the perspective of halakhah must be an oral enumeration of one's transgressions, may be barren. Hence a person must make sure that his heart feels what his mouth is speaking: "Before Torah study he should make a true confession in his heart and not merely say 'I have sinned' with his mouth."

Although Ḥayyim viewed physical needs with contempt,[52] he did not recommend abstinence and asceticism as a way to achieve fear of the Lord. He views enduring pain and experiencing social humiliation, as merely external; but humility must be internal: "For the essence of humility is not only that a person must endure humiliation and suffering and the like, but that he also know in his heart that he is insignificant in comparison to the lowliest of human beings."[53] Nevertheless, he does recommend seeing the torments that are a man's natural lot as a tool for achieving fear of the Lord.[54] He also called on individuals to live simply and rejoice in their lot.[55] This may be the context in which he opposed wearing fine clothes. In his commentary on Pirkei Avot 4:6, where Rabbi Jose says that "He that honors the Law is himself honored," Ḥayyim rejects the idea that people will not respect a scholar who is not well dressed;[56] he counters that respect is not a function of one's clothes, so "there is no need for fine and fancy garments."[57] We see here that Ḥayyim stressed inner humility and attached no importance to external manners and appearance.

Conclusion

All the above leads to the idea that Ḥayyim identified Judaism with Torah study in its classic sense of poring over the Gemara with the goal of determining the halakhah, as well as with observance of the precepts in all their details and minutiae. He included ethical self-improvement, and especially the effort to acquire humility and expel pride, within the ambit of a single precept, fearing the Lord. Fear of the Lord means man's awareness of his nullity vis-à-vis his Creator and his joy that he is able to observe His Torah. This awareness should accompany individuals in every hour, including the time devoted to Torah study; without it they are liable to lose all their learning and hard-acquired knowledge. Even though fear of the Lord is an obligation for every human being and elevates Torah study and observance of the precepts to the level of "for its own sake," Ḥayyim warns against devoting too much time to acquiring it. For him, merely observing the precepts, and, for Jewish men, especially the precept of Torah study, ipso facto causes a person to fear of the Lord; so he should not focus on it alone. Most of a Jewish man's day should be devoted to Torah study; only for a few minutes is he permitted to set aside his study and contemplate his transgressions, lowness, and nullity.

Notes

1. Moshe Shmuel Shmukler, *History of Our Rabbi Hayyim of Volozhin* [Hebrew] (Vilnius: Norber Press, 1909).

2. Allan Nadler, *The Faith of the Mithnagdim: Rabbinic Response to Hasidic Rapture* (Baltimore: Johns Hopkins University Press, 1997), 4–7.

3. Immanuel Etkes, *The Gaon of Vilna: The Man and His Image*, trans. Jeffrey Green (Berkeley: University of California Press, 2002), 151–53.

4. Mordechai Breuer, *The Tents of Torah* [Hebrew] (Jerusalem: Merkaz Zalman Shazar, 2003); Immanuel Etkes and Shlomo Tikochinski, eds., *The Lithuanian Yeshivas—Memoirs* [Hebrew] (Jerusalem: Merkaz Zalman Shazar, 2004); Immanuel Etkes, ed., *Yeshivas and Study Halls* [Hebrew] (Jerusalem: Merkaz Zalman Shazar and the Dinur Center for Research in Jewish History at the Hebrew University of Jerusalem, 2007); Shaul Stampfer, *Lithuanian Yeshivas of the Nineteenth Century: Creating a Tradition of Learning*, trans. Lindsey Taylor-Gutharz (Jerusalem: Magnes Press, 2014); Ben-Tsiyon Klibansky, *Golden Age of Lithuanian Yeshivot in Eastern Europe* [Hebrew] (Jerusalem: Merkaz Zalman Shazar, 2014).

5. Arie Morgenstern, Menachem Friedman, Ya'akov Katz, and Yeshaia Tishbi, "Discussion: The Influence of Messianic Expectations upon Jewish Settlement of Eretz-Israel in the Early 19th Century," *Cathedra* 24 (1982): 51–78; Emmanuel Schieber, "The Theory of the *Pekida* in the Writings of the Vilna Gaon and Its Practical Application by His Followers" [Hebrew], *Daat: A Journal of Jewish Philosophy and Kabbalah*, no. 79/80 (2015): 263–83.

6. Nadler, *The Faith of the Mithnagdim*, 4–7.

7. Jewish women were traditionally forbidden to study Torah. Their role, in addition to observance of the commandments that apply to them, was to help their husbands and sons study Torah.

8. Ezra Kahalani, "The Educational Ideal in the Thought of Rabbi Ḥayyim Volozhiner and Its Actual Realization" [Hebrew], in *On the Patriarchs' Road*, ed. A. Bazak, S. Vigoda, and M. Monitz (Alon Shevut, 2001), 178–79.

9. Etkes, *The Gaon of Vilna*, 178–84; Nadler, *The Faith of the Mithnagdim*, 36–37; Kahalani, "The Educational Ideal," 182–83; Harvey Shapiro, "Contingency, Inquiry, and Effort: The Educational Thought of Rabbi Ḥayyim of Volozhin," *International Journal of Jewish Education Research* 2 (2010): 35–79.

10. Norman Lamm, *Torah Lishmah: Torah for Torah's Sake in the Works of Rabbi Hayyim of Volozhin and His Contemporaries* (New York: Yeshiva University Press, 1989); Jonah Ben Sasson, "The Spiritual World and Educational Philosophy of the Founders of the Lithuanian Yeshiva" [Hebrew], *Ḥinnukh ha-Adam ve-Yiʿudo* 4 (1967): 155–67; Nadler, *The Faith of the Mithnagdim*, 56, 151–52. The first section of *Nefesh ha-Ḥayyim* is devoted mainly to a discussion of the practical precepts; the fourth section focuses on the status of the Torah. See Esti Eisenmann, "Structure and Content in Rabbi Ḥayyim Volozhiner's *Nefesh ha-Ḥayyim*" [Hebrew], in *The Vilna Gaon and His Study Hall*, ed. Moshe Halamish, Yosef Rivlin, and Raphael Shochat (Ramat Gan: Bar-Ilan University, 2003), 185–96.

11. Shapiro, "Contingency, Inquiry, and Effort," 62–70.

12. Etkes, *The Gaon of Vilna*, 164–66.

13. Ḥayyim of Volozin, *Nefesh ha-Ḥayyim* 4.1; Ḥayyim of Volozin, *Nefesh ha-Tzimzum, Rabbi Chaim Volozin's Nefesh HaChaim*, trans. and commentary by Avinoam Fraenkel (Jerusalem: Urim, 2015), 628–32.

14. Ḥayyim of Volozin, *Nefesh ha-Ḥayyim* 4.5; *Nefesh ha-Tzimzum*, 646.

15. Ḥayyim of Volozin, *Nefesh ha-Ḥayyim* 1.5; *Nefesh ha-Tzimzum*, 628–30.

16. BT Shabbat 31a.

17. Ḥayyim of Volozin, *Ruaḥ Ḥayyim* 1.1, 4b; *Nefesh ha-Ḥayyim* 4.4; *Nefesh ha-Tzimzum*, 644.

18. Ḥayyim of Volozin, *Ruaḥ Ḥayyim* 1.1, 4b.

19. Ḥayyim of Volozin, *Ruaḥ Ḥayyim* 1.1, 11b. Cf. Kahalani, "The Educational Ideal," 192–93.

20. Ḥayyim of Volozin, *Nefesh ha-Ḥayyim* 4.9; *Nefesh ha-Tzimzum*, 661.

21. Ḥayyim of Volozin, *Nefesh ha-Ḥayyim*, middle section, 3; *Nefesh ha-Tzimzum*, 593. Cf. *Ruaḥ Ḥayyim* 2.1, 12b: "For the Torah, even if not for its own sake, weakens the [evil] impulse."

22. Ḥayyim of Volozin, *Ruaḥ Ḥayyim* 1.1, 4b–5a.

23. Ḥayyim of Volozin, *Nefesh ha-Ḥayyim*, middle section, 4; *Nefesh ha-Tzimzum*, 601.

24. Ḥayyim of Volozin, *Ruaḥ Ḥayyim* 1.1, 4b.

25. Ḥayyim of Volozin, *Ruaḥ Ḥayyim* 1.1, 5b–6a.

26. Ḥayyim of Volozin, *Nefesh ha-Ḥayyim* 4.5; *Nefesh ha-Tzimzum*, 648.

27. On the amount of time to be spent on this, see above, near note 18.

28. Etkes, *The Gaon of Vilna*, 184–89; Kahalani, "The Educational Ideal," 177–78.

29. Ḥayyim of Volozin, *Ruaḥ Ḥayyim* 4.1, 24a; see also 2.8, 15b, 5.15, 33a. See also 6.1, 37a, s.v. "they reveal the secrets of the Torah to him"; *Nefesh ha-Ḥayyim* 4.5; *Nefesh ha-Tzimzum*, 648.

30. Ḥayyim of Volozin, *Ruaḥ Ḥayyim* 2.1 12a: "Perseverance (*kevi'ut*) is useful in all matters and is the crux of the labor."

31. Shapiro, "Contingency, Inquiry, and Effort," 70–74.

32. Ḥayyim of Volozin, *Ruaḥ Ḥayyim* 1.1, 5a.

33. Ḥayyim of Volozin, *Nefesh ha-Ḥayyim* 4.21; *Nefesh ha-Tzimzum*, 729–33.

34. Ḥayyim of Volozin, *Ruaḥ Ḥayyim* 1.3, 6ab.

35. This is how Ḥayyim explains that the reward for observing the precepts depends on the intention involved, as well as the mishnah in Pirkei Avot (2:1).

36. Ḥayyim of Volozin, *Ruaḥ Ḥayyim* 4.1, 23b.

37. Ḥayyim of Volozin, *Ruaḥ Ḥayyim* 4.1, 24a.

38. Shapiro, "Contingency, Inquiry, and Effort," 52–56.

39. "For the purpose and end of humility is to advance from it to fear of the Lord." Ḥayyim of Volozin, *Ruaḥ Ḥayyim* 6.1, 36a.

40. Ḥayyim of Volozin, *Nefesh ha-Ḥayyim*, middle section, 1; *Nefesh HaTzimzum*, 584.

41. Ḥayyim of Volozin, *Ruaḥ Ḥayyim* 4.4, 26ab.

42. Ḥayyim of Volozin, *Nefesh ha-Ḥayyim* 4.10; *Nefesh ha-Tzimzum*, 663.

43. Ḥayyim of Volozin, *Ruaḥ Ḥayyim* 1.1, 3b.

44. Ḥayyim of Volozin, *Ruaḥ Ḥayyim* 4.1, 23ab. Cf. 3.7, 21ab.

45. "For it was already decreed whether the child will be wise or foolish." Ḥayyim of Volozin, *Ruaḥ Ḥayyim* 2.8, 15b.

46. In his commentary on *Avot* 1:1, he notes, in connection with each link in the chain of transmission—Joshua, the elders, and the prophets—that all of them were humble. See Ḥayyim of Volozin, *Ruaḥ Ḥayyim* 1.1, 4ab.

47. Ḥayyim of Volozin, *Ruaḥ Ḥayyim* 1.1, 3b.

48. Ḥayyim of Volozin, *Ruaḥ Ḥayyim* 1.1, 1b–2b.

49. Ḥayyim of Volozin, letter (on the founding of the yeshiva), published in *Ha-peles* 2 (1901–1902): 140–43.

50. Kahalani, "The Educational Ideal," 182.

51. Ḥayyim of Volozin, *Ruaḥ Ḥayyim* 1.15, 10a.

52. Nadler, *The Faith of the Mithnagdim*, 87.

53. Ḥayyim of Volozin, *Ruaḥ Ḥayyim* 4.1, 24a.

54. Kahalani, "The Educational Ideal," 182.

55. Kahalani, "The Educational Ideal," 197–98.

56. In fact, this is the law as stated by Maimonides, "Laws of the Principles of the Torah," 5.9 in *Mishneh Torah, Book of Knowledge*.

57. Ḥayyim of Volozin, *Ruaḥ Ḥayyim* 4.6, 26b.

Chapter 21

Naḥman of Bratslav

SHAUL MAGID

In onheyb iz geven di emune. (In the beginning there was faith.)

—Elie Wiesel

Where the virtues are required, the vices also may flourish.

—Alasdair MacIntyre, *After Virtue*

The famous Hasidic master Naḥman of Bratslav was born on April 4, the first day of the Hebrew month of Nisan, in 1772.[1] He was born in the town of Medzhibozh, the home of his great-grandfather and founder of Hasidism, Israel Baal Shem Tov. By early adulthood he became one of the most provocative and celebrated Hasidic masters. He died in 1810 of tuberculosis at the age of 38.

What role did Naḥman play in the realm of ethics or virtue ethics? In the case of Naḥman, one of his earliest works, which was only published after his death in 1811, was entitled *Sefer ha-Middot*, loosely translated as "The Book of Character Traits." It is a compilation of aphorisms listed alphabetically that can perhaps best be compared to proverbs, Japanese koans, gnostic wisdom literature, or aphorisms about virtues. *Sefer ha-Middot* is ordered by subject in a fluid Hebrew.[2]

In the introduction we read, "The holy purpose of this work is that it enables the reader to easily access that which he/she can utilize to sanctify themselves. If he/she wants to find a particular remedy (*segulah*) or character trait (*middah*) he/she can easily find it through the alphabetical ordering."[3]

Sefer ha-Middot was likely the work of Naḥman's youth, although scholars think it was an open text that Naḥman began as a young man and continued to develop throughout his life. It was collected and published by Naḥman's erstwhile disciple Nathan Sternhertz of Nemerov (1780–1844) in 1811.[4] *Sefer ha-Middot* differs from other ethical works in that it is more virtue-based, or at least ordered according to what might loosely be called "virtues." It rarely gives any sustained advice on how to *achieve* these virtues, and thus its tie to virtue ethics is ambiguous, as I will discuss below, but it certainly directs its reader toward emotive states, behaviors, and sometimes physical actions to cultivate or avoid states such as joy, anger, depression, conflict, cleanliness, embarrassment, faith, and so on.

Sefer ha-Middot (The Book of Character Traits)

Although written in the later eighteenth or early nineteenth century, *Sefer ha-Middot* is in line with the *musar* or ethical (*hanhagot*) literature of the centuries that preceded it. Hasidic masters were not conversant with the modern philosophical tradition of Kant and Hegel, nor was Naḥman following in the tradition of Moses Maimonides or even in that of pietistic works like Baḥya Ibn Paquda's *Duties of the Heart*.[5] Joseph Dan, for example, suggests that, "in Hasidic literature, religion and ethics were one in the same."[6] On this reading, the distinction between theology and ethics is largely erased in a book such as *Sefer ha-Middot*. One's ethical or relational life is the answer to a divine call rather than a commitment to any human other. Alan Mittleman calls the premodern Jewish ethical pursuit "moral enquiry," that is, serious reflection on the demands of conduct and the ideals of character.[7] *Sefer ha-Middot* could be included in that categorization.

Sefer ha-Middot is a collection of *middot* drawn solely from the classical rabbinic and kabbalistic tradition and thus unoriginal in substance.[8] Aphoristic in style, it offers pithy advice coupled with worldly and heavenly rewards for acting righteously and the dire consequences of acting improperly, sometimes in eyebrow-raising locutions such as, "If one doesn't review his studies and consequently forgets them, his children will die" (*SM*, Children #97).[9] And yet beneath the aphoristic frame and supernatural foundations of *Sefer ha-Middot*, there may be something else happening. At first glance it is a kind of guidebook to classical notions of virtues and vices and the rewards and punishments that accompany them. Yet these sometimes-fantastical aphorisms seem intended to evoke in the reader a state of self-reflection and a meditation on the virtuous life.

Sefer ha-Middot constitutes what I am calling "an ethics of unseen consequences." The founding assumptions are quite traditional: (1) our existence is part of a larger metaphysical plan, (2) divine providence is real and on-going, even if often unseen, and (3) the system of mitzvot constitutes a complex web wherein certain virtues are tied to others as well as to certain vices, constituting a web that is largely unknown to us. By engaging in divine service (*avodat ha-Shem*) one enters this web of mitzvot. One's actions within this web evoke other mitzvot, rewards, and punishments. Thus, one often finds in *Sefer ha-Middot*, "doing x will bring about . . ." or "doing x will rectify y." The connection between x and y is sometimes obvious but often less so. The hermeneutical exercise is to draw conclusions about the symmetry between any x and y by going back to the sources. Naḥman does not cite those sources, however, which is why the annotated editions are so important.

I suggest that the best way to read *Sefer ha-Middot* is devotionally, even contemplatively, its intent being evocative, almost mood inducing, and intentionally deflecting the intellect. We have to keep in mind how much Naḥman believed the intellect was an occupational hazard of the devotional life.[10] By structuring these aphorisms in a way that minimized intellectual distraction, *Sefer ha-Middot* takes its reader into the web of mitzvot, actions and reactions, a kind of labyrinth where everything is intertwined, where virtues and vices share space with Shabbat, the messiah, and dreams, all a part of a living reactive organism called "Torah." What *Sefer ha-Middot* shows the reader is the interconnectedness of it all by looking at it through its operational engine—this will activate that, that will fix this.

In some sense, *Sefer ha-Middot* exhibits a kind of deontological position on ethics—ethics as defined solely by following the rules set forth in the Torah as interpreted by rabbinic tradition. And yet, as opposed to structuring the book in a halakhic way, *Sefer ha-Middot* consists of entries that can loosely be defined as virtues, suggesting, perhaps, that rules are not the sole criteria of behavior but only its superstructure.[11] I don't think all the connections in Naḥman's web of mitzvot need to be smooth or even make clear sense; they are suggestive and evocative. It creates a space for experiencing what it is like to dwell inside the web of Torah through its operational mode of action and reaction.

To illustrate the idiosyncrasy of *Sefer ha-Middot* on the question of virtue, I explore three themes below: faith, the *zaddik*, and money. Faith is the very state that makes ethics, or virtue, possible. Naḥman was an anti-rationalist, a kind a Hasidic fideist in the sense that he believed, not unlike Martin Luther, that reason not only stands in contradistinction to faith but is an impediment to faith.[12] The virtues espoused in *Sefer ha-Middot* are not achieved through reason but through faith in the authority of tradition. Virtues are handed down as a matter of authority. Once they are determined, Naḥman draws on the tradition to present aphoristic aspects of those virtues as the way toward a life of faith, which for him is identical to a life of virtue.

A second theme is the notion of the *zaddik*, or righteous one, a topic that occupies a major place in Naḥman's teachings. Of all the entries in *Sefer ha-Middot* the *zaddik* is by far the most extensive, covering two hundred nine aphorisms in part 1, twenty-one in part 2, and well over a hundred in the additional section that accompanies each entry.[13] For Naḥman there is a difference between righteousness and the *zaddik*. The *zaddik* is not just a righteous figure but an individual who not only merits admiration but also serves as an object of attachment. While the adulation of the *zaddik* is not new in Naḥman, he takes it to new levels and includes it as a central "virtue" in *Sefer ha-Middot*. The *zaddik* as an object becomes the very pillar of faith, out of which all virtue emerges.

The third theme is one's relationship to money. Wealth, or the desire for wealth more generally, is a topic that concerns many ethicists and *musar* thinkers as well. The desire for it, the abuse of it, the way it distorts one's perception of reality are standard tropes. The biblical verse "bribery makes one blind" (Ex. 23:8) permeates Jewish ethical literature. We will see that Naḥman articulates his anti-materialistic form of piety with the recognition that, while poverty increases despondency, wealth increases arrogance.

Virtues: Faith (Emunah)

In *Sefer ha-Middot*, Naḥman does not focus on what one must believe but rather what one might call the "state of belief," that is, what brings one into the orbit of belief, what obstacles prevent it, and what faith itself produces. On the latter point, for example, we read, "Wisdom emerges from faith" (*SM*, Faith #19) and "It is first necessary to believe in God, only after which one can understand God intellectually (*b'sekhel*)" (*SM*, Faith #20). There is nothing remarkable in these comments, one can find them articulated in many classical texts, Jewish or otherwise. For Naḥman, they set the stage for a hierarchy (faith comes before knowledge, faith produces knowledge) that will impact more reactive comments, for example, "faith comes by means of silence" (*SM*, Faith #24) or "faith produces trust (*bitahon*)" (*SM*, Embarrassment #9). Faith in *Sefer ha-Middot* cannot be verified on the basis of evidence; it is both anti-rational and anti-empirical. "One must believe in God through faith and not something verified through a miraculous sign (*mofet*)" (*SM*, Faith #1).

Faith is not based on what we see but rather it helps us to see things aright. "If you see some empirical oddity (*shinui ma'aseh*) do not say it is an accident but rather that it is divinely providential" (*SM*, Faith, #3). The point here is that faith is about the framing and interpretation of sense data; it is a lens through which one experiences the world. Data cannot detract from faith, because faith is totally distinct from the senses. It is a way of viewing the world through the heart and not the mind. "One who does not prepare his/her heart cannot come to faith" (*SM*, Faith #7).

Faith is that which produces a connection to its object, be it the divine or, in some cases, the *zaddik*. "Sometimes faith in God and the *zaddik* are combined. "One who has faith in God brings joy (*naḥat ruaḥ*) to the *zaddik*" (*SM*, *Zaddik* #108). Alternatively, the lack of faith is a disconnect that not only produces alienation but is the very formula of heresy. "One who gains pleasure from the words of a heretic, even if not directly from the heretic, this will bring one to thoughts of idolatry" (*SM*, Faith #5). "One who reads the works of heretics (*minim*) is called an *apikorsus*" (*SM*, Study #58). This is because heresy is the product of reason detached from faith. Heresy is that which disables one's desire for God. "By means of heresy one no longer has a desire to study" (Torah) (*SM*, Study #77). Lack of faith produces a physical repulsion from Torah. "To one who does not have faith, certainly Torah laws (*ḥukot*) will be disgusting (*nimas*)" (*SM*, Faith #39). Reason itself, when it functions alone, is heretical.

Thinking about faith as a virtue in *Sefer ha-Middot*, one might consider that for Naḥman faith is the will that enables the engine of a devotional life to operate. Lack of it produces heresy in its myriad forms, including the natural disgust of truth (Torah). We do find much of the strange action-reaction aphorisms in this entry. But there are some, for example, "Overeating results in a decrease in faith" (*SM*, Faith #11), or "One who raises pigs prevents the redemption" (*SM*, Faith #45). Thus, Torah without faith is heresy, and even reading such heresy is itself an act of heresy. The notion that Torah without faith is heresy is intriguing. In a sense, Naḥman is suggesting that the sanctity of Torah is not self-constituted but is produced via interaction with it through faith in its sanctity. To engage in Torah without a belief in its sanctity turns Torah into its opposite. It may be the most potent kind of heresy. Faith is thus not a virtue in the sense that one who has it is virtuous. Rather, without faith the very possibility of virtue is impossible.

Virtues: The Zaddik

While the doctrine of the *zaddik* is a central theme in Hasidism more generally, in Naḥman's oeuvre the *zaddik* serves as its cornerstone.[14] The *zaddik* is viewed here as a force more than a person, a kind of spiritual treasure (*segulah*) or talisman, and an object of one's submission in order to cultivate a virtuous life. The reason that submission to the *zaddik* cultivates a virtuous life and serves as the source of blessing is that the *zaddik* is a unique reflection of the divine and a portal to divine will and blessing. "Praises that one directs to the *zaddik* are as if praising God" (*SM, Zaddik* #147). "One who disagrees with the *zaddik* . . . has no fear of heaven" (*SM, Zaddik* #200). Thus, belief in the *zaddik* is an extension of belief in God. More strongly, in *Sefer ha-Middot*, it is not quite clear how one gets to God except through the *zaddik*, but this raises a series of other issues that are beyond the scope of this essay.[15]

The virtue of the *zaddik* is not to become one, but to recognize the *zaddik*'s power to be the repository of blessing.[16] The virtue is *proximity* and *submission* to the *zaddik*. "Seeing the face of the *zaddik* sharpens the mind" (*SM, Zaddik* #138). It is a virtue to seek proximity to the *zaddik*, to submit to him as the repository of blessing. By serving the *zaddik* one attains freedom (*ḥerut*), and curses (against one) are nullified (*SM, Zaddik*, part 2, # 14). The point of all this is the experiential and behavioral recognition of the *zaddik* as a portal of virtuousness that can greatly benefit the adept through proximity to him. Proximity to the *zaddik* and his talismanic nature (seeing the face of the *zaddik* is often viewed as more important than hearing Torah from him) is the virtue. How the *zaddik* becomes the *zaddik* is never addressed. The book, and this entry in particular, is not *for* the *zaddik*, but about him. The *zaddik* becomes an object of the virtuous life. While righteousness in general may be the goal of virtue, the *zaddik* is not an exemplar of righteousness in any aspirational sense, but rather an object of devotion by which the reader can maximize his/ her potential as a devotee. If faith is the condition of virtue, the *zaddik* is the object through which faith flows.

Virtues: Money

Aside from the material context of Naḥman's world in which many suffered from abject poverty, the virtue of poverty as well as the advantages of wealth circle through Jewish pietistic literature throughout history.

In *Sefer ha-Middot*, money, livelihood, and wealth are presented as necessary evils, at once desired and yet suspect. Wealth is a mixed blessing, but poverty is a challenge (*nisayon*) for spiritual development. In this entry, we witness much more of the action-reaction motif than in the other two entries. What produces wealth and poverty dominates Naḥman's wisdom here, in sometimes bizarre ways. "Three things bring about poverty: urinating beside one's bed naked, not being careful in washing one's hands, and having one's wife curse him to his face" (*SM*, Money #32). Poverty is viewed as confusing and confounding. "A poor person is as confused as a drunkard" (*SM*, Money #75). Or humiliating. "One who has to borrow from others is like an animal" (*SM*, Money, part 2, #19). Alternatively, poverty is also viewed as potentially beneficial: "Loss of money is an atonement for one's body" (*SM*, Teshuva #91). And the love of money is considered detrimental to one's development. "One who has a desire for money falls from his [spiritual] level" (*SM*, Money #80). "One who hates money will merit a long life" (*SM*, Money #40). Poverty can also be a punishment. "By means of heresy one becomes destitute" (*SM*, Money #81). In the back and forth between praising poverty as a spiritual value and offering advice for attaining wealth, one can see the tension between materiality and spirituality that filters through Nahman's work.[17] What do we make of poverty being a punishment *and* a value; of wealth being a blessing and the cause of one's demise? Yet the rich person seems to also occupy a significant place. "A rich person is like a male and a poor person, a female" (*SM*, Money #102). And yet, "A poor person who is humble, even though he does not give charity, is better than a rich person who gives charity" (*SM*, Haughtiness #31). Naḥman understands that the impoverished suffer. "A person should ask for mercy so as not to become impoverished" (*SM*, Prayer #27). But he cannot quite seem to establish wealth as a value.

Perhaps there is a useful distinction between livelihood (*parnasah*) and wealth (*osher*). The first is a necessity and thus one's behavior should not in any way prevent one from achieving it. The second is a blessing, yet one that comes with considerable hazards. But even livelihood has its hazards. "One who worries day and night about his livelihood will not be successful. The remedy is for him to do teshuva" (*SM*, Money #43). "One's livelihood and opponents prevent a person from reaching one's purpose [in life]" (*SM*, Teshuva #56). What precisely is the virtue being discussed here? On the one hand, poverty is a test, and, on the other hand, an obstacle. One could hardly call it a virtue. The suffering of poverty destroys focus and undermines happiness. The blessing of wealth evokes arrogance and challenges faith. Perhaps each is both a virtue *and* a vice, but in opposite ways. Poverty is a vice that creates opportunities for virtuousness. Wealth is a virtue that creates hazards for vice. The things Naḥman suggests that move one from poverty to virtue and from wealth to vice are sometimes reasonable and sometimes fanciful. But that really doesn't matter. The underlying assumption of all this is that adherence to the dictates of the web of mitzvot enables one to take poverty and make it virtue and to achieve wealth without making it a vice.

This may be the case in *Sefer ha-Middot* more generally. All virtues hold the potential to become vices and all vices hold the potential to become virtues. The categories are fluid by definition. On the one hand, this is obvious. And yet, what *Sefer ha-Middot* tries to do is offer a window into the often unseen consequences of one's behavior, channeled through the web of mitzvot to enable the reader to question one's actions outside the realm of reason. The labyrinth of mitzvot implies everything is connected, but not always logically. Relying on rabbinic literature, Naḥman traces some of those unseen connections to open the reader to the reality that achieving the stated purpose of holiness requires faith in the interconnectedness of all components of the system. *Sefer ha-Middot* is thus a guidebook to enable one to gain some perspective on a Torah action-reaction model of self-perfection.

The Nature of Ethics

"Ethics" for Naḥman is founded on three principles: (1) the interconnectedness of Torah built on a foundation of infinite, often unseen consequences, (2) belief in the *zaddik* as a channel of divine effluence that can aid one in his/her ethical pursuit, not by emulating the *zaddik* but by attaching oneself to him as a devotional act, and (3) preventing reason from making claims about a hierarchy of values and virtues. Virtues are exclusively determined by the dictates of tradition. The cultivation of virtues is never discussed overtly in *Sefer ha-Middot*. There is no evaluative process or behavioral program to follow. In this way *Sefer ha-Middot* differs from traditional and modern *musar* texts. The roadmap of virtues is determined by classical Jewish literature alone. Naḥman was not interested in divulging his sources. In the introduction we read, "The greatness of this book is that there is no need to explain to every knower and seeker of truth and everyone who strives to the way of God. For surely, such an individual will find the meaning in his or her own soul. Happy is the one who attaches themselves to it . . . for the entire book is based on biblical verses and rabbinic teaching, and everything can be known to those who know."[18] To illustrate the template of mitzvot as the backbone of virtue, below is a short excerpt from the second introduction to *Sefer ha-Middot*.[19] It offers us a window into the interconnectedness of mitzvot that stands at the center of Naḥman's theory of virtue:

> Know that every *middah* [virtue/character trait] has many aspects. And every *middah* is in itself a completely self-

> sustaining entity (*kuma shelamah*]. Thus, when a person is missing one aspect of any *middah*, even though the *middah* itself may be complete inside him, because the person is missing [has not integrated] some aspect of that *middah*, it appears as if the *middah* itself is deficient. This is like a person who when h/she has part of a limb missing, the whole body is misaligned, and h/she feels the deficiency in one's entire body. So too when a person is deficient in one aspect of a *middah* it appears as though the entire *middah* is itself deficient.
>
> *Middot* are like neighbors, one *middah* can aid another, as it dwells in proximity to it, as the sages teach "one limb aids another." [For example], when a person eats the limb of an animal, it strengthens that limb in the body. . . . Thus when one wants to go in the holy way h/she must break down all the bad *middot* and achieve all the good *middot*. H/she must constantly inquire into oneself in each *middah* to see if this *middah* is complete inside of them. And when one sees a deficiency in a particular *middah*, one must request aid from a proximate *middah* [to rectify it].[20]

While this doesn't speak directly about the action-reaction motif discussed above, it does affirm the expansive interconnectedness of *middot* more generally, suggesting that a deficiency in one can be completed by another. The author continues, "When one is deficient in humility (*anavah*) there is another *middah* that can aid in humility such as trust (*bitaḥon*). Trust can thus aid one in achieving humility. . . . Sometimes a person already achieved a *middah* but he/she does not use it. That [dormant] *middah* can then be deployed to help achieve another one. To do so one must begin with the *middah* already achieved in order for it to help the one not yet achieved." The idea of using one *middah* as an aid to achieve another is based on the interconnectedness of *middot* more generally. In some way, it serves to explain Naḥman's seemingly arbitrary connection of one *middah* to another. While the connection between trust and humility may not be apparent, although it is not as disparate as some other connections *Sefer ha-Middot* makes, it offers a rendering of how this action-reaction works. When Naḥman tells his reader that x can bring about y without explanation, our author here suggests that this is because the *middah* y (or avoiding the vice y) can function as an aid to achieve x that otherwise eludes him. While never saying so explicitly, the second introduction seems aware of the ostensible arbitrariness of the connections and offers an explanation to suggest the connections may seem arbitrary, but they are in fact part of the complex system of connections whereby one *middah* can help in achieving another.

Ethics and Judaism

How does *Sefer ha-Middot* illustrate Naḥman's views on understanding the tradition more generally? One of the characteristic aspects of Naḥman's hermeneutical project more generally is the notion of *beḥinot,* translated loosely as "aspects," but used as a tool by Naḥman to make seemingly arbitrary connections between one term and another, one word and another, to build an interpretive edifice that serves as the backbone of his homily. The term likely comes from Moses Cordovero's *Pardes Rimonim* in his explanation of the cascading dimensions of divine concatenation that Naḥman deploys to offer a distinctive Hasidic midrashic project.[21]

A similar thing may be happening in *Sefer ha-Middot* in regard to virtues and vices. All virtues and vices are included in an intertwined web of divine will, whose connections can be revealed through the art of interpretation. Engaging in one type of behavior is an attempt to achieve a virtue, or aspire toward a devotional precept, or avoid a vice, and this engagement can be aided by other virtues that can have an impact on one's pursuit. The key to unlock these connections is not through reason, but by the rubrics of the tradition itself. In *Sefer ha-Middot* the interpretive dimension is concealed and what remains is simply the aphorism, the directive, or what one might simply call "advice." Yet *Sefer ha-Middot* is another exemplar of Naḥman's associative project, here it is deployed for devotional purposes and thus the interpretive process is unnecessary.

This is, admittedly, a strange way to approach ethics and certainly a strange way to cultivate virtue. But if one accepts Naḥman's premise that Torah is a web of interconnected points, each of which can impact many others, and those often unseen connections and consequences can be revealed through the interpretive tool of *beḥinot,* it is not so far-fetched to claim that virtue can be achieved by submitting via faith to that idea. It is a way to posit virtue without, even against, reason. The condition of virtue itself is the faith that the Torah holds the key to the virtuous life if one can locate the connections and find an entry point into its unique orbit of sanctity.

Notes

1. Naḥman's messianic pretentions have been the subject of much study. See Arthur Green, *Tormented Master* (Woodstock, VT: Jewish Lights, 1992), 182–220. More extensively, see Tzvi Mark, *Megilat Setarim* (Ramat Gan: Bar Ilan University Press, 2006), 63–158.

2. Not much has been written about *Sefer ha-Middot* in scholarship. See, for example, Zev Gries, *Sifrut ha-Hanhagot* (Jerusalem: Mosad Biyaliḳ, 1989), 249–75; Green, *Tormented Master*, 48–52.

3. Naḥman of Bratslav, *Sefer ha-Middot* (Jerusalem: Yisrael Dov Odesser, n.d.) (*SM*), introduction, 15. I refer to this edition throughout this essay.

4. *SM*, introduction, 11.

5. Maimonides, "Eight Chapters," his introduction to his commentary on Pirkei Avot is often thought to be the quintessence and Jewish ethical literature founded on the principle of Aristotle's *Nicomachean Ethics*.

6. Joseph Dan, *Jewish Mysticism and Jewish Ethics* (Seattle: University of Washington Press, 1986), 111.

7. Alan Mittleman, *A Short History of Jewish Ethics* (Chichester, UK: Wiley-Blackwell, 2012), 1, 2.

8. *SM*, introduction, 9–11. The entries are divided into three parts. The first part is the original aphorisms that were likely written in Naḥman's youth. The second part is additional aphorisms that were written during Naḥman's adulthood. The third part, called "*hashlamot*," is cross-references where the term in the entry is mentioned in other entries. This gives the reader a more complete assessment of the *middah* being discussed.

9. All references to *Sefer ha-Middot* in the body of the text refer to entry and then number.

10. There are many examples of this in Naḥman's *Likkutei Moharan*. For example, *Likkutei Moharan* 2.5, 2.23, 2.44. For a discussion on the casting away of the intellect in Naḥman, see Zvi Mark, *Mysticism and Madness: The Religious Thought of Rabbi Nachman of Bratslav* (New York: Continuum, 2009), 13–24.

11. Claussen suggests a similar negotiation between rules and virtues in his discussion of Simḥah Zissel Ziv. See Geoffrey D. Claussen, *Sharing the Burden: Rabbi Simḥah Zissel Ziv and the Path of Musar* (Albany: State University of New York Press, 2015), 109, 110.

12. Naḥman treats faith in detail in many places in his work. His famous sermon on two types of heresy in *Likkutei Moharan* 1.64 is perhaps his most audacious discussion. See, for example, Green, *Tormented Master*, 285–336; Shaul Magid, "Through the Void: The Absence of God in R. Naḥman of Bratzlav's *Likkutei MoHaRan*," *Harvard Theological Review* 88, no. 4 (1996): 495–519.

13. After each entry there is an additional section called *Haslamah*, which collects the term in question when it is used in other entries.

14. On the *zaddik* more generally, see Immanuel Etkes, "The *Zaddik*: The Interrelationship between Religious Doctrine and Social Organization," in *Hasidism Reappraised*, ed. Ada Rapoport-Albert (London: Littman Library of Jewish Civilization, 1996), 159–68.

15. See, for example, my *Hasidism Incarnate: Hasidism, Christianity, and the Construction of Modern Judaism* (Stanford, CA: Stanford University Press, 2015), where I deal with the incarnational notion of the *zaddik* in a variety of ways.

16. See Moshe Idel, *Hasidism: Between Ecstasy and Magic* (Albany: State University of New York Press, 1995), 189–208.

17. See, for example, in more detail, *Likkutei Moharan* 1.141.

18. *Sefer ha-Middot*, introduction, 10.

19. The attribution of this introduction is a bit unclear. It states, "What I heard from his holy mouth regarding *middot*." It is not clear if this is Nathan or Nemerov recording what he heard from Naḥman, or what the publisher heard for Nathan.

20. *Sefer ha-Middot*, 16. Cf. the first introduction, 9.

21. Harold Bloom uses Cordovero's *beḥinot* as an example of a literary trope of reading against the past by reading out of the past. See Bloom, *Kabbalah and Criticism* (New York: Continuum, 1993), 54ff. Elsewhere I deal with *behinot* in Naḥman's work extensively and suggest that the assumed interconnectedness of all of Torah opens doors whereby one can think the Torah anew through associative reading. One concept can serve as a mirror to another that reflects aspects of the first concept that is not apparent. See Shaul Magid, "Associative Midrash: Reflections on a Hermeneutical Theory in *Likkutei MoHaRan*," in *God's Voice in the Void: Old and New Studies in Bratslav Hasidism* (Albany: State University of New York Press, 2002), 15–66, esp. 43–49. Cf. Arthur Green, *Tormented Master*, 286, 287.

Chapter 22

Isaac Bekhor Amarachi

KATJA ŠMID

Isaac Bekhor Amarachi (?–1888)[1] was a Sephardi author and translator from Salonika. Together with Yosef Ben Meir Sasson, he authored two *musar* works in Ladino, *Sefer Darkhe ha-Adam* and *Musar Haskel* (Salonika, 1843, 1849, and 1892).[2] Between 1845 and 1847, he operated a printing press in Salonika.[3]

Amarachi also translated to Ladino *Ben ha-Melekh ve-ha-Nazir* ("The Prince and the Hermit"; Salonika, 1849), Buddha's story in Ladino, based on Abraham Ibn Ḥasdai's Hebrew translation (Barcelona, thirteenth century); and *Hizzuk Emunah* ("The Strengthening of Faith"; Salonika, 1850), the famous apology of Judaism written in Hebrew by Isaac of Troki (Freiberg, 1681).[4]

Among his translations to Ladino there are three biographical works, written in Hebrew by Abraham Menaḥem Mendel Mohr (1815–1868): *Keter Shem Tov* ("Crown of the Good Name"; Salonika, 1850); Moses Montefiore's biography (Lemberg, 1847); *Tiferet Yisrael* ("The Hope of Israel"; Salonika, 1850), a history of the Rothschild

---

This article has been done in the frame of the Special Intramural Project (PIE) "The Prince and the Hermit: Buddha's story in Judeo-Spanish Version" (ref. 201810I103) of the Spanish National Research Council (CSIC) that was carried out between November 22, 2008, and November 21, 2020. Principal researcher: Katja Šmid.

family (Lemberg, 1843); and *Ḥut ha-Meshulash* ("The Threefold Cord"; Salonika, 1857), a biography of Napoleon III (Lemberg, 1853).[5]

Amarachi wrote a treatise on history and geography of the Holy Land, *Ma'aseh Erets Yisrael* ("The History of the Land of Israel"; Salonika, 1850) in Ladino, based on works by halakhist and geographer Rabbi Yehoseph Schwartz (1804–1865); and the Ladino translation of *Shevile 'olam* ("The Paths of the World"; Salonika, 1853), a Hebrew work on geography of Asia and Africa written by Samson ha-Levi Bloch (Zolkiew, 1822 and 1827).[6]

All the works written or translated by Amarachi are part of his educational and moral life-project that contributed to instruct the Ladino speaking Sephardic readership: on the one hand, his writings teach ethical sensitivity and responsibility, offering practical advice on how to live a moral life; and, on the other hand, they combine relevant topics from Jewish tradition with secular knowledge (universal wisdom, historiography, geography, natural sciences, scientific discoveries, biographies of important Jewish and non-Jewish personalities, etc.) in his quest to educate his readers and to make them wiser and more enlightened.

An Overview of Amarachi's *Musar* Works

The first *musar* works in Ladino had already been published as early as the sixteenth century and became especially popular in the eighteenth and nineteenth when Sephardic rabbis wrote numerous ethical treatises in the vernacular, translations from Hebrew adapted for Ladino readers who did not understand the Holy tongue.[7]

We don't know much about the relationship between Amarachi and Sasson or about the authorship and the part each of them contributed to Ladino ethical works *Sefer Darkhe ha-Adam* and *Musar Haskel*.[8] Yosef Ben Meir Sasson lived between 1810 and 1862 and served as a rabbi in Belgrade between 1851 and 1862. He learned ritual slaughter in Salonika, where he lived for thirty-five years[9] and wrote *Zoveaḥ Todah* (Belgrade, 1860), a guide of Jewish laws for ritual slaughter in Ladino.[10]

The fact that three editions of these two books, printed in Hebrew *Rashi* script, were published in Salonika within a period of only fifty years (1843, 1849, and 1892), testifies to the success these works had among the Ladino readership in the mid-nineteenth century.

Darkhe ha-Adam

Sefer Darkhe ha-Adam ("Book of the Ways of Man") is an original Ladino work whose objectives are didactic, ethical, and entertaining.[11] It was inspired by three Hebrew works, *Sefer ha-Berit* ("The Book of the Covenant"), by Pinḥas Eliyahu Hurwitz (Brünn, 1797),[12] *Seder ha-Dorot* ("The Book of the Generations"), by Yeḥiel Heilprin (Karlsruhe, 1768), and *Shevet Yehudah* ("Scepter of Judah"), by Solomon Ibn Verga (Adrianople, 1550),[13] and it bears ethical, historiographical, and scientific content, as announced on the title page: "Most of its words are from *Sefer ha-Berit* . . . and a little bit of morality and a few stories from *Seder ha-Dorot* and *Shevet Yehudah*." Amarachi and Sasson select the best chapters from the mentioned sources and compile them in this book. In their "Notice to the Readers" in the introduction, they openly acknowledge copying material from these books and note that they add their own ideas:

> Since there are many people who would like to know about the new things [happening] in the world, it seemed appropriate to us to compose this booklet . . . , which contains things taken from some precious books which are not available to everyone, like *Sefer ha-Berit, Shevet Yehudah, Seder ha-Dorot* and other books; and we have translated it to Ladino, so that everyone can understand it, and we only added a few small things of our own, and these are entertaining things that ease the anxiety from our hearts and the sadness by letting us know of what happened to us in the times of Spain.[14]

In three (of six) chapters the authors speak about virtues they consider important to their readers. The first one (1a–14a) opens with an ethical discussion on bad things that can happen to a person as a consequence of his acts, and includes some stories (*ma'asiyot*), based on Maimonides's *Mishneh Torah,* Heilprin's *Seder ha-Dorot,* and other sources. The fourth (29b–52a) and fifth chapters (52a–72a) incorporate the thirteenth chapter from *Sefer ha-Berit*, one of the most powerful moral lessons on loving one's neighbor, a treatise on this universal virtue that was, for the very first time, adapted for Sephardic readers in Ladino.

The other chapters give moral advice exemplified with stories taken from *Shevet Yehudah* such as the *ma'aseh* of King Alfonso's dream (second chapter, 14a–25a),[15] and narratives on blood libels against Jews (sixth chapter, 72a–92b).[16] The third chapter (25a–29b) deals with general history and describes some fascinating episodes about the discovery of the New World;[17] it was inspired by *Sefer ha-Berit* and *Sefer Dibre ha-Yamim le-Malke Tzarfat ve-Otoman* ("Chronicles of the Kings of France and Turkey"; Sabbioneta, 1554), a chronicle written by Yosef ha-Kohen.[18]

Amarachi and Sasson introduce, for the first time, scientific knowledge and historiographic topics taken from general, non-Jewish history, and incorporate them into Ladino ethical literature, an important novelty in the vernacular rabbinic literature in the mid-nineteenth century.[19]

MUSAR HASKEL

Musar Haskel ("Moral Lesson"; Salonika, 1843, 1849, and 1892) is another musar work of varied content by Sasson and Amarachi,[20] which opens with a chapter on scientific knowledge, and compiles some moral, as well as historiographical, chapters, all of them based on classical and more recent Hebrew ethical, scientific, historical, and literary sources. As noted on the cover page, "[the purpose of *Musar Haskel*] is to be read by Jews at night in order to know the ways of God, blessed be He."[21]

Sasson and Amarachi cite all the Hebrew sources they use in a very clear way at the beginning of each paragraph, for example, *Talmud; Tanakh;* Pirkei Avot; *Mishneh Torah*, by Maimonides, especially his "Laws of Character Traits" (*Hilkhot Deot*), on general proper behavior; *Etz ha-Ḥayyim*, by Ḥayyim Vital; *Shevet Yehudah*, by Solomon Ibn Verga (Adrianople, 1550); *Me'il Tzedakah* ("The Robe of Righteousness"; Izmir, 1731), a treatise on the importance of charity, written by Rabbi Eliyahu ha-Kohen, author of *Shevet Musar* ("The Rod of Correction"; Izmir, 1712); *Seder ha-Dorot* (Karlsruhe, 1768), by Lithuanian Rabbi Yeḥiel Heilprin; *Sefer ha-Berit* (Brünn, 1797), written by Pinḥas Eliyahu Hurwitz; and others.

The authors discourse about ethical issues in five (of twelve) chapters (2, 4, 5, 7, 8). Chapter 2 (4a–6a) explains that bad habits and excesses are harmful and cause disease, referring to *Sefer ha-Berit*, and brings a story from *Me'il Tzedakah* with a moral lesson about the virtue of giving charity to the needy. Chapter 4 (12b–17b) is based on "Laws of Character Traits" (*Hilkhot Deot*), the treatise on general proper behavior from Maimonides's *Mishneh Torah* (1170–1180) and mentions Meir Ibn Aldabi's *Shevile Emunah* (1360), an exhaustive treatise on philosophical, scientific, and theological subjects. It explains the importance of being healthy to serve God and gives spiritual advice and tips on how to lead a healthy life regarding eating, drinking, sleeping, bathing, and sexual relations. Chapter 5 (17b–27a), based on Hurwitz's *Sefer ha-Berit*, gives advice on how to raise and educate Jewish sons and teach them righteousness and the right ways to comply with the law in order to be successful in this world and merit the world to come. Chapter 7 (33a–52b), which consists of quotations of Maimonides, passages from *Sefer ha-Berit*, *Tzemaḥ Tzedek* "The Righteous Branch"; Altdorf, 1775), a collection of responsa by Menaḥem Mendel Ben Abraham Krochmal and other sources, deals with man's soul, the power of speech, jealousy, peace, charity, and other virtues that distinguish human beings from animals, exemplified by several stories. Chapter 8 (52b–58a) speaks about the attributes of a wise man contrasted with the defects of a stupid man, exemplified by a story from *Tzemaḥ Tzedek*, and contains quotations from Pirkei Avot, and references to other works.

The other seven chapters (1, 3, 6, 9, 10, 11, 12) deal with scientific and historiographical topics. The book opens with a scientific discussion on the smallpox vaccine inspired by *Sefer ha-Berit* and looks for rational explanations and remedies (chapter 1, 1b–4a).[22] In several chapters the moral content is exemplified with narratives: some parables from the Mishnah, a story of Rabbi Meshulam from *Seder ha-Dorot*, and the story of Bustanay (chapter 3, 6a–12b); three stories taken from *Shevet Yehudah* that relate the experience of Jews in the diaspora in Spain and France (chapter 6, 27a–33a); two more stories from *Shevet Yehudah* about the tensions between Christians and Jews in Spain as well as a discussion on the benefits of science (chapter 9, 58a–64b); and several stories about important rabbis, taken from *Seder ha-Dorot* (chapter 11, 71b–77a). Chapter 10 (64b–71b), exclusively of scientific content, discusses geography, meteorology (using Europe and America as examples), basic astronomy, and describes and explains solar and lunar eclipses of which it includes two illustrations in *Musar Haskel* (68a, 69a).[23] The concluding chapter, entitled *Perek ha-Mashiaḥ* ("The Chapter about the Messiah"), brings an account of the various messianic movements that have disrupted Jewish history, accompanied by many stories and legends about the false messiahs, mainly taken from *Shevet Yehudah* and *Sefer ha-Berit* (chapter 12, 77a–92b).[24] With the themes introduced in these chapters, Amarachi and Sasson managed to "add flavor" to their rabbinic discourse on moral guidance, based on rules of halakhah and musar, and highlight the importance of certain virtues to be practiced in order to be a good person and pursue spiritual improvement, taking into account the experience of suffering during the dark chapters of Jewish history as well as the need to offer Sephardic readers wisdom and worldly knowledge in the vernacular, a task to which Amarachi responded with his varied literary opus.

The use of both traditional and contemporary Hebrew sources that Sasson and Amarachi quote in *Musar Haskel* is much more numerous and diverse than those in *Darkhe ha-Adam*, their first work, in which they combine only three works. The combination of ethical, scientific, and historical passages in *Musar Haskel* incorporates secular knowledge into Sephardic musar literature, and converts Sasson and Amarachi into two of the first Sephardi rabbis to have added an enlightenment agenda to their ethical teachings. This makes their rabbinic discourse diverse, innovative, and unique.

Guidelines for Sephardic Readers on How to Lead an Ethical Life

In both works, the authors discuss various moral virtues and give advice on how to lead an ethical life.

Habits and Virtues to Maintain One's Health

At the beginning of *Darkhe ha-Adam* (1a–6b), Amarachi and Sasson define different kinds of evil and focus on evil caused by man to his fellow man as a consequence of behavior that people themselves have the power to control. Man has a choice to observe the commandments and thus behave in a way that will not harm his fellow man. It is also in his hands to harm himself; therefore the authors give advice on avoiding behavior that may harm his soul: foods that bring all kinds of diseases; physical weakness caused by frequent intercourse; anger and fury; derogatory speech (*lashon ha-ra'*, lit. "evil tongue"); pride and arrogance; and greed. They exemplify the virtues discussed with stories to remind their readers to be careful and moderate in their actions in order to stay healthy. Through proper behavior and the cultivation of these habits and virtues one will avoid harming oneself and others. In short, all physical needs should be satisfied in order to give sustenance to the soul. The authors seek to convince readers to follow their guidance and stay healthy in this world and, in this way, merit the world to come.

In *Musar Haskel* (4a–6a), Sasson and Amarachi, referring to *Sefer ha-Berit*, again point out that eating, having sexual relations, and being angry and jealous in excess are harmful to health, and give a moral lesson on how the virtue of giving charity to the needy at the right moment helps one merit the world to come.

The authors note that in the last generations human bodies are more prone to fall ill; therefore in the fourth chapter of *Musar Haskel* (12b–17b) they offer a Ladino rendition of *Hilkhot De'ot*, the laws of personality development from Maimonides's *Mishneh Torah* (1170–1180). They highlight the importance of being healthy to serve God and give advice on how to lead a healthy life with regard to eating, drinking, sleeping, bathing, and sexual relations. The authors try to convince readers to follow these instructions to stay healthy, and they recommend following a treatment given by a physician in case of illness.

The Virtue of Loving One's Neighbor

Amarachi and Sasson were captivated by *Sefer ha-Berit*, especially by the chapters dealing with neighborly love (*ahavat re'im*). The fourth and fifth chapter of *Darkhe ha-Adam* (29b–72a) are a translation of the penultimate treatise of Hurwitz's *Sefer ha-Berit* that discusses the commandment to love one's fellow man. As noted by Resianne Fontaine,[25] it is divided into thirty-one chapters and offers a definition of neighborly love; a discussion on loving one's neighbor in theory and on how to put it into practice; a discussion on questions about restrictions and priorities in helping one's neighbor; as well as a discussion on the reasons that may prevent the practice of neighborly love. Hurwitz takes an original approach in stressing the love of all human beings, Jews and non-Jews alike, reflecting what David Ruderman describes as his moral cosmopolitanism.[26] In his discourse about senseless hatred, he comments on the tense relations between Sephardim and Ashkenazim in Amsterdam:

> The Sephardim hate the people from Germany and Poland with a great hatred, despite the fact that they live in the same city with Ashkenazim. They praise their own families who are descendants of [the tribe of] Judah and [ask], "What do we have to do with the inferior and despised Tedeschi?" While, in direct opposition, the German and Polish Jews refer to them [the Sephardim] as bitter families in their appearance and in their evil and nasty actions, while "we, the sons of Ephraim, come from an exalted family, from the tribe of Ephraim." Thus this senseless hatred is more difficult than that between one person and his family member or his fellow residents in the same land.[27]

Amarachi translates the meaning of this passage, omits the toponyms and makes it applicable to Sephardim and Ashkenazim of all the eastern Sephardic communities of his time:

> I am amazed about the bad habit present in these generations, most of the people say: "People from that city are mean and liars." And the people from that other city say the same about those of the first city. And there is another bad attribute: most of the Sephardim say that Ashkenazim are bad in their actions and they abhor them, and especially if the Sephardim and Ashkenazim live in the same city, there the enmity is greater. And the Sephardim say that they are from the big family of the tribe of Judah, and the Ashkenazim say of the Sephardim the contrary, that they are bad in their actions and the enmity is much bigger than the abhorrence one feels toward his fellow.[28]

Though the content of the chapter on neighborly love is similar in both works, in the case of Hurwitz it is inserted in a much broader context, since *Sefer ha-Brit* can be read as a compendium of science, as well as a work of kabbalistic musar and even as a spiritual journey to imbibe the Holy Spirit;[29] by contrast, Amarachi in *Darkhe ha-Adam* mainly offers a moral lesson to the Sephardic readership and focuses on the virtue of loving neighbors itself, omitting references to the Kabbalah.[30]

Some years later, in 1847, *Sefer ha-Berit* was translated into Ladino by Ḥayyim Abraham Benveniste Gategno and was published in Salonika in the printing house operated in those years by Isaac Bekhor Amarachi.[31] However, Gategno's translation is not complete and does not include the chapter on loving one's neighbor. Thus, Amarachi and Sasson's translation is the most complete existing version of this treatise in Ladino that the Sephardic readership had the opportunity to read in the vernacular from 1843 on.

In 1870, a shorter version of the treatise on neighborly love appeared in *Pele Yo'etz*, one of the most successful ethical works among Sephardic readers, originally written in Hebrew by Eli'ezer Ben Yitzḥak Papo (Constantinople, 1824),[32] translated into Judeo-Spanish by the author's son, Yeudah Ben Eli'ezer Papo, and published in two volumes (Vienna, 1870–1872, and Salonika, 1899–1900).[33] While Amarachi and Sasson's treatise on neighborly love consists of twenty-two folios in Hebrew Rashi script, Papo's Ladino version is only of seven pages, also in Rashi letters. *Pele Yo'etz* is divided into chapters that are entitled with the virtues themselves and organized in alphabetical order, thus we find Papo's chapter on *Ahavat re'im* under the letter *aleph*.[34] Papo's concise treatise on neighborly love includes a definition of this virtue, that is at the core of the Jewish law, and a deliberation on biblical verses and proverbs dealing with love and friendship of one's fellow man. His sources are moral teachings from the Bible and tannaitic and other rabbinical texts. Like many other Jewish commentators,[35] Papo understands the neighbor to be a fellow Jew: he addresses the Jewish reading public (referring to it with the Ladino expressions such as *la uma yisraelit*, "the Jewish nation," *Yisrael*, "Jews," *los buenos jidios*, "the good Jews"), leaving no doubt that the virtue of loving fellow man applies only to a Jew even though this has not been explicitly stated. Amarachi's writing, by contrast, follows Hurwitz in speaking about love more broadly.

The relationship between virtue and law is obvious in Ladino ethical literature. As noted by Papo, one should fulfill Jewish law with love, because hate is considered a sin; thus, neighborly love derives from love of God. The virtues of being good and fair to one's neighbor, speaking decently about him, and being charitable with the needy are religious obligations.

Amarachi lends special attention to the virtue of neighborly love and offered his Ladino readers, dispersed around the Mediterranean, moral lessons on how to live in peace with themselves, their Sephardi and Ashkenazi brethren who lived in the same area, and with fellow men from other nations and ethno-religious groups.

The Importance of Reading Musar Books

As noted by Hassán,[36] Ladino ethical works offer edifying readings that are not strictly prescriptive and deal with ethical values and concepts, forming a code of conduct that is, in general, aimed to make one a better person and teach what, according to Judaism, one has to do to be a good person.

In the instructive chapter about how parents should educate their children in *Musar Haskel*, we find the following passage discussing the importance of reading books of virtues (musar books) on a daily basis:

> It is also good that a person read one hour every day a book of ethics and books that teach virtues to learn how to deal with other people and put it into practice. . . . And one who wants to learn about [the ways of] ethics and virtues should read *Duties of the Heart* [by Baḥya Ibn Pakuda], *Hilkhot De'ot* by Maimonides, . . . and the second part of *Sefer ha-Berit*. By reading [these] with understanding, he will see that human beings are far behind with these things and realize how many bad habits he has, and by reading and putting these into practice it is certain that it will be pleasing in the eyes of God and people.[37]

As we read in other Ladino musar works,[38] the benefits of reading books of religious edification, either individually or in groups, is a part of the cultivation of the virtues discussed by Sephardic authors. By doing so, readers hear all kinds of narratives (stories, legends, anecdotes, parables, etc.) that exemplify the virtues being deliberated upon, and become acquainted with their exemplars. The protagonists of Ladino ethical works are personalities from the past: biblical figures, Rabbis, kings, and other, either famous or anonymous, individuals. These exemplars of virtues, taken mostly from rabbinical literature, serve as models to be followed and teach the Ladino readership the importance of morality both at individual and communal levels. In some stories of *Darkhe ha-adam* and *Musar Haskel*, groups of diverse ethno-religious backgrounds interact: Sephardim with Ashkenazim and Jews with Christians. Especially in the stories based on *Shevet Yehudah*, by Solomon Ibn Verga, there are several Christian figures: a Roman Pope, the King of Spain, the King of France, King Alfonso from Spain, his son King Manuel, and others. However, they seem to be prototypical or fictional characters used to exemplify virtuous behavior.[39] In both works, we sporadically find protagonists from the Ottoman world, such as the sultan Mahmud and a Turk.

Translators of Jewish virtues to Ladino

Darkhe ha-Adam and *Musar Haskel* are just two examples of numerous ethical books in Ladino that show us what virtues were important to these vernacular speaking rabbis[40] and how the classical Jewish ethical literature was adapted to Ladino readership in the mid-nineteenth century. Amarachi and Sasson aimed to affirm and promulgate religious principles, and were, among many other Sephardic rabbis, educators, who selected the ethical readings, translated and adapted them into Ladino, and offered them to their readers who could then learn from a vernacular ethical literature in which different Hebrew sources came together in a new medium and context. The essential aspect of these books is neither the authors of the Hebrew sources nor their translators to Ladino, but the content itself, as it teaches ethical values and morals. The genre of ethical books was very popular among Ladino readers and therefore the numerous ethical books in Ladino are valuable sources of information about the life and work of pious Sephardi writers and the religious life of the Sephardim scattered in different Jewish communities in the Balkans, their conception of virtues and their local customs and differing ways of living in compliance with Jewish ethics.

Notes

1. Michael Molho, *Tombstones of the Jews Semetery of Salonica* (Tel Aviv, 1974), 568 (in Hebrew). Many thanks to Dr. Dov Cohen for drawing my attention to this book and for helping me with details regarding Amarachi's death. Unfortunately, so far we have not found the year of his birth.

2. Elena Romero, *La creación literaria en lengua sefardí* (Madrid: Mapfre, 1992), 204; David M. Bunis, "Modernization of Judezmo and Hakitia (Judeo-Spanish)," in *The Jews of the Middle East and North Africa in Modern Times*, ed. Reeva Spector Simon, Michael Menachem Laskier, and Sara Reguer (New York: Columbia University Press, 2003), 121; Matthias B. Lehmann, *Ladino Rabbinic Literature and Ottoman Sephardic Culture* (Bloomington: Indiana University Press, 2005), 7; Ana María Riaño López, "La prosa histórica en lengua sefardí," in *Sefardíes: Literatura y lengua de una nación dispersa*, ed. Elena Romero et al. (Cuenca: Universidad de Castilla–La Mancha, 2008), 413, 419.

3. Itshac Emmanuel, "Emprimerias i Empremidores," in *Zikhron Saloniki: Grandeza i destruyicion de Yeruchalayim del Balkan*, ed. David A. Recanati (Tel Aviv: El Commitato por la Edition del Livro Sovre la Communita de Salonique, 1986), 2:242; Lehmann, *Ladino Rabbinic*, 7, 45.

4. Amarachi's name doesn't appear on the title page of the latter as in all the other works he translated. His full name appears "hidden" in an acrostic in biblical verses at the end of the book, probably due to the controversial content of the work.

5. Katja Šmid, "*Sefer ha-Berit* in Ladino: Adaptations and Translations of a Hebrew Best-Seller for the Sephardi Reading Public," in *Ashkenazim and Sephardim: Language Miscellanea*, ed. Andrzej Kątny, Izabela Olszewska, and Aleksandra Twardowska (Frankfurt am Main: Peter Lang, 2019), 111–12.

6. Abraham Menaḥem Mendel Mohr wrote a continuation of Bloch's *Shevile 'olam* with the same title, covering the geography of Europe (Lemberg, 1855–1857). Most likely, again in this case, Amarachi was inspired by Mohr.

7. Lehmann, *Ladino Rabbinic*, 5–6, 12, 35–37.

8. In *Darkhe ha-Adam*, the authors sign Amarachi and Sasson, while in *Musar Haskel* they sign Sasson and Amarachi.

9. Rafael Yosef Ben Sasson, *Zoveaḥ Todah* (Belgrade, 1860), 21a.

10. Ben Sasson, *Zoveaḥ Todah*, 5b; Ženi Lebl, *Do "konačnog rešenja": Jevreji u Beogradu 1521–1942* (Belgrade: Čigoja štampa, 2001), 107–108; Katja Šmid, "Entre la vida y la muerte: Dos obras rabínicas sefardíes impresas en Belgrado," in *Estudios hispánicos en la cultura y ciencia serbia*, ed. Anđelka Pejović et al. (Kragujevac: Universidad de Kragujevac, 2016), 185.

11. Romero, *Creación literaria*, 113; Lehmann, *Ladino Rabbinic*, 177, 179–81, 189–92, 196, 200.

12. David B. Ruderman, *A Best-Selling Hebrew Book of the Modern Era: The Book of the Covenant of Pinhas Hurwitz and Its Remarkable Legacy* (Seattle: University of Washington Press, 2014).

13. Natalia Muñoz Molina, "Versiones judeoespañolas del *Séfer Šébet Yehudá* y los paralelos textuales del *Darjé haadam*," in *La lengua sefardí: Aspectos lingüísticos, literarios y culturales,* ed. Yvette Bürki and Elena Romero (Berlin: Frank and Timme, 2014), 125–34.

14. Isaac Bekhor Amarachi and Yosef Ben Meir Sasson, *Sefer Darkhe ha-Adam* (Salonika: Sa'adi Halevi, 1843), 1b. As mentioned, it is not clear what parts each of the authors contributed to these two publications. It is interesting that sometimes they use the plural form, so it is understood that both were translators of the book. However, occasionally we find the singular form saying, "the translator says." Since it is formulated in singular, it makes us think that Amarachi had a prominent role in these two works.

15. Lehmann, *Ladino Rabbinic,* 178; Natalia Muñoz Molina, "Edición filológica de los diálogos renacentistas de la edición judeoespañola aljamiada del 'Séfer Sebet Yehudá' de Belgrado, 1859" (PhD diss., Complutense University of Madrid, 2014), 54, 72, 219–36.

16. Lehmann, *Ladino Rabbinic,* 104, 178.

17. Lehmann, *Ladino Rabbinic,* 190, 195–96; Katja Šmid, "El descubrimiento del Nuevo Mundo en dos obras rabínicas sefardíes de Salónica (siglo XIX)," *Ars & Humanitas* 11, no. 2 (2017): 261–78.

18. Martin Jacobs, "Joseph ha-Kohen, Paolo Giovio, and Sixteenth-Century Historiography," in *Cultural Intermediaries: Jewish Intellectuals in Early Modern Italy,* ed. David Ruderman and Giuseppe Veltri (Philadelphia: University of Pennsylvania Press, 2004), 67–85.

19. Lehmann, *Ladino Rabbinic,* 189–92.

20. Romero, *Creación literaria,* 113–14; Lehmann, *Ladino Rabbinic,* 7, 45, 104, 177–81, 189–93, 200; Natalia Muñoz Molina, "Pasajes del *Séfer Šébet Yehudá* en la obra judeoespañola *Séfer Musar haskel,*" in *Selected Papers from the Fifteenth British Conference on Judeo-Spanish Studies (29–31 July 2008),* ed. Hilary Pomeroy, Christopher J. Pountain, and Elena Romero (London: Queen Mary University of London, 2012), 143–56; Olga Borovaya, trans., "Isaac Bekhor Amarachi and Joseph ben Meir Sason, *Sefer musar haskel* (Book of Moral Lessons)," in *The Posen Library of Jewish Culture and Civilization,* vol. 6, *Confronting Modernity, 1750–1880,* ed. Elisheva Carlebach and Deborah Dash Moore (New Haven, CT: Yale University Press, 2019), 252–53.

21. Yosef Ben Meir Sasson and Isaac Bekhor Amarachi [Yitzḥak Bekhor Amarachi], *Sefer Musar Haskel* (Salonika: Eliyahu Farachi and Sa'adi Halevi, 1843).

22. Romero, *Creación literaria,* 114; David B. Ruderman, "Some Jewish Responses to Smallpox Prevention in the Late Eighteenth and Early Nineteenth

Centuries: A New Perspective on the Modernization of European Jewry," *Aleph* 2 (2002): 111–44; Lehmann, *Ladino Rabbinic*, 189.

23. Lehmann, *Ladino Rabbinic*, 187–88, 190, 192.

24. Lehmann, *Ladino Rabbinic*, 177, 180–81.

25. Resianne Fontaine, "Love of One's Neighbour in Pinhas Hurwitz's *Sefer ha-Berit*," in *Studies in Hebrew Language and Jewish Culture, Presented to Albert van der Heide on the Occasion of his Sixty-Fifth Birthday*, ed. Martin F. J. Baasten and Reiner Munk (Dordrecht: Springer, 2007), 244–68.

26. Ruderman, *A Best-Selling*, 75–89. See also Fontaine, "Love," 272–76.

27. Ruderman, *A Best-Selling*, 25.

28. Šmid, "*Sefer ha-Berit*," 113–14.

29. Ruderman, *A Best-Selling*, 90.

30. As noted by Šmid, "*Sefer ha-Berit*," 118–19, the passages referring to Kabbalah are omitted from the translation of *Sefer ha-Berit* to Ladino (Salonika, 1847) because, as noted by the translator, except the kabbalists, nobody would understand them. Among the books published in the printing press of Isaac Bekhor Amarachi were *Tiqune ha-Zohar* (1845), *Tiqun Ḥatzot* (1845), and the Ladino translation of Pinḥas Hurwitz's *Sefer ha-Berit* (1847), which might point to Amarachi's kabbalistic background, a matter pending further study.

31. Pinḥas Eliyahu Hurwitz, *Sefer ha-Berit*, trans. Ḥayim Abraham Benveniste Gategno (Salonika, 1847); Lehmann, *Ladino Rabbinic*, 7, 191; Šmid, "*Sefer ha-Berit*," 116–20.

32. Marc D. Angel, *The Essential Pele Yoetz* (New York: Sepher-Hermon, 1991).

33. Yeudah Ben Eli'ezer Papo [Judah Papo, *Pele Yo'etz* (Vienna: Jacob Schlossberg, 1870–1872).

34. Papo, *Pele Yo'etz*, 32–39.

35. Ruderman, *A Best-Selling*, 77–81.

36. Iacob. M. Hassán, "La prosa rabínica," in *Sefardíes: Literatura y lengua de una nación dispersa*, ed. Elena Romero et al. (Cuenca: Universidad de Castilla–La Mancha, 2008), 268, 272.

37. Amarachi and Sasson, *Sefer Musar Haskel*, 21a–21b.

38. Papo, *Pele Yo'etz*, 2: "[T]he real cure for the evil impulse is to read moral books and this is clearly stated in the books."

39. Muñoz Molina, "Edición filológica," 37–38.

40. The term "vernacular rabbis" was coined by Lehmann, *Ladino Rabbinic*, 32, 35, 37–38, 44.

Chapter 23

Israel Salanter

SARAH ZAGER

Rabbi Israel Salanter (1809–1883) is best known as the founder of the modern Musar movement. Though it was nourished by the growth of the modern Yeshivah in Lithuania, the Musar movement also presented a strong religious and social counterpoint to it: Musar rejected the modern Yeshivah's increasingly single-minded focus on Talmud study, instead suggesting that both yeshivah students and *ba'alei batim* (householders) and tradespeople should devote significant time to developing their characters.[1] To do this, Salanter and his followers developed a series of methods for "studying" and thereby improving one's character.

This project developed against a set of religious, political, and social challenges facing Eastern European Jews in the nineteenth century. From the outside, the Czarist regime's economic policies, forced conscription, and increasing imperial control of Jewish educational institutions presented significant threats to Jewish religious culture and practice. At the same time, Hasidism and the Haskalah[2] offered vibrant alternatives to the religious outlook and practices emerging from Lithuanian yeshivot. Salanter's biography was shaped by all of these forces, and his theory of virtue reflects an effort to develop an approach to Jewish life, practice, and ethics that addresses the challenges of poverty and political persecution, while incorporating some of the key strategies of both Hasidism and the Haskalah in the service of keeping young students away from those purportedly damaging influences.

Born in Zagere in 1809, Salanter eventually moved to Salant in 1823, where he studied with Tzvi Hirsch Braude. From there, Salanter rose to prominence in his own right, and, by 1848 was in a prominent enough position to play a leading role in the Jewish community's response to a growing cholera epidemic. Accounts of Salanter's own behavior during the epidemic differ—with some saying that he spoke to the congregation publicly promoting significant halakhic leniencies (including, most famously, eating on Yom Kippur) to help mitigate the effects of the disease. Others report that Salanter himself stood up and made the *kiddush* blessing and ate.[3]

The turning point in Salanter's career came in 1848, when Salanter was offered a position as a teacher in a new government-run seminary, which taught secular subjects alongside a religious curriculum. Rather than accept the post, Salanter moved to Kovno, where he taught at the Nevyozer Kloyz. It is not entirely clear whether this "escape" was as much from the Russian authorities (who likely could have found him in nearby Kovno) or from Jewish leaders who would have impeded his efforts to pursue his novel religious approach.[4] Nonetheless, Salanter's decision seems to be driven by a desire to distance himself and his students from the influence of both Christianity and the Haskalah. A decade later, Salanter seemed to have changed his tack. In 1857, Salanter left Lithuania for Germany and Paris; though the trip was initially for medical reasons, Salanter remained there until his death in order to help educate assimilated Jews in Western European universities.

Salanter's Virtues: A Matter of Survival

The early scholarly reception of Salanter's work suggested that he did not provide a new ethical theory of his own. In his 1928 treatment of Salanter, Louis Ginzberg writes that, "[i]n spite of Salanter's originality, he has not given us a new system of ethics."[5] Versions of this reading of Musar as essentially religiously and ethically conservative have retained their prominence. Over 60 years later, Immanuel Etkes wrote that, "[s]tudy of Salanter's writings reveals that, not only is his underlying theological position completely lacking in innovation, but it even entails a certain degree of retreat. His approach is essentially a return to the classical Rabbinic thought of the Mishnah and the Talmud."[6] In contrast, some of Salanter's more recent scholarly reception has treated him as either laying the groundwork for a form of Jewish antinomianism, or as integrating both traditional and anti-traditional elements.[7] In this chapter, I will suggest that Salanter did offer a novel approach to Jewish ethics, precisely by adopting and manipulating tropes from both earlier Jewish treatments of the virtues and halakhic discourse. This combination of influences leads Salanter to offer a virtue theory that departs from contemporary Aristotelian virtue theories in key ways.

Salanter integrates these various influences in his description of the overall role of the pursuit of the virtues. The "medical metaphor," which treats the vices as "illnesses of the soul" has had a long career in both Jewish and non-Jewish accounts of the virtues; Salanter's reshaping of the medical metaphor provides a helpful window into how he understands the role of the cultivation of the virtues.[8] Maimonides suggests that a person who suffers from an "illness of the soul" should consult a "doctor of the soul" in order to be returned to the path of the mean.[9] As Maimonides describes it, this "illness of the soul" is something that *might* afflict some people in a given situation—some people have sick souls, and others have more or less well ones. Salanter provocatively suggests that everyone suffers from a profound "illness of the soul" that requires substantial "medicine" to overcome.[10] Thus, for Salanter, the project of cultivating the "virtues" is less a project of "character building," "character development," or the pursuit of "human flourishing," than of "curing" our character.

For Salanter, this thoroughgoing illness of the soul obligates us to seek a cure, which can be pursued through a ritualized practice of study, called *limmud musar*. He writes, "A person suffers from a great illness with respect to service of the Holy Blessed One, and it is not easy to make use of the cure of *limmud musar*; one needs a very strong treatment in order to cure such a significant illness."[11] Because Salanter understands this illness to be pervasive, Salanter argues that musar study is obligatory for everyone who experiences this illness, including people he takes to be excluded from the obligation to engage in standard Torah study, such as women and men who are too busy seeking basic subsistence to be able to study.[12] In this way, Salanter rhetorically connects his description of *limmud musar* to the ritualized practice of Torah study, even as he radically expands its scope.

Salanter manipulates standard understandings of Torah study in other ways as well. While some prominent Jewish thinkers of the day treated study as an end in itself, Salanter rejected this view, arguing instead that study in the *Beit Musar* "is not a virtue or an achievement—rather it is absolutely necessary [*hekhraḥi*]. A sick person who is afflicted by sins and transgressions, which will be bitter for him in the end—must go to [the *Beit Musar*] to pour out his soul in *Limmud Musar,* so that he might be saved a bit from his *yetzer,* so that he might overpower it, and so that he will not go in the way of his stubborn heart [Isa. 57:17]."[13] Salanter also recognizes that the process of *limmud musar,* like the process of seeking medical care, is often characterized by a lack of dignity, or even a form of dehumanization. However, people are more willing to accept this form of debasement in the medical case than in the ethical one:

> For physical needs and ailments, a person looks with all his strength for something that will heal him or at least lessen the suffering and wretchedness of his illness. Why does a person not do the same thing for his soul? A sick person is not ashamed to do things that are not commensurate with his dignity, so why does [a person who has a sick] soul complain and look over his shoulder to what others say about him, even to those who do not know anything about what he is? Because it is the way of man to become preoccupied with attending to his physical needs, which distract the heart of man from attending to his eternal end.[14]

Here, Salanter suggests that, like the treatment of a physical illness, the pursuit of virtues can be painful, even destructive; the risks, and even the pain, of the "cure" is warranted by the severity of the "illness" of the soul that Salanter diagnoses in us. In this way, Salanter treats the cultivation of the virtues as a matter of human survival, rather than a tool for the pursuit of human perfection, flourishing, or moral exemplarity, which dominate contemporary virtue theories.

Humility (*Anavah*) and Fear (*Yirah*) as Tools for Moral Repair

Here, I will focus on two virtues that play important and interlocking roles in Salanter's thought: *yirah* (fear of heaven) and *anavah* (humility); analyzing Salanter's use of these virtues can also help us better understand his relationship to contemporary virtue theories.

Yirah plays a central role in Salanter's conception of what it means to live well. *Yirah* is something that can both be cultivated over time and awakened in the heat of the moment—in this sense, it is both a disposition (a disposition to, say, perform mitzvot, or to obey God's overall will) and a set of emotions (a feeling of inadequacy or a felt need, or even a sense of desperation, to improve one's spiritual well-being). For Salanter, *yirah* is fundamentally tied to the reality of divine punishment. *Yirah* is "[f]ear of physical punishment of the body, which exceeds all earthly punishments."[15] Salanter suggests that *yirah* is best cultivated by focusing on the physical details of these punishments and their effects on the individual's physical body. A person who cultivates *yirah* recognizes "that the punishments of the body and soul will not be suffered by a stranger, but instead by the very same person who performs the sins. He himself will suffer a punishment so bitter that he will not be comforted."[16] In turn, this imagined future of physical punishment has an embodied effect in the present; the practice of *limmud musar* leads the soul to be "awakened through the sensation of the limbs."[17]

Cultivating *yirah* is eventually designed to facilitate two kinds of changes in character, called *kibbush ha-yetzer* ("conquering of the will") and *tikkun ha-yetzer* ("rectification of the will"). In the first step of *kibbush ha-yetzer*, Salanter argues, a person must develop the ability to ignore the demands of the evil inclination and the powerful desires that it puts forward. Eventually though, in *tikkun ha-yetzer*, a person will not actually want to act badly; in this process, a person "chang[es] his nature so that he will do good."[18] This distinction roughly tracks the Aristotelian distinction between continent and incontinent actors. Like Aristotle, Salanter expresses a general preference for the latter over the former.[19]

However, Salanter also elaborates this distinction in a way that diverges from the Aristotelian picture, giving humility a central role in the process of *tikkun ha-yetzer*.[20] After distinguishing between *kibbush ha-yetzer* and *tikkun ha-yetzer*, Salanter goes on to divide *tikkun ha-yetzer* into two further types. Salanter writes that, "[t]here are two kinds of *tikkun ha-yetzer*: the first is to rectify [*l'taken*] the powers of the soul they will only desire the good, as determined by the upright intellect, so that [the intellect] will not be overpowered or destroyed by the emotions, as is in the case of most vicious tendencies. And the second is to elevate them to a level that is even higher than the human intellect can understand."[21] This first level follows the Aristotelian view that a person who has been habituated to become temperate will be "most capable of abstaining from pleasures," and who will even derive pleasure from doing so.[22] Salanter also posits that there is a second level of *tikkun ha-yetzer* in which these embodied forces are themselves transformed. However, on this second level, the practitioner "elevates [emotions] to a level that is even higher than the human intellect can understand."[23] Only in this second stage can a person be fully humble. He continues, "Almost all of the foundation of the trait of humility (which is the greatest trait of all, according to Rabbi Yehoshua ben Levi in BT Avodah Zarah 20b) is at a level above the human intellect."[24] The relationship between humility, intellect, and *tikkun ha-yetzer* here is unclear, but Salanter goes on to explain that someone who has successfully learned to desire to only do good (i.e., they have learned to limit their bodily desires to a nearly negligible level), might then be led to think that they are more virtuous than those who have not yet achieved the preliminary level of *tikkun ha-yetzer*; Salanter turns his readers attention to the virtue of humility in order to quell this misconception. To make this point, Salanter quotes a passage from Baḥya Ibn Paquda's *Duties of the Heart*, which suggests that a person ought to see themselves as less virtuous than those around them, even if empirical evidence suggests otherwise.[25] Salanter notes that this way of thinking flies in the face of the intellect, which tends to "seek out and inspect [an issue] from all sides"; on its own, the intellect would say it cannot possibly be that a relatively virtuous person is in fact less virtuous than everyone else on every score.[26] Someone who is able to assume that others are more virtuous, even when the evidence suggests otherwise, is someone who has used the virtue of humility to take the process of *tikkun ha-yetzer* beyond what is possible through the intellect alone.

This allows us to draw out two important contrasts between Salanter's theory of the virtues and Aristotelian and neo-Aristotelian virtue theories. For Salanter, the intellect is a tool used to cultivate the virtues (and, as we will see, a form of study is key to the development of the virtues), but, intellectual excellence does not itself epitomize virtue; instead, to fully achieve the highest level of *tikkun ha-yetzer*, one has to leave the intellect behind in favor of a kind of humility that proceeds against all evidence to the contrary.[27]

The kind of humility that Salanter endorses here requires the practitioner to be perpetually willing to reconsider whether conduct that appears good on intellectual grounds is actually as good as it seems to be; this is especially important when actors compare their own actions to others' behavior. Rather than being almost automatically attracted to the good—as in Iris Murdoch's metaphor of a moral "magnetism"—Salanter suggests that we need to be concerned that our initial attraction to what appears to be good might actually lead us toward away from the good rather than toward it.[28] Salanter's picture of the virtues, then, is a relentlessly self-critical one. While this criticism certainly contains some intellectual elements, it is also grounded in an affective commitment to humility. Achieving *tikkun ha-yetzer* does not thereby allow us to "graduate" from the need to cultivate *yirah*; instead, *yirah* needs to be perpetually reinforced even when it is not obviously rationally grounded.

Limmud Musar as Method for Cultivating the Virtues

As we saw above, one of the main goals of *limmud musar* is to help stimulate an emotional response to the fear of divine punishment, thereby cultivating *yirah*. The practice of *hitpa'alut*, or emotional outpouring, plays a crucial role in this process. Salanter contrasts *hitpa'alut* with intellectually driven modes of Torah study, writing that "[t]he intellect is the power and ability to go broadly, and to seek out and inspect [an issue] from all sides. The same is not true of *hitpa'alut*; it is its tendency to gather together all of the powers of the soul [and focus them] on the thing that the sparks of the *hitpa'alut* point toward, so that almost all of the powers of his soul are forgotten and extinguished for a moment, according to the strength of his *hitpa'alut*."[29] To do this, Salanter suggested that students engage in chanting practices and physical movements that would stimulate this kind of emotional release.

Even as Salanter explicitly contrasts *hitpa'alut* and intellectual analysis, he also models the broad practice of *limmud musar* on Torah study. One of the main ways that *hitpa'alut* can be cultivated, Salanter argues, is by repeating ethical sayings from rabbinic literature. Salanter describes this practice as follows: "What is a person who works hard each day to do? It is an easy thing to do, and it does not require a clear mind or a lot of time, to go over the moral sayings of the Sages a few times, so that his *hitpa'alut* will be awakened in his soul for a short time."[30] This version of study does not require the intellectual training and technical skill that dominant modes of Talmud study practiced in Lithuanian Yeshivot at the time prioritized, but it remains grounded in the rabbinic textual tradition.

Even as Salanter suggests that this practice will be "simple," he also recognizes that it does not always produce the desired effect; even someone who seeks to engage in *hitpa'alut* will not always experience the kind of emotional outpouring that Salanter describes. However, Salanter maintains that this approach nonetheless produces significant effects on the students' subconscious mind.[31] He writes: "A person should not stumble in his *limmud musar* if it does not work and it does not leave a mark in his soul in order to change his ways—it is well-known that even if it is not clear that there is a physical mark, the eyes of the intellect see, over time, with a lot of study, the accumulation of hidden marks, and he will turn into a different person."[32] Here, Salanter endorses something close to an Aristotelian picture of "second nature" in which a person's emotional and psychological habits eventually become consolidated into a set of dispositions that then influence future conduct without much conscious effort from the actor.[33] Thus, for Salanter, "the same is true for *hitpa'alut* of the soul—every act [of *hitpa'alut*] leaves a mark on the subconscious, and when many forms of *hitpa'alut* are consolidated together about a single thing, without a long period between them . . . [this study] creates subconscious forces which are strong enough to produce results."[34] Salanter reshapes the existing practice of Torah study for his own purposes, turning it into a tool for cultivating *yirah*, and, eventually, for *kibbush ha-yetzer* and *tikkun ha-yetzer*.

Salanter also recognizes that cultivating *hitpa'alut* will be much easier to do in a communal environment that is designated especially for the purpose. This leads him to suggest that *limmud musar* should take place in a communal environment, called a *Beit Musar*. This space serves three key functions: first, it provides a designated space for learning practices that might not be otherwise welcome in a traditional *Beit Midrash* and that might not be possible in other spaces. In *Sha'arei Or*, Salanter's students suggest that *limmud musar* will not be at home in other spaces. They write, "Can he really sit in his house and do this? With all of his household surrounding him?

Or in the *Beit Midrash*, where he will disturb those studying *gemara* and halakhah with his learning, with *hitpa'alut* of the soul? Their study may also disturb his study of musar. Also, if *limmud musar* stirs up tears in his eyes, which run like streams of water, he will be too embarrassed and wrapped up in shame to engage in it."[35] Here Salanter's students argue that *limmud musar* requires very specific social conditions—on the one hand, *limmud musar* requires a space where a person can have enough respite from daily life (including family life) in order to concentrate appropriately on one's internal character. At the same time, though, this practice is not a silent form of contemplation or of ascetic isolation from others—musar study is a noisy practice; it is done out loud and among others also engaged in a similar process.

Salanter himself also suggests that the communal atmosphere in the *Beit Musar* will also help students develop a regular habit of *limmud musar*. He writes: "a person will strengthen his fellow, and he will be eager to use strategies so that this time [set aside for musar study] will be proper for him, with no deficiency. And if a person should be absent, or if Satan should take him away from [his study], God forbid, then the matter should be investigated, [and he should] ask for advice and strategies about how to limit his foolishness, and to open his heart with soft words, each person according to his way and his intellect. In this way, he will entrench his moral foundations with a strong stake."[36] In this way, for Salanter, the cultivation of the virtues is an individual, psychological one, but it is one that needs the appropriate communal context in order to succeed. Without an appropriate physical environment, and a set of colleagues who share similar moral goals, it will be difficult to lay the strong psychological foundations for *yirah* and *tikkun ha-yetzer*.

Halakhah and Virtue in Musar

In both its Jewish communal and academic reception, the modern Musar movement is portrayed both as a traditionalist project, designed to help guard Jewish life and practice against the forces of modernity, and a radical reformist one, designed to challenge the fundamental assumptions of Lithuanian methods for Talmud study and the culture of the burgeoning Lithuanian yeshivah.[37] Both of these readings capture something important about Salanter's overall project: on the one hand, Salanter's work was formulated as a response to the perceived threat of both Haskalah and assimilation, but, on the other hand, Salanter modeled the practice of *limmud musar* on the practice of Talmud Torah, borrowing some of the key legal language used to delineate Talmud Torah as a ritualized communal practice. In this way, Salanter's theory of virtue is both deeply rooted in Jewish language, categories, and texts, and, at the same time, critical of some contemporaneous approaches to Judaism that Salanter takes to be mistaken.

We can see this clearly in the way that Salanter describes *limmud musar* as an obligatory practice (a *ḥiyuv*). As we saw above, Salanter thinks that this *ḥiyuv* is grounded in a severe illness of the soul that needs to be cured, rather than in a divine interdiction, but, at the same time, Salanter imagines that we comply with this *ḥiyuv* in much the same way as we comply with the obligation to study Torah. The *Shulḥan Arukh* codifies that "[e]ven a poor person, who goes and begs in doorways, and even one who has a wife and children, is obligated to set times for Talmud Torah, day and night, as it is written 'recite it day and night' [Josh. 1:8]."[38] Similarly, Salanter suggests that one "set aside specific times [for *limmud musar*], each day between the afternoon and evening prayers."[39] This also helps build the communal culture of regular *limmud musar* that we discussed in the previous section.

Salanter's attitude toward halakhah specifically has also been hotly debated in the scholarly literature.[40] Resolving this debate lies well beyond the scope of this chapter, but for our purposes, it is still useful to note that Salanter deployed halakhic terminology frequently in his thought. In one striking example Salanter argues that, while halakhot that address character are usually classified as *mishpatim* rather than *ḥukim*, because they appear to have some grounding in rationality, this misunderstands the role that these commandments have in many people's lives.[41] In fact, Salanter argues, many people need to start off relating to commandments about character as *ḥukim* rather than *mishpatim*. In this way, "[*ḥ*]*ukim* are the rungs by which one ascends the ladder of *mishpatim*. And this is especially true when it comes to the virtues, which are *mishpatim*. All of a person's labor will not be enough to bring them into their correct form and make them upright in their correct boundaries. And so he will have to rely on the human intellect to love the straight path and to hate contortion in his nature (without a warning [*azharah*] in the Torah)."[42] Treating a commandment about a character trait as a *ḥok* or law, actually can help a person achieve *tikkun ha-yetzer.* Salanter continues: "[B]y persistently contemplating the virtues, we will come to understand them as *misphatim* and to understand their true boundaries. And this is what it says in the verse 'And you shall keep My laws [*ḥukkotai*]' [Lev. 18:5], first, and then 'you shall [do] my rules [*mishpatai*].'[43] The force of halakhic norms, even those norms that are not themselves obviously connected to the virtues, nevertheless play a significant role in the process of character development for Salanter. While Salanter does not present a systematic theory of virtue or a systematic philosophy of halakhah, he does manipulate both virtue discourses and the deontic language of halakhah to develop his own pedagogical approach to the virtues. Salanter's virtue theory is at times harsher and more pessimistic than the ones we find in Aristotelian and neo-Aristotelian virtue theories—it focuses on illness more than flourishing—but it also uses deeply deontic language to develop a more concrete and robust set of tools for developing the virtues, even in the face of what might initially seem like a dire diagnosis.

Notes

1. For a discussion of the development of the Lithuanian yeshivah's development see Shaul Stampfer, *Lithuanian Yeshivahs of the Nineteenth Century: Creating a Tradition of Learning* (Oxford: Littman Library of Jewish Civilization, 2014).

2. The "Haskalah," or "Jewish enlightenment," played a significant role in both Western and Eastern European Jewish intellectual life during the eighteenth and nineteenth centuries; it sought to revitalize Jewish culture, philosophy, and literature in order to place it in dialogue with its non-Jewish European counterparts.

3. See Immanuel Etkes, *Rabbi Israel Salanter and the Mussar Movement: Seeking the Torah of Truth* (Philadelphia: Jewish Publication Society, 1993), 169–70.

4. Etkes, *Rabbi Israel Salanter and the Mussar Movement*, 146. See also Shaul Stampfer, *Lithuanian Yeshivas of the Nineteenth Century: Creating a Tradition of Learning* (2012; Oxford: Littman Library of Jewish Civilization, 2014), 261.

5. Louis Ginzberg, "Rabbi Israel Salanter," in *Students, Scholars, and Saints* (Philadelphia: Jewish Publication Society, 1928), 178.

6. Etkes, *Rabbi Israel Salanter and the Mussar Movement*, 93.

7. For the former reading see Shaul Magid, "The Road from Religious Law (Halakha) to the Secular: Constructing the Autonomous Self in the Musar

Tradition and Its Discontents," in *Jewish Spirituality and Social Transformation: Hasidism and Society*, ed. Philip Wexler (New York: Crossroad, 2019), 203–22. For examples of the latter reading see Hillel Goldberg, *Israel Salanter, Text, Structure, Idea: The Ethics and Theology of an Early Psychologist of the Unconscious* (Ktav Publishing House, Inc., 1982), 200; and Geoffrey Claussen, *Sharing the Burden: Rabbi Simhah Zissel Ziv and the Path of Musar* (Albany: State University of New York Press, 2016), 3.

8. For earlier versions of the "medical metaphor," see Plato's *Phaedo* 69a6–c3, as well as Aristotle, *Nicomachean Ethics*, trans. Terence Irwin, 2nd ed. (Indianapolis: Hackett, 1999), 1150b30–35.

9. Maimonides, *Mishneh Torah, Hilkhot De'ot* 2.2.

10. Israel Salanter, *Or Yisrael*, with notes and commentary from Ruben Lichter (Jerusalem: R. Loikhṭer, 2006), letter 6, 123. Translations from *Or Yisrael* are my own, produced in consultation with Zvi Miller, ed., *Ohr Yisrael: The Classic Writings of Rav Yisrael Salanter and His Disciple Rav Yitzchak Blazer*, trans. Eli Linas (Southfield, MI: Targum/Feldheim, 2004).

11. Salanter, *Or Yisrael*, letter 6, 123.

12. Salanter, *Or Yisrael*, letter 3, 72. Salanter writes: "*Limmud musar* is not like other kinds of study. There is no other kind of study whose obligation extends to all people. Women are exempt from *Talmud Torah*, and there is also ample room to exempt those who are downtrodden from their work, and who are not of sound mind because of their horrible hardships, God forbid—each person can be removed from their obligation according to his situation."

13. Salanter, *Or Yisrael*, letter 13, 196.

14. Salanter, *Or Yisrael*, letter 13, 197.

15. Salanter, *Or Yisrael*, letter 9, 172.

16. Salanter, *Or Yisrael*, letter 9, 173.

17. Salanter, *Or Yisrael*, letter 9, 173.

18. Salanter, *Or Yisrael*, letter 17, 225.

19. Aristotle, *Nicomachean Ethics*, 1145b9–14. Notably, while Aristotle reserves the label of "virtuous" for people who do not desire to do bad things, and thus feel no sense of pain at not being able to do them. It is not clear that Salanter ever thinks this is possible for human beings, who remain plagued by even modified or rectified a *yetzer*.

20. Compare this with Aristotle's account of magnanimity, Aristotle, *Nicomachean Ethics*, 1123a35–1123b28.

21. Salanter, *Or Yisrael*, letter 30, 329.

22. Aristotle, *Nicomachean Ethics* 1104b5–9.

23. Salanter, *Or Yisrael*, letter 30, 329.

24. Salanter, *Or Yisrael*, letter 30, 329–30.

25. Salanter, *Or Yisrael*, letter 30, 330–31. Here, Salanter quotes both *Derekh Eretz Zuta* 2 and *Duties of the Heart, Sha'ar Kinah* 10.

26. Salanter, *Or Yisrael*, letter 30, 331.

27. This represents a departure from both the Aristotelian and Maimonidean traditions.

28. Iris Murdoch, *Metaphysics as a Guide to Morals* (1992; London: Penguin, 1994).

29. Salanter, *Or Yisrael*, letter 30, 358–59.

30. Salanter, *Or Yisrael*, letter 30, 366.

31. Though Salanter does not directly thematize "the subconscious" as a single unit, there has been some scholarly debate about whether Salanter's approach to subconscious mental processes was influenced by Freudian psychology. See Hillel Goldberg, "An Early Psychologist of the Unconscious," *Journal of the History of Ideas* 43, no. 2 (1982): 269–84; Goldberg, *Israel Salanter, Text, Structure, Idea: The Ethics and Theology of an Early Psychologist of the Unconscious* (New York: Ktav., 1982).

32. Salanter, *Or Yisrael*, letter 10, 179–80.

33. See Aristotle, *Nicomachean Ethics*, 1144b2–17.

34. Salanter, *Or Yisrael*, letter 6, 126.

35. Isaac Blazer, "*Sha'arei Or*," in *Or Yisra'el*, ed. Isaac Blazer (Vilna, 1900), no. 11, 19. Translations of *Sha'arei Or* are my own.

36. Salanter, *Or Yisrael*, letter 2, 64.

37. For a sense of the range of Musar's scholarly reception see, for example, Etkes, *Rabbi Israel Salanter and the Mussar Movement*; Hillel Goldberg, "Israel Salanter's Suspended Conversation," *Tradition: A Journal of Orthodox Jewish Thought* 22, no. 3 (1986): 31–43; Shaul Magid, "The Road from Religious Law (Halakha) to the Secular: Constructing the Autonomous Self in the Musar Tradition and Its Discontents," in *Jewish Spirituality and Social Transformation: Hasidism and Society*, ed. Philip Wexler (New York: Crossroad, 2019), 203–22; Geoffrey D. Claussen, *Sharing the Burden: Rabbi Simhah Zissel Ziv and the Path of Musar* (Albany: State University of New York Press, 2016).

38. *Shulḥan Arukh*, YD 246.

39. Salanter, *Or Yisrael*, letter 2, 63–64.

40. See, for example, Magid, "The Road from Religious Law (Halakha) to the Secular," and Etkes, *Rabbi Israel Salanter and the Mussar Movement*, 93.

41. In rabbinic interpretation, *misphatim* are laws that parallel rational moral intuitions, while *ḥukim* (sing. "ḥok"), are laws that have no obvious rational basis. For the rabbinic version of this distinction see BT Yoma 67b.

42. Salanter, *Or Yisrael*, letter 31, 399. In rabbinic literature, the term *azharah* is used to refer to an explicit negative commandment in the Torah.

43. Salanter, *Or Yisrael*, letter 31, 403.

Chapter 24

Simḥah Zissel Ziv

GEOFFREY D. CLAUSSEN

Rabbi Simḥah Zissel (Broida) Ziv (1824–1898), also known as the Alter (Elder) of Kelm, was the senior disciple of Rabbi Israel Salanter (see chapter 23) and the leading moral theorist of the Musar movement that Salanter founded. In the 1860's, Simḥah Zissel established a Talmud Torah school in Kelm (Kelmė in modern-day Lithuania), which later grew into a yeshiva, though one that devoted less time to Talmud study than most yeshivas. Simḥah Zissel's Talmud Torah was an institution in which students also devoted significant time to the direct study of *musar*—the study of virtue and character. Additionally, Simḥah Zissel drew inspiration from German neo-Orthodoxy in establishing the Talmud Torah as the first traditionalist yeshiva in Eastern Europe to teach general, non-Jewish studies. After a period in which the Talmud Torah was relocated to Grobin (Grobiņa in modern-day Latvia), Simḥah Zissel established a new Talmud Torah in Kelm in 1886 where elite students studied *musar* and were trained to spread the teachings of the Musar movement throughout Europe and beyond. Most leaders of the Musar movement in the late nineteenth and early twentieth centuries studied with Simḥah Zissel, and were influenced by his approach to virtue.[1]

Wisdom and Musar

When Simḥah Zissel's students compiled his writings for publication after his death, they titled them *Wisdom and Musar* (*Ḥokhmah U-Musar*), referring to the goal of "knowing wisdom and *musar*" articulated at the start of the Book of Proverbs (1:2), and pointing to two central concepts in their teacher's thought. For Simḥah Zissel, *musar* ("moral discipline") describes the process of developing virtue that is the central purpose of human life. That process requires wisdom about human nature as it ordinarily appears, as well as wisdom about the ideal form of the human being and the virtues towards which human beings are called.

What is wisdom about human nature as it ordinarily appears? Employing a medical analogy, Simḥah Zissel teaches that a "physician of the soul" must "recognize the paths of deceptions that flow forth from the evil character traits naturally impressed in the human being" and how "[human] nature is 'simply evil, all the time' [Gen. 6:5]."[2] Like Salanter (and in contrast to thinkers such as Maimonides), Simḥah Zissel views human beings as "naturally" inclined toward deception and evil, and so he calls for "a war against nature, against the brutishness with which the human being is born; and it is a great war to conquer a power as strong and mighty as nature and bring it under the governance of reason."[3] This war—the work of *musar*—is made possible when one understands the human tendency to evil. A person with this understanding may even outwit one's soul by appealing to its corrupt tendencies: for example, when one understands how one's soul selfishly seeks pleasure, one can remind oneself of the inner pleasure associated with virtue and thereby motivate oneself toward virtue.[4]

Simḥah Zissel also points to a second kind of wisdom: wisdom about the human form, the faculty of reason, the true human self—the "true 'I' hidden in the human being."[5] This true self should also be identified with "the image of God," reflecting a capacity to strive for divine virtue. Sometimes using Neoplatonic language to describe this true self as an immaterial entity trapped within the human body, and sometimes using Aristotelian language that describes reason as the form of the human species, Simḥah Zissel teaches that this rational, moral capacity is also part of human nature. In one striking formulation, he describes how "a person is truly an angel"—though, "without learning, he will become an animal."[6] While on the one hand the task of *musar* requires taming one's animal impulses, on the other hand the task of *musar* requires nurturing the intrinsically good side of human nature. *Musar* requires not only an offensive against the evil inclination but also defensive efforts to protect the angelic capacities and the image of God with which all human beings are born.[7]

Human beings must strive to develop stable virtues, so that their emotions, appetites, and imaginations cooperate with reason.[8] Virtues may even become "like second nature," especially when one is trained from one's youth. Simḥah Zissel maintained that educators like himself could train students, for example, to refrain from pernicious speech: "In a place where they train and teach from youth, these things are like second nature, to such an extent that [evil speech] is almost not heard among them."[9]

As human virtue increases and becomes more stable, the correlation between the human and the divine increases: "With every bit more that consistency is found within [a person], his resemblance to the Blessed One will grow greater."[10] And the ideal of virtue toward which one should strive is God's perfect virtue. Therefore, *musar* is an infinite task; no matter how much effort one makes at moral improvement, there will always be more to learn and further to strive toward the divine ideal. Hence, Simḥah Zissel teaches, the greatest of sages are called "disciples of sages" rather than simply "sages": "[F]or all of their days, they are like disciples who are learning."[11] While no one is obligated to go beyond what they are capable of, individuals become obligated to meet higher and higher standards of virtue as their capacities to meet such standards grow. When one expands one's moral capacities, one discovers more ways in which God's Torah will apply to one's life, such that "he will automatically need to be many times more stringent, and the size of the Torah will grow very great for him."[12]

But while recognizing the infinite ideal toward which human beings may strive is a form of wisdom, wisdom also requires recognizing just how weak human reason is, how much human beings resist improvement, and how our natures incline us to be "simply evil, all the time." Even when we seem to make moral progress, our unconscious tendencies rise up and threaten that progress. Even the person who is most habituated to beneficence and lovingkindness "can revert to being reborn with a cruel nature."[13]

Still, for Simḥah Zissel, the persistent difficulty of developing virtue should not lead to despair, but should encourage patient and persistent efforts: "There is no remedy for a human being other than to exert oneself very greatly."[14] A person must "prepare himself to labor in breaking his appetites and character traits, using tremendous force—for a great force and a long time are required if he wants to bend a firm tree which has already been bent to one side and which is [now] to be bent the other way."[15] To overcome evil traits and inclinations, and certainly to aspire toward the heights of virtue, there are no shortcuts: Simḥah Zissel's writings consistently emphasize that the work of *musar* is a slow and arduous process.

Love and Other Virtues

Simḥah Zissel often emphasized virtues including *yirah* (fear of heaven, reverence)[16] and humility (*anavah*),[17] character traits that were also central in Salanter's writings (see chapter 23). He also stressed the importance of equanimity (*menuḥat ha-nefesh* or *yishuv ha-da'at*)—the disposition to see the world calmly, rationally, and clearly, a virtue that he saw as central to the path of Torah as well as to the ancient Greek philosophers whom he often praised.[18] Simḥah Zissel read Aristotle in Hebrew translation, and his reading of Aristotle also encouraged his appreciation of another central virtue: practical wisdom, the disposition to act well in particular moral situations.[19]

Above all, Simḥah Zissel saw love, kindness, and compassion as the central virtues demanded by the Torah. Loving one's fellow as oneself, as Rabbi Akiva recognized (PT Nedarim 41c), is "the foundation of character traits and the great principle of the Torah—that is, for fulfilling the Torah."[20] When Hillel saw the essence of Torah in the commandment to love one's fellow as oneself ("Do not do to your fellow what is hateful to you"; BT Shabbat 31a), he recognized that "the prime foundation in a person's life is that he instill in his heart true love of human beings [*ahavat adam*], whatever religion they may be, because the entire political community is a partnership."[21] As Simḥah Zissel instructed his students, one should "think continually of the positive commandment that 'you should love your fellow as yourself' " and "seek out opportunities for showing lovingkindness to people."[22]

In some passages, Simḥah Zissel emphasizes that love may be demonstrated through simple gestures of good will, as with the Talmudic example of Rabbi Yoḥanan ben Zakkai, who greeted all people in the marketplace "in order to habituate himself to the love of God's creatures [*ahavat ha-beriyyot*]."[23] But other passages emphasize just how demanding love can be. For example, Simḥah Zissel emphasizes that "loving your fellow as yourself" requires being as concerned for others as one is concerned for oneself or one's own family:

> A human being needs to accustom oneself to the character trait of generosity . . . to such an extent that one finds joy in helping and providing for the poor, as if they are truly part of one's family. . . . And this is as the matter of "loving your fellow as yourself." . . . The warning is given to a human being that one should accustom oneself to the character trait of loving God's creatures, slowly, slowly, until one naturally loves the other, and naturally rejoices in the good of the other, just as one naturally rejoices in one's own good and the good of one's children, rather than to fulfill a commandment, for then one's love would not be complete. One's love will only be complete if one loves naturally. And this is the goal of the commandment and the desire of the Blessed One in commanding "loving your fellow as yourself," and in this way one will come to resemble the Blessed One.[24]

One should not love one's fellow as oneself out of a sense of duty to perform the commandment; rather, the disposition to love should be cultivated to a point where one provides for others naturally, easily, and spontaneously, just as one naturally provides for oneself or one's family without being commanded. Human beings must overcome the vice of self-love—the tendency to focus only on oneself—but our tendency to self-love may serve as a model for how one should love others. This ideal is a divine ideal, one impossible for human beings to reach, but an ideal toward which human beings must strive.[25]

Simḥah Zissel also describes the divine ideal of love in far-reaching terms by emphasizing how God's love extends to non-Jews as well as to Jews, to the wicked as well as the righteous, and beyond human beings to include all creatures. For example:

> The [fundamental] quality of God is that He loves all creatures; were it not so, they could not exist in the world. And we find that loving God's creatures is closeness to the Blessed One. . . . Our sages, in their holy way, have taught

> us (BT Sotah 14a): how can a person draw close to the Blessed One? By cleaving to His attributes. And there are no character traits of the Blessed Lord more apparent to us than love of His creatures. "You open up your hand and satisfy the desire of all that lives" (Ps. 145:16)—we see that every single creature receives pleasure and satisfaction for its desire, and this is simply God's love for His creatures. And consequently we find that the prohibition on causing suffering to animals comes from the Torah.[26]

Here, virtue requires emulating God's love for nonhuman animals, especially by heeding the prohibition not to cause them suffering.[27]

Elsewhere, Simḥah Zissel emphasizes that even wicked human beings deserve compassion. "The Torah has compassion for animals, and so (learning from this) we should have compassion for [evildoers] as we do for animals," he teaches.[28] He derives the obligation to love the most wicked of people from traditions about God's compassion for the wicked, such as the midrash in which God silences the angels who were celebrating while Pharaoh's army drowned in the Sea of Reeds (BT Sanhedrin 39b). So too, Simḥah Zissel teaches, God shared the plans for the destruction of Sodom with Abraham (Gen. 18) so that Abraham would see God's compassion for the wicked and seek to emulate it by praying on their behalf. Abraham learned "that one should even have compassion for the wicked, and that one should seek [compassion] for them in prayer."[29] Love for the wicked does not require forgoing their punishment, and it may involve harsh rebuke, but it also requires a commitment to finding goodness within others.[30] And it requires the empathy and compassion that Simḥah Zissel often describes with the phrase "sharing the burden of one's fellow" (or "bearing the burden with one's fellow," *nosei be-ol im ḥaveiro*), a phrase that he uses to describe the highest level of virtue demanded by the Torah. "Sharing the burden of one's fellow," for Simḥah Zissel, is a disposition to see the needs of others, to empathically identify with those in need, and to respond compassionately.

Sharing the Burden and the Example of Moses

While Simḥah Zissel does not believe that it is possible for any human being to fully emulate divine virtue, he often points to biblical and rabbinic heroes (as well as, occasionally, philosophers such as Socrates)[31] who may serve as moral exemplars. Above all, Moses serves as an exemplar. The Torah takes humility to be Moses's exemplary virtue, but Simḥah Zissel sees proper humility as culminating with "sharing the burden of one's fellow," and he sees this as the key trait developed by Moses that allows him to receive the Torah.[32]

"Sharing the burden of one's fellow" appears on a list of forty-eight virtues "by which Torah is acquired," printed in Pirkei Avot, and a medieval midrashic collection links the virtue with Moses witnessing the suffering of the Israelite slaves in Egypt (Exod. 2:11).[33] Building on this tradition, Simḥah Zissel describes how Moses brought the Israelites' suffering "into his heart, so that his heart would feel their pain as if he himself was in this pain." Moses filled his mind with images of the suffering of others, and "habituated himself to seeing these mental images to such an extent that he felt their pain as if he himself was in such pain, and so he came to be sharing their burden."[34] Responding with compassion, he "shares the burden" of a Hebrew slave being beaten by an Egyptian taskmaster, rescuing him from his oppressor (Exod. 2:12); when he sees two slaves fighting (Exod. 2:13), "he shared the burden of the one being oppressed"; so too, he intervenes on behalf of Jethro's daughters in Midian (Exod. 2:17).[35] As a shepherd in Midian (Exod. 3:1), he also habituated himself to mercy for his flock: like Jacob in an earlier generation and David in a later generation, he sought "to share the burden even of animals."[36] When God calls to him from the burning bush (Exod. 3:4), he responds to God's needs, seeing that God is (so to speak) "suffering along with" the enslaved people of Israel.[37] Ultimately, Moses leads Israel out of slavery and to receive the Torah at Mount Sinai, concerned not only for their bodies but also for their souls; his "deep-seated love for Israel joined love for their bodies with love for their souls, just as the love of the Blessed One for His chosen people is for their bodies and for their souls."[38] So too, present-day followers of Moses and God are obligated to show deep concern for their fellows' physical and spiritual well-being.

As Moses witnessed at Sinai, God placed "brickwork" under God's feet (Exod. 24:10) as a visible reminder of Israel's enslavement in Egypt: "The Blessed One does not need this, but it was to proclaim His love for His chosen people, and also to proclaim to humanity the greatness of the obligation of sharing the burden of one's fellow, to experience pain when he is pained and joy when he has joy."[39] But while God may not need a reminder to empathize with Israel, human beings need reminders, and the image of the brickwork shows how images serve as a reminder of the pain of others. Moses was able to share the burden of the Israelite slaves only by habituating himself to mental images of their pain, and so too for later generations: "It is only possible to feel another person's pain and to share his burden with him by utilizing significant mental images, so that with all the pain and suffering and injury which happen to another person, it is as if it happened to oneself."[40]

Developing the capacity to visualize the suffering of others and to stand in their shoes is key to fulfilling the Torah's commandments. For example, the Torah commands lending money to those in poverty, and to adequately fulfill the commandment requires bringing the experience of poverty to mind: the Torah "commands bringing the matter into one's sense-experience so that it is as if you were the poor person, so that then giving the loan will be easy for you."[41] More generally, loving one's fellows and sharing their burdens requires seeing the suffering of others, even those who are not present before our eyes, and responding with compassion.[42]

The Cultivation of Virtue

Simḥah Zissel saw the work of *musar* as requiring continual effort and a wide variety of approaches. He directed his students to employ strategies that might help to cultivate virtue, including engaging in the practices described above: visualization exercises that would help one to see the suffering of others, as well as seeking out opportunities for showing lovingkindness and generosity. Simḥah Zissel also encouraged a number of other practices that were intended to cultivate virtue.

These included practices developed by Israel Salanter of *limmud musar be-hitpa'alut*, the emotionally engaged study of *musar* that generally includes chanting passages from traditional literature to evocative melodies. By engaging the emotions, appetites, and imagination in this process, Simḥah Zissel believed that these passages might be imprinted on the hearts of those who chanted them; and he urged his students to respond to the threat of the evil inclination by raising their voices against it.[43] Following Salanter, he saw the value of separate spaces where one could engage in such exercises without embarrassment, and a communal setting where one could be strengthened by shared dedication to *musar*. The Talmud Torah institutions that Simḥah Zissel directed, highly insular boarding schools that were isolated from the surrounding society, provided ideal settings.[44]

At the Talmud Torahs, Simḥah Zissel also developed a model of peer groups that would provide support for the development of moral character. Some groups dedicated themselves to a particular character trait or practice, while others dedicated each week to focusing on different character traits, and groups met at least once a week to engage in discussion of the traits and practices in question. The groups were intended to function as communities committed to mutual love, respect, and group reflection on moral character and strategies for cultivating virtue.[45]

Some of Simḥah Zissel's disciples, after their time at the Talmud Torah came to an end, continued to belong to peer groups under his guidance that committed to shared practices even while they were physically distanced. One group of close disciples, for example, pledged their love and concern for each other and agreed to take on practices such as the following: to engage in the study of Torah for the sake of heaven; to spend at least half an hour each day (and more on Sabbaths and festivals) engaging in focused *musar* study; to focus on daily prayer as part of the work of *musar*; to accept upon themselves particular assignments pertaining to the particular character traits that they, as individuals, needed to develop; to follow Simḥah Zissel's practice of "tithing days," setting aside every tenth day as a day for special contemplation; to meditate on their own deaths and on God's judgment; to regularly correspond with a partner, and also with Simḥah Zissel.[46] The range of practices listed here include the key practices that Simḥah Zissel recommended for the cultivation of virtue.

In addition to these, Simḥah Zissel also saw the performance of more conventional commandments as inculcating virtue. Taking his cue from Maimonides, he argues that both clearly rational commandments (*mishpatim*) and less obviously rational commandments (*ḥukkim*) have rational purposes and aim at "straightening human character."[47] When Hillel explained that the whole Torah could be summed up in the commandment to love one's fellow as oneself, Simḥah Zissel believed that he was making this same point, connecting the observance of all commandments with the cultivation of virtue.[48] But, while commandments to observe the Sabbath, wear *tzitzit*, or recite blessings aim at virtue, and the fulfillment of these commandments can help to inculcate virtue, performing these activities will not easily produce virtue. Human souls are sufficiently corrupt, in Simḥah Zissel's view, that there are no easy and straightforward paths to virtue; and the Torah ultimately requires much more than might be found on a conventional list of commandments or a conventional code of Jewish law. In Simḥah Zissel's understanding, God is incredibly demanding and requires individuals to do all that they can possibly do to overcome their evil natures, cultivate virtue, and move closer to the divine ideal of perfect virtue.

Notes

1. Geoffrey D. Claussen, *Sharing the Burden: Rabbi Simḥah Zissel Ziv and the Path of Musar* (Albany: State University of New York Press, 2015), 6–40, 183–88; Claussen, "Repairing Character Traits and Repairing the Jews: The Talmud Torahs of Kelm and Grobin in the Nineteenth Century," *Polin: Studies in Polish Jewry* 30, no. 1 (2018): 15–41; Dov Katz, *Tenu'at Ha-Musar*, 2nd ed., vol. 2 (Tel-Aviv: Avraham Tzioni, 1954), 26–219.

2. Simḥah Zissel Ziv, *Sefer Ḥokhmah U-Musar*, vol. 1 (New York, 1957) (hereafter, *ḤuM*), 357, 422. See Claussen, *Sharing the Burden*, 43–44.

3. *ḤuM* 1:57. See Claussen, *Sharing the Burden*, 44.

4. See Claussen, *Sharing the Burden*, 44–45.

5. Simḥah Zissel Ziv, *Sefer Ḥokhmah U-Musar*, vol. 2 (Jerusalem, 1964) (*ḤuM*), 273. See Claussen, *Sharing the Burden*, 45.

6. *Kitvei Ha-Sabba Ve-Talmidav Mi-Kelm*, vol. 1 (Benei Berak: Siftei Ḥakhamim, Va'ad Le-Hafatzat Torah U-Musar, 1997), 5.

7. See Claussen, *Sharing the Burden*, 45–48. For a discussion of these conceptions of human nature in light of contemporary psychology, see Christian B. Miller, "How Contemporary Psychology Supports Central Elements of Simḥah Zissel's Picture of Character," *Journal of Jewish Ethics* 3, no. 1 (2017): 121–24.

8. Claussen, *Sharing the Burden*, 52–55.

9. *Kitvei Ha-Sabba Ve-Talmidav Mi-Kelm*, 1:8. See also *ḤuM* 1:162, 230.

10. *ḤuM* 1:87. See Claussen, *Sharing the Burden*, 113–16.

11. *ḤuM* 1:344. See Claussen, *Sharing the Burden*, 116–20.

12. *ḤuM* 1:422–23. See Claussen, *Sharing the Burden*, 120–24.

13. *ḤuM* 1:91. See Claussen, *Sharing the Burden*, 124–40.

14. *ḤuM* 1:239.

15. *ḤuM* 2:10.

16. See Claussen, *Sharing the Burden*, 29–32, 67–71.

17. See Claussen, *Sharing the Burden*, 57–58, 76, 81, 92, 142.

18. See Claussen, *Sharing the Burden*, 83–86, 142.

19. See Claussen, *Sharing the Burden*, 55–60, 78, 142.

20. *ḤuM* 1:191.

21. *ḤuM* 2:7.

22. *Kitvei Ha-Sabba Mi-Kelm: Pinkas Ha-Kabbalot* (Benei Berak: Siftei Ḥakhamim, Va'ad Le-Hafatzat Torah U-Musar, 1984), 27.

23. *ḤuM* 2:7, with reference to BT Berakhot 17a.

24. *Kitvei Ha-Sabba Mi-Kelm: Inyanei Elul Ve-Yamim Nora'im* (Benei Berak: Siftei Ḥakhamim, Va'ad Le-Hafatzat Torah U-Musar, 1997), 147–48.

25. Claussen, *Sharing the Burden*, 151–56, with reference to the prohibition in BT Bava Metzia 32b.

26. *ḤuM* 1:31.

27. See Geoffrey Claussen, "Jewish Virtue Ethics and Compassion for Animals: A Model from the Musar Movement," *CrossCurrents* 61, no. 2 (2011): 208–16.

28. *ḤuM* 1:59.

29. *ḤuM* 2:193.

30. Claussen, *Sharing the Burden*, 148–51.

31. See Claussen, *Sharing the Burden*, 81–83.

32. See Claussen, *Sharing the Burden*, 158–63.

33. Pirkei Avot 6:6; Pesikta Zutra, Parashat Shemot, 2.

34. *ḤuM* 1:3.

35. *ḤuM* 1:9–10.

36. *ḤuM* 1:8. Cf. *ḤuM* 1:6.

37. *ḤuM* 1:10.

38. *ḤuM* 1:4.

39. *ḤuM* 1:3, with reference to Mekhilta Pisḥa 14.

40. See Claussen, *Sharing the Burden*, 163–66.

41. *ḤuM* 1:56.

42. See Claussen, *Sharing the Burden*, 163–66.

43. See Claussen, *Sharing the Burden*, 17.

44. See Claussen, *Sharing the Burden*, 18–22.

45. See Claussen, *Sharing the Burden*, 17–18, 23–24.

46. *Kitvei Ha-Sabba Mi-Kelm: Pinkas Ha-Kabbalot*, 135–38; Katz, *Tenu'at Ha-Musar*, 2:75–77.

47. *ḤuM* 1:49. See Claussen, *Sharing the Burden*, 87–88.

48. *ḤuM* 2:7. See Claussen, *Sharing the Burden*, 88–89.

Chapter 25

Hermann Cohen

SHIRA BILLET

From 1876 until his retirement in 1912, Hermann Cohen (1842–1918) held a chair in the department of philosophy at the university of Marburg, the only professed Jew in such a position in the Kaiserreich. From Marburg, Cohen became a founding figure of an influential German philosophical movement known as Marburg Neo-Kantianism, centered in the Kantian legacies of philosophy as a science and ethics as the centerpiece of philosophy. From 1888 until his death in 1918, Cohen also produced a remarkable oeuvre of Jewish philosophical writings that are the cornerstone of modern Jewish thought.

Although Jews did not yet officially have legal equality in the Prussia of Cohen's youth, Cohen was born and raised in the small town of Coswig (Anhalt), where Jews were not only tolerated but also respected. Cohen was one of the first Jews to attend the Gymnasium in Dessau, while his father gave him a traditional Jewish education at home. In 1857, Cohen enrolled at the Jüdisch-theologische Seminar in Breslau. Instead of pursuing rabbinic ordination, however, he matriculated at the University of Breslau in 1861 to study philosophy. Although Cohen waded into different philosophical methodologies, a

I am grateful to Leora Batnitzky, Paul Franks, Alan Mittleman, and Sarah Zager for generously commenting on an earlier draft.

primary interest in Plato, Kant, and philosophical idealism emerged early on. Cohen's first book offered a novel interpretation of Kant and launched an improbable academic career (as a Jew) that included the composition of an original neo-Kantian system of philosophy.

While at Marburg, Cohen began to use his unique position to defend Judaism in the context of an unprecedented rise in antisemitism in Germany. Cohen believed that the core of political antisemitism was a philosophical anti-Judaism that professed the incompatibility of Judaism and morality. Cohen's Jewish philosophical writings made the case that Judaism and its historical texts were not only compatible with morality but even offered unique contributions to philosophical ethics. The more Cohen wrote about Judaism, however, the more marginalized he became at the university. Upon retiring in 1912, Cohen relocated to Berlin and taught Jewish philosophy at the Lehranstalt für die Wissenschaft des Judentums. He was still revising the manuscript of *Religion der Vernunft aus den Quellen des Judentums* when he died in 1918.

Cohen believed in what he saw as the moral project of the liberal German nation state and its compatibility with the moral project of Judaism. In a tragic irony, Martha Cohen (his widow) died in a Nazi concentration camp in 1941. Cohen, who experienced virulent antisemitism in his lifetime, has been unfairly reviled for his supposed naivete about Germany. This judgment follows from a misunderstanding of the method of "idealization" characteristic of his philosophical idealism. The Germany Cohen championed was the idealized version of the state that Cohen held up as the moral standard for the flawed actual state of which he was quite critical.[1] Cohen's understanding of the virtues, the subject of this chapter, is inextricably intertwined with his idealism. For Cohen, virtues were essential tools in the endeavor of the ethical individual to come as close as possible to the ideal moral self, and to form ethical communities that strive to progress toward the moral ideal.

Virtue in Cohen's Worldview

Virtue was of central importance to Cohen and to his philosophical understanding of Judaism. The significance and meaning of virtue for Cohen, however, cannot be understood outside of his commitment to

Platonic idealism and his antipathy to Aristotelian accounts of morality and virtue.[2] Although modern virtue theory is associated with Aristotle far more than Plato, Cohen's virtue ethics was decidedly Platonic. Cohen situated himself within a philosophical tradition that began with Plato and, on his account, included Kant and Maimonides.[3]

The Platonic tradition that Cohen claimed was distinguished by two central features: a methodological idealism[4] and a distinction between theoretical and practical philosophy. Aristotelian virtue theory, on Cohen's account, lacked both of these crucial elements. As Cohen read Aristotle, the culmination of human virtue was the attainment of *eudaimonia,* or the joy of leisurely intellectual pursuit.[5] The fatal flaw of Aristotelian virtue ethics lay in its problematic relationship to *eudaimonia*. Dissolving the crucial distinction between theory and praxis, *eudaimonia* conflated the virtues (the realm of moral practice) with morality itself (the realm of moral theory).[6] *Eudaimonia,* as an attainable goal, was fundamentally incompatible with an idealism that posited a never fully realizable ideal toward which human moral effort must always progress.

Plato's account of virtue, grounded in idealism, separated "the idea of the Good" (moral theory) from the virtues themselves (moral praxis). The virtues are enlisted in the infinite task of progressing toward the moral ideal. Cohen criticized Aristotelian virtue, culminating in *eudaimonia,* for failing to overcome the originally naturalistic meanings inherent in the terms for virtue in both Greek (*arete*) and Latin (*virtus*), that is, manliness and power.[7] Cohen thought *eudaimonia* was too easily mistaken for power, a confusion reinforced by the conflation of *eudaimonia* and *arete*/*virtus*. Cohen writes, "In Plato the virtues recede to a preparatory stage of the idea of the Good. The idea of the Good sublimates the virtues, and they shed all of their naturalistic accretion."[8] The Platonic account, in privileging the unattainable "idea of the Good" over the virtues themselves, steered clear of any association between virtue or morality and power by cultivating a profound sense of humility.

At stake for Cohen is the very possibility of moral philosophy. He posits that "[w]ith *eudaimonia* Greek classical philosophy goes to its grave" and "scientific philosophy is dissolved. Where scientific philosophy ends, idealism ends, and . . . the dualism between materialism and spiritualism is unavoidable."[9] Cohen saw Christianity as mired in this Aristotelian legacy, whereas Jewish monotheism offered a path forward with its distinction between God's holiness (morality) and God's actions (the model of human virtue).[10] Judaism, for Cohen, thus anticipated the crucial elements of the Platonic account necessary for any genuinely philosophical ethics. Cohen reads Maimonides in this light.

A passage from Maimonides' *Mishneh Torah* captures, for Cohen, the Maimonidean rejection of Aristotelian virtue in favor of a Platonic-Jewish account:

> The one who serves God out of love is occupied with the pursuit of Torah and its laws, and follows the paths of wisdom, not for the sake of some earthly object, nor for fear of some ill, and not in order to inherit felicity, but rather practices truthfulness for truth's sake . . . and this level [*Stufe* (*ma'alah*); virtue] is a very high level, and not every sage attains it. This is the level of our forefather Abraham [whom God called "the one who loved Him"] . . . that God has commanded us to attain through Moses [as it says, "Love the Lord thy God"].[11]

Cohen reads in this passage an explicit rejection of Aristotelian eudaimonia[12] in favor of a Jewish path to virtue (*ma'alah*) that inclines toward the idea of the Good, exemplified by the notion of "truthfulness for truth's sake." This form of virtue is represented not by Aristotle but by Abraham and Moses, coded through their love of God. We shall see below how religious-philosophical love, virtue, and the virtue of truthfulness in particular, are all interrelated in Cohen's teaching on the virtues.

Cohen reads another passage from Maimonides's *Code* as similarly offering a Jewish (and Platonic) alternative to Aristotelian virtue theory. In "Laws of Character Traits" (*Hilkhot Deot*), 1.1–5, Maimonides describes the Aristotelian "middle path" as the praiseworthy modus operandi of philosophers, but contrasts it with the superior (on Cohen's reading)[13] way of the pious.[14] The pious, rather than settling into a virtuous mean between two extremes, incline toward extreme virtue, exemplified by the virtue of humility. The pious are "exceedingly humble" (*shefal ruaḥ b'yoter*), whereas the philosopher is meek or moderately humble (*anav*).[15] Indeed, Cohen sees humility as the consummate Jewish virtue, intimately intertwined with the love of God. For Cohen, Aristotle's account of virtue as a middle path between two extremes (vices) is tantamount to the claim that "virtue originates from two vices."[16] Cohen takes exception to the idea that the cardinal virtue of courage (*Tapferkeit*), to use his example, "should really be nothing but a maneuver of avoidance" of the two vices of "haughtiness (*Übermut*) and cowardice (*Feigheit*)."[17] Virtue is an inclining toward the idea of the Good rather than a turning away from vice.[18]

Drawing on his reading of Maimonides, Cohen proposes the pursuit of human self-perfection (*Selbstvervollkommnung*) as a replacement for Aristotle's median principle.[19] In keeping with his idealism, the self-perfecting self holds before itself simultaneously the idea of God and the idea of the human being—both ideal concepts related to the idea of the Good.[20] In Maimonides, on Cohen's reading, "the self is therefore not just an expression of the empirical individual but rather represents an ideal concept in ethics, a defining task assigned to the human being. . . . This ethical labor is linked to the idea of God."[21] Cohen explains that "the self finds its model in God. Knowledge of God, as well as love of God, are meaningful exclusively in terms of human ethics, in terms of interpersonal relations, and of a person's relationship to the self."[22]

The ethical aim of self-perfection is encapsulated in the virtue of humility (*Demut*). Avoiding the fundamental error Cohen saw in Aristotelian *eudaimonia*, the human being inclined toward the ideal can never "repose in the proud feeling of his own power, greatness, or purity."[23] As Cohen writes, "[T]he ideal always remains ideal; the task remains a task. . . . In striving toward this aim . . . I practice the virtue which might best be termed the virtue of the self: it is *humility*."[24]

Humility, Fidelity, Courage, and Truthfulness

Cohen's primary philosophical discussion of virtue (*Tugendlehre*) is found in his monograph on ethics, *Ethik des reinen Willens*.[25] Cohen expands upon the *Tugendlehre* and reframes it as a religious (Jewish) doctrine of virtue in his posthumous monograph on religion, *Religion of Reason*.[26] To understand Cohen on the virtues, it is important to consider key components of both discussions.[27]

Cohen posits that virtue is a progressive notion, in the sense that one progresses in one's virtuousness through gradual stages of development, and also in the sense that many of the virtues themselves are on a progressive continuum with one another (i.e., his understanding of the Socratic doctrine of "the unity of the virtues"). In his Jewish writings, Cohen writes that higher levels of virtue are achieved through a pedagogical process of development exemplified in two Hebrew terms for virtues, *middot* (literally, measures), and *ma'alot* (literally, ascending steps).[28] Cohen writes, "The concept of virtue . . . is connected with the development toward higher degrees of approximation toward the divine archetype of morality. Hence the 'step' . . . designates the positive progress in the development."[29]

In Cohen's system of the virtues, explicated in *Ethik des reinen Willens*, there are two ranks or degrees of virtues (*zwei Grade der Tugenden*)[30] corresponding to the two orientations of human ethical consciousness: the individual in relation to humanity as a whole, and in relation to smaller human collectives comprised of individual others.[31] Virtues of the first rank govern humanity as a whole (Cohen's *Allheit*, or totality), whereas virtues of the second rank govern "relative communities" (*die relativen Gemeinschaften*).[32] The primary goal of ethics as Cohen sees it is to enshrine the concept of humanity as a whole (the unity of humanity) into all human political efforts. Philosophical ethics is limited, however, when it comes to theorizing the virtues with respect to intersubjective human relationships, and the relationships between individuals and their various communities. These latter relationships are most fully conceptualized within philosophy of religion, according to Cohen. Cohen's insistence that "the ways of virtue must . . . be directed to these relative communities" opens the door to the crucial role Cohen's Jewish *Tugendlehre* will play in his system of virtue.

Consider the outlines of Cohen's discussions of the virtues in the *Ethik* and in the *Religion*:

Ethik	*Religion*
Truthfulness (*Wahrhaftigkeit*)	Truthfulness
Modesty (*Bescheidenheit*)	Modesty
Humility (*Demut*)	Humility
Courage (*Tapferkeit*)	Justice
Fidelity (*Treue*)	Courage
Justice (*Gerechtigkeit*)	Fidelity
Humanity (*Humanität*)	Peace (*Friede*)

The virtues of the first rank are truthfulness, courage, and justice; modesty, humility, fidelity, humanity, and peace are virtues of the second rank. Virtues of the first rank cannot function properly without virtues of the second rank, which are their necessary complements. Thus, virtues of the second rank are no less important than virtues of the first rank.

In the *Ethik*, Cohen's ordering of the virtues alternates between virtues of the first rank and their complementary second rank virtues. Hence, truthfulness is complemented by modesty (or humility—its more intense form); courage has its complement in fidelity; justice in humanity. But the system is also more fluid: in some ways each virtue of the second rank complements each virtue of the first rank, culminating in what Cohen calls humanity, his term for the ancient Greek virtue of *sophrosyne* (the harmonious integration of the soul).[33] In the *Religion*, Cohen develops the notion of the interrelatedness of the virtues of the second rank into a more robust doctrine of the unity of the virtues. The essential role of the virtues of the second rank becomes starker in the latter work, and instead of each virtue of the first rank having a complementary virtue of the second rank, the second rank virtues become different forms of one another and collaborate to support virtues of the first rank, which are, in turn, also interrelated.

Cohen's discussion of truthfulness and modesty lends clarity to his system of the virtues and the interactions between the two ranks. Kantian that he was, Cohen insisted that the virtue of truthfulness "can never be violated."[34] At the same time, the demands of truthfulness are impossible for humans to heed without assistance. At issue, Cohen says, "is not the casuistry of the necessary lie" but rather the impossibility of achieving certainty regarding what the truth entails:[35] "Truthfulness is based on truth. Who, however, can have certainty about the truth? Can the conditions be fulfilled that are required in each case for the determination of the truth? Truthfulness commands one to intercede in behalf of truth without dismay and to come forward against falsehood without error. Who, however, is able to assert the certainty of his knowledge, which establishes . . . the objective ground of truthfulness?"[36] Cohen laments "[t]he imperfection of human knowledge, the narrowness and dissipation of human consciousness" that "seem to make untenable the condition on which truthfulness depends."[37]

Ethics cannot allow exemption from the absolute virtue of truthfulness, but Cohen argues that the virtue of truthfulness "demands a complement" that can "rescue" it "from the necessity which it suffers."[38] Modesty is "the virtue which truthfully acknowledges the subjective weakness that besets the attainment of truth."[39] While "modesty may not and cannot release me from the virtuous duty of truthfulness," nevertheless "it opens a way out which is not an escape that serves to avoid or veil my subjective inadequacy with regard to objective truth."[40]

We are now in a position to introduce one final crucial aspect of Cohen's system of the virtues. The distinction between virtues of the first rank and those of the second rank is related to a theory of affects. In contrast with Cohen's understanding of Stoic apathy, where virtue is equated with overcoming emotion, in Cohen's *Tugendlehre*, "no virtue can be thought without affect."[41] Honor (*Ehre*) is the primary affect that accompanies virtues of the first rank;[42] love governs virtues of the second rank. In Cohen's discussion of the complementary role of modesty toward truthfulness, modesty requires "forbearance to my weakness, as well as to the weakness of my fellow human being," which "lets love prevail over strict honor" with respect to the absolute demands of truthfulness.[43] While honor demands certainty, love embraces uncertainty. Modesty, powered by love, ever aware that the demands of truthfulness cannot always be met, fosters compassion toward the self and the other.

The most ideal form of the virtue of modesty is humility. Modesty fosters the basic forbearance toward human others that is necessary for the most fundamental forms of human sociality at the core of ethics. Humility, its more perfect form, is achieved only through religion, as it relies on the process of reconciliation with God, the cornerstone of Cohen's mature philosophy of religion. It is worth quoting Cohen at length:

> Love causes forbearance to be exercised in judging my weakness and inadequacy as well as in judging the corresponding deficiencies in the fellow human being. Hence, modesty becomes a support for my love of my fellow human being, as well as for my own moral self-esteem, which I need in various ways for the various stages of my moral self-consciousness, before the great road of repentance finds its conclusion in the reconciliation with God. Upon this great road I must in various ways try to come to terms with myself, and for this I need the self-knowledge of

> modesty, which, in the presence of great questions, leads me to humility. Modesty and humility thus become supports of truthfulness. In them exists the virtue which is relative in comparison with the absolute virtue of truthfulness.[44]

Modesty and humility are forms of self-knowledge. More than "complements" of truthfulness, they are relative forms of it. Since human access to truth is only relative due to the limitations on what we can know made famous by Kant's Critiques, humility and modesty are what we might call, in Kantian terms, the practical forms of truthfulness.

This partial unification of modesty/humility with truthfulness reflects Cohen's doctrine of the unity of the virtues, mentioned above, that was especially developed in the *Religion*. This can be further seen in Cohen's treatment of fidelity (a virtue of the second rank) and its interaction with other virtues of the second rank (humility and modesty) and its support of virtues of the first rank (justice and courage). "Even more than truthfulness is supported by modesty, justice and courage are directly accompanied by fidelity. It is therefore not only a source of temporary assistance or even a substitute but a continuously collaborating supplement."[45] Fidelity plays a special role with respect to justice and courage; the latter can never exist without the former. Furthermore, because it is so profoundly partnered with the other absolute virtues, fidelity "therefore also reaches out to truthfulness." Cohen adds that "modesty itself can be understood as a form of fidelity, namely as a self-examination of the self-consciousness."[46]

Fidelity has a special function in Cohen's moral psychology as the unifier of the moral consciousness. "Unity of consciousness" (often rendered in English "unity of apperception") is an importance principle of Kantian psychology that Cohenian psychology appropriates. In *moral* psychology, Cohen claims that "[w]hat unity means for the psychological consciousness, faithfulness means for the moral consciousness."[47] In Kantian terms, again, we might call fidelity the practical form of the unity of consciousness.

The role fidelity plays in unifying the moral consciousness can be seen in Cohen's discussion of social justice. Poverty, for Cohen always a reflection of "the injustice of the world's economy,"[48] results from a widespread human failure to practice the virtue of justice. The virtue of "[j]ustice brought forth the social legislation of religion," that is, biblical laws designed to alleviate poverty (e.g., debt relief, welfare for the stranger, widow, and orphan) that have their legacy in the modern welfare state.[49] But just as truthfulness required the assistance of modesty, "justice is conscious of the limitations of its own effectiveness. The virtue of the first rank had to call for help from a virtue of the second rank."[50] Cohen describes "almsgiving" as "a form of fidelity" that is specifically necessary as a supplement to justice here. Cohen makes much of the fact that the Hebrew word for justice (*tzedek*) is essentially the same as the word for charity/almsgiving (*tzedakah*).[51]

Furthermore, almsgiving, as a form of fidelity, unifies the moral consciousness; indeed, the human being must give charity "for the coherence of his consciousness":

> The individual consciousness cannot rest satisfied with the legislation of social justice. Too often it is convinced that social justice is only an ideal norm, the actualization of which is very often obstructed and frustrated. If almsgiving were not to assist, the chasm between the social ideal and the political actuality would become a flagrant provocation in the face of which the harmony of human consciousness could not be restored. . . . [Charity,] therefore, becomes the virtue of fidelity in the first place in regard to one's own I, and through it to the fellow human being. All charity expresses fidelity to the human community.[52]

Cohen's account of how the virtue of fidelity involves integrating the self (the I), which in turn integrates the other (the fellow human being) into community with the self, evokes Cohen's description of humility in the monograph on Maimonides.[53] Humility and fidelity are both forms of self-examination that are integral to the human ability to live ethically and to persevere in the infinite task of working toward the moral ideal found in the idea of the Good exemplified in the Maimonidean notion of self-perfection.

Virtue and Jewish Identity

Cohen's conception of the virtues is intimately tied to his understanding of Jewish history and Jewish identity. In his discussion of Maimonides's elevation of the virtue of humility, Cohen reflected that

Judaism had been preserved through the ages, "attesting to its truth in the face of all sorts of worldly pressure," only because it was "the religion of humility."[54] Cohen later expresses the way that humility has preserved Judaism and its truth throughout history by way of his philosophical conception of certain forms of collective suffering as "vicarious suffering" (*Stellvertretung des Leidens*).[55]

In Cohen's philosophy of history, vicarious suffering "is an historical act which the individual does not undertake for his own sake or for the sake of his soul, but in the service of history" and of history's "messianic goal" of unifying all of humanity in ethics.[56] According to Cohen, vicarious suffering, is "for" one's fellow human beings. Cohen's alternative to Aristotelian *eudaimonia*, or happiness, is vicarious suffering. In contrast to Aristotle, Cohen insists that happiness is a life of self-sacrifice accompanied by the awareness that one is part of humanity's progress toward the ideal.[57] Socrates, for Cohen, is the model philosopher who suffers as an outcast in Athens (the gadfly) and then makes the ultimate self-sacrifice in his martyrdom for the sake of the advancement of moral philosophy.[58] Cohen understood the Jewish *Leidensgeschichte* (the long history of Jewish suffering) as a collective version of the self-sacrifice made by Socrates.[59]

Cohen's conception of "vicarious suffering" is intimately tied to his understanding of Judaism's account of justice and courage, on the one hand, and humility and fidelity, on the other. Vicarious suffering unifies all the virtues in the sufferer. Only the person who is well practiced in the virtue of *humility* is capable of suffering in this ideal sense.[60] And, in addition to the crucial connection to justice, Cohen links this calling to the virtue of courage: The virtues of "justice and courage flow together. The martyrdom of justice is at the same time the heroism of courage. Courage is the triumph of humanity, just as justice coupled with love is the embodiment of God's attributes."[61] As we saw above, the virtue of fidelity supports justice and courage to such a profound extent in this work that it is essentially tantamount to them.

In concluding this discussion, it is worth noting that Cohen anticipates an objection to his account of the virtues, and especially to his elevation of humility and fidelity powered by love—virtues that call for self-sacrifice. Modern feminist theory has shown how demanding these sorts of virtues from those who are already oppressed preserves systems of oppression. After the Holocaust, what was seen as

Cohen's philosophical valorization of Jewish martyrdom was critiqued on similar terms. In Cohen's own terms, he anticipates a version of these objections when he admits that "one could view humility in an ambiguous light" if one sees it "as a threat to the ethical individual."[62] Cohen raises the possibility that the elevation of humility is used as a tool by institutions, such as medieval religions and states, to suppress individuality, as a tool for social control. Cohen asks, "What sort of dignity is accorded to the individual, if the church or the state to which he belongs obtains and affirms its own dignity at the individual's expense?"[63] Cohen thinks that the Jewish *Tugendlehre* avoids this problem through a robust conception of divine humility as the model for human humility.

Cohen's situatedness within a certain time, place, and intellectual milieu makes it impossible for his answer to satisfactorily resolve our questions. In his lifetime, Cohen was trying to stretch the minds of his own Christian contemporaries to see that Judaism had a robust and serious philosophical offering. He was trying to get his contemporaries—both Christians and Jews—to ask different questions than the ones they were asking and to seek wisdom from sources and from people they had dismissed. In writing about "the *power* of humility" as a superior alternative "to power (*Macht*), glamour, prosperity, domination (*Herrschaft*), autocracy, [and] imperialism,"[64] Cohen sought to reframe contemporary conversations about power toward an ethics that opposed all forms of human domination. His critique of the virtue theory tradition as having retained the notions of manliness and power embedded in the Greek and Latin (*arete, virtus*) intersects in interesting ways with contemporary feminist accounts of virtue.

While from our vantage point, Cohen does not sufficiently overcome the problematics of elevating humility and fidelity as virtues for an oppressed or marginalized group, we can certainly appreciate that these are virtues that ought to be practiced far more frequently by dominating groups. Cohen's intended audience was not only his coreligionists, but always included his Christian colleagues as well. His interventions were intended as revisions and expansions of philosophy itself and not merely parochial Jewish philosophy. It is a separate question whether Cohen's intended audience was listening, but his Jewish *Tugendlehre* was certainly worthy of their consideration and of ours.

Notes

1. See Steven S. Schwarzschild, "'Germanism and Judaism': Hermann Cohen's Normative Paradigm of the German-Jewish Symbiosis" [1979], reprinted in *The Tragedy of Optimism: Writings on Hermann Cohen*, ed. George Y. Kohler (Albany: State University of New York Press, 2018).

2. I refer in this chapter exclusively to *Cohen's* accounts of Platonic and Aristotelian (and, below, Maimonidean) moral philosophy. It is beyond the scope of this chapter to subject Cohen's readings of these thinkers to the scrutiny and criticism they invite.

3. On Cohen's surprising reading of Maimonides as a Platonist (rather than an Aristotelian), see Leo Strauss, "Cohen und Maimuni," in *Philosophie und Gesetz: Frühe Schriften*, ed. Heinrich Meier (Stuttgart: Metzler, 1997); translated as "Cohen and Maimonides," in *Leo Strauss on Maimonides: The Complete Writings*, ed. Kenneth Hart Green (Chicago: University of Chicago Press, 2013). See also Almut Sh. Bruckstein's commentary (24 and 201n3) in her volume on Cohen's 1908 monograph "Charakteristik der Ethik Maimunis": Hermann Cohen, *Ethics of Maimonides*, trans. with commentary by Almut Sh. Bruckstein (Madison: University of Wisconsin Press, 2003) (henceforth, *EM*). Cohen's original monograph was reprinted in vol. 3 of Bruno Strauss, *Hermann Cohens Jüdische Schriften* (Berlin: Schwetschke, 1924) (henceforth, *JS* 3).

4. Cohen understood his own philosophical system as a form of philosophical idealism, called "critical idealism," based on his Kantian understanding of Plato's *Ideenlehre* (literally doctrine or theory of ideas, but typically translated in English as the theory of forms). On Cohen's account, the Platonic idea anticipated the Kantian regulative ideal. It was a methodological idea, rather than a metaphysical form.

5. *EM* 149; *JS* 3:273. A general note on the use of translations: Where there are published translations of Cohen's writings, I mostly reproduce the cited translators' versions, but on occasion I revise the published translation or replace it with my own where I deem necessary for clarity or accuracy.

6. See Hermann Cohen, *Religion of Reason out of the Sources of Judaism*, trans. Simon Kaplan (New York: Frederick Ungar, 1972) (henceforth, *RoR*), 402–403; Cohen, *Die Religion der Vernunft aus den Quellens des Judentum* (Leipzig: Fock, 1919) (henceforth, *RdV*), 474–75.

7. *EM* 128; *JS* 3:265. *RoR*, 402; *RdV*, 474.

8. *EM* 128; *JS* 3:265–66.

9. *RoR* 403; *RdV* 475.

10. *RoR* 403; *RdV* 476.

11. *Laws of Repentance* (*Hilkhot Teshuva*), 10:2. I provide here an English translation of Cohen's German translation of Maimonides' Hebrew, in *EM*

157–58; *JS* 3:278. Note that the Hebrew term Cohen translates as *Stufe* (level) is one of three Hebrew terms he identifies that mean "virtue" (Tugend). These three are: *ma'alah* (ascending level or step), *middah* (measure), and *shlemut* (perfection).

12. Cohen understands "not every sage attains it" as a reference to Aristotle.

13. *EM* 137; *JS* 3:269. This point is debated in Maimonides scholarship.

14. *EM* 134–35; *JS* 3:269.

15. Maimonides, *Hilkhot Deot* 1.5; cf. 2.3.

16. *EM* 131; *JS* 3:268.

17. *EM* 131; *JS* 3:268.

18. *EM* 131; *JS* 3:268.

19. Cohen associates self-perfection with Maimonides, *Guide* 3.53. See *EM* 153, 155; *JS* 3:276. See also *JS* 1:300 ("Innere Beziehungen der Kantischen Philosophie zum Judentum").

20. See Hermann Cohen, *Ethik des reinen Willens* (Berlin: Cassirer, 1923) (henceforth, *ErW*), chs. 4 and 9.

21. *EM* 148; *JS* 3:272.

22. *EM* 149; *JS* 3:272.

23. *EM* 149; *JS* 3:273.

24. *EM* 153; *JS* 3:275–76.

25. See *ErW*, chs. 10–12, for Cohen's introduction to his *Tugendlehre*.

26. See *RdV*, ch. 18, for Cohen's introduction to his Jewish *Tugendlehre*.

27. My discussion considers the teaching on the virtues in both *ErW* and *RoR* together, to highlight the continuities between them. It is my claim that some of the differences in the later work are a result of Cohen refining certain aspects of the theory in the years between the 1904 initial publication of *ErW* and the penning of the virtue chapters in *RoR*. Nevertheless, it is also important to give each of these discussions a separate consideration, in order to appreciate the differences between them, some of which I highlight here. See the important article by Peter A. Schmid, "Hermann Cohen's Theory of Virtue," in Hermann Cohen's Critical Idealism, ed. Reinier Munk (Dordrecht: Springer, 2005), 231–57, in which the discussions of virtue in *ErW* and *RoR* are treated separately.

28. See *RoR* 408–409; *RdV* 481. See *EM* 129, 156; *JS* 3:266, 276. As noted above, Cohen identified three Hebrew terms for virtue (Tugend): *ma'alah* (ascending level or step), *middah* (measure), and *shlemut* (perfection).

29. *RoR* 408–409; *RdV* 482.

30. *ErW* 460. See *ErW* 450ff.

31. *ErW* 449–50.

32. *ErW* 462.

33. See *ErW* 635. Peace is the Jewish version of this virtue. *RoR* 446; *RdV* 526.

34. *RoR* 424; *RdV* 501.

35. *RoR* 424; *RdV* 501.

36. *RoR* 424; *RdV* 501.

37. *RoR* 424; *RdV* 501.

38. *RoR* 424; *RdV* 501.

39. *RoR* 424; *RdV* 501.

40. *RoR* 424; *RdV* 501.

41. *ErW* 451.

42. Associated with the Hebrew *kavod* (*RoR* 404–405; *RdV* 477), "Honor always means: to honor the equality of humanity" (*ErW* 470).

43. *RoR* 424; *RdV* 501.

44. *RoR* 424; *RdV* 502.

45. *RoR* 445; *RdV* 525.

46. *RoR* 445; *RdV* 525.

47. *RoR* 445; *RdV* 525.

48. *RoR* 265; *RdV* 312.

49. *RoR* 444; *RdV* 523.

50. *RoR* 444; *RdV* 523.

51. *RoR* 432; *RdV* 509. *RoR* 444; *RdV* 523.

52. *RoR* 444; *RdV* 523–24.

53. *EM* 153; *JS* 3:275–76.

54. *EM* 139; *JS* 3:270.

55. See *RoR* 263–65; *RdV* 310–12.

56. *RoR* 439; *RdV* 518.

57. *EM* 149; See *JS* 3:273.

58. See *ErW* 265–67. On Cohen's reception of Socrates, see Shira Billet, "The Philosopher as Witness: Hermann Cohen's Philosophers and the Trials of *Wissenschaft des Judentums*" (PhD diss., Princeton University, 2019).

59. *RoR* 438–39; *RdV* 517.

60. *RoR* 265; *RdV* 312.

61. *RoR* 438; *RdV* 516.

62. *EM* 140–41; *JS* 3:270–71.

63. *EM* 140; *JS* 3:271.

64. *RoR* 265; *RdV* 312.

Chapter 26

Abraham Isaac Kook

DON SEEMAN

"Mystic in a Time of Revolution"[1]

"The science of *musar*" (literally, "ethics"), writes Abraham Isaac Kook (1863–1935), speaks of "the refinement of moral dispositions" (i.e., virtues). But along with their refinement, he insists, we must also discuss "their strengthening and the conceptualization of their specific forms, from which we may derive theoretical and practical teachings."[2] The conceptual study of virtue ethics held a special place for Rabbi Kook as a bridge between some of the many apparent contradictions he hoped to reconcile: tradition and progressive thought, universalism and Jewish particularism, the teachings of philosophers and kabbalists.[3] It may not be entirely incidental in this regard that his father, Zalman Shlomo Ha-Cohen Kook, was a Lithuanian Mitnagged, while his mother, Zlata Perl, descended from the Kapust branch of Chabad Hasidism. Known as a prodigy and autodidact, Kook spent two years at the yeshiva in Volozhin. Later, after the death of his first wife, Batsheva Rabinowitz-Teomim, in 1889, he took a brief sabbatical from his first pulpit in Zaumel (Latvia) to study with the Lithuanian kabbalist Shalom Elyashiv ("Leshem"). He turned down a prestigious position as a teacher of Jewish thought and Musar at the yeshiva in Telz in 1903, but accepted a position the following year as "rabbi of Jaffa and its surrounding settlements," including the nascent "Hebrew city" of Tel-Aviv. Kook wrote prodigiously in both traditional rabbinic and modern literary forms in an explicit attempt to bridge the generational and ideological gaps that beset his Jewish world.[4] He was appointed the first Ashkenazi Chief Rabbi over all of Mandatory Palestine in 1921 and held this position until his death from cancer in 1935.

Virtue and the Scholarly Ambit

"I am eminently aware," Rabbi Kook writes in his youthful collection of sermons *Midbar Shur*, "that though my written halakhic novellae contain correct comments and straight thinking, I cannot claim to have paved any new path that would significantly advance halakhic dialectic [*pilpul*]." On the other hand, "I see that my path in the field of Aggadah and *derush* [homiletics] does represent a new path."[5] Aggadah refers here not just to midrash but to all the nonlegal disciplines of Torah study, "conceptual and critical study [i.e., philosophy], vision and poetry, ethical and homiletical literature, Kabbalah and Hasidism."[6] This is significant because he wants to insist that the function of Aggadah "is to uplift man and his ethical consciousness." Homiletic literature by itself, without these other branches of Aggadah, well may aid in the cultivation of virtue by making ethical and religious ideas accessible to "penetrate the heart, [thus] transforming nature and character traits. "It is not, however, typically thought of as a *generative* literature that also engages the intellect in order to "*broaden* the horizon of ethics, which Kook describes as "the main thing" related to Aggadic literature.[7] Broadening these horizons by embracing the expansive sweep of Aggadic literature that includes philosophy, kabbalah and so forth, became a central task of Kook's own scholarly platform.

Echoing predecessors such as Baḥya Ibn Paquda, Maimonides, Moses Ḥayyim Luzzatto, and Schneur Zalman of Lyady, among others, Kook emphasized the intellectual component of training in moral excellence. "Purification of the moral dispositions (*middot*) through intellect precedes their purification through emotion," he writes, "for if a person does not *know* what is good and what is bad, how will that person arouse themselves emotionally to acquire the good as a possession and to distance what is bad from their habitual dispositions?"[8] For all the importance of knowledge as acquisition, however, he also signals the importance of *thinking* itself as a critical practice related to both study and contemplative worship. His insistence on the expansion of ethical horizons through the study of Aggadah, broadly conceived, evokes Maimonides's attempt to ground an ethics in the progressive and unceasing purification of religious concepts and language, even though this project might seem to complicate conventional piety. One should never confuse the fear of heaven (i.e., piety) with the fear of thinking, Kook writes, because cowardly refusal to "investigate the divine conception and its glory" turns piety itself into a source of narrowness and suffering.[9]

Kook was sensitive to Maimonides's use of parables to convey moral and philosophical lessons.[10] Maimonides interpreted Moses's demand of God, "Show me Thy glory!" for example (see Exod. 33–34), as an expression of the prophet's speculative attempt to know God's essence to the extent humanly possible. God's retort that "Man cannot see me and live," followed by his offer to let Moses see his "back" while causing "all my goodness to pass before thee," is a parable according to Maimonides, for the shift from ontological speculation to the perception and emulation of divine governance, which is at the heart of Maimonidean virtue ethics.[11] "Just as [God] is called merciful, so you too be merciful; just as He is called compassionate, so you too be compassionate, etc."[12] Maimonides's decision to embed this ethico-philosophical teaching in his reading of unfolding Scriptural narrative rather than formulating it in abstract theoretical terms renders it an especially compelling model for the sort of ethical and literary praxis Kook had in mind.[13]

This parable was almost certainly one of the antecedents Kook had in mind when he wrote that the glory of heaven (*kavod shamayim*) which "is lucidly conceptualized [*mosag hasagah behirah*] . . . raises the worth of humanity and of all creatures, and fills them with a consciousness of spiritual grandeur joined to pure humility."[14] Conceptual clarity about God leads here to virtues like humility and appreciation for human dignity. An overly corporeal (*megusham*) understanding of divine glory, by contrast, "tends toward idolatry and debases the dignity (*kavod*) of human beings and all creatures." It transforms the obligation to honor God into "a cruel demand from a [merely] corporeal being that longs for honors without limit, thus degrading every good and refined sentiment." Other modern Jewish thinkers such as Mendelssohn and Levinas also invoked this central Maimonidean theme, but unlike either of them it is clear that Kook also drew substantially on works of Kabbalah, Musar and Hasidism that had already, in some cases, appropriated and partially reframed Maimonides's critique.[15]

Writers like Moses Cordovero (1522–1570) and Joseph Ergas (1685–1730) for example, insisted—as Kook would later do—that misplaced divine corporeality (*hitgashmut*) results from the attempt to grasp God's essence (i.e., glory) directly, without cleaving to the intermediary divine attributes or virtues (*middot*)—which in post-1904 writings Kook begins to refer to in non-Kabbalistic language as "divine ideals."[16] Kabbalists configure these ideals as *sefirot*, which are not just abstract representations of divine governance, as in Maimonides's "attributes of action," but mediating forces and "channels" through which divine vitality and governance are manifest.[17] Their emulation is not only a matter of moral and intellectual perfection, therefore, but also of *tikkun*, or rectification on a cosmic scale. This does not mean, however, that Kabbalah ever wholly eclipsed Kook's strong early interest in the medieval Jewish philosophical tradition. "The old way of choosing one path and following it patiently," he wrote in a 1908 letter, "will not stand. We have grown and developed far beyond this." We must rather "embrace all paths and . . . bind them into a complete and confident harmony."[18]

Kook's curricular recommendations reflect this broad-minded approach and help to distinguish him among his Lithuanian Jewish contemporaries. Proponents of the Musar movement, for example, advocated daily, sometimes ecstatic study of pietistic works and tended to downplay full-blown cosmologies like that associated with the "worlds" and *sefirot* of Lurianic Kabbalah. Despite its inroads into the yeshiva world, some Lithuanian Talmudists expressed skepticism toward Musar for what they perceived as its morbid focus on personal sin. Shouldn't a healthy soul be able to cultivate piety and virtue through more normative pursuits like the study of Talmud and performance of the commandments?[19] Chabad Hasidism, meanwhile, joined Musar in its critique of pure Talmudism, but simultaneously chided Musar for its focus on "the disgusting and abhorrent nature of all bodily and material things," rather than what Hasidim called their "refinement" or "sanctification."[20] It is significant that while Kook echoes each of these approaches at different times, he insists on charting his own distinctive course. Yehudah Mirsky has shown that Kook sought from an early stage to reconcile Musar's deep emphasis on ethical self-cultivation with important trends in Lithuanian Kabbalah influenced by Moses Ḥayyim Luzzatto and the Vilna Gaon (as well as moderate Haskalah).[21] Kook echoed Chabad's critique of both Musar and Talmudism, for example, and called Chabad's contemplative path "exalted and holy," but also opines that Hasidim limit themselves to "a specific style [of devotion] . . . while other ways are closed to them." The attainment of "an exalted universal level," like the one he sought to engender called for reflection upon the whole sweep of Jewish ethical traditions, from philosophy to Kabbalah, and from Hasidism to the teachings of its bitter nemesis, the Vilna Gaon.[22]

Virtue and Nature

Virtue ethics typically require an account of human nature or of the conditions that contribute to human flourishing.[23] One place in which Kook seems to provide this in his discussion of three interdependent levels of penitence or return to God in the first chapter of *Orot Ha-Teshuvah*.

"Natural penitence" includes the return to ways of life that support holistic human vitality as well as *musar kelayot* (literally, "the admonitions of the kidneys") or natural, intuitive ethics.[24] Above that is "traditional penitence," related to the traditional religious idea of repentance from sins that are enumerated in biblical and rabbinic literature. The highest level, which he calls "intellectual penitence," depends on the attainment of a "comprehensive [i.e., all-inclusive, universalistic] worldview."[25] Once again, I believe that a close reading of *Guide* 1.54—particularly the comprehensive revelation of divine governance to Moses—stands somewhere deep in the background of this text. The explicit structure of the chapter, nevertheless, relies more heavily on Ḥayyim of Volozhin's (1749–1821) discussion of penitence as it relates to *nefesh* (embodied vitality), *ruaḥ* (speech), and *neshamah* or *sekhel* (intellect).[26] For Ḥayyim of Volozhin, penitence at each of these levels represents the repair of channels for the unimpeded flow of divine vitality. Sins of speech interrupt vital flow at the level of *ruaḥ*, bodily sins at the level of *nefesh*, and so on. Virtue is not just a privileged set of moral dispositions on this account but a structuring feature of human flourishing and cosmic order.

Kook understood that many of his early twentieth-century readers would have rejected this or any other religious cosmology that seemed incompatible with progressive or scientific worldviews. Some of his most interesting early work sets out to address the moral and epistemological challenges posed by new evolutionary paradigms, the expansion of time into geological epochs, and the increasing recognition of human cultural (which is also to say, ethical) diversity.[27] In a 1905 letter redolent with the contemporary search for a unified field theory in physics, Kook predicts that the unity of "the moral force and the other forces of existence" will one day be recognized.[28] I find it significant, however, that he refrains from offering any definite theory for how this unity will be revealed, suggesting instead that for now science and religion should continue developing their separate (and sometimes apparently contradictory) perspectives.[29] After meeting with him in 1925, Albert Einstein reported that Kook understood his theory of relativity better than most, and recalled that Kook even suggested kabbalistic parallels to the idea of differential rates for the passage of time.[30] Kook's virtue ethics reflect this zeitgeist in his appreciation for the relative moral needs and attainments of different people: the idea that relative vice for one person might be relative virtue for another, and that each historical epoch manifests a natural ethic appropriate to current human achievement.

Unlike more apologetic Orthodox writers, Kook rails against the idea that divine (revealed) ethics must be opposed to, or at least wholly independent from, natural ethics. Those who attempt to defend religion against moral critique, for example, by dismissing the claims of natural ethics tout court are paradoxically responsible for the catastrophic alienation of many Jews from Judaism and the Jewish people, he writes.[31] This does not mean that commandments perceived to be in conflict with natural ethics can simply be set aside, but it does mean that competing claims should be acknowledged and reconciled where possible.[32] Sometimes, taking natural ethics into account can lead to better understanding of the law and its long-term purposes (*ta'amei ha-mitzvot*). In other cases, natural ethics may call attention to the limitations of law as a self-sufficient and all-encompassing framework for human life. Like many other rabbinic writers of his day Kook opposed women's suffrage in the nascent Jewish state, yet it is no accident that a later thinker like Tamar Ross can mine his writing for resources relevant to what she calls "radical feminism and the theology of human autonomy." She invokes Kook, for instance, in support of the idea that "halakhah is not [ideally] meant to be the exclusive conduit to God, detached from worldly experience and the deepest instincts of the human soul."[33] Introducing instinct (moral intuition) and human experience is one way in which a virtue ethics can not only serve as a stabilizing or conservative role in moral life but also one that responds over time to the changing moral ecology of human life.

Kook thought that Jews should be less defensive about the discoveries of modern disciplines like Assyriology, which purport to show parallels between Scripture and the literature of other ancient societies. Such parallels are inevitable, Kook writes, because Judaism's revealed ethics were *always* intended to augment and perfect a universally accessible and preexistent natural ethic that existed among other nations.[34] Characteristically, he also sometimes reverses this polarity, so that "Natural morality, with all its splendor and might . . . may serve as a *basis* for the greatness emanating from the power of Torah."[35] From one perspective, Torah perfects the natural ethic; from another that is equally correct, the natural ethic is the foundation which allows Torah's greatness to become manifest.

Nature may, however, sometimes threaten to overwhelm virtue's limit. This makes perfect sense given Kook's mystical understanding of the virtues (*middot*) not just as personality traits or emotional and psychological dispositions, but also structured media for the modulation of vital flow into and through the world. His writings are replete with appeals to nature and to the Jewish national movement (which puts Jews in contact with nature) as dialectic counterweights to diaspora Judaism's overemphasis on tightly controlled individualistic piety. Despite his own renowned piety and punctilious adherence to halakhah, one comes across startling passages in which Kook also frankly acknowledges that this vital flow cannot remain perfectly calibrated at all times. Vitality that overflows its proper channel is much of what human beings call sin—behaviors that are not necessarily bad in themselves but can cause havoc when the flow is too strong, or the context of its expression is unwise. Indeed, repentance is configured not just as a remorseful response to bad behavior but as a continuous longing for the *correct* modulation of this vital rhythm and flow. Building especially on certain Hasidic teachings, he argues that sometimes the passion that comes with negative personality traits like anger is preferrable to the aridity of someone who is never moved by passion or desire.[36] A "boiling disposition" can at least be sublimated over time into the sustained warmth of prayer. "The greatest sin," in Kook's pointed and dramatic reworking of this theme, "is to conceive of a world that would be [so dry and lifeless as to be] altogether without sin."[37]

Virtue and Law

In his glosses to Luzzatto's *Mesillat Yesharim*, Kook tellingly implies that reflection upon *ta'amei ha-mitzvot* or "reasons for the commandments" contributes to the acquisition of virtue because it allows for reflective alignment with divine purposes.[38] He frequently returns to this theme. In one passage, he describes five different levels of human flourishing through which to analyze the divine rationale for every commandment: (1) health and the body, (2) feelings (including "natural morality" and aesthetics), (3) the nation, (4) the sphere of the "religious" (*dat*), and (5) the intellect (*sekhel*).[39] This multilayered analysis, and in particular his emphasis upon the national dimension, sets Kook apart from other modern writers such as Samuel David Luzzatto (1800–1856), a nineteenth century critic of Maimonides who held that the commandments are almost exclusively devoted to just two virtues: compassion for others and obedience to God.[40] Kook objected to the individualistic focus of Luzzatto's approach as well as the flattening of divine purpose it implies. For Kook, the identification of divine purpose with just one or two virtues—not surprisingly those that resonated most strongly with contemporary bourgeoise European communities—represented in his view a failure of moral imagination. Ethical aspiration should be higher and more radically open-ended.

In one relatively early essay, Kook acknowledges his indebtedness to Baḥya Ibn Paquda's ethical classic *Duties of the Heart*, which argues that, while moral education may begin with the "promptings of the law" (i.e., required behaviors and attitudes), the goal is that these practices should help to generate a subsequent "prompting of the intellect" free-willed moral obligation.[41] A person begins following the law's prompting, for example, by engaging in statutory prayer and reciting the daily blessings. The virtue of gratitude that is cultivated by such practices leads to ever higher appreciation of God's goodness, which prompts us to seek additional means of expression though adherence to law or custom that might cultivate even higher levels of gratitude.[42] Diana Lobel points out that Baḥya's Arabic term *akl,* which medieval Hebrew translators rendered *sekhel,* represents not just intellect in this context, but the perception of a "natural moral instinct" or rational-intuitive apperception of moral duty.[43] That is clearly how Kook also read Baḥya.

Kook's innovation however was to apply this circular relationship between promptings of the law and promptings of the mind across a generational or even evolutionary timeline. An example would be the Torah's prohibition of wearing a garment of mixed wool and linen, which is generally described as a commandment without a reason easily accessible to the human mind. Kook argues that even though the Torah does explicitly allow humans to slaughter and make use of animals for food, clothing and other needs, we can still, even if only slightly, appreciate the fine ethical distinction between clothing made of relatively insensate plants and that which relies upon the "theft" of wool from domestic animals.[44] Under current circumstances this distinction is only strong enough to make a faint impression on most human minds, but many generations of observing the prohibition will ultimately help to generate such concern that the slaughter and even sheering of sheep may *eventually* be phased out, not because the Torah in any way prohibits them, but because human moral sensibilities will have advanced to a point where this comes to seem inevitable. Kook was opposed to early twentieth-century advocacy of mass vegetarianism both because he thought it was premature in human developmental terms and might have a variety of negative repercussions, but it is clear from this example how observance of the law might lead over time to entirely new moral horizons.

Following Naḥmanides among others, Kook looked forward to the "heart of flesh" promised to one day supersede the "heart of stone" that might currently render Torah a source of burden and difficulty to some people.[45] "The root meaning of 'covenant' (*brit*) and of entering into a covenant in its moral sense," he writes, "is that that which is positive and ideal, which flows from the distillation of the most elevated and exalted morality, will be imprinted deeply and strongly in the nature of the human heart and soul." Moral dispositions that seem distant from everyday consciousness today will one day be "fixed firmly in the heart of an upright person," just as "it is fixed firmly in the heart of an upright person [today] to avoid murder . . . which collective morality has already managed to sufficiently internalize."[46] The scriptural model of this achievement was Abraham, whom the rabbis sometimes portray as "fulfilling the entire Torah even before it was given." Abraham was thus an exemplar of natural virtue who had already attained that for which most other people—and the Jewish people as a whole—require the stringencies and disciplines of law brought by Moses. Maimonides also suggested that Moses accomplished through rigor of law what Abraham had tried to bring about purely through kindness.[47] For Kook, the two biblical figures and the styles of ethical comportment they represent must ultimately be unified.[48]

For now, Kook insists that the law represents a floor rather than a ceiling of moral aspiration. While some exemplary acts of kindness are mandated in scripture or by rabbinic decree, neither the rabbis nor the Torah itself made any sustained effort to mandate every potential form in which kindness, for example, could be expressed, because the goal of the law is for people to internalize this demand and seek their own ways of showing kindness to neighbors. The correct proportion between virtue's freedom and law's obligation, Kook once observed, is like the proportion between the scaffolding of a building (law) and the open space in which human activity transpires (virtue).[49] It is in freedom we most closely emulate the divine, even though our very knowledge of divine freedom is learned by extrapolation from our own moral experience, since it is we who are created in God's image.[50]

Virtue and Time

Kook understood that modernity was premised on at least three radical departures from traditional worldviews. Changes in perception of the social order underlay the contemporary European turn to socialism and nationalism; new appreciation for the immensity of the universe challenged medieval notions of anthropocentrism; changes in the perception of time's duration reflected the almost universal adoption of evolutionary historicism in the new understanding of both natural and human affairs.[51] Kook admired Henri Bergson's influential theory of an endlessly creative *élan vital* but also criticized Bergson for his lack of a transcendent divine ideal against which effect of this creative flux might be measured.[52] For Kook, the transcendent ideal and the dynamic *élan vital* correspond to the divine *shelemut* (perfection) and *hishtalmut* (striving for perfection) respectively. Israeli philosopher Hugo Bergman referred to the dynamism of *hishtalmut* as the most radical dimension of Kook's theology, but it is grounded in a reading of Kabbalah that goes back at least to Azriel of Gerona (ca.1160–ca.1238).[53] On this reading, true divine perfection requires not only the perfection associated with infinitude but also the perfections associated with limits and boundedness, which imply the possibility of change, growth, and insufficiency. According to Kook, the complex devotional phenomenology of Jewish life allows expression of both these values and their attendant virtues. *Shelemut* is associated with changelessness and sanctity (*kedusha*), *hishtalmut* with the dynamism and interdependence of blessing (*beracha*).[54] The latter is what allows major kabbalists like Naḥmanides to utter the phrase *avodah tzorekh gavoha*, which means that "human service [i.e., the continuous unfolding of human potential] is a divine need."[55]

Even our understanding of divine law should reflect this unfolding. In his unfinished glosses to the Aggadah of the Babylonian Talmud, Rabbi Kook distinguishes between two distinct interpretive models, which he calls *perush* and *bi'ur*. *Perush* refers to the common rabbinic practice of reasoning by analogy that gives weight to legal precedent and consensus as stabilizing features of Jewish normativity.[56] *Bi'ur* by contrast is identified with practices of "strong reading" conditioned by the ability of certain authorized readers (members of the Sanhedrin for example) to discern the larger divine purposes to which Scripture points—*dorshin taama de-kra*—and accommodate these purposes in their legal rulings.[57] Both forms of reading may exist simultaneously in one historical epoch, but Kook nevertheless suggests that *perush* is most commonly identified with the Jewish people in exile, with legal conservatism, the Babylonian Talmud, and the primacy of reason. *Bi'ur* is associated by contrast with the Palestinian Talmud, with the vitality of the rebuilt nation in its own land, and with the perfection of both intellect and imagination that shade into prophecy.[58] *Bi'ur* thus invites a kind of intuitive phronesis (practical wisdom) that may even succeed in changing the shape of halakhah. A revived Jewish high court or Sanhedrin would have the collective authority to accommodate new moral aspirations and effectively new moral knowledge even at the expense of longstanding Talmudic or post-Talmudic precedent. All they need is a reading of a scriptural verse, he says, and a sufficient reason to consider change.[59]

Finally, though, the most striking aspect of Kook's virtue ethics is his understanding that the sedimentation of new moral knowledge in habitual virtues will, over the long term, transform the very parameters of what we now call nature and the natural ethic. To this end, he cites Moses Ḥayyim Luzzatto's daring formulation: "A person ascends, and the universe ascends with him."[60] Contra Maimonides's reliance on parables to explain prophetic passages like the one in which lions will one day lie down with lambs, Kook holds that this only shows how the natural world too is elevated as humans embody virtue more and more. Ethico-spiritual progress, to put it succinctly, contributes to cosmic *tikkun*. "The self-clarification of my thoughts, my ideas, my virtues, and my feelings," Kook declares, "will encompass the clarification of the whole world. A person should say, *bishvili nivra ha-olam*," which seems to mean in this context that "the world is created by means of the unique path [*shvil*] that channels divine vitality through each individual."[61] In this context, the tumult of confrontation with new ideas and aspirations that seem to confound traditional Jewish virtue ethics may appear less like a confrontation between "Judaism and modernity," and more like an attempt to maintain the equilibrium of virtue and vitality intrinsic to their own ineluctable evolutionary dynamic.

Notes

1. Yehuda Mirsky, *Rav Kook: Mystic in a Time of Revolution* (New Haven, CT: Yale University Press, 2014); also Don Seeman, "Abraham Isaac Kook," in *Oxford Bibliographies in Jewish Studies*, ed. Naomi Seidman (New York: Oxford University Press, 2020).

2. Abraham Isaac Kook, *Arpelei Tohar* (Jerusalem: Machon ha-Yad Tzvi Yehudah, 1983), 31.

3. See Yehudah Mirsky, *Towards the Mystical Experience of Modernity: The Making of Rav Kook, 1865–1904* (Boston: Academic Studies Press, 2021).

4. Abraham Isaac Kook, *Iggerot Ha-Ra'ayah*, vol. 1 (Jerusalem: Mossad Ha-Rav Kook, 1985), 24–27; Yosef Avivi, *The Kabbalah of Rabbi A. I. Kook* (Jerusalem: Yad Ben-Zvi, 2018), 1:40–41.

5. Abraham Isaac Kook, *Midbar Shur* (Jerusalem: Tzvi Yehudah Kook Foundation, 1999), 5–6. Based on the translation by Bezalel Naor, *In the Des-*

ert of Vision: Rabbi Abraham Isaac Kook on the Torah Portion of the Week (Spring Valley, NY: Orot2000), 16–17.

6. From Kook's close associate Shlomo Joseph Zevin, *Le'or ha-halakhah* (Jerusalem: 1977), 281.

7. Kook, *Midbar Shur*, 5–6.

8. Abraham Isaac Kook, *Middot Ha-Ra'ayah*, ed. Tzvi Yehudah Kook (Jerusalem: Mossad HaRav Kook, 1979), 91.

9. Kook, *Middot Ha-Ra'ayah*, 81; see Laurence J. Kaplan, "Rav Kook and the Jewish Philosophical Tradition," in *Rabbi Abraham Isaac Kook and Jewish Spirituality* (New York: New York University Press, 1995), 41–77.

10. For example, *Pinkasei Ha-Ra'ayah* (Jerusalem: Machon Ha-Rav Tzvi Yehudah Kook, 2017) 3:178, 227.

11. Maimonides, *Hilkhot Yesodei Ha-Torah* 1.10; Maimonides, *Guide of the Perplexed* 1.54. See Don Seeman, "Divine Honor as Virtue and Practice in Maimonides," *Journal of Jewish Thought and Philosophy* 16, no. 2 (2008): 195–251.

12. Seeman, "Divine Honor," 229n92, citing *Sifri, Eqev* 13.

13. Seeman, "Divine Honor," 251.

14. Kook, *Middot Ha-Ra'ayah*, 81; Don Seeman, "Violence, Ethics and Divine Honor in Modern Jewish Thought," *Journal of the American Academy of Religion* 73, no. 4 (2005): 1029.

15. For sources on Mendelssohn and Levinas, see respectively Seeman, "Violence, Ethics and Divine Honor," 1036–1042; Don Seeman, "God's Honor, Violence and the State," in *Ploughshares into Swords: Reflections on Religion and Violence*, ed. Robert W. Jenson and Eugene Korn (Center for Jewish-Christian Understanding and Cooperation, 2014), Kindle.

16. Kook, *Middot Ha-Ra'ayah*, 118. See Avivi, *The Kabbalah of Rabbi A. I. Kook*, 79–80, 119.

17. Jonathan Dauber, "Competing Approaches to Maimonides in Early Kabbalah," in *The Cultures of Maimonideanism*, ed. James T. Robinson (Leiden: Brill, 2009), 57–88.

18. Kook, *Iggerot*, 1:112, 142.

19. See Joseph B. Soloveitchik, *Halakhic Man*, trans. Lawrence Kaplan (New York: Jewish Publication Society of America, 1983), 74–76.

20. Yosef Yitzhak Scheersohn, *Kuntres Torat Ha-Hasidut* (New York: Kehot, 1959), 13.

21. Mirsky, *Towards the Mystical Experience of Modernity*.

22. Abraham Isaac Kook, *Kevatsim mi-Ketav Yad Kodsho*, ed. Boaz Ofen (Jerusalem, 2018), 3:24; Kook, *Iggerot Ha-Ra'ayah*, 4:148 (Jerusalem: Mossad Ha-Rav Kook, 2018), 187. From translation by Bezalel Naor, *Legends of Bar Bar Hannah* (New York: Kodesh Press, 2019), 220.

23. See David Novak, *Natural Law in Judaism* (Cambridge: Cambridge University Press, 1998).

24. Abraham Isaac Kook, *Orot Ha-Teshuvah*, with explanations and notes by Yacov Halevy Filber (Jerusalem: 1977), 6–8.

25. Kook, *Orot Ha-Teshuvah* (Jerusalem: 1925), 2–4.10.

26. Ḥayyim of Volozhin, *Nefesh Ha-Hayyim* 1:17.

27. Don Seeman, "Evolutionary Ethics: The *Taamei ha-Mitzvot of Rav Kook*," *Hakira* 26 (2019): 13–55; Seeman, "Anthropology and the Religious Student: Between Love and Respect." *BDD: Journal of Torah and Scholarship* 4 (1997): 5–24. See Novak, *Natural Law*, 137ff.

28. Kook, *Iggerot*, 1:134, 163–64.

29. Kook, *Iggerot*, 1:91, 105; Kook, *Arpelei Tohar*, 40. See Shalom Rosenberg and Gad Freudenthal, "Science and Religion (Torah U-Madda) in Modern Jewish Thought: An Overview," *Aleph* 15, no. 1 (2015): 173.

30. Itzchak Mamorstein, "Ha'Rav Kook: Master of the Lights," *Tikkun* 25, no. 4 (2010): 26–70.

31. Abraham Isaac Kook, *Le-Nevukhei Ha-Dor* (Tel Aviv: Yediot Aharonot, 2014), 124–26 (ch. 22).

32. See Kook, *Orot Ha-Teshuva*, 6–8, and additional sources cited in Seeman, "Evolutionary Ethics."

33. Tamar Ross, "Radical Feminism and a Theology of Jewish Autonomy: An Anatomy of Unexpected Alliances," *Jewish Studies Quarterly* 23, no. 4 (2016): 384.

34. Ross, "Radical Feminism and a Theology of Jewish Autonomy," 170–72.

35. Abraham Isaac Kook, *Orot Ha-Torah*, 12:2–3.

36. See Don Seeman, "Ritual Efficacy, Hasidic Mysticism and 'Useless Suffering' in the Warsaw Ghetto," *Harvard Theological Review* 101 (2008): 474.

37. Kook, *Orot ha-Teshuvah* 5:6; Kook, *'Arpelei Tohar*, 15.

38. Moses Hayyim Luzzatto, *Mesillat Yesharim 'im keitzur Mesillat Yesharim me'et Ha-Ra'ayah Kook* (Jerusalem: Nahum Stepanski, 2006), 93 (ch. 8); Seeman, "Evolutionary Ethics," 50.

39. Kook, *Le-Nevukhei Ha-Dor*, 139–40; Seeman, "Evolutionary Ethics," 47–48.

40. Seeman, "Evolutionary Ethics," 9, 21–27, 41.

41. Seeman, "Evolutionary Ethics," 37–38.

42. Baḥya Ibn Paquda, *Torat Ḥovot Ha-Levavot Maqor Ve-Targum*, ed. Yosef Kapach (Jerusalem: Yad Mahari Kapach, 2001), 136–44.

43. Diana Lobel, *A Sufi-Jewish Dialogue: Philosophy and Mysticism in Baḥya Ibn Paquda's "Duties of the Heart"* (Philadelphia: University of Pennsylvania Press, 2007), 223.

44. For example, Kook, *Ma'amarei Ha-Ra'ayah*, 95–98.

45. See Naḥmanides's commentary to Genesis 26:5.

46. Kook, *Middot Ha-Ra'ayah*, 110–12.

47. Maimonides, *Hilkhot De'ot* 1.7; Maimonides, *Guide of the Perplexed* 2.39.

48. Kook, *Le-Nevukhei Ha-Dor*, 253–54 (ch. 51).

49. Kook, *Iggerot*, 1:89, 92–101.

50. Kook, *For the Perplexed of the Generation* (Jerusalem: Yediot Aharanot, 2014), 27–29. For my reading of Maimonides, see Don Seeman, "Reasons for the Commandments as Contemplative Practice in Maimonides," *Jewish Quarterly Review* 103, no. 3 (2013): 298–327.

51. Abraham Isaac Kook, *Orot Ha-Kodesh*, vol. 2 (*Ma'amar* 5:21), ed. David Cohen (Jerusalem: Mossad Ha-Rav Kook, 1985), 543. See Shmuel H. Bergman, "Torat Ha-Hitpatḥut Ba-Mishnato shel Ha-Rav Kook," in *Shitato shel Ha-Rav Kook Ba-Maḥshavah Ha-Yehudit* (Jerusalem: Ministry of Education, 1963), 59–69; Seeman, "Evolutionary Ethics," 26–27.

52. Kook, *Orot Ha-Kodesh*, vol. 2, 533. Seeman, "Evolutionary Ethics," 20.

53. Samuel Hugo Bergman, *Faith and Reason* (New York: Schoken, 1963), 122–41.

54. Kook, *Orot Ha-Kodesh*, vol. 2, 532–34.

55. See Naḥmanides to Exodus 29:46; Bahya ben Asher to Exod. 29:46 and Num. 15:41; and the whole second part of Meir Ibn Gabbai's *'Avodat Ha-Kodesh*; Seeman, "Divine Honor as Virtue and Practice," 240–41.

56. Abraham Isaac Kook, *'Eyn Ayah, Berakhot*, vol. 1 (Jerusalem: Machon Ha-Rav Tzvi Yehudah Kook, 1993), 15–16 (from the author's introduction); Seeman, "Evolutionary Ethics," 41–42.

57. Ibid. Also *'Eyn Ayah, Shabbat*, vol. 1 (Jerusalem: Machon Ha-Rav Tzvi Yehudah Kook, 2000), 33–34 (ch. 1.52); Abraham Isaac Kook, *Ma'amarei Ha-Ra'ayah*, 543–44.

58. See Avinoam Rosenak, *The Prophetic Halakhah: Rabbi A. I. Kook's Philosophy of Halakhah* [Hebrew] (Jerusalem: Hebrew University Magness Press, 2007).

59. Kook, *Le-Nevuchei Ha-dor*, 83–94. On the acquisition of new moral knowledge see also Luzzatto, *Mesillat Yesharim*, ch. 12.

60. Luzzatto, *Mesillat Yesharim*, ch. 1; Kook, *Orot Ha-Kodesh* 3, 263; Kook, *Arpelei Tohar*, 100; Tamar Ross, "Immortality, Natural Law, and the Role of Human Perceptions in Writings of Rav Kook" in *Rabbi Abraham Isaac Kook and Jewish Spirituality* (New York: New York University Press, 1995), 237–53.

61. Kook, *Arpelei Tohar*, 32. For a precedent to this kind of reading, see for example Levi Yitzchok Rosakov, *Kedushat Levi*, Genesis 1:1.

Chapter 27

Martin Buber

WILLIAM PLEVAN

Martin Buber was born in 1878 in Vienna, Austria. At the age of three, his parents separated when his mother eloped with a Russian solider, a devastating loss that deeply impacted his life and shaped his later work. Martin went to live with his grandparents Salomon and Adele Buber in Lemberg until age fourteen, when he returned to live with his father, Carl, in Vienna. His grandfather, a great Midrash scholar, provided him with a rich education in classical Jewish texts and his grandmother instilled in him a love of languages and literature. In 1899, Buber met and later married Paula Winkler, who would go on to publish several novels and edited much of Buber's work. As a university student in Vienna, Buber became active in the Zionist movement and a leading essayist and speaker in the movement. Having encountered traditional Hasidic communities in his youth with his father and grandfather, Buber composed widely read translations and interpretations of Hasidic tales for a modern audience, leading to him becoming an important figure in Jewish adult education and interfaith dialogue. Beginning with his most celebrated work, *I and Thou*, published in 1923, Buber developed a philosophy of dialogue that made significant contributions to theology, psychology, social sciences, and philosophy. He collaborated with Franz Rosenzweig on an important translation of the Hebrew Bible into German and wrote many significant studies on the theopolitics of the Biblical prophets. In 1938, he left Germany for Jerusalem to become a professor of sociology at the Hebrew University, where he was an outspoken advocate for Arab-Jewish cooperation both before and after the founding of the state of Israel. He died in Jerusalem in 1965.

Character, Wholeness, and Dialogue

Ethical perfection through the development of religious and moral character traits is a central theme in both Buber's Jewish writings and his philosophy of dialogue. His emphasis on interpersonal dialogue, the uniqueness of the individual person, and the momentousness of individual decisions in each unique situation have often led to his work being associated, not unfairly, with existentialism, which tends to obscure the role of the virtues in his thought.[1] Buber does not use the term "virtue," in discussions of character ethics; in this he differs significantly from the classical Aristotelian tradition and its modern variations. However, reading these various texts together offers a distinctively Buberian, dialogical account of the virtues and their role in moral and religious life.

Buber is a humanistic thinker who understands ethical perfection as the self-actualization of each human being's unique personality. His dialogical philosophy, first articulated in *I and Thou,* distinguishes between the I-It and I-You modes of relation to other beings, both human and nonhuman. The I-It mode of utility and instrumentality is both legitimate and indispensable for human life, as it allows human beings to creatively control and manipulate material resources for their benefit. In the I-You mode of dialogical relations, a person relinquishes the instrumentality of the I-It and stands open to the otherness and fullness of other beings. It is in the I-You mode that human beings actualize themselves in their relations to others. Between human beings, an I-You relation involves participating in a shared interpersonal communion that affirms each person's full humanity, or what Buber usually calls wholeness.

Wholeness or unity of self is the key term Buber uses to denote humanistic self-actualization. In *I and Thou,* Buber states that human wholeness is fully actualized within the I-You relation: "The basic word I-You can be spoken only with one's whole being. The concentration and fusion into a whole being can never be accomplished by me, can never be accomplished without me. I require a You to become; becoming I, I say You."[2] For Buber, the very possibility of my selfhood depends on the primordial and ever-recurring encounter I have with other beings who stand against me as other. I-You relations are not always moral in the narrow sense, as they may involve spirited debate or the intimacy of friendship. At the same time, the I-You relation is where human beings become capable of showing genuine care and respect for one another. The actualization of my unique personality requires being fully open to the wholeness of other beings, allowing their unique personality to move or inspire me without my exercising control over them or seeking any utility from them.

Although self-actualization can be achieved in creative work or developing one's expressive capacities, developing a moral character is both indispensable and central to this project. For Buber, having moral character involves one's dialogical responsiveness to each unique person and situation. Distinguishing his view of moral character from classical forms of rule-based or virtue-based ethics, Buber states that

> [t]he great character can be conceived neither as a system of maxims nor as a system of habits. It is peculiar to him to act from the whole of his substance. That is, it is peculiar to him to act in accordance with the uniqueness of every situation which challenges him as an active person. . . . In spite of all similarities every living situation has, like a new-born child, a new face, that has never been before and will never come again. It demands of you a reaction which cannot be prepared beforehand. . . . It demands presence, responsibility; it demands you. I call a great character one who by his actions and attitudes satisfies the claim of situations out of deep readiness to respond with his whole life, and in such a way that the sum of his actions and attitudes expresses at the same time the unity of his being in its willingness to accept responsibility.[3]

Buber goes on to say that moral norms are essential to the moral life, but that such norms should not become "maxims" or "habits." Thus, classical virtues such as justice, compassion, or generosity can serve as educational models for moral character, but Buber's central concern is that moral education should cultivate the capacity of each person to respond to each situation from "the whole of their substance."

Buber describes the actualization of one's own wholeness as unfolding in loving responsibility for others.[4] As he puts it in one of his Hasidic commentaries, in order for a person to live in harmony with others, "he must find his own self, not the trivial ego of the egoistic individual, but the deeper self of the person living in a relationship to the world."[5] Developing moral character begins with striving to actualize one's own unique potential by being responsive to the actual wholeness of others. Being ethical—being just, compassionate, or generous towards others—requires setting aside the I-It mode of instrumentality in relation to others and being fully open to the needs of the other. According to Buber, following maxims or developing habits of virtue, even as applied to concrete situations using practical reason, remains in the I-It mode of relation. Dialogical virtue is thus characterized by spontaneity and responsiveness to concrete situation of other human beings—their unique experiences, their unique situation in life, and their unique suffering. Likewise, one's response to that situation is unique to oneself and thus may differ for each person. There is no way to know in advance of any actual encounter, Buber thinks, what that unique person and unique moment will demand of us.

Buber deploys this dialogical approach to self-actualization in service of a broader critique of modern Western societies. In his view, the pervasiveness of instrumental rationality in modern social and political life obscures the kind of direct, immediate interhuman relations that make human wholeness possible. Buber likewise criticizes rationalistic traditions in Western philosophy, theology, and social thought for failing to provide an account of ethics, politics, and religion that actually promotes human wholeness. Buber presents the ideal of genuine community as the antidote to the spiritual crisis brought on by pervasiveness of I-It relations in modern life. As a sociopolitical project, genuine community seeks to overcome the oppressive features of modern capitalism and centralized nation-states as well as the social alienation common in industrialized urban societies.[6] As an ethical and religious ideal, a genuine community is the locus for actualization of human wholeness, caring relations, and social justice. Buber characterizes genuine community as a social space in which

> individual beings open themselves to one another, disclose themselves to one another, help one another; where immediacy is established between one human being and another; where the sublime stronghold of the individual is unbolted, and man breaks free to meet other man. Where this takes place, where the eternal rises in the Between, the seemingly empty space: that true place of realization is community, and true community is that relationship in which the divine comes to its realization between man and man.[7]

Here and in his later philosophical work, "the between" or "the interhuman" names the ontological reality of the shared social space enacted in dialogue. Buber envisioned the work of creating genuine community in idealistic terms, linking this vision to particular anarchist and socialist experiments in community, such as the Zionist kibbutz.[8] Buber hoped that reorienting social, economic, and political arrangements would foster more direct contact between people in their everyday lives, creating the social conditions for dialogical encounter and human wholeness.

The Virtues of Dialogue

If Buber's ethics has a cardinal virtue, it would be the virtue of dialogical responsiveness and openness, which he connects to the biblical commandment to love one's neighbor.[9] Because a dialogical encounter involves two distinct beings, one cannot assure by one's own actions that such encounters occur. However, Buber thinks that a person can and should strive to remain open to the possibility of a genuine encounter with another and to being responsive to their material needs, their suffering, and their unique voice. In this sense, love of neighbor, and what I am calling dialogical responsiveness, is a feature of all virtues, as they all involve concrete forms of responsiveness to others.

It is not possible, Buber thinks, to sustain responsiveness and openness at all times. A person must also attend to their legitimate needs of safety and security. As an ethical virtue, however, one can be wary of the excessive encroachment of I-It instrumentality in one's life, especially as it limits the possibility for genuine human connection. Cultivating this virtue also involves being engaged in the concrete social work of building a genuine community, participating in common life with neighbors, coworkers, and fellow citizens in a way that promotes genuine community.

Dialogical openness also involves developing spiritual and moral integrity. To actualize one's whole self requires spiritual integrity, that is, knowing what one's potentialities actually are in order to realize them in action. In his essay "Elements of the Interhuman," Buber presents several characteristics of genuine dialogical encounter that amount to variations on the virtue of integrity. For example, Buber discusses the distinction between "being and seeming," meaning presenting ourselves as who we really are as opposed to how we wish to be seen. Buber views "seeming," a common feature of social life, as the source of all forms of disingenuous social relations and the opposite of dialogical relations. The integrity Buber speaks of is related to the importance of honesty and truthfulness, but involves more than just representing facts correctly: "The lie I mean does not take place in relation to particular facts but in relation to existence as such. There are times when a man, to satisfy some stale conceit, forfeits the great chance of a true happening between I and Thou."[10] Buber also discusses the importance of being aware of and affirming the other person as a distinct person, of not imposing one's view on others, and of saying what is on one's mind in order to realize genuine dialogue.

To appreciate Buber's distinctive approach to virtue, it will help to recognize that one of the central themes of his work is the integration of humanistic self-actualization and religious piety. For Buber, one cannot genuinely love God without also loving one's neighbor, and likewise love of one's neighbor is always an expression of love for God. Thus, Buber's account of virtues often integrates the interpersonal and the religious, that is, the divine-human, aspects of a character trait. This feature of Buber's ethics appears in his discussion of acts of hallowing, the elevation of the profane to the sacred through acts done in the spirit of holiness, in his Hasidic commentaries. While Buber himself did not place any importance on ritual observance, he interprets the recitation of blessings and devotional prayers (*kavanot*) of classic Hasidic piety as a ritualized form of a more general spiritual orientation toward the world of people, animals, and things. The hallmark of Hasidic piety is to acknowledge the potential for holiness that resides in all beings and to act in such a way as to invite or enact that holiness to emerge within the world. The act of hallowing "lies in [a person's] preserving the great love of God for all creatures, yes, all things."[11] Hallowing is integral to Buber's humanistic ethic in that it involves actualization of the whole self through openness to the wholeness of others: "The true hallowing of a man is the hallowing of the human in him. Therefore, the Biblical command 'Holy men shall you be unto me' [Lev. 19:2] has received Hasidic interpretation thus: '*Humanly* holy shall you be unto me.' "[12] In Buber's interpretation, Hasidic holiness is this-worldly rather than otherworldly. Becoming "humanly holy" means achieving holiness within everyday human activities such as eating, work, family life, and communal responsibility.

The religious dimension of interhuman encounter also appears in his writings on dialogue: "Above and beyond are bound to one another. The word of him who wishes to speak with men without speaking with God is not fulfilled; but the word of him who wishes to speak with God without speaking with men goes astray."[13] For Buber, the genuine act of dialogical openness is also openness to an encounter with the divine. As we saw in the passage from "The Holy Way" above, where human beings engage in dialogue, "the between," is the place where God enters the world and resides in community.

Buber also discusses humility as a virtue that combines religious and ethical elements. Becoming one's true self does not mean pursuing one's own concerns, good, or salvation at the expense of others. Spiritual development requires the humility to align one's actions with God's concern for all creation. Buber summarizes the teaching of Rabbi Simcha Bunam that the unfolding of history is marked by the tension between the character of the rebellious Korah and that of Moses, "the proud who . . . think of themselves, and the humble, who in all matters think of the world."[14] Buber also describes humility as a virtue possessed by a genuine teacher of moral character: "humility, the feeling of being only one element amidst the fullness of life, only one single existence in the midst of all the tremendous inrush of reality on the pupil."[15] The humble teacher serves as a guide for the student to the realities of the world, particularly with respect to human relations, without imposing themselves or their own understanding on the student.

Buber's discussions of the virtue of justice are found in his interpretation of biblical prophets and his writings on Zionism. For

Buber, the prophetic vision of true community involves the realization of a radically egalitarian form of social and economic justice within the nation. The institution of the sabbatical year served as a signature example of the prophetic project within ancient Israelite society.[16] Buber viewed these biblical commandments as sources for contemporary inspiration, rather than authoritative laws to be interpreted and applied as in the precise formulations of rabbinic halakhah. Buber also embraced the socialist idealism of the Zionist pioneers as an opportunity to reenact the forms of economic sharing found in biblical sources. In returning to the land, Buber envisioned a return to the prophetic task: "The establishment of a true community cannot come unless the agrarian life, a life that draws its strength from the soil, is elevated to a service of God and spreads to the other social classes, binding them, as it were, to God and to the soil."[17] Like other virtues Buber treats, the meaning of justice depends on the concrete relationships of justice between people and not the abstract procedures of institutions. Using Isaiah as a model for modern social criticism, Buber writes that, "[w]hen Isaiah speaks of justice, he is not thinking of institutions, but of you and me, because without you and me the most glorious institution becomes a lie."[18] While institutions to promote and enforce justice are necessary, Buber believes that real justice involves each person giving others their due within mutual relationships.

Evil Urges and Education

Buber viewed moral character development as a person's struggle to achieve wholeness of self against the divided self. This distinction between the divided and the whole self is rooted in his reading of Hasidic teachings about the struggle between the good and evil urges within each human being. Buber interprets these Hasidic teachings as a fusion of the Talmudic doctrine of the two urges with Lurianic Kabbalistic teachings that "fallen sparks" of divine light are hidden within the created world and that human action can redeem these sparks and reunite God and the world from their mutual exile. In Buber's interpretation of Hasidism, the mystical elements of this teaching are transformed and directed towards a worldly and action-oriented approach to moral character development.

Buber emphasizes that in this Hasidic doctrine, evil is not ontologically distinct from the good: "All temptations come from God who clothes Himself in the 'evil' forces . . . evil and good are no longer sundered from one another like two different qualities but like the unformed and the formed material, no longer like left and right, but like above and below, like thornbush and fire. Man must let the thornbush be entirely penetrated by the fire. He must join to God the desire of the temptation itself."[19] Expressing the same idea in his essay about character education, he states: "Good and evil are each other's opposites like right and left. The evil approaches us as a whirlwind, the good as direction."[20] To achieve unity of self means that all of one's motivations are united in purpose. All human beings have desires, urges, and impulses due to their psychobiological makeup or their sociohistorical environment. When a person acts from one of these urges, say for wealth or power, in a way that allows that urge alone to determine action, one is acting as a divided self, as one is allowing one part of their personality to serve as the motivation for the action. The goal in achieving wholeness is to bring all of one's urges, desires, and impulses into a spiritual and ethical unity. Crucial for both Buber's religious thought and his anthropology, a person need not suppress the underlying desires, urges, and impulses that generate actions of the divided self. These urges come from God and can be redeemed and become sources of redemption, liberated like the divine sparks of Lurianic myth. Therefore, the goal of ethical perfection is to channel these urges toward an integrated spiritual and ethical purpose.

Because he believed that each situation and each person demand a unique ethical response, Buber's exemplars of moral perfection are spiritual teachers who respond to their students with dialogical openness and spontaneity. Buber interprets the stories of the Hasidic *tzaddikim* as examples of spiritual leaders who elevate the mundane concerns of their disciples to sacred responsibilities. The "true *tzaddik*" "is the man who hourly measures the depths of responsibility with the sounding lead of his words. . . . Men come to him, and each desires his opinion, his help. . . . And it is this he does for all: *he elevates their need before he satisfies it*."[21] The greatness of the *tzaddikim* is the way they respond and attend to the spiritual task embedded in the mundane material needs of their petitioners. Buber also cites traditions that the *tzaddik* embodies the teachings of Torah and are themselves a

Torah, meaning that their teachings to their disciples are a model for behavior.[22] What they model, as Buber understands it, is a dialogical responsiveness to the unique needs and aspirations of each person.

In his writings on education and philosophical anthropology, Buber discusses the more modest example of the modern humanistic educator. This kind of educator "sees each [individual] as in a position to become a unique, single person, and thus the bearer of a special task of existence which can be fulfilled through him and him alone. He sees every personal life as engaged in such actualization. . . . He cannot wish to impose himself, for he believes in the effect of the actualizing forces, that is, he believes that in every man what is right is established in a single and uniquely personal way."[23] Buber is not valorizing this teacher as a model of spiritual perfection as with the *tzaddik*, but they exemplify the same qualities of openness and attentiveness to the unique situation of the individual in guiding them to their experience of the world. Even instruction in various realms of knowledge requires the teacher to recognize the unique way each student will encounter the world through such knowledge and potentially flourish as a result of their education.

Creation, Revelation, and Redemption

Buber draws on his notion of dialogue to develop a theology of divine imitation that connects his approach to virtue to the images of God found in classical Jewish sources. He interprets the oneness of God and the special name of God—the tetragrammaton—to mean that God is ever-present—continuously available to humanity as a loving, comforting presence in the face of evil and suffering. Created in the divine image, human beings are called upon to realize this divine image through the work of ethical perfection understood as *imitatio dei*.[24] Interpreting a midrash from Genesis Rabbah, Buber states, "We perfect our souls 'toward' God. 'Being like' God is then not something which is unconnected with our earthly life, it is the goal of our life, provided that our life is really a perfecting of our soul 'toward' God."[25] Being "like God," as Buber understands the midrash, is an ethical aspiration, not a static ontological fact. In the same essay he quotes a famous Talmudic statement that the imitation of God consists in imitating divine *middot*, or attributes, of clothing the naked, visiting the sick, comforting mourners, and burying the dead.[26]

Buber also links the humanistic aspiration of wholeness as a religious task to his interpretation of the theological triad of creation, revelation, and redemption. As he cites the great Hasidic master, Rabbi Naḥman of Bratslav (see chapter 21 in this volume): "Every man shall know and consider that in his qualities he is unique in the world and that none like him ever lived, for had there ever before been someone like him, then he could not have needed to exist. But each is in truth a new thing in the world, and he shall make perfect his special characteristics, for it is because they are not perfect that the coming of the Messiah tarries."[27] In Buber's theology, creation teaches that each individual human being, created in the divine image, has unique capacities and potentialities. Revelation provides humanity with the insight, available at every moment, to actualize that potential as a religious task. Drawing on these Hasidic teachings, Buber thought of the actualization of one's individual potential as a religious commandment: not just something we might do, but something we must do. Buber's association of self-actualization with messianic realization suggests that the goal of self-actualization is an ongoing task that one continually strives to achieve without fully achieving it.[28] In general, Buber understands Jewish messianism as continually striving to achieve worldly redemption while always refusing to declare its arrival.[29]

Buber emphasizes the importance of human freedom in his Jewish theology and uses the Jewish concept of *teshuvah*—often translated as "repentance" but more literally, "turning"— to indicate that humanity must and can always strive for ethical perfection. Drawing on the national and communal dimensions of the concept in the biblical prophets, Buber equates *teshuvah* with the process of social and spiritual renewal. To "return" to God means humanity returning to its purpose in its being created in the divine image, which is to bring about peace and harmonious relations within nations and among nations.[30] Buber also understands the individual who strives for wholeness as likewise returning to their true purpose, actualizing their unique potential through living a just and caring life in relation to others.

Buber's humanistic ethic of self-actualization lies at the heart of his vision for Zionism and his critique of rival approaches. Calling his approach to Zionism "Hebrew Humanism," Buber insisted that the task of Zionism was to renew a Jewish commitment to the prophetic task of bringing about a true community that fulfilled God's holy purpose for humanity and could inspire other nations to embrace this task. To say that the people of Israel is chosen by God means that their destiny as a nation depends on their commitment to living whole-heartedly according to truth and righteousness.[31] Buber also intended his studies of Hasidic spirituality to infuse Zionism with religious humanism that placed ethical perfection at its center.[32] As with his account of the virtues, Buber insists that the religious, ethical, and political elements of human social life should be integrated as whole. Indeed, the purpose of Zionism is to aspire to human wholeness and holiness in the daily life of the Jewish people, to share it with the world, and to achieve redemption.

Notes

1. An important exception is Pamela Vermes's study, *Buber on God and the Perfect Man* (London: Littman Library of Jewish Civilization, 1994).

2. Martin Buber, *I and Thou* (New York: Simon and Schuster, 1970), 62.

3. Martin Buber, "Education of Character," in *Between Man and Man* (New York: Macmillian, 1965), 113–14.

4. Buber, *I and Thou*, 66.

5. Martin Buber, "The Way of Man According to the Teachings of Hasidism," in *Hasidism and Modern Man* (Atlantic Highlands, NJ: Humanities Press International, 1988), 151.

6. Cf. Samuel Hayim Brody, *Martin Buber's Theopolitics* (Bloomington: Indiana University Press, 2018), on Buber's anarcho-socialism, and see Lawrence Silberstein, *Martin Buber's Social and Religious Thought* (New York: New York University Press, 1989), on the role of alienation in his thought.

7. Martin Buber, "The Holy Way," in *On Judaism* (New York: Schoken, 1967), 110.

8. See Martin Buber, "The Experiment That Did Not Fail," in *Paths in Utopia* (Syracuse: Syracuse University Press, 1996).

9. Lev. 19:18. Cf. Martin Buber, "Love of God and Love of Neighbor," in *Hasidism and Modern Man*, particularly 230–31; and see Martin Buber, "The Love of God and the Idea of Deity, in *Eclipse of God* (Atlantic Highlands, NJ: Humanities Press International, 1988), 57–58.

10. Martin Buber, "Elements of the Interhuman," in *The Knowledge of Man* (Atlantic Highlands, NJ: Humanities Press International, 1988), 67.

11. Martin Buber, "My Way to Hasidism," in *Hasidism and Modern Man*, 42.

12. Martin Buber, "Hasidism and Modern Man," in *Hasidism and Modern Man*, 23.

13. Martin Buber, "Dialogue," in *Between Man and Man*, 15.

14. Buber, "The Way of Man According to the Teachings of Hasidism," 158.

15. Buber, "Education of Character," 106.

16. Martin Buber, *Moses: The Revelation and the Covenant* (Atlantic Highlands, NJ: Humanities Press International, 1988), 177–81.

17. Buber, "The Holy Way," 144.

18. Martin Buber, "The Demand of the Spirit and Historical Reality," in *Pointing the Way* (Amherst, NY: Humanity Books, 1999), 189.

19. Martin Buber, *Origin and Meaning of Hasidism* (Amherst, NY: Humanity Books, 1988), 80.

20. Buber, "Education of Character," 114.

21. Buber, "My Way to Hasidism," 60–61.

22. Buber, *The Origin and Meaning of Hasidism*, 128–29.

23. Buber, "Elements of the Interhuman," 73.

24. Martin Buber, "The Two Foci of the Jewish Soul," in *Israel and the World: Essays in a Time of Crisis* (Syracuse, NY: Syracuse University Press, 1997), 30–32.

25. Martin Buber, "Imitatio Dei," in *Israel and the World: Essays in a Time of Crisis*, 72. The midrash is attributed to Rabbi Aha as an interpretation of Psalm 100, Genesis Rabbah 49:29.

26. Buber, "Imitatio Dei," 76. The midrash appears in BT Sotah 14a.

27. Martin Buber, "The Life of the Hasidim," in *Hasidism and Modern Man* (Atlantic Highlands, NJ: Humanities Press International, 1988), 103.

28. Cf. Buber, "Two Foci of the Jewish Soul," where Buber presents this interpretation of Jewish messianism.

29. Buber, "The Holy Way," 111.

30. See Martin Buber, "The Faith of Judaism," in *Israel and the World: Essays in a Time of Crisis*, 19–21; "The Spirit of Israel and the World Today," in *Israel and the World: Essays in a Time of Crisis*, 185–86.

31. Martin Buber, "Hebrew Humanism," in *Israel and the World: Essays in a Time of Crisis*, 250–51.

32. Buber, *The Origin and Meaning of Hasidism*, 218.

Chapter 28

Mordecai Kaplan

MATTHEW LAGRONE

Thanks to the work of Mel Scult and others, Mordecai Kaplan's long life is unusually well-documented. Kaplan's lifespan, 1881–1983, looks like a misprint. Born near Vilna, the son of a rabbi, his family moved to the United States when he was young. Later, Kaplan returned to Europe for ordination from Rabbi Isaac Jacob Reines, one of the early rabbinic voices advocating Religious Zionism. Prior to ordination, Kaplan attended the original iteration of the Jewish Theological Seminary (i.e., prior to its reorganization under Solomon Schechter), an institution with which he would have a long, fruitful, and contentious association. He ministered at Kehilath Jeshurun (Kaplan was not yet invested as a rabbi), making him the first JTS graduate to be offered "a large Orthodox pulpit in New York City."[1] Schechter then invited him to be the first dean of JTS's Teachers Institute. Kaplan's career as a public intellectual accelerated when he articulated religious views at variance with the traditional community, which placed him outside Orthodoxy. In 1922, he helped establish the proto-Reconstructionist Society for the Advancement of Judaism, which promoted Kaplan's new theological approaches. His commitment to a thoroughgoing religious revitalization found socio-theological expression in his pioneering *Judaism as a Civilization* (1933) and liturgical expression in a new *Haggadah* and *Sabbath Prayer Book,* both of which were put in *herem* in 1945. From the late 1940s onward, Kaplan's energies were devoted to the creation and development of what would become the Reconstructionist movement in American Judaism.

The Virtues in Kaplan's Worldview

What was Kaplan's worldview and how do the virtues operate within it?

While Kaplan was not an ethicist, he wrote about ethics, if irregularly. Nor was he a philosopher, though at times he thought philosophically.[2] Perhaps it is best, in order later to situate his understanding of the virtues, to describe Kaplan's worldview as a hybrid of pragmatic theology and functionalist sociology. We can then outline his position: Kaplan is a sociologically informed thinker who attempts to rehabilitate traditional Jewish theology in a social-scientific key.[3] While on firmer ground in descriptive sociology, Kaplan confidently mixes God-talk and ethics. Memorably, he defines God, via Matthew Arnold, as "a power that makes for righteousness—not ourselves."[4]

One consistent message in Kaplan's writings is that older religious language can be retained but must be radically redescribed, relocating significance from the world-to-come to this world alone, meeting the community where it is and what it is willing to accept. Language, like religion, evolves. Kaplan's entire project, of course, is keyed to evolutionary metaphors, transferring the terminology of the prestige sciences to the social sciences. For example, salvation becomes "self-fulfillment."[5] Salvation once meant salvation somewhere else and at some other time, thus justifying the inequities of life in the present. For modern Jews, however, salvation must apply to the here and now, with inequities remedied. If salvation means, in the end, returning to God, its new Kaplanian designation as "self-fulfillment" allows us to "identify ourselves with God, and God functions in us. This fact should lead to the conclusion that when we believe in God, we believe that reality . . . is so constituted as to enable man to achieve salvation."[6] The old sense of salvation is untenable, but attraction to the old language remains. Kaplan supplies new breath—frequently in an individualistic, psychological register—to the lungs of exhausted words.

For Kaplan, "religion is a natural social process."[7] It is natural because it is functional; it is a support through life's vicissitudes and a spur to better selves. Religion is a net positive for humanity, but its claims to unchanging truth, hitched to wild supernaturalism, evaporate in confrontation with the tangible successes of modern science. Kaplan adds: "[R]eligion can no longer be a matter of entering into relationship with the supernatural . . . as a reservoir of magic power to be tapped whenever they are aware of their physical limitations."[8] The discovery of unvarying iron, physical laws that administer, indifferently, our world means that we must "accept without reservation the validity of the scientific rather than the authoritative approach to reality."[9] (If the author wanted to respond good-naturedly to this comment, he might ask Kaplan if this means that Monet's painting matters because of the chemical composition of the pigments). The buffered self arises; the porous self closes.[10]

Central to Kaplan's worldview, shared happily or discontentedly by almost all thinkers outside of the more insular Orthodoxies, is that modernity introduces an irreversible break with tradition ("an altogether different universe of discourse"[11]), though earlier habits, customs, and beliefs leak into contemporary Jewish life, sometimes in unexpected ways. In particular, he lit the touch paper to the classical conception of Israel's election.[12] "The aura," Kaplan writes, "of divine election has departed from his people."[13] Phenomenologically, election as an experience has lost its emotional power to compel. Kaplan smashes sharp elbows into the theological and moral content of election, but more: foregoing chosenness is about normalizing Jewish existence. Thus: *Judaism as a Civilization*. Jewish civilization—the whole starter kit of language, history, values, et alia—is beautiful, tragic, and sustaining, an ever-evolving world in miniature. While its origins may not be divine, civilization is also not the result of "deliberate" decisions; instead, its evolutions are spontaneous, part of an emergent order similar to "any living organism."[14] This civilization is like other civilizations, neither superior nor inferior. Be *like* the nations: the Torah's reproof becomes Kaplan's urge toward acceptance.

Virtue ethics, like all theories of ethics, is underpinned by an anthropology of what it means to be human, with the full range of possibilities and limits. The existence of substantive disagreements about the number and content of the virtues, how to apply the principles of those virtues, assumes that such moral sorting is humanly necessary. And, according to Kaplan, in the world of actual human experience, everyone embraces some virtues, even if the term itself goes unused.

Virtue speaks to something natural and rational in us—he calls it an "imperative"[15] that does not emerge from individual preference alone—and desires the good and wishes to forego the bad. Even the one who claims to fully repudiate any virtue, even he experiences moral disgust when he detects some slight against his person: "They resent a 'wrong' done to them and clamour for their 'rights'; they experience a sense of mortification if caught in a lie, regardless of whether they suffer any practical penalties in consequence or not."[16] What Kaplan establishes here is a kind of virtue baseline, as even the denier of virtue experiences guilt after his lie is discovered. This reality suggests that the one who speaks honestly is praiseworthy.

The foregoing offers Kaplan's philosophical guard rails, providing the constraints for how virtue appears in his work. While he did not write systematically about ethics, Kaplan maintains that there is a human nature in which we all share, or at least an inescapable human condition in which we participate. However, it can be a challenge to disentangle Kaplan's convictions about what it means to be virtuous from his guiding sociological considerations. Because his concerns, both scholarly and personal, tilt toward the study of American Jewish society and civic order, his reflections on ethics/virtues ordinarily favor utilitarian explanations and solutions. Nevertheless, the volume and diversity of his writings allow for a sufficiently responsible presentation of those virtues he believes ought to be habitually cultivated and practiced. Such a presentation is more than simply extracting stray passages and flogging them for significance.

The Virtues that Matter

If the preceding rather hazily outlines how virtue ethics relates to Kaplan's thought, this section narrows the focus to some of the virtues that frequently appear in his writings.

Like the medieval rationalists, Kaplan argues that the *mitzvot* train our character, an idea that merges seamlessly with the fundamentals of virtue ethics. He writes: "The development of the traits of kindness, sympathy, and above all, gratitude, is the purpose underlying such precepts as those of loving and honouring parents, refraining from envy, loving our neighbor, treating the stranger with consideration, having pity upon all forms of living creatures. To this category belongs the entire system of ritual observances, the purpose of which may be said to be the evocation of an attitude of thankfulness toward life as a whole."[17] Like principles for virtue ethicists, so the commandments for the observant Jew: they "tell us that what is right is to be a certain kind of person,"[18] nudge us toward virtuous behaviors and attitudes, and cultivate persons who act virtuously.

We place trust in the virtues of others. Kaplan uses the example of one individual loaning money to another with the expectation that the loan will be paid back in a timely manner. The one who does so is trustworthy and honest. The coercive power of the state to enforce contracts can compel the borrower to pay his debt, but perhaps the borrower is out of jurisdiction. Kaplan writes: "But if, despite our inability to enforce our claim and his ability to deny it, we still expect him to pay his debt, we are entertaining an ethical expectation."[19] The virtues, then, are part of our rational nature.

For Kaplan, we elevate our moral lives even while shifting our understanding of the virtues. A virtuous person consciously tries to avoid sin and, when she sins, she seeks to atone for that transgression. Kaplan maintains that modern Jews have a tin ear for those older sounds of sin and atonement, but he recognizes that neither religion nor secular culture can be liberated from notions of sin and atonement, despite the danse macabre of twentieth-century experiments in the evisceration of this part of the human condition. It could not be otherwise: every civilization is, in the end, religious, at least in Tillich's sense. Kaplan is a religious radical but maintains that religion is the binding agent of Jewish civilization. Since religion is a "natural process," it evolves to satisfy the needs of the day, and what is needed now is not the earlier notion of sin as violation of God's law and atonement as retreat into obedience. The ancient version of sin and atonement does not match the evolution of Jewish civilization. However, the circumstances that cause within us a recognition of sin and the urge to seek atonement have not departed. Resorting to one of his favorite literary stratagems, Kaplan asks readers to compare these competing understandings of sin and atonement to the scientific method: "When a scientific hypothesis is proved untenable, a true scientist will always search for a hypothesis which will explain the same phenomena more adequately. We should proceed in the same manner in our religious thinking. *These traditional concepts may have been wrong, but they were rationalizations of deep-seated human needs, and these needs still cry out for an expression which conforms to our present sense of reality."*[20] Shunning sin and seeking atonement when our moral weakness fails to eschew sin nurtures the virtuous life: being, acting, and doing good.

To suggest that virtue ethics, especially compared to deontology, admits some measure of adaptability—even if not to subject it to the scientific method, as Kaplan does—is not to whisper "relativism" sotto voce, a fragile and fraught embrace of the spirit of the age. Yet a historically significant term such as "honor" has surely vacated much of the meaning that, say, Cicero intended by it. It is facile (yet true!) to say that much of what made one honorable in the past fails to qualify one as honorable today—and this is not because the women and men of the past were more (or less) wicked than ourselves—and yet still we do not wish to prune it from the inventory of desirable virtues. Better, then, to rehabilitate it. This was Kaplan's project.

Not all virtues are as historically contingent as honor. Let's consider the key virtue that runs throughout Kaplan's writing: justice. (When Kaplan deliberately promotes the virtuous life, the virtue he advances is unfailingly moral rather than intellectual.) The exceptions are philosophically tedious, so let us acknowledge that a just person is one who deals fairly and transparently with others, untroubled by another's social status or wealth, or lack of either. In advocating for the "the good life," Kaplan summons Micah: "[T]o do one's best is to practice justice and loving kindness, and to be at one's best under all circumstances is to walk humbly with God." And of what does the virtue of justice consist?

> What this implies may be inferred from what Judaism regards as the central problem of human conduct . . . how to prevent man from misusing the power entrusted to him by God. . . . It should not be difficult to group those laws under the categories of justice, loving kindness and walking humbly with God. By noting how each of these three categories is related to the problem of power, we can get at the ethical purpose underlying virtually all the laws in the Torah.[21]

Justice, along with loving-kindness and humility, is a demand that one invested with power—and power is no virtue—act justly, which requires foregoing personal advantage in addition to abandoning power's opiate: the craving to retain and increase one's power.

God's justice is worthy of praise. However, Kaplan argues that our understanding of one who acts justly progresses over time. God as judge is one of the governing biblical and rabbinic representations of the divine. And God as the righteous judge who justly serves the deserts we have earned remains a sustaining metaphor in both daily and *yamim noraim* liturgy. Yet this image, according to Kaplan, needs to be attuned to the ear of the modern Jew. Since, according to Kaplan, we have adjusted our expectations of a righteous judge through time, the older picture of judicial punishment in this world (and, thus, divine reward and punishment in the world-to-come) obscures the portrayal of a just judge who seeks both the public welfare and the offender's rehabilitation. This new picture of acting justly also incorporates Kaplan's sociological thinking and this-worldly religion. The achievements of post-Darwinian science and post-Durkheimian social science underscore the "factors of heredity and environment," factors that move judgment from a bright line test of guilt and innocence, to a multifactorial distribution of liability, one with many moving parts. A good jurist no longer "metes out measure for measure," and now "heaven and hell drop out of the picture"[22] as the compensation and chastisements of supernatural religion recede further into the past of humankind.

Whom Ought I to Emulate?

> During World War I, a student from Germany was arrested by the czarist police and charged with spying for his native land. The defense lawyer asked the Chafetz Chayyim to appear in court as a character witness. Before summoning the rabbi to the witness stand, the lawyer, it is reported, approached the judge and said, "Your honor, the rabbi who is about to testify has an impeccable reputation among his fellow Jews. They tell a story that one day he came home and saw a thief rummaging through his living room. The frightened thief climbed out a window and ran off with some of the rabbi's possessions, and the rabbi ran after him,

> shouting, "I declare all my property ownerless, so that the thief would not be guilty of having committed a crime." The judge looked at the lawyer skeptically. "Do you believe that story really happened?" "I don't know, your honor," the lawyer answered, "but they don't tell stories like that about you and me."[23]

Consequentialism, which shapes the political and social order no matter the particular brand of politics, abstracts us into categories, and not always of our own choosing. Kantianism detaches us from our shared environment. At its healthiest, virtue ethics avoids both the consequentialist affinity for shoving all human reality into classifications and the deontologist uprooting of the web of mutualities in which we are situated. Virtue ethics—again, at its best—regards both the individual and her wider social context. And one of its most attractive features is that individual character ought to be shaped by patterning oneself on virtuous role models, whether living or dead.

Abraham and the prophets are the models for Kaplan's understanding of the good and virtuous life. If such a choice of models is unsurprising, it is for a reason: with his practical wisdom, Abraham's life lends itself to emulation, and the blazing exhortations of the classical prophets commend virtuous action and condemn iniquitous behavior. Both exemplars ask us to be better than we know we are instead of one who follows social rules out of prudence, fear, or worry over status. While broadly rationalist in outlook, Kaplan declines the philosopher's path of intellectual virtues: "[E]thical philosophers are dreamers and creators of utopias. Prophets are practical revolutionaries."[24] And more than that: true prophets, even in moments of reproof, *love* the people to whom God has sent them. Of course, a philosopher *can* love the people, but that requirement is not on the job fact sheet circulated by the HR department.

Abraham's insistence that God act justly with Sodom and Gomorrah because He is just is perhaps the best illustration of virtue ethics in the Torah. In Gen. 18, Abraham implores God to spare the cities if a threshold of righteous people can be found among them, so that the innocent are not destroyed because of the wicked. Abraham pleads, "Far be it from You! Shall not the Judge of all the earth deal justly?" (Gen. 18:25). Kaplan notes that the Rabbis interpret this verse to mean "'that to act unjustly is alien to God.' They thereby indicated that the character of God is necessarily conceived as inherently consistent, integrated. Transferring this attribute of God to human character, we should say that, *if human character is to reflect the divine, it must be integrated and self-consistent. This involves a working synthesis of individual self-expression and social cooperation*" (emphasis in the original).[25] Kaplan always loops any moral lesson back into wider social concerns.

If Abraham's controlling virtue is justice, courage guides the prophets. Exclusive of totalitarian societies, it takes very little courage (or imagination) to denounce one's perceived enemies, but to pour rebuke on the community that you love and in which you live—because you love them and live among them—that takes real courage. It is a virtue that ought to be measured by what it costs the courageous person. But an excess of courage is recklessness, or courage without purpose. The prophets, however, had purpose: "It is inconceivable that the prophets would resort to violent denunciation of their people's ignorance of God's true character, or that they would engage in bitter condemnation of the social injustice that prevailed among their contemporaries, unless those whom they addressed might be expected to know better and to act more ethically."[26]

The Virtues in Kaplan's Interpretation of Tradition and Identity

While advocating for a civilizational profile to understand world and Jewish history, Kaplan is not concerned with ordering civilizations into greater or lesser; each has its own integrity and standards by which it may be judged. This commendable reticence does not mean that Kaplan is unable to identify specific contributions of Jewish civilization to the human project.

Kaplan argues that Jewish civilization was the first to promote conscious ethical living as the priority over the pursuit of wealth and power, especially the latter. Torah and its later rabbinic elaboration serve as wise guides to restrain the human predisposition to misuse power. Tradition urgently teaches the need "to subordinate the use of power to the moral law. *This cardinal doctrine concerning power furnishes the best clue to Judaism's contribution to world ethics*" (emphasis in the original).[27] Additionally, in the economic sphere, ancient Israel made "numerous provisions . . . for honesty, fair dealing and just reward,"[28] organizing a welfare network meant to provide succor across the community, with prophets to remind them when they failed in that obligation.

A culture that nurtures goodness—holstering what Iris Murdoch calls the "fat, relentless ego,"[29] treating others *b'tzelem Elohim* (in the image of God), for example—will transcend the worst features of the nation-state: a bureaucratic regime that ceaselessly monitors its members. Kaplan is not arguing for some libertarian utopia, but instead aspiring toward a virtuous public square, where educational, domestic, civic, and religious institutions sustain and live out the primary goods of the human project: honesty, trustworthiness, charity, self-control, and so on. Like a virtue ethicist, Kaplan accepts principles over rules. The need for rules to govern moral choices is the need for control, to pin those choices like a butterfly's wing to a mounting board. But most moral choices are encoded in a small set of principles (the Aristotelian list of virtues, e.g.) that guide decisions. Kaplan enumerates such principles from Jewish tradition: "There is 'the right and the good,' emphasized by Naḥmanides. There is an ethic of virtue, set out by Maimonides in his "Laws of Character Traits" (*Hilkhot Deot*). There is the concept of *lifnim mishurat ha-din,* acting within or beyond the limits of the law. There is *middat hassidut,* 'saintly conduct,' not required of everyone. There is the general imperative of 'walking in God's ways.'"[30] Many moral rules are bridled by the time and place of their formulation, whereas principles plant within us a disposition to virtuous action.

The foregoing is Kaplan at his most traditionalist. Yet he itched to leave the past and accelerate into modernity, where one of the key questions centers on God's role in shaping the virtuous life. Kaplan does not get lost in a Euthyphro dilemma where "a thing is right and good because God wills it."[31] He rejects this idea as it robs individuals of the autonomy "in the determination of what is right, and [leaves] him entirely at the *mercy of tradition*" (emphasis added).[32] (*Pace* Kaplan, his Seminary colleague and philosophical bête noire, Abraham Joshua Heschel, maintained that "the individual's insight alone is unable to cope with all the problems of living. It is the *guidance of tradition* [emphasis added] on which we must rely, and whose norms we must learn to interpret and to apply.")[33] The virtues generated by tradition are important, but they have a voice and not a veto.

While we can discover moments of virtue ethics' integration within Kaplan's work, in the end he is a fully dressed consequentialist. His promotion of various virtues is authentic, but instruction in the virtuous life does not take precedence over a Baconian "relief of man's estate" consequentialism. It is the triumph of modern science that has removed impediments to self-fulfillment, "our desires and purposes."[34] Kaplan laments that "psychology and the social sciences" have failed to match the feats of the hard sciences that have so altered our experience of the world, yet "we look to these sciences to point the way to the eventual abolition of the inveterate evils of human life."[35] These sentiments don't quite reach the level of scientism, nevertheless we see Kaplan prioritize the observable consequences—the stuff you can count—of the sciences to measure what matters.

Earlier in this section, we considered a passage where Kaplan wrote approvingly of the key principles in a Jewish virtue ethics.[36] But his work walks back the primacy of the virtues and their principles in favor of the utilitarian gesture to rules. He gives the example of what we can learn from Rosh Ha-Shanah about our failures and how to repair our souls. Rather than turning to self-reflection and how we might enhance virtuous living, Kaplan revisits scientific analogies: "Where there is a flaw in a bridge and it breaks under its own weight, the engineer learns to appreciate all the more keenly the law of gravitation upon which he must depend for the security of the bridge he wishes to build."[37] Statements such as this account for the preponderance of Kaplan's meditations on the moral life.

Notes

1. Emanuel Goldsmith and Mel Scult, *Dynamic Judaism: The Essential Writings of Mordecai M. Kaplan* (New York: Fordham University Press), 5.

2. Not all scholars are impressed by Kaplan's philosophical bona fides. See Steven Katz, "Mordecai Kaplan and the Problem of Evil," *Jewish Social Studies* 12, no. 2 (2006): 116ff.

3. See Mel Scult, "The Sociologist as Theologian: The Fundamental Assumptions of Mordecai Kaplan's Thought," *Judaism* 25, no. 3 (1976): 345–52.

4. Mordecai Kaplan, *The Meaning of God in Modern Jewish Religion* (Detroit: Wayne State University Press, 1995), 309.

5. Kaplan, *Meaning of God,* ix.

6. Kaplan, *Meaning of God,* 26.

7. Kaplan, *Meaning of God,* ix.

8. Kaplan, *Meaning of God,* 25.

9. Kaplan, *Meaning of God*, ix–x.

10. See Charles Taylor, *A Secular Age* (Cambridge, MA: Harvard University Press, 2007), ch. 1.

11. Kaplan, *Meaning of God*, 1.

12. See David Novak, "Mordecai Kaplan's Rejection of Election," *Modern Judaism* 15, no. 1 (1995): 1–19.

13. Mordecai Kaplan, *Judaism as a Civilization: Toward a Reconstruction of American-Jewish Life* (Skokie, IL: Varda Books, 2001), 15.

14. Kaplan, *Judaism as a Civilization*, 180.

15. Kaplan, *Meaning of God*, 309.

16. Kaplan, *Meaning of God*, 308–309.

17. Kaplan, *Meaning of God*, 317.

18. David Schmidtz and Matt Zwolinski, "Environmental Virtue Ethics: What It Is and What It Needs To Be," *Cambridge Companion to Virtue Ethics*, ed. Daniel C. Russell (Cambridge: Cambridge University Press, 2013), 221.

19. Kaplan, "A Philosophy of Jewish Ethics," *The Jews: Their History, Culture, and Religion*, 3rd ed., ed. Louis Finkelstein (New York: Harper, 1960), 2:1011.

20. Kaplan, *Meaning of God*, 161.

21. Mordecai Kaplan, "A Philosophy of Jewish Ethics," 1035–36.

22. Kaplan, *Meaning of God*, 7–8.

23. Joseph Telushkin, *Hillel: If Not Now, When?* (New York: Schocken, 2010), 32.

24. Kaplan, *Judaism as a Civilization*, 462.

25. Kaplan, *Meaning of God*, 182–83.

26. Kaplan, "A Philosophy of Jewish Ethics," 1030–31.

27. Kaplan, "A Philosophy of Jewish Ethics," 1034.

28. Kaplan, *Meaning of God*, 317.

29. Iris Murdoch, *The Sovereignty of Good* (London: Routledge and Kegan Paul, 1970), 52.

30. Kaplan, "A Philosophy of Jewish Ethics," 1010.

31. Kaplan, "A Philosophy of Jewish Ethics," 40.

32. Kaplan, "A Philosophy of Jewish Ethics," 40.

33. Abraham Joshua Heschel, *Between God and Man: An Interpretation of Judaism*, ed. Fritz A. Rothchild (New York: Simon and Schuster, 1997), 158. See also, Matthew LaGrone, "Ethical Theories of Mordecai Kaplan and Abraham Joshua Heschel," *The Oxford Handbook of Jewish Ethics and Morality*, ed. Elliot N. Dorff and Jonathan K. Crane (New York: Oxford University Press, 2012), 151–65.

34. Kaplan, *Meaning of God*, 52–53.

35. Kaplan, *Meaning of God*, 52–53.

36. See note 31.

37. Kaplan, *Meaning of God*, 144.

Chapter 29

Eliyahu Eliezer Dessler

ESTHER SOLOMON

Rabbi Eliyahu Eliezer Dessler (1892–1953) was a scion of the Musar movement. From 1905–1928, he studied at the Kelm Musar yeshiva, and then emigrated to England. From 1941, he led the new Gateshead Kollel (yeshiva for married men) and in 1944 founded the Gateshead women's teachers' seminary. In 1949, he moved to Israel, and until his death in 1953 was *mashgiaḥ* (Musar supervisor) of Ponevez Yeshiva in B'nai Brak.[1] His thought was published posthumously as the series *Mikhtav me'Eliyahu*[2] (Epistle of Elijah), which has been reprinted twenty-seven times and which continues to be a fixture of the ḥaredi library.[3]

Cultivation of Character: A Jewish Obligation Promoted by the Musar Movement

Although multiple Jewish sources attest to refinement of virtue[4] as a religious imperative, the Musar movement, founded by Rabbi Israel Salanter (1810–1883; see chapter 23), prioritized it in unprecedented ways. The movement sought to counteract two conceptual, nineteenth-century trends, Enlightenment (Haskalah) and Ḥasidism, which were attracting multitudes of adherents away from Lithuanian-style Orthodoxy.[5] The extreme intellectualism utilized in service of Torah study, particularly in Lithuania,[6] was often alienating to youth, as was conventional practice of the commandments, which for many had become rote behavior.[7] Musar served to reinvigorate Ultra-Orthodox allegiance by injecting new life into ancient practice. Using elements of psychology, Musar demanded that its adherents lead examined lives and systematically work to improve their character. Salanter accepted flawed human nature as given[8] and developed strategies to improve it.[9] Among them were the passionate repetition of verses from Tanakh or Midrash (with "burning lips");[10] the use of visualizations;[11] and, primarily, the setting aside of one hour daily for introspection and the learning of musar texts.[12]

Salanter demonstrated that character development and resultant improved conduct were mandated by the Torah and were, therefore, intrinsic to Jewish observance. He did not advocate character improvement as an end in itself but as the fulfillment of God's directives. In this respect, he equated the development of virtue with keeping the Sabbath and eating kosher food.[13]

Rabbi Simḥah Zissel (Broide) Ziv (1824–1898; see chapter 24) was Salanter's primary disciple and the founder of the Kelm Musar yeshiva where Dessler studied. Like his teacher, he believed that the ultimate human task as determined by God in the Torah, was to achieve elevated ethics and conduct, and that the ideal system for doing so was Musar. Simḥah Zissel further developed Salanter's system by adding various practices, which he implemented at his educational institutions. For instance, he scheduled several daily five-minute learning sessions in order to teach his students the value of time,[14] and he insisted that they keep their possessions neat and orderly, due to his conviction that this was preconditional for an organized mind.[15] An additional tenet of Simḥah Zissel's teachings was frequent deprecation of egocentricity, which he described as the greatest impediment to love of God. He maintained that the development of love for others counteracts self-absorption, thereby leading to Godliness.[16] To that end, he implemented various additional strategies to be practiced by his students, such as thinking constantly about love of one's fellow;[17] learning the accounts of kindness done by people in Tanakh;[18] and performing menial tasks, such as washing the floor of the yeshiva.[19] These enforced practices devolved from Simḥah Zissel's conviction that through nurturing feelings of brotherhood among his students he would enable them to overcome the natural tendency toward selfishness.

Kelm and its precepts exerted a dominant influence on Dessler from his earliest days. As an only child, he spent much time in the company of his father, Rabbi Reuben Dov Dessler (1863–1935), who was educated at the Kelm yeshiva and later became part of its administrative staff, despite his primary occupation as a successful businessman.[20] Eliyahu Eliezer Dessler began his studies at Kelm at the age of thirteen, becoming its youngest student by far.[21] Although Simḥah Zissel had died almost eight years before Dessler's arrival there,[22] the yeshiva had been taken over by his son-in-law, Rabbi Tzvi Hirsch Broide (1865–1913), who was also his nephew. While Simḥah Zissel had innovated regarding strategies for character improvement, his successor did not; instead, he worked at promoting the methodologies developed by his uncle.[23] Like him, Tzvi Hirsch modeled Kelm doctrine, inspiring his students to strive for moral perfection.[24] Kelm ideology forged an indelible impression on Dessler, and its influence could be felt in his conduct throughout his life.[25]

One indicator of this is a letter written by Dessler in 1950, three years before his death. The letter is addressed to Rabbi Shraga Tzvi Grossbard (1917–1993), Rosh Yeshiva of the Ponevez Yeshiva's division for younger boys, as a follow-up to a prior conversation. Dessler wrote in favor of creating a Musar *va'ad*, a type of club designed to improve spirituality for participants. Stipulating that potential group members should be from those who had learned in a Musar yeshiva prior to World War II, he said that they should look for musar works to learn, as well as easily implemented techniques to put into practice, in order to facilitate the larger goal of increased focus on service of God. Dessler added that in his opinion work on self-improvement is holy and is of utmost importance.[26] This letter is a pure reflection of Kelm mentality and its antecedent, the Musar movement as envisioned by Israel Salanter. The starting point is that change is necessary, important, and possible; the methodology is the development of appropriate techniques; and the framework is the working together of a group of like-minded people. That Dessler wrote such a letter in his last years implies that he remained dedicated throughout his life to Kelm principles.

For Dessler, the refinement of virtue represented the highest good, because it had been mandated by God and because it fostered connection to God, the overarching goal of life.[27] Virtue was not relativistically defined; there was no room for debate regarding the definition of virtue as opposed to vice. Instead, the Torah and rabbinic writings were the first and final arbiters of desirable conduct and attitude,[28] and the methodology for attaining perfection was the study of classic texts.

While this perspective was shared by Dessler's predecessors in the Musar movement, he was innovative in his willingness to countenance the use of myriad sources in the formulation of his thought. For instance, because the Musar movement began partially as a reaction to Hasidism, the inclusion of Hasidic ideas in works of the movement is unexpected. Yet, Dessler did include multiple Hasidic and pre-Hasidic[29] writings in his discourse. Additionally, most Musar authorities did not study Kabbalah. The only direct reference to Kabbalah in Salanter's writings is a comment in the margins of a letter to his student Rabbi Eliyahu Levinson, from the year 1850. Apparently referring to one of Luzzatto's books, Salanter wrote: "It has nothing to do with me: I do not involve myself in such things. Nor do I know if this is the right time for them."[30] This would seem to indicate indifference toward Kabbalah. By contrast, Dessler made extensive use of Kabbalistic sources: he studied *Zohar* regularly and sometimes based entire lectures on one Zoharic passage.[31]

Dessler explained his approach, stating that in the post-Holocaust era, with the Ultra-Orthodox world reeling from colossal losses, it could not afford the luxury of internal dissent. In order to create a model of Judaism that would be relevant to a contemporary audience, a synthesis should be made of various elements from within all streams of Ultra-Orthodoxy.[32] Accordingly, in pursuit of a salable construction, Dessler included conceptual elements not generally incorporated in Musar thought. He also dispensed with some practical elements that were: techniques such as repetition of verses or the performance of menial tasks are conspicuous by their absence in Dessler's discourse. From within the practices that comprised his Musar training, he selected self-examination and sustained reflection as crucial for character improvement. However, he did make use of practical methodologies for cultivating what he considered the cardinal virtue: selflessness.

Fostering Giving and Godliness

Starting when he was a student at Kelm, Dessler began to conceptualize his understanding of giving to others and continued to speak about it throughout his life. His conclusions were published as *Kuntres ha-Ḥesed* (Essay on Kindness) and other articles in the *Mikhtav me'Eliyahu* series.[33]

In accordance with the Kelm perspective, Dessler held that selflessness is the key manifestation of Godliness in any individual; giving is an elevated capacity and is among the traits of God, who receives nothing from human beings yet continually provides for them. People were created in the image of God, because they too can act with mercy and altruism;[34] the trait of lovingkindness was developed by the patriarchs and bequeathed to their descendants, the Jewish people.[35] Further, the commandment to "walk in the way of God" necessitates that just as God is indivisible, one should feel at one with fellow Jews.[36] This can be achieved only through developing an attitude of giving.[37]

Beyond the religious obligation to become God-like, Dessler mentioned an additional benefit of becoming a giver: one for whom the material world is uninteresting will be content with his lot. The rabbis describe such a person as rich,[38] because he does not experience lack and as such does not attempt to attain more possessions. Ideally, he feels gratitude to God, which leads to a desire to give.[39] Conversely, materialism disallows interpersonal connection, because all individuals compete for finite resources.[40]

Dessler elaborated regarding the converse of giving, egocentricity, which he, like Simḥah Zissel, viewed as the source of all evil.[41] To Dessler, obviously immoral behavior such as theft, as well as seemingly neutral attitudes such as preferring gifts to purchases, are deplorable for the same reason: both devolve from acquisitiveness.[42] Dessler compared a taker to a pig, which constantly wants to consume and is always hungry. However, he added that the pig has an advantage: it is willing to eat anything and is therefore generally content, because the object of its desires is within reach.[43] By contrast, a person who is motivated by the desire to take, "to inhale that which is outside of himself,"[44] and who focuses on the physical world in pursuit of that goal, will never experience joy: material objects will always remain extraneous to him and will never fill his inner longing.[45] He added that, although we initially think that the acquisition of a specific item will make us happy, we know from experience that after it is ours we invariably crave something else.[46] Yet we refuse to learn from our mistakes.[47]

To Dessler, at any given moment, people are either givers or takers: there is no middle ground. Thus, in every deed, speech or thought, one's perspective is that of either giving or taking, although this is not always observable.[48] According respect to another in order to attain something from him is actually taking, while expressing effusive appreciation for a gift is really giving. Dessler added that all people have an intuitive need to give, which is manifest in the desire for social contact or the desire for children;[49] for Dessler, the acquisition of pets or the adoption of children are proof of this.[50]

Selfishness in Service of Giving

If, as Dessler wrote, a spiritual mindset facilitates altruism, one would assume that it would be the province of an exclusive minority. However, he added that one can become a giver independent of personal spirituality, and listed three methodologies for achieving this: focusing on the fear that self-centeredness will be punished in the next world; realizing the degree to which quality of life is compromised by a materialistic mindset;[51] and identifying with the pain and neediness of others.[52]

The two common elements in these techniques are deep thought regarding one's experience and egocentric motivation for change. The individual attempts to allay his own mental discomfort, either regarding his lot in the next world, or his lived existence as a consumer, or his vicarious experience of another's misfortune. He initially gives to others with the intention of benefitting himself, but he gradually becomes habituated to giving.[53] Thus, although giving should ideally devolve from an elevated appreciation of God's goodness and a resultant desire to emulate God, the process can be reversed: first one gives due to self-interest, which leads to the development of a giving orientation, ultimately allowing the giver to become more God-like.[54]

According to Dessler, love is not conducive to giving; instead, giving leads to love. The desire to give is not the product of love, but rather the catalyst for love's development,[55] because investment of time or effort in anything leads to love for it. This is true for a child, a plant, or an inanimate object: as a person gives, she perceives herself in the recipient of the giving, and, eventually, she loves it because she loves herself.[56] Therefore, subsequent to the initial thought process, Dessler advocated giving as the central methodology for becoming a giver.

Dessler named two individuals as exemplars of giving: Ḥanokh (Enoch), mentioned in the book of Genesis, and the Ḥafetz Ḥayyim, Rabbi Yisrael Meir Kagan (1838–1933). He described Ḥanokh as a shoemaker who, with every stitch, prayed that the shoes he was fashioning would be strong, and that the wearer would derive benefit from them.[57] Similarly, the Ḥafetz Ḥayyim owned a store in which he sold only the best produce, which he weighed in the buyers' favor. Eventually his store had so many patrons that he became concerned for the welfare of other store owners and limited his hours to only a few per day. When he realized that buyers were now timing their purchases to his brief shop hours, he closed his store entirely due to the fear of monetary loss to his competitors.[58] Thus, Dessler's ultimate givers were people whose concern for other people exceeded concern for themselves, to the extent that they forewent their own income in order not to damage that of others. To Dessler, a righteous person does not allow himself to take, so as not to become a taker.[59] As seen regarding the Ḥafetz Ḥayyim, this is true even when not taking actively.

Like his predecessors in Kelm, Dessler discussed the significance of gradual character improvement and utilization of the intellect in its pursuit. These emphases can be discerned in his treatment of topics other than giving. For instance, God's existence and involvement in human affairs were starting points for Dessler, but he believed that received tradition should function only as the initial step in the cultivation of faith.[60] He maintained that it should be followed by sustained thought,[61] without which any level of faith beyond the most rudimentary is unattainable.[62] Through thinking, the student would arrive at a higher level of awareness of God, internalize it, and then restart the process, achieving a slowly deepening recognition of truth.[63] To Dessler, the only impediment to faith is the desire not to see truth:[64] objective intellectualism, unfettered by preconception, would lead naturally to awareness of God.[65] Dessler's attitude to belief in God was similar to that of Simḥah Zissel, who said that without clarity of thought "man is nothing more than a horse." [66]

The same emphasis on gradual change fueled by thought can be seen in Dessler's approach to arrogance, a character trait that he considered intrinsic to human nature[67] and antagonistic to service of

God. As he said, even if a person conceals his righteous behavior from others, he is still in danger of arrogance—arrogance about concealing his actions.[68] Dessler maintained that even the most humble of people is at risk for haughtiness,[69] and that, therefore, one should mentally "bribe the evil inclination" by focusing on the material benefits that accrue to somebody who behaves righteously.[70] Other advice for fighting haughtiness included thinking about one's faults;[71] thinking about the greatness of God and consequent human insignificance;[72] and praying to God for improved character.[73] Again, Dessler's techniques all employ thinking in service of gradual change.

Moving up the Ladder of Perfection

Dessler encouraged his students to take small steps aimed at cultivating character improvement, in order to increase Godliness. He conceived of free choice as highly limited and, in his discussion of the "point of choice," stated that most behaviors are outside the range of personal decision-making. So, for example, for many observant people, slander feels acceptable, whereas Sabbath violation does not. The Torah proscribes both, but, due to habituation, for some individuals the first seems unrestrainable, while the second is emphatically proscribed.[74] Dessler argued that this perception is a true reflection of the individual's present capacity for free choice. Only the most minimal self-restraint is possible in a given area for a person who is habituated otherwise. In this sense, the spectrum of possible behaviors is limited, but, nevertheless, one can make superior or inferior choices within that narrow field. For Dessler, this does not trivialize human choice: choosing correctly within one's subjective continuum represents nothing less than the ultimate human task and determines the individual's spiritual caliber. Thus, seemingly trivial decisions emanate from and lead to closeness to God,[75] investing the mundane with "layers of meaning."[76]

Dessler discussed a person who, despite being born into a society of murderers, chooses to restrict his misconduct to theft: such an individual is considered righteous, because he has made the most moral decision available to him.[77] Thus, the Torah's conceptions of rectitude serve as a framework, within which one is meant to choose the best behavioral options available. Dessler added that the array of choice is not static. Each positive decision serves to push some negative actions out of range and to add positive options to the realm of possibility; every negative choice does the opposite.[78] Implicit in this model is that choice, limited as it may be, is possible and significant. Further, each choice changes the respective range of potential choices for all future generations, adding tremendous import to seemingly inconsequential decisions.[79]

There is much philosophical debate concerning the reconciliation of God's control with the concept of free will. Dessler advanced a theological compromise, wherein human beings maintain free choice regarding a select set of potential actions, but God directly determines everything else.[80] Therefore, to Dessler, God is the only causal force, but cedes control regarding specific domains. While this inconsistency could have led to advanced philosophical discussion, Dessler refrained from it; his analysis of choice centered on where it manifests, not whether it exists.

To Dessler, the goal of Judaism is to gradually improve at service of God and emulation of God. Cultivating the ability to give is seen as prerequisite to this. Dessler suggested various methodologies for becoming a giver, enabling his students to advance in their giving and their consequent Godliness. Working toward steadily evolving virtue was, in Dessler's conception, the central task of all Jews.

Notes

1. Esther Solomon, "Rabbi Dessler's View of Secular Studies and *Wissenschaft des udentums*," *Pardes* 24 (2018): 103–104.

2. Eliyahu Eliezer Dessler, *Mikhtav me'Eliyahu* (Jerusalem: Sifriyati, 1955–1997). In this chapter, *Mikhtav me'Eliyahu* will be cited using the shortform *MM*.

3. Yonoson Rosenblum, *Rav Dessler: The Life and Impact of Rabbi Eliyahu Eliezer Dessler the Michtav m'Eliyahu* (Jerusalem: Feldheim, 2000), v. Rosenblum's book, comprised of personal interviews, documents, and letters, is considered an authoritative text despite having been written for a general (nonacademic) readership. See Noam Green, "The Speculative and Moral Thought of Rabbi Eliyahu Eliezer Dessler: The Crystallization of Ultra-Orthodox Thought in the 20th Century" [Hebrew] (PhD diss., Ben Gurion University, 2016), 3; Jonathan Garb, "*Mussar* as a Modern Movement," lecture, Third International Conference on Modern Religions and Religious Movements in Judaism, Christian-

ity, Islam, and the Bábí-Baháí Faiths, Hebrew University, Jerusalem, March 2011.

4. In this chapter, virtue is defined as moral excellence, positive character traits, and behavior showing high moral standards.

5. Menahem Glenn, *Rabbi Israel Salanter—Religious-Ethical Thinker: The Story of a Religious-Ethical Current in Nineteenth Century Judaism* (New York: Bloch/Dropsie, 1953), 111. Tamar Ross writes that these two causal factors are mentioned by virtually all researchers. See Tamar Ross, "Moral Philosophy in the Writings of Rabbi Salanter's Disciples in the Musar Movement" [Hebrew] (PhD diss., Hebrew University, 1986), 8.

6. Shaul Stampfer, *Families, Rabbis and Education: Traditional Jewish Society in Nineteenth-Century Eastern Europe* (Portland: Littman, 2010), 230; Mordechai Zalkin, "Lithuanian Jewry and the Concept of East European Jewry," in *Jews in the Former Grand Duchy of Lithuania since 1772*, ed. Antony Polonsky, Šarūnas Liekis, and Chaeran Freeze (Oxford: Littman, 2013), 61.

7. Lester Eckman, *The History of the Musar Movement* (New York: Shengold, 1975), 7, 9, 16, 20.

8. Geoffrey Claussen, *Sharing the Burden: Rabbi Simḥah Zissel Ziv and the Path of Musar* (New York: State University of New York Press, 2015), 3.

9. Musar masters and the *mashgiḥim* (Musar supervisors) who followed them were not, according to their own description, trying to create a new philosophy. Rather they were primarily educators striving to lead their charges to better behavior. See Benjamin Brown, "Human Greatness and Human Diminution: Changes in the Mussar Methods in the Slobodka Yeshiva" [Hebrew], in *Yeshivot and Battei Midrash*, ed. Immanuel Etkes (Jerusalem: Zalman Shazar, 2006), 243.

10. Simḥah Zissel Ziv, *Ḥokhmah u-Musar* [Wisdom and Morality], vol. 1 (New York: n.p., 1917), 17; Lester Eckman, *The Teachings of the Fathers of the Musar Movement* (New York: Shengold, 1990), 24. See also Ben-Tsiyon Klibansky, *The Golden Age of the Lithuanian Yeshivot in Eastern Europe* [Hebrew] (Jerusalem: Zalman Shazar, 2014), 314.

11. Immanuel Etkes, *Rabbi Israel Salanter and the Mussar Movement: Seeking the Torah of Truth*, trans. Jonathan Chipman (Jerusalem: Jewish Publication Society, 1993), 105.

12. Kopul Rosen, *Rabbi Israel Salanter and the Musar Movement* (London: Narod Press, 1945), 11.

13. Eckman, *History of the Musar Movement*, 17. See Claussen, *Sharing the Burden*, 3.

14. *Pinkas ha-Kabbalot* [Journal of Resolutions] (B'nai Brak: Siftei Ḥakhamim, 2009), 172.

15. Claussen, *Sharing the Burden*, 24–25.

16. Geoffrey Claussen, "Legacy of the Kelm School of Musar on Questions of Work, Wealth and Poverty," in *Wealth and Poverty in Jewish Tradition,* ed. Leonard Greenspoon (West Lafayette, IN: Purdue University Press, 2015), 156.

17. Ziv, *Ḥokhmah u-Musar,* 1:191; Katz, *Tenu'at ha-Musar,* vol. 2 (Jerusalem: Sifriyati, 1982), 165.

18. Esther Solomon, "Rabbi Eliyahu Eliezer Desser: Not Quite the Musar Traditionalist," *Da'at* 82 (2016): CXXII.

19. Claussen, *Sharing the Burden,* 25.

20. For information on Reuven Dov Dessler see Rosenblum, *Rav Dessler,* 11–25, 111–13, 130, 136–38. See also *Sefer ha-Zikaron Beit Kelm* [Kelm Memorial Volume], vol. 1 (B'nai Brak: Siftei Ḥaim, 2012), 333–88.

21. Kelm Yeshivah catered to mature scholars, many of whom were married. See Rosenblum, *Rav Dessler,* 25.

22. Shlomo Tikochinski, "The Transfer of Lithuanian Yeshivot to the Land of Israel: The Story of *Hebron* and *Ponivez* Yeshivot" [Hebrew], in *Yeshivot and Battei Midrash,* ed. Immanuel Etkes (Jerusalem: Zalman Shazar, 2006), 310.

23. Rosenblum, *Rav Dessler,* 36.

24. Rosenblum, *Rav Dessler,* 80–83.

25. Rosenblum, *Rav Dessler,* 221–31, 296–300.

26. *MM* 5:512.

27. *MM* 1:100–101.

28. For elaboration of this point see Garb, "*Mussar* as a Modern Movement."

29. These include the works of Rabbi Isaac Luria, known as the Ari (1534–1572), whose thought predates Ḥasidism but is the basis of much of the Hasidic thinking that came after him. In a similar relation are the writings of the Maharal, which are also quoted extensively in *Mikhtav me'Eliyahu.* Gershom Scholem saw Maharal as an early version of Ḥasidism. See Aviv Ekroni, "Ha-Maharal Ve-hashkafotav" [Hebrew], Rev. of *Netzach Yisrael,* by Binyamin Gross, *Moznaim* 3, no. 4 (1974): 270–71.

30. Benjamin Brown, " 'It Does Not Relate to Me': Rabbi Israel Salanter and the Kabbalah" [Hebrew], in *And This is for Yehuda,* ed. Maren R. Niehoff, Ronit Meroz, and Jonathan Garb (Jerusalem: Bialik Institute and Mandel Institute, 2012), 423.

31. Solomon, "Not Quite," CXIV. An additional Musar authority who made use of Ḥasidic and Kabbalistic sources was Rabbi Yosef Leib Blokh (1860–1929), of Telshe who quoted from the *Zohar* and from Tanya in his discourses. He did not use other Ḥasidic sources. See Blokh, *Shiurei Da'at,* vols. 1–2 (Jerusalem: Sifriyati, 1964).

32. *MM* 5:39.

33. *MM* 1:32–51, 140–52; *MM* 3:85–104. Regarding the pitfalls of acquisitiveness and the advantages of simplicity, see *MM* 3:18, 49, 72, 332; *MM* 4:241–42; *MM* 5:90.

34. *MM* 1:32, citing Gen. 1:27.

35. *MM* 1:140.

36. *MM* 1:262–63, citing Deut. 28:9.

37. *MM* 1:45.

38. Pirkei Avot 4:1.

39. *MM* 1:50. Dessler wrote that giving leads to gratitude. See *MM* 1:47.

40. Abraham Bik, who sees existentialist ideas in Dessler's *Kuntres ha-Ḥesed*, writes that fetishism disallows connection between people because extreme focus on money and objects ensures that interpersonal connection is made exclusively in service of one's own interests. See Abraham Bik, "Emunat ha'ahava: Rabbi Eliyahu Eliezer Dessler besifro Mikhtav me'Eliyahu" [Faith of Love: R. Eliyahu Eliezer Dessler in his book *Mikhtav Me'Eliyahu*], *Mabua* 15 (2000): 151.

41. *MM* 1:32–33.

42. *MM* 1:33, 47.

43. See discussion of this point in Meir Schlesinger, "Moderation and the Service of God," *Tradition* 24, no. 1 (1988): 6.

44. *MM* 1:41.

45. *MM* 1:42.

46. *MM* 1:42.

47. *MM* 1:40, 42. Materialism was a favorite topic of Dessler. A cursory check reveals that it is addressed on twenty-seven of the first fifty pages of *Mikhtav me'Eliyahu*, with as many as three references per page.

48. *MM* 1:33, 46.

49. *MM* 1:36.

50. *MM* 1:39.

51. *MM* 1:46.

52. *MM* 1:44–45.

53. *MM* 1:45.

54. Manipulative giving does not qualify in this model.

55. *MM* 1:37. Bik describes Dessler's understanding as being similar to that of Erich Fromm. See Bik, "Emunat ha-Ahavah," 153.

56. *MM* 1:36. The related phenomenon of overvaluing an object due to ownership has been called "the endowment effect." See Daniel Kahneman, *Thinking Fast and Slow* (New York: Farrar, Straus and Giroux, 2013), 293–97.

57. *MM* 1:34. Dessler attributes this understanding of Ḥanokh's thoughts to Israel Salanter.

58. *MM* 1:34–35.

59. *MM* 1:46.

60. *MM* 3:177.

61. *MM* 3:177; see Baḥya Ibn Paquda, *Duties of the Heart*, introduction.

62. *MM* 3:161–62, 297. Among his suggested topics were God's personal guidance and the spiritual underpinnings of world affairs. MM 4:29.

63. *MM* 1:171–72.

64. *MM* 3:178.

65. *MM* 1:171.

66. Rosenblum, *Rav Dessler*, 49.

67. *MM* 3:361.

68. *MM* 5:188.

69. *MM* 1:198.

70. *MM* 5:188.

71. *MM* 5:353.

72. *MM* 5:380.

73. *MM* 3:273.

74. *MM* 1:113. In his article on free will, Bentzion Sorotzkin makes reference to Rabbi Shlomo Wolbe's analysis of Dessler's "phenomenal essay on *bechira* [free choice]." Wolbe wrote that in order for a given decision to be within the realm of free choice, there have to be equivalent forces pushing in opposite directions: the individual making the choice must be equally compelled to act on both options before him, and therefore must consciously choose one over the other. When people do something regarding which they do not experience conscious conflict, or if the compelling force on one side is significantly stronger than the other, the fact that they are theoretically able to decide either way does not qualify their actions as expressions of free choice. See Bentzion Sorotzkin, "*Bechira*: How Free Is Free Will?," *Jewish Observer*, April 1996, 18, citing Shlomo Wolbe, *Alei Shur* [Over the Wall], vol. 2 (Be'er Ya'akov: Yeshivat Be'er Ya'akov, 1978), 40.

75. *MM* 1:27, 115–16.

76. *MM* 1:121; *MM* 2:39. See a discussion of this point in Mordechai Mishory, "Toward a Theory of Meaning: Philosophical Basis and Therapeutic Implications," *Tradition* 38, no. 2 (2004): 113. This attitude would have been particularly comforting for Holocaust victims, who had very few observably significant choices available to them. Dessler described any choice that promotes good as Godly, thereby elevating the status of seemingly trivial choices made in the Holocaust.

77. *MM* 1:116.

78. *MM* 1:113.

79. *MM* 1:115.

80. Plantinga calls this stance "weak occasionalism." Alvin Plantinga, "Law, Cause and Occasionalism," in *Reason and Faith: Themes from Richard Swinburne*, ed. Micheal Bergmann and Jeffrey E. Bower (Oxford: Oxford

University Press, 2016), 141. Finkelman refers to Dessler's understanding as occasionalism and says that it is similar to that of Rabbi Ahron Kotler (1892–1962). See Yoel Finkelman, "Milḥama im ha-olam haḥitzoni: HaRav Aharon Kotler" [War against the Outer World: Rabbi Aharon Kotler], in *The Gdoilim: Leaders Who Shaped the Israeli Haredi Jewry*, ed. Benjamin Brown and Nissim Leon (Jerusalem: Magnes, 2017), 422.

Chapter 30

Joseph Soloveitchik

YONATAN Y. BRAFMAN

Joseph Soloveitchik was born in Pruzhana (present-day Belarus) in 1903 to a distinguished family of Lithuanian rabbis. His grandfather, Ḥayyim Soloveitchik, introduced the Brisker Method of Torah learning, which focused on the analysis of rabbinic literature to unearth its governing concepts. He received a traditional Jewish education from communal schools and private instruction. He also attended a Gymnasium in Dubno and the Free Polish University in Warsaw, before moving to the Friedrich-Wilhelm University in Berlin for his doctorate, which he received in 1932. His dissertation was a phenomenological critique of the neo-Kantian epistemology and ontology of Hermann Cohen, in which he argued that it neglected the realist purport of intentionality.[1] Escaping German persecution in 1932, he first settled in Boston where he served as a communal rabbi and the head of a small, advanced seminary before replacing his father, Moses Soloveitchik, as a senior Rosh Yeshivah at Yeshiva University's Rabbi Isaac Elchanan Theological Seminary in 1941. While continuing to reside in Boston, he commuted to Yeshiva University for the next four decades to teach talmudic studies, Jewish philosophy, and practical halakhah. He also served as its official conferrer of ordination as well as the chairman of the Jewish law commission of the Rabbinical Council of America.[2] In these positions, Soloveitchik had an unsurpassed influence on centrist and modern Orthodoxy in America. His hand inscribed its signature positions, specifically the intrinsic value of secular education, the encouragement of talmudic study for women, and the promotion of religious Zionism.[3] Within this community Soloveitchik's authority is such that, even after his death in 1993, many of its debates are less concerned with the merits of a particular position than with what the "Rav" (as he is simply known) would have thought about it.[4]

Soloveitchik's legacy is contested by religious conservatives and liberals within the Orthodox community, who stress different texts within his corpus. The former focus on his talmudic scholarship, while the latter concentrate on his philosophical and theological writings.[5] This essay will only add to this debate by challenging the perception anchored in his most widely read work, *Halakhic Man*, that, under the influence of both the Brisker Method and neo-Kantianism, Soloveitchik held a formal and deontological conception of halakhah. Instead, it suggests that when Soloveitchik's other philosophical and theological writings are read together with his talmudic scholarship, a virtue ethics and jurisprudence emerge.

Centrality of Virtue in Soloveitchik's Thought

Soloveitchik is often associated with a formal and deontological approach to Jewish law (halakhah). On this view, Jewish law is an a priori system of norms, which should be studied and imposed on human nature and the natural world. Taking account of Soloveitchik's broader corpus reveals, however, that, although the commandments and their observance are indeed central, he understands halakhah as a discipline for the cultivation of emotional dispositions. This melding of deontology and virtue ethics indicates an affinity between Soloveitchik and Moses Maimonides: Both view the commandments as fostering virtue, though in different ways. Soloveitchik transcends Maimonides in developing a virtue jurisprudence.

In *Halakhic Man*, Soloveitchik describes Jewish law using neo-Kantian language, as having "a fixed a priori relationship to the whole of reality in all its fine and detailed particulars."[6] This formal conception of halakhah has both theoretical and practical implications: Halakhah is to be explored as a formal system and then used to evaluate reality, as opposed to being subject to revision in view of empirical findings or human experience. Correlatively, halakhah is to be imposed on the natural world and human nature as the realization of the divine command. This motivates a deontological view of halakhah that finds fullest expression in a narrative that Soloveitchik relates about his father, Moses Soloveitchik:

> Once my father was standing on the synagogue platform on Rosh Ha-Shanah, ready and prepared to guide the order of the sounding of the *shofar*. The *shofar*-sounder, a god-fearing Habad Hasid, who was very knowledgeable in the mystical doctrine of the "Alter Rebbe," R. Shneur Zalman of Lyady, began to weep. My father turned to him and said: "Do you weep when you take the lulav? Why then do you weep when you sound the *shofar*? Are not both commandments of God?"[7]

For the elder Soloveitchik, who here represents the halakhic man, the commandments simply prescribe actions to be done. In this, sounding the shofar on Rosh ha-Shanah and taking the lulav on Sukkot do not differ. They thus should both be performed exclusively out of obedience to God. Any emotions, and certainly any differentiation of them according to emotional experience, is beside the point.

While Soloveitchik is certainly describing the view of his eponymous protagonist in this passage, this is not Soloveitchik's own position on halakhah. The reception of *Halakhic Man* has neglected its phenomenological character.[8] In fact, Moses Soloveitchik and Joseph Soloveitchik seem to have a disagreement (*maḥloket*) about the relation between the commandments and emotions, which is realized in specific views about sounding the shofar and waving the lulav. For, in his work of talmudic scholarship, *Shi'urim le-Zekher Abba Mari*, Soloveitchik writes, "[T]his commandment [of rejoicing on the festival] can be fulfilled in many different ways—by eating sacrificial meat, enjoying delicacies, singing in the Temple, and taking the lulav. However, in all these actions the application of one commandment is expressed, [that is,] rejoicing on the festival, whose essence is joy of the heart [*simḥah ba-lev*]."[9] Similarly, in his methodological introduction to Jewish philosophy, *Halakhic Mind*, Soloveitchik writes, "*Kol shofar*, the sound of the shofar, only betokens self-examination and conversion."[10] In the cases of sounding the shofar and taking the lulav, Soloveitchik argues that an emotional experience, joy and contrition, respectively, must accompany the physical performance of the commandments. Whereas Moses Soloveitchik might have held a formal and deontological approach to the commandments, Joseph Soloveitchik argues that at least some of them require emotional experiences.

Because of the prevalence of this type of analysis in Soloveitchik's thought, Aharon Lichtenstein credits him with the development of a novel category of commandment: experiential commandments.[11] Indeed, in a posthumously published essay, "Prayer, Petition, and Crisis," Soloveitchik describes such commandments as follows:

> The Halakhah enters a new dimension of human life, that of subjectivity and inwardness. In contrast to the actional mitzvot [commandments], the experiential mitzvot postulate not a way of doing but of experiencing as well. The Halakhah attempts to regulate not only the body but also the soul. . . . [H]alakhic examination reveals the primary characteristic of that group of mitzvot which finds expression in parallel action. It is that in each mitzvah we must carefully discriminate between *ma'aseh ha-mitzvah* [literally, the action of the commandment] (the piecemeal process of actual execution) and *kiyyum ha-mitzvah* [literally, fulfillment of the commandment], compliance with the norm. *Ma'aseh ha-mitzvah* denotes a religious technique, a series of concrete media through which the execution of the mitzvah is made possible, while *kiyyum ha-mitzvah* is related to the total effect, to the achievement itself, to the structural wholeness of the norm realization.[12]

The physical performance of the commandment is its action (*ma'aseh ha-mitzvah*), while the emotional experience is its fulfilment (*kiyyum ha-mitzvah*). Applied to these cases, the sounding of the shofar and the taking of the lulav are the actions of the commandments; the respective fulfillments are regret and joy.

Soloveitchik, however, seems to be inconsistent in his writings about the relation between the physical action and the emotional fulfillment of the commandment. The actions are described diversely as triggering, expressing, shaping, and realizing the emotions.[13] These descriptions can be harmonized if we understand Soloveitchik as presenting the commandments as a discipline for ethical formation, for then their relationship between the action and the emotion would change over time. While at first the prescribed action would trigger and shape the emotion, over time the emotion would be expressed and realized through the action.

The examples of sounding the shofar and taking the lulav are useful because they illustrate the distance between Soloveitchik and his protagonist in *Halakhic Man*. This analysis in terms of an emotional experience and a physical action is applied to many other commandments, including prayer, the public reading of the Torah, mourning, and perhaps all interpersonal commandments as well as prohibitions.[14] Indeed, it seems that experiential commandments serve as the paradigmatic type of commandment for Soloveitchik.[15] This claim also derives support from a close reading of *Halakhic Mind*. There Soloveitchik argues that the commandments are expressions of religious cognition of reality. The object of these cognitions are values, which are perceived through the emotions. Ultimately, however, such emotions are expressed as theological propositions, religious norms, and concrete behaviors.[16] Drawing these threads together, Soloveitchik's view is that the commandments both express emotional perceptions of value and cultivate these emotional experiences in their practitioners. When the practitioner has been properly disciplined by the commandments so as to have these emotional experiences, he or she is able to perceive the values that the commandments express. Crucially, in Soloveitchik's view, these values are metaphysically real. They are not artifacts of the practice of the commandments; rather, the practice of the commandments enables the individual to see the values that are there in any case.

Placed in the context of types of normative theories, Soloveitchik, then, articulates a virtue ethics, albeit one that also has deontological and consequentialist features. I take the families of normative theories—deontology, consequentialism, and virtue ethics—as differing over the *ultimate* object of ethical evaluation. Deontological positions evaluate actions as right or wrong in view of rules. Consequentialist positions assess states-of-affairs as good or bad depending on whether they instantiate value. Aretaic positions judge dispositions to think, feel, and behave as virtuous or vicious in view of their role in human flourishing. Based on this ultimate object of ethical evaluation, a normative theory can also *derivatively* be concerned with other phenomena, whether dispositions, actions, or states-of-affairs. This is illustrated by rule utilitarianism. As a consequentialist theory, its ultimate object of ethical evaluation are states-of-affairs; however, in view of individuals' ineptitude at anticipating the state-of-affairs that will result from their actions as well as their goodness or badness, it proposes rules to govern individuals' actions. Actions are evaluated by rules, then, like a deontological position, but these rules are justified by whether they generally result in states-of-affairs that instantiate value. So too for each of these objects of ethical evaluation; they can find a derivate role within a theory.

Especially relevant for understanding Soloveitchik's position, rules and values—the main focus of deontology and consequentialism, respectively—can find a place within an aretaic position: Rules can be justified by whether they promote virtuous (and suppress vicious) dispositions. Values can be justified by whether they would be desired by a virtuous person or, alternatively, whether only a vicious person would desire them. Soloveitchik proposes a virtue ethics of halakhah because his focus is on appropriate emotional dispositions; these are expressed and cultivated by the commandments. Moreover, these emotional dispositions are perceptions of value; in this case, joy is the recognition of closeness to God. Certainly, halakhah is the focus of Soloveitchik's thought; but, in contrast to the formal and deontological position often attributed to him, he is concerned with elaborating halakhah's aretaic dimensions.

Love and Holiness

There are many ways to divide the commandments, including between prescriptions and prohibitions (*mitzvot ta'aseh* and *lo-ta'aseh*), between those anchored in the Bible and those instituted by the rabbis (*mitzvot de-'oraita* and *de-rabbanan*), and between those whose reasons are evident and those whose reasons opaque (*mishpatim and ḥukim*). The division between interpersonal and divine-human commandments (*mitzvot bein adam le-ḥavero* and *bein adam le-makom*) is helpful for exploring Soloveitchik's virtue ethics since these encompass the two spheres of human relationships and thus of human flourishing. These other divisions also play a role in the discussion.

Soloveitchik holds that many interpersonal commandments both express and cultivate love. Indeed, in a letter from 1964, he writes:

> All interpersonal commandments (at least the overwhelming majority) correspond to internal emotional instincts that operate in the consciousness of the human being, and were they not given [as commands] they would have been worthy to have been given and we would have derived them from the natural world which surrounds and envelops us, and from our internal world. . . . Thus, the command to love one's neighbor is subsumed under laws that go hand in hand with the natural feeling of justice and mercy. However, when the Jewish people were commanded regarding the rational laws, two new concepts were introduced: (1) An internal-natural instinct was transformed into a divinely revealed command. (2) The normative field of operation was expanded and deepened."[17]

This description of the interpersonal commandment to love your neighbor coheres with Soloveitchik's general account of the commandments. Human beings naturally love others, and so the reason for this commandment is evident (*mishpat*). The commandment to love your neighbor as oneself builds on that love, expanding and concretizing it. Elsewhere, he notes that Maimonides holds in the *Mishneh Torah* ("Laws of Mourning" 14.1) that while various norms regulating interpersonal relationships, including burying the dead, rejoicing with a bride and groom, and escorting guests are rabbinic commandments (*de-rabbanan*), they are encompassed in the biblical commandment (*de-'oraita*) to love your neighbor. Soloveitchik extends this analysis by arguing that while these rabbinic commandments prescribe specific actions toward one's neighbor, they are all instantiations of the biblical commandment to love your neighbor. This biblical commandment requires an emotional response of love for one's neighbor. The rabbinic commandments fix the physical actions of the commandment, while the biblical commandment is its emotional fulfillment.[18] Love for the neighbor is a perception of his or her value. Indeed, in another posthumously published essay, Soloveitchik writes, "[T]he commandment to love incorporates, first of all, the duty to form a positive assessment of the thou and to value him. . . . But the Torah is not content with this passive-contemplative form of love. . . . A person must decant his heartfelt feelings into the external world and give them the concrete form of showing kindness and love to others."[19] Here, too, the integration of dispositions, values, and rules are evident in Soloveitchik's thought. Of course, the commandment to love your neighbor entails specific rules and exhibits the neighbor's value, but its nexus is the disposition to actually love him or her.

Whereas many of the interpersonal commandments convey the value of humanity, some of the divine-human commandments, especially the prohibitions (*lo-ta'aseh*), limit its axiological significance. Soloveitchik also analyzes these commandments in view of their emotional experience. Recognizing human finitude is expressed, according to Soloveitchik, through the emotional process of catharsis, which involves acknowledging human desires but then relinquishing their fulfillment.[20] Soloveitchik describes many prohibitive commandments, including those of certain sex acts, as aimed at achieving catharsis, which he associates with holiness. He writes, "The idea of catharsis through the dialectical movement manifests itself in all Halakhic norms regulating human life."[21] While viewing observance of the commandments as a practice of self-denial might seem opposed to virtue ethics, Soloveitchik clarifies in a posthumously published essay that catharsis brings the human being into alignment with its true nature. He writes, "The human existential experience is intrinsically incomplete; finitude means the absence of wholeness and fullness."[22] Although humans might have delusions of grandeur, they are, in fact, finite. Catharsis is the recognition of this limitation. Indeed, Soloveitchik writes, "By renouncing an unfulfilled wish to God, man finds self-actualization."[23] This self-actualization is a life of holiness.

Love and Holiness thus represent central virtues for Soloveitchik because they permeate the two spheres of human life: interpersonal and divine-human relationships. Both are expressed and cultivated through the commandments; they are also anchored by values—that of humanity and God, respectively.

Halakhic Practice and the Cultivation of Virtue

Soloveitchik holds that virtues are cultivated through the observance of commandments. Virtues, in his view, are emotional dispositions to perceive value in specific circumstances, which are then expressed in action. At the outset of the process of an individual's ethical formation, the commandments stimulate and shape the individual's emotional dispositions in view of their values. Initially, for example, an individual might not perceive the value of his neighbor and love him or her. The commandment to love the neighbor, say, through its implementation as the rabbinic norm of escorting guests, prescribes a behavior that cultivates this emotional disposition and axiological recognition. When an individual has been adequately disciplined by this commandment, however, he or she immediately perceives the value of the neighbor through the emotion of love. This perception and emotion, then, issues in behaviors, like escorting him or her as a guest. Many of the prohibitions work in the same way. The commandment to refrain from certain sex acts prohibits behaviors for which the individual has a desire; it therefore requires the individual to relinquish this desire, affirm his or her own finitude, and recognize a superior value. At first, the individual might simply conform grudgingly. But when the individual has been disciplined by this commandment, he or she might immediately affirm his or her finitude in view of superior values and easily relinquish the desire or not feel it at all. As Soloveitchik is reported as claiming, "[I]n the highest ethical stage, where a person's ethical existence *is* a reality in itself, intention and deed constitute an inseparable oneness."[24]

Because of this bidirectional relation between the commandments and the virtues—the commandments initially cultivate the virtues and ultimately express them—Soloveitchik holds up two exemplars: Abraham and Moses. Abraham, appropriately enough, represents the founder of Judaism. Describing him, Soloveitchik writes, "The charismatic person discovers the ethos himself. As a free personality, he goes out to meet the moral with his full collected being; he chances to find it in himself and to consciously adopt it."[25] For Abraham, the perception of value and emotional response come immediately. He lives, of course, before the giving of the commandments; he is naturally virtuous. In contrast, according to Soloveitchik, Moses "re-educated, retrained, and re-formed himself."[26] Moses is the recipient of the commandments; he must be disciplined to virtue. Through obedience to the commandments, he eventually develops the emotional dispositions and perceives the values. Of these two exemplars, Moses is more practically relevant than Abraham. Abraham represents an individual that can discover virtue within himself and establish an ethical community centered on it. Moses represents an individual that is already part of an ethical community and appropriates virtue to himself.

Also situated within this bidirectional relation yet closer to reality than these two biblical exemplars is the ideal halakhic scholar and decisor. Soloveitchik describes him in a eulogy for his uncle Yitzhak Zev Soloveitchik, who transplanted the Brisker Method to the land of Israel, writing, "When the division between man and Torah shifts entirely from its place not only do the forty-nine gates of halakhic thought and cognition open before him, but also the forty-nine of halakhic vision and feeling. . . . The man of halakhah, to whom the Torah is wed and joined, 'sees' halakhic contents, 'feels' halakhic ideas like they were audial, optical, or olfactory qualities. . . . At this level, the Torah is revealed to this man not only from the perspective of understanding [*binah*], which signifies serene, discriminating, and critical intellectualism, but also by way of the channel of the divine attribute of wisdom [*sefirat ḥakhmah*], from which flows glorious and creative intuition."[27] Marshaling kabbalistic concepts, Soloveitchik here describes a new type of halakhic man. This halakhic man does not comprehend a formal and deontological system as an object of discursive thought; rather, because he has become one with the Torah, he is able to intuitively perceive its contents. Based on this perception, he is able to create and innovate in halakhah. While here Soloveitchik may be describing theoretical Torah study, elsewhere he is reported as saying, "[T]here exist problems which cannot find a clear-cut decision in the Shulḥan Arukh . . . ; one has to decide intuitively."[28] The ideal halakhic scholar and decisor, as a result of sustained practice and study, has fully internalized the Torah. He emotionally perceives its underlying values and is thus able to determine how it should be understood and applied. Indeed, in the few responsa that Soloveitchik wrote, he relies on such intuition about values.[29]

In describing this exemplary halakhic scholar and decisor, Soloveitchik extends his virtue ethics into a virtue jurisprudence. Virtue jurisprudence is the position that the "fundamental notions of legal theory should be virtue and excellence."[30] Like in ethics, the ultimate object of jurisprudence would thus be the virtues and vices of judges. Correct legal determinations are understood in terms of what a virtuous judge would decide. The judge is a *phronimos*, a sage possessed with practical wisdom, who is able to make a prudent judgment for a particular situation. However, as Lawrence B. Solum points out, such a judge gains this wisdom by being a *nomimos*, "someone who grasps the importance of lawfulness and is disposed to act on the basis of the law and norms of his community."[31] It is only by being disciplined by the law that the judge has the virtues to make the law. So too for Soloveitchik's ideal scholar and decisor. Because he is "wed to the Torah," he possesses the virtues to understand and apply it.

A comparison between Maimonides and Soloveitchik is helpful here. Maimonides too sees the inculcation of virtue as a goal of the commandments (*Guide of the Perplexed* 3.31). And, like many proponents of the Brisker Method, Soloveitchik develops his halakhic analysis with reference to Maimonides's *Mishneh Torah*. Still, the distinction between the behavioral action of the commandment and the emotional fulfillment of it is Soloveitchik's innovation. Similarly, Maimonides and Soloveitchik differ on the role of virtue in jurisprudence. Maimonides in the *Mishneh Torah* ("Laws of Judges" 2.1, 7) discusses the theoretical and ethical virtues required of judges. Yet, for him, these are dispositions that are minimally necessary for the judge not to mistake or pervert the law. One who is not "distinguished by wisdom of Torah and possessed of great knowledge" simply will not be able to determine the law correctly. One who does not "despise money" and "love truth," for instance, is susceptible to corruption. This is quite different from Soloveitchik's view in which cultivation by the commandments is necessary to emotionally perceive the value they express, and so properly to comprehend and implement them. Halakhic virtue, for Soloveitchik, is constitutive of correct judgment.[32]

Halakhic Virtue and the Interpretation of the Jewish Tradition

Soloveitchik develops his virtue ethics and virtue jurisprudence of the commandments chiefly through an engagement with halakhic literature, especially the Talmud and the *Mishneh Torah*. He refers to the Hebrew Bible, especially when he discusses Abraham and Moses as two types of exemplars. He also refers to the philosophical tradition, whether directly to Maimonides's *Guide of the Perplexed* or indirectly to Hermann Cohen's *Religion of Reason out of the Sources of Judaism*. In these last cases, his position is often critical. He implies that Maimonides and Cohen subordinate Jewish thought to Aristotelian and Kantian philosophy, respectively, instead of reconstructing it, as he aims to do, out of the commandments.[33] As opposed to Aristotelian knowledge or Kantian ideals, the commandments yield their own values and virtues.

While Soloveitchik seems to be concerned primarily with texts, his focus on virtue expands his conception of the Jewish tradition to include mimetic behavior. In a eulogy for his daughter's mother-in-law, Rebecca Twersky, the Rebbetzin of Talne, he writes:

> People are mistaken in thinking that there is only one *Massorah* [tradition] and one *Massorah* community; the community of the fathers. It is not true. We have two *massorot*, two traditions, two communities, two [chains of reception]—the Massorah community of the fathers and that of the mothers. . . . What is the difference between those two *massorot*, traditions? . . . Father teaches the son the discipline of thought as well as the discipline of action. Father's tradition is an intellectual-moral one. That is why it is identified with *mussar*, which is the Biblical term for discipline. . . . What kind of a Torah does the mother pass on? I admit that I am not able to define precisely the *Massorah* role of the Jewish mother. Only by circumscription I hope to be able to explain it. . . . Most of all I learned . . . that Judaism expresses itself not only in formal compliance with the law but also in a living experience.[34]

Soloveitchik's distinction between an intellectual-moral tradition and experiential tradition can be identified with knowledge and performance of the commandments, on the one hand, and the emotional dispositions and values that they both express and cultivate, on the other. Though, of course, the association of the former with the father and the latter with the mother is gendered, Soloveitchik describes himself as receiving both. Indeed, in his view, it is crucial that he did. For while the intellectual-moral tradition includes the actions of the commandments, the experiential tradition comprises their fulfilment. From the tradition of the fathers, the halakhic virtues can be rationally reconstructed. Through the tradition of the mothers, they can actually be inculcated.

Notes

1. Joseph Soloveitchik (Josef Solowiejczyk), "Das reine Denken und die Seinskonstituierung bei Herman Cohen" [Pure Thought and Constitution of Being according to Hermann Cohen], (diss., Friedrich Wilhelm University, 1932). See Reinier Munk, *The Rationale of Halakhic Man: Joseph B. Soloveitchik's Conception of Jewish Thought* (Amsterdam: Gieben, 1996), for a discussion of its arguments.

2. For more on Soloveitchik's life, see Aaron Rakeffet-Rothkoff, *The Rav: The World of Rabbi Joseph B. Soloveitchik*, ed. Joseph Epstein, 2 vols. (Hoboken, NJ: Ktav, 1999).

3. See Walter Wurzburger, "Rabbi Joseph B. Soloveitchik as Posek of Post-Modern Orthodoxy," in *Exploring the Thought of Rabbi Joseph B. Soloveitchik*, ed. Marc Angel (Hoboken, NJ: Ktav, 1997), 3–24.

4. For example, compare Hershel Schachter, "Women Rabbis?," *Hakirah* 11 (2011): 19–23; and Michael J. Broyde and Shlomo Brody, "Orthodox Women Rabbis? Tentative Thoughts That Distinguish between the Timely and Timeless," *Hakirah* 11 (2011): 25–58.

5. Lawrence Kaplan, "Revisionism and the Rav: The Struggle for the Soul of Modern Orthodoxy," *Judaism* 48, no. 3 (1999): 290–311.

6. Joseph Soloveitchik, *Halakhic Man*, trans. Lawrence Kaplan (Philadelphia: Jewish Publication Society of America, 1983), 23.

7. Soloveitchik, *Halakhic Man*, 60–61.

8. For an identification of Soloveitchik with his protagonist, see David Hartman, "The Halakhic Hero: Rabbi Joseph Soloveitchik, Halakhic Man," *Modern Judaism* 9, no. 3 (1989): 249–73. Cf. Dov Schwartz, *Religion or Halakha: The Philosophy of Rabbi Joseph B. Soloveitchik*, trans. Batya Stein (Leiden: Brill, 2007).

9. Joseph Soloveitchik, *Shi'urim Le-Zecher Abba Mori Zt'l* [Lectures in Memory of My Father, My Teacher, May the Memory of the Righteous Be for a Blessing] (Jerusalem: Akiva Joseph, 1985), 2:204.

10. Joseph Soloveitchik, *The Halakhic Mind: An Essay on Jewish Tradition and Modern Thought* (Ardmore, PA: Seth Press, 1986), 96.

11. Aharon Lichtenstein, "R. Joseph Soloveitchik," in *Great Jewish Thinkers of the Twentieth Century*, ed. Simon Noveck (Washington, DC: B'nai B'rith Books, 1985), 281–98.

12. Joseph Soloveitchik, *Worship of the Heart: Essays on Jewish Prayer*, ed. Shalom Carmy (Jersey City, NJ: Ktav, 2003), 15–18.

13. Alex Sztuden, "Grief and Joy in the Writings of Rabbi Soloveitchik, Part II: Philosophical Aspects of the Ma'aseh/Kiyyum Distinction," *Tradition* 44, no. 1 (2011): 9–32.

14. See Soloveitchik, *Worship of the Heart*, 19–26; and Soloveitchik, *Shi'urim Le-Zecher Abba Mori Zt'l*, 2:229–30.

15. Gerald (Ya'akov) Blidstein, *Society and Self: On the Writings of Rabbi Joseph B. Soloveitchik* (New York: OU Press, 2012), 132.

16. See Yonatan Y. Brafman, "'The Objectifying Instrument of Religious Consciousness': Halakhic Norms as Expression and Discipline in Soloveitchik's Thought," *Diné Israel, Studies in Halakhah and Jewish Law* 32 (2018): 1–38; Brafman, *Critique of Halakhic Reasons*, ch. 1 (forthcoming), for a full defense of these claims.

17. Joseph Soloveitchik, *Community, Covenant and Commitment: Selected Letters and Communications*, ed. Nathaniel Helfgot (Jersey City, NJ: Ktav, 2005), 133.

18. Soloveitchik, *Shi'urim Le-Zecher Abba Mori Zt'l*, 1:71–72.

19. Joseph Soloveitchik, *Halakhic Morality: Essays on Ethics and Masorah*, ed. Joel B. Wolowelsky and Reuven Ziegler (Milford, CT: Maggid Books, 2017), 166.

20. See especially Joseph Soloveitchik, "Catharsis," *Tradition* 17, no. 2 (1978): 38–54.

21. Soloveitchik, "Catharsis," 44–45.

22. Joseph Soloveitchik, *Out of the Whirlwind: Essays on Mourning, Suffering and the Human Condition*, ed. David Shatz, Joel B. Wolowelsky, and Reuven Ziegler (Jersey City, NJ: Ktav, 2003), 155–56.

23. Soloveitchik, *Out of the Whirlwind*, 159. For a concurring view, see Daniel Rynhold and Michael J. Harris, *Nietzsche, Soloveitchik, and Contemporary Jewish Philosophy* (Cambridge: Cambridge University Press, 2018), 170–71.

24. Lawrence Kaplan, *Maimonides: Between Philosophy and Halakhah—Rabbi Joseph B. Soloveitchik's Lectures on the Guide of the Perplexed* (Jerusalem: Ktav, 2016), 217.

25. Joseph Soloveitchik, *The Emergence of Ethical Man*, ed. Michael S. Berger (Jersey City, NJ: Ktav, 2005), 154.

26. Soloveitchik, *The Emergence of Ethical Man*, 186–87.

27. Joseph Soloveitchik, "Mah Dodekh mi-Dod" [How Is Your Beloved Better Than Another?]," in *Be-Sod ha-Yahid ve-ha-Yahad: Mivhar Ketavim 'Ivriyim* [In Aloneness, In Togetherness: Selected Hebrew Writings], ed. Pinchas H. Peli (Jerusalem: Orot, 1976), 219.

28. Joseph Soloveitchik, *The Rav Speaks: Five Addresses on Israel, History, and the Jewish People* (Brooklyn: Judaica Press, 2002), 50.

29. See, for example, Soloveitchik, *Community, Covenant and Commitment*, 24–25.

30. Colin Farrelly and Lawrence B. Solum, "An Introduction to Aretaic Theories of Law," in *Virtue Jurisprudence*, ed. Colin Farrelly and Lawrence B. Solum (New York: Palgrave Macmillan, 2008), 3.

31. Lawrence B. Solum, "Natural Justice: An Aretaic Account of the Virtue of Lawfulness," in *Virtue Jurisprudence*, ed. Colin Farrelly and Lawrence B. Solum (New York: Palgrave Macmillan, 2008), 179.

32. Like many traditional commentators, Soloveitchik alternates between reading his own views into the writings of his predecessors in order to authorize his own claims and presenting "Bloomian" strong reading of them in order to differentiate them. This is evident in his engagement with Maimonides's halakhic positions as well as his philosophy. Compare *Halakhic Mind*, 93–99 and *Maimonides: Between Philosophy and Halakhah.*

33. Soloveitchik, *Halakhic Mind*, 100–102.

34. Joseph Soloveitchik, "A Tribute to the Rebbetzin of Talne," *Tradition* 17, no. 2 (1978): 75–76.

Chapter 31

Hannah Arendt

NED CURTHOYS

— *In memory of Richard King* —

Hannah Arendt was born in 1906 to a Prussian-Jewish family of Russian descent. She grew up in Königsberg, the capital of Eastern Prussia (Kaliningrad in present-day Russia). A gifted child, who read classical philosophy at a young age, Arendt studied philosophy at the University of Freiburg under Martin Heidegger. After a tumultuous affair with the married Heidegger, Arendt moved to the University of Heidelberg in 1926 to do her doctorate under Karl Jaspers, a psychologist turned existential philosopher who was to become a dear friend and mentor throughout her mature life. In 1933, Arendt moved to Berlin, ostensibly to conduct research, in reality seeking evidence of wide-spread antisemitism for the German Zionist organization, under the leadership of her good friend Karl Blumenfeld. Arendt was soon arrested but then shortly thereafter released by the Gestapo and immediately fled to Paris where she worked on behalf of Zionist organizations such as Youth Aliyah, assisting Jewish immigration to mandate Palestine. With the help of contacts, Arendt managed to obtain a visa to the United States where she moved in 1941.

In the afterwar period, Arendt became one of the world's most influential political thinkers with the publication of *The Origins of*

Totalitarianism in 1951. Her other notable works include *The Human Condition* (1958), *Eichmann in Jerusalem* (1963), *On Revolution* (1963), and *Men in Dark Times* (1968). Never parochial or exclusive in her relationship to Judaism, and always attempting to translate her experiences as a Jewish woman and stateless person into concrete political analysis, Arendt sought to enact and articulate the "cosmopolitan role that Jews could fulfill in a global world."[1]

In this essay I shall argue that Arendt's virtue-ethical project participates in a post-Enlightenment tradition of liberal Jewish historical and ethical reflection that is sympathetic to Jewish reinvention and cultural creativity under diasporic conditions, celebrates outsiders to Judaism for enlarging the Jewish contribution to world history, and is suspicious of strains in Judaism that have helped to historically isolate the Jewish people and have dehistoricized their evolving relationship to non-Jewish peoples.[2] In the final section I suggest that Arendt summons a Jewish "pariah tradition" in order to encourage an immanent reading of Jewish history that can provide ethical exemplars of Jewish critical thought and arts of living that interact with the exigencies posed by host societies in the diaspora.

The Importance of Virtue to Arendt

Arendt's wartime experiences were a crucible for her conviction that asking probing and unsettling ethical questions and rediscovering the intersubjective significance of human capacities such as thinking, conscience, judgment, and imagination would prove fundamental to the renewal of critical thought. Arendt felt that the formation of one's distinctive personality, which she considered the responsibility of every individual, was indispensable for ethical conduct. The reason is not difficult to find. Arendt was aghast at the rise of totalitarian systems that had sought to liquidate individual dignity and spontaneity, the ability of each generation to begin something new and to performatively disclose, through speech and action, a unique personality or "who" to a world of engaged spectators. One of the greatest evils of the Nazi criminals, she held, is that they "renounced voluntarily" their personal qualities.[3] As Arendt puts it, anticipating her suggestive conception of the banality of evil, "the greatest evil" that can be perpetrated is precisely that which is committed by nobodies, that is, "human beings who refuse to be persons."[4]

For Arendt, the far-reaching problem was that morality had now been revealed as mere *mores*, as customs or manners that could be exchanged for others. Indeed the more respectable and generally law-abiding the individual, the more outrageous the crimes they were willing to support.[5] The perplexing fact of the matter was that those who held fast to moral norms proved the least reliable to act justly or defend the vulnerable in an emergency situation as moral codes and even the legal system itself proved vulnerable to ethical inversion (though, cunningly, not abandonment) by a murderous regime.[6] Thus the question of ethical deportment arises for Arendt in a more classical guise as a modality of the *care of the self*; the capacity of the self to examine her- or himself, keep her- or himself company, provide her- or himself with resources for solitude, and remain steadfast in her or his principles and promises.[7] Arendt returns to ethics, the cultivation of one's interior life and solicitude toward the quality of one's sensibility, because supposed bulwarks against malfeasance such as religious values, the legal system, and the university's defense of knowledge and rational inquiry, had quickly accommodated themselves to the racial laws of the Nazis. Arendt also realized that we can no longer subscribe to the theological belief in a divinely inspired human conscience that can authentically tell us right from wrong, regardless of the law of the land.[8]

PHILOSOPHY AND THE VIRTUES

With a refreshed attitude toward the past, and with the insidious implications of Europe's ethical degeneration weighing on her mind, Arendt would look at the history of Western philosophy with an acute focus on its inability to value and augment ethical and political virtues, in so doing reviving an Aristotelian emphasis on discriminating intelligence, situated deliberation, and practical wisdom in the conduct of human affairs. Arendt scrutinizes and redescribes the Platonic legacy of idealist metaphysics, noting that a resentful Plato had decided that the death of his master Socrates at the hands of Athenian democracy necessitated the fortification of philosophy as a transcendental mode of metaphysical inquiry that despised opinion in its original sense as situated perspective (*dokei moi*, "it seems to me"). She understood the desire for the realm of immutable ideas as an attempt to preserve the philosophical habitus, the ardent wish shared by Plato and Aristotle for a life of contemplative tranquility protected from the demotic volatility and sporadic anti-intellectualism of Athenian democracy.

Socrates: The Exemplary Philosopher

Arendt decried in Plato that "tyranny of truth" that was opposed to opinion and the plurality of phenomena, the worldly space of appearances that nourishes judgment and common sense. In a variety of essays, Arendt would express a great admiration for Socrates as *the* exemplary philosopher, a courageous, dialogically motivated, and publicly engaged intellectual remembered for his close friendships and concern for the inner life of the people he discourses with.[9] It was Socrates who sought to converse with individuals in small groups in the *polis*. Unlike Plato, Socrates did not forsake the marketplace of ideas but was happy to negotiate with conventional opinion. Lauding Socrates as a philosophical character, Arendt praised Socratic praxis for thinking about all subjects and talking with everybody. Arendt's Socrates is an imagined conversational partner for Arendt in a time of acute distress for philosophy as a mode of comportment, a robust counterweight to the romantic irresponsibility of contemporary intellectuals who "fabricate ideas about everything"[10] yet are predictably obsequious to power.

Arendt values Socrates as a philosophical figure because of the emphasis that he places on interactions with Athenian citizens in an attempt to care for and develop their *logos*, their capacity for discriminating thought and judgment, understood as the deliberative techniques of a worldly self rather than as a purely cognitive orientation; in Plato's Socratic dialogues we are introduced to a Socrates who extols his performative truth-telling function as provocative gadfly, electric ray, generative midwife, and faithful amanuensis for the *logos* of others. It is Kant, Arendt suggests, who will take up the Socratic conception of moral conduct, which seems to "depend primarily upon the intercourse of man with himself."[11] To care for oneself in Socratic terms means to put the duties to oneself ahead of the duties to others; one must not contradict oneself by making an exception in one's own favor, one must not put oneself in a position in which one would to have to despise oneself.

Moral Psychology

There is a moral psychology involved in this internal activity, this Socratic relationship of the self to itself, that in more recent times can be traced back to Enlightenment virtue ethicists such as Adam Smith.[12] Arendt shares with Smith a keen interest in an ethical self that is less concerned with self-abnegating duties toward the other than with its own integrity and the sustaining quality of its internal discourse. Evoking an Aristotelian emphasis on virtue as motivated by the search for human excellence, Arendt criticizes selflessness and "meekness" as the touchstone of ethics and extols "human dignity and even human pride" as salient qualities of the ethical personality.[13] Overthrowing that aspect of Christian morality, love of one's neighbor, that has failed to foster discriminating deliberation and care for the world we inhabit, Arendt affirms a new ethical standard that is skeptical of selflessness, that of "self-respect."[14] As Arendt describes the implications of this conception of developed selfhood, the term "moral personality" is almost a redundancy, for an "individual's personal quality is precisely his 'moral' quality," and this has nothing to do with the "properties, gifts, talents, or shortcomings" with which we are born.[15] In other words, the cultivation of the personality and the character traits one desires to show to the world is the consummate ethical task within reach of every individual.

Arendt and the Resumption of Virtue Ethics

We are now in a position to discuss Arendt's attraction to virtue ethics, which, following Aristotle's profoundly influential treatise the *Nicomachean Ethics*, often embraces self-respecting and self-regarding virtues such as prudence and courage and understands intellectual virtues (*sophia, phronesis, technē*) and rational deliberation as paramount to ethical conduct. The Aristotelian tradition of virtue ethics seeks to improve character and intellect by treating virtue as a skill to be cultivated, "something that we have to do, and that takes focus, effort, and the right kind of practice."[16] Aristotle's *Nicomachean Ethics* also relates virtue to practical intelligence and worldly decision making, the "discriminatory ability (*kritikē*) that involves looking at one's situation from multiple perspectives,"[17] a perspectival account of ethical agency that has a close relationship to Arendt's account of judgment: "[T]he more people's positions I can make present in my thought and hence take into account in my judgment, the more *representative* it will be."[18] Establishing the need for moral philosophy to foster a vigorously energetic internal discourse rather than rely on older verities, Arendt would come to embrace the core Aristotelian conception of virtue (*aretē*) as an excellence predicated on exertion, the repeated action and formative habits that all living things are capable of.[19] Engaging throughout her work in dispersed but significant ruminations on the virtues allowed Arendt to articulate an optimism that we can improve ourselves and the world around us by making discriminating choices and pursuing ends and social goods appropriate to the pluralistic world we inhabit.[20]

Arendt's Central Virtues

When Arendt thinks explicitly about the significance of virtue ethics and particular virtues for the present age, it becomes clear that she associates the cultivation and enactment of virtue with loquacity and logophilia, with that Socratic care to cultivate a dialogical *logos*, a reflective, convivial, and audience-sensitive modality of persuasive and performative speech. Thought itself, as it bears on practical conduct and my relationship with others, is the ability to "actualize the specifically human difference of speech," and this is how "I constitute myself as a person."[21] Arendt's stated conviction that virtue is "eloquent" and adept at "all kinds of predicative or argumentative speech"[22] is to be contrasted with a conception of morality that relies on selfless love of the other or the silence of an elemental goodness (Billy Budd); nor, in partial sympathy with Lionel Trilling, will the practice of virtue truck with the conviction of one's own authenticity, the complacent assumption of an abiding inner self that can ignore or flout social forms.[23]

First Virtue: Love of the World

A signature aspect of Arendt's philosophy is *amor mundi* or caring for a world that is of "inter-est" to us, that is to say, that lies between us, relating and separating us at the very same time. To prize virtue is itself a mark of worldly endeavor allied to the supposition that to practice a virtue is to respect the good of the community of which one is a part. As Alasdair MacIntyre puts it, "[I]t is always within some community with its own specific institutional forms that we learn or fail to learn to exercise the virtues."[24]

As Richard King argues of Arendt's conception of virtue, "Virtue is worldly, made up of those enlightened qualities that preserve the world as it is organized around enlightened self-interest or the common good."[25] For Arendt the cultivation of intellectual and political virtues can be opposed to the disproportionate role of sentiment and imagined solidarity in political decisions. Deborah Nelson analyses the way that Arendt "carefully dissected the 'devastating' effects of compassion in political life."[26] As Douglas Klusmeyer observes, Arendt "rejected any notion of belonging to a people as a matter of love, which she believed should be reserved to the sphere of interpersonal relationships and not applied to abstract collectives."[27] In her famous epistolary exchange with Gershon Scholem, who had accused her of *ahavat Yisrael,* lacking love and empathy for Israel and the Jewish people, Arendt critiques an affective politics that undermines worldly spaces for reflective dialogue and critical dissent, replying to Scholem that the demonstration of "heart" in politics is often an evasive mechanism to conceal factual truth.[28] As Patricia Owens writes, Arendt felt that any other love than love of persons was too vague and politically dangerous, and it is in this more ethically and politically acute sense that "Arendt preferred love of the world." [29]

REALISM, TRUTH-TELLING, AND RECONCILIATION WITH THE WORLD

Another virtue we can infer from Arendt's writing is that of realism, although we must avoid its more cynical, anti-intellectual, and bullishly positivist intonations when thinking about Arendt's idea of the real. As Deborah Nelson argues, Arendt's realism is a motivated posture focused on awareness, receptivity, and attention: "Arendt's most fundamental charge to her readers [is to] to face reality."[30] As Roger Berkowitz suggests, we can think of Arendt's philosophical project as an attempt at reconciliation with what has been given to one, including, in Arendt's case, her Jewish identity, forging a foundational "gratitude" toward the world as it is, which is at the "very core of political judgment."[31]

As Patricia Owens writes, Hannah Arendt was no "straightforward realist," but rather she seeks the cultivation of a character trait in which one can face and "enlarge one's sense of reality" rather than retreat into self-willed fantasy. Arendt urgently sought to address the rise of totalitarianism, which had displayed a frightening, hubristic "contempt for reality."[32] Owens makes the point that for Arendt reality is only discerned through interaction with a world of plural appearances and human perspectives, so that we require the necessity of a strong *public* culture for our sense of the real.[33] As Arendt puts it, "[O]ur feeling for reality depends utterly upon appearance and therefore upon the existence of a public realm into which things can appear."[34] Closely related to the cultivation of a receptiveness to a multifaceted reality that is not just spatiotemporal but constituted by a web of human relationships is Arendt's notion of the *sensus communis* in which we relate to the world and develop a discriminating sense of (aesthetic but also moral) taste through the combined impact of phenomena on our five senses. Owens cites Arendt to the effect that "a thing *is* real only if it shows itself on all sides, is perceived on all sides," such that "there must always be a plurality of individuals or peoples . . . to make reality even possible and guarantee its continuation."[35] With Deborah Nelson, we would also make the point that for Arendt that common sense that integrates us with the world is dialogical and civically minded and thus antithetical to passive apprehension, it is "activity rather than knowledge, something one does, not something one has."[36]

Owens also points to Arendt's emphasis on the role of narrative and storytelling in engendering a sense of the real. As she interprets the critical importance of narration to Arendt, the role of the storyteller is to reconcile us with reality and "to teach acceptance of things as they are."[37] In *Eichmann in Jerusalem*, Arendt points out that Eichmann's lack of meaningful understanding of his actions as a genocidal perpetrator is a function of his deficient narrative abilities and a general remoteness from reality augmented by the reflexive recourse to euphemism and cliché. As Richard King summarizes Arendt's prizing of storytelling and its relationship to the real: "We can no more master the past than we can undo it. But we can reconcile ourselves to it." Storytelling, poetry, and the narrative of historians fulfill the "task of setting this process of narration in motion and involving us in it."[38]

Friendship

Allied to Arendt's rejection of sentimentality is a strong emphasis on *friendship as a virtue* that consistently preserves reference to worldly circumstances. As Arendt reminds us in an essay praising Lessing's "drama of friendship" *Nathan der Weise*, "humanity is exemplified not in fraternity but in friendship," which is not intimately personal but "makes political demands and preserves reference to the world."[39] One of the reasons that Arendt tried to avoid the humbug and hypocrisy to be found in professions of love for human collectives, is because, as Jon Nixon points out, friendship was a vital part of her lived experience and a crucial element of her constantly developing framework of ideas about ethics and political comportment.[40]

As Nixon points out, in keeping with Arendt's virtue-theoretic concern with what Martha Nussbaum has dubbed the "ethical life of the agent,"[41] friendship was a "confirmation rather than surrender of the self," involving a candid relationship that would help to test and modify one's judgments before their exposure to public scrutiny. In the course of Arendt's life, as someone who had suffered considerable trauma, enduring friendship had denied totalitarianism ultimate victory, and stood against the rise of consumerism, the privatization of public life, and a mass culture of immediate gratification.[42]

Arendt was interested in friendship as a certain kind of emotional practice that could enhance one's internal dialogue. Nixon has pointed out that Arendt was interested in Socrates and his *daimon* because of her emphasis on a deliberative technique in which the self divides itself in two in order to deliberate, preserving a relationship of cheerful yet candid friendship between the two interlocutors in order to prevent the drift toward egotistical projection and ideological fantasy.[43] The thinking self is a robust conversation between friendly but candid interlocutors who will never desert each other or resile from their truth-telling capacity: "[C]onscience is the anticipation of the fellow who awaits you if and when you come home."[44]

The Courage to Speak and Appear in Public and the Cultivation of Virtue

Throughout her writings, as we have seen, Arendt identifies the virtues not with interior states of mind but with cultivated habits and the willingness to appear and speak in public. Arendt's revival of Shaftesbury's Stoic-inspired conception of internal dialogue suggests that even our interior life should be robustly dramatized and publicized with the courage and bravura of internal self-mockery and interrogation. The courage to communicate is indispensable to Arendt's conception of ethical and intellectual life. As she puts it: "[B]ecause man exists only in the plural his reason, too, wants communication and is likely to go astray if deprived of it."[45]

The courage to speak, appear, and act are critical ingredients for the cultivation of virtue. Here we need to be mindful of Arendt's signature utterance that one's (largely acquired) personal qualities simply are one's moral qualities, so that the task of the virtue inclined agent is to form a self with a richly dialogical and imaginatively creative interiority, enriched by diverse experiences, alert to the power of ethical example, and willing to perform and display the character traits it wishes to show to the world. Suspicious of any kind of ontology of selfhood, in *The Life of the Mind* Arendt suggests a more dynamic philosophical anthropology, that to be alive is to experience an "urge towards self-display which answers the fact of one's own appearingness."[46] With its theatrical instincts the self does not display and show its "inner self" but itself as an individual.[47] It is an illusion, Arendt insists, to suggest that who we really are is more a matter of our inner life than our external appearances to ourselves and others as social personae, a deft point redolent of Oscar Wilde that is perhaps also a pointed rejoinder to those educated Germans who insisted on their "inner emigration" during the Nazi era.

For Arendt, performative display to oneself and others is key, desiring to set an example and follow the Socratic dictum "*Be* as you wish to appear";[48] as Arendt suggests, the courageous person is not someone whose soul lacks fear but someone who has decided that fear is not what [she or he] wants to show.[49] Courage can then become "second nature or habit," attesting to Arendt's affinities with the Aristotelian tradition of virtue cultivation as self-discipline.[50] Habituation and the desire to shape one's disposition toward virtuous behavior is critical. As Arendt suggests, our ethical decisions are not a reaction to innate qualities given to us but are a deliberate choice among various potentialities for conduct that the world has presented to us.[51] It is out of self-willed acts that character or personality arises, understood as a unity, a comprehensible and "readily identifiable whole."[52] Through a variety of modalities of engaging with the world (friendship, civic engagement, the enjoyment of a world of surfaces and appearances) a virtuous personality emerges, a conception with striking similarities to the cherished post-Aufklärung German-Jewish ideal of *Bildung* or self-culture. As Arendt reminds us, this associative route to an ethical life is indispensable: there is "no abiding self in the flux of inner appearances."[53]

The Power of Examples

Arendt emphasizes the construction of personality through deliberation and judgment. She also insists upon the importance of seeing and beholding examples of the virtues as motivations for thinking and ethical reflection. The examples of courage, justice, and wisdom that one dwells upon need critical and cultural "mediation" so that they can be constructed as ideal types, exemplary figures cut out of the cloth of living beings and endowed with "representative significance," witness Arendt's figure of Socrates as the public philosopher par excellence.[54] The summit of Arendt's reflections on ethical examples is, of course, the biographical portraits in *Men in Dark Times*, a representation of the virtuous words and deeds of individuals that can cast some redemptive "illumination," a "weak and flickering light" no longer provided by theories and concepts.[55] The ethical exemplars discussed therein include her dear friend Karl Jaspers, whose capacities for reinvention and growth can be implicitly contrasted with Heidegger's lack of moral fiber and evasions of reality. Jaspers, writes Arendt, was an "unviolable and unswayable personality," his personally transformative philosophy of communication, influenced by a Socratic and Kantian conception of reasoning in public, saw him emerge as a public intellectual who sought to address Germany's postwar responsibilities. Jaspers's moral education was learnt "as from a model" for what is essential for the whole realm of human affairs, by virtue of a relationship of genuine equality and companionship with his Jewish wife Gertrud Jaspers, née Mayer.[56] Sharing with Kant the conviction that philosophical ideas need to be susceptible to popularization, Jaspers entered into a period of self-reinvention and intellectual productivity because he cheerfully and courageously sought to write and discourse "as if to answer for himself before all of mankind."[57]

Arendt and the Jewish "Pariah Tradition"

As Maria Tamboukou has argued, all four of the Jewish pariahs that appear in Arendt's essay "The Jew as Pariah: A Hidden Tradition" (1944) and who offer a performed resistance to antisemitism and other normative imaginaries are "portrayed as outsiders of their geographies, times and social worlds."[58] These rebellious pariahs, as Tamboukou argues, provide strong analogies with Foucault's preoccupation, in lectures on the hermeneutics of the self in ancient Greece, with the Cynics who mocked artificiality and pretension.[59] In evoking Jewish pariahs from Bernard Lazare to Heinrich Heine and even Charlie Chaplin, who defied stereotypical attributions and assimilationist pressures, Arendt invokes the Socratic legacy of *parrhesia,* where the less powerful speaker has a "specific relationship to the truth through frankness,"[60] openness to danger, preference for criticism rather than flattery, and a conviction of moral duty rather than apathy and self-interest.[61] It is of course this capacity for *parrhesia* that Arendt evokes in her much repeated asseveration that if one is attacked as a Jew one must defend oneself as a Jew.[62] As Douglas Klusmeyer argues, Arendt's "conscious pariah," by contrast to the conformist parvenu, embraces the critical perspective of the outsider among one's people and rebels against injustices inflicted on oppressed peoples more generally, and in doing so models Arendt's own approach to the Jewish question.[63]

Arendt also contributed to Jewish ethical thought with her rejection of an anxious ethnocentrism in Jewish politics that became more salient with the rise of political Zionism. The virtue-ethical tradition of prophetic ethics, which was extolled by German Jewish philosophers such as Hermann Cohen and Ernst Cassirer, redescribes the Jewish prophets themselves as social critics, visionary futurists, and critics of fatalistic and idolatrous tendencies among the Jewish people. Arendt's sympathy for this tradition of thought explains her astounded reaction, in the Scholem exchange, to Golda Meir's claim that she did not believe in God but loved only the Jewish people. Arendt indicates her shock to Scholem, for the greatness of the Jewish people has always been that its belief in God nourished a trust and love towards Him that has surmounted fear. Arendt then ruminates, in a piquant summation of her participation in a liberal Jewish virtue-ethical tradition, that to "love" or "believe" in the Jewish people as a hypostatized collective is an ethical dead-end. Arendt's consequent attention to the crime of genocide, her advocacy on behalf of stateless people for a right to have rights, her attempts to bolster the American republic, and to theorize the world as hospitable to and meaningless without human plurality, indicates a virtuous conception of Jewish advocacy that sustains a vital desire for an ethic of global citizenship.

Notes

1. Natan Sznaider, *Jewish Memory and the Cosmopolitan Order: Hannah Arendt and the Jewish Condition* (Cambridge, UK: Polity, 2011), 5.

2. Ned Curthoys, *The Legacy of Liberal Judaism: Ernst Cassirer and Hannah Arendt's Hidden Conversation* (New York: Berghahn Books, 2013).

3. Hannah Arendt, "Some Questions of Moral Philosophy," in *Responsibility and Judgment*, ed. Jerome Kohn (New York: Schocken, 2003), 111.

4. Arendt, "Some Questions," 111.

5. Hannah Arendt, "Personal Responsibility under Dictatorship," in *Responsibility and Judgment*, 43.

6. Arendt, "Personal Responsibility," 45–46.

7. See Ned Curthoys, "On Active Solitude: Caring for the Self in Hannah Arendt's Moral Philosophy," *Graduate Faculty Philosophy Journal* 38, no. 2 (2017): 325–47.

8. Arendt, "Some Questions," 61.

9. Hannah Arendt, *The Life of the Mind* (London: Secker and Warburg, 1978), 180.

10. "'What Remains? The Language Remains': A Conversation with Günter Gaus," in *The Portable Hannah Arendt*, ed. Peter Baehr (New York: Penguin, 2003), 11.

11. Arendt, "Some Questions," 67.

12. For a superb discussion of Adam Smith as a virtue ethicist see Charles L. Griswold, Jr., *Adam Smith and the Virtues of Enlightenment* (New York: Cambridge University Press, 1999).

13. Arendt, "Some Questions," 67.

14. Arendt, "Some Questions," 67.

15. Arendt, "Some Questions," 79.

16. Daniel C. Russell, "Aristotle on Cultivating Virtue," in *Cultivating Virtue: Perspectives from Philosophy, Theology, and Psychology*, ed. Nancy E. Snow (New York: Oxford University Press, 2015), 27.

17. Russell, "Aristotle on Cultivating Virtue," 29.

18. Arendt, "Some Questions," 141.

19. Russell, "Aristotle on Cultivating Virtue," 21.

20. Russell, "Aristotle on Cultivating Virtue," 23.

21. Arendt, "Some Questions," 95.

22. Arendt, "Some Questions," 76.

23. Hannah Arendt, *On Revolution* (New York: Penguin, 2006).

24. Alasdair MacIntyre, *After Virtue*, 3rd ed. (London: Bloomsbury, 2011), 195.

25. Richard H. King, "Hannah Arendt and the Uses of Literature," *Raritan* 36, no. 4 (2017): 121.

26. Deborah Nelson, "The Virtues of Heartlessness: Mary McCarthy, Hannah Arendt, and the Anesthetics of Empathy," *American Literary History* 18, no. 1 (2006): 87.

27. Douglas B. Klusmeyer, "Law, Narrative and Politics in a Jewish Key: Hannah Arendt and Robert M. Cover in Comparative Perspective," *Law and Humanities* 8, no. 2 (2014): 220.

28. Cited in Nelson, "Virtues of Heartlessness," 92.

29. Patricia Owens, "The Ethic of Reality in Hannah Arendt," in *Political Thought and International Relations*, ed. Duncan Bell (London: Oxford University Press, 2008), 114.

30. Nelson, "Virtues of Heartlessness," 92.

31. Roger Berkowitz, "Reconciling Oneself with Reality, Whatever It May Be: Judgment and Worldliness in Hannah Arendt's Politics," in *Artifacts of Thinking: Reading Hannah Arendt's Denktagebuch*, eds. Roger Berkowitz and Ian Storey (New York: Fordham University Press, 2017), 10.

32. Owens, "Ethic of Reality," 105.

33. Owens, "Ethic of Reality," 106.

34. Cited in Owens, "Ethic of Reality," 106.

35. Cited in Owens, "Ethic of Reality," 115.

36. Nelson, "Virtues of Heartlessness," 91.

37. Cited in Owens, "Ethic of Reality," 113.

38. Cited in King, "Hannah Arendt," 118.

39. Hannah Arendt, *Men in Dark Times* (Orlando, FL: Houghton Mifflin Harcourt, 1983), 25.

40. Jon Nixon, *Hannah Arendt and the Politics of Friendship* (London: Bloomsbury, 2015), viii.

41. Martha Nussbaum, "Virtue Ethics: A Misleading Category," *Journal of Ethics* 3 (1999): 171.

42. Nixon, *Hannah Arendt*, xiii.

43. Nixon, *Hannah Arendt*, 171. For a more developed version of this argument, see Ned Curthoys, "On Active Solitude," 325–47.

44. Arendt, *Life of the Mind*, 191.

45. Arendt, *Life of the Mind*, 99.

46. Arendt, *Life of the Mind*, 21.

47. Arendt, *Life of the Mind*, 29.

48. Arendt, *Life of the Mind*, 37.

49. Arendt, *Life of the Mind*, 36.

50. Arendt, *Life of the Mind*, 36.

51. Arendt, *Life of the Mind*, 37.

52. Arendt, *Life of the Mind*, 37.

53. Arendt, *Life of the Mind*, 39.

54. Arendt, *Life of the Mind*, 169.

55. Arendt, *Men in Dark Times,* ix.

56. Arendt, *Men in Dark Times,* 78.

57. Arendt, *Men in Dark Times,* 75.

58. Maria Tamboukou, "Truth Telling in Foucault and Arendt: Parrhesia, the Pariah and Academics in Dark Times," *Journal of Education Policy* 27, no. 6 (2012): 849.

59. Tamboukou, "Truth Telling," 856.

60. Tamboukou, "Truth Telling," 853, citing Foucault, *Fearless Speech,* ed. Joseph Pearson (Los Angeles: Semiotext(e), 2001), 19.

61. Maria Tamboukou. "Truth Telling," 854.

62. See, for example, Arendt, *Men in Dark Times,* 17–18.

63. Klusmeyer, "Law, Narrative and Politics," 239.

Chapter 32

Emmanuel Levinas

RICHARD A. COHEN

Emmanuel Levinas was born in 1906 into a traditional Litvak home in Kaunas, then part of the Russian empire. In 1923, Levinas left for the University of Strasburg in France, where he matriculated in philosophy. His thesis, published as a prize-winning book in 1930, *The Theory of Intuition in Husserl's Phenomenology*, helped introduce phenomenology to France. He moved to Paris and married Raisa Levi, also from Kaunas. Levinas spent the duration of World War II in Germany in a prisoner-of-war camp, segregated as a Jew, but saved by his French uniform and the Geneva Conventions. His wife and daughter survived in France hidden in a convent. His family in Kaunas was brutally murdered. At war's end Levinas returned to Paris, becoming director of the École Normale Israélite Orientale. Starting in 1961, he also taught philosophy in French universities, retiring in 1976, after three years at the University of Paris-Sorbonne. His two magisterial works of philosophy are *Totality and Infinity* (1961) and *Otherwise than Being or Beyond Essence* (1974). Many of his additional publications address Jews and Jewish topics, including, notably, *Difficult Freedom* (1963; 2nd ed. 1967) and the almost thirty "Talmudic Readings" that Levinas delivered from 1960 to 1989 as keynote addresses at the annual Colloquium of French Speaking Jewish Intellectuals, which he had helped found in postwar Paris. After suffering dementia, Levinas died on December 25, 1995, the eighth day of Chanukah, 5756.

The Importance of Virtue

Two claims distinguish Levinas's philosophy from others. First, *ethics is first philosophy*, meaning ethics as the source of good and evil, justice and injustice, surely, but also of all intelligibility, from sociality, labor, and history, to science, politics, and culture. Second, neither subject nor object, neither being nor language, neither history nor class, but *the other person comes first*. "My neighbor's material needs," Levinas cites Rabbi Israel Salanter, "are my spiritual needs."[1] "The word *I* means *here I am*, answering for everything and for everyone."[2] Ethical responsibility arises as response to the other person, who comes first, whose very vulnerability as a mortal—transforming my very spontaneity into potential murder—is the first command. As such, the face-to-face is not some happenstance or contingent encounter, even one as moving as Buber's I-Thou, but the very origin of the ethical, of responsibilities that beginning with the neighbor encompass all humanity and all of creation.

Levinas's ethics of responsibility, distinctive as it is, can nonetheless be examined in the light of certain parallels and affinities with Aristotelian virtue ethics, such as the following: (1) shared opposition to the *apeiron* ("unlimited"), despite Levinas's insistence that responsibility is "infinite"; (2) similarity of difficulty in the infinite exigency of responsibility and the extremity of the Aristotelean mean; (3) comparability of ever-increasing responsibility and ever refined character development; (4) the dialectic of morality and justice, of sociality and politics, in Levinas, and its counterpart in Aristotle.

(1) Greek philosophy, like Greek art, prefers order, form, and limits to disorder, the amorphous, the unlimited, the *apeiron*, which it opposes as it opposes chaos, confusion, and madness. Such is classicism, at work in Aristotle's virtue ethics, in the cultivation of good character as moderation in all things, striving for the mean ("a state of character concerned with choice, lying in a mean, i.e., the mean relative to us"[3]). Yet Levinas insists on the *infinity* of responsibility, that goodness demands always and ever more and better, in the face of one other person, the neighbor, and no less before others, absent others, hence a never finished politics of justice, but also responsibility before strangers, humanity, all sentient life, and ultimately the universe. "The self is a *sub-jectum*; it is under the weight of the universe, responsible for everything."[4] One can never do enough, the work is never done,

never quits. And yet, unlikely as it may first appear, Levinas's ethics of infinite responsibility opposes the *apeiron* as much as if not even more than the *apeiron* is opposed by Aristotelian virtue ethics. Both are opposed to the *apeiron*. How is this so for Levinas?

The infinite responsibility of the self is not, for Levinas, a dissolution of selfhood, bursting its limits, liquidating personhood, but quite the reverse, the very singularization of the self, devastating, to be sure, but as an *election*, held to its post, as it were, ineluctably, inalienably the one responsible to and for the other who faces and ultimately for all others, an atlas of responsibility holding up the entire universe. Far from dissolution, then, the infinity of responsibility is the greatest possible concentration, singularization, sobriety, not as a for-oneself, however, but as an unrelenting for-the-other, turned inside out. Here we must recall that Levinasian infinity has nothing to do with the "bad infinity" of the *apeiron*, but is modeled instead on the infinity of Descartes's Third Meditation. There, having doubted all things, until finding himself grounded in the indubitability of his now famous *cogito*, Descartes discovers, to his utter amazement, the priority of infinity, perfection, divinity, "that," in Descartes's words, "my perception of the infinite, i.e., God, is in some way prior to my perception of the finite, i.e., myself." The imperfection of finitude, then, is a function of the perfection of the infinite, not the other way around. So too, shifting from epistemology to ethics, for Levinas the infinity of responsibility is the infinite task, the superlative height, of alleviating the suffering of the other person and ultimately of all others. No matter that the work is never done, it needs doing.

Infinity singularizes the self as infinitely responsible, for-the-other before oneself, as rising to oneself despite oneself. "Expiation as uniting identity and alterity."[5] Self as turned inside out for the other, "having-the-other-in-one's skin,"[6] as Levinas writes, "It is a being torn up from oneself for another in the giving to the other of the bread out of one's own mouth."[7] "This inspiration is the psyche."[8] And therefore Levinas radically opposes the *apeiron*, the dissolution of ethical election, ethical sobriety, as irresponsibility itself, whether its seductive corrupting influence comes as the sirens' call of sensationalist Dionysian delirium, the fate of Orestes in Euripides's *Bacchae*, or seduced by a subtler, cooler, cerebral equanimity, beyond good and evil, cog in one Spinozist totality or another, actual or deferred, including the play of poesis. For Levinas, in contrast, the demands of responsibility, like the commands of Judaism, are pressing, concrete, ever increasing, and singularizing "outside of any mysticism."[9] The self is extinguished not by itself or for-itself but in generosity to and for the other, as self-sacrifice.

(2) The infinity of responsibility, and the concomitant difficulty, insufficiency or "guilt" of even the most responsible response to the other, can also be compared to a certain extremity of the Aristotelian mean. Everyone knows that the mean, which is relative to a person and not a mathematical mean or average, requires avoiding extremes of excess or deficiency. The virtue of courage, for instance, lies between cowardice and rashness or foolhardiness. Such a mean, too, is relative to each person, and hence cannot be calculated like a mathematical average. What is too much for one person is not enough for another. What follows, then, is that such a mean, relative to each person, avoiding extremes, is extremely difficult to attain. It is extremely difficult, that is to say, to strike just the right balance, for the path is narrow between too much and too little. Or to put this otherwise, there are far more ways to go wrong, ways made tempting by the allure of pleasures or made off-putting by fears, than the one right way of the middle path. It is this extreme difficulty, then, that, though different, calls to mind the extreme difficulty of a responsibility that, infinite to begin with, can never be fully fulfilled, and yet also increases, as we shall see, to the measure that it is fulfilled. Levinas explicitly calls such ethical responsibility, such election, a "difficult freedom," and entitles one of his books likewise. Aristotle and Levinas both knowingly embrace the difficulty of ethical living.

Levinas therefore elevates "bad conscience" above "good conscience." Not because like a Spinoza, Sade, or Nietzsche he dismisses morality as illusion and ignorance,[10] and would celebrate the dark side, but because he does not flinch from admitting that even our best ethical efforts and accomplishments are never enough. There is always more and better to be done. The day is short, the work long. And so, too, virtue is not a resting on one's laurels, not a mathematical problem solved once and for all, but a matter of character, repeatedly tested, refined, improved time and again, despite its improvements. Nothing is more difficult, then, more taxing, more exacting, more in demand, than responsibility and virtue.

(3) So too, then, we see here identified a third and related parallel: both responsibility and character build upon themselves, grow by

their exercise. Here lies the so-called vicious as well as the virtuous circle, though perhaps one should say spiral, or imagine a snowball rolling down a snow-covered hill, a ball that grows or shrinks by its own usage. Responsibility like good character improves, become more deeply ingrained, is more reliable, farsighted, nuanced, to the measure it is actualized. They are both habits, as it were, which thrive when cultivated and shrivel when abused.

So Levinas writes of "*responsibility increasing in the measure that it is assumed*; duties become greater in the measure that they are accomplished,"[11] as the "deepening of the inner life."[12] Accordingly he distinguishes need, which can be satisfied, from desire, desire for goodness and justice, which cannot, where "the Desired does not fulfill it, but deepens it."[13] The more a person is responsible, the more responsibilities become visible, the more one sees what needs also to be done, so "the more I am just the more guilty I am."[14] Responsibility breeds more responsibility. Only the evil person or the tyrant is complacent, satisfied, finished with responsibility. The faults of a Moses, in contrast, the exemplary man of responsibility, responsible for the entire people of Israel, whom the Bible calls a "servant of God," his faults, though barely visible to lessor men, are punished more severely—he of all people should have known better! Responsibility, as a sort of virtue, increases as it is refined, where fulfillment brings more rather than less responsibilities, recalling an image the rabbis applied to the Ark of the Covenant carried in the desert by Levites: the Levites bore the Ark, but the Ark bore them![15]

(4) Finally, like Aristotle and the entire normative tradition of political philosophy in the West, Levinas distinguishes social and political life, morality and government, the face and law, but treats both, dialectically, under the rule of ethics, of good over evil, and justice over injustice. Responsibility for the neighbor, already infinite, calls forth and is called forth to another infinity—call it "messianism" or "utopianism"—of justice, of responsibility for other others, ultimately for all others. Empowering morality, then, is the task of politics, the state, oriented by justice, "the relationship of the third party is an incessant correction of the asymmetry of proximity."[16] Justice, for its part, if it is to avoid tyranny and dehumanization, must serve morality, must not lose sight in its concern for all, for law, the universal, institutions, of the singular face of each. Levinas distinguishes the first and second persons of morality from the third person of politics, but treats both

as functions of an infinite ethical responsibility. So too for Aristotle, his *Nicomachean Ethics* and his *Politics* are two sides of a single ethics that unites virtue and justice, each supporting the other. Like the Ark and the Levites, again, but no less like the two tablets of a single covenant.

Levinas radically rejects the politics of power, *realpolitik*, which pretends to transcend the transcendence of ethics for the immanence of power. Politics and the state, however, are not simply the suppression and repression of human violence by a stronger violence, as Thrasymachus and Hobbes taught, but rather the rectification of human goodness, the distribution of goodness from one to many, the difficult task of justice. "[T]he face is both the neighbor and the face of faces, visage and visible . . . a terrain common to me and the others where I am counted among them, that is, where subjectivity is a citizen."[17] Justice is difficult because like morality it too is infinite. Just as no one is ever fully responsible even for one other, so too no state is fully just today for all its citizens, or all humanity, today and tomorrow. That justice is *outstanding*, in the double sense of unfinished and excellent, is for Levinas the genuine, the inclusionary sense of Jewish "messianism," and of "monotheistic politics" more broadly.[18] While still outstanding, yet to be accomplished, the borders, the promise of the Promised Land—for all peoples—are already visible: a society in which everyone can act morally without fault, where my responsibility to and for you deprives no one else of their well-being.[19] Justice requires fair laws, fair courts, of course, but it also requires plenty, requires productivity, science, technology, and so forth. Aristotle too recognized and defended a judiciousness of "decency"[20] beyond mere conformity to law, what Levinas describes as judgment "capable of seeing the offense of the offended, or the face," "beyond the justice of universal law."[21] The topic far exceeds the space here available.

Preeminent Virtues: Generosity and Justice

The ancient Greeks highlighted four and the early Christians seven cardinal virtues (and seven "deadly sins"). Levinas has no such list. Nonetheless, two virtues, or two orientations or directions of responsibility, stand out: *generosity* and *justice*. Each is infinite, and infinitely improvable, and each is bound to the other dialectically, or more precisely *diachronically*, as past and future, guilt and struggle.

"No face," Levinas has written, "can be approached with empty hands and closed home."[22] The exigency of generosity is radical, beyond measure, a giving of things, a giving of care, and a giving of oneself, "with all thy heart, and with all thy soul, and with all thy might," according to Deuteronomy 6:5. For Levinas, generosity defines human subjectivity, responsible all the way to the utmost possibility of "dying for . . ."[23] the other person ("God forbid"). It lies as well at the very root of intelligibility, giving rise to meaning, as "a primordial dispossession, a first donation," "speaking the world to the Other . . . the primordial putting in common."[24] "Language does not exteriorize a representation preexisting in me: it puts in common a world hitherto mine . . . the first ethical gesture."[25] Thus, undergirding this or that moral act, a sort of *transcendental* generosity opens up a shared world of meaning, a world at once human and humane, genitive and accusative before nominative, the elevation or priority of *saying* and *hearing*—*shema*—lending a human and humane significance to whatever is *said*.

To be sure, such generosity, at the beginning of the world, transcendental, as it were, cannot be fitted to the Aristotelian mean, because it makes all meaning meaningful, all sense significant in the first place. But the moral agency and political justice it conditions, these can. What is the excess? What the deficiency? At the moral level, the extreme of deficiency is *stinginess*, selfishness, snobbery, "me first," narcissism, shutting the door and gate, depriving, excluding the needy, the suffering, the oppressed. The extreme of excess—too much generosity—is no doubt rarer, though not unknown. To give indiscriminately, without judgment, to the wrong recipients, in the wrong way, or with the wrong priorities, to aid only one's allies, one's friends, to shore up banks and brokerage houses when the mass of ordinary people cannot pay their rents or put food on the table, these would be instances of excess, of profligacy or prodigality, not generosity.

Also there are the excesses of the overly sophisticated. For instance, Nietzsche's "solar solitude," giving without receiving, but really for the giver's self-enhancement alone; Georges Bataille's "visions of excess," "expenditure without reserve," modeled on potlach rites, destroying one's own property as splendorous display, spectacle, to enhance one's own prestige but really in a tantrum of self-destruction, the withering flowers of bourgeois ennui; or the cerebral Parisian host in Pierre Klossowski's novel *Roberte ce soir* (1953), who is convinced that hospitality demands he provide his guests food and drink—and his wife. Such extremes, to which Levinas does not explicitly refer, but which were part of his contemporary Parisian intellectual atmosphere, for all that they subvert the tit-for-tat of economics, are manifestations not of generosity but selfishness.

And what of the political, of government, what are the extremes that ruin justice by excess and deficiency? It turns out that both excesses, however different, ruin justice in the same fundamental way: losing sight of the face of the neighbor for the needs of the state, *realpolitik*, sacrificing each for all, and thereby ruining each and all, an abuse of individual and state at one stroke.

We have already indicated the extreme of excess, the error of Hobbes, which is to reduce justice to "law and order," to legality, to "reasons of State," *della Ragion di Stato*. It is the formula of totalitarian government, the police state, the rigid hegemony of administration, bureaucracy, formalist legalism, conformity, a slavish mass choreography of dancing, marching, and thinking. For Levinas and for Aristotle, however, the law can never be enough, can never be just enough, never sufficiently attentive to the good of each. "The reason," Aristotle says, "is that all law is universal but about some things it is not possible to make a universal statement which shall be correct."[26] Levinas will emphasize another dimension of the law's inadequacy: that it is always approximating but never finishing the work of justice, of providing for the infinite generosity of morality, the face-to-face, which remains, nonetheless, its standard. The work of justice is never done, the law is never just enough, hence an obsessive legalism, the equation of justice and law, is always but a cover for injustice. Levinas invokes Pascal as epigram for *Otherwise than Being or Beyond Essence*: "My place in the sun. There is the beginning and the prototype of the usurpation of the whole world."[27]

As for the extreme of deficiency of justice, it is the rejection of law altogether. Historically it has taken two distinct but related forms. One, fascist, is to substitute the will of the Leader for the rule of law. Such is the infamous "*Fuhrer* principle," that is, what the ruler wills is law, which in fact is no principle at all. Its other form, seemingly more benign, is to substitute society for politics, morality for justice, exalting the "community of virtue" whose goodness, so it is alleged, is stymied by politics. But whether one substitutes law or will, however, in both cases it is justice that is denied and destroyed. We must remember, so Levinas teaches, that justice arises out of morality, as its rectification. No one person can do it all, not only because helping one person is already overwhelming, but because there are more than two people in the world. The other who one faces is also other to others, and these relations, beyond the face-to-face but impinging upon it, as potential dangers to the other by others, extend ultimately to all humanity, indeed to the entire universe, and must also be continually tempered ethically, which is to say, by justice, limiting power, controlling violence, including that of government, laws, institutions, courts, police, businesses, schools, hospitals, and so on, even at their best. Justice, which tempers power, must never forget the human face.

Morality without justice is sentimentality, not morality. Justice without morality is tyranny, not justice. The excesses of each, and even more so the various combinations of such excesses, are monstrous. The topic is also too large for the present essay. We except only the most famous instance of this combination of moral and political deficiency, the biblical city of Sodom (Genesis 18–19), epitome of stinginess and inhospitality.[28] It is often thought that the perversion of Sodom was sodomy, but the truth is that this prosperous and wealthy city preferred such nonfruitful sexuality because it saw children as expenses, as it saw everyone and everything in terms of self-interest, greed, and accumulation. Of all the towns mentioned in the Bible, only such a city—prosperous and wealthy, yet stingy and inhospitable—merited divine destruction, "a hail of fire and brimstone."[29]

For both Levinas and Aristotle, politics is not simply about power, but power serving justice, power in the service of morality. Levinas would therefore endorse Aristotle's insight in *Politics* that "a state's purpose is not merely to provide a living but to make a life that is good . . . to have an eye to the virtue and vice of the citizens."[30]

The Cultivation of Virtues

Regarding the cultivation of morality, we have already mentioned the virtuous circle of responsibility, which increases to the measure that it is taken up. The more one is responsible, the more one is responsive to the needs of others, the more one appreciates how much more is demanded of responsibility. And this "more" is both quantitative and qualitative.

Regarding the cultivation of justice, Levinas believes that the best possible political regime, which means the best chance for a better future, is democracy. Democracy because the pacific transfer of power by means of periodic elections is the best guarantee, the best safeguard, however imperfect, against tyranny, the tyrannies of property, privilege, and power. I cite:

> By admitting its imperfection, by arranging for a recourse for the judged, justice is already questioning the State. This is why democracy is the necessary prolongation of the State. It is not one regime possible among others, but the only suitable one. This is because it safeguards the capacity to improve or to change the law by changing—unfortunate logic!—tyrants, these personalities necessary to the State despite everything. Once we choose another tyrant, we imagine, of course, that he will be better than his predecessor. We say this with each election![31]

Neither optimistic nor pessimistic, such is the politics of justice, where the status quo is never good enough, never just enough. Justice, we can also say, is always future, today oriented by a better tomorrow. Patriotism is therefore never complacency but always protest, for a better future, for all, including yet unborn generations to come.

Virtue and Jewish Identity

Levinas freely acknowledges that Judaism is too rich, too varied, too profound, and too ancient to be reduced to a philosophy or, for that matter, a set of beliefs. For Levinas, it is the ethical grandeur of Judaism, however, that is central and determinative, the highest sense of *holiness*. Holiness, Judaism is an ethical way of life, "an inner morality, not an outer dogmatism,"[32] but not an inner morality in a contemplative sense, but a morality active in the world, loving the neighbor, feeding the hungry, struggling for justice. For Levinas, Judaism's universality is not reductive or leveling but inclusive, all-embracing, welcoming all. So, for instance, for Levinas the significance of the new State of Israel, which is to say, the meaning of "Zionism," lies not in securing yet another "State of Caesar," a state ruled by egoism and aggrandizing power, but a "State of David," a state ruled by justice, justice tempered by mercy, despite the considerable difficulties. Such an Israel, such a Zionism, alone is *worthy* of Judaism's heritage and its election. Ethics includes and colors all of Judaism, permeating and uplifting its prayers and rituals, its family mores, its sociality, its political activism, everyone and everything enters into the exigencies of ethical responsibility, teaching, reinforcing, instituting the imperatives of generosity and hospitality, the serious life of responsibility.

Levinas shows in all aspects of Judaism's complex multi-layered life the highest ethical significance. We have already seen one instance, with the notion of "election." Instead of signifying an arbitrary privilege, a favoritism, which would only reinforce arrogance and resentment, for Levinas the true sense of election lies in the singularizing nonsubstitutability of responsibility. Responsibility is election, the privilege of service to others. So too "*hineni*," "here I am"—the biblical response of Abraham, Jacob, Moses, Samuel, and Isaiah—stripped of all hagiography is the very formula of responsible selfhood, good character: here I am ready to help you. So too with "Love your neighbor as yourself": no longer raising the neighbor to second place after oneself, but to first place, loving the neighbor is oneself. So, too, as we have seen, "messianism" and "Zionism" are—consistent with a deep understanding of Judaism—envisioned as struggles for justice, for Jews, for Israel, but also for all humankind. This is a small sampling.

Levinas envisions Judaism as "a religion for adults,"[33] radically opposed to the credulities and seductions of myth or blind faith. "Judaism appeals to a humanity devoid of myths," Levinas has written, "not because the marvelous is repugnant to its narrow soul but because myth, albeit sublime, introduces into the soul that troubled element, that impure element of magic and sorcery and that drunkenness of the Sacred and of war that prolong the animal within the civilized."[34] Judaism is not some otherworldly escapism, not a fantasy or make-believe, not a childish ignorance. Responsibility is serious, deep and deepening, holy. "Everything that cannot be restored to an interhuman relation," Levinas has written in *Totality and Infinity*, "represents not the superior form but the forever primitive form of religion."[35] "The relation to God," Levinas has written, "is already ethics; or, as Isaiah 58 would have it, the proximity to God, devotion itself, is devotion to the other man."[36] "Ethics is not the corollary of the vision of God, it is that very vision."[37] "To know God is to know what must be done."[38]

A final word about Levinas's writings. One can divide them between the philosophical and the Jewish. Some commentators have mistaken their rhetorical difference for an essential one, segregating philosophical from "confessional" writings, perpetrating a divide more appropriate to Christianity. This is a mistake. All of Levinas's writings teach the very same lessons: the priority of the other person as moral obligation for me, the infinity of responsibility, responsibility as morality, responsibility requiring justice, and so on. There is harmony between claiming "ethics as first philosophy"[39] and understanding of Judaism as "a religion for adults." On this score, what divides Levinas's writings is their intended audience. The so-called Jewish writings are intended for a Jewish audience, assume a certain familiarity, a shorthand regarding shared terminology, texts, experiences, traditions, history, sufferings, and all the specifics that constitute and differentiate one community—in this case an ancient community, a people "as old as the world"[40]—from others, *but* without thereby in any way excluding anyone. One can equally say that the philosophical writings assume a certain familiarity with the Western philosophical canon, which is also not intended to exclude anyone. Whether they—philosophical or Jewish—are successful at such ethical inclusiveness, is for readers to decide.

Notes

1. Emmanuel Levinas, "Judaism and Revolution," in *Nine Talmudic Readings*, trans. Annette Aronowicz (Bloomington: Indiana University Press, 1990), 99.

2. Emmanuel Levinas, *Otherwise than Being or Beyond Essence*, trans. Alphonso Lingis (Pittsburgh: Duquesne University Press, 1998), 114. Levinas's "here I am," formula of self as responsibility, in French "*me voici*," is of course also the biblical Hebrew "*heneni*."

3. Aristotle, *Nicomachean Ethics*, trans. David Ross (London: Oxford University Press, 1961), 1106b36.

4. Levinas, *Otherwise than Being*, 116.

5. Levinas, *Otherwise than Being*, 118.

6. Levinas, *Otherwise than Being*, 115.

7. Levinas, *Otherwise than Being*, 142.

8. Levinas, *Otherwise than Being*, 114.

9. Levinas, *Otherwise than Being*, 115.

10. Levinas, *Otherwise than Being*, 126: "It is time the abusive confusion of foolishness with morality were denounced."

11. Emmanuel Levinas, *Totality and Infinity*, trans. Alphonso Lingis (Pittsburgh: Duquesne University Press, 2003), 244.

12. Levinas, *Totality and Infinity*, 246.

13. Levinas, *Totality and Infinity*, 34.

14. Levinas, *Totality and Infinity*, 244.

15. BT Sotah 35a.

16. Levinas, *Otherwise than Being*, 158.

17. Levinas, *Otherwise than Being*, 158.

18. See, Emmanuel Levinas, "The State of Caesar and the State of David," in *Beyond the Verse: Talmudic Readings and Lectures*, trans. Gary D. Mole (New York: Continuum, 2007), 171–81, 208–209.

19. Micah 4:4: "Everyone shall sit under their own vine and fig tree, and no one shall make them afraid." Quoted by Amanda Gorman, American poet laureate, in "The Hill We Climb," read at the inauguration of President Joe Biden on January 20, 2021.

20. Aristotle, *The Politics*, trans. T. A. Sinclair, revised and re-presented by Trevor J. Saunders (Harmondsworth, UK: Penguin, 1982), 3.9.

21. Levinas, *Totality and Infinity*, 247.

22. Levinas, *Totality and Infinity*, 172.

23. See, Emmanuel Levinas, "Dying for . . . ," in *Entre Nous: On Thinking-of-the-Other*, trans. Michcael B. Smith and Barbara Harshav (New York: Columbia University Press, 1998), 207–17.

24. Levinas, *Totality and Infinity*, 173.

25. Levinas, *Totality and Infinity*, 174.

26. Aristotle, *Nicomachean Ethics*, 1137b11, et passim.

27. Levinas, *Entre Nous*, 231, and Levinas, *Otherwise than Being*, vii.

28. See, for example, Ezekiel (16:49: "This was the guilt of your [Jerusalem's] sister Sodom: pride, abundance of bread and prosperous ease, but she did not aid the poor and needy"); BT Sanhedrin 109a; Genesis Rabbah 49.

29. For a more developed Levinasian discussion of the devastation of Sodom and the Cities of the Plain, compared and contrasted with the later destruction of Gibeah and the Tribe of Benjamin, see, Richard A. Cohen, "Judges 19–21: The Disasters of the Community of Virtue," *Religions* 11, no. 10, article 531 (2020), https://doi.org/10.3390/rel11100531.

30. Aristotle, *Politics*, 3.9.

31. Jill Robbins, ed., *Is It Righteous to Be? Interviews with Emmanuel Levinas* (Stanford, CA: Stanford University Press, 2001), 194.

32. Levinas, "Being a Westerner," in *Difficult Freedom*, 49.

33. Emmanuel Levinas, "A Religion for Adults," in *Emmanuel Levinas, Difficult Freedom,* trans. Sean Hand (Baltimore: Johns Hopkins University Press, 1970), 11–26.

34. Levinas, "Being a Westerner," 48.

35. Levinas, *Totality and Infinity,* 79.

36. Emmanuel Levinas, "On Jewish Philosophy," in *Emmanuel Levinas, In the Time of the Nations,* trans. Michael B. Smith (Bloomington: Indiana University Press, 1994), 171.

37. Levinas, "A Religion for Adults," 17.

38. Levinas, "A Religion for Adults," 17.

39. Emmanuel Levinas, "Ethics as First Philosophy," in *The Levinas Reader,* ed. Sean Hand (Oxford: Blackwell, 2005), 75–87.

40. See Emmanuel Levinas, "As Old as the World?" in *Nine Talmudic Readings,* 70–93.

Chapter 33

Abraham Joshua Heschel

EINAT RAMON

Abraham Joshua Heschel (1907–1973) was one of the pivotal non-Orthodox Jewish thinkers of the twentieth century. Now widely known as a progressive colleague of Martin Luther King, Jr., and an opponent of US involvement in the Vietnam War, Heschel was a dissenter in the service of truth who aimed to disturb the complacency of the bourgeoisie, both Jewish and Christian. Heschel was born and raised in Warsaw; both of his parents came from "dynasties" of rabbis, linking him to the founders of Hasidism.[1] He was educated and first ordained by his Hasidic uncle. Though he was expected to marry his cousin and take over the Hasidic community of his father, who had passed away when he was 11,[2] he turned first to a secular high school education in Lithuania and then moved to Berlin to study at the *Hochschule,* the liberal rabbinic seminary, and at the University of Berlin.[3] Following the rise of the Nazis, Heschel was saved by Professor Julian Morgenstern, the president of Hebrew Union College at the time, who brought him to teach at HUC in Cincinnati in 1940.[4] There he met his future wife, Sylvia, a pianist.[5] In 1945, they moved to New York, where he taught at the Jewish Theological Seminary, his spiritual home until the end of his life. A prolific theologian, Heschel wrote influential works in Yiddish, Hebrew, German, and English.

The Importance of Virtues to Heschel's Thought

Heschel's view of virtue is rooted in both his traditional Eastern European Jewish education, which he cherished, and his observation that the "solution" to social problems cannot be found in political systems. These problems stem from human greed, materialism, and the worship of technology, and promote a horrific civilization rooted in ancient idolatry. In Heschel's mind, his response to Western technological culture, in all its various expressions and political guises, is rooted in classical Jewish sources—the Bible, rabbinic tradition, Jewish philosophy, Kabbalah, and Hasidism. The remedy for humanity's waywardness is likewise rooted in the vision of God's love for humans and in the law and lore He gave to them, which embodies the spirit of Jewish life in its various manifestations throughout the ages.

A concern for the traditional Jewish concept of improvement or perfection of one's personal virtues (*tikkun ha-middot*) is implied in all of Heschel's discussions of the purpose of the laws revealed by God.

Just as he was opposed to a technical obedience to halakhah, Heschel rejected a technocratic worldview, one that relies on technology to solve all of humanity's existential problems. At the same time, he thought that abiding by and internalizing the ethos embedded in the Jewish system of *mitzvot*—the laws presented by God as commandments that were given at Sinai to Jews and to non-Jews alike—could save the world from the potential calamities caused by humanity, which did not end with World War II. Humanity's problem, as it was exposed in the Shoah and the totalitarian communist regimes that followed it, is that, according to Heschel, "We are impressed by the towering buildings of New York City. Yet not the rock of Manhattan nor the steel of Pittsburgh, but the law that came from Sinai is their ultimate foundation."[6] So writes Heschel in his first systematic theology, *Man Is Not Alone* (1951).

A few years later, in *God in Search of Man* (1955), Heschel was more explicit as to why this is the case: "The law, stiff with formality, is a cry for creativity; a call for nobility concealed in the form of commandments. It is not designed to be a yoke, a curb, a strait jacket for human action. Above all, the Torah asks for *love*: thou shalt love thy God: thou shalt love thy neighbor. All observance is training in the art of love. To forget that love is the purpose of all mitzvot is to vitiate their meaning. . . . Both body and soul must participate in carrying out a ritual, a law, an imperative, a *mitzvah*. Thoughts, feelings ensconced in the inwardness of man, deeds performed in the absence of the soul are incomplete."[7] A careful reader of Heschel must be aware that, whereas love of God and humans is the goal of all of human existence, *love does not come easy*! God's love towards humans, humans' love toward each other, and humans' love of God as endorsed by Jewish tradition is not a spontaneous emotion that emerges from one's feelings but rather a state of mind that involves many implicit and explicit actions, that is, the commandments. Love involves a constant inner labor, informed and guided by the Torah, that requires a tremendous effort of working upon one's virtues and one's emotions.

Thus, Heschel derives virtues from the long list of the 613 commandments for Jews, and the seven commandments for non-Jews. He blames not only a single modern political philosophy, but all of humanity, for the mass killings of the twentieth century. The virtues that Heschel wishes to cultivate through education are found in—and derived from—the content of Sinai's commandments. That is because "the quest for right living . . . has been the main theme of Jewish literature, from the prophets till the times of Hasidism."[8]

As I argued earlier, Heschel's entire corpus of thought responds to the horrors and mass murders that have colored human history, but above all to the great dictatorial ideologies of the twentieth century, Nazism and Communism. In his essay, "The Meaning of the War," which was published in *Liberal Judaism* in 1944 in the midst of the Holocaust, Heschel—already an immigrant in the US—reminds humanity that Hitler and the Nazis were not the only source of evil: "Let fascism not serve as an alibi for our conscience. We have failed to fight for right, for justice, for goodness."[9] In a 1949 essay, following the Holocaust and the establishment of the State of Israel, he reminds all of his listeners and readers that, "[w]hen the annual congress of the Nazi Party convened in Nuremberg in 1937, journalists from all over the world, such as the *Times of London*, described with enthusiasm the demonstrations of the Nazi organization."[10] Thus, he blames all of Western industrial society for exploiting its military power, technology, and propaganda to perpetuate the evils of war in modern times. Given the abject failure of human societies to identify and stop the Nazi, fascist, communist, and other imperialist horrors, it is not a surprise that Heschel turned his attention to individuals, the human beings who can make the world a better place by keeping and performing commandments. Where large societies and civilizations fail, perhaps individuals and small communities can morally prevail. Through cultivating and demonstrating noble virtues, individuals may save lives, become "dissidents," and act as firm and silent protesters who might stop, even partially, the crimes and the horrors.

In an autobiographical statement found in the introduction to his first theological work, his PhD dissertation, *The Prophets* (published as an extended study in the US in 1962), Heschel revealed the driving force and motivation behind his theological writings.[11] The following is a glimpse into how the state of moral urgency that accompanied him throughout his life emerged in his thought while he was studying in Germany in the late 1930s:

> What drove me to study the prophets? In the academic environment in which I spent my student years philosophy had become an isolated, self-subsisting, self-indulgent entity, a *Ding an sich,* encouraging suspicion instead of love of wisdom. The answers offered were unrelated . . . , indifferent to a situation, in which good and evil became irrelevant, in which man became increasingly callous to catastrophe and ready to suspend sensitivity in the face of truth. I was slowly led to the realization that some of the terms, motivations, and concerns which dominate our thinking may prove destructive of the roots of human responsibility and treasonable to the ultimate ground of human solidarity.[12]

Cultivating the virtues that Heschel mentions—love of wisdom, sensitivity, responsibility, solidarity, and truth-seeking—could, he hoped, prevent the terrible calamities that humanity has the potential to impose on itself through idolatrous thinking.

How is the root of evil embedded in idolatry? Heschel explains this in various passages: "The root of all evil is, according to Isaiah, man's . . . pride, arrogance, and presumption." Since the dawn of human history, imperialistic cultures have been "full of arrogance, pride, insolence, and false boasts." But the "design of the Lord" is "to humble the pride of all glory, to dishonor all the honored of the earth."[13] And whereas "pagans exalt sacred things, prophets extol sacred deeds."[14] "The prophets were the first men in history to regard a nation's reliance upon force as evil."[15] These passages explain why Heschel was not as fully optimistic as his JTS colleague Mordecai Kaplan and others were following the victory of the United States and its allies in World War II and the establishment of the State of Israel in 1948.

In his lectures to academicians and scientists at Stanford (published as the book *Who Is Man?* in 1965), Heschel quoted Sir Arthur Keith, a Darwinian scientist who believed that "[n]ature keeps her human orchard healthy by pruning. War is her pruning hook." He ended that passage with a quote from Heinrich von Treitschke, who said that "God will see to it that war always occurs as a drastic medicine for the human race."[16] Killing as a "moral" advancement of the ecosystem and human civilization is, according to him, the root cause of the mass killings of modernity.[17] Heschel's concern was very specific and precise: "One of the most frightening prospects we must face is that this earth may be populated by a race of Homo sapiens according to biology, devoid of the quality distinguished from the rest of organic nature."[18] In his last book, *A Passion for Truth,* about Kierkegaard and the Kotzker Rebbe (published posthumously in 1973), Heschel deepened his analysis of the state of humanity in that same spirit. "It is ironic," he wrote, "that the natural sciences have long since abandoned the assumption that man is the center of nature and ultimate end of the evolutionary process." According to the natural sciences, the world and all the creatures in it, including human beings, are small machines, parts of a deterministic larger machine that man will eventually conquer and master. Heschel critiques the natural sciences' disinterest in the miraculous aspect of creation, their neglect of the Creator and of such basic elements of human existence as humility, an awareness of God, and the other aspects of what amounts to cherishing human life as unique and the "crown of creation." Therefore, the scientific-materialistic view of man was, along with antisemitism, at the root of the Holocaust:

> [T]he Holocaust did not take place suddenly. It was in the making for several generations. It had its origin in a lie: that the Jew was responsible for all social ills, for all personal frustrations. Decimate the Jews and all problems could be solved. The Holocaust was initiated by demonic thoughts' savage words. What is the state of mankind today? Has

> the mind been purged, have the words been cleansed of corrupt deceit? How shall we prevent genocide in the years to come? Has mankind become less cruel, less callous?[19]

And what did Heschel learn from the Kotzker Rebbe that points out the direction we must take in life, as a response to the grim view of humanity embodied in his recognition that vile lies currently run the world? The Kotzker Rebbe "taught us never to say farewell to *Truth*."[20] Thus, we can see why seeking the truth was a major virtue in Heschel's thought.

A central dilemma faced, according to Heschel, by living persons in the face of a scientific and mechanistic view of humanity and nature, is whether the ultimate transcendence is alive or not. How can we actually relate to the living God in the face of scientific skepticism? If we allow for the ultimacy of "being as being, then the status of man as a living being becomes precarious—if the ultimate is sheer being, then the living human has nothing to relate himself to as living. He can only relate himself to nothing. What surrounds him is a void, where all life is left behind."[21] In this sentence, Heschel is hinting that the modern denial of God's ultimate reality and his intimate relationship with humans is dangerous to people. A consequence of the virtue of truth-seeking is to see the potential remedy to humanity's decay in the commandments that God gave to humans at Sinai. That voice encapsulates the only possible response to the tremendous intellectual and moral challenge of the mechanistic-scientific paradigm.[22]

One might argue that by asserting so strongly that there is no remedy to humanity's ills other than following God's commandments, Heschel may be alienating his materialist and scientifically minded readers. Although Heschel's non-Orthodox hermeneutics of the Torah could appeal to such readers, Heschel was not willing to yield to materialistic skepticism concerning the authenticity of God's true revelation to humans, and he was consistently impatient with the skeptic. As Neil Gillman has argued, Heschel insisted that "the evidence for the reality of God is all about us. We can learn to see it in nature and in history."[23] In Heschel's own words: "[T]he prophet seems to have realized how hard it is not to be perverse, not to be an abomination."[24] Being a prophet and a pious human being is difficult when faced with "the modern version of the Golden Rule: *Suspect thy neighbor as thyself*," "the hysteria of suspicion" that "holds many of us in spell."[25]

Piety, Truth-Seeking, and Reverence for Parents

In Heschel's view, the commandments revealed at Sinai that are essential for the world's continuity are many. Virtues, in Heschel's thought, are embedded in God's commandments, which train humans in the art of loving God. If we search for a common denominator among all the virtues that Heschel lists in his various writings, we discover that they are all linked to piety. These virtues, and the commandments that lead to their attainment, help us become pious people.

What are the characteristics of piety? At the end of *Who Is Man?*, Heschel mentions a list of virtues by which the moral God-loving human must abide: "Significant living" is the attempt to adjust to what is expected and required of a human being. This kind of living is achieved through "sensitivity to demands as inherent in being human as physiological functions are in human beings"; "responsibility," "love," "the capacity to praise," and most of all "embarrassment"—which is the guarantee of humility—all of these virtues are "the touchstone of religious commitment."[26] One might wonder about the connection between the virtues of "love," "humility," and "embarrassment" according to Heschel, who regards the entire "project" of God's commandments as training in the art of love. Perhaps the answer to this question lies in the idea of the pious man's "pattern of life" in the image of God and with God, performing God's commandments.[27] With that kind of humble consciousness put into practice through the Torah,[28] one lives in a consciousness wherein every act and thought sanctified by the commandments increases humans' ability to love: to sense the significant in small things, to develop an interest in in the ultimate value of all acts.[29]

As indicated above, the virtue of seeking the truth is also essential to Heschel's thought. This virtue requires unmasking deep lies and struggling for the Truth. Heschel follows the Talmudic saying (BT Shabbat 55a) that God's identifying imprint (on the world) is Truth; but how is its expression translated into everyday life? Consider the following statements from *Man Is Not Alone*: "The pious man lays no claim to reward. He hates show, or being conspicuous in any way and is shy of displaying his qualities even to his own mind"; and "piety desires not merely to learn faith's truth, but to agree with it."[30] The pious man, according to Heschel, detests "hypocrisy and pretense of devoutness." Heschel brings an example of hypocrisy and lies: "[M]onuments of worldly glory are repulsive to him when they are built by the sweat and tears of suffering slaves."[31] These descriptions of the pious man's detestation of hypocrisy explain what exactly Heschel means when he writes that seeking the truth is a virtue that must determine the direction of our lives. Rather than engaging in a detailed philosophy of morals, Heschel introduces the pious man to us. The virtuous individual who lives in an awareness "of ever living under the watchful eye of God" is living a "life compatible with God's presence."[32] Heschel does not engage in a philosophical discussion of the virtues, their hierarchy, or how to resolve potential conflicts between them; rather he introduces us to the pious man—his unique way of thinking, believing, behaving, being in the world. We, Heschel's readers, can strive to resemble him (which is the purpose of Heschel's writing) rather than analyzing his ideas. The man (or woman) who abides by the law of truth knows that "he has no claim to anything with which he is endowed"; and "his thankfulness being stronger than his wants and desires."[33] As we are introduced to the features of the pious man's personality, we become aware of what truth-seeking means as a virtue, a characteristic of the heart, rather than an abstract idea that must be implemented.

Another commandment that could be regarded as a source of virtue in Heschel's thought is "revere thy father and thy mother." "Without profound reverence for father and mother, our ability to observe the other commandments is dangerously impaired," Heschel wrote.[34] As he explained in an interview a few months before his death in 1973, in response to journalist Carl Stern's question "Do you have a message for young people?":

> I would say that in spite of the negative qualities they may discover in their fathers, they should remember one thing, and the most important thing—the most important thing is to ponder the mystery of their own existence.
>
> The people who represent the mystery of my existence: father and mother. And the less I have reverence for the mystery of my existence, regardless of the special faults of my parents, I'm simply not human. Because to be human consists of a number of qualities or sensibilities. One of the central sensibilities is a sense of mystery of my own existence. Without it I cease to be human. I may be a human being, but I'm not being human. . . .

> Shouldn't a child realize how much his parents have done for him, for their children, in bringing them up? How much sacrifice, how many efforts, how many sleepless nights, how much love. Isn't it scandalous not to appreciate the sacrifice of parents?[35]

Heschel's statement here is very indicative as to what could be, in his eyes, the human response to the ills of human civilization. In his final, direct message to young people in general and young Jews in particular, in the midst of the American "hippie rebellion" of the '60s, Heschel explained that the essence of their humanity lies in their awe and reverence for the mystery of human birth (reverence for God's laws and His presence in Nature), and for the essence of human identity (reverence for God's presence in history, as told through the Bible). Honoring our father and mother teaches us awe of God, love, and respect for the Torah—the source of the virtues that we received through our father and mother. It points to Heschel's idea that the human sense of the ineffable, and our radical amazement, starts with the miracle of our birth.[36]

In order to understand the centrality of honoring one's father and mother, one must understand Heschel's philosophy of education. According to Heschel's approach to the education of children, which he inherited from his Hasidic upbringing, Judaism is "not merely a matter of external forms" (as he wrote in 1956), "it is also a matter of inner living."[37] "Our task, then, must be to teach Judaism as a subject of the deepest personal significance."[38] Although Heschel discusses adult Jewish education in post–World War II America, the idea of receiving from one's parents and teachers an education that emphasizes the inner meaning of mitzvah is implied in a statement in *God in Search of Man*, where Heschel explains that "a mitzvah is an act which God and man have in common."[39] As Heschel's response to Carl Stern indicates, this type of internalized perception of commandments begins at home. "Honor thy father and thy mother" embodies, in Judaism, the celebration of our teachers of Torah: "The teacher," he explains in his essay on Jewish education, "is the central pillar of Jewish living, past, present, and future. According to Jewish tradition, God Himself teaches."[40] One's mother and father are thus one's primary teachers, those from whom one learns about the inner connection of the human being and God.

The Cultivation of Virtues through Mitzvot and Exemplars

Heschel argues that "[t]he idea of mitzvah occupies the focus of the Jew's attention"; "the mitzvoth are hidden brilliance."[41] Thus, Heschel draws upon the Torah's commandments as the source for human values. This is his response to a dynamic he describes as follows: "We only graft goodness upon selfishness, and relish self-indulgence in all values; that we cannot but violate truth with evasion. Honesty is held to be wishful thinking, purity the squaring of the circle of human nature. The hysteria of suspicion has made us unreliable to ourselves, trusting neither our aspirations nor our convictions. Suspiciousness, not skepticism, is the beginning of our thinking."[42] If a denial of the possibility of commitment to virtue is the rule of a modern "suspicious" society as Heschel describes it in this passage, we can see which virtues he cherishes and how they are related to the system of *mitzvot*. In illustrating how virtues are embodied in *mitzvot*, Heschel explains: "Jewish Law is sacred prosody, for the divine sings in our deeds, the divine is disclosed in our deeds."[43] Hence among those virtues that are translated to deeds, Heschel mentions in the above passage purity and faith, aspiration and conviction, to which he often adds the (obvious) virtue of his commitment to God and to the Jewish people. This commitment to the Jewish people is the overriding paradigm of the virtue of commitment found in Heschel's thought; he considered it a "spiritual order": "[L]iving *in* the Jews of the past and *with* the Jews of the present . . . we do a mitzvah 'in the name of all of Israel.' We act both as individuals and as the community of Israel. . . . All generations are present, as it were, in every moment."[44]

We see, then, that Heschel portrayed in his various writings a wide variety of virtues, translated into the deeds (commandments) and engraved on the hearts of Jews. But Heschel chose not to create "lists" of those virtues—his theological writings were antithetical to "lists," and were not constructed that way. For Heschel, theology was supposed to express the features of poetry. Theology, as he learned from the biblical prophets, can influence only if it is inspiring—the medium of poetic language is part of the message. Heschel was, therefore, extremely conscious of the aesthetic quality of his works, which he intended to attract an audience that was initially suspicious of or even hostile towards Judaism. In this context, crafting lists of virtues or commandments would have missed the point.

Heschel also published spiritual biographies of Jewish role models from biblical times until modernity, putting into practice his belief that our teachers teach us how to implement commandment-based virtues in our lives. In a world lacking virtues and values, we can determine how these virtues might operate in our daily lives if we are able to learn about those who lived in accordance with them: the prophets, Rabbi Akiva and Rabbi Ishmael (the heroes of his main book in Hebrew, *Torah min Hashamyim*), Maimonides and other medieval rabbis, and various Hasidic teachers including the Baal Shem Tov and the Kotzker Rebbe.

Virtues in Heschel's Thought in the Context of his Interpretation of the Jewish Tradition

The cultivation of noble virtues as demonstrated in the lives of Jewish spiritual leaders throughout the generations is an important theme in Heschel's thought, and a major component of his theological/educational goal to teach his readers how the centrality of God's commandments ought to be implemented in a human being's life. Virtues are a central piece of the "Heschelian theological project"; and yet they emerge here in a nonsystematic manner that almost marginalizes them. It seems to me that Heschel addresses this problem in his claim that "so much of what is given out as Jewish thinking is obsolete liberalism or narrow parochialism." There are dissenters in Judaism today," yet "those who are authentic speak in a small still voice which the Establishment is unable to hear."[45]

Heschel's response to the modern and postmodern human situation is that "[o]urs is a Godless world. We Jews dance around the Golden Calf. We have forgotten that we live in a world that is treyf [impure]."[46] In the face of such a reality, Heschel took upon himself the role of a "dissenter" who speaks "in a small still voice," hoping as a teacher—like teachers of Judaism throughout the generations—that that "small still voice" would be heard and echoed by those who strive to follow the path set forth for humanity at Sinai.

Notes

1. Edward K. Kaplan, *Abraham Joshua Heschel: Prophetic Witness* (New Haven, CT: Yale University Press, 1998), vii, xi, xii, xiii.

2. Kaplan, *Prophetic Witness*, 45–55.

3. Kaplan, *Prophetic Witness*, 77–120.

4. Edward K. Kaplan, *Spiritual Radical: Abraham Joshua Heschel in America, 1940–1972* (New Haven, CT: Yale University Press, 2007), 5–7.

5. Kaplan, *Spiritual Radical*, 83–86.

6. Abraham Joshua Heschel, *Man Is Not Alone: A Philosophy of Religion* (New York: Farrar, Straus and Giroux, 1951), 147.

7. Abraham Joshua Heschel, *God in Search of Man: A Philosophy of Judaism* (New York: Farrar, Straus and Giroux, 1955), 307.

8. Heschel, *Man Is Not Alone*, 269.

9. Abraham Joshua Heschel, *Moral Grandeur and Spiritual Audacity: Essays*, ed. Susannah Heschel (New York: Farrar, Straus and Giroux, 1996), 210.

10. Heschel, *Moral Grandeur*, 58–59.

11. Einat Ramon, "Idolatry and the Dazzle of the Enlightenment in Abraham Joshua Heschel's Thought" [Hebrew], *Daat*, no. 71 (2011): 105–31.

12. Abraham Joshua Heschel, *The Prophets* (New York: Jewish Publication Society, 1982), xviii.

13. Heschel, *The Prophets*, 165.

14. Abraham Joshua Heschel, *The Earth Is the Lord's: The Inner World of the Jew in East Europe* (New York: Abelard-Schuman, 1950), 14.

15. Heschel, *The Prophets*, 166.

16. Heschel, *Who Is Man?* (Stanford, CA: Stanford University Press, 1965), 3–4.

17. Abraham Joshua Heschel, *The Insecurity of Freedom* (New York: Farrar, Straus and Giroux, 1966), 24, likely referring to the eighteenth-century book by La Mettrie, *Man a Machine*.

18. Heschel, *Insecurity of Freedom*, 29.

19. Abraham Joshua Heschel, *A Passion for Truth* (Woodstock, VT: Jewish Lights, 1995), 322.

20. Heschel, *A Passion for Truth*, 323. My emphasis.

21. Heschel, *Who Is Man?*, 69.

22. James Hyman, "Meaningfulness, the Ineffable and the Commandments in the Thought of Abraham Joshua Heschel," *Conservative Judaism* 50, no. 2–3 (1998): 84–99.

23. Neil Gillman, *Sacred Fragments: Recovering Theology for the Modern Jew* (Philadelphia: Jewish Publication Society, 1990), 134.

24. Heschel, *God in Search of Man*, 391.

25. Heschel, *God in Search of Man*, 389.

26. Hyman, "Meaningfulness," 106–107.
27. Heschel, *Man Is Not Alone,* 269.
28. Heschel, *Man Is Not Alone,* 270.
29. Heschel, *Man Is Not Alone,* 278.
30. Heschel, *Man Is Not Alone,* 281.
31. Heschel, *Man Is Not Alone,* 283.
32. Heschel, *Man Is Not* Alone, 283.
33. Heschel, *Man Is Not Alone,* 287.
34. Heschel, *Insecurity of Freedom,* 39.
35. Heschel, *Moral Grandeur,* 404.
36. Abraham Joshua Heschel, *Abraham Joshua Heschel: Essential Writings,* ed. Susannah Heschel (Maryknoll, NY: Orbis, 2011), 54–56.
37. Heschel, *Moral Grandeur,* 149.
38. Heschel, *Moral Grandeur,* 149.
39. Heschel, *God in Search of Man,* 287.
40. Heschel, *Moral Grandeur,* 152.
41. Heschel, *Moral Grandeur,* 77.
42. Heschel, *Moral Grandeur,* 6.
43. Heschel, *Moral Grandeur,* 79.
44. Heschel, *God in Search of Man,* 423–24.
45. Heschel, *Essential Writings,* 107.
46. Heschel, *Essential Writings,* 79.

Chapter 34

Jewish Feminism

REBECCA J. EPSTEIN-LEVI

Jewish feminism, like other feminisms, covers a lot of ground. Beneath the aegis of "Jewish feminism," broadly conceived, one can find liberal and radical streams, streams that emphasize Jewish text, ritual, or theology, streams that eschew more recognizably "religious" aspects of Judaism but are steeped in some form of Jewish cultural identity, and streams that may not explicitly identify themselves as Jewish but are shaped to a significant extent by some aspects of a thinker's Jewishness.

By "Jewish feminism," I mean, broadly speaking, thought and practice that challenge the subordination and oppression of women and, increasingly, other gender minorities (1) as Jews, (2) in Jewish contexts, and/or (3) in some way that is significantly formed by Jewish experience, identity, thought, or practice. While here I focus to some extent on academic Jewish feminism, this definition also includes nonacademic clergy, liturgists and artists, activists, and community members.

While there is notable work that predates this, such as the writing and activism of figures like Bertha Pappenheim (1859–1936) and Rabbi Regina Jonas (1902–1944), generally speaking, scholars of Jewish studies are likely to trace Jewish feminist thought, *named* as such, to the 1970s, when thinkers like Rachel Adler[1] and Trude

Weiss-Rosmarin[2] drew explicit attention to Jewish women's social, ritual, theological, and halakhic subordination *as Jews*, within Jewish contexts. The subsequent decades saw a flourishing of feminist publications like *Lilith*, feminist ritual and liturgical innovations, the ordination of women rabbis by the Reform, Reconstructionist, and Conservative movements in American Judaism, and the publication of key works of Jewish feminist thought, such as Blu Greenberg's *On Women and Judaism: A View from Tradition*, Judith Plaskow's *Standing Again at Sinai*, and Rachel Adler's *Engendering Judaism*. More recently, Jewish feminist thought has increasingly come to embrace queer and transgender liberation, and it has also begun to grapple with race in a more substantive way, although the "official" Jewish feminist canon remains deeply and perniciously white.[3]

How Is Virtue Important to Jewish Feminism?

How is virtue important to Jewish feminism? The answer to this will depend a great deal on how we choose to define "virtue ethics." Broadly speaking, virtue ethics is a family of theories that are united by their primary focus on virtues, or desirable character traits, the practices or disciplines by which persons and communities cultivate and strengthen those traits, and the cultivation of the practical wisdom needed to evaluate, understand, and respond well in a given situation.

At first, it seems tricky to apply this framework to the field of "Jewish feminism," because, as Judith Plaskow notes, "very little Jewish feminist work comes with the label 'ethics.'"[4] If this is true of "ethics" in general, it is true of "virtue ethics" even more so. And yet, just as Plaskow goes on to say that "Jewish feminism, for all its internal diversity, is fundamentally about ethics [because f]eminists' insistence that women's subordination in Judaism and the larger society [is] real and unjust, and that change is urgent and necessary are the common threads that . . . define Jewish feminism's ethical core,"[5] I think it is also true that there is something about Jewish feminisms, taken together, that is fundamentally about *virtue ethics*. After all, one of the major foci of the family of ethical theories collected under the aegis of "virtue ethics" is not just "desirable character traits," but the processes and disciplines by which those traits are formed and reinforced.

Virtue ethics, in other words, concerns not just static qualities, but active character formation and commitments to particular ways of being. And, just as Plaskow notes that central to any Jewish feminism is a commitment to naming and correcting injustice that is fundamentally ethical in character, similarly central to any proposed remedy for the injustices Jewish feminism names is some kind of call to *form different habits.*

Thus, when virtue ethics asks, "What are the disciplines we ought to cultivate? Which habits of thought or behavior, which practices, which ways of being are desirable, and which habits are characteristic of the particular affinities or communities in question?" it becomes relevant and recognizable to several of the core questions that Jewish feminisms, broadly speaking, are asking. To interrogate the ways gender-based oppression works within a family of traditions that share an overwhelming focus on the ways participants live their day-to-day lives and a particular set of attitudes toward shared texts and daily rituals entails reexamining those attitudes and ways of being, asking how they reinforce or subvert gendered hierarchies, and modifying them or replacing them as necessary. Both the objects of this interrogation and repair *and* the processes of interrogation and repair themselves fall squarely within the domain of virtue ethics.

Some Jewish Feminist Disciplines

Understood in the terms I've articulated above, there are a number of virtues and disciplines one could identify as characteristic of Jewish feminism. Here, I focus on three areas of Jewish feminist discipline: reinterpretation, citation, and recanonization.

REINTERPRETATION

The story and interpretation of written and oral Torah has been at the center of normative rabbinic Judaism for the vast majority of its existence, so developing reparative, subversive, or revisionist interpretive approaches to the canon is an obvious strategy for Jewish feminists. The fact that women have been excluded from these practices for most of Jewish history only makes their power more apparent. Furthermore, normative rabbinic Judaism has valued these interpretive practices not only for the textual insights they might yield but for the ways they shape the people and communities who engage in them. To learn Torah in the proper ways is to partake in a discipline that cultivates specific virtues. Various forms of feminist reinterpretation, similarly, become more than merely ways of understanding the mechanics of oppression or of ameliorating any given text—they, too, become disciplines that shape feminist Jewish readers in particular ways and cultivate virtues.

There are a number of streams of feminist interpretive practice, but they can be roughly divided into what we might call critical approaches and (re)constructive approaches. Critical approaches, broadly speaking, seek to identify and analyze the ways gendered oppression works within a given text, or how a given text is deployed to perpetuate gendered oppression. (Re)constructive approaches, broadly speaking, seek to *remedy* gendered oppression in some way through their interpretation of a text or texts.

Tamar Ross, in her pivotal work of Orthodox feminist thought, *Expanding the Palace of Torah,* offers a taxonomy of Jewish feminist approaches to text, all of which are squarely (re)constructive.[6] Ross identifies several distinct "tracks" or streams, each of which has certain defining traits, themes, and/or practices. Thus, for example, "historical restorativists," such as Judith Hauptman and Tikva Frymer-Kensky use feminist historical methodologies to situate core texts within their cultural and historical contexts, arguing that in this light they actually represent improvements in women's status.[7] Thinkers who deploy what she calls "golden thread methodology" try to "depatriarchalize" core texts, arguing that "a good restorativist reading simply entails peeling off the centuries of androcentric interpretation that have accrued to the original text."[8] "Multiple thread restorativists" like Daniel Boyarin search out and highlight potentially reparative counternarratives to the prevailing sexism within classical texts, often borrowing methodologies from literary studies, psychoanalysis, feminist and queer theory, and postcolonial theory to do so.[9]

Each of these approaches focuses on different interpretive virtues. Whereas historical restorativists and golden thread revisionists, for example, are likelier to ground their arguments in a return to some original core of the tradition, making a virtue of returning to a "source" or of age, multiple thread restorativists tend to highlight the innovative and even subversive potential of their readings. Marla Brettschneider, for example, uses the "alternative system of complex hierarchies" she finds in particular Talmudic passages as a "counter-text" that can "disrupt [regnant] oppressive categorizations."[10]

Ross's taxonomy, however, is not exhaustive. Many feminist rabbinics scholars, for example, offer detailed critical approaches to analyzing and understanding gendered hierarchies in the classical rabbinic canon, as well as careful (re)constructive approaches that cannot fit neatly into any of Ross's categories. Charlotte Fonrobert's classic study of rabbinic menstrual purity discourse, for example, offers a clear-eyed analysis of the rabbis' rhetorical constructions and uses of imagined female bodies as tools to reinscribe their epistemic authority.[11] Julia Watts Belser's work on gender and disability in the context of rabbinic accounts of ecological and political catastrophe combines careful text-historical work with theoretical tools from queer and crip studies to examine the intersection of multiple hierarchies, at once using the oppressive strands in the texts to illuminate aspects of present-day systems and the potentially liberative strands as subversive tools, without disproportionately emphasizing either.[12] Elizabeth Shanks Alexander traces the rabbinic canon's linguistic, ritual, and pedagogical axes, painting a sober portrait of its overarching gender politics, while simultaneously arguing that when people who have been excluded or marginalized from this canon on the basis of gender gain the skills to play in these texts' arenas, that in itself is a reparative discipline.[13] For all of these scholars, to read carefully and critically, with attention to the structural details of gendered oppression, and to then consciously engage, reread, and reinterpret toward reparative or liberatory ends, is a practiced discipline that asks a scholar to navigate between the claims and pressures of the extant bodies of tradition and the exigencies of their own positionality. Such a discipline requires hermeneutic, historical, political, and affective fluency.

Canonical texts, of course, are not the only possible objects of feminist reinterpretive disciplines. Thinkers, artists, and activists like Brettschneider,[14] Katya Gibel Mevorach,[15] Melanie Kaye/Kantrowitz,[16] Naomi Zack,[17] Chanda Prescod-Weinstein,[18] and Aurora Levins Morales,[19] for example, reinterpret constructions of Jewish peoplehood, race, and political objectives, challenging regnant images of American Jews as uniformly white and Ashkenazi and the conflation of Zionism with Jewish identity and self-preservation in ways that highlight the connections between these structures and gendered hierarchies. Here, too, these scholars bring practices of historically and politically incisive critical reading and structural analysis together with skill at affective navigation and constructive rereading and retelling toward liberatory ends.

Citation

Citation is a practice that shapes scholars, canons, and entire fields, something that feminist scholars have recognized clearly. Citations, as Sara Ahmed argues, "can be feminist bricks; they are the materials through which, from which, we create our dwellings."[20] Whom we cite—whose work we recognize as worth acknowledging—conditions whom we will continue to acknowledge going forward, as do the choices we make, consciously and unconsciously, about to whom we attribute key ideas, commentaries, and practices. Citation has the power to shape whom we understand as having built a field. It tells us whom we are expected to take seriously.

If attention to citation is a keystone virtue of feminist scholarship more generally, one can argue that it is also a characteristic virtue of Jewish thought, inasmuch as such can be clearly defined. Certainly there are styles of citation that can help us identify some texts and ways of reasoning as recognizably Jewish. One example of this is the characteristic *memra* chains in classical rabbinic text: "Rabbi Ammi, and some say Rabbi Assi, said in the name of Rabbi Yohanan in the name of Rabbi . . ." Another example is the invocation of having learned x or y tradition or practice from one's ancestors or from members of one's community—admired figures who are both sources of knowledge and models for others' behavior. Citation substantially forms Jewish intellectual and ritual communities and genealogies. It alerts us to the ways in which Jewish practice is itself a form of reproduction. Indeed, as Alexander has argued, rabbinic text study—marked as it is by these genealogical citations—itself becomes a key mechanism by which Judaism has constructed gendered categories and reproduced gendered hierarchies, "facilitat[ing] the construction of a world in which fathers reproduced their social and covenantal identity in the next generation."[21]

If "official" Jewish citation practices have served to reinscribe androcentrism and patriarchy, what do Jewish feminist citation practices look like? What habits do they cultivate, and what dwellings do they build? To begin with, Jewish feminists tend to cite other Jewish feminists. As Jewish feminist thought grows as a field, these citations build up like Ahmed's bricks—and not wholly unlike memra chains, either ("Epstein-Levi said in the name of Plaskow in the name of Adler . . ."). These citation practices also cross boundaries between genres, such as academic writing and *psak*; for example, the very first citation in rabbinics scholar and Conservative rabbi Gail Labovitz's 2020 *teshuva* on egalitarian marriage is of Rachel Adler's germinal work *Engendering Judaism: An Inclusive Theology and Ethics*.[22]

Jewish feminists are also likely to cite thinkers who otherwise might not have been considered as dialogue partners for Jewish thought, putting non-Jewish feminism, as well as theoretical tools from a range of disciplines, in dialogue with Jewish sources and ways of thinking. Ross identifies "multiple thread" restorativism as particularly likely to be in explicit interdisciplinary conversation, but such interdisciplinary work is by no means limited to this subset of thinkers; indeed, Ross herself, like many feminist thinkers who are committed to working within the halakhic tradition in some form—notably Rachel Adler—makes extensive use of legal scholar Robert Cover's understanding of laws as situated in and substantially constituted by the narratives held by the communities they bind.[23]

Repeating these citation practices, in clear awareness of their political impact as such, as they build upon each other, is thus both strategy and *habitus*. It inclines the individual reader to ask, "Who is and is not being cited, and why?" It inclines the reader to think about the ways other disciplines, and other hierarchies and identities, might be entangled in questions of Jewishness and gender, and to make effort to cite thinkers who have been marginalized by those entangled hierarchies. Collectively, it works to build communities in which these citation practices, and the cultivation of the virtues that come with them, are expected.

RECANONIZATION

This is perhaps hard to separate from citation, and perhaps is better thought of as a "next step" of it, since citations are part of what builds a canon. Another part of building a canon, however, is explicitly naming sources as canonical and challenging boundaries of what we consider normative. If citations are, in Ahmed's words, bricks that build walls, then canons are one type of wall. And how we construct our walls, where we put them, and whether and where we place portals in them both reflect how we have been formed as moral actors *and* influence how we will continue to be formed. For, like citations, our canons shape us even as we shape them. The sources—textual, ritual, behavioral—we treat as authoritative significantly condition us as moral agents and as communities. They reflect and reinscribe who is inside or outside the boundaries of the community, who may and may not hold various kinds of explicit and implicit authority, and whom we point to as models after whose moral, intellectual, and ritual examples we ought to strive.

The walls of normative Jewish thought, a basic feminist critique easily tells us, have overwhelmingly been built and sited by and for men—and men within a particular set of intellectual, cultural, and ritual traditions, at that. Classical rabbinic texts especially, as well as regnant halakhic traditions, mystical traditions, and a particular set of mostly Euro-American, mostly male Jewish philosophers (Hermann Cohen, Martin Buber, Franz Rosenzweig, Emmanuel Levinas, Joseph Soloveitchik, Abraham Joshua Heschel, Gershom Scholem, and so forth (some accounts might include Hannah Arendt or even Judith Plaskow if they are feeling particularly magnanimous) have overwhelmingly formed the canon of academic Jewish thought. This is not just a problem of representation. As Andrea Dara Cooper notes in her incisive and important bibliographic roundup of key texts in gender and modern Jewish thought, "[F]orm tends to mirror content in the formation and maintenance of such canons. . . . It is not simply a matter of adding women-identified and nonbinary voices to the canon (although any heterogeneity is preferable to none), but of attending to critiques informed by gender and feminist analysis in order to uncover viewpoints and frameworks that have been overlooked."[24]

Challenging the boundaries of this canon is a recurring practice within a range of Jewish feminist scholarship. One notable example of this is Chava Weissler's classic work on *tkhines*—early modern collections of Yiddish prayers and devotional literature largely intended for women that told stories about women as moral exemplars, and at least some of which were written *by* women, as well. The *tkhines*, and the ways women interacted with them, Weissler argues, "reveal [women's] intensely lived religious life, and a richly imagined spiritual world."[25] The *tkhines* represent a rich textual tradition in which women are centered and can act as exemplars and sources of moral, ritual, spiritual, and practical knowledge, Weissler argues, and deserve equal scholarly attention to "canonical" sources. Additionally, studying the *tkhines* helps readers understand the ways women's subordination is connected to larger hierarchies of gender, class, and disability: vernacular devotional and moral literature like the *tkhines* tended to be targeted not just toward women but also men who are not learned—for potentially a range of reasons—and who are therefore "like women."[26] Attending to this body of work, in other words, provides opportunities not only to expand the range of whose texts and experiences we take seriously, but also helps us become better and more careful readers of the ways oppressive hierarchies are entangled with one another.

The movement toward recanonization goes beyond expanding which *texts* are included in the canon, actively questioning whether the canon should be text-centered at all. Michal S. Raucher, for example, calls for Jewish ethics to not merely include but to *center* ethnography, especially that which highlights the lives and experiences of women and gender minorities. Indeed, Raucher argues, ethnography "is both a more ethical approach for Jewish ethics and a historically accurate way of determining an ethical response in Jewish thought . . . not only because it appreciates context but because it is attentive to feminist critiques of religious ethics."[27] While, as Raucher notes, constructive Jewish ethicists have been slow to pick up on the potential and, indeed, imperative of ethnographic sources, Jewish feminist scholarship more broadly has been more attentive to this call. Works such as Raucher's own study of Haredi women's reproductive agency, Susan Starr Sered's study of the ritual expertise of elderly Kurdish and Yemenite women,[28] Vanessa L. Ochs's studies of Jewish women's ritual innovations,[29] Tova Hartman and Naomi Marmon's study of Orthodox women's *niddah* practice,[30] and Katya Gibel Mevorach's pivotal study of the experiences of Black American Jews[31] all work powerfully to broaden regnant understandings of who Jews are, what Jews do, what kinds of agency, knowledge, and power Jewish women, gender and sexual minorities, and nonwhite and non-Ashkenazi Jews in fact already possess, and the range of exemplars for thought and practice that exist in the Jewish world. Such broadening, which requires scholars and readers to question regnant accounts of where authority and collective identities are grounded and to resituate themselves and their place in their communities based on what they learn, is fundamentally and inextricably character work at both individual and collective levels.

Recanonization might also mean reconsidering just whom we read as a "Jewish" thinker. Brettschneider, for example, devotes significant space to reading the Black Jewish novelist Jamaica Kincaid as a Jewish thinker through her meditations on otherness and diaspora and her use of biblical motifs.[32] Or, as Joyce Antler has covered in depth, a disproportionate number of figures in the US radical feminist movements of the second half of the twentieth century were Jewish.[33] Shall we read these figures as Jewish feminists, or as feminists who happen to be Jewish? What would it mean, for example, to read the pivotal feminist thinker Shulamith Firestone as a Jewish thinker?

Recanonization also applies to the rereading of liturgy, and to the reworking of extant liturgies and the creation of new ones. This might take the form of inventing new rituals, as well as scholarship that takes these new rituals seriously and bolsters their place within the tradition, as Vanessa Ochs's *Inventing Jewish Ritual* demonstrates.[34] It might take the form of feminist curation of and commentary on extant liturgy, the composition of new liturgies that directly address gendered experiences and concerns, and anything in between; indeed, most works of feminist liturgy do some of both. Noteworthy examples include Rachel Adler's *brit ahuvim* ceremony, intended as structurally egalitarian, historically grounded alternative to the practice of *kiddushin* in which a groom acquires his bride,[35] and Catherine Madsen and Joy Ladin's "Ritual for Gender Transition," which weaves Ladin's poetry together with elements from extant rituals for conversion, death, birth and naming, and coming of age to create ritual space and acknowledgment for transgender Jews.[36] Indeed, Adler's *brit ahuvim* has become so firmly canonical within significant streams of Jewish practice that it itself has become a basis for further liturgical and legal innovation—for example, for officially sanctioned queer marriage rites in Conservative Judaism.[37]

Virtue, Identity, and Agency

"I am a Jewish feminist and a feminist Jew," writes Judith Plaskow in the introduction to her field-defining work *Standing Again at Sinai*, "in every moment of my life." To separate her Jewish self from her feminist self, Plaskow argues, was to "[hand] over to a supposedly monolithic Jewish tradition the power and the right to define Judaism for the past and for the future . . . [to deny] my own power as a Jew to help shape what Judaism will become."[38] To write *Standing Again at Sinai*, she continues, was to cease relinquishing that power.

In this, Plaskow has drawn together the ways Jewish feminist virtue and Jewish feminist identity are inextricably linked. To be a Jewish feminist, for all the ground that category covers, is to assert that Jews who have been oppressed and excluded from full Jewish participation on the basis of their gender in fact rightly possess agency and power to articulate stories about who they are, what Judaism has been and can be, and where they are situated within it. To claim this power when the weight of precedent denies it is a discipline. It requires one to decide to keep it up. It entails other, linked disciplines, such as the ones I have covered in this chapter. It requires the support of a community that acknowledges that keeping up the discipline of claiming power, cultivating linked virtues like critical insight, audacity, and courage to push against the walls of regnant power is *difficult*, that it ought *not* be up to the oppressed to be better than their oppressors.

Yet ironically, in this way, to keep up the often-exhausting disciplines necessary to continue claiming the power of full participation and self-articulation is one thing that makes Jewish feminism especially Jewish, or so it seems to me. For, as Plaskow writes, one can understand Torah "to be the partial record of the 'Godwrestling' of part of the Jewish people, [which again and again] has felt itself called by and accountable to a power not of its own making, a power that seemed to direct its destiny and give meaning to its life."[39] To relate as a Jew to that power has been to simultaneously struggle with it and be indelibly shaped by it. And at its best, Jewish feminism shows us how that struggle, and the way it shapes its participants, can be part of a strange and wending journey toward a more just and compassionate world.

Notes

1. Rachel Adler, "The Jew Who Wasn't There: Halacha and the Jewish Woman," *Response: A Contemporary Jewish Review*, Summer 1973, 77–82.

2. Trude Weiss-Rosmarin, "The Unfreedom of Jewish Women," *Jewish Spectator*, October 1970, 2–6.

3. For more analysis of which, see, for example, Marla Brettschneider, "Critical Attention to Race: Race Segregation and Jewish Feminism," *Bridges* 15, no. 2 (2010), 20–33.

4. Judith Plaskow, "Jewish Feminist Ethics," in *The Oxford Handbook of Jewish Ethics*, ed. Elliot N. Dorff and Jonathan K. Crane (Oxford: Oxford University Press, 2013), 272.

5. Plaskow, "Jewish Feminist Ethics."

6. Tamar Ross, *Expanding the Palace of Torah: Orthodoxy and Feminism* (Waltham, MA: Brandeis University Press, 2004), ch. 6. It's important to note that Ross is critical of most of these streams; for what it's worth, I agree with substantial parts of her critique. But critical or otherwise, her taxonomy is helpful for descriptive purposes alone.

7. Judith Hauptman, *Rereading the Rabbis: A Woman's Voice* (New York: Routledge, 1998, 2018); Tikva Frymer-Kensky, *In the Wake of the Goddesses: Women, Culture, and the Biblical Transformation of Pagan Myth* (New York: Ballantine, 1992). See Ross, *Expanding the Palace of Torah*, 105–106.

8. Ross, *Expanding the Palace of Torah*, 108. See, for example, Judith Antonelli, *In the Image of God: A Feminist Commentary on the Torah* (Lanham, MD: Rowman and Littlefield, 1995).

9. Daniel Boyarin, *Carnal Israel: Reading Sex in Talmudic Culture* (Berkeley: University of California Press, 1993); Boyarin, *Unheroic Conduct: The Rise of Heterosexuality and the Invention of the Jewish Man* (Berkeley: University of California Press, 1997). See Ross, *Expanding the Palace of Torah*, 108–109.

10. Marla Brettschneider, *Jewish Feminism and Intersectionality* (Albany: State University of New York Press, 2016), 25.

11. Charlotte Fonrobert, *Menstrual Purity: Rabbinic and Christian Reconstructions of Biblical Gender* (Stanford, CA: Stanford University Press, 2000).

12. Julia Watts Belser, *Rabbinic Tales of Destruction: Gender, Sex, and Disability in the Ruins of Jerusalem* (Oxford: Oxford University Press, 2018); *Power, Ethics, and Ecology in Jewish Late Antiquity: Rabbinic Responses to Drought and Disaster* (Cambridge: Cambridge University Press, 2015).

13. Elizabeth Shanks Alexander, *Gender and Timebound Commandments in Judaism* (Cambridge: Cambridge University Press, 2013).

14. Brettschneider, *Jewish Feminism and Intersectionality*; "Critical Attention to Race,"; Brettschneider, *The Family Flamboyant: Race Politics, Queer Families, Jewish Lives* (Albany: State University of New York Press, 2006).

15. Katya Gibel Mevorach, *Black, Jewish, and Interracial: It's Not the Color of Your Skin but the Race of Your Kin, and Other Myths of Identity* (Durham, NC: Duke University Press, 1997).

16. Melanie Kaye/Kantrowitz, *The Colors of Jews: Racial Politics and Radical Diasporism* (Bloomington: Indiana University Press, 2007).

17. Naomi Zack, "On Being and Not Being Black and Jewish," in *The Multiracial Experience: Racial Borders as the New Frontier*, ed. Maria P. P. Root (Thousand Oaks, CA: Sage, 1996), 140–51.

18. Chanda Prescod-Weinstein, "Black and Palestinian Lives Matter: Black and Jewish America in the Twenty-First Century," in *On Antisemitism: Solidarity and the Struggle for Justice*, ed. Jewish Voice for Peace (Chicago: Haymarket Books, 2017), 31–42.

19. Aurora Levins Morales, *Medicine Stories: Essays for Radicals*, rev. and expanded (Durham, NC: Duke University Press, 2019); "Who Am I to Speak?," in *On Antisemitism: Solidarity and the Struggle for Justice*, ed. Jewish Voice for Peace (Chicago: Haymarket Books, 2017), 103–10.

20. Sara Ahmed, *Living a Feminist Life* (Durham, NC: Duke University Press, 2017), 16.

21. Alexander, *Gender and Timebound Commandments in Judaism*, 19.

22. Gail Labovitz, "With Righteousness and Justice, With Goodness and Mercy: Options for Egalitarian Marriage Within Halakhah," Rabbinical Assembly, Committee on Jewish Law and Standards, 2020, Even Ha-Ezer 27:1, https://www.rabbinicalassembly.org/sites/default/files/2020-05/Labovitz EgalitarianMarriage.pdf.

23. Ross, *Expanding the Palace of Torah*, 149–61; Rachel Adler, *Engendering Judaism: An Inclusive Theology and Ethics* (Philadelphia: Jewish Publication Society, 1998), 34–36.

24. Andrea Dara Cooper, "Gender and Modern Jewish Thought," in *Jewish Studies*, ed. Naomi Seidman, Oxford Bibliographies Online, https://www.oxfordbibliographies.com/view/document/obo-9780199840731/obo-9780199840731-0204.xml.

25. Chava Weissler, *Voices of the Matriarchs: Listening to the Prayers of Early Modern Jewish Women* (Boston: Beacon, 1998), 7.

26. Weissler, *Voices of the Matriarchs*, 54.

27. Michal Raucher, *Conceiving Agency: Reproductive Agency among Haredi Women* (Bloomington: Indiana University Press, 2020), 19.

28. Susan Starr Sered, *Women as Ritual Experts: The Religious Lives of Elderly Jewish Women in Jerusalem* (Oxford: Oxford University Press, 1992).

29. Vanessa L. Ochs, *Inventing Jewish Ritual* (Philadelphia: Jewish Publication Society, 2007).

30. Tova Hartman and Naomi Marmon, "Lived Regulations, Systemic Attributions: Menstrual Separation and Ritual Immersion in the Experience of Orthodox Jewish Women," *Gender and Society* 18, no. 3 (2004), 389–408.

31. Mevorach, *Black, Jewish, and Interracial.*

32. Brettschneider, *Jewish Feminism and Intersectionality*, 41–60.

33. Joyce Antler, *Jewish Radical Feminism: Voices from the Women's Liberation Movement* (New York: New York University Press, 2018).

34. Ochs, *Inventing Jewish Ritual.*

35. Adler, *Engendering Judaism,* 169–208.

36. Catherine Madsen and Joy Ladin, "Ritual for Gender Transition (Male to Female)," in *Balancing on the Mechitza: Transgender in the Jewish Community,* ed. Noach Dzmura (Berkeley, CA: North Atlantic Books, 2010), 85–92.

37. Elliot N. Dorff, Daniel Nevins, and Avram Reisner, "Rituals and Documents of Marriage and Divorce for Same-Sex Couples," Rabbinical Assembly, Committee on Jewish Law and Standards, 2012, https://www.rabbinicalassembly.org/sites/default/files/public/halakhah/teshuvot/2011-2020/same-sex-marriage-and-divorce-appendix.pdf.

38. Judith Plaskow, *Standing Again at Sinai: Judaism from a Feminist Perspective* (New York: Harper Collins, 1990), xi–xii.

39. Plaskow, *Standing Again at Sinai,* 33.

Chapter 35

Jewish Environmentalism

HAVA TIROSH-SAMUELSON

Environmental virtue ethics is a moral theory that applies the principles of virtue ethics to environmentalism. A strand of environmental ethics, environmental virtue ethics shifts the focus from consideration of rules, duties, rights, and consequences to the cultivation of character. By focusing on the excellences of character, the virtues, environmental virtue ethics cultivates the personality that treats nature with awe, respect, and love. This posture is also shared by world religions, especially the Abrahamic traditions, that responded to the environmental crisis by reminding us that the world is God's creation and humanity must take care of what belongs to God. Caring for God's creation requires the cultivation of a character that stands in the appropriate relationship with God, with other human beings, and with the natural world. The virtues Judaism extols—humility, modesty, temperance, simplicity, generosity, and compassion—are environmentally significant because they ensure that humans will treat nature with awe, respect, and love rather than with greed, selfishness, and violence. In his *Nicomachean Ethics,* Aristotle explained that virtues can be acquired only through habitual practice in the mean between excess and deficiency. In Judaism the virtuous character emerges through observance of the commandments that include duties toward the natural world. Maimonides, who was most responsible for integrating Aristotle's virtue ethics with rabbinic Judaism, has been the major inspiration for Jewish environmental virtue ethics, but modern Jewish philosophers including Hermann Cohen, Abraham Joshua Heschel, and Joseph Soloveitchik have also been relevant.

Environmental Virtue Ethics

Environmental ethics emerged in the early 1970s in response to the growing awareness of the ecological crisis in the 1960s.[1] At first, environmental philosophers held that standard theories of moral philosophy (e.g., deontology, consequentialism, and utilitarianism) are sufficient to ground environmental ethics in response to the eco-crisis by focusing or the rights of animals and their liberation from suffering on the intrinsic value of nature that compels respond for nature. While these approaches expanded the scope of ethics, most ethicists concerned with environmental degradation found them insufficient because they were too anthropocentric. Instead, environmental ethicists sought a new paradigm rooted in a nonindividualistic ontology that takes into consideration ecological wholes, inclusive of human and nonhuman biota and the abiotic environment. In the 1970s and 1980s, environmental ethicists debated the universal ground(s) for environmental values and the debate crystallized in two major schools of environmental ethics—Deep Ecology and Social Ecology.[2] The former was non-anthropocentric (also referred to as "biocentric' or "ecocentric"), whereas the latter was anthropocentric, but the debates about these perspectives and the possibility of reconciling them continued well into the 1990s, constituting environmental metaethics.

In 1983, Thomas E. Hill introduced a new consideration into the debate when he claimed that neither the language of rights nor the language of utility explain how people behave in regard to the natural environment, for example, when a person chooses to cut down and pave over an entire wooded lot.[3] Hill showed "how traditional (rights-based) deontological and (utilitarian) teleological theories can fail to track our moral intuitions regarding environmental issues."[4] Instead, Hill asked a simple question: "What kind of person would do such a thing?" That question launched environmental virtue ethics, because it indicated that actions toward the natural environment flow from one's character, the key concept of virtue ethics. Character consists of long-term stable dispositions to act in distinctive ways. The virtues are the excellences of character that embody our conception of the good, enabling a person to act well and do the right thing. Since the virtuous person expresses his or her virtue through action, right action flows from the goodness of character. Hill's intervention reflected the revival of virtue ethics since 1958 and the emergence of environmental virtue ethics as a distinct discourse within environmental ethics.[5]

Creation Care: The Complementarity of Duties and Virtues

As environmental ethics came into its own, so did the discourse on religion and ecology.[6] It emerged in the early 1970s in response to the bold charges of Lynn White, Jr., that "Christianity is the most anthropocentric religion," and that responsibility for our ecological crisis lies squarely at the door of the Judeo-Christian tradition.[7] The Bible was to blame, because its creation narrative gave humans the mandate to "have dominion" over nature, exploiting it for its own benefit. In response to White's charges, Jewish and Christian theologians began to examine their traditions in light of the environmental crisis.[8] Jewish theologians, scholars, and spiritual leaders insisted that Genesis 1:26–28, the main proof text of White's critique, by no means summarizes the Judaic approach to the natural world. In truth, Scripture does not sanction human domination of the Earth, because it severely curtails human activities concerning the natural world. Moreover, Scripture entrusts humanity "to serve and protect" the Earth (Gen. 2:15) by specifying how to treat the soil, vegetation, and animals to ensure the just management of God's created Earth and its enduring fecundity.[9] As Jews began to interpret Judaism with the eco-crisis in mind, they demonstrated that the Judaic tradition articulates not only a deep concern for the well-being of God's creation but also an obligation to protect it from human destruction. Caring for God's creation is a religious obligation constituted by the covenant between Israel and God.

Jewish environmentalists have shown that biblical environmental ethics coheres with concerns for sustainability, biodiversity, future generations, curbing consumption of animals, attentiveness to the suffering of animals, and commitment to ecological justice.[10]

However, the centrality of halakhah in Jewish self-understanding dictated that Jewish environmental discourse focused first on legal principles, precepts, and norms that govern the relationship of humanity and nature.[11] Much attention has been given to the precept

"Do Not Destroy" (*bal tashchit*) derived from the biblical prohibition on cutting down fruit-bearing trees in time of siege (Deut. 20:19).[12] This verse was invoked by Tannaitic and Amoraic sources to justify a broad range of environmental prohibitions, including the prohibition on cutting off water supplies to trees, overgrazing, unjustifiably killing animals or feeding them noxious foods, hunting animals for sport, species extinction and the destruction of cultivated plant varieties, pollution of the air and water, overconsumption of anything, and squandering minerals and other resources.[13]

Eilon Schwartz, a leading Jewish environmentalist, demonstrated that "there is no one Jewish approach to *bal tashchit* and its application, but rather multiple approaches that are debated from within the tradition."[14] The precept can be interpreted minimally to focus on human needs and wants or maximally "to have human wants counterbalanced with the legitimate claims of the natural world."[15] Tanhum S. Yoreh's recent reexamination of the entire halakhic discourse on *bal tashchit* from antiquity to the present also concludes that "*bal tashchit* continues to prove itself to be a highly nuanced concept."[16] However, he argues that the diverse interpretations focus not so much on protection of the environment but on the prevention of self-harm. If so, the precept of *bal tashchit* is more anthropocentric than Jewish environmentalists have been willing to admit. Examining contemporary rulings on environmental related issues in Israel, Yoreh argues that highlighting the connection between environmental degradation and self-harm will motivate Orthodox Jews to become more environmentally engaged.

The legal discourse related to the environment does not exhaust the notion of creation care. To care about, care for, and take care of God's created world involves not only prescribed actions but also emotions, attitudes, values, and experiences all of which constitute human flourishing. The Bible makes clear that if Israel observes divine commands, the land of Israel is abundant and fertile, producing grain, oil, and wine, the necessities of human life, and the foundation of human flourishing. Flourishing manifests the inherent righteousness of the person who observes the commandments and who stands in the right relationship with God and with all of creation. The opening hymn of the book of Psalms expresses this foundational insight of Judaism: the righteous person (*tzaddik*) who lives by God's Torah flourishes "like a tree planted on streams of water, which yields its fruit in season, whose foliage never fades and whatever it produces thrives" (Ps. 1:3).[17] The righteous person possesses the admirable character traits that enables him or her to act rightly toward other people and toward all of creation. Those who possess the virtues fulfill their divine obligations to God's created world and as a result they thrive.

The ideal of justice (*tzedek*) captures the complementarity of duty and virtue in Judaism. It is environmentally significant that in the Bible justice is expressed in the obligation to care for the poor (Deut. 15:7–8), the widow, the orphan and the stranger (Exod. 22:20–21), the Levite (Det. 12:17–19), and the landless. Care for the socially vulnerable and care for the well-being of the land and all those dependent on it is most evident in the laws of the Sabbatical Year (Exod. 23:10–11; Lev. 25:2–7, 25:20–22; Deut. 15:1–3). If their needs are taken care of, the land is fecund and the society flourishes, but when greed, viciousness, and lust for power prevail so as to trample the needy members of the society, the land becomes impoverished as well, unable to sustain its people.[18] Justice then is not only a social ideal of fair distribution of resources, it is also an environmental commitment to treat the land properly, avoiding exploitation of natural resources, preventing wanton destruction of habitats, and ensuring biodiversity. Justice is an environmental virtue.[19] Zalman Schachter-Shalomi and Arthur Waskow, the visionaries of Jewish environmentalism, coined and popularized the concept of Eco-Kashrut, which links observance of the dietary laws with social justice and environmental justice.[20] Kashrut should not be reduced to punctilious observance of the dietary laws; no less crucial is the just treatment of the laborers who produce the food, or the just use of the economic value accrued from all forms of labor. Although Eco-Kashrut does not explicitly appeal to the concept of virtue, justice implies the presence of the virtue of righteousness (*tzedakah*). To be holy as God is holy (Lev. 19:2), Israel must possess the virtue of righteousness.

Cultivating Environmentally Virtuous Jews

During the 1990s several Jewish philosophers paid attention to the revival of virtue ethics in contemporary moral philosophy,[21] but it was Moshe Sokol, the co-organizer of the conference called "Judaism and the Natural World," who first applied it to Jewish environmentalism.[22] Noting some shortcomings of Jewish eco-theology, Sokol (similarly to

Thomas Hill) sought to shift the direction of Jewish environmentalism by focusing on virtue ethics. Sokol asked: "Are there specific moral virtues and sensibilities which characterize the individual who shows care and concern for the natural world? What justifies their cultivation? How do they relate to other virtues? What are their implications for engaging the natural world?" His own list of environmental virtues included "a deep sense of humility . . . the capacity for gratitude; the capacity to experience awe and sublimity; the virtues of temperance, continence, and respectfulness, among others."[23] Although Sokol did not relate environmental virtue ethics to the larger discourse on human flourishing, or happiness,[24] he charted a fruitful path for Jewish environmental ethics.

A major inspiration to Jewish environmentalism was Abraham Joshua Heschel, who highlighted the importance of wonder. Already in 1955 Heschel stated: "[A]s civilization advances, the sense of wonder declines. Such decline is an alarming symptom of our state of mind. Humankind will not perish for want of information; but only for want of appreciation."[25] Heschel correctly identified the root of our environmental crisis: the loss of wonder, awe, and appreciation and their replacement by indifference, greed, and domination. Heschel's "radical amazement" called on us to restore the sense of awe, wonder, and reverence to the mystery of life and the feeling of respect and gratitude for what is given.[26] Wonder, for Heschel, was no adoration of nature. Indeed, Heschel makes clear that, "to Judaism, the adoration of nature is as absurd as the alienation from nature is unnecessary."[27] Rather, Heschel's "radical amazement" appreciates the sublime mystery of nature, while affirming "the reality of God as distinct from, though intimately present to, the world that God creates and loves."[28] Heschel's theology of nature was neither mere poetic musing nor mere speculation; rather, it "requires practical action, as do the revealed laws of ritual and ethical mitzvot."[29] Heschel inspired many Jewish environmentalists,[30] whereas secular and Christian environmentalists took their cue from Rachel Carson, promoting wonder and reverence for life as the virtues that facilitate environmental consciousness.[31] Wonder is not just an emotion, but the basis of environmental spirituality rooted in the virtue of humility.[32]

Humility (*anavah*) is a central virtue of Judaism, and many Jewish philosophers and theologians have elaborated on its importance.[33] For Maimonides, who systematically fused Aristotle's virtue ethics with rabbinic Judaism, virtue lies in the mean between extremes of excess and deficiency. The wise person who possesses the moral and intellectual virtues is disposed to act in the "middle path" by cultivating humility.[34] Daniel H. Frank has argued that the virtue of humility disrupts the Aristotelian ethics of moderation, because it calls one for supererogation, thus introducing a two-tiered morality: the pious person (*ḥasid*) is of a higher moral rank than the wise person.[35]

What matters for us is not how Maimonides deviated from Aristotle but how humility pertains to the natural world. For Maimonides, humility is cultivated by contemplating the natural world God had created. By observing the very structure, orderliness, and regularity of the created world, we become aware of God's caring management of the world that sustains its existence.[36] Centuries later Joseph B. Soloveitchik brilliantly analyzed the dialectics of majesty and humility that exists on both divine and human levels.[37] Translating these insights into environmental parlance, we could say that humility enables us to contemplate Earth's biodiversity, which in turn arouses in us guilt and shame about environmental degradation and the diminishment of the Earth's fecundity.[38]

The virtue of humility is closely related to the virtue of modesty (*tzni'ut*); namely, the avoidance of extroverted, self-centered behavior is another environmentally significant virtue. Contrasted with the vices of frivolity and lewdness, the virtue of modesty has been applied primarily to sexual ethos, but even some feminists have recognized that modesty should be regarded as a virtue, because it encourages feminist change. Hermann Cohen, yet another modern interpreter of Maimonides, held that "modesty provides an indispensable condition for morality," although Cohen differentiated between modesty and humility and his understanding of humility evolved over time.[39] Cohen's insight that "modesty is self-respect just as much as respect for the Other" is most relevant to environmentalism, since modesty leads to "awareness of and sensitivity to the effects of everyday behaviors on vulnerable others."[40] Such an attitude is relevant to creation care, because it prevents us from carelessly exploiting the gifts of nature for our benefits or by pretending that we know all there is to know about the workings of nature. Cohen's focus on compassion (*Mitleid*) as the response to suffering has obvious environmental implications, since compassion toward animals (*tza'ar ba'alei ḥayyim*) is a key aspect of Jewish environmentalism.[41] Whereas Maimonides did see the causal link between the proper treatment of animals and virtue,[42] Cohen did not draw these environmental implications.[43]

To cultivate humility and modesty we must exercise self-control and self-restraint (*kibbush ha-yetzer*), because we are naturally disposed to follow our desires. If for Aristotle virtue ethics was an elaborate program for the "training of desire," for Maimonides that function was accomplished by the Law.[44] Temperance (*metinut*) or moderation is the virtue that emerges when we control immediate urges and think through the implications of our temptations before acting on them. Temperance is a balance between the extremes of overindulgence, on the one hand, and self-destructive abstinence, on the other hand. By cultivating temperance one can responsibly enjoy bodily pleasures, which is part of human flourishing. The relevance of temperance to environmentalism is self-evident since much of the environmental crisis is due to overconsumption, especially in regard to food. In this context, temperance means "knowing where our food comes from, how it impacts the earth's ecosystems, what creatures have suffered to bring it to us, and which of our neighbors are not getting what they need."[45] Temperance in regard to eating entails taking responsibility of our own eating in a broader social and cultural context.[46] Gluttony, the opposite of temperance, is not only an individual vice but a vice that contributes to environmentally harmful consumerism. As much as temperance has environmental significance,[47] Eco-Kashrut covers a range of social values and political activities that require self-restraint.

Although virtues are character traits of individuals, they are expressed socially and publicly. Overconsumption, indulgence, and the greed of individuals or collectives greatly contribute to environmental degradation. Not surprisingly, the virtue of simplicity (*pashtut*) has received a lot of attention from environmentalists. Joshua Gambrel and Philip Cafaro noted that simplicity "furthers human flourishing, both individual and social, and sustains nature's ecological flourishing."[48] The virtue of simplicity, of course, was promoted by the ancient Stoics and Cynics as well as by the ancient rabbis.[49] The ability to be satisfied with one's portion in life rather than greedily pursue wealth and pleasures is clearly an environmental virtue. Environmental values such as stewardship, reverence for life, and responsibility are all virtues that promote creation care. Loyalty, trust, and generosity, all of which are central in Jewish ethics, have also been recognized as environmental virtues.[50] In short, to engage in creation care we need to cultivate moral and intellectual virtues that "motivate [us] to know the truth and to apply our knowledge at the right time, in the right circumstances and in the right way."[51]

Conclusion

Beginning with the Bible, Judaism has articulated an environmental virtue ethics that offers us a meaningful response to the current environmental crisis, brought about not by the Bible (as Lynn White, Jr., has charged) but rather by people who have ignored the environmental message of the Bible as well as its social ethos. In the Judaic environmental ethics, duty and virtue are intertwined, calling for the cultivation of a personality type that will stand in relation to God and engage in the pursuit of justice for humans and for all created beings. Jewish environmental virtue ethics has much in common with secular ethical discourses, especially with virtue ethics and with feminist ethics of care,[52] as well as with Christian environmentalism that focuses on creation care and the cultivation of character.[53] The severity of the environmental crisis compels us to integrate secular and religious discourses and bridge barriers between religious traditions and within strands of a given religious tradition. The environmental crisis also demands that we make the cultivation of environmentally virtuous Jews the goal of Jewish moral education. An environmentally oriented moral education could enable Jews to care about others, both humans and nonhuman, biotic and abiotic, including future generations, illustrating that social justice is eco-justice. Jews who are environmentally virtuous are moved by the needs of others rather than by selfishness, self-centeredness, or pride, and they appreciate and respond the wonder of creation that they are tasked to protect. Making environmental virtue ethics central to Jewish education will enable us to meaningfully respond to the environmental crisis and chart a path for a more sustainable future.

Notes

1. For the main strands, debates, and key texts in environmental ethics see Andrew Light and Holmes Rolston III, eds., *Environmental Ethics: An*

Anthology (Malden, MA: Blackwell, 2003); David R. Keller, ed., *Environmental Ethics: The Big Questions* (Malden, MA: Wiley-Blackwell, 2010). For major themes of environmental ethics, see Dale Jamieson, ed., *A Companion to Environmental Philosophy* (Malden, MA: Blackwell, 2001).

2. The shared ground and differences of these approaches are best summarized in Steve Chase (ed.), *Defending the Earth: A Debate Between Murray Bookchin and Dave Foreman* (Montreal: Black Rose Books, 1991).

3. Thomas E. Hill, "Ideals of Human Excellence and Preserving Natural Environments," *Environmental Ethics* 5, no. 3 (1983): 211–24.

4. Matt Zwolinsky and David Schmidtz, "Environmental Virtue Ethics: What It Is and What It Needs to Be," in *The Cambridge Companion to Virtue Ethics*, ed. Daniel C. Russell (Cambridge: Cambridge University Press, 2013), 221–33, quote on 224.

5. See Geoffrey B. Frasz, "Environmental Virtue Ethics: A New Direction for Environmental Ethics," *Environmental Ethics* 15, no. 3 (1993): 259–74; Louke van Wensveen, *Dirty Virtues: The Emergence of Ecological Virtue Ethics* (Amherst, NY: Humanity Books, 2000); Wensveen, "The Emergence of Ecological Virtue Language," in *Environmental Virtue Ethics*, ed. Ronald L. Sandler and Philip Cafaro (Lanham, MD: Rowman and Littlefield, 2005), 15–30; Philip Cafaro, *Thoreau's Living Ethics: Walden and the Pursuit of Virtue* (Athens, GA: University of Georgia Press, 2004); Ronald L. Sandler, *Character and Environment: A Virtue Oriented Approach to Environmental Ethics* (New York: Columbia University Press, 2007); Philip Cafaro and Ronald Sandler, eds., *Virtue Ethics and the Environment* (Dordrecht: Springer, 2010); Brian Treanor, *Emplotting Virtue: A Narrative Approach to Environmental Ethics* (Albany: State University of New York Press, 2014); Philip Cafaro, "Environmental Virtue Ethics," in *The Routledge Companion to Virtue Ethics* (London: Routledge, 2015), 427–44; Jason Kawall, ed., *The Virtues of Sustainability* (Oxford: Oxford University Press, 2021).

6. See John Grim and Mary Evelyn Tucker, *Ecology and Religion* (Washington, DC: Island Press, 2014); Grim and Tucker, "The Movement of Religion and Ecology: Emerging Field and Dynamic Force," in *Routledge Handbook of Religion and Ecology*, ed. Willis Jenkins, Mary Evelyn Tucker, and John Grim (New York: Routledge, 2017), 2–12.

7. Lynn White, Jr., "The Religious Roots of Our Ecologic Crisis," *Science* 155 (1967): 1204–1207.

8. For annotated bibliography of Jewish environmentalism, see Hava Tirosh-Samuelson, "Judaism and the Environment," in *Jewish Studies*, ed. Naomi Seidman, Oxford Bibliographies Online, 2015, https://doi.org/10.1093/OBO/9780199840731-0118. For an overview of Christian environmentalism consult Ernst M. Conradie, "Christianity: An Ecological Critique of Christianity and a Christian Critique of Ecological Destruction," in *Routledge Handbook of Religion and Ecology*, 70–78, and the literature cited there.

9. See Hava Tirosh-Samuelson, "Jewish Environmental Ethics: The Imperative of Responsibility," in *The Wiley-Blackwell Companion of Religion and Ecology*, ed. John Hart (Malden, MA: Willey-Blackwell, 2017), 179–94.

10. See Jeremy Benstein, *The Way into Judaism and the Environment* (Woodstock, VT: Jewish Lights, 2006).

11. See Manfred Gerstenfeld, *Judaism, Environmentalism and the Environment: Mapping and Analysis* (Jerusalem: Jerusalem Institute for Israel Studies, 1998); Gerstenfeld, *The Environment in the Jewish Tradition: A Sustainable World* (Jerusalem: Jerusalem Institute for Israel Studies, 2002); Walter Jacob and Moshe Zemer, eds., *The Environment in Jewish Law: Essays and Responsa* (New York: Berghahn Books, 2003); Ora Sheinson and Shai Spetgang, eds., *Compendium of Sources in Halacha and the Environment* (Jerusalem: Canfei Nesharim, 2005).

12. See Eilon Schwartz, "*Bal Tashchit*: A Jewish Environmental Precept," in *Judaism and Environmental Ethics: A Reader* (Lanham, MD: Lexington Books, 2001), 230–49; David Nir, "A Critical Examination of the Jewish Environmental Law of *Bal Tashchit*," *Georgetown International Environmental Law Review* 18, no. 2 (2006): 335–53; Ellen Cohn, "Growing an Environmental Ethics: The Conceptual Roots of *Bal Tashchit*," in *Compendium of Sources in Halacha and the Environment*, 38–44.

13. The relevant Tannaitic and Amoraic sources are analyzed in Tanhum S. Yoreh, *Waste Not: A Jewish Environmental Ethics* (Albany: State University of New York Press, 2019).

14. Schwartz, "*Bal Tashchit*," 244.

15. Schwartz, "*Bal Tashchit*," 244.

16. Yoreh, *Waste Not*, 230.

17. I developed this point in, Hava Tirosh-Samuelson, *Happiness in Premodern Judaism: Virtue, Knowledge, and Well-Being* (Cincinnati: Hebrew Union College Press, 2003), ch. 2.

18. The Sabbatical Year (*shemitah*) has become the driving inspiration of Jewish environmentalism. See Adrienne Crone, "A Shemita Manifesto: A Radical Sabbatical Approach to Jewish Food Reform in the United States," *Scripta Instituti Donneriani Aboensis* 26 (2015): 303–25; David Krantz, "The Shemitah Revolution: The Reclamation and Reinvention of the Sabbatical Year," *Religions* 7, no. 8 (2016), https://doi.org/10.3390/rel7080100. In Israel the environmental organization Teva Ivry has spearhead the revival of *Shemitah* as critique of consumerism, secularism, and technological oversaturation.

19. In contemporary virtue ethics, the virtue of justice has been associated with the capabilities approach promoted by Martha Nussbaum and Amartya Sen. See Jay Drydyk, "A Capability Approach to Justice as a Virtue," *Ethical Theory and Moral Practice* 15, no. 1 (2012): 23–38. On justice as environmental virtue see Paul Haught, "Environmental Virtues and Environmental Justice," *Environmental Ethics* 33, no. 4 (2011): 357–75.

20. See Arthur Waskow and Rebecca T. Alpert, "Toward Ethical Kashrut," *The Reconstructionist*, March–April, 1987, 9–13; Arthur Waskow, "What Is Eco-Kosher?," in *This Sacred Earth: Religion, Nature, Environment*, ed. Roger S. Gottlieb (New York: Routledge, 1996), 297–300.

21. Walter S. Würzburger, *Ethics of Responsibility: Pluralistic Approaches to Covenantal Ethics* (Philadelphia: Jewish Publication Society, 1994); Daniel Statman and Avi Sagi, *Religion and Morality* (Amsterdam: Rodopi, 1995); Daniel Statman, *Virtue Ethics* (Edinburgh: Edinburgh University Press, 1997); Yitzchak Blau, "The Implications of Jewish Virtue Ethics," *Torah U-Madda Journal* 9 (2000): 19–41.

22. Held in 1997 this conference was part of the series of conferences on Religions of the World and Ecology organized by Mary Evelyn Tucker and John Grim. The proceedings of the conference on Judaism and additional essays were published in *Judaism and Ecology: Created World and Revealed Word*, ed. Hava Tirosh-Samuelson (Harvard University Press, 2002).

23. Moshe Sokol, "What Are the Ethical Implications of Jewish Theological Conceptions of the Natural World," in Tirosh-Samuelson, *Judaism and Ecology*, 283–303, quote on 278. That Sokol refers to virtues as "capacities" indicates his indebtedness to Nussbaum's "capabilities approach."

24. Tirosh-Samuelson, *Happiness in Premodern Judaism*, traced that discourse in Judaism but without dealing with environmental concerns.

25. Abraham Joshua Heschel, *God in Search of Man: A Philosophy of Judaism* (New York: Farrar Straus, and Cudahy, 1955), 46.

26. See Edward K. Kaplan, "Reverence and Responsibility: Abraham Joshua Heschel on Nature and the Self," in Tirosh-Samuelson, *Judaism and Ecology*, 407–22.

27. Heschel, *God in Search of Man*, 90.

28. John C. Merkle, "Heschel's Monotheism vis-à-vis Pantheism and Panentheism," *Studies in Christian-Jewish Relations* 2, no. 2 (2007): 26–33, quote on 27.

29. Kaplan, "Reverence and Responsibility," 415.

30. For example, Benstein, *The Way into Judaism and the Environment*; Eilon Schwartz, "Mastery and Stewardship, Wonder and Connectedness: A Typology of Relations to Nature in Jewish Text and Tradition," in Tirosh-Samuelson, *Judaism and Ecology*, 93–106.

31. See Philip Cafaro, "Rachel Carson Environmental Ethics," in *Rachael Carson: Legacy and Challenge*, ed. Lisa H. Sideris and Kathleen Dean Moore, 60–78 (Albany: State University of New York Press, 2008).

32. See Robert C. Fuller, *Wonder: From Emotion to Spirituality* (Chapel Hill: University of North Carolina Press, 2006).

33. See Daniel Nelson, "The Virtue of Humility in Judaism: A Critique of Rationalist Hermeneutics," *Journal of Religious Ethics* 13, no. 2 (1985): 298–311.

This essay persuasively critiques the Rawlsian interpretation of the virtue of humility by Ronald Green, "Jewish Ethics and the Virtue of Humility," *Journal of Religious Ethics* 1 (1973): 53–63.

34. For exposition of Maimonides's ethics, see Marvin Fox, *Interpreting Maimonides: Studies in Methodology, Metaphysics and Moral Philosophy* (Chicago: University of Chicago Press, 1990); Raymond Weiss, *Maimonides' Ethics: The Encounter of Philosophic and Religious Morality* (Chicago: University of Chicago Press, 1991).

35. Daniel Frank, "Humility as a Virtue: A Maimonidean Critique of Aristotelian Virtue," in *Moses Maimonides and His Time*, ed. Eric L. Ormsby (Washington, DC: Catholic University of America Press, 1989), 89–99. Frank highlights the tension between Judaic supererogatory piety and the Aristotelian virtue ethics, but for the Jewish followers of Maimonides in the late Middle Ages there was no tension between Aristotle's "greatness of soul" and Judaic morality. See Tirosh-Samuelson, *Happiness in Premodern Judaism*, ch. 9.

36. Eliezer Haddad, *The Torah and Nature in Maimonides' Writings* [Hebrew] (Jerusalem: Magness Press of the Hebrew University, 2011).

37. Joseph B. Soloveitchik, "Majesty and Humility," *Tradition: A Journal of Orthodox Jewish Thought* 17, no. 2 (1978): 25–37.

38. On humility as environmental virtue, see Lisa Gerber, "Standing Humbly before Nature," *Ethics and the Environment* 7, no. 1 (2002): 39–53; Matthew Pianalto, "Humility and Environmental Virtue Ethics," in *Virtues in Action*, ed. M. W. Austin (London: Palgrave Macmillan, 2013), 132–49.

39. Robert Erlewine, "Herman Cohen, Maimonides, and the Jewish Virtue of Humility," *Journal of Jewish Thought and Philosophy* 18, no. 1 (2010): 27–47, quote on 34.

40. Laura M. Hartman, "Environmental Modesty: Reclaiming an Ancient Virtue," *Journal of Religious Ethics* 43, no. 3 (2015): 475.

41. See Richard H. Schwartz, "Jewish Traditions," in *Animals and World Religions*, ed. Lisa Kemmerer (Oxford: Oxford University Press, 2012), 169–204.

42. See Lenn E. Goodman, "Respect for Nature in the Jewish Tradition," in Tirosh-Samuelson, *Judaism and Ecology*, 227–59.

43. Benjamin Cleveland Ricciardi, "Herman Cohen on Compassion: A Cognitivist Take on the Peculiarly Religious Emotion," *Journal of Jewish Ethics* 5, no. 2 (2019): 207–27.

44. Weiss, *Maimonides' Ethics*, 62–69.

45. Kathryn D. Blanchard and Kevin J. O'Brien, *Introduction to Christian Environmentalism: Ecology, Virtue, and Ethics* (Waco, TX: Baylor University Press, 2017), 71.

46. For elaboration of this point, see Jonathan K. Crane, *Eating Ethically: Religion and Science for a Better Diet* (New York: Columbia University Press, 2017).

47. A good example how a traditional virtue can be interpreted environmentally is offered by Louke van Wensveen, "Attunement: An Ecological Spin on the Virtue of Temperance," *Philosophy in the Contemporary World* 8, no. 1 (2001): 67–78.

48. Joshua Colt Gambrel and Philip Cafaro, "The Virtue of Simplicity," in Cafaro and Sandler, *Virtue Ethics and the Environment*, 85–108, quote on 85.

49. Tirosh-Samuelson, *Happiness in Premodern Judaism*, 101–42; Jonathan Wyn Schofer, *The Making of a Sage: A Study in Rabbinic Ethics* (Madison: University of Wisconsin Press, 2005).

50. See Jennifer Welchman, "Virtue of Stewardship," *Environmental Ethics* 21 (1999): 411–23; Jason Kawall, "Reverence for Life as a Viable Environmental Virtue," *Journal of Ethics* 7 (2009): 365–92.

51. Sue P. Stafford, "Intellectual Virtue in Environmental Virtue Ethics," *Environmental Ethics* 32, no. 4 (2010): 339–59. Stafford discusses loyalty, trust, and benevolence as intellectual virtues that are environmentally relevant. In "Virtue of Stewardship," Welchman analyzes loyalty, benevolence, and charity as environmental virtues.

52. See Hava Tirosh-Samuelson, "Ethics of Care and Responsibility Bridging Secular and Religious Cultures," in *Environmental Ethics: Cross-cultural Explorations*, ed. Monika Kirloskar-Steinbach and Madalina Diaconu (Freiburg: Verlag Karl Alber, 2020), 29–57.

53. A good example is Steven Bouma-Prediger, *Earthkeeping and Character: Exploring Christian Ecological Virtue Ethics* (Grand Rapids, MI: Baker Academic, 2020).

Afterword

ALAN L. MITTLEMAN

The materials made thematic in this book may well be described as constituting a tradition. A tradition, broadly speaking, is that which has been handed down from the past.[1] Expansive definitions of tradition, such as that of Edward Shils, would include such phenomena as language, architectural styles, even physical artifacts crafted in the past and still in use. Tradition, on this expansive definition, does not require the internal awareness of someone participating in the tradition that she is doing so. To talk of tradition, it is sufficient that the inheritance in the past lives on into the present. Nonetheless, it is often the case that those who inherit traditions know that they have done so; they take a certain attitude toward their traditions, whether that of esteem or criticism. They take them seriously enough to interpret them, to situate their own thought and action within or with respect to them.[2]

The ongoing concern for moral character that courses through Judaism over the millennia constitutes both an expansive tradition and, more tightly, a substantive one. From the biblical literature to the twenty-first century, Jewish religious and other texts have asked Jews to work on their souls, so to speak. The texts have offered a vision of how one should live, of what the best life for Jews is, of how one's mode of being should relate to the end or purpose of being. The texts have propounded visions of a normative anthropology in relation to normative teleology. Ideals and norms of character have sometimes been defended in a theoretical voice, as in Maimonides or Gersonides. Sometimes they have been embedded in a rich, metaphysical mythopoesis, as in the *Zohar* and some Hasidic figures. Sometimes they are offered in the mode of practical advice, as in the Proverbs and in many musar teachers. Sometimes the justification for a set of virtues has been tacit and implied, while, at other times, it has been articulate and discursive. It is not that every author or body of literature cited in this volume needs consciously to position him or herself vis-à-vis a predecessor in order to participate in tradition. Tradition is an objective social reality, partly constitutive of a social world as such.

Focus on character and its excellences, that is, on the virtues as an important dimension of Jewish moral reflection begins in the Bible. Its concerns have had to do with how a Jew (and sometimes, at least implicitly, a human being as such) should live, what ideals a Jew should strive for, what a normative Jewish personality is like. The catalog of what constitutes the virtues is not fixed, nor does it necessarily map onto those of other great traditions. The tradition, like most if not all literary traditions, is internally pluralistic and argumentative. It is not that the participants in the tradition agree with one another about specific virtues or the weighing of them or their centrality to a good, proper, just, or holy life. They agree on the basic claim that character matters and that virtue is constitutive of character. The participants in the tradition argue with one another within a framework that structures moral reasoning. They share a basic, orienting text—the Bible—but they differ, unsurprisingly, over how to interpret it. Some of the differences in interpretation come from the very different cultures in which the historical interpreters lived—Talmudic Babylonia is not Hellenistic Alexandria, nor is medieval Ashkenaz medieval Catalonia. None of them are Wilhelmine Germany, twentieth-century America, or post–World War II France. The use of philosophical and other cultural materials from the environing society creates strong differences of emphasis in the ethical visions of the various authors. If common reference to the biblical legacy provides centripetal force, philosophy and culture provide a centrifugal one.

Nor does the matter of the tradition's internal pluralism end there. The heterogeneity of the Hebrew Bible itself drives differences in interpretation. The Bible presents different normative images of an ideal Israelite—prophet, sage, military hero, political leader. These are not entirely commensurable with one another. The Bible also provides different portrayals of God, in whose ways the Jew is to walk (Deut. 28:9). For some authors, Jewish virtue ethics comprises the commitment to imitate God. "You shall be holy, for I, the LORD your God am holy!" (Lev. 19:2). Yet what characterization of God is one encouraged to emulate? Surely not the God who is a "consuming fire" (Deut. 4:24), who wreaks judgment on the pagan nations and, most especially, on his own erring nation. It is the God of mercy, patience, and compassion whom Jews have been urged to emulate. But that image of God sits uneasily alongside others. One must already bring an ethical sensitivity to the biblical text in order to draw morally cogent norms and ideals from it. As in Aristotle's metaphor of the racetrack (*Nicomachean Ethics* 1095b), the ethical person does not start at the beginning of the course but in the middle; an ethical formation is already required in order to be sensitive to moral norms. The status of a preexisting moral normativity vis-à-vis the Torah is itself debated in the Jewish sources.

Jewish virtue ethics often points to biblical figures in order to exemplify an ideal of conduct and character. Moses, for example, is ideally humble. It relies as well on the ideality of the divine, whom Jews are to emulate. In this, it is perfectionist. For Stanley Cavell, who popularized the term, moral perfectionism has to do with a vision of the self as on a journey "described as education or cultivation."[3] Jewish virtue texts have concern for the individual, call on him or her to cultivate certain excellences, see the soul or self as enroute, and identify a vision of human perfection as the goal.

Although what an individual thinker means by perfection (*shleimut*) might vary, that Jewish virtue ethics per se is perfectionist seems clear. In this context, moral perfectionism means that the good life for human beings is understood in terms of excellence (rather than, say, happiness, welfare, or desire-satisfaction). The authors often claim or at least imply that there are reliable standards of intellectual and practical excellence inherent in Jewish life and the revealed sources on which it is based. A serious, worthy life is one dedicated to excellence. While serious lives can cultivate plural goods, there always seems to be a sense that the time is short and the work is great. There are endless distractions but no time to waste. One should be strenuous in cultivating the virtues.

Virtue, however, is seldom an end in itself. In much of the pious literature discussed in this volume, the end is communion with God. Virtue is a means to that end. Neither eudaemonia—the Aristotelian goal—nor human well-being as such are intrinsic values. Being human means being radically flawed, imperfect, refractory—virtue ethics is a project of mastering the human such that humanity can approach divinity. Humans are to become holy, as God is holy. Human potential holiness will always be distant from divine actual holiness. But the tradition aims at something more than eudaemonia as the final end of ethical striving.

How particularistic is Jewish virtue ethics? The Bible and, to an extent, subsequent Jewish thought, especially in periods of high culture and social tolerance, has a universalistic horizon. The Bible speaks of *all* human beings as created in the "image of God" (Gen. 1:27). Its prophetic texts know of international norms of behavior, of decency. Its wisdom texts use international norms of sage-like phronesis (*ḥokhma*). Nonetheless, the audience and the authorship of the Jewish moral tradition is mostly the Jews. The particularism is unmistakable, especially in the ages of persecution. The Jewish virtues do not necessarily map onto the Hellenic ones.

Conspicuously underdeveloped, for example, is a valorization of courage, a virtue central to the classical Greek tradition. There are courageous biblical heroes, as well as later figures, sometimes martyrs, such as Rabbi Akiva, but courage is less an epitome of human excellence, than a sacrifice of humanity for the sake of God (or, in Hermann Cohen, for humanity itself). The original Greek sense of courage as manliness is de minimis. Except for thinkers immersed in classical Greco-Roman culture, such as Philo or at the edge of religious Judaism, such as Spinoza or Arendt, courage entails too high a valuation of human greatness. In a tradition where humility—the intentional diminution of oneself before God—is often the greatest virtue, the exaltation of heroic humanity through courage would be discordant. If humility is human diminution before God, its positive counterpart is holiness, a distant approximation of God's separateness from the world. Perfectionism in a religious key, the way of Susan Wolf's devalued "moral saint," is likely not attractive to modern people.[4] Particularism may be problematic, too. What can such a particularism, its universal horizon notwithstanding, say to modern persons?

Who, then, beyond some in the Jewish community, can Jewish virtue ethics speak to today? Presumably, communitarians, especially if they are religiously committed, would be more sympathetic to this millennial tradition than liberal cosmopolitans. The communitarians could prize this tradition based on the richness of its moral resources, its capacity to orient the whole of individual and communal life in a well-grounded way. They would celebrate its thickness, as opposed to the Rawlsian thinness that liberals desire. Nor would they fret over much about the seeming arbitrariness of its grounds. We have nothing more fundamental, they might claim, than our communities and the identities and correlative practices that they impart. A good tradition, on such an account, is also one with the critical resources to correct itself. The Jewish tradition, partly originating in the work of the great biblical prophets, is hardly deficient in those resources. For religiously committed communitarians, that the tradition is ultimately grounded in divine revelation also gives it a universality that undergirds and contextualizes its particularity.

It is harder to see how the Jewish tradition of virtue ethics might speak to liberal cosmopolitans. For it to do so, we need to recall that virtue, as Joseph Story said, "is never a matter of indifference."[5] A free republic, so the theory went, requires self-disciplined, self-restraining people such that the state need not control too much of its citizens' lives in its pursuit of ordered liberty. The people must have the capacity to order themselves. For this, the traditions, practices, and institutions of civil society need to form citizens whose personal virtues can serve public, democratic purposes. Even though it is not, as in a classical republic, the business of the political community to coerce citizens to virtue, it is not a matter of indifference. The state can help facilitate civil society's formation of moral persons. This view of the founders is not popular among liberals today, but it is not obvious that the view is false.

A friend of Jewish virtue ethics might argue that liberalism, as a thin view of ethics vis-à-vis the public sphere, needs thickly constituted moral traditions. It needs particularism and perfectionism. Liberalism has tended to take its sense of what is right, appropriate, and practicable in the public life of a modern secular state and project it onto the normative traditions that antedate liberalism. It has tended, in the words of the late political theorist Jean Bethke Elshtain, to impose a "monistic liberalism."[6] That can't be good for ethics, politics, or liberalism. Learning from older, fuller traditions of virtue might enrich liberalism and enhance its prospects for survival in our increasingly uncertain world.

The tradition of Jewish virtue ethics can help us appreciate how moral orientations from other times and places can still form persons who bring such virtues as compassion, justice, responsibility, humility, prudence, self-control, and, yes, holiness to contemporary life. These and others contribute to the goodness of personal life, as well as to political well-being, even in a secular and a liberal society.

Afterword

1. Edward Shils, *Tradition* (Chicago: University of Chicago Press, 1981), 12.

2. Shils calls this "substantive traditionality" and deems it a "major pattern of human thought." Shils, *Tradition*, 21.

3. Stanley Cavell, *Cities of Words* (Cambridge, MA: Harvard University Press, 2004), 26. For further explication of Cavell's concept of perfectionism, see Richard Eldridge, ed., *Stanley Cavell* (New York: Cambridge University Press, 2003), 39.

4. Susan Wolf, "Moral Saints," *Journal of Philosophy* 79, no. 8 (1982): 419–39.

5. Joseph Story, *Commentaries on the Constitution* (1833), cited in Peter Berkowitz, ed., *Never a Matter of Indifference* (Stanford, CA: Hoover Institution Press, 2003), front matter.

6. Jean Bethke Elshtain, "The Liberal Social Contract and the Privatization of Religion," in *Religion as a Public Good*, ed. Alan Mittleman (Lanham, MD: Rowman and Littlefield, 2003), 21.

Contributors

Julia Annas is Regents Professor Emerita at the University of Arizona. She is an Honorary Fellow of St. Hugh's College, Oxford, a Member of the American Academy of Arts and Sciences, and was President of the Pacific Division of the American Philosophical Association 2004–2005. She has published sixteen books (eight edited or translations) and many articles, mainly on ethics in the ancient Greco-Roman world and contemporary virtue ethics.

Deborah Barer is Associate Professor of Religious Studies at Towson University. Her research explores different models of decision-making in the Babylonian Talmud and their application to contemporary issues in Jewish law and ethics.

Shira Billet is Assistant Professor of Jewish Thought and Ethics at the Jewish Theological Seminary. Her research is in nineteenth- and early twentieth-century German Jewish philosophy. She coedited *Spinoza, Hermann Cohen, and the Legacies of German Idealism* (a special issue of *Jewish Studies Quarterly,* 2018) and is the author of "Between Jewish Law and State Law: Rethinking Hermann Cohen's Critique of Spinoza." She has several forthcoming articles and translations and is completing a manuscript on Hermann Cohen.

Harris Bor is a Research Fellow at the London School of Jewish Studies and barrister (trial advocate) specializing in international arbitration and commercial litigation. He is the author of *Staying Human: A Jewish Theology for the Age of Artificial Intelligence* (2021), and contributor to *New Perspectives on the Haskalah* (2001). He holds a PhD from Cambridge University, is a rabbinic scholar with the Montefiore Endowment, and has been a visiting scholar at Harvard University and University College London.

Yonatan Y. Brafman is Assistant Professor of Modern Judaism and Neubauer Faculty Fellow in the Department of Religion at Tufts University. He is the coeditor, with Leora Batnitzky, of *Jewish Legal Theories: Writings on State, Religion, and Morality* and the author of *Critique of Halakhic Reasons: Divine Commandments and Social Normativity* (forthcoming). His research focuses on Jewish law in the context of moral, legal, and political philosophy.

Geoffrey D. Claussen is Lori and Eric Sklut Scholar in Jewish Studies, Associate Professor of Religious Studies, and Chair of the Department of Religious Studies at Elon University. He is the author of *Sharing the Burden: Rabbi Simhah Zissel Ziv and the Path of Musar* (SUNY Press, 2015) and *Modern Musar: Contested Virtues in Jewish Thought* (2022).

Richard A. Cohen is Professor of Jewish Thought at the University at Buffalo (SUNY), and Director of the annual Levinas Philosophy Summer Seminar. His most recent books are *Out of Control: Confrontations between Spinoza and Levinas* (2016) and *Levinasian Meditations: Ethics, Philosophy and Religion* (2010). More recently he coedited a volume on contemporary political theory and praxis, contra authoritarian governance, *The Politics of Humanity* (2021). He has translated, edited, and introduced four books by Levinas.

Ned Curthoys is Senior Lecturer in English and Literary Studies at the University of Western Australia. His fields of research include Jewish and Holocaust studies, the thought of Hannah Arendt, German-Jewish intellectual history, postcolonial and Middle Eastern studies, and historical fiction. He has published widely on Hannah Arendt as a humanis public intellectual. His monograph *The Legacy of Liberal Judaism: Erns Cassirer and Hannah Arendt's Hidden Conversation* was published in 2013 With Isabelle Hesse, he is the editor of *Literary Representations of th Palestine/Israel Conflict after the Second Intifada* (2022).

Esti Eisenmann studies Jewish thought over the generations. He research deals with the concept of divinity, biblical exegesis, ethic and the interpretation of Jewish tradition in light of Greek philosophy, with special attention to the Jewish contribution to the development of the sciences. She is currently investigating the commentaries on Aristotle's *Physics* written in Hebrew by Gersonides. She teaches courses on Jewish philosophy and mysticism at the Open University of Israel, the Hebrew University, and Herzog College.

Rebecca J. Epstein-Levi is Assistant Professor of Jewish Studies and Gender and Sexuality Studies at Vanderbilt University. She works on the ethics of sex and sexuality, disability, and neurodiversity in dialogue with rabbinic text. Her book, *When We Collide: Sex, Social Risk, and Jewish Ethics* is forthcoming in 2023. In her copious free time, she enjoys cooking unnecessarily complicated meals and sharpening her overly large collection of kitchen knives.

Eitan Fishbane is Associate Professor of Jewish Thought at The Jewish Theological Seminary in New York City. His books include *As Light Before Dawn: The Inner World of a Medieval Kabbalist* (2009), *The Art of Mystical Narrative: A Poetics of the Zohar* (2018), and, most recently, *Embers of Pilgrimage: Poems* (2021).

Alexander Green is Visiting Associate Professor at SUNY, University at Buffalo, in the Department of Jewish Thought. His research is on medieval and early modern Jewish philosophy, ethics, and the history of biblical interpretation. He is the author of two books: *The Virtue Ethics of Levi Gersonides* (2016) and *Power and Progress: Joseph Ibn Kaspi and the Meaning of History* (SUNY Press, 2019).

Jonathan Jacobs is Associate Professor in the Department of Bible at Bar-Ilan University. His main research interest is medieval biblical exegesis. He is the author of three books and numerous scholarly articles. His forthcoming book will deal with the Byzantine exegesis in the Bible.

Patrick Benjamin Koch is Emmy Noether Research Group Leader at the Institute for Jewish Philosophy and Religion at the University of Hamburg, where he directs the project "Jewish Moralistic Writings of the Early Modern Period" funded by the German Research Foundation. His research interests include Jewish intellectual history with a particular focus on Kabbalah and *musar*. He has published widely on these topics, inter alia in the *Jewish Quarterly Review* and the *Harvard Theological Review*.

Baruch Frydman-Kohl is Rabbi Emeritus of Beth Tzedec Congregation, Toronto, and Senior Rabbinic Fellow of the Shalom Hartman Institute. In addition to his academic publications in medieval Jewish thought and philosophy of law, he has co-led multifaith Path of Abraham missions to the Holy Land, serves as a member of the Catholic-Jewish Consultation of Canada and is Vice-Chair of the Canadian Rabbinic Caucus. He is a Member of the Order of Canada.

Matthew LaGrone is the Program Head, Liberal Studies, at the University of Guelph–Humber in Toronto.

Carlos Lévy is Professor Emeritus of Roman Literature and Philosophy in the University of Paris–Sorbonne. He is a member of the French Académie des Inscriptions et Belles Lettres. His main fields of research are philosophy and rhetoric both in the Hellenistic and the Roman world, as well as the reception of these philosophical doctrines in contemporary philosophers, as Michel Foucault. His many publications include *Les philosophies hellénistiques* (1997), *Philon d'Alexandrie et le langage de la philosophie* (editor) (1998), *Michel Foucault et la philosophie antique* (2003), and *Les scepticismes* (2018).

Joseph Isaac Lifshitz is Senior Lecturer in the Interdisciplinary Program in Philosophy and Jewish Thought, Shalem College. His fields of research are political philosophy, philosophy of law, Jewish philosophy and Jewish medieval history. Among his publications are *Rabbi Meir of Rothenberg and the Foundations of Jewish Political Thought* (2015) and *One God; Many Images: Dialectical Thought in Hasidei Ashkenaz* (Hebrew) (2015).

Diana Lobel, Associate Professor of Religion at Boston University, is author of *Moses and Abraham Maimonides: Encountering the Divine* (2021), *Philosophies of Happiness* (2017), *The Quest for God and the Good* (2011), *A Sufi-Jewish Dialogue: Philosophy and Mysticism in Baḥya Ibn Paquda's Duties of the Heart* (2007), and *Between Mysticism and Philosophy: Sufi Language of Religious Experience in Judah Halevi's Kuzari* (2000).

Shaul Magid is Professor of Jewish Studies at Dartmouth College and Kogod Senior Research Fellow at the Shalom Hartman Institute of North America. His work includes early modern Kabbalah, Hasidism, and Modern Judaism.

Eugene D. Matanky is a doctoral candidate (ABD) at Tel Aviv University. His doctorate, entitled "Esoteric Labor: A Material Reception of Cordoverean Kabbalah," explores the different labors—material, intellectual-cultural, and hermeneutical—involved in forming Cordoverean Kabbalah. This research touches upon issues of manuscript and print culture, the sociology and transmission of knowledge, and processes of canonization. He was recently awarded the Nathan Rotenstreich Scholarship for outstanding PhD students in the humanities.

Amanda Beckenstein Mbuvi, Vice President for Academic Affairs at the Reconstructionist Rabbinical College, is a Hebrew Bible scholar with an interest in identity and community in the biblical texts and among their readers. In addition to numerous scholarly articles, Mbuvi is author of the 2016 book *Belonging in Genesis: Biblical Israel and the Politics of Identity Formation*.

Alan Mittleman is the Aaron Rabinowitz and Simon H. Rifkind Professor Jewish Philosophy at the Jewish Theological Seminary in New York. He specializes in modern Jewish thought, ethics, and political theory. His most recent book is *Does Judaism Condone Violence?*

Clifford Orwin is Professor of Political Science, Classics, and Jewish Studies at the University of Toronto. He is also Distinguished Visiting Fellow at the Hoover Institution of Stanford University and a Founding Senior Fellow of the Berlin/Bochum Thucydides Center in Germany. He is the author of *The Humanity of Thucydides* (1994; 5th ed. 2020; Mandarin translation 2015) and of many articles on the history of political thought as well as essays and columns on current issues. His major current project is a book on Josephus.

Sarah Pessin is Professor of Philosophy and Interfaith Chair at the University of Denver. She is the author of *Ibn Gabirol's Theology of Desire* (2013) and the editor of the "Jewish Tradition" section of *Medieval Philosophy: A Multicultural Reader* (2019). She has also authored chapters for key reference works including the *Stanford Encyclopedia of Philosophy*, the *Cambridge History of Jewish Philosophy*, the *Cambridge History of Medieval Philosophy*, the *Cambridge Companion to Medieval Jewish Philosophy*, and the *Routledge Companion to Islamic Philosophy*. She is currently completing a manuscript on pardon in early Levinas.

William Plevan teaches modern Jewish thought, theology, and ethics at the Jewish Theological Seminary, Gratz College, and the Reconstructionist Rabbinical College. His essay "Exile and Alienation in Martin Buber's Philosophical Anthropology" is due to be published this year. He is also the editor of a Festschrift, *Personal Theology: Essays in Honor of Neil Gillman*.

Einat Ramon is Senior Lecturer of Jewish Thought at the Schechter Institute of Jewish Studies. She is the founder of the Marpeh Program, the only academic program for the training of spiritual caregivers in Israel. Dr. Ramon's book *A New Life: Religion, Motherhood and Supreme Love in the Thought of A. D. Gordon* was published in 2007. In addition, she has published numerous articles on various modern Jewish thinkers.

Heidi M. Ravven, PhD, is Professor of Religious Studies at Hamilton College and Senior Fellow at the Carter School of Peace and Conflict Resolution, George Mason University. Ravven, in 2005, received an unsolicited grant from the Ford Foundation of $500,000. She published *The Self Beyond Itself: An Alternative History of Ethics, the New Brain Sciences, and the Myth of Free Will* (2013; Chinese edition 2017). Her current research is *Remaking American Civil Religion*.

Elias Sacks is Director of the Program in Jewish Studies and Associate Professor of Religious Studies at the University of Colorado Boulder, and is the Incoming Director of the Jewish Publication Society. He has published on medieval and modern thinkers such as Maimonides, Spinoza, Moses Mendelssohn, Nachman Krochmal, Franz Rosenzweig, and Jacob Taubes, including the 2017 book *Moses Mendelssohn's Living Script* and some of the first English translations of Mendelssohn's Hebrew writings.

Don Seeman is Associate Professor in the Department of Religion and the Tam Institute for Jewish Studies at Emory University. H serves on the editorial boards of *Prooftexts: Journal of Jewish Literary History* and the *Journal of Contemplative Studies* and is coeditor of the series in Contemporary Anthropology of Religion at Palgrave. Recent publications include a coedited volume on *Hasidism, Suffering and Renewal* (SUNY Press, 2021) and another on *Existential Anthropology and the Academic Study of Religion* (forthcoming).

Ken Seeskin is Emeritus Professor of Philosophy and Emeritus Philip M. and Ethel Klutznick Professor of Jewish Civilization at Northwestern University. He specializes in the rationalist tradition in Jewish philosophy with an emphasis on Maimonides. Publications include *Maimonides on the Origin of the World* (2005), *Jewish Messianic Thoughts in an Age of Despair* (2012), *Thinking about the Torah: A Philosopher Reads the Bible* (2016), and *Thinking about the Prophets: A Philosopher Reads the Bible* (2020).

Katja Šmid holds a PhD in Linguistics from the University of Ljubljana. Currently, she is a Distinguished Researcher in Sephardic studies at the Spanish National Research Council (CSIC). Her fields of expertise are Ladino language and literature with a special focus on Judeo-Spanish rabbinic writings, Ottoman Sephardic women, and the Jewish-Balkan cultural legacy. She is author of a scientific edition of Eliezer Papo's late nineteenth-century Judezmo rabbinical treatise, focusing on the habits and customs relating to Sabbath observance among the Sephardim of Bosnia (2012).

Esther Solomon recently received her doctorate in Jewish Thought from Bar Ilan University. She has written several articles about Rabbi Dessler, including "Toward a Presentation of Rabbinic Unity: Explication of Interpretative Discrepancy in the Thought of Rabbi Eliyahu Eliezer Dessler" (2022), "R. Dessler's View of Secular Studies and *Wissenschaft des Judentums*" (2018), and "Rabbi Eliyahu Eliezer Dessler: Not Quite the Musar Traditionalist" (2016).

Hava Tirosh-Samuelson is Regents Professor of History, Irving and Miriam Lowe Professor of Modern Judaism, and Director of Jewish Studies at Arizona State University. She specializes in Jewish intellectual history, religion, science, and technology, and religion and ecology. She is the editor of *Judaism and Ecology: Created World and Revealed*

Word (2002) and the author of *Happiness in Premodern Judaism: Virtue, Knowledge, and Well-Being* (2003) and *Religion and Environment: The Case of Judaism* (2020).

Roslyn Weiss is Professor Emerita of Philosophy at Lehigh University. She holds a PhD in Philosophy (Columbia University) and an MA in Jewish Studies (Baltimore Hebrew University). She is the author of four books on Plato's dialogues and sixty articles on Greek philosophy, Jewish philosophy, ethics, and philosophy of religion. She has published the first complete English translation of Ḥasdai Crescas's *Or Hashem* (Light of the Lord) (2018).

Shira Weiss is Assistant Director of the Sacks-Herenstein Center for Values and Leadership of Yeshiva University and teaches Jewish Philosophy at Bernard Revel Graduate School of Jewish Studies. She is the author of *Joseph Albo on Free Choice* (2017), *Ethical Ambiguity in the Hebrew Bible* (2018), and articles in academic journal and anthologies, as well as coauthor of *The Protests of Job: An Interfaith Dialogue* (2022).

Sarah V. Zager is a scholar of ethics and Jewish thought. She received her PhD in Religious Studies and Philosophy from Yale University in 2022. She is currently a fellow at the Katz Center for Advanced Jewish Studies at the University of Pennsylvania.

Index

Adler, Rachel, 469, 470, 475, 478
afterlife, *see* world to come
al-Ghazālī, 66, 69
Albo, Joseph, 2, 173–183, 198n56; *Sefer ha-Ikkarim* (*Book of Principles*), 173–180, 198n56
Amarachi, Isaac Bekhor, 3, 5, 297–310; hour a day, 5; neighborly love, 303–306; *Musar Haskel*, 297–298, 300–302, 303, 307; *Sefer Darkhe ha-Adam*, 297–300, 302, 307
anger, 52, 57, 85, 99, 101, 102–103, 104, 107, 112, 114, 115, 119, 120, 127, 146, 171, 201, 220, 261, 284, 302, 360
antisemitism, 26, 338, 425, 435–436, 459
Aquinas, St. Thomas, 38
Arama, Isaac, 2, 185–198; *Akedat Yitsḥak*, 185–186, 187, 188; *Ḥazut Kashah*, 185, 187; *Yad Avshalom*, 185, 194–195
Arendt, Hannah, xii, 3, 5, 425–439, 476, 500; courage, 433–434; *Eichmann in Jerusalem*, 426, 432; friendship, 432–433; historically grounded storytelling, 5, 432; love of the world, 430–431; *Men in Dark Times*, 426, 435; realism, 5, 431–432; *The Life of the Mind*, 434
Aristotle, xi–xii, 2, 10, 26, 38, 39, 52, 59, 62n7, 66, 67, 68, 81, 89, 90, 91, 98, 100–104, 107, 108n2, 108n13, 138, 144, 147n3, 149, 150, 159, 175, 176, 181n10, 186, 187, 189, 191, 192, 321, 326, 328, 339, 340, 349n2, 370, 392, 420, 427, 429, 433, 442, 444, 446, 448, 449, 488–490, 495n35; anger, 103; continence, 315, 322n19; *De Anima*, 153; divine, 101, 102, 150; equity (*epeikeia*), 189; four causes, 150; friendship, 139, 189, 191, 196n22; *Generation of Animals*, 154; great souled man (*megalopsychos*), 100, 495n35; habits, 99, 318, 326, 430, 434, 483; human flourishing or *eudaimonia*, 52, 139, 143, 341, 347, 499; moral virtues, 150, 157, 192, 316; *Nicomachean Ethics*, 99, 101, 103, 104, 150, 156, 159, 178, 187, 196n13, 196n24, 294n4, 429–430, 446, 483, 499; the mean, xi, 55, 60, 62n4, 68, 99, 101, 104–105, 107, 150, 157, 169, 178, 189, 234, 340–341, 442, 444, 447, 483, 489; *Poetics*, 145; *Politics*, 446, 449; practical wisdom, 175, 196n18, 328, 427, 429; soul, 99
arrogance, *see* pride

asceticism, 33, 60, 65, 66, 68, 71–72, 77n16, 234, 277, 319
Averroes, 149, 150, 153, 160n14; *Commentary on Aristotle's Nicomachean Ethics*, 150
Azriel of Gerona, 363
awe, *see* fear

Baal Shem Tov, 283, 465
Bialik, Ḥayyim Naḥman, 227
Brethren of Purity (*Ikhwān aṣ-Ṣafā*), 66, 83, 84
Buber, Martin, 5, 93, 94, 369–381, 442, 476; dialogical responsiveness, 5, 370–376; *I and Thou*, 369, 370

Cassirer, Ernst, 266n16, 436
Christianity, 38, 52, 62n3, 81, 89, 113, 123, 174, 179, 181n6, 185–186, 187, 189, 196n14, 213–214, 256, 301, 307, 312, 339, 348, 429, 446, 452, 455, 485, 488, 491
Cicero, 388
Cohen, Hermann, 3, 337–351, 409, 419–420, 436, 476, 484, 489–490, 500; fidelity, 345–346; humility, 324–347; truthfulness, 343–344, 345
commandment/s, *mitzvah*/*mitzvot* (also precept), xii, 5, 11, 67, 71, 72–73, 74, 98, 120, 124–126, 129–130, 133, 134n11, 155, 165, 168, 169, 175, 176, 178, 185, 189, 190, 192, 229, 230, 268n65, 270, 272, 273, 274, 278, 285–286, 291, 302, 315, 321, 329, 332, 333, 356, 358, 376, 379, 386–387, 396, 410–420, 456–457, 458, 460, 461, 462, 463, 464, 465, 483, 486, 488
Communism, 457
compassion or mercy, 57, 60, 61, 85, 89, 100, 101, 106–107, 112, 118, 120, 140, 144–146, 147n4, 148n16, 152–153, 177, 201, 202, 205, 206, 207, 328, 330, 331, 332, 344, 355, 360, 362, 371, 372, 415, 479, 483, 489, 499, 501
contentment, 85, 99
consequentialism or utilitarianism, xi, 2, 138, 147n3, 390, 392–393, 413–414, 484
Cordovero, Moses, 3, 199–211, 295n21, 356; *Pardes Rimonim* (*Orchard of Pomegranates*), 199, 200, 205, 293; *Tomer Devorah* (*The Palm Tree of Deborah*), 200–204, 205, 206, 233
courage, 1, 4, 26–27, 41, 62n4, 68, 85, 99, 157, 167, 175, 177–178, 180, 182n27, 341, 342–343, 345, 347, 391, 428, 429, 433–434, 435, 444, 500
covenant, 11, 13, 15, 17, 117, 194, 361, 485
Crescas, Ḥasdai, 2, 163–172, 173, 176, 180n3, 214; four perfections, 164–165; happiness, 164; *Light of the Lord*, 163–171, 180; *Refutation of the Principles of the Christians* (*Bittul Ikkarei ha-Notzerim*), 163; *Sermon on the Passover*, 163; virtues of character, 167–168; virtues of conduct, 165–167

Descartes, René, 214, 443
Dessler, Eliyahu, Eliezer 3, 5, 395–408; generosity or giving to others, 5, 398–402; responsibility,
devekut, cleaving, 128–129, 134n8, 140, 235n10, 244, 247, 275, 330, 356

disputation, 123; Barcelona, 123; Tortosa, 173–174
Douglas, Mary, 14

Einstein, Albert, 358
Elazar of Worms, 3, 5, 111–122; *Book of the Name*, 120; *Sefer ha-Rokeaḥ*, 111, 120; virtue of modesty, 112–121
empathy, 5, 144, 148n16, 203, 204, 330, 332, 431
environmentalism, xi, 4, 483–496; compassion towards animals, 28, 112, 330, 331, 361, 484–486, 489–490; "Do Not Destroy" (*bal tashchit*), 486
equanimity, 61, 257, 262–263, 264, 328, 443
esotericism, 3, 75, 128, 142, 143, 159, 200, 205, 233, 273

faith, 44, 118, 186, 187, 189, 190, 192, 193–195, 197n25, 283n1, 284, 286–288, 293–294, 401
fear, awe, reverence, 1, 4, 62n4, 69–70, 120, 126, 157, 165, 171, 176, 177, 178, 179, 180, 186, 187, 189, 190, 192, 194, 197n44, 198n56, 229, 230–231, 237n30, 259, 270–278, 314–317, 318, 319, 328, 355, 400, 436, 444, 462–463, 483, 488
feminism, 4, 5, 347, 348, 359, 469–482, 489; citation, 5, 474–475; recanonization, 475–478; reinterpretation, 471–474
fidelity, loyalty, 11, 13, 15, 16, 21n3–4, 43, 185, 187, 190, 194, 341–346, 490, 496n51
flourishing or felicity, 4, 12, 52, 62, 139, 143, 144, 145, 164, 186, 189, 190, 192, 194, 197n44, 242, 313, 339, 340, 341, 347, 357, 358, 360, 413, 414, 486, 488, 490, 499, 500
forgiveness, 114, 120, 139, 146, 177–178, 190
Foucault, Michel, 436
Franklin, Benjamin, 255, 257, 258, 264
free choice, free will, 172n11, 177–179, 192, 220, 221, 250–251, 289, 379, 402, 403, 407n74
friendship, 4, 139, 188, 191, 262, 428, 432–433, 434, 447

generosity, 1, 4, 5, 85, 99, 167, 192, 272, 329, 332, 371, 372, 388, 396, 398–402, 444, 446–448, 451, 483, 490
Gersonides, 2, 5, 149–162, 176, 186, 214, 497; Agent Intellect, 150; *Book of Animals*, 154, 160n14; *Commentary on the Torah*, 155–156, 198n56; God, 150–152, 154–155; immortality of the soul, 151–152, 159; kingship, 159; narrative, 5, 155–156; practical intellect, 151, 153, 159; priesthood, 159; *Supercommentary on De Anima*, 153; virtues of altruism, 154–155, 156; virtues of physical preservation, 152–154, 156; *Wars of the Lord* (*Sefer Milḥamot Hashem*), 150, 180
gratitude, 67, 71, 72, 73, 139, 361, 386, 387, 399, 406n39, 431, 462, 488
greed, 85, 303, 449, 456, 483, 487, 488, 490

habits, habituation, xi, 42, 99, 107, 175, 188, 191, 230, 233, 243, 259–262, 301, 302–304, 306, 316,

habits, habituation *(continued)* 318–319, 326, 327, 328–329, 331, 332, 354–355, 364, 371–372, 385, 386, 400, 402, 430, 433, 434, 445, 471, 474, 483

Ḥafetz Ḥaim (Kagan, Israel Meir), 389, 401

halakhah or Jewish law, 54–55, 58, 67, 123, 124, 174, 200, 206, 208n9, 208n10, 241, 247–248, 250, 251, 270, 272, 277, 278, 286, 302, 313, 319, 320–321, 354, 358–359, 361, 362, 363, 376, 409, 410–420, 456, 463, 464, 476, 485, 486, 488, 490

happiness, *see* flourishing

Haredi Judaism, 3, 395, 477

Hasidism, 3, 139, 228, 264, 269, 272, 283, 284, 286, 288, 293, 311, 353, 354, 356, 360, 369, 372, 374–375, 376–377, 379, 380, 395, 398, 405n29, 405n31, 411, 455, 456, 457, 463, 465, 498; *tzaddik*, 377–378

Haskalah, 3, 228, 255, 259, 311–312, 320, 321n2, 357, 388, 395

hate, 76, 85, 89, 257, 304, 305, 328

Ḥayyim of Volozhin, 3, 269–281, 357–358; "fear of the Lord," 270–278; humility, 274–278, 280n39, 281n46; *Nefesh ha-Ḥayyim*, 270, 279n10; Moses, 276–277; perseverance (*kevi'ut*), 272–273, 280n30; *Ruaḥ ha-Ḥayyim*, 270, 271

Hebrew Bible, 2, 9–22, 71, 72, 81, 88, 97, 117, 123, 124, 125, 138, 150, 152, 155–156, 163, 165, 185, 187, 205, 300, 345–346, 376, 379, 389, 415, 420, 456, 465, 478, 485, 486, 491, 497, 498, 500, 501; Aaron, 44, 115, 117, 119, 132, 133; Abel, 140, 141, 156–157, 252; Abraham, 5–6, 12, 25, 27, 31, 32–33, 43, 44, 72, 115, 131, 139, 141, 142, 157–158, 167, 178–179, 193–194, 198n53, 202, 276, 330, 340, 362, 390–391, 417, 419, 451; Adam, 89, 141, 170, 172n10, 203, 250–252; Cain, 140, 141, 156–157, 203, 252; I–II Chronicles, 131; covenant, 11, 13, 15, 17; David, 16–18, 20, 46, 75, 83, 115, 131, 232, 331; Deuteronomy, 5, 11, 14–16, 21n3, 21n4, 44, 101, 124, 126, 127, 128, 129, 130, 134n4, 134n12, 134n14, 167, 169, 193, 196n23, 229, 248, 264, 447, 486, 487, 498, 499; Ecclesiastes, 87, 116, 124, 126, 131, 181n12, 185, 197n44; Enoch, 401; Esau, 28; Esther, 185; Exodus, 18, 20, 44, 56, 87, 101, 106, 129, 130, 132, 133, 134n14, 166, 177, 189, 201–202, 247–250, 276, 331, 355, 487; Eve, 89, 141, 252; family, 11, 14; Garden of Eden, 32, 89, 169–170, 172n9, 250–252; Genesis, 11, 12, 32, 119, 131, 134n13, 156–158, 169–170, 172n9, 179, 190, 250–251, 276, 326, 330, 390, 449, 485, 500; Gideon, 116; Isaac, 33, 131, 179, 194; Isaiah, 117, 119, 141, 178, 314, 376, 451, 458; Jacob, 12, 25, 28–29, 33, 34n5, 139, 158–149, 331, 451; Jethro, 331; Jeremiah, 109n18; Job, 72, 124, 131; Joseph, 20, 25, 29, 44, 46, 139; Josiah, 117, 119; Joshua, 320; Judges, 115; I–II Kings, 117, 119; Korah, 375; Laban, 33; Lamentations, 185; Leah, 25; Levi, 28; Leviticus, 11, 14, 21n7, 54, 63n12, 101, 117, 119, 124–125, 129, 130–131, 134n4, 134n12, 166, 321, 375, 487, 499; Lot, 125; memory, 12–13, 14, 18; Micah, 201–202, 388; Miriam, 115; Moses, 5, 20, 2[illegible] 27, 29, 41–42, 43, 44–46, 58, 92,

100, 101, 104, 105, 106, 107, 108, 115, 131–133, 134n14, 139, 167, 229, 238n42, 276–277, 331–332, 340, 355, 357, 362, 375, 417, 419, 445, 451, 499; Noah, 125, 170, 172n10, 193; Numbers, 44, 100, 115, 132, 133, 134n14; Pharaoh, 29, 132, 158, 177, 178, 330; Potiphar, 29; priestly, 11–12, 13, 18, 21n7; Proverbs, 125, 185, 187–188, 189, 190, 191, 192, 326, 498; Psalms, 75, 83, 99–100, 113, 115, 116, 117, 119, 120, 131, 175, 176, 232, 238n43, 270, 330, 486, 487; Rachel, 24–25; Reuben, 28; Ruth, 185; Samuel, 13, 43, 46, 128, 451; Sarah, 25–26; Saul, 13, 16–18, 20, 46; *shema*, 13, 14–15; Solomon, 46, 87, 192; Song of Songs, 185; Tabernacle, 13–14; *toledot*, 12, 18; Tower of Babel, 156–157; wisdom, *ḥokhmah*, 13; Zechariah, 100

Hegel, Georg Wilhelm Friedrich, 284

Heidegger, Martin, 425, 435

Heschel, Abraham Joshua, 3, 392, 455–467, 476, 484, 488; *A Passion for Truth*, 459; *God in Search of Man*, 456–457, 463; *Man Is Not Alone*, 456, 461–462; *The Prophets*, 458–459; *Who Is Man?*, 459

Hobbes, Thomas 214, 446, 448

holiness, 1, 4, 124–126, 291, 340, 374–375, 380, 416, 450–451, 487, 498, 500, 502

Holocaust, 347–348, 407n76, 459–460

honesty, 112, 130–131, 216–217, 218, 219, 222, 223, 374, 387, 391, 392, 464

hope, 27, 32, 176–177, 180, 188

humanity (virtue of), *humanität*, 342–343, 347; *philanthrōpia*, 27–28, 41

humility, 1, 4, 44, 45–46, 66, 68, 71, 85, 88, 92, 99, 100, 101, 102, 107, 112, 114, 115, 117, 118, 119, 121, 126–127, 128–129, 131–133, 134n14, 139, 167, 188, 203, 229, 231, 257, 274–278, 280n39, 281n46, 290, 292, 314–317, 328, 331, 340–341, 342–347, 348, 375, 388, 399, 458, 459, 461, 483, 488–490, 495n33, 499, 500, 501

Hurwitz, Eliyahu, *Sefer ha-Berit*, 299, 300, 301, 303–304, 305, 306, 310n30

Ibn Ezra, Abraham, 209n18

Ibn Gabirol, Solomon, 2, 5, 66, 81–95; *On the Improvement of the Moral Qualities*, 81, 83; *Kingdom's Crown*, 81; *The Fountain of Life*, 81, 84; virtue of receptivity, 93–94

Ibn Paquda, Baḥya, 2, 5, 65–79, 180, 232, 233, 284, 306, 316, 354, 360–361; asceticism (*zuhd*), 66–67, 68, 71; "duties of the heart," 5, 66, 67, 68, 72–74

Ibn Verga, Solomon, *Shevet Yehudah*, 299, 300, 301, 302, 307

image of God (*tzelem Elohim*), 119, 139, 146, 326, 362, 378, 379, 392, 399, 500

imitatio dei, 82, 83, 92, 93, 101, 264, 327, 378, 499

jealousy, 85, 88, 92, 133, 157, 301, 303

Jewish Theological Seminary, 383, 455, 459

Josephus, Flavius, 2, 37–49; *Against Apion*, 37, 38, 40, 41; *Antiquities of the Jews*, 37, 38, 39, 44–46; civic virtue, 41; *Jewish War*, 38, 40, 41, 49n36; martyrdom, 42; Moses,

Josephus, Flavius *(continued)* 41–42, 43, 44–46; piety, 41, 43; regime (*politeuma*), 39, 40, 41; theocracy, 42
joy, 85, 104, 165, 178, 219, 223, 284, 287, 329, 331, 411, 412
Joseph Karo, 199
Judah Halevi, 66, 72, 121, 176, 180
Judah He-Hasid, 111–112, 113–115, 116; *Sefer Hasidim*, 111–112, 113–114
justice, 1, 4, 6, 26, 27, 29, 41, 63n26, 68, 88, 99, 131, 133, 152, 154, 167, 188, 196n23, 206, 216, 244, 342–343, 345, 347, 371, 372, 375, 376, 379, 388–389, 391, 415, 435, 442, 445–451, 452, 457, 479, 485, 487, 498, 501

Kabbalah, 3, 123, 137, 140, 145, 163, 199–207, 209n15, 233, 264, 270, 276, 284, 305, 310, 354, 356, 357, 358, 363, 398, 405n31, 418, 456
Kant, Immanuel and Kantianism, xi, 138, 147n3, 255, 284, 337, 338, 339, 343, 345, 349n4, 390, 410, 420, 428, 435
Kaplan, Mordechai, 3, 6, 383–394, 459; Jewish civilization, 385, 387, 391–392; justice, 388–389, 391
Kelm Musar yeshiva, 325, 395–397
Kierkegaard, Soren, 459
Kook, Abraham Isaac, 3, 353–367
Kotzker Rebbe, 459–460, 465

land of Israel, 3, 123, 127, 137, 145, 167, 298, 418, 486
Lefin, Menaḥem Mendel, 3, 5, 255–268; charting one's progress, 5, 257, 263; *Ḥeshbon ha-Nefesh*, 256, 259–265
Levinas, Emmanuel, 3, 5, 94, 356, 441–454, 476; generosity, 5, 444, 446–448, 451; holiness, 450–451; justice, 442, 445–451, 452; responsibility, 5, 442–446, 449, 451–452
liberalism, 42, 214, 338, 426, 465, 469, 500–502
lifnim mishurat ha-din, 392
Locke, John, 255, 257, 258–259, 261; sensationalism, 258–259; *Some Thoughts concerning Education*, 258
love, 1, 4, 11, 16, 27, 59, 60, 62, 66, 67, 68–69, 70, 71, 73, 76, 85, 89, 103, 114, 115, 128, 139, 140, 142, 144–146, 147n4, 148n16, 154–155, 157, 165, 168, 169, 171, 178, 179, 180, 186, 188, 189, 192, 196n22, 198n46, 201, 206, 223, 229, 230, 241, 251, 300, 303–306, 327, 328–329, 331, 332, 333, 340–341, 344, 347, 373, 374–375, 378, 386, 388, 390, 391, 396, 399, 400–401, 414–417, 429, 430–431, 433, 436, 450, 451, 456–457, 458, 461, 483, 488
loyalty, *see* fidelity
Luria, Isaac and Lurianic Kabbalah, 199, 227, 356, 376, 377, 405n29
Luzzatto, Moses Ḥayyim, 3, 227–239, 354, 357, 364, 398; *Derekh ha-Shem*, 228, 230, 234; *Mesillat Yesharim*, 228–234, 360
Luzzatto, Samuel David, 360

MacIntyre, Alasdair, 38, 283, 430
Maharal, 405n29
Maimonides, Moses, 2, 38, 44, 62n7 69, 97–109, 121, 149, 150, 159, 16 176, 180n3, 181n10, 193, 198n46, 201, 209n15, 214, 216, 223, 250, 284, 300, 313, 326, 333, 339, 340–

341, 346, 349n2, 354, 355, 356, 360, 362, 364, 410, 419–420, 423n32, 465, 483–484, 488–490, 495n35, 497; imagination, 89; "Eight Chapters," 98–102, 159, 169, 178, 294n4; *Guide of the Perplexed*, 97, 98, 104, 105–107, 150, 163, 180, 181n10, 186, 198n56, 201, 223, 256, 357, 419; mean, 99–105, 107, 313, 350n19, 489; *Mishneh Torah*, 97, 98, 101, 102–105, 159, 164, 281n56, 299, 300, 301, 303, 306, 340–341, 392, 415, 419; repentance, 103–104; *Treatise on Logic*, 245
martyrdom, 42, 59–60, 168, 347–348
Mendelssohn, Moses, 3, 5, 241–254, 255, 356; *Bi'ur*, 244, 247–250; *Commentary on Maimonides's* Treatise on Logic, 245; "On Evidence in Metaphysical Sciences," 241–243, 244; poetry and music, 5, 246–250
messiah and messianism, 33, 59, 64n29, 181n5, 190, 194, 228, 231, 285, 302, 347, 379, 381n28, 445, 446, 451
miracles, 44–45, 176, 182n16, 186, 193, 287, 463
moderation, *see* temperance
modesty, 5, 101, 112–121, 342–345, 483, 489–490
Musar movement, 3, 256, 264, 311, 319, 325, 356, 395
mysticism, 3, 66, 68, 112, 120, 128, 133, 134n8, 134n10, 137, 138, 145, 264, 353, 359, 376, 476

Naḥman of Bratslav, 3, 5, 283–295, 379; faith (*emunah*), 286–288; money, 286, 289–291; *Sefer ha-Middot*, 283–294; *zaddik*, 5, 286–289, 291
Naḥmanides, 3, 121, 123–135, 176, 209n18, 250, 361, 363, 392; "Beyond the Letter of the Law," 129–131; humility, 126–127, 128–129, 131–133, 134n14; *Iggeret ha-Musar* (*Epistle on Ethics*), 127, 128–129, 134n7; intimacy with God, 127–129; "You Shall Be Holy," 124–126, 128–129, 133
Nazirite, 106, 125
Nazi, 338, 426, 427, 434, 455, 457
Neoplatonism, 2, 66, 81, 82, 90, 91, 326; emanation, 82, 84, 90, 92, 94
Nietzsche, Friedrich, 444, 447
Nissim ben Reuben Gerondi (Ran), 163, 176
nobility, 26, 27
Nussbaum, Martha, 139, 144, 146, 147n3, 147n4, 433, 493n19

Ochs, Vanessa 477, 478

pardes, 56
parrhesia, 436
Pascal, Blaise, 448
patience, 104, 257, 259, 263, 327, 356, 499
perseverance, 67, 272–273, 280n30, 346
Philo of Alexandria, xii, 2, 23–35, 38, 500; courage, 26–27; *De ebrietate*, 28; *De Fuga et inuentione*, 33; *De Josepho*, 29; *De sacrificiis*, 28; *De somniis*, 29; *De vita Mosis*, 27, 30; humanity (*philanthrōpia*), 27–28; *Legatio ad Gaium*, 24; nobility, 26, 27; *On the Contemplative Life* (*De vita contemplativa*), 33; *On the Creation* (*De opificio mundi*),

Philo of Alexandria *(continued)* 32–33; *Quod omnis probus liber sit,* 24; repentance, 26, 27; *Treatise of Virtues* (*De virtutibus*), 26–28
piety, 4, 41, 43, 59, 68, 100–101, 102, 112, 118, 119, 120, 139, 229–230, 232, 286, 340, 355, 356, 359, 374–375, 461–462, 489, 499
Plaskow, Judith, 470–471, 476, 478–479
Plato, or Platonic, xii, 2, 10, 26, 30, 31, 39, 68, 83, 89, 90, 94, 144, 218, 228, 245, 338, 339, 340, 349n2, 349n4, 427, 428; *Euthyphro,* 392; *Phaedo,* 247; *Theaetetus,* 31; *Timaeus,* 30, 84, 92
practical wisdom, 26, 52, 54, 60, 155, 157–158, 175, 188, 190, 196n18, 328, 363, 390, 418, 427, 429, 470, 500, 502
prayer, 18, 59, 67, 74, 189, 413, 451; Shema, 59, 71, 447
pride, 46, 71, 85, 88, 89, 100, 101, 102, 112–115, 119, 127, 132, 167, 171, 231, 247–248, 276, 278, 286, 290, 302–303, 341, 344, 375, 401–402, 431, 451, 458, 491

Rabbinic, 2, 5, 51–64, 66, 68, 71, 115, 117, 163, 165, 187, 269, 284, 291, 389, 409, 456, 471, 489; *Avot de Rabbi Nathan,* 52–53; Babylonian Talmud, 53, 54, 56, 60, 62n1, 108n13, 115, 123, 124, 158, 173, 189, 200, 236n16, 270, 271, 273–274, 300, 313, 316, 318, 328–329, 330, 363, 419, 461, 473; *Baraita,* 229, 236n16; Ben Zoma, 275; discipleship, 53; Eliezer ben Pedat, 54; Elisha ben Abuyah, 60, 63n26; Genesis Rabbah, 378; Hillel the Elder, 115, 116, 328, 333; legal argumentation, 5, 53–55; Mishnah, 51, 62n2, 301, 313; Palestinian Talmud, 51, 236n16, 328, 363; Pirkei Avot, 52–53, 55, 69, 98, 100, 116, 126, 196n24, 270, 273, 275–276, 278, 280n35, 281n46, 294n4, 300, 301, 331; Rabban Gamliel, 60; Rabbi Abba, 140–141, 143; Rabbi Akiva, 52, 55–60, 62, 63n24, 328, 465, 500; Rabbi Elazar ben Azariah, 55–56, 63n19; Rabbi Eliezer ben Horkanus, 55–57; Rabbi Jose, 278; Rabbi Joshua, 56; Rabbi Levitas of Yavne, 275; Rabbi Meir, 54; Rabbi Shimon bar Yoḥai, 60, 137, 138, 143, 145, 203; Rabbi Yehoshua ben Levi, 316; Rabbi Yishmael, 58–59, 63n24, 118, 465; Rabbi Yoḥanan, 54; Rabbi Yoḥanan ben Zakkai, 273, 328–329; Resh Lakish, 54, 60; righteousness, 59–60; Talmud study, 311, 318, 319, 325; Tosefta, 51, 62n2
Rashi, 132, 270
Reconstructionist Judaism, 3, 383–384, 470
repentance, 26, 27, 71, 82, 86, 100, 103, 104, 141, 142, 177, 189, 190, 203, 205, 207, 262, 274, 290, 344, 357, 359–360, 379
responsibility, 5, 19, 22n19, 32, 89, 120, 298, 371, 372, 375, 377, 426, 442–446, 452n2, 458, 461, 485, 490, 501
reverence, *see* fear
righteousness, 31, 52, 58–61, 72, 83, 103, 105, 116–118, 131, 139, 141–142, 175, 188, 193, 196n23, 257, 263, 286, 289, 301, 380, 384, 389, 401, 402, 486–487
Rosenzweig, Franz, 369, 476
Ross, Tamar, 472–473, 475, 480n6

Saadya Gaon, 66, 68, 72, 73, 180

Salanter, Israel, 3, 5, 256, 311–324, 325, 328, 442; fear, 314–317, 318, 319; *hitpa'alut* (emotional outpouring), 317–318; humility, 314–317; *limmud musar*, 317–319
Samuel ben Judah of Marseilles, 150
Scholem, Gershom, 405n29, 431, 436, 476
sefirot, 138–139, 142, 200–207, 208n8, 233, 356; *Arikh Anpin* (*The Long Countenance*), 201–202; *Binah*, 203, 205, 207, 418; *ein sof*, 202, 211n42; *Gevurah*, 203; *Keter*, 202, 203, 207; *Shekhinah* or *Malkhut*, 128–129, 139, 142, 144, 203–204, 205, 231; *Tiferet*, 142, 203, 205
shame, 53, 57, 69–70, 86, 88, 89, 116, 273–274
Shmuel He-Hasid, 111
Shneur Zalman of Lyady, 354, 411
Shulḥan Arukh, 320, 418
simplicity, 43, 483, 490
Smith, Adam, 429
Socrates, 6, 68, 241, 247, 331, 342, 347, 427, 428, 430, 433, 434, 435, 436
solidarity, 431, 458
Soloveitchik, Joseph, 3, 264, 409–423, 476, 484, 489; *Halakhic Man*, 410–414; *Halakhic Mind*, 411, 413; love, 414–417
Spinoza, Baruch, xii, 3, 213–225, 443, 444, 500; desire, 218–219; *Ethics*, 213, 214, 215–223; freedom, 213, 214–215, 219–223; *Theological Political Treatise*, 214, 215, 217, 219, 223–224; *Tractatus Politicus*, 213; *Treatise on the Emendation of the Intellect*, 217, 219
Stoic, Stoicism, 2, 26, 27–28, 30, 31, 344, 433
storytelling, 5, 14–15, 432
temperance, 1, 4, 26, 41, 52, 59–60, 68, 99, 175, 316, 442, 483, 488, 490, 502
Theophrastus, 39
Tosafists, 123, 270
trust, 67, 68, 71, 74, 176–177, 180, 287, 292, 387, 392, 436, 490
truthfulness, 341–346, 374

Vilna Gaon, 269, 277, 357
Vital, Ḥayyim, 300

walk in God's ways (Deut. 28:9), 101, 229, 264, 388, 399, 498
wisdom, 1, 4, 13, 68, 82, 118, 139, 143–144, 188, 189, 190, 197n39, 246, 260, 263, 270, 271, 275, 276, 301, 326, 327, 348, 418, 419, 435, 458, 489
world to come, 4, 33, 52, 62, 64n29, 119, 151–152, 159, 164, 168, 170, 176, 190, 384, 389, 400

Xenophon, 39

yirah, *see* fear, awe, reverence

Ziv, Simḥah Zissel, 3, 5, 325–336, 396, 397, 399, 401; love, mercy and compassion, 328–330; Moses, 331–332; sharing the burden, empathy, 5, 330–332
Zionism, 224, 369, 373, 375, 376, 379–380, 383, 410, 425, 436, 450–451, 457, 459, 473
Zohar, 3, 6, 137–148, 199–202, 205, 206, 227, 398, 405n31, 498; forgiveness, 146; Other Side, 141, 146; *ḥokhmat ha-nistar* (wisdom of the hidden), 143–144; love and compassion, 144–146; *tzedek*, *tzedakah*, 142

www.ingramcontent.com/pod-product-compliance
Lightning Source LLC
Chambersburg PA
CBHW021937250225
22368CB00008B/18
9781438493909